MICROECONOMICS

ROGER A. ARNOLD

CALIFORNIA STATE UNIVERSITY
SAN MARCOS

9 E

SOUTH-WESTERN
CENGAGE Learning·

Australia · Brazil · Japan · Korea · Mexico · Singapore · Spain · United Kingdom · United States

SOUTH-WESTERN
CENGAGE Learning™

Microeconomics, 9E
Roger A. Arnold

Vice President of Editorial, Business: Jack W. Calhoun

Vice President/Editor-in-Chief: Alex von Rosenberg

Senior Acquisitions Editor: Michael W. Worls

Senior Developmental Editors: Jennifer E. Thomas, Laura Bofinger

Editorial Assistant: Lena Mortis

Marketing Manager: John Carey

Marketing Communications Manager: Sarah Greber

Senior Content Project Manager: Kim Kusnerak

Media Editor: Deepak Kumar

Senior Manufacturing Buyer: Sandee Milewski

Production Service: Macmillan Publishing Solutions

Compositor: Macmillan Publishing Solutions

Senior Art Director: Michelle Kunkler

Cover/Internal Designer: Ke Design/Mason, Ohio

Cover Image: © Digital Vision Photography

Rights Account Manager—Text: Mollika Basu

Photography Manager: Deanna Ettinger

Photo Researcher: Susan Van Etten

For product information and technology assistance, contact us at **Cengage Learning Customer & Sales Support, 1-800-354-9706**

For permission to use material from this text or product, submit all requests online at **www.cengage.com/permissions**
Further permissions questions can be emailed to **permissionrequest@cengage.com**

ExamView® is a registered trademark of eInstruction Corp. Windows is a registered trademark of the Microsoft Corporation used herein under license. Macintosh and Power Macintosh are registered trademarks of Apple Computer, Inc. used herein under license.

Library of Congress Control Number: 2008938431
ISBN-13: 978-0-324-78549-4
ISBN-10: 0-324-78549-6
Instructor's Edition ISBN 13: 978-0-324-78564-7
Instructor's Edition ISBN 10: 0-324-78564-X

South-Western Cengage Learning
5191 Natorp Boulevard
Mason, OH 45040
USA

Cengage Learning products are represented in Canada by Nelson Education, Ltd.

For your course and learning solutions, visit www.cengage.com
Purchase any of our products at your local college store or at our preferred online store **www.ichapters.com**

Printed in the United States of America
1 2 3 4 5 6 7 12 11 10 09 08

To
Sheila, Daniel,
and David

BRIEF CONTENTS

CONTENTS

CHAPTER 2   ECONOMIC ACTIVITIES: PRODUCING AND TRADING   33

CHAPTER 3   SUPPLY AND DEMAND: THEORY   53

MICROECONOMICS

PART 2 MICROECONOMIC FUNDAMENTALS

CHAPTER 5 ELASTICITY   113

CHAPTER **6** CONSUMER CHOICE: MAXIMIZING UTILITY AND BEHAVIORAL ECONOMICS   140

ECONOMICS 24/7

Who Would Spend $16,000 for a Peanut Butter and Jelly Sandwich?
143

How You Pay for Good Weather
147

Which Is Better: A Tax Rebate or a Tax Bonus?
150

To Accept or Reject the Money
153

OFFICE HOURS

"Is There an Indirect Way of Proving the Law of Diminishing Marginal Utility?"
154

APPENDIX C: BUDGET CONSTRAINT AND INDIFFERENCE CURVE ANALYSIS   158

PART 3 PRODUCT MARKETS AND POLICIES

CHAPTER **11** GOVERNMENT AND PRODUCT MARKETS: ANTITRUST AND REGULATION   272

PART 4 FACTOR MARKETS AND RELATED ISSUES

CHAPTER **12** FACTOR MARKETS: WITH EMPHASIS ON THE LABOR MARKET   295

PART 5 MARKET FAILURE AND PUBLIC CHOICE

THE GLOBAL ECONOMY

PART 6 INTERNATIONAL ECONOMICS AND GLOBALIZATION

CHAPTER **19** INTERNATIONAL FINANCE 446

CHAPTER **20** GLOBALIZATION AND INTERNATIONAL IMPACTS
ON THE ECONOMY 475

PRACTICAL ECONOMICS

PART 7 FINANCIAL MATTERS

CHAPTER **21** STOCKS, BONDS, FUTURES, AND OPTIONS   503

WEB CHAPTER

PART 8 WEB CHAPTER

CHAPTER **22** AGRICULTURE: PROBLEMS, POLICIES, AND UNINTENDED EFFECTS   524

Roger Arnold
YOUR PARTNER FOR SUCCESS

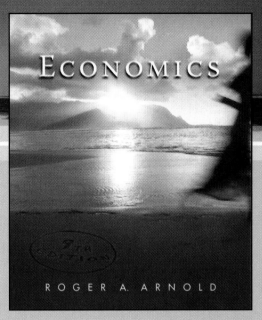

ECONOMICS

9TH EDITION

ROGER A. ARNOLD

Let Roger Arnold's *Economics* be your partner for success. With innovative new pedagogical features, increased coverage of globalization, easy customization, and fully integrated digital options, *Economics* may be your perfect solution. Packed with intriguing pop culture examples, the text illustrates that economics is both a huge factor in how the world works, and an integral part of the day-to-day experiences of the average college student.

What Matters to You in the 9th Edition?

Office Hours

This new feature seeks to emulate the kinds of questions you bring to Economics instructors after class. *Office Hours* explores key concepts such as how the money supply works; the purpose of the PPF; marginal revenue and marginal costs; and the purpose of the *AD/AS* framework.

Enhanced "Thinking Like an Economist"

This classic feature now rotates through the narrative along with two new features: *Finding Economics* and *Common Misconceptions*. Incorporating *Thinking Like an Economist* into the narrative of each chapter helps to better emphasize the importance of developing this skill—to view the world through the lens of economic analysis.

- **Finding Economics** illustrates the economics around us, such as how a technological advance in farming may end up resulting in more attorneys, accountants, or teachers.

- **Common Misconceptions** illuminates murky questions like whether one person's profit is another person's loss, and whether the wealthy really pay a lower percentage of taxes than others.

Enhanced Globalization Coverage

This chapter has been significantly expanded, revised and updated. It now offers a total picture of how globalization affects the U.S., and how economies interact throughout the world.

Many New Applications

The Ninth Edition of *Economics* includes many new applications in the proven favorite—Economics 24/7 features. Here are just a few of the applications that are new to the Ninth Edition, demonstrating Arnold's emphasis on current events that are relevant to your lives:

- Which is better, a tax rebate or a tax bonus?
- Is economics at work in the plastic surgeon's office?
- What economic concepts are illustrated in the popular ABC television series, *Lost*?
- Is the law of demand at work for iPods?
- How can we accurately compare GDP between different countries?
- How does the government spend taxpayers' money?

**TOMLINSON
ECONOMICS
VIDEOS**

Tomlinson Economics Videos

Award winning teacher, actor and professional communicator, Steven Tomlinson (Ph.D. Economics, Stanford) walks you through all of the topics covered in principles of economics in an online video format. Segments are organized to follow the organization of the Arnold text and most videos include class notes that you can download and quizzes for you to test your understanding.

Find out more at
www.cengage.com/economics/tomlinson.

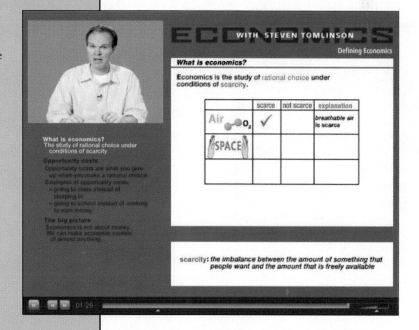

Arnold's Study Guide – Your Partner for Success

Study Guide

Written and updated by Roger Arnold, this thorough Study Guide helps you to gain a solid understanding of chapter material. The Study Guide reinforces learning with a list of key concepts and terms, review questions and problems, short-answer exercises asking "what is wrong" or "what has been overlooked" in a list of statements, and multiple-choice, true/false, and fill-in-the-blank practice questions. Reading and completing the Study Guide exercises for each chapter further explains chapter concepts, assists in the review of key terms and ideas, and prepares you for testing on the content. Visit **www.ichapters.com** to purchase the print Study Guide.

In Appreciation

This book could not have been written and published without the generous expert assistance of many people. A deep debt of gratitude is owed to the reviewers of the first through eighth editions and to the reviewers of this edition, the ninth.

First Edition Reviewers

Jack Adams
University of Arkansas, Little Rock

William Askwig
University of Southern Colorado

Michael Babcock
Kansas State University

Dan Barszcz
College of DuPage, Illinois

Robert Berry
Miami University, Ohio

George Bohler
Florida Junior College

Tom Bonsor
Eastern Washington University

Michael D. Brendler
Louisiana State University

Baird Brock
Central Missouri State University

Kathleen Bromley
Monroe Community College, New York

Douglas Brown
Georgetown University

Ernest Buchholz
Santa Monica Community College, California

Gary Burbridge
Grand Rapids Junior College, Michigan

Maureen Burton
California Polytechnic University, Pomona

Carol Carnes
Kansas State University

Paul Coomes
University of Louisville, Kentucky

Eleanor Craig
University of Delaware

Wilford Cummings
Grosmont College, California

Diane Cunningham
Glendale Community College, California

Douglas C. Darran
University of South Carolina

Edward Day
University of Southern Florida

Johan Deprez
University of Tennessee

James Dietz
California State University, Fullerton

Stuart Dorsey
University of West Virginia

Natalia Drury
Northern Virginia Community College

Lu Ann Duffus
California State University, Hayward

John Eckalbar
California State University, Chico

John Elliot
University of Southern California

Charles Fischer
Pittsburg State University, Kansas

John Gemello
San Francisco State University

Carl Guelzo
Cantonsville Community College, Maryland

Jan Hansen
University of Wisconsin, Eau Claire

John Henderson
Georgia State University

Ken Howard
East Texas Baptist University

Mark Karscig
Central Missouri State University

Stanley Keil
Ball State University, Indiana

Richard Kieffer
State University of New York, Buffalo

Gene Kimmett
William Rainey Harper College, Illinois

Luther Lawson
University of North Carolina

Frank Leori
College of San Mateo, California

Kenneth Long
New River Community College, Virginia

Michael Magura
University of Toledo, Ohio

Bruce McCrea
Lansing Community College, Michigan

Gerald McDougall
Wichita State University, Kansas

Kevin McGee
University of Wisconsin, Oshkosh

Francois Melese
Auburn University, Alabama

Herbert Miliken
American River College, California

Richard Miller
Pennsylvania State University

Ernest Moser
Northeast Louisiana University

Farhang Niroomand
University of Southern Mississippi

Eliot Orton
New Mexico State University

Marty Perline
Wichita State University, Kansas

Harold Petersen
Boston College

Douglas Poe
University of Texas, Austin

Joseph Rezney
St. Louis Community College, Missouri

Terry Ridgway
University of Nevada, Las Vegas

Thomas Romans
State University of New York, Buffalo

Robert Ross
Bloomsburg State College, Pennsylvania

Keith A. Rowley
Baylor University, Texas

Anandi Sahu
Oakland University, Michigan

Richard Scoggins
California State University, Long Beach

Paul Seidenstat
Temple University, Pennsylvania

Shahram Shafiee
North Harris County College, Texas

Alan Sleeman
Western Washington University

John Sondey
University of Idaho

Robert W. Thomas
Iowa State University

Richard L. Tontz
California State University, Northridge

Roger Trenary
Kansas State University

Bruce Vanderporten
Loyola University, Illinois

Thomas Weiss
University of Kansas

Richard O. Welch
University of Texas at San Antonio

Donald A. Wells
University of Arizona

John Wight
University of Richmond, Virginia

Thomas Wyrick
Southwest Missouri State University

Second Edition Reviewers

Scott Bloom
North Dakota State University

Thomas Carroll
University of Nevada, Las Vegas

Larry Cox
Southwest Missouri State University

Diane Cunningham
Los Angeles Valley College

Emit Deal
Macon College

Michael Fabritius
University of Mary Hardin Baylor

Frederick Fagal
Marywood College

Ralph Fowler
Diablo Valley College

Bob Gilette
Texas A&M University

Lynn Gillette
Indiana University, Indianapolis

Simon Hakim
Temple University

Lewis Karstensson
University of Nevada, Las Vegas

Abraham Kidane
California State University, Dominguez Hills

W. Barbara Killen
University of Minnesota

J. David Lages
Southwest Missouri State University

Anthony Lee
Austin Community College

Marjory Mabery
Delaware County Community College

Bernard Malamud
University of Nevada, Las Vegas

Michael Marlow
California Polytechnic State University, San Luis Obispo

Phil J. McLewin
Ramapo College of New Jersey

Tina Quinn
Arkansas State University

Terry Ridgway
University of Nevada, Las Vegas

Paul Snoonian
University of Lowell

Paul Taube
Pan American University

Roger Trenary
Kansas State University

Charles Van Eaton
Hillsdale College

Mark Wheeler
Bowling Green State University

Thomas Wyrick
Southwest Missouri State University

Third Edition Reviewers

Carlos Aguilar
University of Texas, El Paso

Rebecca Ann Benakis
New Mexico State University

Scott Bloom
North Dakota State University

Howard Erdman
Southwest Texas Junior College

Arthur Friedberg
Mohawk Valley Community College

Nancy A. Jianakoplos
Colorado State University

Lewis Karstensson
University of Nevada, Las Vegas

Rose Kilburn
Modesto Junior College

Ruby P. Kishan
Southeastern Community College

Duane Kline
Southeastern Community College

Charles A. Roberts
Western Kentucky University

Bill Robinson
University of Nevada, Las Vegas

Susan C. Stephenson
Drake University

Charles Van Eaton
Hillsdale College

Richard O. Welch
The University of Texas at San Antonio

Calla Wiemer
University of Hawaii at Manoa

Fourth Edition Reviewers

Uzo Agulefo
North Lake College

Kari Battaglia
University of North Texas

Scott Bloom
North Dakota State University

Harry Ellis, Jr.
University of North Texas

Mary Ann Hendryson
Western Washington University

Eugene Jones
Ohio State University

Ki Hoon Him
Central Connecticut State University

James McBrearty
University of Arizona

John A. Panagakis
Onondaga Community College

Bill Robinson
University of Nevada, Las Vegas

George E. Samuels
Sam Houston State University

Ed Scahill
University of Scranton

Charles Van Eaton
Hillsdale College

Thomas Wyrick
Southwest Missouri State University

Fifth Edition Reviewers

Kari Battaglia
University of North Texas

Douglas A. Conway
Mesa Community College

Lee A. Craig
North Carolina State University

Harry Ellis, Jr.
University of North Texas

Joe W. Essuman
University of Wisconsin, Waukesha

Dipak Ghosh
Emporia State University

Shirley J. Gideon
The University of Vermont

Mary Ann Hendryson
Western Washington University

Calvin A. Hoerneman
Delta College

George H. Jones
University of Wisconsin, Rock County

Donald R. Morgan
Monterey Peninsula College

John A. Panagakis
Onondaga Community College

Bill Robinson
University of Nevada, Las Vegas

Steve Robinson
The University of North Carolina at Wilmington

David W. Yoskowitz
Texas Tech University

Sixth Edition Reviewers

Hendrikus J.E.M. Brand
Albion College

Curtis Clarke
Dallas County Community College

Andrea Gorospe
Kent State University, Trumbull

Mehrdad Madresehee
Lycoming College

L. Wayne Plumly
Valdosta State University

Craig Rogers
Canisius College

Uri Simonsohn
Carnegie Mellon University

Philip Sprunger
Lycoming College

Lea Templer
College of the Canyons

Soumya Tohamy
Berry College

Lee Van Scyoc
University of Wisconsin, Oshkosh

Seventh Edition Reviewers

Pam Coates
San Diego Mesa College

Peggy F. Crane
Southwestern College

Richard Croxdale
Austin Community College

Harry Ellis, Jr.
University of North Texas

Craig Gallet
California State University, Sacramento

Kelly George
Embry-Riddle Aeronautical University

Anne-Marie Gilliam
Central Piedmont Community College

Richard C. Schiming
Minnesota State University, Mankato

Lea Templer
College of the Canyons

Jennifer VanGilder
California State University, Bakersfield

William W. Wilkes
Athens State University

Janice Yee
Wartburg College

Eighth Edition Reviewers

Dr. Clive R. Belfied
Queens College, City University of New York

Barry Bomboy
J. Sargeant Reynolds Community College

James Bryan
North Harris Montgomery Community College

Peggy F. Crane
Southwestern College

Richard Croxdale
Austin Community College

Harry Ellis, Jr.
University of North Texas

Kelly George
Embry Riddle Aeronautical University

Alan Kessler
Providence College

Denny Myers
Oklahoma City Community College

Charles Newton
Houston Community College

Ahmad Saranjam
Northeastern University

Jennifer VanGilder, PhD
California State University Bakersfield

Janice Yee
Wartburg College

Ninth Edition Reviewers

Bart Allen
Northern Oklahoma College

Nand Arora
Cleary University

Fathollah Bagheri
University of North Dakota

Mohammad Bajwa
Northampton Community College

Atin Basuchoudhary
Virginia Military Institute

Susan Bell
Seminole Community College

Douglas Campbell
University of Memphis

Franny Chan
Mt. San Antonio College

Stephen B. Davis
Southwest Minnesota State University

William L. Davis
University of Tennessee, Martin

James Dulgeroff
California State University, San Bernandino

Dr. J. Pat Fuller
Brevard Community College

Dr. Robert Garnett
Texas Christian University

Lynde Gilliam
Metropolitan State College of Denver

Judith A. Grenkowicz
Kirtland Community College

Pablo Hernandez
Hollins University

Philip L. Hersch
Wichita State University

Michael Heslop
Northern Virginia Community College (NOVA)

Chandrea Hopkins
College of Lake County

Brian K. Jackson
Oklahoma Wesleyan University

Bun Song Lee
Northwestern State University

Joanne Leoni
Johnson & Wales University

Michael L. Marlow
California Polytechnic State University

Peter Mavrokordatos
Tarrant County Community College

Dominic F. Minadeo
Troy University

Dr. Barbara B. Murray
Baltimore City Community College

Bernard J. Sharkey, Jr.
Louisiana State University

Joe Silverman
MiraCosta College

Martha Stuffler
Irvine Valley College

Vicky Tucker
Lewis University

Mary Louis White
Albright University

I would like to thank Peggy Crane of Southwestern College, who revised the Test Bank, and Jane Himarios of the University of Texas at Arlington, who revised the Instructor's Manual. I owe a dept of gratitude to all the fine and creative people I worked with at South-Western/Cengage Learning. These persons include Jack Calhoun; Alex von Rosenberg; Michael Worls, Executive Editor for Economics; Jennifer Thomas, Senior Developmental Editor; Kim Kusnerak, Senior Content Project Manager; John Carey, Senior Marketing Manager; Michelle Kunkler, Senior Art Director; and Sandee Milewski, Senior Frontlist Buyer.

My deepest debt of gratitude goes to my wife, Sheila, and to my two sons, David, eighteen years old, and Daniel, twenty one years old. They continue to make all my days happy ones.

Roger A. Arnold

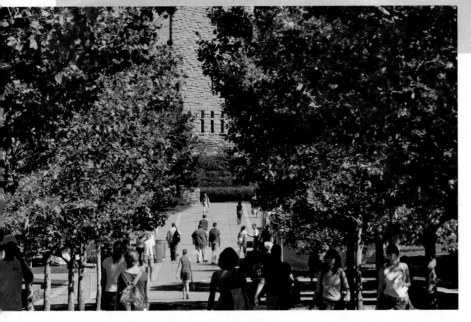

CHAPTER 1

WHAT ECONOMICS IS ABOUT

Introduction You are about to begin your study of economics. Before we start discussing particular topics in economics, we think it best to give you an overview of *what economics is* and of some of the *key concepts* in economics. These key concepts can be compared to musical notes: just as musical notes repeat themselves in any song (you hear the musical note G over and over again), so do the key concepts in economics repeat themselves. Some of the key concepts we discuss include scarcity, opportunity cost, efficiency, marginal decision making, and exchange.

A DEFINITION OF ECONOMICS

In this section, we discuss a few key economic concepts; then we incorporate knowledge of these concepts into a definition of economics.

Goods and Bads

Economists talk about *goods* and *bads*. A **good** is anything that gives a person **utility** or satisfaction. Here is a partial list of some goods: a computer, a car, a watch, a television set, friendship, and love. You will notice from our list that a good can be either tangible or intangible. A computer is a tangible good; friendship is an intangible good. Simply put, for something to be a good (whether tangible or intangible), it simply has to give you utility or satisfaction.

A **bad** is something that gives a person **disutility** or dissatisfaction. If the flu gives you disutility or dissatisfaction, then it is a bad. If the constant nagging of an acquaintance is something that gives you disutility or dissatisfaction, then it is a bad.

People want goods and they do not want bads. In fact, they will pay to get goods ("Here is $1,000 for the computer"), and they will pay to get rid of bads they currently have ("I'd be willing to pay you, doctor, if you can prescribe something that will shorten the time I have the flu").

Good
Anything from which individuals receive utility or satisfaction.

Utility
The satisfaction one receives from a good.

Bad
Anything from which individuals receive disutility or dissatisfaction.

Disutility
The dissatisfaction one receives from a bad.

1

Can something be a *good* for one person and a *bad* for another person? Well, because a good is something that gives one utility and a bad is something that gives one disutility, this question is simply asking whether something can give utility to one person and disutility to another. Can you identify such a thing? What about cigarette smoking? For some people, smoking cigarettes gives them utility; for other people, it gives them disutility. We conclude that smoking cigarettes can be a good for some people and a bad for others. This must be why the wife tells her husband, "If you want to smoke, you should do it outside." In other words, get those *bads* away from me.

Resources

Goods do not just appear before us when we snap our fingers. It takes resources to produce goods. (Sometimes *resources* are referred to as *inputs* or *factors of production*.)

Generally, economists divide resources into four broad categories: *land, labor, capital,* and *entrepreneurship*. **Land** includes natural resources, such as minerals, forests, water, and unimproved land. For example, oil, wood, and animals fall into this category. (Sometimes economists refer to this category simply as *natural resources*.)

Labor consists of the physical and mental talents people contribute to the production process. For example, a person building a house is using his or her own labor.

Capital consists of produced goods that can be used as inputs for further production. Factories, machinery, tools, computers, and buildings are examples of capital. One country might have more capital than another. This means that it has more factories, machinery, tools, and so on.

Entrepreneurship refers to the particular talent that some people have for organizing the resources of land, labor, and capital to produce goods, seek new business opportunities, and develop new ways of doing things.

Scarcity and a Definition of Economics

We are now ready to define a key concept in economics: *scarcity*. **Scarcity** is the condition in which our wants (for goods) are greater than the limited resources (land, labor, capital, and entrepreneurship) available to satisfy those wants. In other words, we want goods, but there are just not enough resources available to provide us with all the goods we want.

Look at it this way: Our wants (for goods) are infinite, but our resources (which we need to produce the goods) are finite. Scarcity is our infinite wants hitting up against finite resources.

Many economists say that if scarcity didn't exist, neither would economics. In other words, if our wants weren't greater than the limited resources available to satisfy them, there would be no field of study called economics. This is similar to saying that if matter and motion didn't exist, neither would physics or that if living things didn't exist, neither would biology. For this reason, we define **economics** in this text as the science of scarcity. More completely, *economics is the science of how individuals and societies deal with the fact that wants are greater than the limited resources available to satisfy those wants.*

Land
All natural resources, such as minerals, forests, water, and unimproved land.

Labor
The physical and mental talents people contribute to the production process.

Capital
Produced goods that can be used as inputs for further production, such as factories, machinery, tools, computers, and buildings.

Entrepreneurship
The particular talent that some people have for organizing the resources of land, labor, and capital to produce goods, seek new business opportunities, and develop new ways of doing things.

Scarcity
The condition in which our wants are greater than the limited resources available to satisfy those wants.

Economics
The science of scarcity; the science of how individuals and societies deal with the fact that wants are greater than the limited resources available to satisfy those wants.

 Thinking like AN ECONOMIST

Scarcity Affects Everyone

Everyone in the world has to face scarcity, even billionaires. Take, for example, Bill Gates, the cofounder of Microsoft and one of the richest people in the world. He may be able to satisfy more of his wants for tangible goods (houses, cars) than most people, but this doesn't mean he has the resources to satisfy all his wants. His wants might include more time with his children, more friendship, no disease in the world, peace on earth, and a hundred other things that he does not have the resources to "produce."

LOST

*L*ost is an ABC television series; the pilot for the show aired on September 22, 2004. The show is about people who have survived a plane crash (Oceanic flight 815) and now inhabit a mysterious tropical island.

The tropical island is unlike any island anyone has ever seen or visited before. We'll show you just how later, but before we do, let's return to our discussion of scarcity, goods, and resources. We know that scarcity is a condition where our wants for goods are greater than the resources available to satisfy those wants.

Now ask: If you didn't need resources to produce goods—if you didn't need *anything* to produce goods—would you have overcome scarcity? Would you have defeated scarcity?

The answer is yes. Obviously the only reason you cannot have all the goods you want is because resources are needed to produce goods, and there are a finite number of resources in the world. Wood is needed to produce a chair, labor is needed to produce a computer, and capital is needed to produce a car. If you didn't need wood, labor, or capital to produce any good—if you didn't need *anything* to produce goods—then you could have all the goods you desire. And if you could have all the goods you desire, you would have defeated or overcome scarcity. Make sense?

With this as background, listen to the words of Ben, one of the characters on *Lost*. In the third season of *Lost*, Episode 13 ("The Man from Tallahassee"), he speaks the following words to John Locke, one of the survivors of the plane crash.

© 2007 AMERICAN BROADCASTING COMPANY, INC.

I can show you things. Things I know you want to see very badly. Let me put it so you'll understand. Picture a box. You know something about boxes, don't you John? What if I told you that somewhere on this island there's a very large box . . . and whatever you imagined . . . whatever you wanted to be in it . . . when you opened that box, there it would be. What would you say about that, John?

They key words are, "there's a very large box . . . and whatever you imagined . . . whatever you wanted to be in it . . . when you opened that box, there it would be." In other words, if you wish for a good—any good—there it will be. You do not have to produce the good, you do not need any resources before you can produce the good. All you have to do is wish for it and "there it would be."

In other words, the box on the *Lost* island is all anyone needs, and then with that box, anything you wish for will be yours. That is a setting in which scarcity is no more. And because scarcity is no more, neither is choice, which is one of the effects of scarcity. There is no need to decide between good X and Y, you can have both. And what about the cost of these goods? Is there a cost to them? Certainly not, for if you don't have to give up one thing to get something else (which is the case in real life), the opportunity cost of what you get is zero. Wishing for X at 10:05 doesn't mean you have given up the chance to get Y, because with a magic box, you can wish for Y at 10:05 and one second.

In conclusion, the *Lost* island is truly an unusual and very different island. It is an island where for some people scarcity, choices, and costs are no more. You just might say that it is a make-believe island.

THINKING IN TERMS OF SCARCITY'S EFFECTS Scarcity has effects. Here are three: (1) the need to make choices, (2) the need for a rationing device, and (3) competition. We describe each.

Choices People have to make choices because of scarcity. Because our unlimited wants are greater than our limited resources, some wants must go unsatisfied. We must choose which wants we will satisfy and which we will not. Jeremy asks: Do I go to Hawaii or do I pay off my car loan earlier? Ellen asks: Do I buy the new sweater or two new shirts?

Rationing Device
A means for deciding who gets what of available resources and goods.

Need for a Rationing Device A **rationing device** is a means of deciding who gets what. It is scarcity that implies the need for a rationing device. If people have infinite wants for goods and there are only limited resources to produce the goods, then a rationing device must be used to decide who gets the available quantity of goods. Dollar price is a rationing device. For example, there are 100 cars on the lot and everyone wants a new car. How do we decide who gets what quantity of the new cars? The answer is "use the rationing device dollar price." Those people who pay the dollar price for the new car end up with a new car.

Is dollar price a fair rationing device? Doesn't it discriminate against the poor? After all, the poor have fewer dollars than the rich, so the rich can get more of what they want than can the poor. True, dollar price does discriminate against the poor. But then, as the economist knows, every rationing device discriminates against someone.

Suppose that dollar price could not be used as a rationing device tomorrow. Some rationing device would still be necessary because scarcity would still exist. How would we ration gas at the gasoline station, food in the grocery store, or tickets for the Super Bowl? Let's consider some alternatives to dollar price as a rationing device.

Suppose first come, first served is the rationing device. For example, suppose there are only 40,000 Super Bowl tickets. If you are one of the first 40,000 in line for a Super Bowl ticket, then you get a ticket. If you are person number 40,001 in line, you don't. Such a method discriminates against those who can't get in line quickly. What about slow walkers or people with a disability? What about people without cars who can't drive to where the tickets are distributed?

Or suppose brute force is the rationing device. For example, if there are 40,000 Super Bowl tickets, then as long as you can take a ticket away from someone who has a ticket, the ticket is yours. Who does this rationing method discriminate against? Obviously, it discriminates against the weak and non-aggressive.

Or suppose beauty is the rationing device. The more beautiful you are, the better your chance of getting a Super Bowl ticket. Again, the rationing device discriminates against someone.

These and many other alternatives to dollar price could be used as a rationing device. However, each discriminates against someone, and none is clearly superior to dollar price.

In addition, if first come, first served, brute force, beauty, or another alternative to dollar price is the rationing device, what incentive would the producer of a good have to produce the good? With dollar price as a rationing device, a person produces computers and sells them for money. He then takes the money and buys what he wants. But if the rationing device were, say, brute force, he would not have an incentive to produce. Why produce anything when someone will end up taking it away from you? In short, in a world where dollar price isn't the rationing device, people are likely to produce much less than in a world where dollar price is the rationing device.

Scarcity and Competition Do you see much competition in the world today? Are people competing for jobs? Are states and cities competing for businesses? Are students competing for grades? The answer to all these questions is yes. The economist wants to know why this competition exists and what form it takes. First, the economist concludes, *competition exists because of scarcity.* If there were enough resources to satisfy all our seemingly unlimited wants, people would not have to compete for the available but limited resources.

Second, the economist sees that competition takes the form of people trying to get more of the rationing device. If dollar price is the rationing device, people will compete to earn dollars. Look at your own case. You are a college student working for a degree. One reason (but perhaps not the only reason) you are attending college is to earn a higher income after graduation. But why do you want a higher income? You want it because it will allow you to satisfy more of your wants.

Suppose muscular strength (measured by lifting weights) were the rationing device instead of dollar price. People with more muscular strength would receive more resources and goods than people with less muscular strength would receive. In this situation, people would compete for muscular strength. (Would they spend more time at the gym lifting weights?) The lesson is simple: *Whatever the rationing device, people will compete for it.*

Finding ECONOMICS

At the Campus Book Store

To learn economics well, you must practice what you learn. One of the ways of "practicing economics" is to find economics in everyday scenes of life. With this in mind, consider the following scene: You are in the campus book store buying a book for your computer science course. You are currently handing over $65 to the cashier. Can you find the economics in this simple scene? Before you read on, think about it for a minute.

Let's work backward to find the economics. You are currently handing the cashier $65. We know that dollar price is a rationing device. But let's now ask ourselves why we would need a rationing device to get the book. The answer is scarcity. In other words, scarcity is casting its long shadow there in the book store when you buy a book. We have found one of the key economic concepts—scarcity—in the campus book store. (If you also said that a book is a good, then you have found even more economics in the book store. Can you find more than scarcity and a good?)

SELF-TEST

(Answers to Self-Test questions are in the Self-Test Appendix.)

1. Scarcity is the condition of finite resources. True or false? Explain your answer.
2. How does competition arise out of scarcity?
3. How does choice arise out of scarcity?

KEY CONCEPTS IN ECONOMICS

There are numerous key concepts in economics—concepts that define the field. We discuss a few of these concepts next.

Opportunity Cost

So far we have established the fact that people must make choices because scarcity exists. In other words, because our seemingly unlimited wants push up against limited resources, some wants must go unsatisfied. We must therefore *choose* which wants we will satisfy and which we will not. The most highly valued opportunity or alternative forfeited when a choice is made is known as **opportunity cost**. Every time you make a choice, you incur an opportunity cost. For example, you have chosen to read this chapter. In making this choice, you denied yourself the benefits of doing something else. You could have watched television, emailed a friend, taken a nap, eaten a few slices of pizza, read a novel, shopped for a new computer, and so on. Whatever you *would have chosen* to do had you decided not to read this chapter is the opportunity cost of your reading this chapter. For example,

Opportunity Cost
The most highly valued opportunity or alternative forfeited when a choice is made.

if you would have watched television had you chosen not to read this chapter—if this was your next best alternative—then the opportunity cost of reading this chapter is watching television.

Common MISCONCEPTIONS

Think "No Free Lunch"

Economists are fond of saying that *there is no such thing as a free lunch*. This catchy phrase expresses the idea that opportunity costs are incurred when choices are made. Perhaps this is an obvious point, but consider how often people mistakenly assume there *is* a free lunch. For example, some parents think education is free because they do not pay tuition for their children to attend public elementary school. Sorry, but that is a misconception. Free implies no sacrifice and no opportunities forfeited, which is not true in regard to elementary school education. Resources that could be used for other things are used to provide elementary school education.

Consider the people who speak about free medical care, free housing, free bridges ("there is no charge to cross it"), and free parks. Sorry, again, but free medical care, free housing, free bridges, and free parks are misconceptions. The resources that provide medical care, housing, bridges, and parks could have been used in other ways.

Opportunity Cost and Behavior

Economists believe that a change in opportunity cost can change a person's behavior. For example, consider Ryan, who is a sophomore at Cornell University in Ithaca, New York. He attends classes Monday through Thursday of every week. Every time he chooses to go to class, he gives up the opportunity to do something else, such as the opportunity to earn $10 an hour working at a job. The opportunity cost of Ryan spending an hour in class is $10.

Now let's raise the opportunity cost of attending class. On Tuesday, we offer Ryan $70 to skip his economics class. He knows that if he attends his economics class, he will forfeit $70. What will Ryan do? An economist would predict that as the opportunity cost of attending class increases relative to the benefits of attending class, Ryan is less likely to attend class.

This is how economists think about behavior, whether it is Ryan's or your own. *The higher the opportunity cost of doing something, the less likely it will be done.* This is part of the economic way of thinking.

Before you continue, look at Exhibit 1, which summarizes some of the things about scarcity, choice, and opportunity cost up to this point.

exhibit 1

Scarcity and Related Concepts

WHY DIDN'T JESSICA ALBA GO TO COLLEGE?

Jessica Alba, the actress, was born on April 28, 1981. After graduating from high school, Jessica Alba chose not to go to college. But why didn't she go to college? It's not because she couldn't get into a college or couldn't afford college. Jessica Alba did not go to college because it was costlier for her to go to college than it is for most 18- to 25-year-olds to attend college.

To understand, think of what it costs you to attend college. If you pay $2,000 tuition a semester for eight semesters, the full tuition amounts to $16,000. However, $16,000 is not the full cost of your attending college because if you were not a student, you could be earning income working at a job. For example, you could be working at a full-time job earning $25,000 annually. Certainly, this $25,000, or at least part of it if you are currently working part time, is forfeited because you attend college. It is part of the cost of your attending college.

Thus, the *tuition* cost may be the same for everyone who attends your college, but the *opportunity cost* is not. Some people have higher opportunity costs for attending college than others do. Jessica Alba had high

© AP PHOTO/MATT SAYLES

opportunity costs for attending college. She would have to give up the income she earned from commericals, TV shows, and movies.

This discussion illustrates two related points made in this chapter. First, *the higher the opportunity cost of doing something, the less likely it will be done.* The opportunity cost of attending college is higher for Jessica Alba than it (probably) is for you, and that is why you are in college and Jessica Alba did not go to college.

Second, according to economists, *individuals think and act in terms of costs and benefits and only undertake actions if they expect the benefits to outweigh the costs.* Jessica Alba was likely to see certain benefits to attending college—just as you see certain benefits to attending college. However, those benefits were insufficient for her to attend college because benefits are not all that matter. Costs matter too. For Jessica Alba, the costs of attending college were much higher than the benefits, and so she chose not to attend college. In your case, the benefits are higher than the costs, and so you have decided to attend college.

Benefits and Costs

If it were possible to eliminate air pollution completely, should all air pollution be eliminated? If your answer is yes, then you are probably focusing on the *benefits* of eliminating air pollution. For example, one benefit might be healthier individuals. Certainly, individuals who do not breathe polluted air have fewer lung disorders than people who do breathe polluted air.

But benefits rarely come without costs. The economist reminds us that although there are benefits to eliminating pollution, there are costs too. To illustrate, one way to eliminate all car pollution tomorrow is to pass a law stating that anyone caught driving a car will go to prison for 40 years. With such a law in place, and enforced, very few people would drive cars, and all car pollution would be a thing of the past. Presto! Cleaner air! However, many people would think that the cost of obtaining that cleaner air is too high. Someone might say, "I want cleaner air, but not if I have to completely give up driving my car. How will I get to work?"

What distinguishes the economist from the non-economist is that the economist thinks in terms of *both* costs *and* benefits. Often, the non-economist thinks in terms of one or the other. There are benefits from studying, but there are costs too. There are benefits from coming to class, but there are costs too. There are costs to getting up early each morning and exercising, but let's not forget that there are benefits too.

Decisions Made at the Margin

It is late at night and you have already studied three hours for your biology test tomorrow. You look at the clock and wonder if you should study another hour. How would you summarize your thinking process? What question or questions do you ask yourself to decide whether or not to study another hour?

Perhaps without knowing it, you think in terms of the costs and benefits of further study. You probably realize that there are certain benefits from studying an additional hour (you may be able to raise your grade a few points), but there are costs too (you will get less sleep or have less time to watch television or talk on the phone with a friend). Thinking in terms of costs and benefits, however, doesn't tell us *how* you think in terms of costs and benefits. For example, when deciding what to do, do you look at the total costs and total benefits of the proposed action, or do you look at something less than the total costs and benefits? According to economists, for most decisions, you think in terms of *additional,* or *marginal,* costs and benefits, not *total* costs and benefits. That's because most decisions deal with making a small, or additional, change.

To illustrate, suppose you just finished eating a hamburger and drinking a soda for lunch. You are still a little hungry and are considering whether or not to order another hamburger. An economist would say that in deciding whether or not to order another hamburger, you will compare the additional benefits of the additional hamburger to the additional costs of the additional hamburger. In economics, the word *marginal* is a synonym for *additional.* So we say that you will compare the **marginal benefits** of the (next) hamburger to the **marginal costs** of the (next) hamburger. If the marginal benefits are greater than the marginal costs, you obviously expect a net benefit to ordering the next hamburger, and therefore, you order the next hamburger. If, however, the marginal benefits are less than the marginal costs, you obviously expect a net cost to ordering the next hamburger, and therefore, you do not order the next hamburger.

Condition	Action
MB of next hamburger > MC of next hamburger	Buy next hamburger
MB of next hamburger < MC of next hamburger	Do not buy next hamburger

What you don't consider when making this decision are the total benefits and total costs of hamburgers. That's because the benefits and costs connected with the first hamburger (the one you have already eaten) are no longer relevant to the current decision. You are not deciding between eating two hamburgers and eating no hamburgers; your decision is whether to eat a second hamburger after you have already eaten a first hamburger.

According to economists, when individuals make decisions by comparing marginal benefits to marginal costs, they are making **decisions at the margin**. The president of the United States makes a decision at the margin when deciding whether or not to talk another 10 minutes with the speaker of the House of Representatives, the employee makes a decision at the margin when deciding whether or not to work two hours overtime, and the economics professor makes a decision at the margin when deciding whether or not to put an additional question on the final exam.

Efficiency

What is the right amount of time to study for a test? In economics, the "right amount" of anything is the "optimal" or "efficient" amount, and the efficient amount is the amount

Marginal Benefits
Additional benefits. The benefits connected to consuming an additional unit of a good or undertaking one more unit of an activity.

Marginal Costs
Additional costs. The costs connected to consuming an additional unit of a good or undertaking one more unit of an activity.

Decisions at the Margin
Decision making characterized by weighing the additional (marginal) benefits of a change against the additional (marginal) costs of a change with respect to current conditions.

for which the marginal benefits equal the marginal costs. Stated differently, you have achieved **efficiency** when the marginal benefits equal the marginal costs.

Suppose you are studying for an economics test, and for the first hour of studying, the marginal benefits (*MB*) are greater than the marginal costs (*MC*):

$$MB \text{ studying first hour} > MC \text{ studying first hour}$$

Given this condition, you will certainly study for the first hour. After all, it is worthwhile: The additional benefits are greater than the additional costs, so there is a net benefit to studying.

Suppose for the second hour of studying, the marginal benefits are still greater than the marginal costs:

$$MB \text{ studying second hour} > MC \text{ studying second hour}$$

You will study for the second hour because the additional benefits are still greater than the additional costs. In other words, it is worthwhile studying the second hour. In fact, you will continue to study as long as the marginal benefits are greater than the marginal costs. Exhibit 2 graphically illustrates this discussion.

The marginal benefit (*MB*) curve of studying is downward sloping because we have assumed that the benefits of studying for the first hour are greater than the benefits of studying for the second hour and so on. The marginal cost (*MC*) curve of studying is upward sloping because we assume that it costs a person more (in terms of goods forfeited) to study the second hour than the first, more to study the third than the second, and so on. (If we assume the additional costs of studying are constant over time, the *MC* curve is horizontal.)

In the exhibit, the marginal benefits of studying equal the marginal costs at three hours. So three hours is the efficient length of time to study in this situation. At fewer than three hours, the marginal benefits of studying are greater than the marginal costs; thus, at all these hours, there are net benefits from studying. At more than three hours, the marginal

Efficiency
Exists when marginal benefits equal marginal costs.

Efficiency

MB = marginal benefits and *MC* = marginal costs. In the exhibit, the *MB* curve of studying is downward sloping and the *MC* curve of studying is upward sloping. As long as *MB* > *MC*, the person will study. The person stops studying when *MB* = *MC*. This is where efficiency is achieved.

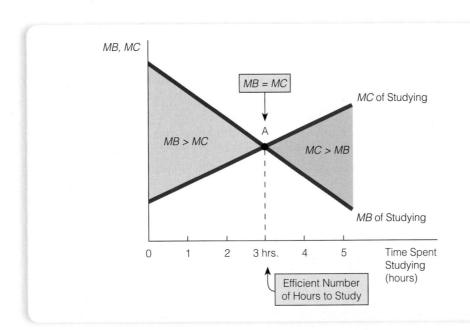

costs of studying are greater than the marginal benefits, and so it wouldn't be worthwhile to study beyond three hours.

MAXIMIZING NET BENEFITS Take another look at Exhibit 2. Suppose you had stopped studying after the first hour (or after the 60th minute). Would you have given up anything? Yes, you would have given up the net benefits of studying longer. To illustrate, notice that between the first and the second hour, the marginal benefits (*MB*) curve lies above the marginal costs (*MC*) curve. This means there are net benefits to studying the second hour. But if you hadn't studied that second hour—if you had stopped after the first hour—then you would have given up the opportunity to collect those net benefits. The same analysis holds for the third hour. We conclude that by studying three hours (but not one minute longer), you have maximized net benefits. In short, efficiency (which is consistent with *MB* = *MC*) is also consistent with maximizing net benefits.

Thinking like AN ECONOMIST

No $10 Bills on the Sidewalk

An economist says that people try to maximize their net benefits. You ask for proof. The economist says, "You don't find any $10 bills on the sidewalk." What is the economist getting at by making this statement? Well, keep in mind that the reason you don't find any $10 bills on the sidewalk is because if there were a $10 bill on the sidewalk, the first person to see it would pick it up, so that when you came along it wouldn't be there. But why would the first person to find the $10 bill pick it up? Because people don't pass by net benefits, and picking up the $10 bill comes with net benefits. The *benefits* of having an additional $10 are obvious; the *costs* of obtaining the additional $10 bill are simply what you give up during the time you are stooping down to pick it up. In short, the marginal benefits are likely to be greater than the marginal costs (giving us net benefits) and that is why the $10 bill is picked up. Saying there are no $10 bills on the sidewalk is the same as saying no one leaves net benefits on the sidewalk; instead, people try to maximize net benefits.

Unintended Effects

Economists think in terms of unintended effects. Consider an example. Andres, 16 years old, currently works after school at a grocery store. He earns $6.50 an hour. Suppose the state legislature passes a law specifying that the minimum dollar wage a person can be paid to do a job is $8.50 an hour. The legislators' intention in passing the law is to help people like Andres earn more income.

Will the $8.50 an hour legislation have the intended effect? Perhaps not. The manager of the grocery store may not find it worthwhile to continue employing Andres if she has to pay him $8.50 an hour. In other words, Andres may have a job at $6.50 an hour but not at $8.50 an hour. If the law specifies that no one will earn less than $8.50 an hour and the manager of the grocery store decides to fire Andres rather than pay this amount, then an unintended effect of the $8.50 an hour legislation is Andres' losing his job.

As another example, let's analyze mandatory seatbelt laws to see if they have any unintended effects. States have laws that require drivers to wear seatbelts. The intended effect is to reduce the number of car fatalities by making it more likely drivers will survive an accident.

Could these laws have an unintended effect? Some economists think so. They look at accident fatalities in terms of this equation:

Total number of fatalities = Number of accidents × Fatalities per accident

For example, if there are 200,000 accidents and 0.10 fatalities per accident, the total number of fatalities is 20,000.

The objective of a mandatory seatbelt program is to reduce the total number of fatalities by reducing the fatalities per accident. Many studies have found that wearing seatbelts does just this. If you are in an accident, you have a better chance of not being killed if you are wearing a seatbelt.

Let's assume that with seatbelts, there are 0.08 instead of 0.10 fatalities per accident. If there are still 200,000 accidents, this means that the total number of fatalities falls from 20,000 to 16,000. Thus, there is a drop in the total number of fatalities if fatalities per accident are reduced and the number of accidents is constant.

Number of Accidents	Fatalities per Accident	Total Number of Fatalities
200,000	0.10	20,000
200,000	0.08	16,000

However, some economists wonder if the number of accidents stays constant. Specifically, they suggest that seatbelts may have an unintended effect: *The number of accidents may increase.* This happens because wearing seatbelts may make drivers feel safer. Feeling safer may cause them to take chances that they wouldn't ordinarily take—such as driving faster or more aggressively, or concentrating less on their driving and more on the music on the radio. For example, if the number of accidents rises to 250,000, then the total number of fatalities is 20,000.

Number of Accidents	Fatalities per Accident	Total Number of Fatalities
200,000	0.10	20,000
250,000	0.08	20,000

We conclude the following: If a mandatory seatbelt law reduces the number of fatalities per accident (intended effect) but increases the number of accidents (unintended effect), it may, contrary to popular belief, not reduce the total number of fatalities. In fact, some economic studies show just this.

What does all this mean for you? You may be safer if you know that this unintended effect exists and you adjust accordingly. To be specific, when you wear your seatbelt, your chances of getting hurt in a car accident are less than if you don't wear your seatbelt. But if this added sense of protection causes you to drive less carefully than you would otherwise, then you could unintentionally offset the measure of protection your seatbelt provides. To reduce the probability of hurting yourself and others in a car accident, *the best policy is to wear a seatbelt and to drive as carefully as you would if you weren't wearing a seatbelt.* Knowing about the unintended effect of wearing your seatbelt could save your life.

Exchange

Exchange or **trade** is the process of giving up one thing for something else. Economics is sometimes called the "science of exchange" because so much that is discussed in economics has to do with exchange.

We start with a basic question: Why do people enter into exchanges? The answer is that they do so to make themselves better off. When a person voluntarily trades $100 for a jacket, she is saying, "I prefer to have the jacket instead of the $100." And of course, when the seller of the jacket voluntarily sells the jacket for $100, he is saying, "I prefer to have the $100 instead of the jacket." In short, through trade or exchange, each person gives up something he or she values less for something he or she values more.

Exchange (Trade)
The process of giving up one thing for another.

ECONOMICS IN A COSMETIC SURGEON'S OFFICE?

According to the American Society for Aesthetic Plastic Surgery, cosmetic surgery is on the rise. In 1997, there were approximately 2.09 million surgical and non-surgical cosmetic procedures. In 2005, that number had risen to 11.42 million procedures. If we consider only surgical cosmetic procedures, the number was 972,996 in 1997, rising to 2.1 million in 2005. In 2006, the top five surgical cosmetic procedures (in order) were lipoplasty (liposuction), breast augmentation, eyelid surgery, rhinoplasty (nose reshaping), and abdominoplasty (tummy tuck). The top non-surgical procedure: Botox® injections.

But enough of the facts and figures of cosmetic surgery. In this chapter we have discussed a few key economic concepts. One way to test how many of these concepts we are learning is to try to find them in different settings. You are in a store buying a shirt. How many economic concepts can you find in the store? You are driving to work. How many economic concepts can you find on your drive? Or, as we have done here, someone has just brought up the subject of cosmetic surgery. How many economic concepts can you find that are relevant to cosmetic surgery?

One thing is that cosmetic surgery gives some people utility, so for those persons it is a good. (Could cosmetic surgery ever be a bad? Well, it might be if the surgery does not turn out the way a person intended.)

We know that goods do not fall from the sky, just waiting to be picked up. It takes resources to produce a good. What resources are needed to produce cosmetic surgery? Certainly there is the surgeon's labor and his or her use of some capital goods (such as scalpels).

Does cosmetic surgery have anything to do with rationing devices? People usually get cosmetic surgery to improve their appearance. But why would people want to improve their appearance? One reason might be to feel better about themselves. Another could be to use their improved looks to get more of what they may want in life. Whether it's true or not, if they believe that only the best looking people get into the entertainment industry, or only the best looking people get the job promotions, or only the best looking people get the choice of whom they will date, then cosmetic surgery might be the means for them to get what they want, in much the same way that money (a definite rationing device) might be necessary to buy a computer, a car, or a vacation to Barbados.

Is there an opportunity cost to cosmetic surgery? Whatever would have been done with the money paid for the surgery, and whatever would be done with the time spent during the surgery and recovery constitutes the opportunity cost of the cosmetic surgery.

How might benefits and costs be relevant to surgery? Probably no one undertakes cosmetic surgery unless he or she believes the benefits will be greater than the costs.

What about the economic concept of exchange or trade? The person getting the cosmetic surgery turns over dollars to the cosmetic surgeon and in return the cosmetic surgeon performs lipoplasty, rhinoplasty, or some other procedure on that person. The person getting the cosmetic surgery implicitly says through his actions that he values the cosmetic procedure more than the money he pays, and the cosmetic surgeon obviously values the money more than the time and labor he has to expend to perform the surgery.

Finally, consider the economic concept of efficiency. In this chapter we learned that efficiency has to do with the marginal benefits and the marginal costs of an activity. The efficient amount of an activity is that amount at which the marginal benefits of the activity equal the marginal costs. Obviously, the efficient amount of the activity will change as the marginal benefits and/or marginal costs change. For example, if you raise the marginal benefits of studying, and the marginal costs remain constant, the efficient amount of studying will rise.

Earlier in this feature we learned that the number of cosmetic procedures is on the rise. While the number of surgical and non-surgical cosmetic procedures was 2.09 million in 1997 that number had risen to 11.42 procedures in 2005. Either the marginal benefits of cosmetic procedures had risen during this time, or the marginal costs had fallen, or both had changed in the stated directions.

Some persons have suggested that the main variable that has changed is the marginal cost of cosmetic surgery. It has fallen during the time period specified earlier. Not in dollar terms, but in terms of how acceptable cosmetic surgery has become. Consumer surveys show that over time cosmetic surgery has become more acceptable, as evidenced by the number of surveyed persons who say they would "not be embarrassed" to have cosmetic surgery. In 2006, 82 percent of women and 79 percent of men said that they would have cosmetic surgery if they felt they needed it.

You can think of trade in terms of utility or satisfaction. Imagine a utility scale that goes from 1 to 10, with 10 being the highest utility you can achieve. Now suppose you currently have $40 in your wallet and you are at 7 on the utility scale. A few minutes later, you are in a store looking at some new CDs. The price of each is $10. You end up buying four CDs for $40.

Before you made the trade, you were at 7 on the utility scale. Are you still at 7 on the utility scale after you traded your $40 for the four CDs? The likely answer is no. If you expected to have the same utility after the trade as you did before, it is unlikely you would have traded your $40 for the four CDs. The only reason you entered into the trade is that you *expected* to be better off after the trade than you were before the trade. In other words, you thought trading your $40 for the four CDs would move you up the utility scale from 7 to, say, 8.

SELF-TEST

1. Give an example to illustrate how a change in opportunity cost can affect behavior.

2. There are both costs and benefits of studying. If you continue to study (say, for a test) as long as the marginal benefits of studying are greater than the marginal costs and stop studying when the two are equal, will your action be consistent with having maximized the net benefits of studying? Explain your answer.

3. You stay up an added hour to study for a test. The intended effect is to raise your test grade. What might be an unintended effect of staying up an added hour to study for the test?

ECONOMIC CATEGORIES

Economics is sometimes broken down into different categories according to the type of questions economists ask. Four common economic categories are positive economics, normative economics, microeconomics, and macroeconomics.

Positive and Normative Economics

Positive economics attempts to determine *what is*. **Normative economics** addresses *what should be*. Essentially, positive economics deals with cause-effect relationships that can be tested. Normative economics deals with value judgments and opinions that cannot be tested.

Many topics in economics can be discussed within both a positive framework and a normative framework. Consider a proposed cut in federal income taxes. An economist practicing positive economics would want to know the *effect* of a cut in income taxes. For example, she may want to know how a tax cut will affect the unemployment rate, economic growth, inflation, and so on. An economist practicing normative economics would address issues that directly or indirectly relate to whether the federal income tax *should* be cut. For example, she may say that federal income taxes should be cut because the income tax burden on many taxpayers is currently high.

This book mainly deals with positive economics. For the most part, we discuss the economic world as it is, not the way someone might think it should be. Keep in mind, too, that no matter what your normative objectives are, positive economics can shed some light on how they might be accomplished. For example, suppose you believe that absolute poverty should be eliminated and the unemployment rate should be lowered. No doubt you have ideas as to how these goals can be accomplished. But will your ideas work? For example, will a greater redistribution of income eliminate absolute poverty? Will lowering taxes lower the unemployment rate? There is no guarantee that the means

Positive Economics
The study of "what is" in economic matters.

Normative Economics
The study of "what should be" in economic matters.

you think will bring about certain ends will do so. This is where sound positive economics can help. It helps us see what is. As someone once said, "It is not enough to want to do good; it is important also to know how to do good."

Microeconomics and Macroeconomics

It has been said that the tools of microeconomics are microscopes, and the tools of macroeconomics are telescopes. Macroeconomics stands back from the trees to see the forest. Microeconomics gets up close and examines the tree itself, its bark, its limbs, and its roots. **Microeconomics** is the branch of economics that deals with human behavior and choices as they relate to relatively small units—an individual, a firm, an industry, a single market. **Macroeconomics** is the branch of economics that deals with human behavior and choices as they relate to an entire economy. In microeconomics, economists discuss a single price; in macroeconomics, they discuss the price level. Microeconomics deals with the demand for a particular good or service; macroeconomics deals with aggregate, or total, demand for goods and services. Microeconomics examines how a tax change affects a single firm's output; macroeconomics looks at how a tax change affects an entire economy's output.

Microeconomists and macroeconomists ask different types of questions. A microeconomist might be interested in answering such questions as:

- How does a market work?
- What level of output does a firm produce?
- What price does a firm charge for the good it produces?
- How does a consumer determine how much of a good he or she will buy?
- Can government policy affect business behavior?
- Can government policy affect consumer behavior?

On the other hand, a macroeconomist might be interested in answering such questions as:

- How does the economy work?
- Why is the unemployment rate sometimes high and sometimes low?
- What causes inflation?
- Why do some national economies grow faster than other national economies?
- What might cause interest rates to be low one year and high the next?
- How do changes in the money supply affect the economy?
- How do changes in government spending and taxes affect the economy?

Microeconomics
The branch of economics that deals with human behavior and choices as they relate to relatively small units—an individual, a firm, an industry, a single market.

Macroeconomics
The branch of economics that deals with human behavior and choices as they relate to highly aggregate markets (e.g., the goods and services market) or the entire economy.

"I DON'T BELIEVE THAT EVERY TIME A PERSON DOES SOMETHING, HE COMPARES THE MARGINAL BENEFITS AND COSTS"

Student:

In class yesterday you said that individuals compare the marginal benefits (*MB*) of doing something (say, exercising) with the marginal costs (*MC*), and if the marginal benefits are greater than the marginal costs, they exercise; but if the marginal costs are greater than the marginal benefits, they don't. Here is what I am having a problem with: I don't believe that every time a person does something, he compares the marginal benefits and costs. I think people do some things without thinking of benefits and costs; they do some things instinctively or because they have always done them.

Instructor:

Can you give an example?

Student:

I don't think of the benefits and costs of eating breakfast in the morning, I just eat breakfast. I don't think of the benefits and costs of doing my homework, I just do the homework before it is due. For me, so many of my activities are automatic; I do them without thinking.

Instructor:

It doesn't necessarily follow that you are not considering benefits and costs when you do something automatically. All you have to do is "sense" whether doing something comes with net benefits (benefits greater than costs) or net costs (costs greater than benefits); all you have to do is "sense" whether something is likely to make you better off or worse off. You eat breakfast in the morning because you have "decided" that it makes you better off. But making you better off is no different than saying that you receive net benefits from eating breakfast, which is no different than saying that the benefits of eating breakfast are greater than the costs. In other words, better off = net benefits = benefits greater than costs.

Student:

I see what you're saying. But then how would you explain the fact that Smith smokes cigarettes and Jones does not. If both Smith and Jones consider the benefits and costs of smoking cigarettes, then it seems that both would have to either smoke, or both would have to not smoke. The fact that different people do different things tells me that not everyone is considering the costs and benefits of their actions, because if everyone did consider the costs and benefits of their actions, they would all do the same thing.

Instructor:

I disagree. Not everyone sees the costs and benefits of the same thing the same way. Jim and Bob may not see the benefits or costs of smoking the same way. For Jim, the benefits of smoking may be high, but for Bob they may be low. It is no different than saying different people estimate the benefits of playing chess, or eating a doughnut, or riding a bicycle differently. The same holds for costs. Not everyone will estimate the costs of playing chess, or eating a doughnut, or riding a bicycle the same way. The costs of a person with diabetes eating a doughnut are much higher than the costs of a person without diabetes eating a doughnut.

Student:

Let me see if I have this right. You are making two points. First, not everyone has the same benefits and costs of, say, running a mile. Second, everyone who does run a mile believes the benefits are greater than the costs and everyone who does not run a mile believes the costs are greater than the benefits.

Instructor:

Yes, that's it. It is really no different than saying that everybody is trying to make himself better off (reap net benefits), but not everybody will do X because not everybody will be made better off by doing X.

Points to Remember

1. If you undertake those actions for which you expect to receive net benefits, then you are "thinking" in terms of costs and benefits. Specifically, you expect the marginal benefits to be greater than the marginal costs.

2. The costs and benefits of doing any activity are not necessarily the same for everybody. Smith may expect higher benefits than Jones when it comes to doing X; Jones may expect higher costs than Smith when it comes to doing X.

a reader asks | What's in Store for an Economics Major?

This is my first course in economics. The material is interesting, and I have given some thought to majoring in economics. Please tell me something about the major and about job prospects for an economics graduate. What courses do economics majors take? What is the starting salary of economics graduates? Do the people who run large companies think highly of people who have majored in economics?

If you major in economics, you will certainly not be alone. Economics is one of the top majors at Yale, Harvard, Brown, the University of California at Berkeley, Princeton, Columbia, Cornell, Dartmouth, and Stanford. For the 2003–2004 academic year, the number of economics degrees granted by U.S. colleges and universities increased 40 percent from five years previously.

The popularity of economics is probably based on two major reasons. First, many people find economics an interesting course of study. Second, what you learn in an economics course is relevant and applicable to the real world.

Do executives who run successful companies think highly of economics majors? Well, a *BusinessWeek* survey found that economics was the second favorite undergraduate major of chief executive officers (CEOs) of major corporations. Engineering was their favorite undergraduate major.

An economics major usually takes a wide variety of economics courses, starting with introductory courses—principles of microeconomics and principles of macroeconomics—and then studying intermediate microeconomics and intermediate macroeconomics. Upper division electives usually include such courses as public finance, international economics, law and economics, managerial economics, labor economics, health economics, money and banking, environmental economics, public choice, and more.

According to the National Association of Colleges and Employers Salary Survey in Summer 2007, the average starting salary for a college graduate in economics was $48,483. For a college graduate in finance, the average starting salary was $47,239, and for a college graduate in accounting, the average starting salary was $46,718. The average starting salary for a college graduate in computer science was $53,396.

Finally, in the June 16, 2008, edition of *Forbes* magazine, an article reported on median salary by undergraduate major. The second highest median salary by major was economics (computer engineering was the first). Specifically, after 10–20 years of work experience, the median salary for persons who had majored in economics at college was higher than for persons who had completed a major in the following areas: electricial engineering, computer science, mechanical engineering, finance, mathematics, civil engineering, political science, marketing, accounting, history, business management, communications, english, biology, sociology, graphic design, psychology, and criminal justice.

Chapter Summary

GOODS, BADS, AND RESOURCES

- A good is anything that gives a person utility or satisfaction.
- A bad is anything that gives a person disutility or dissatisfaction.
- Economists divide resources into four categories: land, labor, capital, and entrepreneurship.
- Land includes natural resources, such as minerals, forests, water, and unimproved land.
- Labor refers to the physical and mental talents that people contribute to the production process.

- Capital consists of produced goods that can be used as inputs for further production, such as machinery, tools, computers, trucks, buildings, and factories.
- Entrepreneurship refers to the particular talent that some people have for organizing the resources of land, labor, and capital to produce goods, seek new business opportunities, and develop new ways of doing things.

SCARCITY

- Scarcity is the condition in which our wants are greater than the limited resources available to satisfy them.

- Scarcity implies choice. In a world of limited resources, we must choose which wants will be satisfied and which will go unsatisfied.

- Because of scarcity, there is a need for a rationing device. A rationing device is a means of deciding who gets what quantities of the available resources and goods.

- Scarcity implies competition. If there were enough resources to satisfy all our seemingly unlimited wants, people would not have to compete for the available but limited resources.

OPPORTUNITY COST

- Every time a person makes a choice, he or she incurs an opportunity cost. Opportunity cost is the most highly valued opportunity or alternative forfeited when a choice is made. The higher the opportunity cost of doing something, the less likely it will be done.

COSTS AND BENEFITS

- What distinguishes the economist from the non-economist is that the economist thinks in terms of *both* costs and benefits. Asked what the benefits of taking a walk may be, an economist will also mention the costs of taking a walk. Asked what the costs of studying are, an economist will also point out the benefits of studying.

DECISIONS MADE AT THE MARGIN

- Marginal benefits and costs are not the same as total benefits and costs. When deciding whether to talk on the phone one more minute, an individual would not consider the total benefits and total costs of speaking on the phone. Instead, the individual would compare only the marginal benefits (additional benefits) of talking on the phone one more minute to the marginal costs (additional costs) of talking on the phone one more minute.

EFFICIENCY

- As long as the marginal benefits of an activity are greater than its marginal costs, a person gains by continuing to do the activity—whether the activity is studying, running, eating, or watching television. The net benefits of an activity are maximized when the marginal benefits of the activity equal its marginal costs. Efficiency exists at this point.

UNINTENDED EFFECTS

- Economists often think in terms of causes and effects. Effects may include both intended effects and unintended effects. Economists want to denote both types of effects when speaking of effects in general.

EXCHANGE

- Exchange or trade is the process of giving up one thing for something else. People enter into exchanges to make themselves better off.

ECONOMIC CATEGORIES

- Positive economics attempts to determine what is; normative economics addresses what should be.

- Microeconomics deals with human behavior and choices as they relate to relatively small units—an individual, a firm, an industry, a single market. Macroeconomics deals with human behavior and choices as they relate to an entire economy.

Key Terms and Concepts

Good	Capital	Marginal Benefits	Normative Economics
Utility	Entrepreneurship	Marginal Costs	Microeconomics
Bad	Scarcity	Decisions at the Margin	Macroeconomics
Disutility	Economics	Efficiency	
Land	Rationing Device	Exchange (Trade)	
Labor	Opportunity Cost	Positive Economics	

Questions and Problems

1 The United States is considered a rich country because Americans can choose from an abundance of goods and services. How can there be scarcity in a land of abundance?

2 Give two examples for each of the following: (a) an intangible good, (b) a tangible good, (c) a bad.

3 Give an example of something that is a good for one person and a bad for someone else.

4 What is the difference between the resource labor and the resource entrepreneurship?

5 Can either scarcity or one of the effects of scarcity be found in a car dealership? Explain your answer.

6 Explain the link between scarcity and each of the following: (a) choice, (b) opportunity cost, (c) the need for a rationing device, (d) competition.

7 Is it possible for a person to incur an opportunity cost without spending any money? Explain.

8 Discuss the opportunity costs of attending college for four years. Is college more or less costly than you thought it was? Explain.

9 Explain the relationship between changes in opportunity cost and changes in behavior.

10 Smith says that we should eliminate all pollution in the world. Jones disagrees. Who is more likely to be an economist, Smith or Jones? Explain your answer.

11 A friend pays for your lunch. Is this an example of a "free lunch"? Why or why not?

12 A layperson says that a proposed government project simply costs too much and therefore shouldn't be undertaken. How might an economist's evaluation be different?

13 Economists say that individuals make decisions at the margin. What does this mean?

14 How would an economist define the efficient amount of time spent playing tennis?

15 Ivan stops studying before the point at which his marginal benefits of studying equal his marginal costs. Is Ivan forfeiting any net benefits? Explain your answer.

16 What does an economist mean if she says there are no $10 bills on the sidewalk?

17 A change in X will lead to a change in Y; the predicted change is desirable, so we should change X. Do you agree or disagree? Explain.

18 Why do people enter into exchanges?

19 When two individuals enter an exchange, you can be sure that one person benefits and the other person loses. Do you agree or disagree with this statement? Explain your answer.

20 What is the difference between positive economics and normative economics? between microeconomics and macroeconomics?

21 Would there be a need for a rationing device if scarcity did not exist? Explain your answer.

22 Jackie's alarm clock buzzes. She reaches over to the small table next to her bed and turns it off. As she pulls the covers back up, Jackie thinks about her 8:30 American history class. Should she go to the class today or sleep a little longer? She worked late last night and really hasn't had enough sleep. Besides, she's fairly sure her professor will be discussing a subject she already knows well. Maybe it would be okay to miss class today. Is Jackie more likely to miss some classes than she is to miss other classes? What determines which classes Jackie will attend and which classes she won't attend?

23 If you found $10 bills on the sidewalk regularly, we might then conclude that individuals don't try to maximize net benefits. Do you agree or disagree with this statement? Explain your answer.

24 The person who smokes cigarettes cannot possibly be thinking in terms of costs and benefits because it has been proven that cigarette smoking increases one's chances of getting lung cancer. Do you agree or disagree with the part of the statement that reads "the person who smokes cigarettes cannot possibly be thinking in terms of costs and benefits"? Explain your answer.

25 Janice decides to go out on a date with Kyle instead of Robert. Do you think Janice is using some kind of "rationing device" to decide who she dates? If so, what might that rationing device be?

WORKING WITH DIAGRAMS

A picture is worth a thousand words. With this familiar saying in mind, economists construct their diagrams or graphs. With a few lines and a few points, much can be conveyed.

TWO-VARIABLE DIAGRAMS

Most of the diagrams in this book represent the relationship between two variables. Economists compare two variables to see how a change in one variable affects the other variable.

Suppose our two variables of interest are *consumption* and *income.* We want to show how consumption changes as income changes. Suppose we collect the data in Table 1. By simply looking at the data in the first two columns, we can see that as income rises (column 1), consumption rises (column 2). Suppose we want to show the relationship between income and consumption on a graph. We could place *income* on the horizontal axis, as in Exhibit 1, and *consumption* on the vertical axis. Point A represents income of $0 and consumption of $60, point B represents income of $100 and consumption of $120, and so on. If we draw a straight line through the various points we have plotted, we have a picture of the relationship between income and consumption, based on the data we collected.

Notice that our line in Exhibit 1 slopes upward from left to right. Thus, as income rises, so does consumption. For example, as you move from point A to point B, income rises from $0 to $100 and consumption rises from $60 to $120. The line in Exhibit 1 also shows that as income falls, so does consumption. For example, as you move from point C to point B, income falls from $200 to $100 and consumption falls from $180 to $120. When two variables—such as consumption and income—change in the same way, they are said to be **directly related**.

Now let's take a look at the data in Table 2. Our two variables are *price of compact discs (CDs)* and *quantity demanded of CDs.* By simply looking at the data in the first two columns, we see that as price falls (column 1), quantity demanded rises (column 2).

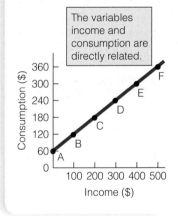
table 1

(1) When Income Is:	(2) Consumption Is:	(3) Point
$ 0	$ 60	A
100	120	B
200	180	C
300	240	D
400	300	E
500	360	F

table 2

(1) When Price of CDs Is:	(2) Quantity Demanded of CDs Is:	(3) Point
$20	100	A
18	120	B
16	140	C
14	160	D
12	180	E

Inversely Related
Two variables are inversely related if they change in opposite ways.

Independent
Two variables are independent if as one changes, the other does not.

Slope
The ratio of the change in the variable on the vertical axis to the change in the variable on the horizontal axis.

exhibit 2

A Two-Variable Diagram Representing an Inverse Relationship

In this exhibit, we have plotted the data in Table 2 and then connected the points with a straight line. The data represent an inverse relationship: as one variable (price) falls, the other variable (quantity demanded) rises.

The variables price and quantity demanded are inversely related.

Suppose we want to plot these data. We could place *price* (of CDs) on the vertical axis, as in Exhibit 2, and *quantity demanded* (of CDs) on the horizontal axis. Point A represents a price of $20 and a quantity demanded of 100, point B represents a price of $18 and a quantity demanded of 120, and so on. If we draw a straight line through the various points we have plotted, we have a picture of the relationship between price and quantity demanded, based on the data in Table 2.

Notice that as price falls, quantity demanded rises. For example, as price falls from $20 to $18, quantity demanded rises from 100 to 120. Also as price rises, quantity demanded falls. For example, when price rises from $12 to $14, quantity demanded falls from 180 to 160.

When two variables—such as price and quantity demanded—change in opposite ways, they are said to be **inversely related**.

As you have seen so far, variables may be directly related (when one increases, the other also increases), or they may be inversely related (when one increases, the other decreases). Variables can also be **independent** of each other. This condition exists if as one variable changes, the other does not.

In Exhibit 3(a), as the X variable rises, the Y variable remains the same (at 20). Obviously, the X and Y variables are independent of each other: as one changes, the other does not.

In Exhibit 3(b), as the Y variable rises, the X variable remains the same (at 30). Again, we conclude that the X and Y variables are independent of each other: as one changes, the other does not.

SLOPE OF A LINE

It is often important not only to know *how* two variables are related but also to know *how much* one variable changes as the other variable changes. To find out, we need only calculate the slope of the line. The **slope** is the ratio of the change in the variable on the vertical axis to the change in the variable on the horizontal axis. For example, if Y is on the vertical axis and X on the horizontal axis, the slope is equal to $\Delta Y/\Delta X$. (The symbol "Δ" means "change in.")

$$\text{Slope} = \frac{\Delta Y}{\Delta X}$$

Exhibit 4 shows four lines. In each case, we have calculated the slope. After studying (a)–(d), see if you can calculate the slope in each case.

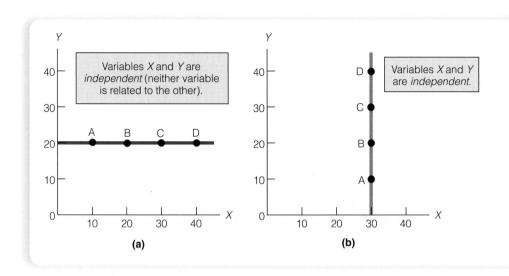

exhibit 3

Two Diagrams Representing Independence Between Two Variables

In (a) and (b), the variables X and Y are independent: as one changes, the other does not.

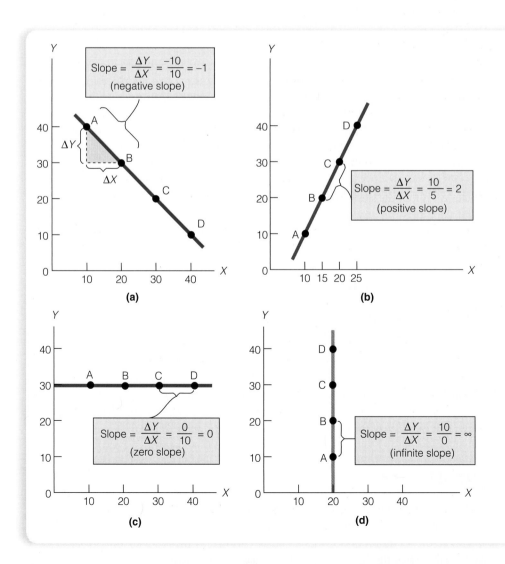

exhibit 4

Calculating Slopes

The slope of a line is the ratio of the change in the variable on the vertical axis to the change in the variable on the horizontal axis. In (a)–(d), we have calculated the slope.

Calculating the Slope of a Curve at a Particular Point

The slope of the curve at point A is 0.67. This is calculated by drawing a line tangent to the curve at point A and then determining the slope of the line.

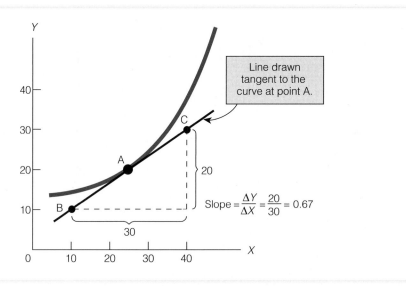

SLOPE OF A LINE IS CONSTANT

Look again at the line in Exhibit 4(a). We computed the slope between points A and B and found it to be −1. Suppose that instead of computing the slope between points A and B, we had computed the slope between points B and C or between points C and D. Would the slope still be −1? Let's compute the slope between points B and C. Moving from point B to point C, the change in Y is −10 and the change in X is +10. So the slope is −1, which is what the slope was between points A and B.

Now let's compute the slope between points A and D. Moving from point A to point D, the change in Y is −30 and the change in X is +30. Again the slope is −1. Our conclusion is that the slope between any two points on a (straight) line is always the same as the slope between any other two points. To see this for yourself, compute the slope between points A and B and between points A and C using the line in Exhibit 4(b).

The 45-Degree Line

Any point on the 45-degree line is equidistant from each axis. For example, point A is the same distance from the vertical axis as it is from the horizontal axis.

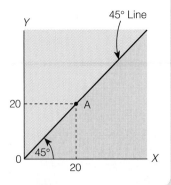

SLOPE OF A CURVE

Economic graphs use both straight lines and curves. The slope of a curve is not constant throughout as it is for a straight line. The slope of a curve varies from one point to another.

Calculating the slope of a curve at a given point requires two steps, as illustrated for point A in Exhibit 5. First, draw a line tangent to the curve at the point (a tangent line is one that just touches the curve but does not cross it). Second, pick any two points on the tangent line and determine the slope. In Exhibit 5 the slope of the line between points B and C is 0.67. It follows that the slope of the curve at point A (and only at point A) is 0.67.

THE 45-DEGREE LINE

Economists sometimes use a *45-degree line* to represent data. This is a straight line that bisects the right angle formed by the intersection of the vertical and horizontal axes (see Exhibit 6). As a result, the 45-degree line divides the space enclosed by the two axes into *two equal parts*. We have illustrated this by shading the two equal parts in different colors.

exhibit 7

A Pie Chart

The breakdown of activities for Charles Myers during a typical 24-hour weekday is represented in pie chart form.

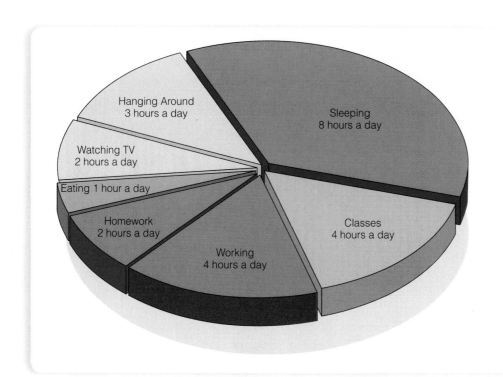

The major characteristic of the 45-degree line is that any point that lies on it is equidistant from both the horizontal and vertical axes. For example, point A is exactly as far from the horizontal axis as it is from the vertical axis. It follows that point A represents as much *X* as it does *Y*. Specifically, in the exhibit, point A represents 20 units of *X* and 20 units of *Y*.

PIE CHARTS

In numerous places in this text, you will come across a *pie chart*. A pie chart is a convenient way to represent the different parts of something that when added together equal the whole.

Let's consider a typical 24-hour weekday for Charles Myers. On a typical weekday, Charles spends 8 hours sleeping, 4 hours taking classes at the university, 4 hours working at his part-time job, 2 hours doing homework, 1 hour eating, 2 hours watching television, and 3 hours doing nothing in particular (we'll call it "hanging around"). Exhibit 7 shows the breakdown of a typical weekday for Charles in pie chart form.

Pie charts give a quick visual message as to rough percentage breakdowns and relative relationships. For example, it is easy to see in Exhibit 7 that Charles spends twice as much time working as doing homework.

BAR GRAPHS

The *bar graph* is another visual aid that economists use to convey relative relationships. Suppose we wanted to represent the gross domestic product for the United States in different years. The **gross domestic product (GDP)** is the value of the entire output produced annually within a country's borders. A bar graph can show the actual GDP for each year and can also provide a quick picture of the relative relationships between the GDP in

Gross Domestic Product (GDP)
The value of the entire output produced annually within a country's borders.

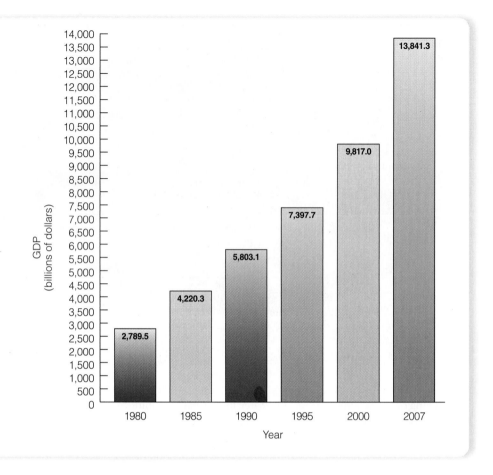

exhibit 8

A Bar Graph

U.S. gross domestic product for different years is illustrated in bar graph form.

Source: Bureau of Economic Analysis

different years. For example, it is easy to see in Exhibit 8 that the GDP in 1990 was more than double what it was in 1980.

LINE GRAPHS

Sometimes information is best and most easily displayed in a *line graph*. Line graphs are particularly useful for illustrating changes in a variable over some time period. Suppose we want to illustrate the variations in average points per game for a college basketball team in different years. As you can see from Exhibit 9(a), the basketball team has been on a roller coaster during the years 1996–2009. Perhaps the message transmitted here is that the team's performance has not been consistent from one year to the next.

Suppose we plot the data in Exhibit 9(a) again, except this time we use a different measurement scale on the vertical axis. As you can see in (b), the variation in the performance of the basketball team appears much less pronounced than in (a). In fact, we could choose some scale such that if we were to plot the data, we would end up with close to a straight line. Our point is simple: Data plotted in line graph form may convey different messages depending on the measurement scale used.

Sometimes economists show two line graphs on the same axes. Usually, they do this to draw attention to either (1) the *relationship* between the two variables or (2) the *difference* between the two variables. In Exhibit 10, the line graphs show the variation and trend in projected federal government expenditures and tax receipts for the years 2008–2013 and draw attention to what has been happening to the "gap" between the two.

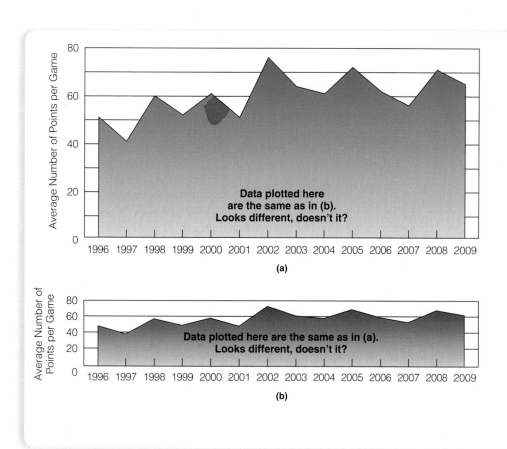

exhibit 9

The Two Line Graphs Plot the Same Data

In (a) we plotted the average number of points per game for a college basketball team in different years. The variation between the years is pronounced. In (b) we plotted the same data as in (a), but the variation in the performance of the team appears much less pronounced than in (a).

Year	Average Number of Points per Game
1996	50
1997	40
1998	59
1999	51
2000	60
2001	50
2002	75
2003	63
2004	60
2005	71
2006	61
2007	55
2008	70
2009	64

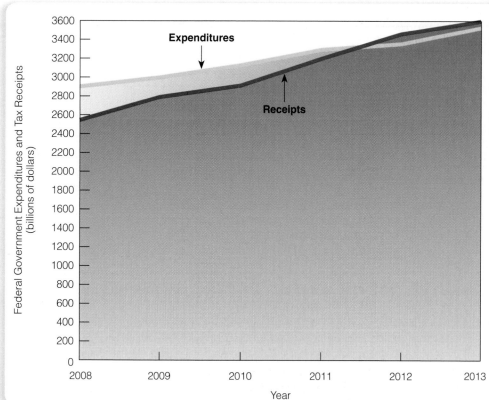

exhibit 10

Projected Federal Government Expenditures and Tax Receipts, 2008–2013

Projected federal government expenditures and tax receipts are shown in line graph form for the period 2008–2013.

Source: Congressional Budget Office

Appendix Summary

- Two variables are directly related if one variable rises as the other rises.
- An upward-sloping line (left to right) represents two variables that are directly related.
- Two variables are inversely related if one variable rises as the other falls.
- A downward-sloping line (left to right) represents two variables that are inversely related.
- Two variables are independent if one variable rises as the other remains constant.
- The slope of a line is the ratio of the change in the variable on the vertical axis to the change in the variable on the horizontal axis. The slope of a (straight) line is the same between every two points on the line.

- To determine the slope of a curve at a point, draw a line tangent to the curve at the point and then determine the slope of the tangent line.
- Any point on a 45-degree line is equidistant from the two axes.
- A pie chart is a convenient way to represent the different parts of something that when added together equal the whole. A pie chart visually shows rough percentage breakdowns and relative relationships.
- A bar graph is a convenient way to represent relative relationships.
- Line graphs are particularly useful for illustrating changes in a variable over some time period.

Questions and Problems

1   What type of relationship would you expect between the following: (a) sales of hot dogs and sales of hot dog buns, (b) the price of winter coats and sales of winter coats, (c) the price of personal computers and the production of personal computers, (d) sales of toothbrushes and sales of cat food, (e) the number of children in a family and the number of toys in a family.

2   Represent the following data in bar graph form.

Year	U.S. Money Supply (billions of dollars)
2003	1,273
2004	1,344
2005	1,371
2006	1,374
2007	1,369

3   Plot the following data and specify the type of relationship between the two variables. (Place "price" on the vertical axis and "quantity demanded" on the horizontal axis.)

Price of Apples ($)	Quantity Demanded of Apples
0.25	1,000
0.50	800
0.70	700
0.95	500
1.00	400
1.10	350

4   In Exhibit 4(a), determine the slope between points C and D.

5   In Exhibit 4(b), determine the slope between points A and D.

6   What is the special characteristic of a 45-degree line?

7   What is the slope of a 45-degree line?

8   When would it be preferable to illustrate data using a pie chart instead of a bar graph?

9   Plot the following data and specify the type of relationship between the two variables. (Place "price" on the vertical axis and "quantity supplied" on the horizontal axis.)

Price of Apples ($)	Quantity Supplied of Apples
0.25	350
0.50	400
0.70	500
0.95	700
1.00	800
1.10	1,000

SHOULD YOU MAJOR IN ECONOMICS?

You are probably reading this textbook as part of your first college course in economics. You may be taking this course because you need it to satisfy the requirements in your major. Economics courses are sometimes required for students who plan to major in business, history, liberal studies, social science, or computer science. Of course, you may also be taking this course because you plan to major in economics.

If you are like many college students, you may complain that not enough information is available to students about the various majors at your college or university. For example, students who major in business sometimes say they are not quite certain what a business major is all about, but then they go on to add that majoring in business is a safe bet. "After all," they comment, "you are pretty sure of getting a job if you have a business degree. That's not always the case with other degrees."

Many college students choose their majors based on their high school courses. History majors sometimes say that they decided to major in history because they "liked history in high school." Similarly, chemistry, biology, and math majors say they chose chemistry, biology, or math as a college major because they liked studying chemistry, biology, or math in high school. In addition, if a student had a hard time with chemistry in high school and found it boring, then he doesn't usually want to major in chemistry in college. If a student found both math and economics easy and interesting in high school, then she is likely to major in math or economics.

Students also often look to the dollars at the end of the college degree. A student may enjoy history and want to learn more history in college but tell herself that she will earn a higher starting salary after graduation if she majors in computer science or engineering. Thus, when choosing a major, students often consider (1) how much they enjoy studying a particular subject, (2) what they would like to see themselves doing in the future, and (3) income prospects.

Different people may weight these three factors differently. But no matter what weights you put on each of the factors, it is always better to have more information than less information, *ceteris paribus.* (We note *"ceteris paribus"* because it is not necessarily better having more information than less information if you have to pay more for the additional information than the additional information is worth. Who wants to pay $10 for a piece of information that only provides $1 in benefits?)

We believe this appendix is a fairly low-cost way of providing you with more information about an economics major than you currently have. We start by dispelling some of the misinformation you might possess about an economics major. Stated bluntly, some things that people think about an economics major and about a career in economics are just not true. For example, some people think that economics majors almost never study social relationships; instead, they only study such things as inflation, interest rates, and unemployment. Not true. Economics majors study some of the same things that sociologists, historians, psychologists, and political scientists study. We also provide you with some information about the major that you may not have.

Next, we tell you the specifics of the economics major—what courses you study if you are an economics major, how many courses you are likely to have to take, and more.

Finally, we tell you something about a career in economics. Okay, so you have opted to become an economics major. But the day will come when you have your degree in hand. What's next? What is your starting salary likely to be? What will you be doing? Are you going to be happy doing what economists do? (If you never thought economics was about happiness, you already have some misinformation about economics. Contrary to what most laypeople think, economics is not just about money. It is about happiness too.)

FIVE MYTHS ABOUT ECONOMICS AND AN ECONOMICS MAJOR

Myth 1: Economics Is All Mathematics and Statistics

Some students choose not to major in economics because they think economics is all mathematics and statistics. Math and statistics are used in economics, but at the undergraduate degree level, the math and statistics are certainly not overwhelming. Economics majors are usually required to take one statistics course and one math course (usually an introductory calculus course). Even students who say, "Math isn't my subject" are sometimes happy with the amount of math they need in economics. Fact is, at the undergraduate level at many colleges and universities, economics is not a very math-intensive course of study. There are many diagrams in economics, but there is not a large amount of math.

A proviso: The amount of math in the economics curriculum varies across colleges and universities. Some economics departments do not require their students to learn much math or statistics, but others do. Speaking for the majority of departments, we still hold to our original point that there isn't really that much math or statistics in economics at the undergraduate level. The graduate level is a different story.

Myth 2: Economics Is Only About Inflation, Interest Rates, Unemployment, and Other Such Things

If you study economics at college and then go on to become a practicing economist, no doubt people will ask you certain questions when they learn your chosen profession. Here are some of the questions they ask:

- Do you think the economy is going to pick up?
- Do you think the economy is going to slow down?
- What stocks would you recommend?
- Do you think interest rates are going to fall?
- Do you think interest rates are going to rise?
- What do you think about buying bonds right now? Is it a good idea?

People ask these kinds of questions because most people believe that economists only study stocks, bonds, interest rates, inflation, unemployment, and so on. Well, economists do study these things. But these topics are only a tiny part of what economists study. It is not hard to find many economists today, both inside and outside academia, who spend most of their time studying anything but inflation, unemployment, stocks, bonds, and so on.

As we hinted earlier, much of what economists study may surprise you. There are economists who use their economic tools and methods to study crime, marriage, divorce, sex, obesity, addiction, sports, voting behavior, bureaucracies, presidential elections, and much more. In short, today's economics is not your grandfather's economics. Many more topics are studied today in economics than were studied in your grandfather's time.

Myth 3: People Become Economists Only if They Want to "Make Money"

A while back we asked a few well-respected and well-known economists what got them interested in economics. Here is what some of them had to say:[1]

Gary Becker, the 1992 winner of the Nobel Prize in Economics, said: "I got interested in economics when I was an undergraduate in college. I came into college with a strong interest in mathematics, and at the same time with a strong commitment to do something to help society. I learned in the first economics course I took that economics could deal rigorously, à la mathematics, with social problems. That stimulated me because in economics I saw that I could combine both the mathematics and my desire to do something to help society."

Vernon Smith, the 2002 winner of the Nobel Prize in Economics, said: "My father's influence started me in science and engineering at Cal Tech, but my mother, who was active in socialist politics, probably accounts for the great interest I found in economics when I took my first introductory course."

Alice Rivlin, an economist and former member of the Federal Reserve Board, said: "My interest in economics grew out of concern for improving public policy, both domestic and international. I was a teenager in the tremendously idealistic period after World War II when it seemed terribly important to get nations working together to solve the world's problems peacefully."

Allan Meltzer said: "Economics is a social science. At its best it is concerned with ways (1) to improve well being by allowing individuals the freedom to achieve their personal aims or goals and (2) to harmonize their individual interests. I find working on such issues challenging, and progress is personally rewarding."

Robert Solow, the 1987 winner of the Nobel Prize in Economics, said: "I grew up in the 1930s and it was very hard not to be interested in economics. If you were a high school student in the 1930s, you were conscious of the fact that our economy was in deep trouble and no one knew what to do about it."

Charles Plosser said: "I was an engineer as an undergraduate with little knowledge of economics. I went to the University of Chicago Graduate School of Business to get an MBA and there became fascinated with economics. I was impressed with the seriousness with which economics was viewed as a way of organizing one's thoughts about the world to address interesting questions and problems."

Walter Williams said: "I was a major in sociology in 1963 and I concluded that it was not very rigorous. Over the summer I was reading a book by W.E.B. DuBois, *Black Reconstruction,* and somewhere in the book it said something along the lines that blacks could not melt into the mainstream of American society until they understood economics, and that was something that got me interested in economics."

Murray Weidenbaum said: "A specific professor got me interested in economics. He was very prescient: He correctly noted that while lawyers dominated the policy-making process up until then (the 1940s), in the future economics would be an important tool for developing public policy. And he was right."

Irma Adelman said: "I hesitate to say because it sounds arrogant. My reason [for getting into economics] was that I wanted to benefit humanity. And my perception at the time was that economic problems were the most important problems that humanity has to face. That is what got me into economics and into economic development."

Lester Thurow said: "[I got interested in economics because of] the belief, some would see it as naive belief, that economics was a profession where it would be possible to help make the world better."

---

1. See various interviews in Roger A. Arnold, *Economics,* 2d ed. (St. Paul, MN: West Publishing Company, 1992).

Myth 4: Economics Wasn't Very Interesting in High School, So It's Not Going to Be Very Interesting in College

A typical high school economics course emphasizes consumer economics and spends much time discussing this topic. Students learn about credit cards, mortgage loans, budgets, buying insurance, renting an apartment, and other such things. These are important topics because not knowing the "ins and outs" of such things can make your life much harder. Still, many students come away from a high school economics course thinking that economics is always and everywhere about consumer topics.

However, a high school economics course and a college economics course are usually as different as day and night. Simply leaf through this book and look at the variety of topics covered compared to the topics you might have covered in your high school economics course. Go on to look at texts used in other economics courses—courses that range from law and economics to history of economic thought to international economics to sports economics—and you will see what we mean.

Myth 5: Economics Is a Lot Like Business, But Business Is More Marketable

Although business and economics have some common topics, much that one learns in economics is not taught in business and much that one learns in business is not taught in economics. The area of intersection between business and economics is not large.

Still, many people think otherwise. And so thinking that business and economics are pretty much the same thing, they often choose to major in the subject they believe has greater marketability—which they believe is business.

Well, consider the following:

1. A few years ago *BusinessWeek* magazine asked the chief executive officers (CEOs) of major companies what they thought was the best undergraduate degree. Their first choice was engineering. Their second choice was economics. Economics scored higher than business administration.

2. The National Association of Colleges and Employers undertook a survey in 2007 in which they identified the average starting salary offers in different disciplines. The average starting salary in economics was $48,483. Here are average starting salaries for some other fields: computer science, $53,396; accounting, $46,718; finance, $47,239; civil engineering, $47,718; marketing, $41,323; electrical engineering, $54,599; and chemical engineering, $60,054.

WHAT AWAITS YOU AS AN ECONOMICS MAJOR?

If you become an economics major, what courses will you take? What are you going to study?

At the lower-division level, economics majors must take both the principles of macroeconomics course and the principles of microeconomics course. They usually also take a statistics course and a math course (usually calculus).

At the upper-division level, they must take intermediate microeconomics and intermediate macroeconomics, along with a certain number of electives. Some of the elective courses include: (1) money and banking, (2) law and economics, (3) history of economic thought, (4) public finance, (5) labor economics, (6) international economics, (7) antitrust and regulation, (8) health economics, (9) economics of development, (10) urban and regional economics, (11) econometrics, (12) mathematical economics, (13) environmental economics, (14) public choice, (15) global managerial economics, (16) economic approach to politics and sociology, (17) sports economics, and many more courses. Most economics majors take between 12 and 15 economics courses.

One of the attractive things about studying economics is that you will acquire many of the skills employers highly value. First, you will have the quantitative skills that are important in many business and government positions. Second, you will acquire the writing skills necessary in almost all lines of work. Third, and perhaps most importantly, you will develop the thinking skills that almost all employers agree are critical to success.

A study published in the 1998 edition of the *Journal of Economic Education* ranked economics majors as having the highest average scores on the Law School Admission Test (LSAT). Also, consider the words of the Royal Economic Society: "One of the things that makes economics graduates so employable is that the subject teaches you to think in a careful and precise way. The fundamental economic issue is how society decides to allocate its resources: how the costs and benefits of a course of action can be evaluated and compared, and how appropriate choices can be made. A degree in economics gives a training in decision making principles, providing a skill applicable in a very wide range of careers."

Keep in mind, too, that economics is one of the most popular majors at some of the most respected universities in the country. As of this writing, economics is the top major at Harvard, Princeton, Columbia, Stanford, the University of Pennsylvania, and the University of Chicago. It is the second most popular major at Brown, Yale, and the University of California at Berkeley. It is the third most popular major at Cornell and Dartmouth.

WHAT DO ECONOMISTS DO?

Employment for economists is projected to grow between 21 and 35 percent between 2000 and 2010. According to the *Occupational Outlook Handbook*:

> Opportunities for economists should be best in private industry, especially in research, testing, and consulting firms, as more companies contract out for economic research services. The growing complexity of the global economy, competition, and increased reliance on quantitative methods for analyzing the current value of future funds, business trends, sales, and purchasing should spur demand for economists. The growing need for economic analyses in virtually every industry should result in additional jobs for economists.

Today, economists work in many varied fields. Here are some of the fields and some of the positions economists hold in those fields:

Education
College professor
Researcher
High school teacher

Journalism
Researcher
Industry analyst
Economic analyst

Accounting
Analyst
Auditor
Researcher
Consultant

General Business
Chief executive officer
Business analyst
Marketing analyst
Business forecaster
Competitive analyst

Government
Researcher
Analyst
Speechwriter
Forecaster

Financial Services
Business journalist
International analyst

Newsletter editor
Broker
Investment banker

Banking
Credit analyst
Loan officer
Investment analyst
Financial manager

Other
Business consultant
Independent forecaster
Freelance analyst
Think tank analyst
Entrepreneur

Economists do a myriad of things. For example, in business, economists often analyze economic conditions, make forecasts, offer strategic planning initiatives, collect and analyze data, predict exchange rate movements, and review regulatory policies, among other things. In government, economists collect and analyze data, analyze international economic situations, research monetary conditions, advise on policy, and much more. As private consultants, economists work with accountants, business executives, government officials, educators, financial firms, labor unions, state and local governments, and others. Median annual wage and salary earnings of economists were $77,010 in May 2006. The middle 50 percent earned between $55,740 and $103,500. The lowest 10 percent earned less than $42,280, and the highest 10 percent earned more than $136,550.

PLACES TO FIND MORE INFORMATION

If you are interested in an economics major and perhaps a career in economics, here are some places where you can go and some people you can speak with to acquire more information:

- To learn about the economics curriculum, we urge you to speak with the economics professors at your college or university. Ask them what courses you would have to take as an economics major. Ask them what elective courses are available. In addition, ask them why they chose to study economics. What is it about economics that interested them?

- For more information about salaries and what economists do, you may want to visit the *Occupational Outlook Handbook* website at http://www.bls.gov/oco/.

- For starting salary information, you may want to visit the National Association of Colleges and Employers website at http://www.naceweb.org/.

- To see a list of famous people who have majored in economics, go to http://www.marietta.edu/~ema/econ/famous.html.

CONCLUDING REMARKS

Choosing a major is a big decision and therefore should not be made too quickly and without much thought. In this short appendix, we have provided you with some information about an economics major and a career in economics. Economics may not be for everyone (in fact, economists would say that if it were, many of the benefits of specialization would be lost), but it may be right for you. Economics is a major where many of today's most marketable skills are acquired—the skills of good writing, quantitative analysis, and thinking. It is a major in which professors and students daily ask and answer some very interesting and relevant questions. It is a major that is highly regarded by employers. It may just be the right major for you. Give it some thought.

CHAPTER 2

ECONOMIC ACTIVITIES: PRODUCING AND TRADING

Introduction In the last chapter you learned about various economic concepts—such as scarcity, choice, and opportunity cost. In this chapter we develop a graphical framework of analysis with which to understand these concepts and more. Specifically, we develop the production possibilities frontier. Next we go on to discuss one of the most important topics in economics—trade.

THE PRODUCTION POSSIBILITIES FRONTIER

This section discusses the production possibilities frontier (PPF) and numerous economic concepts that can be illustrated by it.

The Straight-Line PPF: Constant Opportunity Costs

Assume the following:

1. Only two goods can be produced in an economy: computers and television sets.

2. The opportunity cost of one television set is one computer.

3. As more of one good is produced, the opportunity cost between television sets and computers is constant.

In Exhibit 1(a), we have identified six combinations of computers and television sets that can be produced in our economy. For example, combination A is 50,000 computers and 0 television sets, combination B is 40,000 computers and 10,000 television sets, and so on. We plotted these six combinations of computers and television sets in Exhibit 1(b). Each combination represents a different point in Exhibit 1(b). For example, the combination of 50,000 computers and 0 television sets is represented by point A. The line that connects points A–F is the production possibilities frontier. A **production possibilities frontier (PPF)** represents the combination of two goods that can be produced in a certain period of time under the conditions of a given state of technology and fully employed resources.

Production Possibilities Frontier (PPF)
Represents the possible combinations of two goods that can be produced in a certain period of time under the conditions of a given state of technology and fully employed resources.

exhibit 1

Production Possibilities Frontier (Constant Opportunity Costs)

The economy can produce any of the six combinations of computers and television sets in part (a). We have plotted these combinations in part (b). The production possibilities frontier in part (b) is a straight line because the opportunity cost of producing either good is constant: for *every* 1 computer not produced, 1 television set is produced.

Combination	Computers	Television Sets	Point in Part (b)
A	50,000	0	A
B	40,000	10,000	B
C	30,000	20,000	C
D	20,000	30,000	D
E	10,000	40,000	E
F	0	50,000	F

(a)

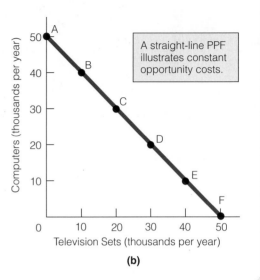

A straight-line PPF illustrates constant opportunity costs.

(b)

The production possibilities frontier is a straight line in this instance because the opportunity cost of producing computers and television sets is constant.

Straight-line PPF = Constant opportunity costs

For example, if the economy were to move from point A to point B, from B to C, and so on, the opportunity cost of each good would remain constant at 1 for 1. To illustrate, at point A, 50,000 computers and 0 television sets are produced. At point B, 40,000 computers and 10,000 television sets are produced.

We conclude that for every 10,000 computers not produced, 10,000 television sets are produced—a ratio of 1 to 1. The opportunity cost—1 computer for 1 television set—that exists between points A and B also exists between points B and C, C and D, D and E, and E and F. In other words, opportunity cost is constant at 1 computer for 1 television set.

The Bowed-Outward (Concave-Downward) PPF: Increasing Opportunity Costs

Assume two things:

1. Only two goods can be produced in an economy: computers and television sets.

2. As more of one good is produced, the opportunity cost between computers and television sets changes.

In Exhibit 2(a), we have identified four combinations of computers and television sets that can be produced in our economy. For example, combination A is 50,000 computers and 0 television sets, combination B is 40,000 computers and 20,000 television sets, and so on. We plotted these four combinations of computers and television sets in Exhibit 2(b).

exhibit 2

Production Possibilities Frontier (Increasing Opportunity Costs)

The economy can produce any of the four combinations of computers and televisions sets in part (a). We have plotted these combinations in part (b). The production possibilities frontier in part (b) is bowed outward because the opportunity cost of producing television sets increases as more television sets are produced.

Combination	Computers	Television Sets	Point in Part (b)
A	50,000	0	A
B	40,000	20,000	B
C	25,000	40,000	C
D	0	60,000	D

(a)

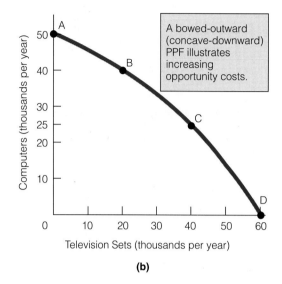

A bowed-outward (concave-downward) PPF illustrates increasing opportunity costs.

(b)

Each combination represents a different point. The curved line that connects points A–D is the production possibilities frontier.

In this case, the production possibilities frontier is bowed outward (concave downward) because the opportunity cost of television sets increases as more sets are produced.

Bowed-outward PPF = Increasing opportunity costs

To illustrate, let's start at point A, where the economy is producing 50,000 computers and 0 television sets, and move to point B, where the economy is producing 40,000 computers and 20,000 television sets.

What is the opportunity cost of a television set over this range? We see that 20,000 more television sets are produced by moving from point A to point B but *at the cost of 10,000 computers.* This means for every 1 television set produced, 1/2 computer is forfeited. Thus, the opportunity cost of 1 television set is 1/2 computer.

Now let's move from point B, where the economy is producing 40,000 computers and 20,000 television sets, to point C, where the economy is producing 25,000 computers and 40,000 television sets.

Point B: 40,000 computers, 20,000 television sets

Point C: 25,000 computers, 40,000 television sets

What is the opportunity cost of a television set over this range? In this case, 20,000 more television sets are produced by moving from point B to point C *but at the cost of 15,000 computers.* This means for every 1 television set produced, 3/4 computer is forfeited. Thus, the opportunity cost of 1 television set is 3/4 of a computer.

What statement can we make about the opportunity costs of producing television sets? Obviously, as the economy produces more television sets, the opportunity cost of producing television sets increases. This gives us the bowed-outward production possibilities frontier in Exhibit 2(b).

Law of Increasing Opportunity Costs

We know that the shape of the production possibilities frontier depends on whether opportunity costs (1) are constant or (2) increase as more of a good is produced. In Exhibit 1(b), the production possibilities frontier is a straight line; in Exhibit 2(b), it is bowed outward (curved). In the real world, most production possibilities frontiers are bowed outward. This means that for most goods, the opportunity costs *increase* as more of the good is produced. This is referred to as the **law of increasing opportunity costs.**

But why (for most goods) do the opportunity costs increase as more of the good is produced? The answer is because people have varying abilities. For example, some people are better suited to building houses than other people are. When a construction company first starts building houses, it employs the people who are most skilled at house building. The most skilled persons can build houses at lower opportunity costs than others can. But as the construction company builds more houses, it finds that it has already employed the most skilled builders, so it must employ those who are less skilled at house building. These (less skilled) people build houses at higher opportunity costs. Where three skilled house builders could build a house in a month, as many as seven unskilled builders may be required to build it in the same length of time. Exhibit 3 summarizes the points in this section.

Law of Increasing Opportunity Costs

As more of a good is produced, the opportunity costs of producing that good increase.

exhibit 3

A Summary Statement About Increasing Opportunity Costs and a Production Possibilities Frontier That Is Bowed Outward (Concave Downward)

Many of the points about increasing opportunity costs and a production possibilities frontier that is bowed outward are summarized here.

We start with the assumption that not all people can build houses at the same opportunity cost.

→ When houses are first built, only the people who *can* build them at (relatively) low opportunity costs *will* build them.

→ As increasingly more houses are built, people with higher opportunity costs of building houses will start building houses.

→ This is the same as saying that as more houses are built, the opportunity cost of building houses increases.

And this is why the PPF for houses and good X is bowed outward (concave downward). See diagram at left.

Notice that when we go from building 60 to 70 houses (10 more houses), we forfeit 5 units of good X; but when we go from building 110 to 120 houses (again, 10 more houses), we forfeit 20 units of good X.

Economic Concepts Within a PPF Framework

The PPF framework is useful for illustrating and working with economic concepts. This section discusses seven economic concepts in terms of the PPF framework (see Exhibit 4).

SCARCITY Recall that scarcity is the condition where wants (for goods) are greater than the resources available to satisfy those wants. The finiteness of resources is graphically portrayed by the PPF in Exhibit 5. The frontier (itself) tells us: "At this point in time, that's as far as you can go. You cannot go any farther. You are limited to choosing any combination of the two goods on the frontier or below it."

The PPF separates the production possibilities of an economy into two regions: (1) an attainable region, which consists of the points on the PPF itself and all points below it (this region includes points A–F) and (2) an unattainable region, which consists of the points above and beyond the PPF (such as point G). Recall that scarcity implies that some things are attainable and others are unattainable. Point A on the PPF is attainable, as is point F; point G is not.

Choice and opportunity cost are also shown in Exhibit 5. Note that within the attainable region, individuals must choose the combination of the two goods they want to produce. Obviously, hundreds of different combinations exist, but let's consider only two, represented by points A and B. Which of the two will individuals choose? They can't be at both points; they must make a choice.

Opportunity cost is illustrated as we move from one point to another on the PPF in Exhibit 5. Suppose we are at point A and choose to move to point B. At A, we have 55,000 television sets and 5,000 cars, and at point B, we have 50,000 television sets and 15,000 cars. What is the opportunity cost of a car? Because 10,000 *more* cars come at a cost of 5,000 *fewer* television sets, the opportunity cost of 1 car is 1/2 television set.

PRODUCTIVE EFFICIENCY Economists often say that an economy is **productive efficient** if it is producing the maximum output with given resources and technology. In Exhibit 5, points A, B, C, D, and E are all productive efficient points. Notice that all these points lie on the production possibilities frontier. In other words, we are getting the most (in terms of output) from what we have (in terms of available resources and technology).

It follows that an economy is **productive inefficient** if it is producing less than the maximum output with given resources and technology. In Exhibit 5, point F is a productive inefficient point. It lies below the production possibilities frontier; it is below the outer limit of what is possible. In other words, we could produce more goods with the resources we have available to us. Or we can get more of one good without getting less of another good.

To illustrate, suppose we move from inefficient point F to efficient point C. We produce more television sets and no fewer cars. What if we move from F to D? We produce more television sets and more cars. Finally, if we move from F to E, we produce more cars and no fewer television sets. Thus, moving from F can give us more of at least one good and no less of another good. In short, productive inefficiency implies that gains are possible in one area without losses in another.

UNEMPLOYED RESOURCES When the economy exhibits productive inefficiency, it is not producing the maximum output with the available resources and technology.

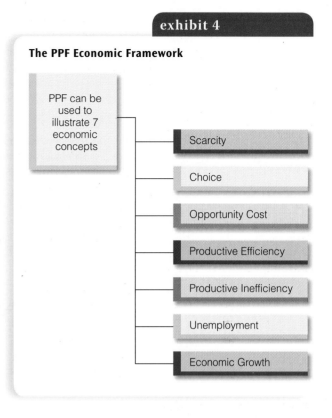

exhibit 4

The PPF Economic Framework

PPF can be used to illustrate 7 economic concepts
- Scarcity
- Choice
- Opportunity Cost
- Productive Efficiency
- Productive Inefficiency
- Unemployment
- Economic Growth

Productive Efficiency
The condition where the maximum output is produced with given resources and technology.

Productive Inefficiency
The condition where less than the maximum output is produced with given resources and technology. Productive inefficiency implies that more of one good can be produced without any less of another good being produced.

exhibit 5

The PPF and Various Economic Concepts

The PPF can illustrate various economic concepts: (1) Scarcity is illustrated by the frontier itself. Implicit in the concept of scarcity is the idea that we can have some things but not all things. The PPF separates an attainable region from an unattainable region. (2) Choice is represented by our having to decide among the many attainable combinations of the two goods. For example, will we choose the combination of goods represented by point A or by point B? (3) Opportunity cost is most easily seen as movement from one point to another, such as movement from point A to point B. More cars are available at point B than at point A, but fewer television sets are available. In short, the opportunity cost of more cars is fewer television sets. (4) Productive efficiency is represented by the points on the PPF (such as A–E), while productive inefficiency is represented by any point below the PPF (such as F). (5) Unemployment (in terms of resources being unemployed) exists at any productive inefficient point (such as F), whereas resources are fully employed at any productive efficient point (such as A–E).

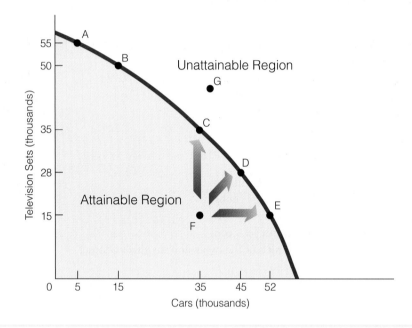

One reason may be that the economy is not using all its resources; that is, some of its resources are unemployed, as at point F in Exhibit 5.

When the economy exhibits productive efficiency, it is producing the maximum output with the available resources and technology. This means it is using all its resources to produce goods; its resources are fully employed, and none are unemployed. At the productive efficient points A–E in Exhibit 5, there are no unemployed resources.

ECONOMIC GROWTH Economic growth refers to the increased productive capabilities of an economy. It is illustrated by a shift outward in the production possibilities frontier. Two major factors that affect economic growth are (1) an increase in the quantity of resources and (2) an advance in technology.

With an increase in the quantity of resources (e.g., through a new discovery of resources), it is possible to produce a greater quantity of output. In Exhibit 6, an increase in the quantity of resources makes it possible to produce both more military goods and more civilian goods. Thus, the PPF shifts outward from PPF_1 to PPF_2.

Technology refers to the body of skills and knowledge concerning the use of resources in production. An advance in technology commonly refers to the ability to produce more output with a fixed quantity of resources or the ability to produce the same output with a smaller quantity of resources.

Technology
The body of skills and knowledge concerning the use of resources in production. An advance in technology commonly refers to the ability to produce more output with a fixed amount of resources or the ability to produce the same output with fewer resources.

Suppose an advance in technology allows more military goods and more civilian goods to be produced with the same quantity of resources. As a result, the PPF in Exhibit 6 shifts outward from PPF_1 to PPF_2. The outcome is the same as when the quantity of resources is increased.

Finding ECONOMICS

In an Attorney's Office

An attorney is sitting in his office working. Where is the economics?

Let's back up and first talk about farmers and a change in technology. During the twentieth century, many farmers left farming because farming experienced major technological advances. Where farmers once farmed with minimal capital equipment, today they use computers, tractors, pesticides, cellular phones, and much more. In 1910, the United States had 32.1 million farmers; today there are around 4.8 million farmers. Where did all the farmers go?

Because of technological advancements, fewer farmers were needed to produce food and so many farmers left the farmers for the cities, where they entered the manufacturing and service industries. In other words, people who were once farmers (or whose parents and grandparents were farmers) began to produce cars, airplanes, television sets, and computers. They became attorneys, accountants, and police officers.

What we learn here is that a technological advancement in one sector of the economy can have ripple effects throughout the economy. We also learn that a technological advancement can affect the composition of employment.

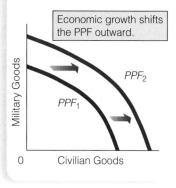

exhibit 6

Economic Growth Within a PPF Framework

An increase in resources or an advance in technology can increase the production capabilities of an economy, leading to economic growth and a shift outward in the production possibilities frontier.

> Economic growth shifts the PPF outward.

SELF-TEST

(Answers to Self-Test questions are in the Self-Test Appendix.)

1. What does a straight-line production possibilities frontier (PPF) represent? What does a bowed-outward PPF represent?

2. What does the law of increasing costs have to do with a bowed-outward PPF?

3. A politician says, "If you elect me, we can get more of everything we want." Under what condition(s) is the politician telling the truth?

4. In an economy, only one combination of goods is productive efficient. True or false? Explain your answer.

EXCHANGE OR TRADE

Exchange (trade) is the process of giving up one thing for something else. Usually, money is traded for goods and services. Trade is all around us; we are involved with it every day. Few of us, however, have considered the full extent of trade.

Periods Relevant to Trade

There are three time periods relevant to the trading process. We discuss these relevant time periods next.

Exchange (Trade)
The process of giving up one thing for something else.

THE PPF AND YOUR GRADES

You have your own PPF, you just may not know it. Suppose you are studying for two upcoming exams. You have only a total of eight hours before you have to take the first exam, after which you will immediately proceed to take the second exam. Time spent studying for the first exam (in economics) takes away from time that could be spent studying for the second exam (in math), and vice versa. Also, time studying

©PIXLAND/JUPITER IMAGES

is a resource in the production of a good grade; less time studying for the economics exam and more time spent studying for the math exam means a higher grade in math and a lower grade in economics. For you, the situation may look as it does in Exhibit 7(a). We have identified four points in the exhibit (1–4) corresponding to the four combinations of two grades (one grade in economics and one grade in English).

You will notice also that each grade comes with a certain amount of time studying. This time is specified under the grade.

Given the resources you currently have (your labor and time) you can achieve any of the four combinations. For example, you can spend six hours studying for economics and get a B (point 1), but this means you study math for zero hours and get an F in that course.

Or you can spend four hours studying for economics and get a C (point 2), leaving you two hours to study for math, in which you get a D.

What do you need to get a higher grade in one course without getting a lower grade in the other course? You need more resources, which in this case is more time. If you have eight hours to study, your PPF shifts rightward, as in Exhibit 7(b). Now point 5 is possible (whereas it was not possible before you got more time). At point 5, you can get a C in economics and in math, which was an impossible combination of grades when you had less time (a PPF closer to the origin).

exhibit 7

(a)

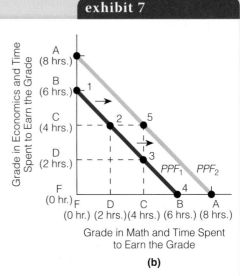

(b)

Ex Ante
Phrase that means "before," as in before a trade.

BEFORE THE TRADE Before a trade is made, a person is said to be in the **ex ante** position. For example, suppose Ramona has the opportunity to trade what she has, $2,000, for something she does not have, a plasma television set. In the ex ante position, she wonders if she will be better off with (1) the television set or with (2) $2,000 worth of other goods. If she concludes that she will be better off with the television set than with $2,000 worth of other goods, she will make the trade. Individuals will make a trade only if they believe ex ante (before) the trade that the trade will make them better off.

TRADING PRISONERS

Earlier we said that no one enters into a trade unless he expects to be made better off by the trade. Let's now translate Rag this into *utility* (which we discussed in Chapter 1).

Suppose Bob has a radio and Jim has a book. The two men come together and trade: Bob gives Jim the radio in exchange for the book. Now ask yourself this question: For this trade to occur, what condition must hold? The answer for Bob is that the book must give him more utility than the radio.

For Bob: Utility of book (10 utils) > Utility for radio (8 utils)

The answer for Jim is that the radio must give him more utility than the book.

For Jim: Utility of radio (10 utils) > Utility for book (8 utils)

In other words, no one enters a trade unless he expects to be made better off (gain utility). In our example, each person is made better off by (or gains) 2 utils.

Economists assume that the one thing individuals want to do is maximize their utility. In other words, they want as much utility as possible. To help them in this endeavor, they trade. In fact, their desire for utility is so great that individuals will even end up trading with their enemies sometimes. To illustrate, in April 2007, the Israelis and Hezbollah were negotiating for prisoners, as were the Taliban and the government of Afghanistan. In both cases (Israeli-Hezbollah and Taliban-Afghani government) it wasn't the actual trade of prisoners that was being called into question, it was the *terms of trade*. In other words, all sides had agreed to a trade, it was simply how many prisoners would be traded on one side for prisoners on the other side.

AT THE POINT OF TRADE Suppose Ramona now gives $2,000 to the person in possession of the television set. Does Ramona still believe she will be better off with the television set than with the $2,000? Of course she does. Her action testifies to this fact.

AFTER THE TRADE After a trade is made, a person is said to be in the **ex post** position. Suppose two days have passed. Does Ramona still feel the same way about the trade as she did before the trade and at the point of trade? Maybe. Maybe not. She may look back on the trade and regret it. She may say that if she had it to do over again, she would not trade the $2,000 for a plasma television set. In general, though, people expect a trade to make them better off, and usually, the trade meets their expectations. But there are no guarantees that a trade will meet expectations because no one in the real world can see the future.

Ex Post
Phrase that means "after," as in after a trade.

Trade and the Terms of Trade

Trade refers to the process whereby "things" (money, goods, services, etc.) are given up to obtain something else. The **terms of trade** refer to *how much* of one thing is given up for *how much* of something else. For example, if $30 is traded for a bestselling book, the terms of trade are 1 bestseller for $30. If the price of a loaf of bread is $2.50, the terms of trade are 1 loaf of bread for $2.50. Buyers and sellers can always think of more advantageous terms of exchange. Buyers prefer lower prices, whereas sellers prefer higher prices.

Terms of Trade
How much of one thing is given up for how much of something else.

Thinking like AN ECONOMIST

It's Always Possible to Imagine Better Terms of Trade

A person buys a pair of shoes for $100. Later that day, the person says that he was "ripped off" by the shoe store owner; specifically, he says he paid too much for the shoes. Is this person arguing against trade or against the terms of trade? The economist knows that sometimes what sounds like a person arguing "against trade" is really his argument against the "terms of trade." Everyone can think of better terms of trade for himself. You buy a book for $40. Are there better terms of trade for you? Sure, you would have rather paid $30 for the book instead of $40. Sometimes, when it sounds as if we are arguing against trade, what we are really saying is this: "I wish I could have bought the good or service at better terms of trade than I did."

Costs of Trades

As always, economists consider both benefits and costs. They want to determine what costs are involved in a trade and whether the costs may prevent a trade from taking place.

UNEXPLOITED TRADES Suppose Smith wants to buy a red 1965 Ford Mustang in excellent condition. The maximum price she is willing and able to pay for the Mustang is $30,000. Also suppose that Jones owns a red 1965 Ford Mustang in excellent condition. The minimum price he is willing and able to sell the Mustang for is $23,000. Obviously, Smith's maximum buying price ($30,000) is greater than Jones's minimum selling price ($23,000), so a potential trade or exchange exists.

Transaction Costs
The costs associated with the time and effort needed to search out, negotiate, and consummate an exchange.

Will the potential trade between Smith and Jones become an actual exchange? The answer to this question may depend on the transaction costs. **Transaction costs** are the costs associated with the time and effort needed to search out, negotiate, and consummate a trade. To illustrate, neither Smith nor Jones may know that the other exists. Suppose Smith lives in Roanoke, Virginia, and Jones lives 40 miles away in Blacksburg, Virginia. Each needs to find the other, which may take time and money. Perhaps Smith can put an ad in the local Blacksburg newspaper stating that she is searching for a 1965 Ford Mustang in mint condition. Alternatively, Jones can put an ad in the local Roanoke newspaper stating that he has a 1965 Ford Mustang to sell. The ad may or may not be seen by the relevant party and then acted upon. Our point is a simple one: Transaction costs sometimes keep potential trades from turning into actual trades.

Consider another example. Suppose Kurt hates to shop for clothes because shopping takes too much time. He has to get in his car, drive to the mall, park the car, walk into the mall, look in different stores, try on different clothes, pay for the items, walk to and get back in his car, and drive home. Suppose Kurt spends an average of two hours when he shops, and he estimates that an hour of his time is worth $30. It follows, then, that Kurt incurs $60 worth of transaction costs when he buys clothes. Usually, he is not willing to incur the transaction costs necessary to buy a pair of trousers or a shirt.

Now, suppose we ask Kurt if he would be more willing to buy clothes if shopping was easier. Suppose, we say, the transaction costs associated with buying clothes could be lowered from $60 to less than $10. At lower transaction costs, Kurt says that he would be willing to shop more often.

How can transaction costs be lowered? Both people and computers can help lower the transaction costs of trades. For example, real estate brokers lower the transaction costs of selling and buying a house. Jim has a house to sell but doesn't know how to find a buyer. Karen wants to buy a house but doesn't know how to find a seller. Enter the real estate broker, who brings buyers and sellers together. In so doing, she lowers the transaction costs of buying and selling a house.

As another example, consider e-commerce on the Internet. Ursula can buy a book by getting in her car, driving to a bookstore, getting out of her car, walking into the bookstore, looking at the books on the shelves, taking a book to the cashier, paying for it, leaving the store, getting back in her car, and returning home. Or Ursula can buy a book over the Internet. She can click on one of the online booksellers, search for the book by title, read a short description of the book, and then click once to buy. Buying on the Internet has lower transaction costs than shopping at a store because online buying requires less time and effort. Before online book buying and selling, were there potential book purchases and sales that weren't being turned into actual book purchases and sales? There is some evidence that there were.

TURNING POTENTIAL TRADES INTO ACTUAL TRADES Some people are always looking for ways to earn a profit. It would seem that one way to earn a profit is to turn potential trades into actual trades by lowering transaction costs. Consider the following example. Buyer Smith is willing to pay a maximum price of $400 for good X; Seller Jones is willing to accept a minimum price of $200 for good X. Currently, the transaction costs of the exchange are $500, evenly split between Buyer Smith and Seller Jones.

Buyer Smith thinks, "Even if I pay the lowest possible price for good X, $200, I will still have to pay $250 in transaction costs, bringing my total to $450. The maximum price I am willing to pay for good X is $400, so I will not make this purchase."

Seller Jones thinks, "Even if I receive the highest possible price for good X, $400, I will still have to pay $250 in transaction costs, leaving me with only $150. The minimum price I am willing to accept for good X is $200, so I will not make this sale."

This potential trade will not become an actual trade unless someone can lower the transaction costs. One role of an entrepreneur is to try *to turn potential trades into actual trades by lowering transaction costs*. Suppose Entrepreneur Brown can lower the transaction costs for Buyer Smith and Seller Jones to $10 each, asking $60 from each person for services rendered. Also, Entrepreneur Brown negotiates the price of good X at $300. Will the potential exchange become an actual exchange?

Buyer Smith thinks, "I am willing to pay a maximum of $400 for good X. If I purchase good X through Entrepreneur Brown, I will pay $300 to Seller Jones, $10 in transaction costs, and $60 to Brown. This is a total of $370, leaving me better off by $30. It is worthwhile for me to purchase good X."

Seller Jones thinks, "I am willing to sell good X for a minimum of $200. If I sell good X through Entrepreneur Brown, I will receive $300 from Buyer Smith and will have to pay $10 in transaction costs and $60 to Brown. That will leave me with $230, or $30 better off. It is worthwhile for me to sell good X."

Thinking like AN ECONOMIST

Profit Motivates Action

In the example just given, Buyer Smith and Seller Jones were made better off by Entrepreneur Brown. Keep in mind that it was profit that motivated Entrepreneur Brown to turn a potential exchange into an actual exchange and, in the process, make both Smith and Jones better off. Simply put, the desire for profit (to help ourselves) can often prompt us to assist others. Thus, an entrepreneur can earn a profit by finding a way to lower transaction costs. As a result, a potential exchange turns into an actual exchange.

Trades and Third-Party Effects

Consider two trades. In the first, Harriet pays 80 cents to Taylor for a pack of chewing gum. In this trade, both Harriet and Taylor are made better off (they wouldn't have traded otherwise), and no one is made worse off.

In the second trade, Bob pays $5 to George for a pack of cigarettes. Bob takes a cigarette, lights it, and smokes it. It happens that he is near Caroline when he smokes the cigarette, and she begins to cough because she is sensitive to cigarette smoke. In this trade, both Bob, who buys the cigarettes, and George, who sells the cigarettes, are made better off. But Caroline, who had nothing to do with the trade, is made worse off. In this exchange, a third party, Caroline, is adversely affected by the exchange between George and Bob.

These examples show that some trades affect only the parties involved in the exchange, and some trades have *third-party effects* (someone other than the parties involved in the exchange is affected). In the cigarette example, the third-party effect was negative; there was an adverse effect on Caroline, the third party. Sometimes economists call adverse third-party effects *negative externalities*. A later chapter discusses this topic in detail.

SELF-TEST

1. What are transaction costs? Are the transaction costs of buying a house likely to be greater or less than those of buying a car? Explain your answer.

2. Smith is willing to pay a maximum of $300 for good X, and Jones is willing to sell good X for a minimum of $220. Will Smith buy good X from Jones?

3. Give an example of a trade without third-party effects. Next, give an example of a trade with third-party effects.

PRODUCTION, TRADE, AND SPECIALIZATION

The first section of this chapter discusses production; the second section discusses trade. From these two sections, you might conclude that production and trade are unrelated activities. However, they are not: Before you can trade, you need to produce something. This section ties production and trade together and also shows how the benefits one receives from trade can be affected by how one produces.

Producing and Trading

To show how a change in production can benefit traders, we eliminate anything and everything extraneous to the process. Thus, we eliminate money and consider a barter, or moneyless, economy.

In this economy, there are two individuals, Elizabeth and Brian. They live near each other, and each engages in two activities: baking bread and growing apples. Let's suppose that within a certain period of time, Elizabeth can produce 20 loaves of bread and no apples, or 10 loaves of bread and 10 apples, or no bread and 20 apples. See Exhibit 8. In other words, three points on Elizabeth's production possibilities frontier correspond to 20 loaves of bread and no apples, 10 loaves of bread and 10 apples, and no bread and 20 apples. As a consumer, Elizabeth likes to eat both bread and apples, so she decides to produce (and consume) 10 loaves of bread and 10 apples.

exhibit 8

Elizabeth		Brian	
Bread	**Apples**	**Bread**	**Apples**
20	0	10	0
10	10	5	15
0	20	0	30

Production by Elizabeth and Brian

This exhibit shows the combinations of goods each can produce individually in a given time period.

Within the same time period, Brian can produce 10 loaves of bread and no apples, or 5 loaves of bread and 15 apples, or no bread and 30 apples. In other words, these three combinations correspond to three points on Brian's production possibilities frontier. Brian, like Elizabeth, likes to eat both bread and apples, so he decides to produce and consume 5 loaves of bread and 15 apples. See Exhibit 8.

Elizabeth thinks that both she and Brian may be better off if each specializes in producing only one of the two goods and trading it for the other. In other words, Elizabeth should produce either bread or apples but not both. Brian thinks this may be a good idea but is not sure which good each person should specialize in producing.

An economist would advise each to produce the good that he or she can produce at a lower cost. In economics, a person who can produce a good at a lower cost than another person is said to have a **comparative advantage** in the production of that good.

Exhibit 8 shows that for every 10 units of bread Elizabeth does not produce, she can produce 10 apples. In other words, the opportunity cost of producing 1 loaf of bread (B) is 1 apple (A):

$$\text{Opportunity costs for Elizabeth: } 1B = 1A$$
$$1A = 1B$$

Comparative Advantage
The situation where someone can produce a good at lower opportunity cost than someone else can.

As for Brian, for every 5 loaves of bread he does not produce, he can produce 15 apples. So for every 1 loaf of bread he does not produce, he can produce 3 apples. It follows, then, that for every 1 apple he chooses to produce, he forfeits 1/3 loaf of bread.

$$\text{Opportunity costs for Brian: } 1B = 3A$$
$$1A = \tfrac{1}{3}B$$

Comparing opportunity costs, we see that Elizabeth can produce bread at a lower opportunity cost than Brian can. (Elizabeth forfeits 1 apple when she produces 1 loaf of bread, whereas Brian forfeits 3 apples when he produces 1 loaf of bread.) On the other hand, Brian can produce apples at a lower opportunity cost than Elizabeth can. We conclude that Elizabeth has a comparative advantage in the production of bread, and Brian has a comparative advantage in the production of apples.

Suppose each person specializes in the production of the good in which he or she has a comparative advantage. This means Elizabeth produces only bread and produces 20 loaves. Brian produces only apples and produces 30 apples.

Now suppose that Elizabeth and Brian decide to trade 8 loaves of bread for 12 apples. In other words, Elizabeth produces 20 loaves of bread and then trades 8 of the loaves for 12 apples. After the trade, Elizabeth consumes 12 loaves of bread and 12 apples.

exhibit 9

Consumption for Elizabeth and Brian With and Without Specialization and Trade

A comparison of the consumption of bread and apples before and after specialization and trade shows that both Elizabeth and Brian benefit from producing the good in which each has a comparative advantage and trading for the other good.

		No Specialization and No Trade	Specialization and Trade	Gains from Specialization and Trade
Elizabeth	Consumption of Loaves of Bread	10	12	+2
	Consumption of Apples	10	12	+2
Brian	Consumption of Loaves of Bread	5	8	+3
	Consumption of Apples	15	18	+3

Compare this situation with what she consumed when she didn't specialize and didn't trade. In that situation, she consumed 10 loaves of bread and 10 apples. Clearly, Elizabeth is better off when she specializes and trades than when she does not. But what about Brian?

Brian produces 30 apples and trades 12 of them to Elizabeth for 8 loaves of bread. In other words, he consumes 8 loaves of bread and 18 apples. Compare this situation with what he consumed when he didn't specialize and didn't trade. In that situation, he consumed 5 loaves of bread and 15 apples. Thus, Brian is also better off when he specializes and trades than when he does not.

Exhibit 9 summarizes consumption for Elizabeth and Brian. It shows that both Elizabeth and Brian make themselves better off by specializing in the production of one good and trading for the other.

Finding ECONOMICS

At the Airport

You wake up in the morning and drive to the airport. Curbside at the airport you have your bags checked. You tip the person who checks your luggage. You then line up to go through security. Once on the plane you hear the pilot telling you the flying time for today's flight. Later in the flight, the flight attendant brings you a soft drink and a snack. What you see at the airport and on board the plane is different people performing different tasks. The pilot is flying the plane and the customer service person at the check-in counter is receiving your luggage, and so on. Can you find the economics? Think about it for a minute before you read on.

What you see at the airport and on board the plane is specialization. The pilot isn't flying the plane and checking your luggage too. He is only flying the plane. The flight attendant isn't serving you food and checking you through security too. He is only serving you food. Why do people specialize? Largely, it's because individuals have found that they are better off specializing than not specializing. And usually what people specialize in is that activity in which they have a comparative advantage.

economics 24/7

JERRY SEINFELD, THE DOORMAN, AND ADAM SMITH

Oh, I get it. Why waste time making small talk with the doorman? I should just shut up and do my job, opening the door for you.
—The doorman, speaking to Jerry, in an episode of *Seinfeld*

In a Seinfeld episode, Jerry comes across a doorman (played by actor Larry Miller) who seems to have a chip on his shoulder. While waiting for the elevator, Jerry sees the doorman reading a newspaper. Jerry looks over and says, "What about those Knicks?" (a reference to the New York Knicks professional basketball team). The doorman's response is, "What makes you think I wasn't reading the Wall Street page? Oh, I know, because I'm the uneducated doorman."

This exchange between the doorman and Jerry would be unlikely if Jerry had not lived in New York City or in some other large city. That's because doormen are usually found only in large cities. If you live in a city with a population less than 100,000, you may not find a single doorman in the entire city. There are few doormen even in cities with a population of one million.

© NBC TV/THE KOBAL COLLECTION

This observation is not unique to us. It goes back to Adam Smith, who said that there is a direct relationship between the degree of specialization and the size of the market. Smith said: "There are some sorts of industry, even of the lowest kind, which can be carried on nowhere but in a great town. A porter, for example, can find employment and subsistence in no other place. A village is by much too narrow a sphere for him; even an ordinary market town is scarce large enough to afford him constant occupation."[1]

Smith's observation that "some sorts of industry . . . can be carried on nowhere but in a great town" seems true. Some occupations and some goods can only be found in big cities. Try to find a doorman in North Adams, Michigan (population 514), or restaurant chefs who only prepare Persian, Yugoslavian, or Caribbean entrées in Ipswich, South Dakota (population 943).

---

[1] Smith, Adam. *An Inquiry into the Nature and Causes of the Wealth of Nations.* Edwin Cannan, ed. New York: Modern Library, 1965.

Profit and a Lower Cost of Living

The last column of Exhibit 9 shows the gains from specialization and trade. One way to view these gains is in terms of Elizabeth and Brian being better off when they specialize and trade than when they do not specialize and do not trade. In short, specialization and trade make people better off.

Another way to view these gains is in terms of profit and a lower cost of living. To illustrate, let's look again at Elizabeth. Essentially, Elizabeth undertakes two actions by specializing and trading. The first action is to produce more of one good (loaves of bread) than she produces when she does not specialize. The second action is to trade, or "sell," some of the bread for a "price" higher than the cost of producing the bread. Specifically, she "sells" 8 of the loaves of bread (to Brian) for a "price" of 12 apples. In other words, she "sells" each loaf of bread for a "price" of 1 1/2 apples. But Elizabeth can produce a loaf of bread for a cost of 1 apple. So she "sells" the bread for a "price" (1 1/2 apples) that's higher than her cost of producing the bread (1 apple). The difference is her profit.

Common MISCONCEPTIONS

About Profits and Winners and Losers

Many people think that one person's profit is another person's loss. In other words, because Elizabeth earns a profit by specializing and trading, Brian must lose. But we have showed that this is not the case. The cost to Brian of producing a loaf of bread is 3 apples. But he "buys" bread from Elizabeth for a "price" of only 1 1/2 apples. In other words, while Elizabeth is earning a profit, Brian's cost of living (what he has to forfeit to get a loaf of bread) is declining.

A Benevolent and All-Knowing Dictator Versus the Invisible Hand

Suppose a benevolent dictator governs the country where Brian and Elizabeth live. We assume that this benevolent dictator knows everything about almost every economic activity in his country. In other words, he knows Elizabeth's and Brian's opportunity costs of producing bread and apples.

Because the dictator is benevolent and because he wants the best for the people who live in his country, he orders Elizabeth to produce only loaves of bread and Brian to produce only apples. Next, he tells Elizabeth and Brian to trade 8 loaves of bread for 12 apples.

Afterward, he shows Exhibit 9 to Elizabeth and Brian. They are both surprised that they are better off having done what the benevolent dictator told them to do.

Now in the original story about Elizabeth and Brian, there was no benevolent, all-knowing dictator. There were only two people who were guided by their self-interest to specialize and trade. In other words, self-interest did for Elizabeth and Brian what the benevolent dictator did for them.

Adam Smith, the eighteenth-century Scottish economist and founder of modern economics, spoke about the *invisible hand* that "guided" individuals' actions toward a positive outcome that they did not intend. That is what happened in the original story about Elizabeth and Brian. Neither intended to increase the overall output of society; each intended only to make himself or herself better off.

SELF-TEST

1. If George can produce either (a) 10X and 20Y or (b) 5X and 25Y, what is the opportunity cost to George of producing one more X?

2. Harriet can produce either (a) 30X and 70Y or (b) 40X and 55Y; Bill can produce either (c) 10X and 40Y or (d) 20X and 20Y. Who has a comparative advantage in the production of X? of Y? Explain your answers.

"WHAT PURPOSE DOES THE PPF SERVE?"

Student:

It seems that economists have many uses for the production possibilities frontier (PPF). For example, they can talk about scarcity, choice, opportunity costs, and many other topics in terms of the PPF. Beyond this, what purpose does the PPF serve?

Instructor:

One purpose is to ground us in reality. For example, the frontier (or boundary) of the PPF represents scarcity, which is a fact of life. In other words, the frontier of the PPF is essentially saying, "Here is scarcity. Work with it." One of the important effects of acknowledging this fact is that we come to understand *what is* and *what is not* possible. For example, if the economy is currently on the frontier of its PPF, producing 100 units of X and 200 units of Y, it follows that it's possible to get more of X, but it's impossible to get more of X without getting less of Y. In other words, the frontier of the PPF grounds us in reality: More of one thing means less of something else.

Student:

But isn't this something that we already knew?

Instructor:

We understand that more of X means less of Y once someone makes this point, but think of how often we might act as if we don't know it. John thinks he can work more hours at his job and get a good grade on his upcoming chemistry test. Well, he might be able to get a good grade (say, a 90), but this ignores how much higher the grade could have been (say, five points higher) if he hadn't worked more hours at his job. The frontier of the PPF reminds us that there are trade-offs in life. That is an important reality to be aware of. We ignore it at our own peril.

Student:

I've also heard that the PPF can show us what is necessary before the "average person" in a country can become richer. Is this true? And what kind of richer do we mean here?

Instructor:

We are talking about becoming richer in terms of having more goods and services. It's possible for the "average person" to become richer through economic growth. In other words, the average person in society becomes richer if the PPF shifts rightward by more than the population grows. To illustrate, suppose that a 100-person economy is currently producing 100 units of X and 200 units of Y. It follows that

the average person can have 1 unit of X and 2 units of Y. Now suppose there is economic growth (shifting the PPF to the right) and the economy can now produce more of both goods, X and Y. It produces 200 units of X and 400 units of Y. If the population has not changed (if it is still 100 people), then the average person can now have 2 units of X and 4 units of Y. The average person is richer in terms of two goods, X and Y. If we change things, and let the population grow from 100 persons to, say, 125 persons, it is still possible for the average person to have more through economic growth. With a population of 125 people, the average person now has 1.6 units of X and 3.2 units of good Y. In other words, as long as the productive capability of the economy grows by a greater percentage than the population, it is possible for the average person to become richer (in terms of goods and services).

Student:

Just because the economy is producing more of both goods (X and Y), it doesn't necessarily follow that the average person is better off in terms of goods and services, does it? Can't all the extra output end up in the hands of only a few people instead of being evenly distributed across the entire population?

Instructor:

That's correct. What we are assuming when we say the "average person" can be made better off is that if we took the extra output and divided it evenly across the population, then the average person would be better off in terms of having more goods and services. By the way, this is what economists mean when they say that the output (goods and services) per capita in a population has risen.

Points to Remember

1. The production possibilities frontier (PPF) grounds us in reality. It tells us *what is* and *what is not* possible in terms of producing various combinations of goods and services.

2. The PPF tells us that when we have efficiency (we are at a point on the frontier itself), more of one thing means less of something else. In other words, the PPF tells us there are trade-offs in life.

3. If the PPF shifts rightward and the population does not change, then output per capita rises.

a reader asks | How Will Economics Help Me if I'm a History Major?

I'm a history major taking my first course in economics. But quite frankly, I don't see how economics will be of much use in my study of history. Any thoughts on the subject?

Economics often plays a major role in historical events. For example, many social scientists argue that economics played a large role in the collapse of communism. If communism had been able to produce the quantity and variety of goods and services that capitalism produces, perhaps the Soviet Union would still exist.

Fact is, understanding economics may help you understand many historical events or periods. If, as a historian, you study the Great Depression, you will need to know something about the stock market, tariffs, and more. If you study the California Gold Rush, you will need to know about supply, demand, and prices. If you study the history of prisoner-of-war camps, you will need to know about how and why people trade and about money. If you study the Boston Tea Party, you will need to know about government grants of monopoly and about taxes.

Economics can also be useful in another way. Suppose you learn in your economics course what can and cannot cause inflation. We'll say you learn that X can cause inflation and that Y cannot. Then, one day, you read an article in which a historian says that Y caused the high inflation in a certain country and that the high inflation led to a public outcry, which was then met with stiff government reprisals. Without an understanding of economics, you might be willing to accept what the historian has written. But with your understanding of economics, you know that events could not have happened as the historian reports because Y, which the historian claims caused the high inflation, could not have caused the high inflation.

In conclusion, a good understanding of economics will not only help you understand key historical events but will also help you discern inaccuracies in recorded history.

Chapter Summary

AN ECONOMY'S PRODUCTION POSSIBILITIES FRONTIER

- An economy's production possibilities frontier (PPF) represents the possible combinations of two goods that the economy can produce in a certain period of time under the conditions of a given state of technology and fully employed resources.

INCREASING AND CONSTANT OPPORTUNITY COSTS

- A straight-line PPF represents constant opportunity costs: Increased production of one good comes at constant opportunity costs.
- A bowed-outward (concave-downward) PPF represents the law of increasing opportunity costs: Increased production of one good comes at increased opportunity costs.

THE PRODUCTION POSSIBILITIES FRONTIER AND VARIOUS ECONOMIC CONCEPTS

- The PPF can be used to illustrate various economic concepts. Scarcity is illustrated by the frontier itself. Choice is illustrated by our knowing that we have to locate at some particular point either on the frontier or below it. In short, of the many attainable positions, one must be chosen. Opportunity cost is illustrated by a movement from one point on the PPF to another point on the PPF. Unemployed resources and productive inefficiency are illustrated by a point below the PPF. Productive efficiency and fully employed resources are illustrated by a point on the PPF. Economic growth is illustrated by a shift outward in the PPF.

EXCHANGE OR TRADE

- The three time periods relevant to the trading process are (1) the ex ante period, which is the time before the trade is made, (2) the point of trade, and (3) the ex post period, which is the time after the trade has been made.
- There is a difference between trade and the terms of trade. Trade refers to the act of giving up one thing for something else. For example, a person may trade money for a car. The terms of trade refer to *how much* of one thing is traded for *how much* of something else. For example, how much money ($25,000? $30,000?) is traded for one car.

TRANSACTION COSTS

- Transaction costs are the costs associated with the time and effort needed to search out, negotiate, and consummate a trade. Some potential exchanges are not realized because of high transaction costs. Lowering transaction costs can turn a potential exchange into an actual exchange.

- One role of an entrepreneur is to try to lower transaction costs.

COMPARATIVE ADVANTAGE AND SPECIALIZATION

- Individuals can make themselves better off by specializing in the production of the good in which they have a comparative advantage and then trading some of that good for other goods. A person has a comparative advantage in the production of a good if he or she can produce the good at a lower opportunity cost than another person can.

- Individuals gain by specializing and trading. Specifically, they earn a profit by specializing in the production of the goods in which they have a comparative advantage.

Key Terms and Concepts

Production Possibilities Frontier (PPF)	Productive Efficiency	Exchange (Trade)	Terms of Trade
Law of Increasing Opportunity Costs	Productive Inefficiency	Ex Ante	Transaction Costs
	Technology	Ex Post	Comparative Advantage

Questions and Problems

1 Describe how each of the following would affect the U.S. production possibilities frontier: (a) an increase in the number of illegal immigrants entering the country, (b) a war that takes place on your country's soil, (c) the discovery of a new oil field, (d) a decrease in the unemployment rate, and (e) a law that requires individuals to enter lines of work for which they are not suited.

2 Explain how the following can be represented in a PPF framework: (a) the finiteness of resources implicit in the scarcity condition, (b) choice, (c) opportunity cost, (d) productive efficiency, and (e) unemployed resources.

3 What condition must hold for the production possibilities frontier to be bowed outward (concave downward)? to be a straight line?

4 Give an example to illustrate each of the following: (a) constant opportunity costs and (b) increasing opportunity costs.

5 Why are most production possibilities frontiers for goods bowed outward (concave downward)?

6 Within a PPF framework, explain each of the following: (a) a disagreement between a person who favors more domestic welfare spending and one who favors more national defense spending, (b) an increase in the population, and (c) a technological change that makes resources less specialized.

7 Explain how to derive a production possibilities frontier. For instance, how is the extreme point on the vertical axis identified? How is the extreme point on the horizontal axis identified?

8 If the slope of the production possibilities frontier is the same between any two points, what does this imply about costs? Explain your answer.

9 Suppose a nation's PPF shifts inward as its population grows. What happens, on average, to the material standard of living of the people? Explain your answer.

10 "A nation may be able to live beyond its means, but the world cannot." Do you agree or disagree? Explain your answer.

11 Can a technological advancement in sector X of the economy affect the number of people who work in sector Y of the economy? Explain your answer.

12 Use the PPF framework to explain something in your everyday life that was not mentioned in the chapter.

13 Describe the three time periods relevant to the trading process.

14 Are all exchanges or trades beneficial to both parties in the ex post position? Explain your answer.

15 A person who benefits from a trade can be disgruntled over the terms of trade. Do you agree or disagree? Explain your answer.

16 Give a numerical example that illustrates high transaction costs preventing an exchange or trade from taking place.

17 Give an example of a negative third-party effect (negative externality).

18 On any given day, 16 million items in 27,000 different categories are listed on sale on eBay.com. What does eBay do? It brings buyers and sellers together. But how does it do this?

19 Bob and Susan are married. Instead of splitting the various tasks in the home equally (you cook half the meals and I'll cook the other half of the meals), they end up specializing in certain tasks. For example, Susan does the cooking and Bob washes the dishes; Susan does the laundry and Bob mows the lawn. Why might Bob and Susan find it better to specialize in certain tasks instead of equally splitting each task?

20 Is it always possible to imagine better terms of trade? Give an example of why it is or why it is not.

21 "A profit for one person does not necessarily imply a loss for someone else." Do you agree or disagree? Explain your answer with an example.

22 What does it mean to say that someone has a comparative advantage in the production of good X?

23 The frontier or boundary of the PPF says "Here is scarcity." What does this mean?

24 Why might there be more people working as doormen in New York City than Topeka, Kansas?

Working with Numbers and Graphs

1 Tina can produce any of the following combinations of goods X and Y: (a) 100X and 0Y, (b) 50X and 25Y, and (c) 0X and 50Y. David can produce any of the following combinations of goods X and Y: (a) 50X and 0Y, (b) 25X and 40Y, and (c) 0X and 80Y. Who has a comparative advantage in the production of good X? of good Y? Explain your answer.

2 Using the data in problem 1, prove that both Tina and David can be made better off through specialization and trade.

3 Exhibit 6 represents an advance in technology that made it possible to produce more of both military and civilian goods. Represent an advance in technology that makes it possible to produce more of only civilian goods. Does this indirectly make it possible to produce more military goods? Explain your answer.

4 In the following figure, which graph depicts a technological breakthrough in the production of good X only?

5 In the preceding figure, which graph depicts a change in the PPF that is a likely consequence of war?

6 If PPF_2 in the following graph is the relevant production possibilities frontier, then which points are unattainable? Explain your answer.

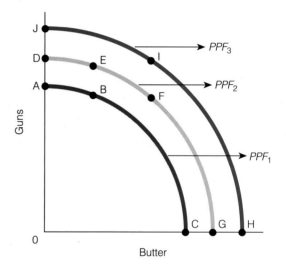

7 If PPF_1 in the preceding figure is the relevant production possibilities frontier, then which point(s) represent productive efficiency? Explain your answer.

(1)   (2)   (3)   (4)

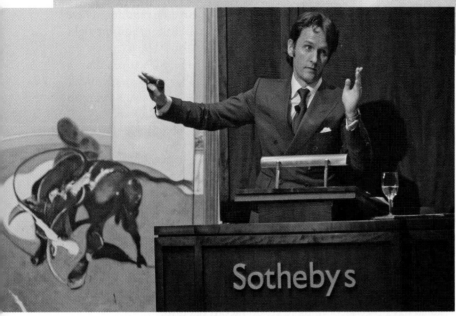

CHAPTER 3

SUPPLY AND DEMAND: THEORY

Introduction Psychologists sometimes use a technique called word association to learn more about their patients. The psychologist says a word, then the patient says the first word that comes into his or her head: morning, night; boy, girl; sunrise, sunset. If a psychologist ever happened to say "supply" to an economist, the response would undoubtedly be "demand." To economists, supply and demand go together. (Thomas Carlyle, the historian and philosopher, said that "it is easy to train economists. Just teach a parrot to say Supply and Demand." Not funny, Carlyle.) Supply and demand have been called the "bread and butter" of economics. In this chapter, we discuss them, first separately and then together.

A NOTE ABOUT THEORIES

Economists often build theories. They build a **theory** to answer questions that do not have obvious answers. For example, they might build a theory to understand why interest rates rise at some times and fall at others, why the price of a car is $25,000 and not $27,000, or why some countries have higher economic growth rates than other countries. When building theories, economists omit certain variables or factors when trying to explain or understand something. To understand why, consider an analogy. Suppose you were to draw a map for a friend, showing him how to get from his house to your house. Would you draw a map that showed *every single thing* your friend would see on the trip from his house to yours, or would you simply draw the main roads and one or two landmarks? If you'd do the latter, you would be abstracting from reality; you would be omitting certain things.

You would "omit certain variables or factors" for two reasons. First, to get your friend from his house to yours, you don't need to include everything on your map. Simply noting main roads may be enough. Second, if you did note everything on your map, your friend might get confused. Giving too much detail could be as bad as giving too little.

Theory
An abstract representation of the real world designed with the intent to better understand the world.

(Back in Chapter 1, you learned there is an efficient amount of almost everything. There is also an efficient amount of detail. There can be too much, too little, or just the right amount. Just the right amount is the efficient amount.)

When economists build a theory, they do the same thing you do when you draw a map. They abstract from reality; they leave out certain things. They focus on the major factors or variables that they believe will explain the phenomenon they are trying to understand.

This chapter deals with the theory of supply and demand. The objective of the theory is to try to understand why prices are what they are—for instance, why bread's price is $2 a loaf and not $20 a loaf or why a computer's price is $1,000 and not $10,000.

WHAT IS DEMAND?

Market

Any place people come together to trade.

A **market** is any place people come together to trade. Economists often say that there are *two* sides to every market: a buying side and a selling side. The buying side of the market is usually referred to as the *demand* side; the selling side of the market is usually referred to as the *supply* side. Let's begin with a discussion of *demand*.

Demand

The willingness and ability of buyers to purchase different quantities of a good at different prices during a specific time period.

The word **demand** has a precise meaning in economics. It refers to:

1. the willingness and ability of buyers to purchase different quantities of a good
2. at different prices
3. during a specific time period (per day, week, etc.).[1]

For example, we can express part of John's demand for magazines by saying that he is willing and able to buy 10 magazines a month at $4 per magazine and that he is willing and able to buy 15 magazines a month at $3 per magazine.

Remember this important point about demand: Unless both willingness and ability to buy are present, there is no demand, and a person is not a buyer. For example, Josie may be willing to buy a computer but be unable to pay the price; Tanya may be able to buy a computer but be unwilling to do so. Neither Josie nor Tanya demands a computer, and neither is a buyer of a computer.

The Law of Demand

Law of Demand

As the price of a good rises, the quantity demanded of the good falls, and as the price of a good falls, the quantity demanded of the good rises, *ceteris paribus*.

Will people buy more units of a good at lower prices than at higher prices? For example, will people buy more shirts at $10 a shirt than at $70 a shirt? If your answer is yes, you instinctively understand the law of demand. The **law of demand** states that as the price of a good rises, the quantity demanded of the good falls, and as the price of a good falls, the quantity demanded of the good rises, *ceteris paribus*. Simply put, the law of demand states that the price of a good and the quantity demanded of the good are inversely related, *ceteris paribus*:

$$P \uparrow Q_d \downarrow$$
$$P \downarrow Q_d \uparrow ceteris\ paribus$$

where P = price and Q_d = quantity demanded.

Quantity demanded is the number of units of a good that individuals are willing and able to buy at a particular price during some time period. For example, suppose individuals

---

1. Demand takes into account *services* as well as goods. A few examples of goods: shirts, books, and television sets. A few examples of services: dental care, medical care, an economics lecture. To simplify the discussion, we refer only to goods.

are willing and able to buy 100 TV dinners per week at a price of $4 per dinner. Therefore, 100 units is the quantity demanded of TV dinners at $4.

A warning: We know that the words "demand" and "quantity demanded" sound alike. But keep in mind that they do not speak to the same thing. Demand is different than quantity demanded. You need to keep that in mind as you continue to read this chapter. For now, remind yourself that demand speaks to the willingness and ability of buyers to buy different quantities of a good at different prices. Quantity demanded speaks to the willingness and ability of buyers to buy a specific quantity (say, 100 units of a good) at a specific price (say, $10 per unit).

What Does *Ceteris Paribus* Mean?

When we defined the law of demand, we used the term **ceteris paribus**. This is a Latin term that means *all other things held constant* or *nothing else changes*. For example, an economist might say: "As the price of Pepsi-Cola rises, the quantity demanded of Pepsi-Cola falls, *ceteris paribus*." Translated: If we raise the price of Pepsi-Cola, and nothing else changes—in other words, people's preferences stay the same, the recipe for Pepsi-Cola stays the same, and so on—then in response to the higher price of Pepsi-Cola, people will buy less Pepsi-Cola.

But some people ask, "Why would economists want to assume that when the price of Pepsi-Cola rises, nothing else changes? Don't other things change in the real world? Why assume things that we know are not true?"

Economists do not specify *ceteris paribus* because they want to say something false about the world. They specify it because they want to clearly define what they believe to be the real-world relationship between two variables. Look at it this way. If you drop a ball off the roof of a house, it will strike the ground *unless someone catches it.* This statement is true, and probably everyone would willingly accept it as true. But saying "unless someone catches it" is really no different than saying "assuming nothing else changes" or "*ceteris paribus.*"

Ceteris Paribus
A Latin term meaning "all other things constant" or "nothing else changes."

Thinking like An Economist

The Ceteris Paribus *Mindset*

Suppose John has eaten fat-free ice cream for the past two months but hasn't lost any weight. Does that mean that eating fat-free ice cream (instead of regular ice cream) won't help you lose weight? Not at all. We know that eating fat-free ice cream will help you lose weight "assuming nothing else changes" or "*ceteris paribus.*" In other words, if you were eating one bowl of regular ice cream twice a week, and you now replace it with one bowl of fat-free ice cream twice a week, and you change nothing else—you don't change how much you exercise, or how much you eat, or how much you sleep, and so on—then replacing regular ice cream with fat-free ice cream will cause you to lose weight. Of course, if you eat twice as much fat-free ice cream as regular ice cream, and stop exercising, and start eating more cookies (because you think you can take on more cookie calories because you are taking in fewer ice cream calories per serving), then you're not going to lose weight.

To the economist, all she is saying when she adds "*ceteris paribus*" to the end of a sentence (e.g., as the price of Pepsi-Cola rises, the quantity demanded of Pepsi-Cola falls, *ceteris paribus*) is the point we made in our ice cream example—namely, that if you change one thing (like eating fat-free ice cream and not regular ice cream), and nothing else changes, then you can expect a particular outcome (you will lose weight). The economist is not trying to get the results she wants by saying "*ceteris paribus*"; she is just trying to tell you what the relationship is between two variables.

Demand Schedule
The numerical tabulation of the quantity demanded of a good at different prices. A demand schedule is the numerical representation of the law of demand.

Demand Curve
The graphical representation of the law of demand.

Absolute (Money) Price
The price of a good in money terms.

Relative Price
The price of a good in terms of another good.

---

exhibit 1

Demand Schedule and Demand Curve

Part (a) shows a demand schedule for good X. Part (b) shows a demand curve, obtained by plotting the different price-quantity combinations in part (a) and connecting the points. On a demand curve, the price (in dollars) represents price per unit of the good. The quantity demanded, on the horizontal axis, is always relevant for a specific time period (a week, a month, and so on).

Demand Schedule for Good X

Price (dollars)	Quantity Demanded	Point in Part (b)
4	10	A
3	20	B
2	30	C
1	40	D

(a)

(b)

Four Ways to Represent the Law of Demand

Here are four ways to represent the law of demand.

- *In Words.* We can represent the law of demand in words; we have done so already. Earlier we said that as the price of a good rises, quantity demanded falls, and as price falls, quantity demanded rises, *ceteris paribus*. That was the statement (in words) of the law of demand.

- *In Symbols.* We can also represent the law of demand in symbols, which we have also done earlier. In symbols, the law of demand is:

$$P\uparrow\ Q_d\downarrow$$
$$P\downarrow\ Q_d\uparrow\ ceteris\ paribus$$

- *In a Demand Schedule.* A **demand schedule** is the numerical representation of the law of demand. A demand schedule for good X is illustrated in Exhibit 1(a).

- *As a Demand Curve.* In Exhibit 1(b), the four price-quantity combinations in part (a) are plotted and the points connected, giving us a (downward-sloping) demand curve. A (downward-sloping) **demand curve** is the graphical representation of the inverse relationship between price and quantity demanded specified by the law of demand. In short, a demand curve is a picture of the law of demand.

 Finding ECONOMICS

In a Visit Home to See Mom

A friend tells you that she only flies home to see her mother once a year. You ask why. She says, "Because the price of the ticket to fly home is $1,100." She then adds, "If the price were, say, $600 instead of $1,100, I'd fly home twice a year instead of once." Can you find any economics in what she says? If you listen closely to what she says, she has identified two points on her demand curve for air travel home: one point corresponds to $1,100 and one ticket (home) and the other point corresponds to $600 and two tickets home.

Two Prices: Absolute and Relative

In economics, there are absolute (or money) prices and relative prices. The **absolute (money) price** is the price of the good in money terms. For example, the absolute price of a car might be $30,000. The **relative price** is the price of the good *in terms of another good.* For example, suppose the absolute price of a car is $30,000 and the absolute price of a computer is $2,000. The relative price of the car—that is, the price of the car *in terms of computers*—is 15 computers. A person gives up the opportunity to buy 15 computers when he or she buys a car.

$$\text{Relative price of a car (in terms of computers)} = \frac{\text{Absolute price of a car}}{\text{Absolute price of a computer}}$$
$$= \frac{\$30,000}{\$2,000}$$
$$= 15$$

Thus, the relative price of a car in this example is 15 computers.

Now let's compute the relative price of a computer—that is, the price of a computer in terms of a car:

$$\text{Relative price of a computer (in terms of cars)} = \frac{\text{Absolute price of a computer}}{\text{Absolute price of a car}}$$

$$= \frac{\$2,000}{\$30,000}$$

$$= \frac{1}{15}$$

Thus, the relative price of a computer in this example is 1/15 of a car. A person gives up the opportunity to buy 1/15 of a car when he or she buys a computer.

Now consider this question: What happens to the relative price of a good if its absolute price rises and nothing else changes? For example, if the absolute price of a car rises from $30,000 to $40,000, what happens to the relative price of a car? Obviously, it rises from 15 computers to 20 computers. In short, if the absolute price of a good rises and nothing else changes, then the relative price of the good rises too.

Thinking like AN ECONOMIST

Higher Price Can Mean Cheaper

The economist knows that it is possible for a good to go up in price at the same time as it becomes cheaper. (How can this happen?) To illustrate, suppose the absolute price of a pen is $1 and the absolute price of a pencil is 10 cents. The relative price of 1 pen, then, is 10 pencils. Now let the absolute price of a pen rise to $1.20 at the same time that the absolute price of a pencil rises to 20 cents. As a result, the relative price of 1 pen falls to 6 pencils. In other words, the absolute price of pens rises (from $1 to $1.20) at the same time as pens become relatively cheaper (in terms of how many pencils you have to give up to get a pen). Who would have thought it?

Why Does Quantity Demanded Go Down as Price Goes Up?

The law of demand states that price and quantity demanded are inversely related. This much you know. But you do know *why* quantity demanded moves in the opposite direction of price? We identify two reasons. The first reason is that *people substitute lower priced goods for higher priced goods.*

Often, many goods serve the same purpose. Many different goods will satisfy hunger, and many different drinks will satisfy thirst. For example, both orange juice and grapefruit juice will satisfy thirst. On Monday, the price of orange juice equals the price of grapefruit juice, but on Tuesday, the price of orange juice rises. As a result, people will choose to buy less of the relatively higher priced orange juice and more of the relatively lower priced grapefruit juice. In other words, a rise in the price of orange juice will lead to a decrease in the quantity demanded of orange juice.

The second reason for the inverse relationship between price and quantity demanded has to do with the **law of diminishing marginal utility**, which states that for a given time period, the marginal (additional) utility or satisfaction gained by consuming equal successive units of a good will decline as the amount consumed increases. For example, you may receive more utility or satisfaction from eating your first hamburger at lunch than from eating your second and, if you continue, more utility from your second hamburger than from your third.

What does this have to do with the law of demand? Economists state that the more utility you receive from a unit of a good, the higher the price you are willing to pay for it;

Law of Diminishing Marginal Utility
For a given time period, the marginal (additional) utility or satisfaction gained by consuming equal successive units of a good will decline as the amount consumed increases.

TICKET PRICES AT DISNEY WORLD

The Walt Disney Company operates two major theme parks in the United States: Disneyland in California and Disney World in Florida. Every year, millions of people visit each site. The ticket price for visiting Disneyland or Disney World differs depending on how many days a person visits the theme park. For example, Disney World sells one- to ten-day tickets. Here are the ticket prices:

Ticket	Price
1 day	$71
2 day	$139
3 day	$203
4 day	$212
5 day	$215
6 day	$217
7 day	$219
8 day	$221
9 day	$223
10 day	$225

Now if we take the price of a one-day ticket and multiply it by 2, we get $142, but oddly enough, the price of a two-day ticket is not $142 but $139. Of course, if we take the price of a one-day ticket and multiply it by 10, we get $710, but Disney World doesn't charge $710

for a ten-day ticket, it charges $225, which is $485 less than $710. Why does Disney World charge less than double the price of a one-day ticket for a two-day ticket, and why does Disney World charge less than 10 times the price of a one-day ticket for a ten-day ticket?

Disney World is effectively telling visitors that if they want to visit the theme park for one day, they have to pay $71. But if they want to visit the theme park for additional days they don't have to pay $71 for each additional day. They pay less for additional days. But why?

An economic concept, the law of diminishing marginal utility, is the reason. The law of diminishing marginal utility states that as a person consumes additional units of a good, eventually the utility from each additional unit of the good decreases. Assuming the law of diminishing marginal utility holds for Disney World, individuals will get more utility from the first day at Disney World than from, say, the second, third, or tenth day. The less utility or satisfaction a person gets from something, the lower the dollar amount he is willing to pay for it. Thus, a person would not be willing to pay as much for the second day at Disney World as the first, and he would not be willing to pay as much for the tenth day as the ninth and so on. Disney World knows this and therefore prices its tickets differently depending on how many days one wants to visit Disney World.

the less utility you receive from a unit of a good, the lower the price you are willing to pay for it. According to the law of diminishing marginal utility, individuals obtain less utility from additional units of a good. It follows that they will only buy larger quantities of a good at lower prices. And this is the law of demand.

Individual Demand Curve and Market Demand Curve

There is a difference between an individual demand curve and a market demand curve. An individual demand curve represents the price-quantity combinations of a particular good for a *single buyer*. For example, a demand curve could show Jones's demand for CDs. A market demand curve represents the price-quantity combinations of a particular good for *all buyers*. In this case, the demand curve would show all buyers' demand for CDs.

A market demand curve is derived by "adding up" individual demand curves, as we show in Exhibit 2. The demand schedules for Jones, Smith, and other buyers are shown in part (a). The market demand schedule is obtained by adding the quantities demanded at each price. For example, at $12, the quantities demanded are 4 units for Jones, 5 units for Smith, and 100 units for other buyers. Thus, a total of 109 units are demanded at $12.

exhibit 2

Deriving a Market Demand Schedule and a Market Demand Curve

Part (a) shows four demand schedules combined into one table. The market demand schedule is derived by adding the quantities demanded at each price. In (b), the data points from the demand schedule are plotted to show how a market demand curve is derived. Only two points on the market demand curve are noted.

Price	Quantity Demanded							All Buyers
	Jones		**Smith**		**Other Buyers**			**All Buyers**
$15	1		2		20			23
14	2		3		45			50
13	3		4		70			77
12	4	+	5	+	100	=		109
11	5	+	6	+	130	=		141
10	6		7		160			173

(a)

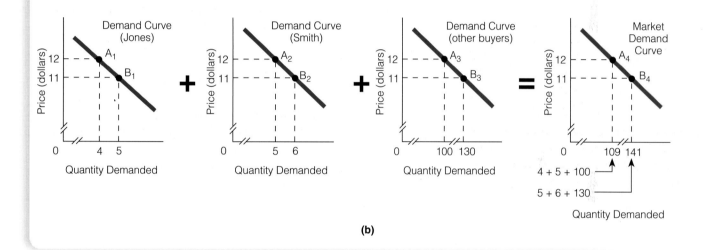

(b)

In part (b), the data points for the demand schedules are plotted and added to produce a market demand curve. The market demand curve could also be drawn directly from the market demand schedule.

A Change in Quantity Demanded Versus a Change in Demand

Economists often talk about (1) a change in quantity demanded and (2) a change in demand. As we stated earlier, although "quantity demanded" may sound like "demand," they are not the same. In short, a "change in quantity demanded" *is not* the same as a "change in demand." (Read the last sentence at least two more times.) We use Exhibit 1 to illustrate the difference between "a change in quantity demanded" and "a change in demand."

A CHANGE IN QUANTITY DEMANDED   Look at the horizontal axis in Exhibit 1, which is labeled "quantity demanded." Notice that quantity demanded is a *number*—such as 10, 20, 30, 40, and so on. More specifically, it is the number of units of a good that individuals are willing and able to buy at a particular price during some time period. In

Exhibit 1, if the price is $4, then quantity demanded is 10 units of good X; if the price is $3, then quantity demanded is 20 units of good X.

Quantity demanded = The *number* of units of a good that individuals are
willing and able to buy at a particular price

Now, again looking at Exhibit 1, what can change quantity demanded from 10 (which it is at point A) to 20 (which it is at point B)? Or what has to change before quantity demanded will change? The answer is on the vertical axis of Exhibit 1. The only thing that can change the quantity demanded of a good is the price of the good, which is called **own price**.

Own Price

The price of a good. For example, if the price of oranges is $1, this is its own price.

Change in quantity demanded = A *movement* from one point to another point
on the same demand curve *caused* by a change
in the price of the good

A CHANGE IN DEMAND Let's look again at Exhibit 1, this time focusing on the demand curve. Demand is represented by the *entire* curve. When an economist talks about a "change in demand," he or she is actually talking about a change—or shift—in the entire demand curve.

Change in demand = Shift in demand curve

Demand can change in two ways: Demand can increase, and demand can decrease. Let's look first at an *increase* in demand. Suppose we have the following demand schedule.

Demand Schedule A	
Price	Quantity Demanded
$20	500
$15	600
$10	700
$ 5	800

The demand curve for this demand schedule will look like the demand curve labeled D_A in Exhibit 3(a).

What does an increase in demand mean? It means that individuals are willing and able to buy more units of the good at each and every price. In other words, demand schedule A will change as follows:

Demand Schedule B (increase in demand)	
Price	Quantity Demanded
$20	~~500~~ 600
$15	~~600~~ 700
$10	~~700~~ 800
$ 5	~~800~~ 900

Whereas individuals were willing and able to buy 500 units of the good at $20, now they are willing and able to buy 600 units of the good at $20; whereas individuals were willing and able to buy 600 units of the good at $15, now they are willing and able to buy 700 units of the good at $15; and so on.

exhibit 3

Shifts in the Demand Curve

In part (a), the demand curve shifts rightward from D_A to D_B. This shift represents an increase in demand. At each price, the quantity demanded is greater than it was before. For example, the quantity demanded at $20 increases from 500 units to 600 units. In part (b), the demand curve shifts leftward from D_A to D_C. This shift represents a decrease in demand. At each price, the quantity demanded is less. For example, the quantity demand at $20 decreases from 500 units to 400 units.

D_A: Based on demand schedule A

D_A to D_B: Increase in demand (rightward shift in demand curve).

D_B: Based on demand schedule B

(a)

D_C: Based on demand schedule C

D_A to D_C: Decrease in demand (leftward shift in demand curve).

D_A: Based on demand schedule A

(b)

As shown in Exhibit 3(a), the demand curve that represents demand schedule B lies to the right of the demand curve that represents demand schedule A. We conclude that *an increase in demand is represented by a rightward shift in the demand curve and means that individuals are willing and able to buy more of a good at each and every price.*

Increase in demand = Rightward shift in the demand curve

Now let's look at a decrease in demand. What does a decrease in demand mean? It means that individuals are willing and able to buy less of a good at each and every price. In this case, demand schedule A will change as follows:

Demand Schedule C (decrease in demand)	
Price	Quantity Demanded
$20	~~500~~ 400
$15	~~600~~ 500
$10	~~700~~ 600
$ 5	~~800~~ 700

As shown in Exhibit 3(b), the demand curve that represents demand schedule C obviously lies to the left of the demand curve that represents demand schedule A. We conclude that a *decrease in demand is represented by a leftward shift in the demand curve and means that individuals are willing and able to buy less of a good at each and every price.*

Decrease in demand = Leftward shift in the demand curve

economics 24/7

iPODS AND THE LAW OF DEMAND

The law of demand holds that the price of a good and the quantity demanded of the good are inversely related. But does the law of demand hold for an individual when it comes to a good like an iPod? Will the individual buy more iPods at $10 than at $200? Perhaps she will, if only to give some iPods to friends.

But suppose we assume that the person doesn't want to give away any iPods as gifts. She wants only an iPod for herself. How many more than one iPod does she need? Probably none since there is little use of buying two iPods if one iPod holds all the songs you want. In other words, instead of having a downward-sloping demand curve for iPods, an individual might have a demand curve that looks like the one in Exhibit 4(a). This curve says the individual will buy one iPod no matter what the price is between zero and $300. But if the price is above $300, she will not buy an iPod since the demand curve doesn't extend that high.

Suppose no person has a downward-sloping demand curve. Is it still possible for the *market demand curve* to be downward-sloping? The answer is yes. To understand why, let's suppose there is another person's demand

©AP PHOTO/PAUL SAKUMA

curve for an iPod shown in Exhibit 4(b). This demand curve says she is willing and able to buy one iPod if the price is anywhere between zero and $200, but she won't buy an iPod if the price is higher than $200.

If we horizontally sum the two demand curves in panels (a) and (b) to get the market demand curve, we see that at a price of $300, one iPod will be purchased, and at $200, two iPods will be purchased. This is shown in Exhibit 4(c). Notice that this gives us a downward-sloping demand curve: More iPods are bought at a lower price than at a higher price.

exhibit 4

What Factors Cause the Demand Curve to Shift?

We know what an increase and decrease in demand mean: An increase in demand means consumers are willing and able to buy more of a good at every price. A decrease in demand means consumers are willing and able to buy less of a good at every price. We also know that an increase in demand is graphically portrayed as a rightward shift in a demand curve and a decrease in demand is graphically portrayed as a leftward shift in a demand curve.

But what factors or variables can increase or decrease demand? What factors or variables can shift demand curves? We identify and discuss these factors or variables in this section.

INCOME As a person's income changes (increases or decreases), his or her demand for a particular good may rise, fall, or remain constant.

ADVERTISING AND THE DEMAND CURVE

A company produces a good that it hopes to sell. To help sell its product, the company hires an advertising firm to work up an advertising campaign. It takes out ads in magazines and newspapers and on the radio and television.

Now ask if the seller of a good would prefer the demand for its good to be high or low? Obviously, the answer is high. All other things being equal, the higher the demand for the good, the higher the equilibrium price of the good. But to change a low demand into a high demand, one or more of the factors that demand is dependent upon (income, preferences, price of related goods, and so on) will have to change.

Which of these demand factors does advertising try to change? An ad runs in a magazine stating that good X is just like good Y except it is priced lower. Obviously here the company placing the ad is comparing the price of a substitute (Y) with the good it sells (X). We know that if X and Y are substitutes, then the higher the price of Y, the higher the demand for X.

Some ads inform the public of a good it may not know about. When ads do this, which of the demand factors is the company placing the ad trying to change? Obviously it is trying to change the number of buyers: the more buyers, the higher the demand curve. By informing people of a good they may not be aware of, it is possible to change nonbuyers into buyers.

Some ads try to persuade—they try to change preferences in favor of a particular good. If they are successful, the demand for the good being advertised rises. It is perhaps this kind of advertising (the kind designed to persuade) that we reject as manipulative. People might argue: "Advertisers simply create a demand for certain goods that would not ordinarily exist. They get us to buy things we don't really want to buy. No one has a demand for a cell phone with 100 different ringtones."

Can advertising persuade? At times, probably. But is it wrong to persuade? Our guess is that you weren't born with a demand for higher education. No doubt your parents, high school teachers, and friends might have influenced your decision to attend college. Were they manipulating you when they were telling you about the advantages of college?

Here's a controversial issue to discuss or think about. Person X tries to raise your demand for higher education and attending the opera. Person Y tries to raise your demand for cocaine. In some sense, both persons are "advertising" the benefits of different goods. Is advertising all right if it is truthful and the good being advertised is "good for you" but not all right if the good is "bad for you"? Next controversial issue: Who decides what is good and bad for you?

For example, suppose Jack's income rises. As a consequence, his demand for CDs rises. For Jack, CDs are a normal good. For a **normal good**, as income rises, demand for the good rises, and as income falls, demand for the good falls.

Normal Good
A good the demand for which rises (falls) as income rises (falls).

$$X \text{ is a normal good: If income} \uparrow \text{ then } D_X \uparrow$$
$$\text{If income} \downarrow \text{ then } D_X \downarrow$$

Now suppose Marie's income rises. As a consequence, her demand for canned baked beans falls. For Marie, canned baked beans are an inferior good. For an **inferior good**, as income rises, demand for the good falls, and as income falls, demand for the good rises.

Inferior Good
A good the demand for which falls (rises) as income rises (falls).

$$Y \text{ is an inferior good: If income} \uparrow \text{ then } D_y \downarrow$$
$$\text{If income} \downarrow \text{ then } D_y \uparrow$$

Finally, suppose when George's income rises, his demand for toothpaste neither rises nor falls. For George, toothpaste is neither a normal good nor an inferior good. Instead,

exhibit 5

Substitutes and Complements

(a) Coca-Cola and Pepsi-Cola are substitutes: The price of one and the demand for the other are directly related. As the price of Coca-Cola rises, the demand for Pepsi-Cola increases. (b) Tennis rackets and tennis balls are complements: The price of one and the demand for the other are inversely related. As the price of tennis rackets rises, the demand for tennis balls decreases.

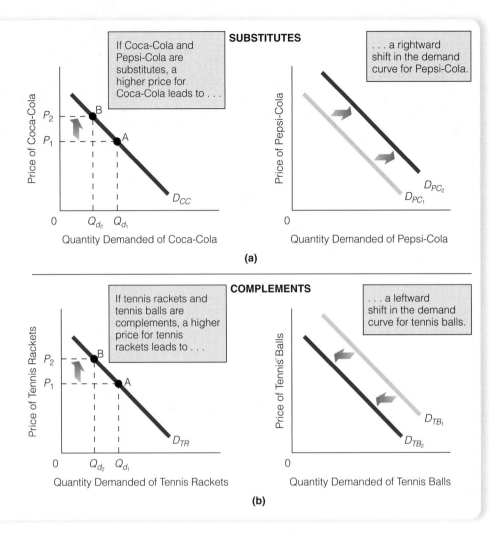

Neutral Good
A good the demand for which does not change as income rises or falls.

it is a neutral good. For a **neutral good**, as income rises or falls, the demand for the good does not change.

PREFERENCES People's preferences affect the amount of a good they are willing to buy at a particular price. A change in preferences in favor of a good shifts the demand curve rightward. A change in preferences away from the good shifts the demand curve leftward. For example, if people begin to favor Elmore Leonard novels to a greater degree than previously, the demand for Elmore Leonard novels increases, and the demand curve shifts rightward.

Substitutes
Two goods that satisfy similar needs or desires. If two goods are substitutes, the demand for one rises as the price of the other rises (or the demand for one falls as the price of the other falls).

PRICES OF RELATED GOODS There are two types of related goods: substitutes and complements. Two goods are **substitutes** if they satisfy similar needs or desires. For many people, Coca-Cola and Pepsi-Cola are substitutes. If two goods are substitutes, as the price of one rises (falls), the demand for the other rises (falls). For instance, higher Coca-Cola prices will increase the demand for Pepsi-Cola as people substitute Pepsi for the higher-priced Coke [Exhibit 5(a)]. Other examples of substitutes are coffee and tea, corn chips and potato chips, two brands of margarine, and foreign and domestic cars.

X and Y are substitutes: If $P_X \uparrow$ then $D_Y \uparrow$
If $P_X \downarrow$ then $D_Y \downarrow$

Two goods are **complements** if they are consumed jointly. For example, tennis rackets and tennis balls are used together to play tennis. If two goods are complements, as the price of one rises (falls), the demand for the other falls (rises). For example, higher tennis racket prices will decrease the demand for tennis balls, as Exhibit 5(b) shows. Other examples of complements are cars and tires, light bulbs and lamps, and golf clubs and golf balls.

NUMBER OF BUYERS   The demand for a good in a particular market area is related to the number of buyers in the area: more buyers, higher demand; fewer buyers, lower demand. The number of buyers may increase owing to a higher birthrate, increased immigration, the migration of people from one region of the country to another, and so on. The number of buyers may decrease owing to a higher death rate, war, the migration of people from one region of the country to another, and so on.

EXPECTATIONS OF FUTURE PRICE   Buyers who expect the price of a good to be higher next month may buy the good now—thus increasing the current (or present) demand for the good. Buyers who expect the price of a good to be lower next month may wait until next month to buy the good—thus decreasing the current (or present) demand for the good. For example, suppose you are planning to buy a house. One day, you hear that house prices are expected to go down in a few months. Consequently, you decide to delay your purchase of a house for a few months. Alternatively, if you hear that prices are expected to rise in a few months, you might go ahead and purchase a house now.

Movement Factors and Shift Factors

Economists often distinguish between (1) factors that can move us along curves and (2) factors that can shift curves.

The factors that move us along curves are sometimes called *movement* factors. In many economic diagrams—such as the diagram of the demand curve in Exhibit 1—the movement factor (price) is on the vertical axis.

The factors that actually shift the curves are sometimes called *shift* factors. The shift factors for the demand curve are income, preferences, the price of related goods, and so on. Often, the shift factors do not appear in the economic diagrams. For example, in Exhibit 1, the movement factor—price—is on the vertical axis, but the shift factors do not appear anywhere in the diagram. We just know what they are and that they can shift the demand curve.

When you see a curve in this book, first ask what factor will move us along the curve. In other words, what is the movement factor? Second, ask what factors will shift the curve. In other words, what are the shift factors? Exhibit 6 summarizes the shift factors that can change demand and the movement factors that can change quantity demanded.

Finding ECONOMICS

Soft Drinks Go on Sale

Karen buys more soft drinks when soft drinks go on sale. Two people interpret this action differently. John says that if Karen buys more soft drinks when soft drinks go on sale, Karen's demand curve has shifted to the right. Laura says that if Karen buys more soft drinks when soft drinks go on sale, Karen is simply "moving down" her given demand curve. "In short," says Laura, "Karen's quantity demanded of soft drinks has increased." Who is right? Laura is. Saying that soft drinks went on sale is no more than saying that the price of soft drinks declined. As price declines, quantity demanded (not demand) increases.

Complements
Two goods that are used jointly in consumption. If two goods are complements, the demand for one rises as the price of the other falls (or the demand for one falls as the price of the other rises).

exhibit 6

A Change in Demand Versus a Change in Quantity Demanded

(a) A change in demand refers to a shift in the demand curve. A change in demand can be brought about by a number of factors (see the exhibit and text). (b) A change in quantity demanded refers to a movement along a given demand curve. A change in quantity demanded is brought about only by a change in (a good's) own price.

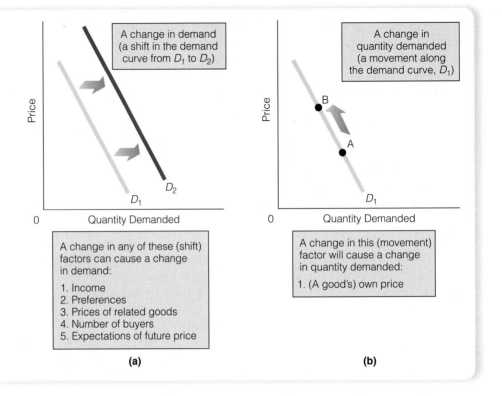

(a)   (b)

SELF-TEST

(Answers to Self-Test questions are in the Self-Test Appendix.)

1. As Sandi's income rises, her demand for popcorn rises. As Mark's income falls, his demand for pre-paid telephone cards rises. What kinds of goods are popcorn and telephone cards for the people who demand each?

2. Why are demand curves downward sloping?

3. Give an example that illustrates how to derive a market demand curve.

4. What factors can change demand? What factors can change quantity demanded?

SUPPLY

Just as the word *demand* has a specific meaning in economics, so does the word *supply*. **Supply** refers to

Supply
The willingness and ability of sellers to produce and offer to sell different quantities of a good at different prices during a specific time period.

1. the willingness and ability of sellers to produce and offer to sell different quantities of a good

2. at different prices

3. during a specific time period (per day, week, etc.).

Law of Supply
As the price of a good rises, the quantity supplied of the good rises, and as the price of a good falls, the quantity supplied of the good falls, *ceteris paribus.*

The Law of Supply

The **law of supply** states that as the price of a good rises, the quantity supplied of the good rises, and as the price of a good falls, the quantity supplied of the good falls, *ceteris paribus.* Simply put, the price of a good and the quantity supplied of the good are directly related, *ceteris paribus.* (Quantity supplied is the number of units sellers are willing and able to produce and offer to sell at a particular price.) The (upward-sloping) **supply curve** is the graphical representation of the law of supply (see Exhibit 7). The law of supply can be summarized as follows:

$$P\uparrow Q_S\uparrow$$
$$P\downarrow Q_S\downarrow \text{ ceteris paribus}$$

where P = price and Q_S = quantity supplied.

The law of supply holds for the production of most goods. It does not hold when there is no time to produce more units of a good. For example, suppose a theater in Atlanta is sold out for tonight's play. Even if ticket prices increased from $30 to $40, there would be no additional seats in the theater. There is no time to produce more seats. The supply curve for theater seats is illustrated in Exhibit 8(a). It is fixed at the number of seats in the theater, 500.[2]

The law of supply also does not hold for goods that cannot be produced over any period of time. For example, the violin maker Antonio Stradivari died in 1737. A rise in the price of Stradivarius violins does not affect the number of Stradivarius violins supplied, as Exhibit 8(b) illustrates.

Why Most Supply Curves Are Upward Sloping

Think back to the discussion of the *law of increasing opportunity costs* in Chapter 2. That discussion shows that if the production possibilities frontier (PPF) is bowed outward, increasing costs exist. In other words, increased production of a good comes at increased opportunity costs. An upward-sloping supply curve simply reflects the fact that costs rise when more units of a good are produced.

THE MARKET SUPPLY CURVE An individual supply curve represents the price-quantity combinations for a single seller. The market supply curve represents the price-quantity combinations for all sellers of a particular good. Exhibit 9 shows how a market supply curve can be derived by "adding" individual supply curves. In part (a), a **supply schedule**, the numerical tabulation of the quantity supplied of a good at different prices, is given for Brown, Alberts, and other suppliers. The market supply schedule is obtained by adding the quantities supplied at each price, *ceteris paribus.* For example, at $11, the

Supply Curve
The graphical representation of the law of supply.

A Supply Curve

The upward-sloping supply curve is the graphical representation of the law of supply, which states that price and quantity supplied are directly related, *ceteris paribus.* On a supply curve, the price (in dollars) represents price per unit of the good. The quantity supplied, on the horizontal axis, is always relevant for a specific time period (a week, a month, and so on).

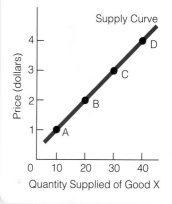

Supply Schedule
The numerical tabulation of the quantity supplied of a good at different prices. A supply schedule is the numerical representation of the law of supply.

exhibit 8

Supply Curves when There Is No Time to Produce More or No More Can Be Produced

The supply curve is not upward-sloping when there is no time to produce additional units or when additional units cannot be produced. In those cases, the supply curve is vertical.

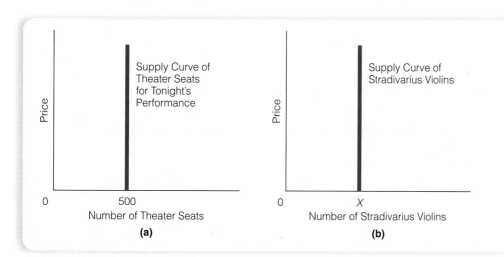

(a) (b)

---

2. The vertical supply curve is said to be *perfectly inelastic.*

exhibit 9

Deriving a Market Supply Schedule and a Market Supply Curve

Part (a) shows four supply schedules combined into one table. The market supply schedule is derived by adding the quantities supplied at each price. In (b), the data points

from the supply schedules are plotted to show how a market supply curve is derived. Only two points on the market supply curve are noted.

| Price | Quantity Supplied | | | |
	Brown	Alberts	Other Suppliers	All Suppliers
$10	1	2	96	99
11	2 +	3 +	98 =	103
12	3 +	4 +	102 =	109
13	4	5	106	115
14	5	6	108	119
15	6	7	110	123

(a)

(b)

quantities supplied are 2 units for Brown, 3 units for Alberts, and 98 units for other suppliers. Thus, a total of 103 units are supplied at $11. In part (b), the data points for the supply schedules are plotted and added to produce a market supply curve. The market supply curve could also be drawn directly from the market supply schedule.

Changes in Supply Mean Shifts in Supply Curves

Just as demand can change, so can supply. The supply of a good can rise or fall. What does it mean if the supply of a good increases? It means that suppliers are willing and able to produce and offer to sell more of the good at all prices. For example, suppose that in January sellers are willing and able to produce and offer for sale 600 shirts at $25 each and that in February they are willing and able to produce and sell 900 shirts at $25 each. An increase in supply shifts the entire supply curve to the right, as shown in Exhibit 10(a).

The supply of a good decreases if sellers are willing and able to produce and offer to sell less of the good at all prices. For example, suppose that in January sellers are willing and able to produce and offer for sale 600 shirts at $25 each and that in February they are willing and able to produce and sell only 300 shirts at $25 each. A decrease in supply shifts the entire supply curve to the left, as shown in Exhibit 10(b).

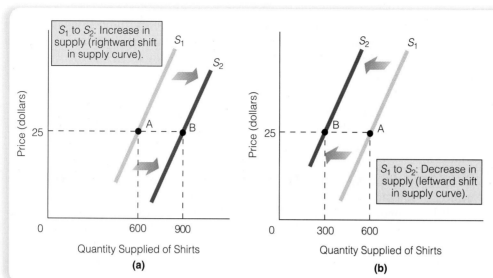

exhibit 10

Shifts in the Supply Curve

(a) The supply curve shifts rightward from S_1 to S_2. This represents an increase in the supply of shirts: At each price the quantity supplied of shirts is greater. For example, the quantity supplied at $25 increases from 600 shirts to 900 shirts. (b) The supply curve shifts leftward from S_1 to S_2. This represents a decrease in the supply of shirts: At each price the quantity supplied of shirts is less. For example, the quantity supplied at $25 decreases from 600 shirts to 300 shirts.

What Factors Cause the Supply Curve to Shift?

We know the supply of any good can change. But what causes supply to change? What causes supply curves to shift? The factors that can change supply include (1) prices of relevant resources, (2) technology, (3) prices of other goods, (4) number of sellers, (5) expectations of future price, (6) taxes and subsidies, and (7) government restrictions.

PRICES OF RELEVANT RESOURCES Resources are needed to produce goods. For example, wood is needed to produce doors. If the price of wood falls, it becomes less costly to produce doors. How will door producers respond? Will they produce more doors, the same number of doors, or fewer doors? With lower costs and prices unchanged, the profit from producing and selling doors has increased; as a result, there is an increased (monetary) incentive to produce doors. Door producers will produce and offer to sell more doors at each and every price. Thus, the supply of doors will increase, and the supply curve of doors will shift rightward. If the price of wood rises, it becomes more costly to produce doors. Consequently, the supply of doors will decrease, and the supply curve of doors will shift leftward.

TECHNOLOGY In Chapter 2, technology is defined as the body of skills and knowledge concerning the use of resources in production. Also, an advance in technology refers to the ability to produce more output with a fixed amount of resources, thus reducing per-unit production costs. To illustrate, suppose it currently takes $100 to produce 40 units of a good. The per-unit cost is therefore $2.50. If an advance in technology makes it possible to produce 50 units at a cost of $100, then the per-unit cost falls to $2.00.

If per-unit production costs of a good decline, we expect the quantity supplied of the good at each price to increase. Why? The reason is that lower per-unit costs increase profitability and therefore provide producers with an incentive to produce more. For example, if corn growers develop a way to grow more corn using the same amount of water and other resources, it follows that per-unit production costs will fall, profitability will increase, and growers will want to grow and sell more corn at each price. The supply curve of corn will shift rightward.

PRICES OF OTHER GOODS Think of a farmer who is producing wheat. Suddenly, the price of something he is not producing (say, corn) rises relative to wheat. It is possible that the farmer may shift his farming away from wheat to corn. In other words, as the price of corn rises relative to wheat, the farmer switches from wheat production to corn production. We conclude that a change in the price of one good can lead to a change in the supply of another good.

NUMBER OF SELLERS If more sellers begin producing a particular good, perhaps because of high profits, the supply curve will shift rightward. If some sellers stop producing a particular good, perhaps because of losses, the supply curve will shift leftward.

EXPECTATIONS OF FUTURE PRICES If the price of a good is expected to be higher in the future, producers may hold back some of the product today (if possible, but perishables cannot be held back). Then they will have more to sell at the higher future price. Therefore, the current supply curve will shift leftward. For example, if oil producers expect the price of oil to be higher next year, some may hold oil off the market this year to be able to sell it next year. Similarly, if they expect the price of oil to be lower next year, they might pump more oil this year than previously planned.

TAXES AND SUBSIDIES Some taxes increase per-unit costs. Suppose a shoe manufacturer must pay a $2 tax per pair of shoes produced. This tax leads to a leftward shift in the supply curve, indicating that the manufacturer wants to produce and offer to sell fewer pairs of shoes at each price. If the tax is eliminated, the supply curve shifts rightward.

    Subsidies have the opposite effect. Suppose the government subsidizes the production of corn by paying corn farmers $2 for every bushel of corn they produce. Because of the subsidy, the quantity supplied of corn is greater at each price, and the supply curve of corn shifts rightward. Removal of the subsidy shifts the supply curve of corn leftward. A rough rule of thumb is that we get more of what we subsidize and less of what we tax.

GOVERNMENT RESTRICTIONS Sometimes, government acts to reduce supply. Consider a U.S. import quota on Japanese television sets. An import quota, or quantitative restriction on foreign goods, reduces the supply of Japanese television sets in the United States. It shifts the supply curve leftward. The elimination of the import quota allows the supply of Japanese television sets in the United States to shift rightward.

    Licensure has a similar effect. With licensure, individuals must meet certain requirements before they can legally carry out a task. For example, owner-operators of day-care centers must meet certain requirements before they are allowed to sell their services. No doubt, this reduces the number of day-care centers and shifts the supply curve of day-care centers leftward.

A Change in Supply Versus a Change in Quantity Supplied

It is important to remember that a change in *supply* is not the same as a change in *quantity supplied*. A change in supply refers to a shift in the supply curve, as illustrated in Exhibit 11(a). For example, saying that the supply of oranges has increased is the same as saying that the supply curve for oranges has shifted rightward. The factors that can change supply (shift the supply curve) include prices of relevant resources, technology, prices of other goods, number of sellers, expectations of future price, taxes and subsidies, and government restrictions.

    A change in quantity supplied refers to a movement along a supply curve, as in Exhibit 11(b). The only factor that can directly cause a change in the quantity supplied of a good is a change in the price of the good, or own price.

Subsidy
A monetary payment by government to a producer of a good or service.

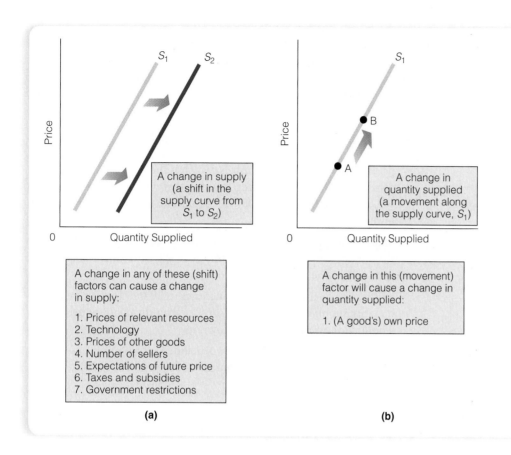

exhibit 11

A Change in Supply Versus a Change in Quantity Supplied

(a) A change in supply refers to a shift in the supply curve. A change in supply can be brought about by a number of factors (see the exhibit and text). (b) A change in quantity supplied refers to a movement along a given supply curve. A change in quantity supplied is brought about only by a change in (a good's) own price.

SELF·TEST

1. What would the supply curve for houses (in a given city) look like for a time period of (a) the next ten hours and (b) the next three months?

2. What happens to the supply curve if each of the following occurs?

   a. There is a decrease in the number of sellers.

   b. A per-unit tax is placed on the production of a good.

   c. The price of a relevant resource falls.

3. "If the price of apples rises, the supply of apples will rise." True or false? Explain your answer.

THE MARKET:
PUTTING SUPPLY AND DEMAND TOGETHER

In this section, we put supply and demand together and discuss the market. The purpose of the discussion is to gain some understanding about how prices are determined.

Supply and Demand at Work at an Auction

Imagine you are at an auction where bushels of corn are bought and sold. At this auction, the auctioneer will adjust the corn price to sell all the corn offered for sale. The supply curve of corn is vertical, as in Exhibit 12. It intersects the horizontal axis at

exhibit 12

Supply and Demand at Work at an Auction

Q_d = quantity demanded; Q_s = quantity supplied. The auctioneer calls out different prices, and buyers record how much they are willing and able to buy. At prices of $9.00, $8.00, and $7.00, quantity supplied is greater than quantity demanded. At prices of $4.25 and $5.25, quantity demanded is greater than quantity supplied. At a price of $6.10, quantity demanded equals quantity supplied.

40,000 bushels; that is, quantity supplied is 40,000 bushels. The demand curve for corn is downward sloping. Furthermore, suppose each potential buyer of corn is sitting in front of a computer that immediately registers the number of bushels he or she wants to buy. For example, if Nancy Bernstein wants to buy 5,000 bushels of corn, she simply keys "5,000" into her computer. The auction begins. (Follow along in Exhibit 12 as we relay what is happening at the auction.) The auctioneer calls out the price:

- $9.00. The potential buyers think for a second, and then each registers the number of bushels he or she is willing and able to buy at that price. The total is 10,000 bushels, which is the quantity demanded of corn at $9.00. The auctioneer, realizing that 30,000 bushels of corn (40,000 − 10,000 = 30,000) will go unsold at this price, decides to lower the price per bushel to:

- $8.00. The quantity demanded increases to 20,000 bushels, but still the quantity supplied of corn at this price is greater than the quantity demanded. The auctioneer calls out:

- $7.00. The quantity demanded increases to 30,000 bushels, but the quantity supplied at $7.00 is still greater than the quantity demanded. The auctioneer drops the price down to:

- $4.25. At this price, the quantity demanded jumps to 60,000 bushels, but that is 20,000 bushels more than the quantity supplied. The auctioneer calls out a higher price:

- $5.25. The quantity demanded drops to 50,000 bushels, but buyers still want to buy more corn at this price than there is corn to be sold. The auctioneer calls out:

- $6.10. At this price, the quantity demanded of corn is 40,000 bushels and the quantity supplied of corn is 40,000 bushels. The auction stops. The 40,000 bushels of corn are bought and sold at $6.10 per bushel.

Surplus (Excess Supply)
A condition in which quantity supplied is greater than quantity demanded. Surpluses occur only at prices above equilibrium price.

Shortage (Excess Demand)
A condition in which quantity demanded is greater than quantity supplied. Shortages occur only at prices below equilibrium price.

Equilibrium Price (Market-Clearing Price)
The price at which quantity demanded of the good equals quantity supplied.

Equilibrium Quantity
The quantity that corresponds to equilibrium price. The quantity at which the amount of the good that buyers are willing and able to buy equals the amount that sellers are willing and able to sell, and both equal the amount actually bought and sold.

The Language of Supply and Demand: A Few Important Terms

If quantity supplied is greater than quantity demanded, a **surplus** or **excess supply** exists. If quantity demanded is greater than quantity supplied, a **shortage** or **excess demand** exists. In Exhibit 12, a surplus exists at $9.00, $8.00, and $7.00. A shortage exists at $4.25 and $5.25. The price at which quantity demanded equals quantity supplied is the **equilibrium price (market-clearing price)**. In our example, $6.10 is the equilibrium price. The quantity that corresponds to the equilibrium price is the **equilibrium quantity**. In our example, it is 40,000 bushels of corn. Any price at which quantity demanded is not equal to quantity supplied is a **disequilibrium price**.

A market that exhibits either a surplus $(Q_s > Q_d)$ or a shortage $(Q_d > Q_s)$ is said to be in **disequilibrium**. A market in which quantity demanded equals quantity supplied $(Q_d = Q_s)$ is said to be in **equilibrium** (identified by the letter E in Exhibit 12).

Moving to Equilibrium: What Happens to Price when There Is a Surplus or a Shortage?

What did the auctioneer do when the price was $9.00 and there was a surplus of corn? He lowered the price. What did the auctioneer do when the price was $5.25 and there was a shortage of corn? He raised the price. The behavior of the auctioneer can be summarized this way: If a surplus exists, lower the price; if a shortage exists, raise the price. This is how the auctioneer moved the corn market into equilibrium.

Not all markets have auctioneers. (When was the last time you saw an auctioneer in the grocery store?) But many markets act *as if* an auctioneer were calling out higher and lower prices until equilibrium price is reached. In many real-world auctioneer-less markets, prices fall when there is a surplus and rise when there is a shortage. Why?

WHY DOES PRICE FALL WHEN THERE IS A SURPLUS? In Exhibit 13, there is a surplus at a price of $15: Quantity supplied (150 units) is greater than quantity demanded (50 units). Suppliers will not be able to sell all they had hoped to sell at $15. As a result, their inventories will grow beyond the level they hold in preparation for demand changes. Sellers will want to reduce their inventories. Some will lower prices to do so, some will cut back on production, others will do a little of both. As shown in the exhibit, there is a tendency for price and output to fall until equilibrium is achieved.

WHY DOES PRICE RISE WHEN THERE IS A SHORTAGE? In Exhibit 13, there is a shortage at a price of $5: Quantity demanded (150 units) is greater than quantity supplied (50 units). Buyers will not be able to buy all they had hoped to buy at $5. Some buyers will bid up the price to get sellers to sell to them instead of to other buyers. Some sellers, seeing buyers clamor for the goods, will realize that they can raise the price

Disequilibrium Price
A price other than equilibrium price. A price at which quantity demanded does not equal quantity supplied.

Disequilibrium
A state of either surplus or shortage in a market.

Equilibrium
Equilibrium means "at rest." Equilibrium in a market is the price quantity combination from which there is no tendency for buyers or sellers to move away. Graphically, equilibrium is the intersection point of the supply and demand curves.

---

exhibit 13

Moving to Equilibrium

If there is a surplus, sellers' inventories rise above the level they hold in preparation for demand changes. Sellers will want to reduce their inventories. As a result, price and output fall until equilibrium is achieved. If there is a

shortage, some buyers will bid up price to get sellers to sell to them instead of to other buyers. Some sellers will realize they can raise the price of the goods they have for sale. Higher prices will call forth added output. Price and output rise until equilibrium is achieved.

(Note: Recall that price, on the vertical axis, is price per unit of the good, and quantity, on the horizontal axis, is for a specific time period. In this text, we do not specify this on the axes themselves, but consider it to be understood.)

Price	Q_s	Q_d	Condition
$15	150	50	Surplus
10	100	100	Equilibrium
5	50	150	Shortage

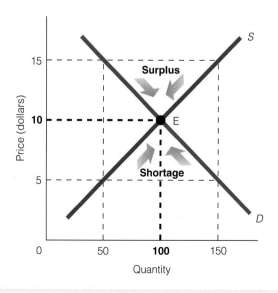

A Summary Exhibit of a Market (Supply and Demand)

This exhibit ties together the topics discussed so far in this chapter. A market is composed of both supply and demand, as shown. Also shown are the factors that affect supply and demand and therefore indirectly affect the equilibrium price and quantity of a good.

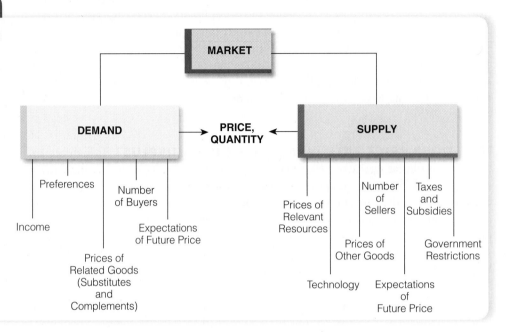

of the goods they have for sale. Higher prices will also call forth added output. Thus, there is a tendency for price and output to rise until equilibrium is achieved.

Take a look at Exhibit 14. It brings together much of what we have discussed about supply and demand.

Speed of Moving to Equilibrium

On July 16, 2008, at 12:00 p.m. (Eastern time), the price of a share of IBM stock was approximately $123. A few minutes later, the price had risen to $124. Obviously, the stock market is a market that equilibrates quickly. If demand rises, then initially there is a shortage of the stock at the current equilibrium price. The price is bid up, and there is no longer a shortage. All this happens in seconds.

Now consider a house offered for sale in any city in the United States. It is not uncommon for the sale price of a house to remain the same even though the house does not sell for months. For example, a person offers to sell her house for $400,000. One month passes, no sale; two months pass, no sale; three months pass, no sale; and so on. Ten months later, the house has still not sold, and the price is still $400,000.

Is $400,000 the equilibrium price of the house? Obviously not. At the equilibrium price, there would be a buyer for the house and a seller of the house (quantity demanded would equal quantity supplied). At a price of $400,000, there is a seller of the house but no buyer. The price of $400,000 is above equilibrium price. At $400,000, there is a surplus in the housing market; equilibrium has not been achieved.

Some people may be tempted to argue that supply and demand are at work in the stock market but not in the housing market. A better explanation, though, is that *not all markets equilibrate at the same speed.* While it may take only seconds for the stock market to go from surplus or shortage to equilibrium, it may take months for the housing market to do so.

economics 24/7

THE DOWRY AND MARRIAGE MARKET DISEQUILIBRIUM

It is generally accepted by men and women that monogamy is the ideal marriage practice. In other words, polygyny (the practice of one man being able to have more than one wife) is not the ideal marriage practice, and therefore should be deemed illegal. Some anthropologists and evolutionary biologists challenge orthodoxy by arguing that polygyny gives women greater choice. Here is how they structure their argument. Suppose there are 1,000 men and 1,000 women. Suppose each of the men and each of the women is given a ranking of between 1 and 1,000. The number 1 man is ranked higher than the number 2 man (and so on) in terms of a variety of characteristics. The same holds for women.

Currently the number 1 man is matched up with the number 1 woman, the number 2 man with the number 2 woman, and so on. The woman marries the man with whom she shares the same ranking. Now suppose the 404th-ranked woman (who is scheduled to marry the 404th-ranked man) prefers to be the second wife of the 40th-ranked man rather than the only wife of the 404th man. If polygyny were allowed, the 404th-ranked woman can marry the 40th-ranked man and share him with another wife. If polygyny is outlawed, she can't.

Now let's put things into economic terms. We know that a shortage exists if the quantity demanded of a good is greater than the quantity supplied. Think of the situation we have just discussed, where two women might want to marry the same man. Quantity supplied of the man is one, but the quantity demanded (of him) is two. This sounds like a shortage of the man, unless polygyny is permitted, because in that case it is possible for the two women to be married to the same man.

But suppose polygyny is not permitted, even though the two women still want to be married to the same man. Now we have the problem of a shortage (of this particular man) that cannot be eliminated through the adoption of polygyny. But what other way remains to eliminate the shortage? Normally we think of money as eliminating a shortage, and this is exactly what might be the purpose of the dowry. A dowry is a transfer of assets from the bride's family to the groom's family (usually) before the marriage takes place. If two women want to be married to the same man, but only one can be legally married to him, then the dowry may effectively take the place of polygyny (in eliminating the shortage of the man). All other things being equal, the prospective bride's family that offers the better dowry to the groom's family ends up with the groom as their son-in-law. This is consistent with the findings of anthropologists Gaulin and Boster, who have shown that the dowry is almost exclusively found in societies where monogamy has been imposed (and polygyny outlawed).

Moving to Equilibrium: Maximum and Minimum Prices

The discussion of surpluses illustrates how a market moves to equilibrium, but there is another way to demonstrate this. Exhibit 15 shows the market for good X. Look at the first unit of good X. What is the *maximum price buyers would be willing to pay* for it? The answer is $70. This can be seen by following the dotted line up from the first unit of the good to the demand curve. What is the *minimum price sellers need to receive before they would be willing to sell* this unit of good X? It is $10. This can be seen by following the dotted line up from the first unit to the supply curve. Because the maximum buying price is greater than the minimum selling price, the first unit of good X will be exchanged.

What about the second unit? For the second unit, buyers are willing to pay a maximum price of $60, and sellers need to receive a minimum price of $20. The second unit of good X will be exchanged. In fact, exchange will occur as long as the maximum buying price is greater than the minimum selling price. The exhibit shows that a total of four units of good X will be exchanged. The fifth unit will not be exchanged because the maximum buying price ($30) is less than the minimum selling price ($50).

exhibit 15

Moving to Equilibrium in Terms of Maximum and Minimum Prices

As long as the maximum buying price is greater than the minimum selling price, an exchange will occur. This condition is met for units 1–4. The market converges on equilibrium through a process of mutually beneficial exchanges.

Units of Good X	Maximum Buying Price	Minimum Selling Price	Result
1st	$70	$10	Exchange
2d	60	20	Exchange
3d	50	30	Exchange
4th	40	40	Exchange
5th	30	50	No Exchange

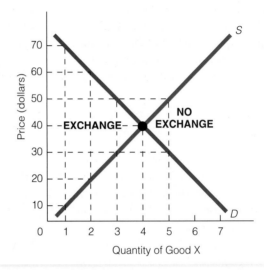

In the process just described, buyers and sellers trade money for goods as long as both benefit from the trade. The market converges on a quantity of 4 units of good X and a price of $40 per unit. This is equilibrium. In other words, mutually beneficial trade drives the market to equilibrium.

Equilibrium in Terms of Consumers' and Producers' Surplus

Equilibrium can be viewed in terms of two important economic concepts: consumers' surplus and producers' (or sellers') surplus. **Consumers' surplus** is the difference between the maximum buying price and the price paid by the buyer.

Consumers' Surplus (CS)
The difference between the maximum price a buyer is willing and able to pay for a good or service and the price actually paid. CS = Maximum buying price − Price paid.

Consumers' surplus = Maximum buying price − Price paid

For example, if the highest price you would pay to see a movie is $10 and you pay $7 to see the movie, then you have received $3 consumers' surplus. Obviously, the more consumers' surplus consumers receive, the better off they are. Wouldn't you have preferred to pay, say, $4 to see the movie instead of $7? If you had paid only $4, your consumers' surplus would have been $6 instead of $3.

Producers' (Sellers') Surplus (PS)
The difference between the price sellers receive for a good and the minimum or lowest price for which they would have sold the good. PS = Price received − Minimum selling price.

Producers' (sellers') surplus is the difference between the price received by the producer or seller and the minimum selling price.

Producers' (sellers') surplus = Price received − Minimum selling price

Suppose the minimum price the owner of the movie theater would have accepted for admission is $5. But she doesn't sell admission for $5; she sells it for $7. Her producers' or sellers' surplus is $2. A seller prefers a large producers' surplus to a small one. The theater owner would have preferred to sell admission to the movie for $8 instead of $7 because then she would have received $3 producers' surplus.

Total surplus is the sum of the consumers' surplus and producers' surplus.

Total surplus = Consumers' surplus + Producers' surplus

Total Surplus (TS)
The sum of consumers' surplus and producers' surplus. $TS = CS + PS$.

In Exhibit 16(a), consumers' surplus is represented by the shaded triangle. This triangle includes the area under the demand curve and above the equilibrium price. According to the definition, consumers' surplus is the highest price buyers are willing to pay (maximum buying price) minus the price they pay. For example, the window in (a) shows that buyers are willing to pay as high as $7 for the 50th unit but only pay $5. Thus, the consumers' surplus on the 50th unit of the good is $2. If we add the consumers' surplus on each unit of the good between and including the first and the 100th units (the equilibrium quantity), we obtain the shaded consumers' surplus triangle.

In Exhibit 16(b), producers' surplus is represented by the shaded triangle. This triangle includes the area above the supply curve and under the equilibrium price. Keep in mind the definition of producers' surplus—the price received by the seller minus the lowest price the seller would accept for the good. For example, the window in (b) shows that sellers would have sold the 50th unit for as low as $3 but actually sold it for $5. Thus, the producers' surplus on the 50th unit of the good is $2. If we add the producers' surplus on each unit of the good between and including the first and the 100th unit, we obtain the shaded producers' surplus triangle.

exhibit 16

Consumers' and Producers' Surplus

(a) Consumers' surplus. As the shaded area indicates, the difference between the maximum or highest amount buyers would be willing to pay and the price they actually pay is consumers' surplus. (b) Producers' surplus. As the shaded area indicates, the difference between the price sellers receive for the good and the minimum or lowest price they would be willing to sell the good for is producers' surplus.

(a)

Consumers' Surplus (CS)

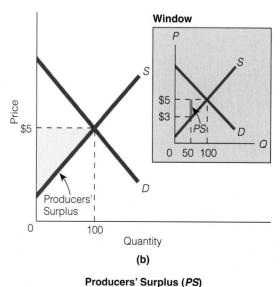

(b)

Producers' Surplus (PS)

Equilibrium, Consumers' Surplus, and Producers' Surplus

Consumers' surplus is greater at equilibrium quantity (100 units) than at any other exchangeable quantity. Producers' surplus is greater at equilibrium quantity than at any other exchangeable quantity. For example, consumers' surplus is areas $A + B + C$ at 75 units, but areas $A + B + C + D$ at 100 units. Producers' surplus is areas $E + F + G$ at 75 units, but areas $E + F + G + H$ at 100 units.

Quantity (units)	Consumers' Surplus	Producers' Surplus
25	A	E
50	$A + B$	$E + F$
75	$A + B + C$	$E + F + G$
100 (Equilibrium)	$A + B + C + D$	$E + F + G + H$

(a)

(b)

Now consider consumers' surplus and producers' surplus at the equilibrium quantity. Exhibit 17 shows that consumers' surplus at equilibrium is equal to areas $A + B + C + D$, and producers' surplus at equilibrium is equal to areas $E + F + G + H$. At any other exchangeable quantity, such as at 25, 50, or 75 units, both consumers' surplus and producers' surplus are less. For example, at 25 units, consumers' surplus is equal to area A, and producers' surplus is equal to area E. At 50 units, consumers' surplus is equal to areas $A + B$, and producers' surplus is equal to areas $E + F$.

Is there a special property to equilibrium? At equilibrium, both consumers' surplus and producers' surplus are maximized. In short, total surplus is maximized.

What Can Change Equilibrium Price and Quantity?

Equilibrium price and quantity are determined by supply and demand. Whenever demand changes, supply changes, or both change, equilibrium price and quantity change. Exhibit 18 illustrates eight different cases where this occurs. Cases (a)–(d) illustrate the four basic changes in supply and demand, where either supply or demand changes. Cases (e)–(h) illustrate changes in both supply and demand.

- (a) Demand rises (the demand curve shifts rightward from D_1 to D_2), and supply is constant (the supply curve does not move). As a result of demand rising and supply remaining constant, equilibrium price rises from P_1 to P_2 and equilibrium quantity rises from 10 units to 12 units. Now let's see if you can identify what has happened to quantity supplied (not supply) as price has risen from P_1 to P_2. (Remember, quantity supplied changes if *price* changes.) As price rises from P_1 to P_2, quantity supplied rises from 10 to 12 units. We see this as a movement up the supply curve from point 1 to point 2, which corresponds (on the horizontal axis) to a change from 10 to 12 units.

exhibit 18

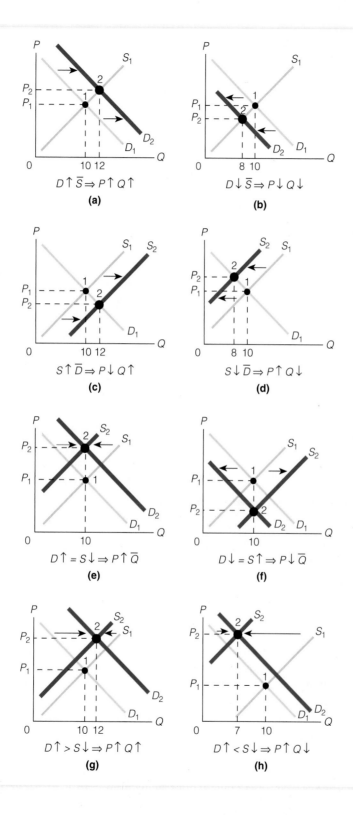

Equilibrium Price and Quantity Effects of Supply Curve Shifts and Demand Curve Shifts

The exhibit illustrates the effects on equilibrium price and quantity of a change in demand, a change in supply, or change in both. Below each diagram the condition leading to the effects is noted, using the following symbols: (1) a bar over a letter means *constant* (thus, $\bar{S}$ means that supply is constant); (2) a downward-pointing arrow ($\downarrow$) indicates a fall; (3) an upward-pointing arrow ($\uparrow$) indicates a rise. A rise (fall) in demand is the same as a rightward (leftward) shift in the demand curve. A rise (fall) in supply is the same as a rightward (leftward) shift in the supply curve.

OVERBOOKING AND THE AIRLINES

Airlines often overbook flights; that is, they accept more reservations than there are seats available on a flight. They do this because they know that a certain (usually small) percentage of individuals with reservations will not show up. An empty seat means that the airline's cost per actual passenger on board is higher than it would be if the seat were occupied by a paying passenger. So airlines try to make sure there are few empty seats. One way to reduce the number of empty seats is to overbook.

A while back, when an airline was confronted with more people with reservations showing up for a flight than there were seats available, it would simply "bump" passengers. In other words, the airline would tell some passengers that they could not fly on a particular flight. Obviously, the bumped passengers were disappointed and angry.

One day while shaving, economist Julian Simon (1932–1998) came up with a better way to deal with overbooking. He argued that the airline should enter into a market transaction with those persons who had reserved seats for an overbooked flight. Instead of bumping people randomly, an airline should ask passengers to sell their seats back to the airline. Passengers who absolutely had to get from one city to another would not sell their seats, but passengers who did not have to get from one city to another right away might be willing to sell their ticket for a given flight.

Simon wrote the executives of various airlines and outlined the details of his plan. He even told them that the first airline that enacted the plan would likely reap larger sales. It could, after all, guarantee its passengers that they would not get bumped. Most airline executives wrote back and told him it was a reasonably good idea but unworkable.

Simon contacted various economists asking them to support his idea publicly. Some did; some didn't. For years, Simon pushed his idea with airline executives and government officials.

Then Alfred Kahn, an economist, was appointed chairman of the Civil Aeronautics Board. Simon contacted Kahn with his plan, and Kahn liked it. According to Simon, "Kahn announced something like the scheme in his first press conference. He also had the great persuasive skill to repackage it as a 'voluntary' bumping plan, and at the same time to increase the penalties that airlines must pay to involuntary bumpees, a nice carrot-and-stick combination."[1]

The rest, as people say, is history. Simon's plan has been in operation since 1978. Simon wrote, "The volunteer system for handling airline oversales exemplifies how markets can improve life for all concerned parties. In case of an oversale, the airline agent proceeds from lowest bidder upwards until the required number of bumpees is achieved. Low bidders take the next flight, happy about it. All other passengers fly as scheduled, also happy. The airlines can overbook more, making them happy too."[2]

---

1. See Julian Simon, "Origins of the Airline Oversales Auction System," at http://www.cato.org/pubs/regulation/regv17n2/reg17n2-simon.html.

2. Ibid.

- (b) Demand falls (the demand curve shifts leftward from D_1 to D_2), and supply is constant. As a result, equilibrium falls from P_1 to P_2 and equilibrium quantity falls from 10 units to 8 units. Now ask: Has quantity supplied (not supply) changed? Yes it has. As a result of price falling from P_1 to P_2, we move down the supply curve from point 1 to point 2, and quantity supplied falls from 10 units to 8 units.

- (c) Supply rises (the supply curve shifts rightward from S_1 to S_2), and demand is constant. As a result, equilibrium price falls from P_1 to P_2 and equilibrium quantity rises from 10 units to 12 units. Now ask: Has quantity demanded (not demand) changed? Yes it has. As a result of price falling from P_1 to P_2, we move down the demand curve from point 1 to point 2, and quantity demanded rises from 10 to 12 units.

- (d) Supply falls (the supply curve shifts leftward from S_1 to S_2), and demand is constant. As a result, equilibrium price rises from P_1 to P_2 and equilibrium quantity falls from 10 to 8 units. One last time: Has quantity demanded (not demand) changed? Yes it has. As a result of price rising from P_1 to P_2, we move up the demand curve from point 1 to point 2, and quantity demanded falls from 10 to 8 units.

- (e) Demand rises (the demand curve shifts from D_1 to D_2) and supply falls (the supply curve shifts leftward from S_1 to S_2) by an equal amount. As a result, equilibrium price rises from P_1 to P_2 and equilibrium quantity remains constant at 10 units.

- (f) Demand falls (the demand curve shifts leftward from D_1 to D_2) and supply rises (the supply curve shifts rightward from S_1 to S_2) by an equal amount. As a result, equilibrium price falls from P_1 to P_2 and equilibrium quantity is constant at 10 units.

- (g) Demand rises (the demand curve shifts rightward from D_1 to D_2) by a greater amount than supply falls (the supply curve shifts leftward from S_1 to S_2). As a result, equilibrium price rises from P_1 to P_2 and equilibrium quantity rises from 10 to 12 units.

- (h) Demand rises (the demand curve shifts rightward from D_1 to D_2) by a smaller amount than supply falls (the supply curve shifts leftward from S_1 to S_2). Equilibrium price rises from P_1 to P_2 and equilibrium quantity falls from 10 to 7 units.

DEMAND AND SUPPLY AS EQUATIONS

You are used to seeing demand and supply as curves. Let's now look at demand and supply as equations. Here is a demand equation:

$$Q_d = 1,500 - 32P$$

To see what this equation says, we let price (P) in the equation equal $10 and then solve for quantity demanded (Q_d). We get 1,180.

$$Q_d = 1,500 - 32(10) = 1,180$$

So this equation says that if price is $10, it follows that quantity demanded is 1,180 units. We could find other quantities demanded by plugging in different dollar amounts for price (P).

Now here is a supply equation:

$$Q_s = 1,200 + 43P$$

To find what quantity supplied (Q_s) equals at a particular price, we let $5 equal price ($P$) and solve for quantity supplied. We get 1,415.

$$Q_s = 1,200 + 43(5) = 1,415$$

Now suppose we want to find equilibrium price and quantity given our demand and supply equations. How would we do it?

First, we know that in equilibrium the quantity demanded (Q_d) of a good is equal to the quantity supplied (Q_s), so let's set the two equations equal to each other this way:

$$1,500 - 32P = 1,200 + 43P$$

Now we can solve for P. We add $32P$ to both sides of the equal sign and subtract 1,200 from both sides. We are left with:

$$75P = 300$$

It follows then that $P = 300/75$ or $4.00.

Once we know equilibrium price is $4.00, we can place this value in either the demand or supply equation to find the equilibrium quantity. Let's place it in the demand equation:

$$Q_d = 1,500 - 32(4.00) = 1,372$$

Just to make sure that 1,372 is also the quantity supplied, we put the equilibrium price of $4.00 into the supply equation:

$$Q_s = 1,200 + 43(4.00) = 1,372$$

In summary, given our demand and supply equations, equilibrium price is $4.00 and equilibrium quantity is 1,372.

SELF-TEST

1. When a person goes to the grocery store to buy food, there is no auctioneer calling out prices for bread, milk, and other items. Therefore, supply and demand cannot be operative. Do you agree or disagree? Explain your answer.

2. The price of a given-quality personal computer is lower today than it was five years ago. Is this necessarily the result of a lower demand for computers? Explain your answer.

3. What is the effect on equilibrium price and quantity of the following?

    a. A decrease in demand that is greater than the increase in supply

    b. An increase in supply

    c. A decrease in supply that is greater than the increase in demand

    d. A decrease in demand

4. At equilibrium quantity, what is the relationship between the maximum buying price and the minimum selling price?

5. If the price paid is $40 and the consumers' surplus is $4, then what is the maximum buying price? If the minimum selling price is $30 and producers' surplus is $4, then what is the price received by the seller?

PRICE CONTROLS

Because scarcity exists, there is a need for a rationing device—such as dollar price. But price is not always permitted to be a rationing device. Sometimes, price is controlled. There are two types of price controls: price ceilings and price floors. In the discussion of price controls, the word *price* is used in the generic sense. It refers to the price of an apple, for example, the price of labor (wage), the price of credit (interest rate), and so on.

Price Ceiling: Definition and Effects

Price Ceiling
A government-mandated maximum price above which legal trades cannot be made.

A **price ceiling** is a government-mandated maximum price above which legal trades cannot be made. For example, suppose the government mandates that the maximum price at which good X can be bought and sold is $8. It follows that $8 is a price ceiling. If $8 is below the equilibrium price of good X, as in Exhibit 19, any or all of the following effects may arise.[3]

SHORTAGES At the $12 equilibrium price in Exhibit 19, the quantity demanded of good X (150) is equal to the quantity supplied (150). At the $8 price ceiling, a shortage exists. The quantity demanded (190) is greater than the quantity supplied (100). When a shortage exists, there is a tendency for price and output to rise to equilibrium. But when a price ceiling exists, this tendency cannot be realized because it is unlawful to trade at the equilibrium price.

FEWER EXCHANGES At the equilibrium price of $12 in Exhibit 19, 150 units of good X are bought and sold. At the price ceiling of $8, 100 units of good X are bought and sold. (Buyers would prefer to buy 190 units, but only 100 are supplied.) We conclude that price ceilings cause fewer exchanges to be made.

Notice in Exhibit 19 that the demand curve is above the supply curve for all quantities less than 150 units. (At 150 units, the demand curve and the supply curve intersect and thus share the same point in the two-dimensional space.) This means the maximum buying price is greater than the minimum selling price for all units less than 150. In particular, the maximum buying price is greater than the minimum selling price for units 101 to 149. For example, buyers might be willing to pay $17 for the 110th unit, and sellers might be willing to sell the 110th unit for $10. But no unit after the 100th unit (not the 110th unit, not the 114th unit, not the 130th unit) will be produced and sold because of the price ceiling. In short, the price ceiling prevents mutually advantageous trades from being realized.

NONPRICE RATIONING DEVICES If the equilibrium price of $12 fully rationed good X before the price ceiling was imposed, it follows that a (lower) price of $8 can only partly ration this good. In short, price ceilings prevent price from rising to the level sufficient to ration goods fully. But if price is responsible for only part of the rationing, what accounts for the rest? The answer is some other (nonprice) rationing device, such as first come, first served (FCFS).

In Exhibit 19, 100 units of good X will be sold at $8, although buyers are willing to buy 190 units at this price. What happens? Possibly, good X will be sold on an FCFS basis for $8 per unit. In other words, to buy good X, a person must not only pay $8 per unit but also be one of the first people in line.

BUYING AND SELLING AT A PROHIBITED PRICE Buyers and sellers may regularly circumvent a price ceiling by making their exchanges "under the table." For example, some buyers may offer some sellers more than $8 per unit for good X. No

exhibit 19

A Price Ceiling

The price ceiling is $8 and the equilibrium price is $12. At $12, quantity demanded = quantity supplied. At $8 quantity demanded > quantity supplied. (Recall that price, on the vertical axis, always represents price per unit. Quantity, on the horizontal axis, always holds for a specific time period.)

A price ceiling creates a shortage.

---

3. If the price ceiling is above the equilibrium price (say, $8 is the price ceiling and $4 is the equilibrium price), it has no effects. Usually, however, a price ceiling is below the equilibrium price.

doubt, some sellers will accept the offers. But why would some buyers offer more than $8 per unit when they can buy good X for $8? The answer is because not all buyers can buy the amount of good X they want at $8. As Exhibit 19 shows, there is a shortage. Buyers are willing to buy 190 units at $8, but sellers are willing to sell only 100 units. In short, 90 fewer units will be sold than buyers would like to buy. Some buyers will go unsatisfied. How, then, does any one buyer make it more likely that sellers will sell to him or her instead of to someone else? The answer is by offering to pay a higher price. Because it is illegal to pay a higher price, the transaction must be made "under the table."

TIE-IN SALES In Exhibit 19, the maximum price buyers would be willing and able to pay per unit for 100 units of good X is $18. (This is the price on the demand curve at a quantity of 100 units.) The maximum legal price, however, is $8. This difference between these two prices often prompts a **tie-in sale**, a sale whereby one good can be purchased only if another good is also purchased. For example, if Ralph's Gas Station sells gasoline to customers only if they buy a car wash, the two goods are linked together in a tie-in sale. Suppose that the sellers of good X in Exhibit 18 also sell good Y. They might offer to sell buyers good X at $8 only if the buyers agree to buy good Y at, say, $10. We choose $10 as the price for good Y because $10 is the difference between the maximum per-unit price buyers are willing and able to pay for 100 units of good X ($18) and the maximum legal price ($8).

In New York City and other communities with rent-control laws, tie-in sales sometimes result from rent ceilings on apartments. Occasionally, to rent an apartment, an individual must agree to buy the furniture in the apartment.

Tie-in Sale
A sale whereby one good can be purchased only if another good is also purchased.

Common MISCONCEPTIONS

About the Prices That Buyers Prefer

Do buyers prefer lower prices to higher prices? "Of course," someone might say, "buyers prefer lower prices to higher prices. What buyer would want to pay a higher price for anything?" But wait a minute. Price ceilings are often lower than equilibrium prices. Does it follow that buyers prefer price ceilings to equilibrium prices? Not necessarily. Price ceilings have effects that equilibrium prices do not: shortages; use of first come, first served as a rationing device; tie-in sales; and so on. A buyer could prefer to pay a higher price (an equilibrium price) than to pay a lower price and have to deal with the effects of a price ceiling. All we can say for certain is that buyers prefer lower prices to higher prices, *ceteris paribus*. As in many cases, the *ceteris paribus* condition makes all the difference.

Thinking like AN ECONOMIST

Look for the Unintended Effects

Economists think in terms of unintended effects. For example, a price ceiling policy intended to lower prices for the poor may cause shortages, the use of nonprice rationing devices, illegal market transactions, and tie-in sales. When we consider both the price ceiling and its effects, it is not clear that the poor have been helped. The economist knows that wanting to do good (for others) is not sufficient. It is important to know how to do good too.

exhibit 20

A Price Floor

The price floor is $20 and the equilibrium price is $15. At $15, quantity demanded = quantity supplied. At $20, quantity supplied > quantity demanded.

Price Floor: Definition and Effects

A **price floor** is a government-mandated minimum price below which legal trades cannot be made. For example, suppose the government mandates that the minimum price at which good X can be sold is $20. It follows that $20 is a price floor (see Exhibit 20). If the price floor is above the equilibrium price, the following two effects arise.[4]

SURPLUSES At the $15 equilibrium price in Exhibit 20, the quantity demanded of good X (130) is equal to the quantity supplied (130). At the $20 price floor, a surplus exists.

The quantity supplied (180) is greater than the quantity demanded (90). A surplus is usually a temporary state of affairs. When a surplus exists, there is a tendency for price and output to fall to equilibrium. But when a price floor exists, this tendency cannot be realized because it is unlawful to trade at the equilibrium price.

FEWER EXCHANGES At the equilibrium price in Exhibit 20, 130 units of good X are bought and sold. At the price floor, 90 units are bought and sold. (Sellers want to sell 180 units, but buyers buy only 90.) We conclude that price floors cause fewer exchanges to be made.

Price Floor
A government-mandated minimum price below which legal trades cannot be made.

SELF-TEST

1. Do buyers prefer lower prices to higher prices?
2. When there are long-lasting shortages, there are long lines of people waiting to buy goods. It follows that the shortages cause the long lines. Do you agree or disagree? Explain your answer.
3. Who might argue for a price ceiling? a price floor?

---

4. If the price floor is below the equilibrium price (say, $20 is the price floor and $25 is equilibrium price), it has no effects. Usually, however, a price floor is above the equilibrium price.

"I THOUGHT PRICES EQUALED COSTS PLUS 10 PERCENT"

Student:

My uncle produces and sells lamps. I asked him once how he determines the price he sells his lamps for. He said he takes his costs and adds on 10 percent. In other words, if it cost him $200 to make a lamp, he sells it for a price of $220. If all sellers do the same thing, then prices aren't being determined by supply and demand, are they?

Instructor:

Supply and demand could still be at work even given what your uncle said. For example, it could be that $220 is the (supply-and-demand determined) equilibrium price for the type of lamps your uncle is producing and selling. Look at it this way: If your uncle could sell the lamps for, say, $250 each, then he would have told you that he takes his cost (of $200) and adds on 25 percent ($50) to get "his price" of $250.

Student:

Is the point that what looks like *cost plus 10 percent* to me could really be supply and demand?

Instructor:

Yes, that's the point. But there is something else we can add to make the point stronger. Think of the housing market for a minute. Are the prices of houses determined by *cost plus 10 percent* or by supply and demand? Let's see if we can think through an example together. Suppose you buy a house for $400,000 in one year and then decide to sell that house ten years later. What price do you charge for the house? Do you charge the (market) equilibrium price for that house, or do you charge what you paid for the house ($400,000) plus 10 percent (plus $40,000) for a total of $440,000?

Student:

Oh, I think I see what you mean. You mean that if the equilibrium price for the house happened to be $650,000, there would be no way I would charge only $440,000.

Instructor:

Exactly. In other words, the supply-and-demand-determined price would take precedence over the cost plus 10 percent price. Now going back to your uncle, he might have just thought that he was charging a price of cost plus 10 percent because the equilibrium price for the goods he produced and sold happened to be 10 percent higher than his cost. But as stated before, if that equilibrium price had been

25 percent higher, your uncle would have told you his price was determined by his taking his costs and adding on 25 percent. It was the equilibrium price that was determining what percentage your uncle said he added to costs, and not simply his picking a percentage out of thin air.

Points to Remember

1. What looks like cost plus 10 percent (cost plus some markup) could instead be supply and demand at work.

2. Supply and demand are obviously determining prices at, say, an auction. There is one good for sale (say, a painting) and numerous buyers. The bidding stops when there is only one buyer left. At the price the last bidder bid, the quantity demanded (of the painting) equals the quantity supplied and both equal one. Just because you might not see supply and demand at work in non-auction settings, it doesn't necessarily follow that supply and demand are not at work determining prices.

a reader asks | How Does Knowing About Supply and Demand Help Me?

Some things are interesting but not useful. Other things are useful but not interesting. For example, supply and demand are interesting but not useful. Learning how to fix a car is useful but not particularly interesting. Am I wrong? Have I missed something? Is knowledge of supply and demand useful? If it is, what can you do with it?

A knowledge of supply and demand can be used both to explain and to predict. Let's look at the issue of prediction first. Suppose you learn that the federal government is going to impose a quota on imported television sets. What will happen when the quota is imposed? With your knowledge of supply and demand, you can predict that the price of television sets will rise. In other words, you can use your knowledge of supply and demand to predict what *will happen*. Stated differently, you can use your knowledge of supply and demand to see into the *future*. Isn't the ability to see into the future useful?

Supply and demand also allows you to develop richer and fuller explanations of events. To illustrate, suppose there is a shortage of

apples in country X. The cause of the shortage, someone says, is that apple growers in the country are simply growing too few apples. Well, of course, it's true that apple growers are growing "too few" apples compared to the number of apples consumers want to buy. But does this explanation completely account for the shortage of apples? Your knowledge of supply and demand will prompt you to ask *why* apple growers are growing too few apples. When you understand that quantity supplied is related to price, you understand that apple growers will grow more apples if the price of apples is higher. What is keeping the price of apples down? Could it be a price ceiling? Without a price ceiling, the price of apples would rise, and apple growers would grow (and offer to sell) more apples. The shortage of apples will vanish.

In other words, without a knowledge of supply and demand, you may have been content to explain the shortage of apples by saying that apple growers are growing too few apples. With your knowledge of supply and demand, you delve deeper into *why* apple growers are growing too few apples.

Chapter Summary

DEMAND

- The law of demand states that as the price of a good rises, the quantity demanded of the good falls, and as the price of a good falls, the quantity demanded of the good rises, *ceteris paribus*. The law of demand holds that price and quantity demanded are inversely related.
- Quantity demanded is the total number of units of a good that buyers are willing and able to buy at a particular price.
- A (downward-sloping) demand curve is the graphical representation of the law of demand.
- Factors that can change demand and cause the demand curve to shift include income, preferences, prices of related goods (substitutes and complements), number of buyers, and expectations of future price.
- The only factor that can directly cause a change in the quantity demanded of a good is a change in the good's own price.

ABSOLUTE PRICE AND RELATIVE PRICE

- The absolute price of a good is the price of the good in money terms.

- The relative price of a good is the price of the good in terms of another good.

SUPPLY

- The law of supply states that as the price of a good rises, the quantity supplied of the good rises, and as the price of a good falls, the quantity supplied of the good falls, *ceteris paribus*. The law of supply asserts that price and quantity supplied are directly related.
- The law of supply does not hold when there is no time to produce more units of a good or when goods cannot be produced at all (over any period of time).
- The upward-sloping supply curve is the graphical representation of the law of supply. More generally, a supply curve (no matter how it slopes) represents the relationship between price and quantity supplied.
- Factors that can change supply and cause the supply curve to shift include prices of relevant resources, technology, prices of other goods, number of sellers, expectations of future price, taxes and subsidies, and government restrictions.

- The only factor that can directly cause a change in the quantity supplied of a good is a change in the good's own price.

THE MARKET

- Demand and supply together establish equilibrium price and equilibrium quantity.
- A surplus exists in a market if, at some price, quantity supplied is greater than quantity demanded. A shortage exists if, at some price, quantity demanded is greater than quantity supplied.
- Mutually beneficial trade between buyers and sellers drives the market to equilibrium.

CONSUMERS' SURPLUS, PRODUCERS' SURPLUS, AND TOTAL SURPLUS

- Consumers' surplus is the difference between the maximum buying price and price paid by the buyer.

    Consumers' surplus = Maximum buying price − Price paid

- Producers' (or sellers') surplus is the difference between the price the seller receives and minimum selling price.

    Producers' surplus = Price received − Minimum selling price

- The more consumers' surplus that buyers receive, the better off they are. The more producers' surplus that sellers receive, the better off they are. Total surplus is the sum of consumers' surplus and producers' surplus.
- Total surplus (the sum of consumers' surplus and producers' surplus) is maximized at equilibrium.

PRICE CEILINGS

- A price ceiling is a government-mandated maximum price. If a price ceiling is below the equilibrium price, some or all of the following effects arise: shortages, fewer exchanges, nonprice rationing devices, buying and selling at prohibited prices, and tie-in sales.
- Consumers do not necessarily prefer (lower) price ceilings to (higher) equilibrium prices. They may prefer higher prices and none of the effects of price ceilings to lower prices and some of the effects of price ceilings. All we can say for sure is that consumers prefer lower prices to higher prices, *ceteris paribus.*

PRICE FLOORS

- A price floor is a government-mandated minimum price. If a price floor is above the equilibrium price, the following effects arise: surpluses and fewer exchanges.

Key Terms and Concepts

Theory	Law of Diminishing Marginal	Law of Supply	Disequilibrium Price
Market	Utility	Supply Curve	Disequilibrium
Demand	Own Price	Supply Schedule	Equilibrium
Law of Demand	Normal Good	Subsidy	Consumers' Surplus
Ceteris Paribus	Inferior Good	Surplus (Excess Supply)	Producers' (Sellers') Surplus
Demand Schedule	Neutral Good	Shortage (Excess Demand)	Total Surplus
Demand Curve	Substitutes	Equilibrium Price (Market-	Price Ceiling
Absolute (Money) Price	Complements	Clearing Price)	Tie-in Sale
Relative Price	Supply	Equilibrium Quantity	Price Floor

Questions and Problems

1   When economists build theories they abstract from reality. What does this mean?

2   What is wrong with this statement: Demand refers to the willingness of buyers to purchase different quantities of a good at different prices during a specific time period.

3   What is the difference between *demand* and *quantity demanded*?

4   True or false? As the price of oranges rises, the demand for oranges falls, *ceteris paribus.* Explain your answer.

5   What does *ceteris paribus* mean, and how is it used in terms of the law of demand?

6   "The price of a bushel of wheat, which was $3.00 last month, is $3.70 today. The demand curve for wheat must have shifted rightward between last month and today." Discuss.

7 "Some goods are bought largely because they have 'snob appeal.'" For example, the residents of Beverly Hills gain prestige by buying expensive items. In fact, they won't buy some items unless they are expensive. The law of demand, which holds that people buy more at lower prices than higher prices, obviously doesn't hold for the residents of Beverly Hills. The following rules apply in Beverly Hills: "high prices, buy; low prices, don't buy." Discuss.

8 "The price of T-shirts keeps rising and rising, and people keep buying more and more. T-shirts must have an upward-sloping demand curve." Identify the error.

9 With respect to each of the following changes, identify whether the demand curve will shift rightward or leftward:

a. an increase in income (the good under consideration is a normal good)

b. a rise in the price of a substitute good

c. a fall in the price of a complementary good

d. a fall in the number of buyers

10 What does a sale on shirts have to do with the law of demand (as applied to shirts)?

11 What is wrong with this statement: "As the price of a good falls, the supply of that good falls, *ceteris paribus*"?

12 In the previous chapter, you learned about the law of increasing opportunity costs. What does this law have to do with an upward-sloping supply curve?

13 How might the price of corn affect the supply of wheat?

14 What is the difference between supply and quantity supplied?

15 Predict what would happen to the equilibrium price of marijuana if it were legalized.

16 Compare the ratings for television shows with prices for goods. How are ratings like prices? How are ratings different from prices? (Hint: How does rising demand for a particular television show manifest itself?)

17 At equilibrium in a market, the maximum price buyers would be willing to pay for the good is equal to the minimum price sellers need to receive before they are willing to sell the good. Do you agree or disagree with this statement? Explain your answer.

18 Must consumers' surplus equal producers' surplus at equilibrium price? Explain your answer.

19 Many movie theaters charge a lower admission price for the first show on weekday afternoons than they do for a weeknight or weekend show. Explain why.

20 A Dell computer is a substitute for a Hewlett-Packard computer. What happens to the demand for Hewlett-Packard computers and the quantity demanded of Dell computers as the price of a Dell falls?

21 Describe how each of the following will affect the demand for personal computers: (a) a rise in incomes (assuming computers are a normal good), (b) a lower expected price for computers, (c) cheaper software, and (d) computers become simpler to operate.

22 Describe how each of the following will affect the supply of personal computers: (a) a rise in wage rates, (b) an increase in the number of sellers of computers, (c) a tax placed on the production of computers, and (d) a subsidy placed on the production of computers.

23 The law of demand specifies an inverse relationship between price and quantity demanded, *ceteris paribus*. Is the "price" in the law of demand absolute price or relative price? Explain your answer.

24 Use the law of diminishing marginal utility to explain why demand curves slope downward.

25 Explain how the market moves to equilibrium in terms of shortages and surpluses and in terms of maximum buying prices and minimum selling prices.

26 Identify what happens to equilibrium price and quantity in each of the following cases:

a. Demand rises and supply is constant

b. Demand falls and supply is constant

c. Supply rises and demand is constant

d. Supply falls and demand is constant

e. Demand rises by the same amount that supply falls

f. Demand falls by the same amount that supply rises

g. Demand falls by less than supply rises

h. Demand rises by more than supply rises

i. Demand rises by less than supply rises

j. Demand falls by more than supply falls

k. Demand falls by less than supply falls

27 Many of the proponents of price ceilings argue that government-mandated maximum prices simply reduce producers' profits and do not affect the quantity supplied of a good on the market. What must the supply curve look like before a price ceiling does not affect quantity supplied?

28 When speeding tickets were $100, there were usually 500 speeders on the roads each month in a given city; when ticket prices were raised to $250, there were usually 215 speeders on the roads in the city each month. Can you find any economics in this observation?

29 James lives in a rent-controlled apartment and has for the past few weeks been trying to get the supervisor to fix his shower. What does waiting to get one's shower fixed have to do with a rent-controlled apartment?

30 On most days there are more people who want to see the taping of the *Tonight Show with Jay Leno* (in Burbank, California) than there are seats in the studio where Jay Leno tapes the show. What might explain this shortage?

31 Explain why there are fewer exchanges made when a disequilibrium price (below equilibrium price) exists than when equilibrium price exists.

32 Buyers always prefer lower prices to higher prices. Do you agree or disagree with this statement? Explain your answer.

33 What is the difference between a price ceiling and a price floor? What effect is the same for both a price ceiling and a price floor?

Working with Numbers and Graphs

1 If the absolute price of good X is $10 and the absolute price of good Y is $14, then what is (a) the relative price of good X in terms of good Y and (b) the relative price of good Y in terms of good X?

2 Price is $10, quantity supplied is 50 units, and quantity demanded is 100 units. For every $1 rise in price, quantity supplied rises by 5 units and quantity demanded falls by 5 units. What is the equilibrium price and quantity?

3 Using numbers explain how a market demand curve is derived from two individual demand curves.

4 Draw a diagram that shows a larger increase in demand than the decrease in supply.

5 Draw a diagram that shows a smaller increase in supply than the increase in demand.

6 At equilibrium in the following figure, what area(s) does consumers' surplus equal? producers' surplus?

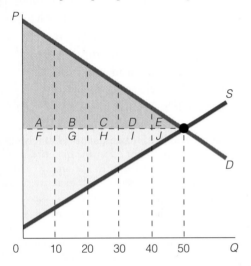

7 At what quantity in the preceding figure is the maximum buying price equal to the minimum selling price?

8 In the following figure, can the movement from point 1 to point 2 be explained by a combination of an increase in the price of a substitute and a decrease in the price of nonlabor resources? Explain your answer.

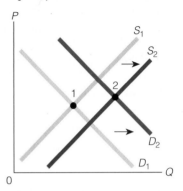

9 The demand curve is downward sloping, the supply curve is upward sloping, and the equilibrium quantity is 50 units. Show on a graph that the difference between the maximum buying price and minimum selling price is greater at 25 units than at 33 units.

10 Determine equilibrium price and quantity for the following supply and demand equations:

a. $Q_d = 1,800 - 60P$; $Q_s = 400 + 10P$

b. $Q_d = 950 - 23P$; $Q_s = 900 + 27P$

c. $Q_d = 2,250 - 12P$; $Q_s = 1,200 + 13P$

11 Using each of the supply and demand equations in problem 10, identify quantity demanded and quantity supplied if price equals $15.

12 Diagrammatically show and explain why a price ceiling that is above the equilibrium price will not prompt a tie-in sale.

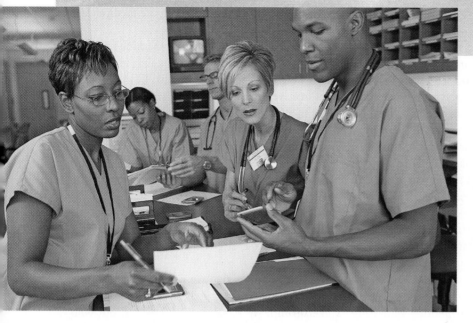

CHAPTER 4

SUPPLY AND DEMAND: APPLICATIONS

Introduction In the last chapter we discussed the theory of supply and demand. In this chapter it is time to work with supply and demand. This is a chapter of applications. Each application has something to do with one of the topics we discussed in the last chapter. Many applications deal with supply and demand, some deal with price, and others deal with price ceilings and price floors.

The theory of supply and demand is not very useful to you unless you can use it to explain some of the things you see around you in everyday life. In this chapter we discuss medical care, changing house prices, college classes at 10 a.m., driving on a freeway, standardized tests (such as the SAT), college athletes, and more—all within the general framework of supply and demand.

APPLICATION 1: WHY IS MEDICAL CARE SO EXPENSIVE?

Think of the way you buy groceries. You go to the grocery store, place certain products in your basket, and then pay for them (usually with cash) at the cash register.

Now think of the way you buy medical care. You go to the doctor or hospital, give the doctor's office or hospital your health insurance card, perhaps pay a copayment of $10 or $20, and then receive medical care. Your doctor or the hospital ends up billing your insurance company for the bulk of your expenses.

Now what is the difference between the way you buy groceries and the way you buy medical care? Well, in the grocery store example there are only two parties: you (the buyer) and the grocery store (the seller). In the medical care example, there are three parties: you, the doctor or hospital, and the insurance company. The insurance company is often referred to as the "third party." So, we can put things this way: There is no third party in the grocery store example but there is a third party in the medical care example.

What the existence of a third party does is separate the buying of something from the paying for something. In the grocery store example, the person who bought the groceries and the person who paid for the groceries were the same person (you). In the medical care example, the person who bought and received the medical care (you) was different from the person or entity that paid for the medical care (the insurance company).

But wait a minute, you say. You indirectly pay for your medical care by paying monthly insurance premiums to the medical insurance company. Yes, that is partly true, but it is similar to what happens at a buffet. You pay a set dollar price for the buffet and then you can eat all you want. Our guess is that you will end up eating more food at the buffet than you would if you had to pay for each item at the buffet.

The same often happens with medical care. You pay a set premium to the insurance company (let's say $250 a month) and then you enter the health care buffet line. Might you end up buying more health care than you would if each item of the health care buffet were priced separately?

Before we continue on, there are perhaps two points that we need to get out of the way. You might say: But I don't buy medical care in the medical care buffet line as I buy food in the food buffet line. I like shrimp, steak, salads, and desserts, but who likes getting x-rays taken, being prodded and poked by doctors, and taking medicine? It is ridiculous to think that a person will buy shrimp cocktails the same way he or she buys MRIs.

That is true, of course. But that is not the point we are making. The point is that once you get sick, and go to the doctor or hospital, the existence of a third party (who pays for the medical care you receive) may give you, your doctor, and the hospital options for more medical examinations/procedures/care than you need. A conversation in your doctor's office may go like this:

> **Doctor:** I think you have condition X but just to be sure let's order some blood tests and get an MRI too.
>
> **You:** Whatever you think is best.

Now ask yourself what you might say if you had to pay—out of your pocket—for the blood test and MRI. You might ask, "How much is this going to cost me, doctor? And is all this really necessary?"

Our point is a simple one: Once you have paid your insurance premium, the price you pay for medical care amounts only to your copayment (which is usually minimal). For all practical purposes, the dollar amount you have to pay, out of pocket, to get medical care is zero. That is a fairly low price for health care. We can expect that the quantity demanded of medical care would be greater at zero than at some positive dollar amount.

Now let us link the *quantity demanded* of medical care (which will be high if the price of medical care is zero) with the *demand for specific items* that make up medical care. (In our buffet food example, it would be similar to linking the *quantity demanded* of food with the *demand* for specific food items—shrimp, chocolate ice cream, or a Caesar's salad.)

If the quantity demanded of medical care is higher at a zero price than at some positive price, then we would expect the demand for those *specific items* that make up health care to be higher than it would be if the quantity demanded of health care were lower. We show this diagrammatically in Exhibit 1. In Exhibit 1(a), we show the demand for medical care as downward sloping. Notice that if the price is zero for health care, then the quantity demanded of medical care is 100 units. But if the price is some positive dollar amount (such as P_1), then the quantity demanded of medical care is 50 units.

exhibit 1

The Price of Medical Care and the Demand for X-rays

(a) If the price of medical care is low (say, zero), the quantity demanded of medical care is 100 units. If the price of medical care for you is P_1, the quantity demanded of medical care is 50 units. (b) The lower the price of medical care and the higher the quantity demanded of medical care in panel (a), then the higher the demand curve for x-rays in (b). (c) The higher the demand for x-rays, the higher the price of x-rays.

(a)

(b)

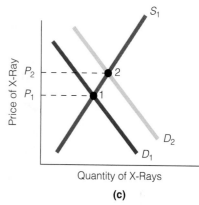

(c)

In Exhibit 1(b), we do not show the demand for medical care in general, but instead show the demand for a specific item of medical care—the demand for x-rays. There are two demand curves in panel (b). The first demand curve (D_1) is the demand that exists for x-rays if the *quantity demanded of medical care* is 50 units in panel (a). Stated differently, it is the demand for x-rays if the price for medical care (shown in panel a) is P_1. The second demand curve (D_2) is the demand curve that exists for x-rays if the *quantity demanded of medical care* is 100 units in panel (a). Stated differently, it is the demand for x-rays if the price for medical care (shown in panel a) is zero.

In a nutshell, what we are saying is this: The lower the price of medical care, the higher the quantity demanded of medical care, and the higher the demand for x-rays. The higher the price of medical care, the lower the quantity demanded of medical care, and the lower the demand for x-rays.

Price of medical care is low → Quantity demanded of medical care is high → Demand for x-rays is high

Price of medical care is high → Quantity demanded of medical care is low → Demand for x-rays is low

We have come to the point in the analysis where we must ask what does a high demand for x-rays end up doing to the price of an x-ray? Obviously, it pushes up the price of an x-ray. See Exhibit 1(c).

As a result, the health insurance company finds itself paying more for the x-rays (you receive). Can you see what will happen next? That's right, the health insurance company will make the argument that with rising medical costs, the premiums for your health insurance coverage will need to rise too.

Why is health insurance as expensive as it is, you ask. You now have a large part of the answer. Think buffet.

SELF-TEST

(Answers to Self-Test questions are in the Self-Test Appendix.)

1. Suppose food insurance exists. You pay the food insurance company a certain dollar amount each month and then you purchase all the food you want to purchase from your local grocery store. The grocery store sends the bill to your food insurance company. What will happen to the price of food and to the premium you pay for food insurance?

2. In Exhibit 1(a), suppose that the price a person has to pay for medical care is between P_1 and zero. Where would the demand for x-rays in panel (b) be in relationship to D_1 and D_2?

APPLICATION 2: WHERE WILL HOUSE PRICES CHANGE THE MOST?

At one point in time you notice that house prices are rising. You also notice that house prices rise more in some areas of the country than in other areas. You wonder why. At another point in time you notice that house prices are falling. You also notice that house prices fall more in some areas of the country than in other areas. You wonder why.

Your knowledge of why prices change might lead you to say this: Obviously supply and demand changes are different in different areas of the country and that is why price changes are different too. To illustrate, in one area of the country the demand for houses rises by more than in another area and this explains why house prices rise by more in one area than in another area.

But suppose the demand for houses rises by the same in all areas of the country. What then? Well, the answer may have to do with the supply curve. To illustrate, look at the two supply curves in Exhibit 2. You will notice that we have drawn S_1 as steeper than S_2. Suppose S_1 represents the supply of houses in area 1 of the country and S_2 represents the supply of houses in area 2. Obviously, if the demand for houses rises in both areas by the same amount—identified by a shift in the demand curve from D_1 and D_2—we notice

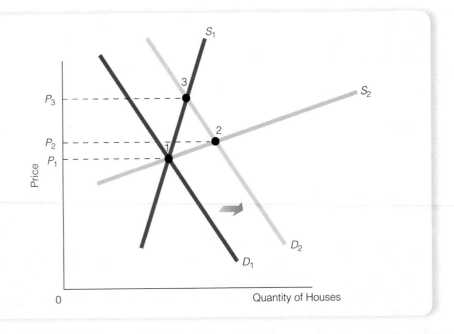

exhibit 2

Where Will Prices Change the Most?

We start with two supply curves (S_1 and S_2) and one demand curve (D_1). If we increase demand from D_1 to D_2, you will notice that price rises no matter which supply curve is operational. However, price rises more the steeper the supply curve is. Since S_1 is steeper than S_2, price rises more using S_1 than it does using S_2. The same holds for a decrease in demand. If we decrease demand from D_2 to D_1, we see that price falls more along S_1 than S_2.

that house prices rise by more in area 1 (moving from P_1 to P_3) than in area 2 (moving from P_1 to P_2). We conclude that the shape of the supply curve affects how high price will rise for a given increase in demand. (In a later chapter, we will discuss the topic of price elasticity of supply, which is not the same as the steepness of the supply curve, but indirectly relates to it.)

The shape of the supply curve will also affect how low price will fall for a given decrease in demand. Using the same exhibit, suppose demand falls from D_2 to D_1. We notice that price falls more (from P_3 to P_1) if S_1 is the operational supply curve than if S_2 is the operational supply curve (from P_2 to P_1).

SELF-TEST

1. In city 1 the supply curve of housing is steeper than in city 2. Given an equal decrease in demand for housing in both cities, in which city will the price of housing fall by less?

2. In city 1 the supply curve of housing is steeper than in city 2. Given an equal increase in demand for housing in both cities, in which city will the (equilibrium) quantity of houses increase less?

APPLICATION 3: WHY DO COLLEGES USE GPAS, ACTS, AND SATS FOR PURPOSES OF ADMISSION?

At many colleges and universities, a student pays part of the price of his or her education (by way of tuition payments), and taxpayers and private donors pay part (by way of tax payments and charitable donations, respectively). Thus, the tuition that students pay to attend colleges and universities is usually less than the equilibrium tuition. To illustrate, suppose a student pays tuition T_1 at a given college or university. As shown in Exhibit 3, T_1 is below the equilibrium tuition, T_E. At T_1, the number of students who want to attend the university (N_1) is greater than the number of openings at the university (N_2); that is, quantity demanded is greater than quantity supplied. The university receives more applications for admission than there are places available. Something has to be done. But what?

The college or university is likely to ration its available space by a combination of money price and some other nonprice rationing devices. The student must pay the tuition, T_1, *and* meet the standards of the nonprice rationing devices. Colleges and universities usually use such things as GPAs (grade point averages), ACT scores, and SAT scores as rationing devices.

Thinking like AN ECONOMIST

Identifying Rationing Devices

The layperson sees a university that requires a GPA of 3.8 and an SAT score of 1,900 or better for admission. An economist sees a rationing device. The economist then goes on to ask why this particular nonprice rationing device is used. He reasons that there would be no need for a nonprice rationing device if (dollar) price were fully rationing the good or service.

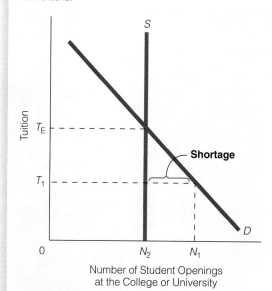

exhibit 3

College and University Admissions

If the college or university charges T_1 in tuition (when T_E is the equilibrium tuition), a shortage will be generated. The college or university will then use some nonprice rationing device, such as GPAs, ACTs, and SATs, as admission criteria.

Number of Student Openings
at the College or University

SELF-TEST

1. Suppose the demand rises for admission to a university but both the tuition and the number of openings in the entering class remain the same. Will this affect the admission standards of the university? Explain your answer.

2. Administrators and faculty at state colleges and universities often say that their standards of admission are independent of whether there is a shortage or surplus of openings at the university. Do you think this is true? Do you think that faculty and administrators ignore surpluses and shortages of openings when setting admission standards? Explain your answer.

APPLICATION 4: SUPPLY AND DEMAND ON A FREEWAY

What does a traffic jam on a busy freeway in any large city have to do with supply and demand? Actually, it has quite a bit to do with supply and demand. Look at it this way: There is a demand for driving on the freeway and a supply of freeway space. The supply of freeway space is fixed (freeways do not expand and contract over a day, week, or month). The demand, however, fluctuates. It is higher at some times than at other times. For example, we would expect the demand for driving on the freeway to be higher at 8 a.m. (rush hour) than at 11 p.m. But even though the demand may vary, the money price for driving on the freeway is always the same—zero. A zero money price means that motorists do not pay tolls to drive on the freeway.

Exhibit 4 shows two demand curves for driving on the freeway: $D_{8\,a.m.}$ and $D_{11\,p.m.}$ We have assumed the demand at 8 a.m. is greater than at 11 p.m. We have also assumed that at $D_{11\,p.m.}$ and zero money price the freeway market clears: Quantity demanded of freeway space equals quantity supplied of freeway space. At the higher demand, $D_{8\,a.m.}$, however, this is not the case. At zero money price, a shortage of freeway space exists: Quantity demanded of freeway space is greater than quantity supplied of freeway space. The shortage appears in the form of freeway congestion and bumper-to-bumper traffic. One way to eliminate the shortage is through an increase in the money price of driving on the freeway at 8 a.m. For example, as Exhibit 4 shows, a toll of 70 cents would clear the freeway market at 8 a.m.

If charging different prices (tolls) at different times of the day on freeways sounds like an unusual idea, consider how Miami Beach hotels price their rooms. They charge different prices for their rooms at different times of the year. During the winter months when the demand for vacationing in Miami Beach is high, the hotels charge higher prices than when the demand is (relatively) low. If different prices were charged for freeway space at different times of the day, freeway space would be rationed the same way Miami Beach hotel rooms are rationed.

Before we leave this topic, let's consider the three alternatives usually proposed for freeway congestion. Some people propose tolls, some propose building more freeways, and others propose encouraging carpooling. Tolls deal with the congestion problem by adjusting price to its equilibrium level, as shown in Exhibit 4. Building more freeways deals with the problem by increasing supply. In Exhibit 4, it would be necessary to shift the supply curve of freeway space to the right so there is no longer any shortage of space at 8 a.m. More carpooling

© DAVID PAUL MORRIS/GETTY IMAGES

deals with the problem by decreasing demand. Two people in one car take up less space on a freeway than two people in two cars. In Exhibit 4, if through carpooling the demand at 8 a.m. begins to look like the demand at 11 p.m., then there is no longer a shortage of freeway space at 8 a.m.

A final note: A fee to drive in the Central London area was introduced in 2003. Anyone going into or out of the Central London area between 7:00 a.m. and 6:30 p.m., Monday through Friday, must pay a fee of approximately $15. (Not everyone has to pay the fee. For example, taxi drivers, ambulance drivers, police vehicles, motorcycle drivers, and bicyclists do not have to pay the fee. The residents who live in the area receive a 90 percent discount.) Many people have claimed the fee a success because it has cut down on traffic and travel times and reduced pollution in the area.

Some people have urged New York City to institute a similar fee program to drive on certain streets in the city. On any given day in New York City, there are approximately 800,000 cars on the streets south of 60th Street in Manhattan. According to many, the city is "choking in traffic." We will have to wait to see if New York City goes the way of London.

Thinking like AN ECONOMIST

It's One of Three

The economist knows that when there are buyers and sellers of anything (bread, cars, or freeway space), only three conditions are possible—equilibrium, shortage, or surplus. When the economist sees traffic congestion, the first thing that comes to mind is that there is a shortage of road space. But why is there a shortage? The economist knows that shortages occur at prices below equilibrium price. In other words, price is too low.

exhibit 4

Freeway Congestion and Supply and Demand

The demand for driving on the freeway is higher at 8 a.m. than at 11 p.m. At zero money price and $D_{11 p.m.}$, the freeway market clears. At zero money price and $D_{8 a.m.}$, there is a shortage of freeway space, which shows up as freeway congestion. At a price (toll) of 70 cents, the shortage is eliminated and freeway congestion disappears.

SELF-TEST

1. In Exhibit 4, at what price is there a surplus of freeway space at 8 a.m.?

2. If the driving population increases in an area and the supply of freeway space remains constant, what will happen to freeway congestion? Explain your answer.

APPLICATION 5: PRICE CEILINGS IN THE KIDNEY MARKET

Just as there are people who want to buy houses, computers, and books, there are people who want to buy kidneys. These people have kidney failure and either will die without a new kidney or will have to endure years of costly and painful dialysis. This demand for kidneys is shown as D_K in Exhibit 5.

The supply of kidneys is shown as S_K in Exhibit 5. Notice that at $0 price, the quantity supplied of kidneys is 350. These kidneys are from people who donate their kidneys

exhibit 5

The Market for Kidneys

We have identified the demand for kidneys as D_K and the supply of kidneys as S_K. Given the demand for and supply of kidneys, the equilibrium price of a kidney is P_1. It does not follow, though, that simply because there is an equilibrium price, people will be allowed to trade at this price. Today, it is unlawful to buy and sell kidneys at any positive price. In short, there is a price ceiling in the kidney market and the ceiling is $0. At the price ceiling, there is a shortage of kidneys, a nonprice rationing device for kidneys (first-come-first-served), fewer kidney transplants (than there would be at P_1), and illegal purchases and sales of kidneys.

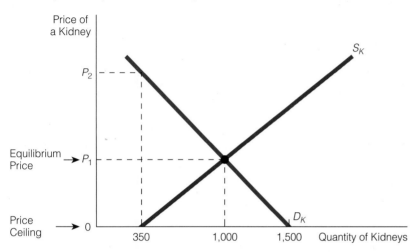

to others, asking nothing in return. They may donate their kidneys upon their death or may donate one of their two kidneys while living. We have drawn the supply curve as upward sloping because we assume that some people who today are unwilling to donate a kidney for $0 might be willing to do so for some positive dollar amount. Specifically, we assume that as the price of a kidney rises, the quantity supplied of kidneys will rise.

If there were a free market in kidneys, the price of a kidney would be P_1 in Exhibit 5. At this price, 1,000 kidneys would be purchased and sold—1,000 kidney transplants would occur.

Today, there is no free market in kidneys. Buying or selling kidneys is illegal at any dollar amount. In essence, then, there is a price ceiling in the kidney market, and the ceiling is set at $0. What is the effect of this price ceiling?

If the demand curve for kidneys and the supply curve of kidneys intersected at $0, there would be neither a surplus nor a shortage of kidneys. But there is evidence that the demand and supply curves do not intersect at $0; they look more like those shown in Exhibit 5. In other words, there is a shortage of kidneys at $0: The quantity supplied of kidneys is 350 and the quantity demanded is 1,500. (Although these are not the actual numbers of kidneys demanded and supplied at $0, they are representative of the current situation in the kidney market.)

The last chapter described the possible effects of a price ceiling set below equilibrium price: shortages, nonprice rationing devices, fewer exchanges, tie-in sales, and buying and selling at prohibited prices (in other words, illegal trades). Are any of these effects occurring in the kidney market?

First, there is evidence of a shortage. In almost every country in the world, there are more people on national lists who want a kidney than there are kidneys available. Some of these people die waiting for a kidney.

Second, as just indicated, the nonprice rationing device used in the kidney market is (largely) first come, first served. A person who wants a kidney registers on a national waiting list. How long one waits is a function of how far down the list one's name appears.

Third, there are fewer exchanges; not everyone who needs a kidney gets a kidney. With a price ceiling of $0, only 350 kidneys are supplied. All these kidneys are from people who freely donate their kidneys. If P_1 were permitted, some people who are unwilling to supply a kidney (at $0) would be willing to do so. In short, monetary payment would provide the incentive for some people to supply a kidney. At P_1, 1,000 kidneys are demanded and supplied, so more people would get kidney transplants when the price of a kidney is P_1 (1,000 in total) than when the price of a kidney is $0 (350 in total). More transplants, of course, means fewer people die waiting for a kidney.

Fourth, kidneys are bought and sold at prohibited prices. People buy and sell kidneys today; they just do so illegally. There are stories of people paying between $25,000 and $200,000 for a kidney.

Some people argue that a free market in kidneys would be wrong. Such a system would place the poor at a disadvantage. Think of it: A rich person who needed a kidney could buy the kidney, but a poor person could not. The rich person would get a second chance at life, whereas the poor person would not. No one particularly enjoys contemplating this stark reality.

But consider another stark reality. If it is unlawful to pay someone for a kidney, fewer kidneys will be forthcoming. In other words, the quantity supplied of kidneys is less at $0 than at, say, $20,000. Fewer kidneys supplied mean fewer kidney transplants. And fewer kidney transplants mean more people will die from kidney failure.

Finding ECONOMICS

Not Getting a Kidney Transplant

A person dies because she does not receive a much-needed kidney transplant in time. Where is the economics here? To most people, this is simply a very sad fact of life. How unfeeling it might seem, then, when the economist points out that the person might have died because of a long string of events that started with a disequilibrium price. The economist's story goes like this: (1) The current price in the kidney market is a disequilibrium price (below equilibrium price). (2) As a result, the quantity supplied of kidneys is less than it would be if the equilibrium price existed in the kidney market. (3) It follows that there will be fewer kidneys supplied for transplants, and some people who might have gotten a kidney but don't now will end up dying.

SELF-TEST

1. A shortage of kidneys for transplants is a consequence of the price of a kidney being below equilibrium price. Do you agree or disagree? Explain your answer.

2. Assume the price ceiling in the kidney market is $0. Will there be a shortage of kidneys? Explain your answer.

APPLICATION 6: THE MINIMUM WAGE LAW

Recall that a price floor is a legislated minimum price below which trades cannot legally be made. The *minimum wage* is a price floor—a government-mandated minimum price for labor. It affects the market for unskilled labor. In Exhibit 6, we assume the minimum wage is W_M and the equilibrium wage is W_E. At the equilibrium wage, N_1 workers are employed. At the higher minimum wage, N_3 workers want to work but only N_2 actually do work. There is a surplus of workers equal to $N_3 - N_2$ in this unskilled labor market. In addition, fewer workers are working at the minimum wage (N_2) than at the equilibrium wage (N_1). Overall, the effects of the minimum wage are (1) a surplus of unskilled workers and (2) fewer workers employed.

Suppose two economists decide to test the theory that as the minimum wage rises, some unskilled workers will lose their jobs. They look at the number of unskilled workers before and after the minimum wage is raised, and surprisingly, they find that the number of unskilled workers is the same. Is this sufficient evidence to conclude that an increase in the minimum wage does not cause some workers to lose their jobs? We'll leave that question hanging while we consider whether or not the economists have adequately tested their theory. Instead of focusing on the number of people who lose their jobs, suppose they look at the people who keep their jobs but have their hours reduced as a result of the higher minimum wage. Let's look at an example. Suppose a local hardware store

exhibit 6

Effects of the Minimum Wage

At a minimum wage of W_M an hour, there is a surplus of workers and fewer workers are employed than would be at the equilibrium wage W_E.

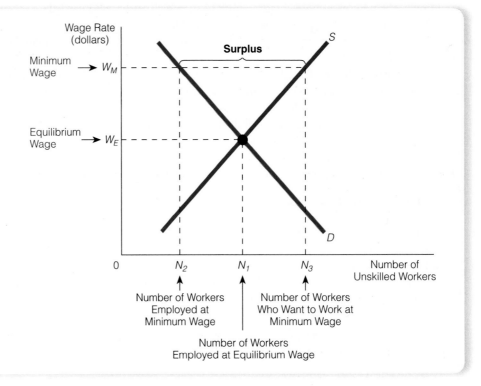

currently employs David and Francesca to work after school cleaning up and stocking shelves. The owner of the store pays each of them the minimum wage of, say, $6.55 an hour. Then, the minimum wage is raised to $8.25 an hour. Will either David or Francesca lose their jobs as a result? Not necessarily. Instead, the owner of the store could reduce the number of hours he employs the two workers. For example, instead of having each of them work 20 hours a week, he might ask each to work only 14 hours a week.

Now, let's reconsider our original question: Has the higher minimum wage eliminated jobs? In a way, no. It has, however, reduced the number of hours a person works in a job. (Of course, if we define a job as including both a particular task and a certain number of hours completing that task, then the minimum wage increase has eliminated "part" of the job.) This discussion argues for changing the label on the horizontal axis in Exhibit 6 from "Number of Unskilled Workers" to "Number of Unskilled Labor Hours."

Thinking like AN ECONOMIST

Direction Versus Magnitude

In economics, some questions relate to "direction" and some to "magnitude." For example, suppose someone asks, "If the demand for labor is downward sloping and the labor market is competitive, how will a minimum wage (above the equilibrium wage) affect employment?" This person is asking a question that relates to the direction of the change in employment. Usually, these types of questions can be answered by applying a theory. Applying the theory of demand, an economist might say, "At higher wages, the quantity demanded of labor, or the employment level, will be lower than at lower wages." The word *lower* speaks to the *directional change* in employment.

(continued)

Thinking Like An Economist (continued)

Now suppose someone asks, "How much will employment decline?" This person is asking a question that relates to *magnitude*. Usually, questions that deal with magnitude can be answered only through some kind of empirical (data-collecting and analyzing) work. In other words, we would have to collect employment figures at the equilibrium wage and at the minimum wage and then find the difference.

SELF-TEST

1. When the labor supply curve is upward sloping, a minimum wage law that sets the wage rate above its equilibrium level creates a surplus of labor. If the labor supply curve is vertical, does a surplus of labor still occur? Explain your answer.

2. Someone says that an increase in the minimum wage will not cause firms to hire fewer workers. What is this person assuming?

APPLICATION 7: PRICE FLOORS AND WINNERS AND LOSERS

Exhibit 7 shows the demand for and supply of an agricultural foodstuff (corn, wheat, soybeans, etc.). If the market is allowed to move to equilibrium, the equilibrium price will be P_1, and the equilibrium quantity will be Q_1. Consumers' surplus will equal the area under the demand curve and above the equilibrium price: areas $1 + 2 + 3$. Producers' surplus will equal the area under the equilibrium price and above the supply curve: areas $4 + 5$. Total surplus, of course, is the sum of consumers' surplus and producers' surplus: areas $1 + 2 + 3 + 4 + 5$.

Now suppose that the suppliers of the foodstuff argue for (and receive) a price floor, P_F. At this higher price, consumers do not buy as much as they once did. They now buy Q_2, whereas they used to buy Q_1. In addition, consumers' surplus is now only area 1, and producers' surplus is areas $2 + 4$.

Obviously, consumers have been hurt by the new higher (government-mandated) price of P_F; specifically, they have lost consumers' surplus equal to areas $2 + 3$.

How have suppliers fared? Whereas their producers' surplus was equal to areas $4 + 5$ at P_1, it is now equal to areas $2 + 4$. (Area 2, which used to be part of consumers' surplus, has been transferred to producers and is now part of producers' surplus.) Whether or not producers are better off depends on whether or not area 2 (what they gain from P_F) is larger than area 5 (what they lose from P_F). Visually, we can tell that area 2 is larger than area 5, so producers are better off.

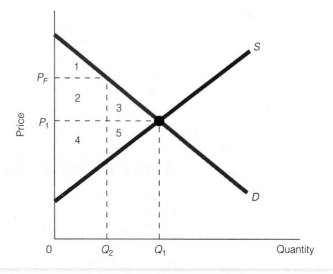

exhibit 7

Agricultural Price Floors

The demand for and supply of an agricultural foodstuff are shown in this exhibit. The equilibrium price is P_1; consumers' surplus (*CS*) is areas $1 + 2 + 3$; producers' surplus is areas $4 + 5$. A price floor of P_F effectively transfers some of the consumers' surplus to producers in the form of a gain in producers' surplus. Specifically, at P_F, consumers' surplus is area 1 and producers' surplus is areas $2 + 4$. Consumers are net losers because consumers' surplus has decreased by areas $2 + 3$. Producers are net gainers because producers' surplus has increased from areas $4 + 5$ to areas $2 + 4$ and area 2 is larger than area 5. Overall, the economic pie of *CS* + *PS* has decreased from areas $1 + 2 + 3 + 4 + 5$ to areas $1 + 2 + 4$.

What is the overall effect of the price floor? Have producers gained more than consumers have lost, or have consumers lost more than producers have gained? To answer this question, we note that consumers lose areas 2 + 3 in consumers' surplus; producers gain area 2 in producers' surplus and lose area 5 in producers' surplus. So the gains and losses are:

Losses to consumers: areas 2 + 3

Gains to producers: area 2

Losses to producers: area 5

Part of the loss to consumers is offset by the gain to producers (area 2), so net losses amount to areas 3 + 5. In other words, total surplus—the sum of consumers' surplus and producers' surplus—is lower than it was. Whereas it used to be areas 1 + 2 + 3 + 4 + 5, it now is areas 1 + 2 + 4. The total surplus lost is areas 3 + 5.

In short, (1) consumers lose, (2) producers gain, and (3) society (which is the sum of consumers and producers) loses.

You can think of this example in terms of a pie. Initially, the pie was made up of areas 1 + 2 + 3 + 4 + 5. This rather large pie registered all the gains of consumers and producers. After the price floor of P_F was imposed, the pie shrank to areas 1 + 2 + 4; in other words, the pie was smaller by areas 3 + 5.

Deadweight Loss
The loss to society of not producing the competitive, or supply-and-demand-determined, level of output.

A loss in total surplus—in our example, areas 3 + 5—is sometimes called a **deadweight loss**. It is the loss to society of not producing the competitive, or supply-and-demand-determined, level of output. In terms of Exhibit 7, it is the loss to society of producing Q_2 instead of producing Q_1.

 Common MISCONCEPTIONS

About Gains and Losses

Some persons argue that a price floor creates a situation in which (a) someone wins and someone loses and (b) the gains for the winner are equal to the losses for the loser (e.g., $5 is lost by one person and $5 is won by another person). A quick look at Exhibit 7 tells us that (b) is not true. The losses (for consumers) are not offset by the gains (for producers). A price ceilings ends with a *net loss* or *deadweight loss* of areas 3 + 5. Now think of how hard it would have been to identify this deadweight loss without the tools of supply, demand, consumers' surplus, and producers' surplus. Economic tools often have the ability to make what is invisible visible.

SELF-TEST

1. Look at the area equal to areas 3 + 5 in Exhibit 7. If there is a price floor, this area ends up being a deadweight loss. It is the loss to society of not producing Q_1. Are there mutually beneficial trades that exist between Q_2 and Q_1, and if so, how do you know this?

2. Why might producers argue for a price floor if it ends up making society worse off?

APPLICATION 8: ARE RENTERS BETTER OFF?

We begin with an analysis of two laws related to eviction of a renter. Under law 1, a renter has 30 days to vacate an apartment after being served with an eviction notice. Under law 2, the renter has 90 days to vacate.

Landlords will find it less expensive to rent apartments under law 1 than under law 2. Under law 1, the most money a landlord can lose after serving an eviction notice is 30 days' rent. Under law 2, a landlord can lose 90 days' rent. Obviously, losing 90 days' rent is more costly than losing 30 days' rent.

A different supply curve of apartments exists under each law. The supply curve under law 1 (S_1 in Exhibit 8) lies to the right of the supply curve under law 2 (S_2 in the exhibit). Again, that's because it is less expensive to supply apartments under law 1 than under law 2.

If the supply curve is different under the two laws, the equilibrium rent will be different too. As shown in Exhibit 8, the equilibrium rent will be lower under law 1 (R_1) than under law 2 (R_2).

In conclusion, under law 1, a renter pays lower rent (good) and has fewer days to vacate the apartment (bad). Under law 2, a renter pays a higher rent (bad) and has more days to vacate the apartment (good). Who pays for the additional days to vacate the apartment under law 2? The renter pays for these additional days by paying higher rent.

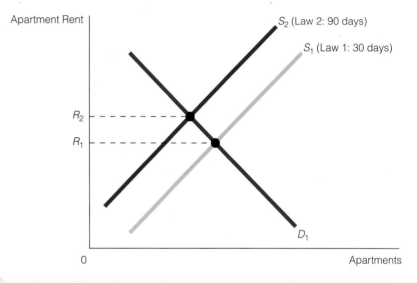

exhibit 8

Apartment Rent and the Law

Under law 1, a renter has 30 days to leave an apartment after receiving an eviction notice from his or her landlord. Under law 2, a renter has 90 days to leave an apartment after receiving an eviction notice from his or her landlord. The cost to the landlord of renting an apartment is higher under law 2 than law 1, and so the supply curve of apartments under law 1 lies to the right of the supply curve of apartments under law 2. Different supply curves mean different rents. Apartment rent is higher under law 2 (R_2) than under law 1 (R_1).

Finding ECONOMICS

In an HMO

You may frequently hear people complain about their health maintenance organizations (HMOs). The complaints are diverse and wide-ranging. One common complaint is that patients cannot sue their HMOs in state courts for denial of benefits and poor-quality care. Some people argue that patients should have the right to sue their HMOs.

Let's consider two settings: one in which patients cannot sue their HMOs and one in which patients can sue. If patients cannot sue, an HMO's liability cost is lower than if patients can sue. A difference in liability costs will be reflected in different supply curves.

To illustrate, recall that any single point on a supply curve is the minimum price sellers need to receive for them to be willing and able to sell that particular unit of a good. Suppose when patients cannot sue, an HMO is willing and able to provide health care to John for $300 a month. If patients can sue, is the HMO still willing and able to provide health care to John for $300 a month? Not likely. Because of the higher liability cost due to the patient's ability to sue, the HMO is no longer willing and able to provide health care to John for $300 month. It will, however, be willing and able to provide health care to John for, say, $350 a month.

Saying a seller's minimum price for providing a good or service rises is the same as saying the seller's supply curve has shifted upward and to the left. In other words, the supply curve of HMO-provided health care will shift upward and to the left if patients have the right to sue. This is the same way the supply curve of apartments moved in Exhibit 4.

(continued)

Finding Economics (continued)

Will a difference in supply curves affect the price patients pay for their HMO-provided health care coverage? Yes. One effect of moving from a setting where patients do not have the right to sue to one where patients do have the right to sue is that patients will have to pay more for their HMO-provided health care coverage.

Economists don't determine whether a patient having the right to sue is good or bad or right or wrong. Economists use their tools (in this instance, supply and demand) to point out that things people want, such as the right to sue their HMOs, often come with price tags. Individuals must decide whether the price they pay is worth what they receive in return.

SELF-TEST

1. Economists often say, "There is no such thing as a free lunch." How is this saying related to patients moving from a system where they cannot sue their HMOs to one where they can?

2. A professor tells her students that they can have an extra week to complete their research papers. Under what condition are the students better off with the extra week? Can you think of a case where the students would actually be worse off with the extra week?

APPLICATION 9: DO YOU PAY FOR GOOD WEATHER?

Some places in the country are considered to have better weather than other places. For example, most people would say the weather in San Diego, California, is better than the weather in Fargo, North Dakota. Often, a person in San Diego will say, "You can't beat the weather today. And the good thing about it is that you don't have to pay a thing for it. It's free."

In one sense, the San Diegan is correct: There is no weather market. Specifically, no one comes around and asks San Diegans to pay a certain dollar amount for the weather on a given day.

But in another sense, the San Diegan is incorrect. The fact is that San Diegans indirectly pay for their good weather. How do they pay? To enjoy the weather in San Diego

on a regular basis, you have to live in San Diego—you need to have housing. There is a demand for housing in San Diego just as there is a demand for housing in other places. Is the demand for housing in San Diego higher than it would be if the weather were not so good? Without the good weather, living in San Diego would not be as pleasurable, and therefore, the demand to live there would be lower. See Exhibit 9. In short, the demand for housing in San Diego is higher because San Diego enjoys good weather. It follows that the price of housing is higher too (P_2 as opposed to P_1 in Exhibit 9). Thus, San Diegans indirectly pay for their good weather because they pay higher housing prices than they would if San Diego had bad weather.

Was our representative San Diegan right when he said the good weather was free?

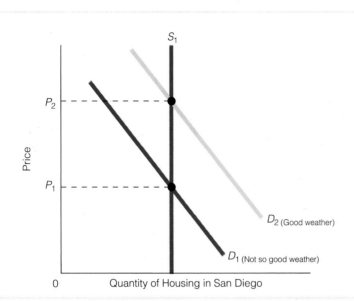

exhibit 9

The Price of Weather and Housing Prices

We show two demand curves, D_1 and D_2. D_1 represents the demand for housing in San Diego if the weather were not so good. The higher demand curve D_2 shows the demand for housing in San Diego if the weather is good. Notice that the price of housing in San Diego is higher if the weather is good than not so good. Lesson learned: You pay for good weather (in San Diego) in terms of higher house prices.

Finding ECONOMICS

Good Schools and House Prices

There are two neighborhoods, A and B. The kids who live in neighborhood A go to school A and the kids who live in neighborhood B go to school B. Currently, school A has a much better academic reputation than school B. Can you find the economics?

This is really no more than a disguised version of our good weather example. If school A is better than school B, then the equilibrium price of houses in neighborhood A is likely to be higher than the equilibrium price of (similar) houses in neighborhood B. Just as we pay for good weather in terms of house prices, we pay for good schools in terms of house prices too.

SELF-TEST

1. Give an example to illustrate that someone may "pay" for clean air in much the same way that she "pays" for good weather.

2. If people pay for good weather, who ultimately receives the "good-weather payment"?

APPLICATION 10: COLLEGE SUPERATHLETES

Let's consider a young man, 17 years old, who is one of the best high school football players in the country. As a superathlete, the young man will be recruited by many college and university football coaches. Every one of those colleges and universities will likely want its coach to be successful at getting the young athlete; after all, at many universities, athletics is a moneymaker.

Our superathlete decides to attend college A, where he receives a "full ride"—a full scholarship. How should this full scholarship be viewed? One way is to say the superathlete is charged zero tuition to attend the college. (In other words, whereas some students pay a price of $10,000 a year to attend the college, the superathlete pays nothing.)

The College Athlete

The exhibit shows the demand for and supply of a college athlete. If the market wage for the college athlete is $15,000, then the buyer of the athlete—in this case, the college— receives consumers' surplus equal to area A. If the wage can be held down to the tuition cost of attending the college—$10,000 in this example— then the college receives consumers' surplus of areas A + B.

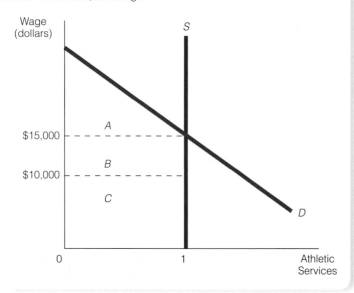

Another way to view the full scholarship involves a two-step process. First, the college pays the super-athlete a dollar amount equal to the full tuition. Second, it then charges the superathlete the full tuition. (In other words, the college gives the athlete $10,000 with one hand and then collects the $10,000 with the other hand.)

Although it ends up being the same for the athlete regardless of which way we view the full scholarship, for purposes of our analysis, let's view the full scholarship the second way: as a payment to the athlete combined with full price being charged. This way of viewing the scholarship leads to two important questions:

1. Can the college pay the athlete more than the full tuition of the college? In other words, if the full tuition is $10,000 a year, can the college pay the athlete, say, $15,000 a year?

2. Is the superathlete being paid what he is worth?

Because of NCAA rules, the answer to the first question is essentially no. The NCAA states that a college or university cannot pay a student to attend, and for all practical purposes, the NCAA views payment as anything more than a full scholarship. The NCAA takes the position that college athletes are amateurs, and amateurs cannot be paid to play their sport.

How does the NCAA rule affect our second question? What if the athlete's worth to the college or university is greater than the dollar amount of the full tuition? For example, suppose the athlete will increase the revenues of the college by $50,000 a year, and the full tuition is only $10,000 a year. In this case, the NCAA rule sets a price ceiling for the college. It sets a ceiling on what the college can pay an athlete. What is the effect of this price ceiling?

Let's consider the demand (on the part of various colleges) for a single superathlete and the supply of this single superathlete (see Exhibit 10). We assume that the supply curve is vertical at 1 "athletic services."

Now suppose the representative college charges tuition of $10,000. Because of the NCAA rule, this dollar amount is the effective price ceiling (or wage ceiling). Furthermore, let's suppose that the single college athlete's market equilibrium wage is $15,000. So, if the NCAA rule did not exist, the athlete's wage would rise to $15,000. This dollar amount is equal to areas B + C in Exhibit 10. What is the consumers' surplus for the college that buys the athlete's services for $15,000? Obviously, it is equal to area A.

However, the NCAA rule stipulates that the college cannot pay the athlete more than $10,000 (full tuition). So, the athlete's payment falls from $15,000 to $10,000, or from areas B + C to simply area C. The college's consumers' surplus increases to areas A + B. Essentially, the NCAA rule transfers part of the athlete's income—area B—to the college in the form of greater consumers' surplus.

Just as the price floor in Application 7 leads to a transfer (from consumers to producers), a price ceiling leads to a transfer. The price ceiling set by the NCAA rule results in a transfer from the athlete to the college. In short, the athlete loses and the college gains. Moreover, in this case, the college gain in consumers' surplus equals the income loss for the athlete.

SELF-TEST

1. University X is a large university with a major football team. A new field house and track were just added to the university. How is this related to the discussion in this application?

2. Sometimes it is argued that if colleges paid student athletes, the demand for college sports would decline. In other words, the demand for college sports is as high as it is because student athletes are not paid (the way athletes in professional sports are paid). How would the analysis in this application change if we assume this argument is true?

APPLICATION 11: 10 A.M. CLASSES IN COLLEGE

Suppose an economics class is offered in the same classroom at 10 a.m. in the morning and at 8 p.m. at night. Most students would prefer the 10 a.m. class to the 8 p.m. class. Notice in Exhibit 11 that the supply of seats in the class is the same at each time, but the demand to occupy those seats is not. Because the demand is greater for the 10 a.m. class than for the 8 p.m. class, the equilibrium price for the 10 a.m. class is higher than the equilibrium price for the 8 p.m. class.

But the university or college charges the same tuition no matter what time students choose to take the class. The university doesn't charge students a higher tuition if they enroll in 10 a.m. classes than if they enroll in 8 p.m. classes.

Suppose tuition of T_1 is charged for all classes, and T_1 is the equilibrium tuition for 8 p.m. classes (see Exhibit 11). It follows that T_1 is below the equilibrium tuition for 10 a.m. classes. At T_1, the quantity demanded of seats for 10 a.m. classes will be greater than the quantity supplied; more students will want the 10 a.m. class than there is space available.

How will the university allocate the available seats? It may do it the same way that airlines ration aisle seats—that is, on a first come, first served basis. Students who are first to register get the 10 a.m. class; the latecomers have to take the 8 p.m. class. Or the university could ration these "high-demand classes" by giving their upper-class students (seniors) first priority.

Thinking like AN ECONOMIST

Remembering Price

The layperson sees students clamoring to get 10 a.m. classes and concludes that the demand is high for classes at this time. He then wonders why the university doesn't schedule more 10 a.m. classes. The economist knows that what the layperson sees is as much an effect of price as of demand. The demand for 10 a.m. classes may be high, but the quantity demanded may not be if the price is high enough. In fact, even though the demand for various classes at various times may be different, there is some set of prices that will make the quantity demanded of each class the same.

exhibit 11

The Supply and Demand for College Classes at Different Times

A given class is offered at two times, 10 a.m. and 8 p.m. The supply of seats in the classroom is the same at both times; however, the student demand for the 10 a.m. class is higher than the demand for the 8 p.m. class. The university charges the same tuition, T_1, regardless of which class a student takes. At this tuition, there is a shortage of seats for the 10 a.m. class. Seats are likely to be rationed on a first-come-first-served (first to register) basis or on seniority (seniors take precedence over juniors, etc.).

Supply of Seats at 10 a.m. and 8 p.m.

Shortage of Seats for 10 a.m. Class

T_1

Tuition

Demand for 10 a.m. Class

Demand for 8 p.m. Class

0

Number of Seats in Class

SELF·TEST

1. Suppose college students are given two options. With option A, the price a student pays for a class is always the equilibrium price. For example, if the equilibrium price to take Economics 101 is $600 at 10 a.m. and is $400 at 4 p.m., then students pay more for the 10 a.m. class than they do for the 4 p.m. class. With option B, the price a student pays for a class is the same regardless of the time the class is taken. When given the choice between options A and B, many students would say they prefer option B to option A. Is this the case for you? If so, why would this be your choice?

2. How is the analysis of the 10 a.m. class similar to the analysis of a price ceiling in the kidney market?

APPLICATION 12: WHAT WILL HAPPEN TO THE PRICE OF MARIJUANA IF THE PURCHASE AND SALE OF MARIJUANA ARE LEGALIZED?

In the United States, the purchase or sale of marijuana is unlawful. However, there is still a demand for and supply of marijuana. There is also an equilibrium price of marijuana. Let's say that price is P_1.

Suppose that beginning tomorrow, the purchase and sale of marijuana become legal. Will P_1 rise, fall, or remain the same?

The answer, of course, depends on what we think will happen to the demand for and supply of marijuana. If the purchase and sale of marijuana are legal, then some people currently producing corn and wheat will likely choose instead to produce and sell marijuana. So the supply of marijuana will rise. If nothing else changes, the price of marijuana will fall.

But something else is likely to change. If marijuana consumption is no longer illegal, then the number of people who want to buy and consume marijuana will likely rise. In other words, there will be more buyers of marijuana. This will increase the demand for marijuana.

Thus, decriminalizing the purchase and sale of marijuana is likely to shift both the marijuana demand and supply curves to the right. What happens to the price of marijuana depends on how much the curves shift. Three possibilities exist:

1. The demand curve shifts to the right by the same amount as the supply curve shifts to the right. In this case, the price of marijuana will not change. (Try to visualize the demand and supply curves shifting.)

2. The demand curve shifts to the right by more than the supply curve shifts to the right. In this case, the price of marijuana will rise. (Try to visualize the demand curve shifting to the right by more than the supply curve shifts to the right. Can you see the higher price on the vertical axis?)

3. The supply curve shifts to the right by more than the demand curve shifts to the right. In this case, the price of marijuana will fall.

If you can't visualize the shifts of the demand and supply curves for the three possibilities, draw the original demand and supply curves, then draw the shift in each curve, and finally, identify the new equilibrium price.

"DOESN'T HIGH DEMAND MEAN HIGH QUANTITY DEMANDED?"

Student:

The other day in class you said, "The demand for 10 a.m. classes may be high, but the quantity demanded may not be if the price is high enough." In other words, you were saying that high demand doesn't necessarily mean high quantity demanded. But I thought it did. Could you explain?

Instructor:

Let me explain what is going on by first showing you the demand schedule for two goods, A and B.

Good A Demand Schedule

Price	Quantity Demanded
$6	100
7	80
8	60
9	40

Good B Demand Schedule

Price	Quantity Demanded
$6	200
7	150
8	125
9	90

As you can see from the two demand schedules, the demand for good B is greater than the demand for good A. In other words, if we were to derive a demand curve for each good (based on its demand schedule) the demand curve for good B would lie farther to the right than the demand curve for good A.

Now suppose we look at quantity demanded for each good at the price of $6. The quantity demanded of good A (the low demand good) is 100 units and the quantity demanded of good B (the high demand good) is 200 units. What can we conclude? Namely, a*t the same price for each good* ($6), quantity demanded is higher when demand is higher.

But now let's consider quantity demanded for each good when the price of good A is $6 and the price of good B is $9. The quantity demanded of good A (the low demand good) is 100 units and the quantity demanded of good B (the high demand good) is 90 units. In other words, if the price is high enough for good B (the high demand good), the quantity demanded of good B may end up being lower than the quantity demanded of good A (the low demand good).

Now let's go back and repeat the statement I made in class: "The demand for 10 a.m. classes may be high, but the quantity demanded may not be if the price is high enough." Now do you understand what I was saying?

Student:

Yes, I think I do. You were saying that high demand doesn't necessarily mean high quantity demanded if we are dealing with different prices.

Instructor:

Yes, that's it.

Points to Remember

1. High demand means high quantity demanded, but only "necessarily so" if the price for the high demand good and the low demand good are the same. From our example: At a price of $6, quantity demanded for the high demand good B is greater than quantity demanded for the low demand good A.

2. Quantity demanded for the low demand good can be higher than quantity demanded for the high demand good if the prices for the two goods are not the same and the price for the high demand good is high enough. From our example: At a price of $9 for good B (the high demand good), quantity demanded is lower than quantity demand is for good A (the low demand good) at a price of $6.

a reader asks | How Do I Find My Own Supply-and-Demand Applications?

I can understand an economist's applications of supply and demand, but I don't know how to apply supply and demand myself. How do I find my own supply-and-demand applications?

You can proceed in several ways, two of which we discuss here. First, you can heed the words of Robert Solow: "I am a supply-and-demand economist. When I come across something, I ask myself what is being transferred here and where does the supply come from and where does the demand come from."[1]

We can reformulate what Solow has said into a single question: Is trade involved? This is the relevant supply-and-demand question because supply and demand are about trade. In other words, when you observe something, simply ask: Is this about trade? If you are driving on a freeway, ask: Is driving on a freeway about trade? Specifically, is something being "bought" and "sold"? If so, what? If you are applying to college, ask: Is this about trade? What is being bought and sold?

A second way to proceed is to look for surpluses and shortages around you. Surpluses and shortages are manifestations of market

disequilibrium. If you find them, you can be fairly sure that supply and demand are relevant. If you are sitting in a classroom with empty seats, ask: Is there a surplus or shortage here? In this case, of course, there is a surplus, which should lead you to think about price. Surpluses exist when prices are too high. Why is the price too high? If you observe more people applying to a particular college than the college will admit, ask: Is there a surplus or shortage here? In this case, there is a shortage, which again should lead you to think about price. Shortages exist when prices are too low. Why is price too low?

The key to finding your own supply-and-demand applications is to (1) observe things around you and then (2) ask questions about the things you observe. If you are sitting in a restaurant eating a meal, ask questions about what you observe. Is trade involved here? Yes. Is the restaurant filled to capacity, and is there a line of people waiting to get in? Yes. Are there more people who want to eat at this restaurant than there are spaces to accommodate them? Yes. Is there a shortage here? Yes. Why do shortages exist? Prices are too low. Why doesn't the restaurant raise its prices and eliminate the shortage?

The process isn't that hard, is it?

1. Interview with Robert Solow. The entire interview is in *Economics* by Roger A. Arnold (St. Paul, MN: West Publishing Company, 1992).

Chapter Summary

WHY IS MEDICAL CARE SO EXPENSIVE?

- When it comes to medical care, often there is the person who sells medical care, the person who buys medical care, and the person who (directly) pays for the medical care (the third party).

- Once a person has paid her (medical) insurance premium, the price she pays for medical care may amount to no more than her copayment (which is usually minimal). For all practical purposes, then, the dollar amount she has to pay out of pocket to get medical care is zero. We expect the quantity demanded of medical care to be greater than at some positive dollar amount.

WHERE WILL HOUSE PRICES CHANGE THE MOST?

- The supply curve for housing is steeper in city 1 than city 2. For an equal increase in demand for housing in each city, house prices will rise more in city 1. For an equal decrease in demand for housing in each city, house prices will fall more in city 2.

WHY DO COLLEGES USE GPAs, ACTs, AND SATs FOR PURPOSES OF ADMISSION?

- Colleges and universities charging students less than the equilibrium tuition for admission create a shortage of spaces at the colleges or universities. Consequently, colleges and universities have to impose some nonprice rationing device, such as GPAs or ACT or SAT scores.

SUPPLY AND DEMAND ON A FREEWAY

- The effect of a disequilibrium price for driving on a freeway is a traffic jam. If the price to drive on a freeway is $0 and at this price the quantity demanded of freeway space is greater than the quantity supplied, then there will be a shortage of freeway space that will manifest itself as freeway congestion.

PRICE CEILING IN THE KIDNEY MARKET

- Currently, there is a price ceiling in the kidney market, and the price is set at $0. Many of the effects of a price ceiling (shortages, fewer exchanges, etc.) are seen in the kidney market.

THE MINIMUM WAGE LAW

- A minimum wage (above equilibrium wage) reduces the number of unskilled workers working or reduces the number of unskilled labor hours purchased by employers.

PRICE FLOORS AND WINNERS AND LOSERS

- A price floor placed on an agricultural foodstuff ends up lowering consumers' surplus, raising producers' surplus, and creating a deadweight loss. In short, a price floor can transfer "surplus" from consumers to producers and leave society (as a whole) worse off too.

ARE RENTERS BETTER OFF?

- The supply curve of apartments will shift upward and to the left if renters have 90 days as opposed to 30 days to vacate an apartment. As a result, renters will pay higher rent when they have 90 days to vacate and apartment.

DO YOU PAY FOR GOOD WEATHER?

- If good weather gives people utility, then the demand for and the price of housing will be higher in a city with good weather than in a city with bad weather. Conclusion: People who buy houses in good-weather locations indirectly pay for the good weather.

COLLEGE SUPERATHLETES

- If a college superathlete receives a full scholarship to play a sport at a university and if the full scholarship is less than the equilibrium wage for the superathlete (because of a prohibition mandating that the athlete cannot be paid the difference between his higher equilibrium wage and the dollar amount of his full scholarship), then the university gains at the expense of the athlete.

10 A.M. CLASSES IN COLLEGE

- Colleges usually charge the same tuition for a class no matter when the class is taken. The supply of seats in the class may be the same at each time, but the demand for the class may be different at different times. At least for some classes, the quantity demanded of seats (in the class) will be greater than the quantity supplied. Thus, some nonprice rationing device will have to be used to achieve equilibrium.

LEGALIZATION OF MARIJUANA

- If the purchase and sale of marijuana are legalized, the price of marijuana may rise, fall, or remain the same. The price will depend on whether the rise in the demand for marijuana is more than, less than, or equal to the rise in the supply of marijuana.

Key Terms and Concepts

Deadweight Loss

Questions and Problems

1 If there were no third parties in medical care, medical care prices would be lower. Do you agree or disagree? Explain your answer.

2 What does the shape of the supply curve have to do with how much price will rise given an increase in demand?

3 Harvard, Yale, and Princeton all charge relatively high tuition. Still, each uses ACT and SAT scores as admission criteria. Are charging a relatively high tuition and using standardized test scores (as admission criteria) inconsistent? Explain your answer.

4 Suppose the purchase and sale of marijuana are legalized and the price of marijuana falls. What explains the lower price of marijuana?

5 The minimum wage in year 1 is $1 higher than the equilibrium wage. In year 2, the minimum wage is increased so that it is $2 above the equilibrium wage. We observe that the same number of people are working at the minimum wage in year 2 as in year 1. Does it follow that an increase in the minimum wage does not cause some workers to lose their jobs? Explain your answer.

6 In our discussion of the kidney market, we represent the demand curve for kidneys as downward sloping and the supply curve of kidneys as upward sloping. At the end of the discussion, we state, "If it is unlawful to pay someone for a kidney, fewer kidneys will be forthcoming. In other words, the quantity supplied of kidneys is less at $0 than at, say, $20,000. Fewer kidneys supplied mean fewer kidney

transplants." Would there be fewer kidney transplants if the supply curve of kidneys is vertical? Explain your answer.

7 What do the applications about freeway congestion and 10 a.m. classes have in common?

8 Economics has been called the "dismal science" because it sometimes "tells us" that things are true when we would prefer they were false. For example, although there are no free lunches, might we prefer that there were? Was there anything in this chapter that you learned was true that you would have preferred to be false? If so, identify it. Then explain why you would have preferred it to be false.

9 In the discussion of health care and the right to sue your HMO, we state, "Saying a seller's minimum price for providing a good or service rises is the same as saying the seller's supply curve has shifted upward and to the left." Does it follow that if a seller's minimum price falls, the supply curve shifts downward and to the right? Explain your answer.

10 Application 9 explains that even though no one directly and explicitly pays for good weather ("Here is $100 for the good weather"), it is still possible to pay for good weather indirectly, such as through housing prices. Identify three other things (besides good weather) that you believe people pay for indirectly.

11 Suppose there exists a costless way to charge drivers on the freeway. Under this costless system, tolls on the freeway would be adjusted according to traffic conditions. For example, when traffic is usually heavy, such as from 6:30 a.m. to 9:00 a.m. on a weekday, the toll to drive on the freeway would be higher than the toll would be when traffic is light. In other words, freeway tolls would be used to equate the demand for freeway space and the supply of freeway space. Would you be in favor of such a system to replace our current (largely, zero-price) system? Explain your answer.

12 Wilson walks into his economics class ten minutes late because he couldn't find a place to park. Because of his tardiness, he doesn't hear the professor tell the class there will be a quiz at the next class session. At the next class session, Wilson is unprepared for the quiz and ends up failing it. Might Wilson's failing the quiz have anything to do with the price of parking?

13 University A charges more for a class for which there is high demand than for a class for which there is low demand. University B charges the same for all classes. All other things being equal between the two universities, which university would you prefer to attend? Explain your answer.

14 Explain and diagrammatically represent how a price floor can bring about a transfer from consumers to producers.

15 Suppose the equilibrium wage for a college athlete is $40,000, but because of NCAA rules, the university can offer him only $22,000 (full tuition). How might the university administrators, coaches, or university alumni lure the college athlete to choose their school over others?

16 Consider the theater in which a Broadway play is performed. If tickets for all seats are the same price (say, $70), what economic effect might arise?

17 What is the relationship between the probability of a person being admitted to the college of his choice and the tuition the college charges?

18 Samantha is flying from San Diego, California, to Arlington, Texas, on a commercial airliner. She asks for an aisle seat but only middle-of-the-row seats are left. Why aren't any aisle seats left? (Hint: The airlines charges the same price for an aisle seat as a middle-of-the-row seat.)

Working with Numbers and Graphs

1 The price to drive on a freeway is $0 at all times of the day. This price establishes equilibrium at 3 a.m. but is too low to establish equilibrium at 5 p.m. There is a shortage of freeway space at 5 p.m.

a. Graphically show and explain how carpooling may eliminate the shortage.

b. Graphically show and explain how building more freeways may eliminate the shortage.

2 Diagrammatically show and explain why there is a shortage of classroom space for some college classes and a surplus for others.

3 Smith has been trying to sell his house for six months, but so far, there are no buyers. Draw the market for Smith's house.

CHAPTER 5

ELASTICITY

Introduction In New York City, a Broadway play is performed in a theater with 1,500 seats. Will the play take in more revenue if the average ticket price for a performance is $70 or if it is $120? If you said $120, consider some other questions: Will the play take in more revenue if the average price is $120 or $180? Will it take in more revenue if the average price is $180 or $250? Are you beginning to get suspicious? Perhaps the highest ticket price won't generate the greatest amount of revenue, but then which ticket price will. The answer may surprise you. As we begin our discussion of microeconomics, we need to take some time to discuss what microeconomics is about and how best to study it.

HOW TO APPROACH THE STUDY OF MICROECONOMICS

Microeconomics is the branch of economics that deals with human behavior and choices as they relate to relatively small units: an individual, a firm, an industry, a single market. Microeconomics involves some key players—players we see time and again. These are:

1. consumers,

2. business firms, and

3. factor (or resource) owners.

Each of these three microeconomic players has an objective (or goal), faces some constraints, and has to make choices. In a way, all of microeconomics is really about:

1. objectives,

2. constraints, and

3. choices.

Let's discuss the three players in terms of their objectives, constraints, and choices.

Consumers

Consumers buy goods and services produced by firms, thereby advancing their *objective* of trying to maximize their utility or satisfaction. Yet very few people can buy all the goods they might like to consume. Consumers' purchases are *constrained* by their limited incomes and by the positive prices for each good. Each purchase subtracts from the consumer's available income and eventually nothing remains. Given limited purchasing ability, the consumer attempts to gain as much utility as possible from each dollar spent. In practice, this is done by *choosing* to use *marginal analysis* in making consumption decisions—by comparing the additional (or marginal) benefits and additional (or marginal) costs of each purchase.

Firms

Firms *hire* productive factors or resources, combine them in a certain way to *produce* a final good, and then *sell* that good to consumers. In short, firms play two roles in the economy: They are the buyers of factors and the sellers of goods.

FIRMS AS BUYERS When firms hire workers and other productive factors, the objective is to maximize profit. Among other things, this objective implies that they will hire a mix of factors that will minimize their costs of producing the desired amount of output. Their hiring decisions are constrained by the positive price of factors and by the need to cover opportunity costs. Firms achieve their objectives by choosing to hire only factors that contribute more at the margin to the firm's output and sales receipts than the additional cost of employing them.

FIRMS AS SELLERS The *objective* in this role is to maximize profit. In their attempt to maximize profit, firms (as sellers) have to *choose* what quantity of the good or service to produce and *choose* what price to charge. The *constraints* placed on sellers comes from consumers, who search for lower prices and higher quality, and from competitors, who attempt to undercut prices charged by other sellers or produce a more desirable good or service.

Factor Owners

Factor (or resource) owners sell the factors or resources to firms, which firms then use to produce goods and services. The *objective* of factor owners is to maximize the income they earn from selling their factors. Since factors are not infinite, factor owners are *constrained* by the prices paid for their services in the marketplace and by the finite amount of factors they have to sell. For example, you, as the owner of your labor, can sell only as much labor as you have in a 24-hour day (where approximately 8 hours each day are needed for sleep). Factor owners achieve their objective by *choosing* to sell those units (of the factor) for which the additional (marginal) benefits, in terms of price offered for the resource, are greater than or equal to the additional (marginal) cost. For example, how much of your labor you choose to sell will depend on the value you place on what you could be doing if you didn't work (your opportunity costs) in relation to the price you are offered for one hour's worth of your labor.

The Choices Made in Market Settings

Consumers, firms, and factor owners make their choices not in a vacuum, but in market settings, and not all market settings are alike. In other words, the setting (or environment) in which consumers, firms, and factor owners make choices may differ from one time to the next. To illustrate, consumers might make choices in one market setting that has many buyers and many sellers and later make choices in a market setting that has many buyers and only a few sellers. Much of our discussion of microeconomics focuses on the various market settings in which choices are made.

Recap

What should you look for as you begin your study of microeconomics?

1. You should look for the different players—consumers, firms, and factor owners.
2. You should identify the objective of each.
3. You should identify the constraints that each faces.
4. You should focus on how the economic player chooses within those constraints.
5. You should keep in mind the environment—or the market setting—in which all this takes place.

ELASTICITY: PART 1

The law of demand states that price and quantity demanded are inversely related, *ceteris paribus*. But it doesn't tell us by what percentage the quantity demanded changes as price changes. Suppose price rises by 10 percent. As a result, quantity demanded falls, but by what percentage does it fall? The notion of price elasticity of demand can help answer this question. The general concept of elasticity provides a technique for estimating the response of one variable to changes in another variable. It has numerous applications in economics.

Price Elasticity of Demand

If you have ever watched the TV shopping networks, such as QVC or the Home Shopping Network, every now and then you see computers for sale. For example, QVC often offers Dell computers for sale, making an assertion like, "Today, we're offering this Dell computer, along with a printer, digital camera, flat-panel monitor, and scanner all for the unbelievable price of $1,700."

No matter how many computers QVC sells with its offer, one question almost always pops into the minds of the top managers of both QVC and Dell: How many more computers could they have sold if the price had been, say, $100 lower? Similarly: How many fewer computers would they have sold if the price had been, say, $100 higher? Specifically, QVC and Dell managers want to know the *price elasticity of demand* for the computer being offered for sale. **Price elasticity of demand** is a measure of the responsiveness of quantity demanded to changes in price. More specifically, it addresses the percentage change in quantity demanded for a given percentage change in price.

Let's say that QVC raises the price of the computer by 10 percent, and as a result quantity demanded for the computer falls by 20 percent. The percentage change in quantity demanded—20 percent—divided by the percentage change in price—10 percent—is called the *coefficient of price elasticity of demand (E_d)*.

Price Elasticity of Demand
A measure of the responsiveness of quantity demanded to changes in price.

$$E_d = \frac{\text{Percentage change in quantity demanded}}{\text{Percentage change in price}} = \frac{\%\Delta Q_d}{\%\Delta P}$$

In the formula, E_d = coefficient of price elasticity of demand, or simply elasticity coefficient, % = percentage, and Δ stands for "change in."

If we carry out the calculation in our simple example—where quantity demanded changes by 20 percent and price changes by 10 percent—we get the number 2. An economist would say either, "The coefficient of price elasticity of demand is 2" or, more simply,

"Price elasticity of demand is 2." Either expression means that the percentage change in quantity demanded will be 2 times any percentage change in price.[1] If price changes 5 percent, quantity demanded will change 10 percent; if price changes 10 percent, quantity demanded will change 20 percent.

WHERE IS THE MISSING MINUS SIGN? You know that price and quantity demanded move in opposite directions: When price rises, quantity demanded falls; when price falls, quantity demanded rises. In our example, when price rises by 10 percent, quantity demanded falls by 20 percent. Now, when you divide a *minus 20 percent* by a *positive 10 percent,* you don't get 2; you get –2. Instead of saying that the price elasticity of demand is 2, you might think the price elasticity of demand is –2. However, by convention, economists usually simplify things by speaking of the absolute value of the price elasticity of demand; thus they drop the minus sign.

FORMULA FOR CALCULATING PRICE ELASTICITY OF DEMAND Using percentage changes to calculate price elasticity of demand can lead to conflicting results depending on whether price rises or falls. Therefore, economists use the following formula to calculate price elasticity of demand.[2]

$$E_d = \frac{\dfrac{\Delta Q_d}{Q_{d\,\text{Average}}}}{\dfrac{\Delta P}{P_{\text{Average}}}}$$

In the formula, ΔQ_d stands for the absolute change in Q_d. For example, if Q_d changes from 50 units to 100 units, then ΔQ_d is 50 units. ΔP stands for the absolute change in price. For example, if price changes from $12 to $10, then ΔP is $2. $Q_{d\,\text{Average}}$ stands for the average of the two quantities demanded, and P_{Average} stands for the average of the two prices.

For the price and quantity demanded data in Exhibit 1, the calculation is

$$E_d = \frac{\dfrac{50}{75}}{\dfrac{2}{11}} = 3.67$$

Because we use the average price and average quantity demanded in our price elasticity of demand equation, 3.67 may be considered the price elasticity of demand at a point *midway between the two points identified on the demand curve.* For example, in Exhibit 1, 3.67 is the price elasticity of demand between points A and B on the demand curve.

Elasticity Is Not Slope

There is a tendency to think that slope and price elasticity of demand are the same, but they are not. Suppose we identify a third point on the demand curve in Exhibit 1. The following table shows the price and quantity demanded for our three points.

Point	Price	Quantity Demanded
A	$12	50
B	10	100
C	8	150

---

1. This assumes we are changing price from its current level.

2. This formula is sometimes called the midpoint formula for calculating price elasticity of demand.

To calculate the *price elasticity of demand* between points A and B, we divide the percentage change in quantity demanded (between the two points) by the percentage change in price (between the two points). Using the price elasticity of demand formula, we get 3.67.

The *slope of the demand curve* between points A and B is the ratio of the change in the variable on the vertical axis to the change in the variable on the horizontal axis.

$$\text{Slope} = \frac{\Delta \text{Variable on vertical axis}}{\Delta \text{Variable on horizontal axis}} = \frac{-2}{50} = -0.04$$

Now let's calculate the price elasticity of demand and the slope between points B and C. The price elasticity of demand is 1.80; the slope is still −0.04.

From Perfectly Elastic to Perfectly Inelastic Demand

Look back at the equation for the elasticity coefficient and think of it as

$$E_d = \frac{\text{Percentage change in quantity demanded}}{\text{Percentage change in price}} = \frac{\text{Numerator}}{\text{Denominator}}$$

Focusing on the numerator and denominator, we realize that (1) the numerator can be greater than the denominator, (2) the numerator can be less than the denominator, or (3) the numerator can be equal to the denominator. These three cases, along with two peripherally related cases, are discussed in the following paragraphs. Exhibits 2 and 3 provide summaries of the discussion.

ELASTIC DEMAND ($E_d > 1$) See Exhibit 3(a). If the numerator (percentage change in quantity demanded) is greater than the denominator (percentage change in price), the elasticity coefficient is greater than 1 and demand is elastic. This is **elastic demand**; that is, quantity demanded changes proportionately more than price changes. A 10 percent increase in price causes, say, a 20 percent reduction in quantity demanded ($E_d = 2$).

Percentage change in quantity demanded > Percentage change in price →

$E_d > 1 \rightarrow$ Demand is elastic

INELASTIC DEMAND ($E_d < 1$) See Exhibit 3(b). If the numerator (percentage change in quantity demanded) is less than the denominator (percentage change in price), the elasticity coefficient is less than 1 and demand is inelastic. This is **inelastic demand**;

Elastic Demand
The demand when the percentage change in quantity demanded is greater than the percentage change in price. Quantity demanded changes proportionately more than price changes.

Inelastic Demand
The demand when the percentage change in quantity demanded is less than the percentage change in price. Quantity demanded changes proportionately less than price changes.

exhibit 2

Price Elasticity of Demand	Demand may be elastic, inelastic, unit elastic, perfectly elastic, or perfectly inelastic.	
Elasticity Coefficient	**Responsiveness of Quantity Demanded to a Change in Price**	**Terminology**
$E_d > 1$	Quantity demanded changes proportionately more than price changes: $\%\Delta Q_d > \%\Delta P$.	Elastic
$E_d < 1$	Quantity demanded changes proportionately less than price changes: $\%\Delta Q_d < \%\Delta P$.	Inelastic
$E_d = 1$	Quantity demanded changes proportionately to price change: $\%\Delta Q_d = \%\Delta P$.	Unit elastic
$E_d = \infty$	Quantity demanded is extremely responsive to even very small changes in price.	Perfectly elastic
$E_d = 0$	Quantity demanded does not change as price changes.	Perfectly inelastic

exhibit 3

Graphical Representation of Price Elasticity of Demand

(a) The percentage change in quantity demanded is greater than the percentage change in price: $E_d > 1$ and demand is elastic. (b) The percentage change in quantity demanded is less than the percentage change in price: $E_d < 1$ and demand is inelastic. (c) The percentage change in quantity demand is equal to percentage change in price: $E_d = 1$ and demand is unit elastic. (d) A small change in price reduces quantity demanded to zero: $E_d = \infty$ and demand is perfectly elastic. (e) A change in price does not change quantity demanded: $E_d = 0$ and demand is perfectly inelastic.

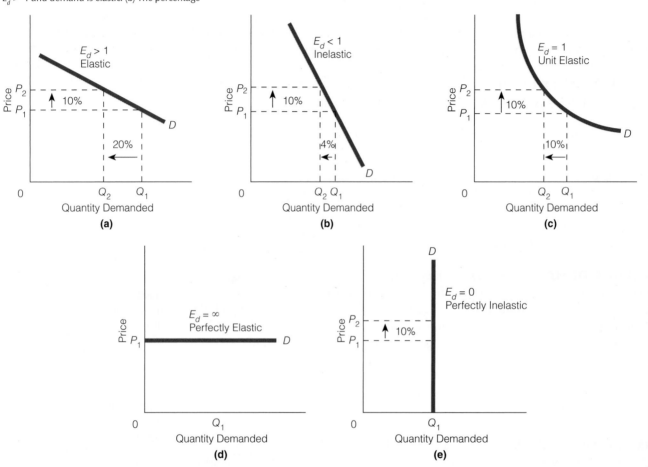

that is, quantity demanded changes proportionately less than price changes. A 10 percent increase in price causes, say, a 4 percent reduction in quantity demanded ($E_d = 0.4$).

Percentage change in quantity demanded < Percentage change in price →

$E_d < 1 \rightarrow$ Demand is inelastic

UNIT ELASTIC DEMAND ($E_d = 1$) See Exhibit 3(c). If the numerator (percentage change in quantity demanded) equals the denominator (percentage change in price), the elasticity coefficient is 1. This is **unit elastic demand**; that is, quantity demanded changes proportionately to price changes. For example, a 10 percent increase in price causes a 10 percent decrease in quantity demanded ($E_d = 1$). In this case, demand exhibits unitary elasticity, or is unit elastic.

Unit Elastic Demand
The demand when the percentage change in quantity demanded is equal to the percentage change in price. Quantity demanded changes proportionately to price changes.

Percentage change in quantity demanded = Percentage change in price →

$E_d = 1 \rightarrow$ Demand is unit elastic

PERFECTLY ELASTIC DEMAND ($E_d = \infty$)   See Exhibit 3(d). If quantity demanded is extremely responsive to changes in price, the result is **perfectly elastic demand**. For example, buyers are willing to buy all units of a seller's good at $5 per unit but nothing at $5.10. A small percentage change in price causes an extremely large percentage change in quantity demanded (from buying all to buying nothing). The percentage is so large, in fact, that economists say it is infinitely large.

PERFECTLY INELASTIC DEMAND ($E_d = 0$)   See Exhibit 3(e). If quantity demanded is completely unresponsive to changes in price, the result is **perfectly inelastic demand**. A change in price causes no change in quantity demanded. For example, suppose the price of Dogs Love It dog food rises 10 percent (from $10 to $11), and Jeremy doesn't buy any less of it per week for his dog. It follows that Jeremy's demand for Dogs Love It dog food is perfectly inelastic between a price of $10 and $11.

PERFECTLY ELASTIC AND PERFECTLY INELASTIC DEMAND CURVES
Even though you are used to seeing downward-sloping demand curves, Exhibit 3 shows two demand curves that are not downward sloping. The question is, aren't all demand curves supposed to be downward sloping because, according to the law of demand, an inverse relationship exists between price and quantity demanded? The answer is that in the real world, no demand curves are perfectly elastic (horizontal) or perfectly inelastic (vertical) at all prices. Thus, the perfectly elastic and perfectly inelastic demand curves in Exhibit 3 should be viewed as representations of the extreme limits between which all real-world demand curves fall.

However, a few real-world demand curves do *approximate* the perfectly elastic and inelastic demand curves in Exhibit 3(d) and (e); that is, they come very close. For example, the demand for a particular farmer's wheat approximates the perfectly elastic demand curve in (d). A later chapter discusses the perfectly elastic demand curve for firms in perfectly competitive markets.

Finding ECONOMICS

At the Local Coffee Bar

You buy seven coffees at the local coffee bar each week when the price of a cup of coffee is $2 and you buy five coffees a week when the price is $2.50. Where is the economics here? Actually, economics appears in two places. First, the law of demand is visible because you buy fewer cups of coffee at the higher price. Second, it is easy to calculate your price elasticity of coffee between the lower and higher prices. It is 1.5, which means your demand for coffee is elastic.

Price Elasticity of Demand and Total Revenue (Total Expenditure)

Total revenue (*TR*) of a seller equals the price of a good times the quantity of the good sold.[3] For example, if the hamburger stand down the street sells 100 hamburgers today at $1.50 each, its total revenue is $150.

Suppose the hamburger vendor raises the price of hamburgers to $2 each. What do you predict will happen to total revenue? Most people say it will increase in the widespread

Perfectly Elastic Demand
The demand when a small percentage change in price causes an extremely large percentage change in quantity demanded (from buying all to buying nothing).

Perfectly Inelastic Demand
The demand when the quantity demanded does not change as price changes.

Total Revenue (*TR*)
Price times quantity sold.

---

3. In this discussion, *total revenue* and *total expenditure* are equivalent terms. Total revenue equals price times the quantity sold. Total expenditure equals price times the quantity produced. If something is sold, it must be purchased, making total revenue equal to total expenditure. The term *total revenue* is used when looking at things from the point of view of the sellers in a market. The term *total expenditure* is used when looking at things from the point of view of the buyers in a market. Buyers make expenditures; sellers receive revenues.

belief that higher prices bring higher total revenue. However, total revenue may increase, decrease, or remain constant. Suppose price rises to $2, but because of the higher price, the quantity of hamburgers sold falls to 50. Total revenue is now $100 (whereas it was $150). Whether total revenue rises, falls, or remains constant after a price change depends on whether the percentage change in quantity demanded is less than, greater than, or equal to the percentage change in price. Thus, price elasticity of demand influences total revenue.

ELASTIC DEMAND AND TOTAL REVENUE If demand is elastic, the percentage change in quantity demanded is greater than the percentage change in price. Given a price rise of, say, 5 percent, quantity demanded falls by more than 5 percent—say, 8 percent—having an effect on total revenue. Because quantity demanded falls, or sales fall off, by a greater percentage than the percentage rise in price, total revenue decreases. In short, if demand is elastic, a price rise decreases total revenue.

$$\text{Demand is elastic: } P\uparrow \rightarrow TR \downarrow$$

What happens to total revenue if demand is elastic and price falls? In this case, quantity demanded rises (price and quantity demanded are inversely related) by a greater percentage than the percentage fall in price, causing total revenue to increase. In short, if demand is elastic, a price fall increases total revenue.

$$\text{Demand is elastic: } P\downarrow \rightarrow TR \uparrow$$

Exhibit 4(a) may help you see the relationship between a change in price and total revenue if demand is elastic. The exhibit shows elastic demand between points A and B on the demand curve. At point A, price is P_1 and quantity demanded is Q_1. Total revenue is equal to the rectangle $0P_1AQ_1$. Now suppose we lower price to P_2. After the price decline, total revenue is now the rectangle $0P_2BQ_2$, which, as you can see, is larger than rectangle $0P_1AQ_1$. In other words, if demand is elastic and price declines, total revenue will rise.

Of course, when price moves in the opposite direction, rising from P_2 to P_1, then the total revenue rectangle becomes smaller. In other words, if demand is elastic and price rises, total revenue will fall.

INELASTIC DEMAND AND TOTAL REVENUE If demand is inelastic, the percentage change in quantity demanded is less than the percentage change in price. If price rises, quantity demanded falls but by a smaller percentage than the percentage rise in price. As a result, total revenue increases. So if demand is inelastic, a price rise increases total revenue. However, if price falls, quantity demanded rises by a smaller percentage than the percentage fall in price, and total

---

exhibit 4

Price Elasticity of Demand and Total Revenue

In (a) demand is elastic between points A and B. A fall in price, from P_1 to P_2, will increase the size of the total revenue rectangle from $0P_1AQ_1$ to $0P_2BQ_2$. A rise in price, from P_2 to P_1, will decrease the size of the total revenue rectangle from $0P_2BQ_2$ to $0P_1AQ_1$. In other words, when demand is elastic, price and total revenue are inversely related. In (b) demand is inelastic between points A and B. A fall in price, from P_1 to P_2, will decrease the size of the total revenue rectangle from $0P_1AQ_1$ to $0P_2BQ_2$. A rise in price, from P_2 to P_1, will increase the size of the total revenue rectangle from $0P_2BQ_2$ to $0P_1AQ_1$. In other words, when demand is inelastic, price and total revenue are directly related.

(a)

(b)

DRUG BUSTS AND CRIME

Most people agree that the sale or possession of drugs such as cocaine and heroin should be illegal, but sometimes laws may have unintended effects. Do drug laws have unintended effects? Let's analyze the enforcement of drug laws in terms of supply, demand, and price elasticity of demand.

© AP PHOTO/CP/NATHAN DENETTE

Suppose for every $100 of illegal drug sales, 60 percent of the $100 paid is obtained by illegal means. That is, buyers of $100 worth of illegal drugs obtain $60 of the purchase price from criminal activities such as burglaries, muggings, and similar activities.

We assume the demand for and supply of cocaine in a particular city are represented by D_1 and S_1 in Exhibit 5. The equilibrium price of $50 an ounce and the equilibrium quantity of 1,000 ounces give cocaine dealers a total revenue of $50,000. If 60 percent of this total revenue is obtained by the criminal activities of cocaine buyers, then $30,000 worth of crime has been committed to purchase the $50,000 worth of cocaine.

Now suppose there is a drug bust in the city, reducing the supply of cocaine. The supply curve shifts leftward from S_1 to S_2, the equilibrium price rises to $120 an ounce, and the equilibrium quantity falls to 600 ounces. The demand for cocaine is inelastic between the two prices, at 0.607. When demand is inelastic, an increase in price will raise total revenue. The total revenue received by cocaine dealers is now $72,000. If, again, we assume that 60 percent of the total revenue paid comes from criminal activity, then $43,200 worth of crime has been committed to purchase the $72,000 worth of cocaine.

Our conclusion: If the demand for cocaine is inelastic and people commit crimes to buy drugs, then a drug bust can actually increase the amount of drug-related crime. Obviously, this is an unintended effect of the enforcement of drug laws.

exhibit 5

Drug Busts and Drug-Related Crime

In the exhibit, P = price of cocaine, Q = quantity of cocaine, and TR = total revenue from selling cocaine. At a price of $50 for an ounce of cocaine, equilibrium quantity is 1,000 ounces and total revenue is $50,000. If $60 of every $100 cocaine purchase is obtained through crime, then $30,000 worth of crime is committed to purchase $50,000 worth of cocaine. As a result of a drug bust, the supply of cocaine shifts leftward; the price rises and the quantity falls. Because we have assumed the demand for cocaine is inelastic, total revenue rises to $72,000. Sixty percent of this comes from criminal activities, or $43,200.

	P	Q	TR	Dollar Amount of TR Obtained Through Crime
Before Drug Bust	$50	1,000	$50,000	$30,000
After Drug Bust	120	600	72,000	43,200

Elasticities, Price Changes, and Total Revenue

If demand is elastic, a price rise leads to a decrease in total revenue (*TR*), and a price fall leads to an increase in total revenue. If demand is inelastic, a price rise leads to an increase in total revenue and a price fall leads to a decrease in total revenue. If demand is unit elastic, a rise or fall in price does not change total revenue.

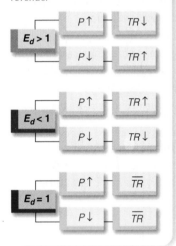

revenue decreases. If demand is inelastic, a price fall decreases total revenue. If demand is inelastic, price and total revenue are directly related.

$$\text{Demand is inelastic: } P\uparrow \rightarrow TR\uparrow$$
$$\text{Demand is inelastic: } P\downarrow \rightarrow TR\downarrow$$

You can see the relationship between inelastic demand and total revenue in Exhibit 4(b), where demand is inelastic between points A and B on the demand curve. If we start at P_1 and lower price to P_2, the total revenue rectangle goes from $0P_1AQ_1$ to the smaller total revenue rectangle $0P_2BQ_2$. In other words, if demand is inelastic and price falls, total revenue will fall.

Moving from the lower price, P_2, to the higher price, P_1, does just the opposite. If demand is inelastic and price rises, the total revenue rectangle becomes larger; that is, total revenue rises.

UNIT ELASTIC DEMAND AND TOTAL REVENUE If demand is unit elastic, the percentage change in quantity demanded equals the percentage change in price. If price rises, quantity demanded falls by the same percentage as the percentage rise in price. Total revenue does not change. If price falls, quantity demanded rises by the same percentage as the percentage fall in price. Again, total revenue does not change. If demand is unit elastic, a rise or fall in price leaves total revenue unchanged.

For a review of the relationship between price elasticity of demand and total revenue, see Exhibit 6.

 Common MISCONCEPTIONS

About Price and Total Revenue

Ask some people what will happen if a seller raises the selling price of a product, and they will tell you that total revenue is bound to rise: "Sellers want higher prices because they take in more money at higher prices than at lower prices." As you have just learned, this is not always true. If demand is inelastic and price rises, then total revenue rises too. But if demand is elastic and price rises, then total revenue falls. Finally, if demand is unit elastic and price rises, then total revenue remains unchanged. Simply put, it is a myth that total revenue always rises as sellers raise prices.

 Common MISCONCEPTIONS

About the Effects of Earthquakes in Los Angeles

Suppose an earthquake in Los Angeles destroys 10 percent of the apartment stock. As a result, we can expect the average rent for an apartment in the city to rise. Some people go further and argue that, because of the earthquake, landlords will end up taking in more total revenue than they did before the earthquake, but this is not necessarily true. To illustrate, suppose the rent before the earthquake is $2,000 and 100,000 apartments are rented. The monthly total revenue is $200 million. Now suppose the earthquake occurs, reducing the number of apartments to 90,000. As a result of a lower supply of apartments, the average rent rises to, say, $2,100 a month. At this higher rent per month, the monthly total revenue (from apartments) is $189 million. We get a lower total revenue because demand for apartments between the lower rent and the higher rent is elastic. As we have learned, if demand is elastic and price rises, total revenue falls.

SELF-TEST

(Answers to Self-Test questions are in the Self-Test Appendix.)

1. On Tuesday, price and quantity demanded are $7 and 120 units, respectively. Ten days later, price and quantity demanded are $6 and 150 units, respectively. What is the price elasticity of demand between the $7 and $6 prices?

2. What does a price elasticity of demand of 0.39 mean?

3. Identify what happens to total revenue as a result of each of the following:

   a. Price rises and demand is elastic.

   b. Price falls and demand is inelastic.

   c. Price rises and demand is unit elastic.

   d. Price rises and demand is inelastic.

   e. Price falls and demand is elastic.

4. Alexi says, "When a seller raises his price, his total revenue rises." What is Alexi implicitly assuming?

ELASTICITY: PART 2

This section discusses the elasticity ranges of a straight-line downward-sloping demand curve and the determinants of price elasticity of demand.

Price Elasticity of Demand Along a Straight-Line Demand Curve

The price elasticity of demand for a straight-line downward-sloping demand curve varies from highly elastic to highly inelastic. To illustrate, consider the price elasticity of demand at the upper range of the demand curve in Exhibit 7(a). Whether the price falls from $9 to $8 or rises from $8 to $9, using the price elasticity of demand formula (identified earlier in the chapter), we calculate price elasticity of demand as 5.66.[4]

Now consider the price elasticity of demand at the lower range of the demand curve in Exhibit 7(a). Whether the price falls from $3 to $2 or rises from $2 to $3, we calculate the price elasticity of demand as 0.33.

In other words, along the range of the demand curve we have identified, price elasticity goes from being greater than 1 (5.66) to being less than 1 (0.33). Obviously, on its way from being greater than 1 to being less than 1, price elasticity of demand must be equal to 1. In

exhibit 7

Price Elasticity of Demand Along a Straight-Line Demand Curve

In (a), the price elasticity of demand varies along the straight-line downward-sloping demand curve. There is an elastic range to the curve (where $E_d > 1$) and an inelastic range (where $E_d < 1$). At the midpoint of any straight-line downward-sloping demand curve, price elasticity of demand is equal to 1 ($E_d = 1$).

Part (b) shows that in the elastic range of the demand curve, total revenue rises as price is lowered. In the inelastic range of the demand curve, further price declines result in declining total revenue. Total revenue reaches its peak when price elasticity of demand equals 1.

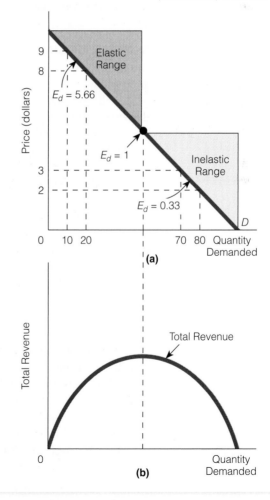

4. Keep in mind that our formula uses the average of the two prices and the average of the two quantities demanded. You may want to look back at the formula to refresh your memory.

Exhibit 7(a), we have identified price elasticity of demand as equal to 1 at the *midpoint* of the demand curve.[5]

What do the elastic and inelastic ranges along the straight-line downward-sloping demand curve mean in terms of total revenue? If we start in the elastic range of the demand curve in Exhibit 7(a) and lower price, total revenue rises, as shown in Exhibit 7(b). That is, as price is coming down within the elastic range of the demand curve in (a), total revenue is rising in (b).

When price has fallen enough that we move into the inelastic range of the demand curve in (a), further price declines simply lower total revenue, as shown in (b). Therefore, total revenue is at its highest—its peak—when price elasticity of demand equals 1.

Determinants of Price Elasticity of Demand

The four factors that are relevant to the determination of price elasticity of demand are:

1. number of substitutes,
2. necessities versus luxuries,
3. percentage of one's budget spent on the good, and
4. time.

Because all four factors interact, we hold all other things constant as we discuss each.

NUMBER OF SUBSTITUTES Suppose good A has 2 substitutes and good B has 15 substitutes. Assume that each of the 2 substitutes for good A is as good a substitute (or a good enough substitute) for that good as each of the 15 substitutes is for good B.

Let the price of each good rise by 10 percent. The quantity demanded of each good decreases. Will the percentage change in quantity demanded of good A be greater or less than the percentage change in quantity demanded of good B? That is, will quantity demanded be more responsive to the 10 percent price rise for the good that has 2 substitutes (good A) or for the good that has 15 substitutes (good B)? The answer is the good with 15 substitutes, good B. The reason is that the greater the opportunities are for substitution (there is more chance of substituting a good for B than of substituting a good for A), the greater the cutback in the quantity of the good purchased will be as its price rises. When the price of good A rises 10 percent, people can turn to 2 substitutes. Quantity demanded of good A falls, but not by as much as if 15 substitutes had been available, as there are for good B.

The relationship between the availability of substitutes and price elasticity is clear:

The more substitutes there are for a good, the higher the price elasticity of demand will be; the fewer substitutes for a good, the lower the price elasticity of demand.

For example, the price elasticity of demand for Chevrolets is higher than the price elasticity of demand for all cars because there are more substitutes for Chevrolets than there are for cars. Everything that is a substitute for a car (taking a bus, getting on a train, walking, bicycling, etc.) is also a substitute for a specific type of car, such as a Chevrolet, but some substitutes for a Chevrolet (Ford, Toyota, Chrysler, Mercedes-Benz, etc.) are not substitutes for a car. Instead, they are simply types of cars.

Thus, the preceding relationship above can be restated as:

The more broadly defined the good is, the fewer the substitutes it will have; the more narrowly defined the good, the more the substitutes.

---

5. For any straight-line downward-sloping demand curve, price elasticity of demand equals 1 at the midpoint of the curve.

There are more substitutes for this economics textbook than there are for textbooks. There are more substitutes for Coca-Cola than there are for soft drinks.

NECESSITIES VERSUS LUXURIES Generally, the more that a good is considered a luxury (a good that we can do without) rather than a necessity (a good that we can't do without), the higher the price elasticity of demand will be. For example, consider two goods: jewelry and a medicine for controlling high blood pressure. If the price of jewelry rises, it is easy to cut back on purchases; no one really needs jewelry to live. However, if the price of the medicine for controlling one's high blood pressure rises, it is not so easy to cut back. We expect the price elasticity of demand for jewelry to be higher than the price elasticity of demand for high blood pressure medicine.

PERCENTAGE OF ONE'S BUDGET SPENT ON THE GOOD Claire Rossi has a monthly budget of $3,000. Of this monthly budget, she spends $3 per month on pens and $400 per month on dinners at restaurants. In percentage terms, she spends 0.1 percent of her monthly budget on pens and 13 percent of her monthly budget on dinners at restaurants. Suppose both the price of pens and the price of dinners at restaurants double. Would Claire be more responsive to the change in the price of pens or to the change in the price of dinners at restaurants? The answer is the change in the price of dinners at restaurants because Claire feels a doubling in the price of a good on which she spends 0.1 percent of her budget a lot less than a doubling in price of a good on which she spends 13 percent. Claire is more likely to ignore the doubling in the price of pens than she is to ignore the doubling in the price of dinners at restaurants. Buyers are (and thus quantity demanded is) more responsive to price as the percentage of their budget that goes for the purchase of the good increases.

> *The greater the percentage of one's budget that goes to purchase a good, the higher the price elasticity of demand will be; the smaller the percentage of one's budget that goes to purchase a good, the lower the price elasticity of demand.*

TIME As time passes, buyers have greater opportunities to be responsive to a price change. If the price of electricity went up today and you knew about it, you probably would not change your consumption of electricity today as much as you would three months from today. As time passes, you have more chances to change your consumption by finding substitutes (natural gas), changing your lifestyle (buying more blankets and turning down the thermostat at night), and so on. We conclude:

> *The more time that passes (since the price change), the higher the price elasticity of demand for the good will be; the less time that passes, the lower the price elasticity of demand for the good.*

In other words, price elasticity of demand for a good is higher in the long run than in the short run.

Finding ECONOMICS

In Apples and Pens

Parker buys a lot more apples when their price falls, but he doesn't buy many more pens when the price of pens falls. Where is the economics here? Obviously, Parker's price of elasticity of demand is different for apples than for pens. We don't have any percentage changes to compare, but from the little information given, Parker's price elasticity of demand for apples seems to be greater than his price elasticity of demand for pens.

WHY IS JACK BAUER EATING A CALORIEMATE BLOCK IN JAPAN?

Many companies hire celebrities to advertise their products. In the past, Shaquille O'Neal was hired to advertise Burger King, Shakira was hired to advertise Pepsi, Jerry Seinfeld to advertise American Express, Celine Dion to advertise Chrysler, Tim McGraw to advertise Anheuser-Busch, and Michael Jordan to advertise products such as Gatorade and Nike. Why do companies hire celebrities to pitch their wares? The obvious answer is to get the attention of consumers. When people see a sports star, television star, model, or movie star talking about a product, they are likely to take notice.

But there are other ways to get the attention of consumers; so maybe another factor is involved. Some economists have hypothesized that the other factor is related to price elasticity of demand and total revenue.

Consider the case of actor Kiefer Sutherland, who, as the TV show *24* character Jack Bauer, has advertised the product CalorieMate in Japan. (The product Sutherland advertises is a bar-shaped cookie, called a CalorieMate block, that one eats for a needed energy boost. Check out YouTube if you want to see one of the CalorieMate commercials with Sutherland.) In showing Jack Bauer eating a CalorieMate block, Otsuka Pharmaceutical Company (the company that makes CalorieMate block) may have been trying to convey the following message: For Jack Bauer, there is only one high-energy block—no substitutes.

© FOX TV/THE KOBAL COLLECTION

If the Japanese buying public accepts this message—if buyers believe there are no substitutes for a CalorieMate block or if they want to do what Jack Bauer does—then the price elasticity of a CalorieMate block declines. The fewer substitutes that are perceived, the lower the price elasticity of demand will be.

And if it is possible to get the demand for CalorieMate block to become inelastic (at least for a short range of the demand curve above current price), then Otsuka Pharmaceutical can raise both price and total revenue. Remember, if demand is inelastic, an increase in price leads to higher total revenue.

Does Otsuka Pharmaceutical want to increase its total revenue? Under the conditions stated, it certainly does. Of course, at a higher price, fewer CalorieMate blocks will be sold, but profit is the objective, not the number of CalorieMate blocks sold. Profit is the difference between total revenue and total cost. If the demand for a CalorieMate block is inelastic, a price increase will raise total revenue and mean fewer CalorieMate blocks sold, which will lower costs. If revenues rise and costs decline, profits rise.

The concluding point: The discussion of price elasticity of demand in this chapter isn't as far removed from the discussions in the offices of major companies and advertising firms around the world.

SELF-TEST

1. If there are 7 substitutes for good X and demand is inelastic, does it follow that, if there are 9 substitutes for good X, demand will be elastic? Explain your answer.

2. Price elasticity of demand is predicted to be higher for which good of the following combinations of goods? Explain your answers.

    a. Dell computers or computers.

    b. Heinz ketchup or ketchup.

    c. Perrier water or water.

OTHER ELASTICITY CONCEPTS

This section looks at three other elasticities: cross elasticity of demand, income elasticity of demand, and price elasticity of supply.

Cross Elasticity of Demand

Cross elasticity of demand measures the responsiveness in the quantity demanded of one good to changes in the price of another good. It is calculated by dividing the percentage change in the quantity demanded of one good by the percentage change in the price of another good.

$$E_c = \frac{\text{Percentage change in quantity demanded of one good}}{\text{Percentage change in price of another good}}$$

where E_c stands for the coefficient of cross elasticity of demand, or elasticity coefficient.

This concept is often used to determine whether two goods are substitutes or complements and the degree to which one good is a substitute for or a complement to another. Consider two goods: Skippy peanut butter and Jif peanut butter. Suppose that when the price of Jif increases by 10 percent, the quantity demanded of Skippy increases by 45 percent. The cross elasticity of demand for Skippy with respect to the price of Jif is written

$$E_c = \frac{\text{Percentage change in quantity demanded of Skippy}}{\text{Percentage change in price of Jif}}$$

In this case, the cross elasticity of demand is a positive 4.5. When the cross elasticity of demand is positive, the percentage change in the quantity demanded of one good (numerator) moves in the same direction as the percentage change in the price of another good (denominator). This is a characteristic of goods that are substitutes. As the price of Jif rises, the demand curve for Skippy shifts rightward, causing the quantity demanded of Skippy to increase at every price.[6] We conclude that if $E_c > 0$, the two goods are substitutes.

$$E_c > 0 \rightarrow \text{Goods are substitutes}$$

If the elasticity coefficient is negative, $E_c < 0$, then the two goods are complements.

$$E_c < 0 \rightarrow \text{Goods are complements}$$

A negative cross elasticity of demand occurs when the percentage change in the quantity demanded of one good (numerator) and the percentage change in the price of another good (denominator) move in opposite directions. For example, suppose the price of cars increases by 5 percent, and the quantity demanded of car tires decreases by 10 percent. Calculating the cross elasticity of demand, we have -10 percent $\div 5$ percent $= -2$. Cars and car tires are complements.

The concept of cross elasticity of demand can be very useful. A company that sells cheese might ask, what goods are substitutes for cheese? The answer would help the company identify its competitors. The company could find out which goods are substitutes for cheese by calculating the cross elasticity of demand between cheese and other goods. A positive cross elasticity of demand would indicate that the two goods were substitutes, and the higher the cross elasticity of demand is, the greater the degree of substitution will be.

Income Elasticity of Demand

Income elasticity of demand measures the responsiveness of quantity demanded to changes in income. It is calculated by dividing the percentage change in quantity demanded of a good by the percentage change in income.

---

6. Recall that if two goods are substitutes, a rise in the price of one good causes the demand for the other good to increase.

economics 24/7

WILL HIGH TAXES ON CIGARETTES REDUCE SMOKING?

In recent years, there have been attempts to raise the taxes on cigarettes. The stated purpose of the increase in taxes is to make smoking more expensive, and the hope is that people will quit smoking, reduce the amount they smoke, or never start smoking.

Will higher taxes on cigarettes cause millions of smokers to stop or cut back on smoking? Will higher taxes prevent teenagers from starting to smoke and reduce the number of teenagers who are smoking? If the demand curve for cigarettes is downward sloping, higher cigarette prices (brought about by higher taxes) will decrease the quantity demanded of cigarettes. The question is, by how much? Thus, price elasticity of demand is needed for the analysis.

To take an extreme case, suppose the demand curve for cigarettes is perfectly inelastic between the current price and the new higher price brought about through higher taxes. In this case, the quantity demanded of cigarettes will not change. If the demand curve is inelastic (but not perfectly inelastic), the percentage decline in the quantity demanded of cigarettes will be less than the percentage increase in the price of cigarettes.

The antitobacco lobby prefers that the demand curve for cigarettes be highly elastic. In this case, the percentage change in the quantity demanded of cigarettes will be greater than the percentage change in price; that is, many more people will stop smoking if cigarette demand is elastic than if it is inelastic.

Another consideration is that the elasticity of demand for cigarettes may be different for adults than it is for teenagers. In fact, some studies show that teenagers are much more sensitive to cigarette price than adults are. In other words, the elasticity of demand for cigarettes is greater for teenagers than for adults. One study found the elasticity of demand for cigarettes to be 0.35 (in the long run), but the study did not separate adult smoking and teenage smoking. Another study looked at only teenage smoking and concluded that for every 10 percent rise in price, quantity demanded would decline by 12 percent. In other words, the teenage demand for cigarettes is elastic.

For those who want to use higher cigarette taxes as a means of curtailing teenage smoking, that is encouraging news.

$$E_y = \frac{\text{Percentage change in quantity demanded}}{\text{Percentage change in income}}$$

where E_y = coefficient of income elasticity of demand, or elasticity coefficient.

Income elasticity of demand is positive, $E_y > 0$, for a *normal good*. Recall that a normal good is one whose demand and thus whose quantity demanded increase, given an increase in income. Thus, for a normal good, the variables in the numerator and denominator in the income elasticity of demand formula move in the same direction.

$$E_y > 0 \rightarrow \text{Normal good}$$

In contrast to a normal good, the demand for an *inferior good* decreases as income increases. Income elasticity of demand for an inferior good is negative, $E_y < 0$.

$$E_y < 0 \rightarrow \text{Inferior good}$$

To calculate the income elasticity of demand for a good, we use the same approach that we used to calculate price elasticity of demand.

$$E_y = \frac{\dfrac{\Delta Q_d}{Q_{d\,\text{Average}}}}{\dfrac{\Delta Y}{Y_{\text{Average}}}}$$

where $Q_{d\,\text{Average}}$ is the average quantity demanded, and Y_{Average} is the average income.

GREENHOUSE GASES AND GAS-EFFICIENT CARS

Here is an often heard argument: (1) Greenhouse gases generated by human activity, such as driving cars, are causing global warming. (2) If the car industry were forced to produce more gas-efficient cars, we would burn less gas. (3) Therefore fewer greenhouses gases would be emitted.

To this argument an economist might respond, "It's not guaranteed to turn out that way." To illustrate, suppose the price of a gallon of gasoline is $3.80, one car gets 16 miles to a gallon, and another car gets 32 miles a gallon. Lyle, who owns the car that gets 16 miles to a gallon, travels an average of 160 miles a week; so he needs to buy 10 gallons of gasoline each week for a total cost of $38. His price for driving each mile is 24 cents (10 gallons × $3.80 = $38 and $38 ÷ 160 miles = 24 cents per mile).

Lyle trades in his car for one that gets 32 miles a gallon. If he continues to travel an average of 160 miles a week, he now needs to buy only 5 gallons of gasoline each week. With less gas purchased, less gas is used (to drive his car), and fewer greenhouse gases are emitted. Things work out just as the argument said they would.

But one thing is being overlooked. The cost of driving a mile is lower for Lyle when he drives the 32-mile-per-gallon car than when he drives the 16-mile-per-gallon car. When he drives the 16-mile-per-gallon car, he pays 24 cents to drive a mile. When he drives the 32-mile-per-gallon car, he pays only 12 cents to drive a mile (5 gallons × $3.80 = $19 and $19 ÷ 160 miles = 12 cents per mile). Lyle must still drive 160 miles to and from work each week, but he doesn't necessarily continue to drive only 160 miles each week when the price of driving a mile drops to 12 cents. If Lyle's demand curve for driving is downward sloping, we can expect him to drive more miles at the lower price per mile.

Suppose Lyle's demand for driving is elastic. In other words, the percentage change in the miles Lyle drives is greater than the percentage change in the price of driving. Let's say that, as the price of driving falls from 24 cents to 12 cents a mile, Lyle increases his driving from 160 miles a week to 370 miles a week. At 24 cents a mile and 160 miles a week, Lyle used to purchase and use 10 gallons of gas. At 12 cents a mile and at 370 miles a week, Lyle purchases and uses 11.56 gallons of gas (370 miles ÷ 32 miles per gallon = 11.56 gallons). Because more greenhouse gases are emitted using 11.56 gallons of gas a week than when using 10 gallons of gas a week, we can see that Lyle's gas-efficient car doesn't really lower greenhouse gas emissions. In fact, if everyone is like Lyle, gas-efficient cars will actually increase greenhouse gases in the atmosphere. (Obviously, things don't have to turn out this way; Lyle's demand for driving could be inelastic.)

Suppose income increases from $500 to $600 per month, and as a result quantity demanded of good X increases from 20 units to 30 units per month. We have

$$E_y = \frac{\frac{10}{25}}{\frac{100}{550}} = 2.2$$

E_y is a positive number; so good X is a normal good. Also, because $E_y > 1$, demand for good X is said to be **income elastic**. In other words, the percentage change in quantity demanded of the good is greater than the percentage change in income. If $E_y < 1$, the demand for the good is said to be **income inelastic**. If $E_y = 1$, then the demand for the good is **income unit elastic**.

Income Elastic
The condition when the percentage change in quantity demanded of a good is greater than the percentage change in income.

Income Inelastic
The condition when the percentage change in quantity demanded of a good is less than the percentage change in income.

Income Unit Elastic
The condition when the percentage change in quantity demanded of a good is equal to the percentage change in income.

Price Elasticity of Supply

Price Elasticity of Supply
A measure of the responsiveness of quantity supplied to changes in price.

Price elasticity of supply measures the responsiveness of quantity supplied to changes in price. It is calculated by dividing the percentage change in quantity supplied of a good by the percentage change in the price of the good.

$$E_s = \frac{\text{Percentage change in quantity supplied}}{\text{Percentage change in price}}$$

where E_s stands for the coefficient of price elasticity of supply, or elasticity coefficient. We use the same approach to calculate price elasticity of supply that we used to calculate price elasticity of demand.

In addition, supply can be classified as elastic, inelastic, unit elastic, perfectly elastic, or perfectly inelastic (Exhibit 8). Elastic supply ($E_s > 1$) refers to a percentage change in quantity supplied that is greater than the percentage change in price.

Percentage change in quantity supplied > Percentage change in price →

$E_s > 1$ → Elastic supply

exhibit 8

Price Elasticity of Supply

(a) The percentage change in quantity supplied is greater than the percentage change in price: $E_s > 1$ and supply is elastic. (b) The percentage change in quantity supplied is less than the percentage change in price: $E_s < 1$ and supply is inelastic. (c) The percentage change in quantity supplied is equal to the percentage change in price: $E_s = 1$ and supply is unit elastic. (d) A small change in price changes quantity supplied by an infinite amount: $E_s = \infty$ and supply is perfectly elastic. (e) A change in price does not change quantity supplied: $E_s = 0$ and supply is perfectly inelastic.

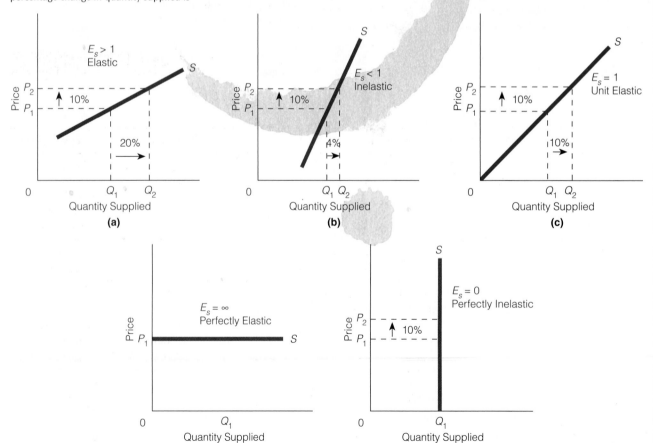

Inelastic supply ($E_s < 1$) refers to a percentage change in quantity supplied that is less than the percentage change in price.

$$\text{Percentage change in quantity supplied} < \text{Percentage change in price} \rightarrow$$
$$E_s < 1 \rightarrow \text{Inelastic supply}$$

Unit elastic supply ($E_s = 1$) refers to a percentage change in quantity supplied that is equal to the percentage change in price.

$$\text{Percentage change in quantity supplied} = \text{Percentage change in price} \rightarrow$$
$$E_s = 1 \rightarrow \text{Unit elastic supply}$$

Perfectly elastic supply ($E_s = \infty$) represents the case where a small change in price changes quantity supplied by an infinitely large amount (and thus the supply curve, or a portion of the overall supply curve, is horizontal). Perfectly inelastic supply ($E_s = 0$) represents the case where a change in price brings no change in quantity supplied (and thus the supply curve, or a portion of the overall supply curve, is vertical).

See Exhibit 9 for a summary of the elasticity concepts.

Price Elasticity of Supply and Time

The longer the period of adjustment is to a change in price, the higher the price elasticity of supply will be. (We are referring to goods whose quantity supplied can increase with time, a characteristic of most goods. It does not, however, cover original Picasso paintings.) The obvious reason for this is that additional production takes time.

exhibit 9

Summary of the Four Elasticity Concepts

Type	Calculation	Possibilities	Terminology
Price elasticity of demand	$\dfrac{\text{Percentage change in quantity demanded}}{\text{Percentage change in price}}$	$E_d > 1$ $E_d < 1$ $E_d = 1$ $E_d = \infty$ $E_d = 0$	Elastic Inelastic Unit elastic Perfectly elastic Perfectly inelastic
Cross elasticity of demand	$\dfrac{\text{Percentage change in quantity demanded of one good}}{\text{Percentage change in price of another good}}$	$E_c < 0$ $E_c > 0$	Complements Substitutes
Income elasticity of demand	$\dfrac{\text{Percentage change in quantity demanded}}{\text{Percentage change in income}}$	$E_y > 0$ $E_y < 0$ $E_y > 1$ $E_y < 1$ $E_y = 1$	Normal good Inferior good Income elastic Income inelastic Income unit elastic
Price elasticity of supply	$\dfrac{\text{Percentage change in quantity supplied}}{\text{Percentage change in price}}$	$E_s > 1$ $E_s < 1$ $E_s = 1$ $E_s = \infty$ $E_s = 0$	Elastic Inelastic Unit elastic Perfectly elastic Perfectly inelastic

For example, suppose that the demand for new housing increases in your city and that the increase occurs all at once on Tuesday, placing upward pressure on the price of housing. The number of houses supplied won't be much different on Saturday than it was on Tuesday. It will take time for suppliers to determine whether the increase in demand is permanent. If they decide it is a temporary state, not much will change. If contractors decide it is permanent, they need time to move resources from the production of other things into the production of new housing. Simply put, the change in quantity supplied of housing is likely to be different in the long run than in the short run, given a change in price. This effect translates into a higher price elasticity of supply in the long run than in the short run.

Thinking like AN ECONOMIST

Think Ratios

In a way, this chapter is about ratios. A ratio describes how one thing changes (the numerator) relative to a change in something else (the denominator). For example, when we discuss price elasticity of demand, we investigate how quantity demanded changes as price changes; when we discuss income elasticity of demand, we explore how quantity demanded changes as income changes. Economists often think in terms of ratios because they are often comparing the change in one variable to the change in another.

THE RELATIONSHIP BETWEEN TAXES AND ELASTICITY

Before discussing how elasticity affects taxes and tax revenues, we explore how supply and demand determine who pays a tax.

exhibit 10

Who Pays the Tax?

A tax placed on the sellers of DVDs shifts the supply curve from S_1 to S_2 and raises the equilibrium price from $15.00 to $15.50. Part of the tax is paid by buyers through a higher price paid ($15.50 instead of $15.00), and part of the tax is paid by sellers through a lower price kept ($14.50 instead of $15.00).

Who Pays the Tax?

Many people think that if government places a tax on the seller of a good, the seller actually pays the tax. However, the *placement* of a tax is not the same as its *payment*, and placement does not guarantee payment.

Suppose the government imposes a tax on sellers of music DVDs. Sellers are taxed $1 for every DVD they sell: Sell a DVD, send $1 to the government. This government action changes equilibrium in the DVD market. To illustrate, in Exhibit 10, before the tax is imposed, the equilibrium price and quantity of DVDs are $15 and Q_1, respectively. The tax per DVD shifts the supply curve leftward from S_1 to S_2. The vertical distance between the two supply curves represents the $1-per-DVD tax.

The vertical distance between the two curves represents the $1-per-DVD tax because what matters to sellers is how much they keep for each DVD sold, not how much buyers pay. For example, if sellers are keeping $15 per DVD for Q_1 DVDs before the tax is imposed, then they want to keep $15 per DVD for Q_1 DVDs after the tax is imposed. But if the tax is $1, the only way they can keep $15 per DVD for Q_1 DVDs is to receive $16 per DVD. They receive $16 per DVD from buyers, turn over $1 to the government, and keep $15. In other words, each quantity on the new supply curve, S_2, corresponds to a $1 higher price than it did on the old supply curve, S_1.

However, the new equilibrium price will not necessarily be $1 higher than the old equilibrium price. The new equilibrium is at a price of $15.50 and quantity of Q_2. Buyers pay $15.50 per DVD (after the tax is imposed), as opposed to $15.00 (before the tax was imposed). The difference between the new price and the old price is the amount of the $1.00 tax that buyers pay per DVD. In this example, buyers pay 50 cents, or one-half of the $1.00 tax per DVD.

> Before the tax, buyers pay $15.00.
>
> After the tax, buyers pay $15.50.

The sellers receive $15.50 per DVD from buyers (after the tax is imposed), as opposed to $15.00 per DVD (before the tax was imposed), but they do not get to keep $15.50 per DVD. One dollar has to be turned over to the government, leaving the sellers with $14.50. Before the tax was imposed, however, sellers received and kept $15.00 per DVD. As noted, it is the price that sellers get to keep that is relevant to them. The difference between $15.00 and $14.50 is the amount of the tax per DVD that sellers pay. In this example, the sellers pay 50 cents, or one-half of the $1.00 tax per DVD.

> Before the tax, sellers receive $15.00 and keep $15.00.
>
> After the tax, sellers receive $15.50 and keep $14.50.

So, although the full tax was *placed* on the sellers, they *paid* only one-half of it, whereas, although none of the tax was placed on buyers, they paid one-half of it too. The lesson is that government can place a tax on whomever it wants, but the laws of supply and demand determine who actually ends up paying it.

 Thinking like AN ECONOMIST

Placement Can Be Different from Payment

According to a layperson, if the government places a tax on A, then A pays the tax. The economist knows that the placement and the payment of a tax are two different things. Government may determine the placement of a tax, but supply and demand determine the payment of a tax.

Elasticity and the Tax

In our tax example, buyers paid half of the $1 tax and sellers paid half, but this result does not occur in every situation. The buyer can pay more than half the tax. In fact, the buyer can pay the full tax if demand for the good is perfectly inelastic, as in Exhibit 11(a). The tax shifts the supply curve from S_1 to S_2, and the equilibrium price rises from $15.00 to $16.00. In other words, if demand is perfectly inelastic and a tax is placed on the sellers of a good, buyers pay the full tax as part of a higher price.

Parts (b)–(d) of Exhibit 11 show other cases. In part (b), demand is perfectly elastic. The tax shifts the supply curve from S_1 to S_2, but there is no change in equilibrium price. Sellers must therefore pay the full tax if demand is perfectly elastic. In part (c), supply is perfectly elastic, and buyers pay the full tax. In part (d), a change in price causes no change in quantity supplied. If sellers try to charge a higher price than $15 for their good

exhibit 11

Different Elasticities and Who Pays the Tax

Four extreme cases are illustrated here. If demand is perfectly inelastic (a) or if supply is perfectly elastic (c), buyers pay the full tax even though the tax may be placed entirely on sellers. If demand is perfectly elastic (b) or if supply is perfectly inelastic (d), the full tax is paid by the sellers.

(and thus try to get buyers to pay some of the tax), a surplus will result, driving the price back down to $15. In this case, sellers pay the full tax. Although it is not shown in the exhibit, sellers would receive $15, turn over $1 to the government, and keep $14 for each unit sold.

Degree of Elasticity and Tax Revenue

Suppose there are two sellers: A and B. Seller A faces a perfectly inelastic demand for her product and is currently selling 10,000 units a month. B faces an elastic demand for his product and is currently selling 10,000 units a month. Government is thinking about placing a $1 tax per unit of product sold on one of the two sellers. If government's objective is to maximize tax revenues, it should tax seller A, because that seller is facing the inelastic demand curve.

To illustrate, in Exhibit 12, the demand curve facing seller A is D_1; the demand curve facing seller B is D_2. S_1 represents the supply curve for both firms. Currently, both firms are at equilibrium at point A, selling 10,000 units.

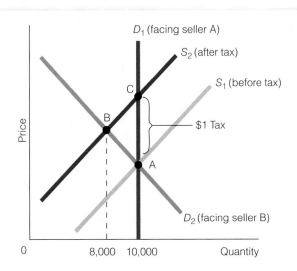

exhibit 12

Maximizing Tax Revenues

Two sellers, A and B, are each currently selling 10,000 units of their good. A faces the demand curve D_1 and B faces D_2. If the objective is to maximize tax revenues with a $1 tax per unit of product sold and only one seller can be taxed, taxing A will maximize tax revenues and taxing B will not. Note that after the tax has been placed, the supply curve shifts from S_1 to S_2. A is in equilibrium at point C, selling 10,000 units, and B is in equilibrium at point B, selling 8,000 units. Because tax revenues equal the tax per unit times the quantity of output sold, taxing A raises $10,000 in tax revenues whereas taxing B raises $8,000.

If government places a $1 tax per unit sold on seller A, the supply curve shifts to S_2, and equilibrium is now at point C. Because demand is perfectly inelastic, A still sells 10,000 units. Tax revenue equals the tax ($1) times 10,000 units, or $10,000.

If government places the $1 tax per unit sold on seller B, tax revenue will be only $8,000. When the tax shifts the supply curve to S_2, equilibrium moves to point B, where only 8,000 units are sold.

The lesson: Given the $1 tax per unit sold, tax revenues are maximized by placing the tax on the seller who faces the more inelastic (less elastic) demand curve.

SELF-TEST

1. What does an income elasticity of demand of 1.33 mean?

2. What does perfectly inelastic supply signify?

3. Why will government raise more tax revenue if it applies a tax to a good with inelastic demand than if it applies the tax to a good with elastic demand?

4. Under what condition would a per-unit tax placed on the sellers of computers be fully paid by the buyers of computers?

"WHAT IS THE RELATIONSHIP BETWEEN DIFFERENT PRICE ELASTICITIES OF DEMAND AND TOTAL REVENUE?"

Student:

I'm still not sure I understand the relationship between price elasticity of demand and total revenue.

Instructor:

Let's use some numbers to illustrate the relationship. Here we have identified two points on a demand curve:

Price	Quantity Demanded
$10	110
$12	100

The price elasticity of demand between these two points is 0.52, which means that demand is inelastic. Now let's find the total revenue at each price. If we assume we are in equilibrium (at which quantity demanded is equal to quantity supplied), then total revenue at $10 is $1,100. (We get this amount by multiplying $10 times 110.) When price is $12, total revenue is $1,200. We conlude that if price elasticity of demand is less than 1 (demand is inelastic), a price rise will raise total revenue. Therefore, if we lower price (from $12 to $10), total revenue will decline.

Now let's change one of the numbers in the table. We change 100 to 80. We now have this:

Price	Quantity Demanded
$10	110
$12	80

If we compute the new price elasticity of demand, we get 1.73, meaning that demand is elastic. Now let's compute total revenue at each price. At $10, total revenue is $1,100. At the higher price of $12, total revenue is $960. We conclude that if price elasticity is greater than 1 (demand is elastic) and if price rises, total revenue falls. And, of course, if price falls (from $12 to $10), total revenue will rise.

Student:

So in the first example, when demand was inelastic, we raised price, and total revenue increased. But in the second example, when demand was elastic and we raised price, total revenue decreased.

Instructor:

Yes, that is correct. When demand is inelastic, the directional change in price brings about the same directional change in total revenue: When price rises, total revenue rises; when price falls, total revenue falls. But in the case where demand is elastic, the directional change in price brings about an opposite directional change in total revenue: When price rises, total revenue falls; when price falls, total revenue rises.

Points to Remember

1. When demand is inelastic, price and total revenue move in the same direction.
2. When demand is elastic, price and total revenue move in opposite directions.

a reader asks | Is the Type of Thinking Inherent in Elasticity Useful?

The elasticity concepts in this chapter are interesting, and I'm sure they're useful to business firms. But I don't really see how thinking about elasticities helps me in any fundamental way. Any comments?

Elasticity (price, income, supply, cross) relates to a change in one thing relative to a change in something else. Thinking in terms of these types of relationships can help you gain insight into certain phenomena. For example, if a company is forced to pay its employees higher hourly wage rates ($20 instead of $18), will the higher wage rate result in the company's paying a larger total amount in wages (say, $500,000 a month instead of $400,000)? The answer most people will give is yes. They reason this way: Multiplying a given number of hours worked by $20 results in a greater total dollar amount than multiplying the number of hours by $18.

However, thinking elastically, we know that changing one thing can lead to a change in something else. Specifically, we know that an increase in wage rates can affect the number of hours worked. Companies may not hire as many employees or may not have their employees work as many hours if the hourly wage is $20 than if it is $18. In short, hours worked are likely to fall as wage rates rise. Whether the total amount the firm pays in wages rises, falls, or remains constant depends on the percentage rise in wage rates relative to the percentage fall in hours worked. For example, if the percentage increase in wage rates is less than the percentage decline in hours worked, the total amount paid in wages will decline.

We could not have easily come up with this conclusion had we not looked at the percentage change in one thing relative to the percentage change in something else. This type of thinking, of course, is inherent in the elasticity concepts discussed in this chapter.

Chapter Summary

PRICE ELASTICITY OF DEMAND

- Price elasticity of demand is a measure of the responsiveness of quantity demanded to changes in price.
- If the percentage change in quantity demanded is greater than the percentage change in price, demand is elastic.
- If the percentage change in quantity demanded is less than the percentage change in price, demand is inelastic.
- If the percentage change in quantity demanded is equal to the percentage change in price, demand is unit elastic.
- If a small change in price causes an infinitely large change in quantity demanded, demand is perfectly elastic.
- If a change in price causes no change in quantity demanded, demand is perfectly inelastic.
- The coefficient of price elasticity of demand (E_d) is negative, signifying the inverse relationship between price and quantity demanded. For convenience, however, the absolute value of the elasticity coefficient is used.

TOTAL REVENUE AND PRICE ELASTICITY OF DEMAND

- Total revenue equals price times quantity sold. Total expenditure equals price times quantity purchased. Total revenue equals total expenditure.
- If demand is elastic, price and total revenue are inversely related: As price rises (falls), total revenue falls (rises).

- If demand is inelastic, price and total revenue are directly related: As price rises (falls), total revenue rises (falls).
- If demand is unit elastic, total revenue is independent of price: As price rises (falls), total revenue remains constant.

DETERMINANTS OF PRICE ELASTICITY OF DEMAND

- The more substitutes for a good, the higher the price elasticity of demand; the fewer substitutes for a good, the lower the price elasticity of demand.
- The more that a good is considered a luxury instead of a necessity, the higher the price elasticity of demand is.
- The greater the percentage of one's budget that goes to purchase a good, the higher the price elasticity of demand will be; the smaller the percentage of one's budget that goes to purchase a good, the lower the price elasticity of demand.
- The more time that passes (since a price change), the higher the price elasticity of demand will be; the less time that passes, the lower the price elasticity of demand.

CROSS ELASTICITY OF DEMAND

- Cross elasticity of demand measures the responsiveness in the quantity demanded of one good to changes in the price of another good.

- If $E_c > 0$, two goods are substitutes. If $E_c < 0$, two goods are complements.

INCOME ELASTICITY OF DEMAND

- Income elasticity of demand measures the responsiveness of quantity demanded to changes in income.
- If $E_y > 0$, the good is a normal good. If $E_y < 0$, the good is an inferior good.
- If $E_y > 1$, demand is income elastic. If $E_y < 1$, demand is income inelastic. If $E_y = 1$, demand is income unit elastic.

PRICE ELASTICITY OF SUPPLY

- Price elasticity of supply measures the responsiveness of quantity supplied to changes in price.
- If the percentage change in quantity supplied is greater than the percentage change in price, supply is elastic.
- If the percentage change in quantity supplied is less than the percentage change in price, supply is inelastic.
- If the percentage change in quantity supplied is equal to the percentage change in price, supply is unit elastic.
- Price elasticity of supply is higher in the long run than in the short run.

TAXES AND ELASTICITY

- There is a difference between the placement and the payment of a tax. For example, a tax may be placed on the seller of a good, and both the seller and buyer end up paying the tax.
- In this chapter, we discuss a per-unit tax that was placed on the seller of a specific good (DVDs). This tax shifted the supply curve of DVDs leftward. The vertical distance between the old supply curve (before the tax) and the new supply curve (after the tax) was equal to the per-unit tax.
- If a per-unit tax is placed on the seller of a good, both the buyer and the seller will pay part of the tax if the demand curve is downward sloping and the supply curve is upward sloping.
- The more inelastic the demand is, the larger the percentage of the tax is that the buyer will pay.
- The more elastic the demand, the smaller the percentage of the tax is that the buyer will pay.
- When demand is perfectly inelastic or supply is perfectly elastic, buyers pay the full tax.
- When demand is perfectly elastic or supply is perfectly inelastic, sellers pay the full tax.

Key Terms and Concepts

Price Elasticity of Demand	Perfectly Elastic Demand	Income Elasticity of Demand	Income Unit Elastic
Elastic Demand	Perfectly Inelastic Demand		Price Elasticity of Supply
Inelastic Demand	Total Revenue (*TR*)	Income Elastic	
Unit Elastic Demand	Cross Elasticity of Demand	Income Inelastic	

Questions and Problems

1 Explain how a seller can determine whether the demand for his or her good is inelastic, elastic, or unit elastic between two prices.

2 For each of the following, identify where demand is elastic, inelastic, perfectly elastic, perfectly inelastic, or unit elastic:
   a. Price rises by 10 percent, and quantity demanded falls by 2 percent.
   b. Price falls by 5 percent, and quantity demanded rises by 4 percent.
   c. Price falls by 6 percent, and quantity demanded does not change.
   d. Price rises by 2 percent, and quantity demanded falls by 1 percent.

3 Prove that price elasticity of demand is not the same as the slope of a demand curve.

4 Suppose the current price of gasoline at the pump is $3 per gallon and that 1 million gallons are sold per month. A politician proposes to add a 10-cent tax to the price of a gallon of gasoline. She says the tax will generate $100,000

tax revenues per month (1 million gallons × $0.10 = $100,000). What assumption is she making?

5 Identify whether total revenue rises, falls, or remains constant for each of the following:
   a. Demand is inelastic, and price falls.
   b. Demand is elastic, and price rises.
   c. Demand is unit elastic, and price rises.
   d. Demand is inelastic, and price rises.
   e. Demand is elastic, and price falls.

6 Suppose a straight-line downward-sloping demand curve shifts rightward. Is the price elasticity of demand higher, lower, or the same between any two prices on the new (higher) demand curve than on the old (lower) demand curve?

7 Suppose Austin, Texas, is hit by a tornado that destroys 25 percent of the housing in the area. Would you expect the total expenditure on housing after the tornado to be greater than, less than, or equal to what it was before the tornado? Explain your answer.

8 In each of the following pairs of goods, which has the higher price elasticity of demand?

   a. Airline travel in the short run or airline travel in the long run.

   b. Television sets or Sony television sets.

   c. Cars or Toyotas.

   d. Telephones or AT&T telephones.

   e. Popcorn or Orville Redenbacher's popcorn.

9 How might you determine whether toothpaste and mouthwash manufacturers are competitors?

10 Assume the demand for product A is perfectly inelastic. Further, assume that the buyers of A get the funds to pay for it by stealing.

   a. If the supply of A decreases, what happens to its price?

   b. What happens to the amount of crime committed by the buyers of A?

11 Suppose you learned that the price elasticity of demand for wheat is 0.7 between the current price for wheat and a price $2 higher per bushel. Do you think farmers collectively would try to reduce the supply of wheat and drive the price up $2 higher per bushel? Why? Assuming that they would try to reduce supply, what problems might they have in actually doing so?

12 In 1947, the U.S. Department of Justice brought a suit against the DuPont Company (which at the time sold 75 percent of all the cellophane in the United States) for monopolizing the production and sale of cellophane. In court, the DuPont Company tried to show that cellophane was only one of several goods in the market in which it was sold. It argued that its market was not the cellophane market but the flexible packaging materials market, which included (besides cellophane) waxed paper, aluminum foil, and other such products. DuPont pointed out that it had only 20 percent of all sales in this more broadly defined market. Using this information, discuss how the concept of cross elasticity of demand would help establish whether DuPont should have been viewed as a firm in the cellophane market or as a firm in the flexible packaging materials market.

13 It has been said that, if government wishes to tax certain goods, it should tax goods that have inelastic rather than elastic demand. What is the rationale for this statement?

14 A tax is placed on the sellers of a good. What happens to the percentage of this tax that buyers pay as the price elasticity of demand for the good decreases? Explain your answer.

Working with Numbers and Graphs

1 A college raises its annual tuition from $2,000 to $2,500, and its student enrollment falls from 4,877 to 4,705. Compute the price elasticity of demand. Is demand elastic or inelastic?

2 As the price of good X rises from $10 to $12, the quantity demanded of good Y rises from 100 units to 114 units. Are X and Y substitutes or complements? What is the cross elasticity of demand?

3 The quantity demanded of good X rises from 130 to 145 units as income rises from $2,000 to $2,500 a month. What is the income elasticity of demand?

4 The quantity supplied of a good rises from 120 to 140 as price rises from $4 to $5.50. What is the price elasticity of supply?

5 In the following figure, what is the price elasticity of demand between the two prices on D_1? on D_2?

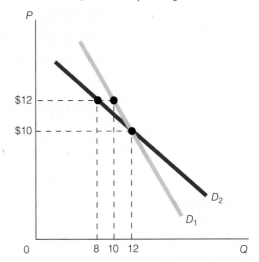

CHAPTER 6

CONSUMER CHOICE: MAXIMIZING UTILITY AND BEHAVIORAL ECONOMICS

Introduction Just before purchasing a computer, a book, or an iPod, what do you think about? Do you say, "Do I want this or not?" Many people would give this answer. Economists have taken this response, put it under a microscope, and concluded that it is as if you say to yourself, "The marginal utility of this item divided by its price is greater than the marginal utility of other items divided by their prices; so I am going to make this purchase because it will increase my overall utility." You may not believe now that you or anyone else would think this way, but you may believe it after reading this chapter.

UTILITY THEORY

Water is cheap, and diamonds are expensive. But water is necessary to life and diamonds are not. Isn't it odd—even paradoxical—that what is necessary to life is cheap and what is not necessary is expensive? Eighteenth-century economist Adam Smith wondered about this question. He observed that often things that have the greatest value in use (or that are the most useful) have a relatively low price, and things that have little or no value in use have a high price. Smith's observation came to be known as the **diamond-water paradox**, or the paradox of value. The paradox challenged economists, and they sought a solution to it. This section begins to develop parts of the solution they found.

Utility: Total and Marginal

Saying that a good gives you **utility** is the same as saying that it has the power to satisfy your wants or that it gives you satisfaction. For example, suppose you buy your first unit of good X, and you get a certain amount of utility, say, 10 **utils** from it. (Utils are an artificial construct used to measure utility; we realize you have never seen a util—no one has.) You buy a second unit of good X, and, once again, you get a certain amount of utility from this second unit, say, 8 utils. You purchase a third unit and receive 7 utils. The sum

Diamond-Water Paradox
The observation that things with the greatest value in use sometimes have little value in exchange and things with little value in use sometimes have the greatest value in exchange.

Utility
A measure of the satisfaction, happiness, or benefit that results from the consumption of a good.

Util
An artificial construct used to measure utility.

of the amount of utility you obtain from each of the 3 units is the total utility you receive from purchasing good X: 25 utils. **Total utility** is the total satisfaction one receives from consuming a particular quantity of a good (in this example, 3 units of good X).

Total utility is different from marginal utility. **Marginal utility** is the *additional* utility gained from consuming an additional unit of good X. Marginal utility is the change in total utility divided by the change in the quantity consumed of a good:

$$MU = \frac{\Delta TU}{\Delta Q}$$

where the change in the quantity consumed of a good is usually equal to 1 unit.

To illustrate, suppose you receive 10 utils of total utility from consuming 1 apple and 19 utils of total utility from consuming 2 apples. The marginal utility of the second apple (the additional utility of consuming an additional apple) is 9 utils. As a person consumes more apples, total utility rises, but marginal utility (additional utility received from the additional apple) falls. In other words, total utility rises as marginal utility falls.

Thinking like AN ECONOMIST

Total Utility and Marginal Utility Can Move in Opposite Directions

The economist knows that marginal utility and total utility can move in opposite directions. Stated differently, a rise in total utility doesn't mean that marginal utility is rising too. To illustrate, look at the table:

(1) Number of Apples Consumed	(2) Total Utility (utils)	(3) Marginal Utility (utils)
1	10	10
2	19	9
3	27	8

As we move from one to two to three apples, total utility rises, but marginal utility falls.

Law of Diminishing Marginal Utility

Do you think the marginal utility of the second unit is greater than, less than, or equal to the marginal utility of the first unit? Consider the difference in marginal utility between the third unit and the second unit or between the fifth unit and the fourth unit (had we extended the number of units consumed). In general, the question is whether the marginal utility of the following unit is greater than, less than, or equal to that of the preceding unit.

Economists have generally answered "less than." The **law of diminishing marginal utility** states that for a given time period, the marginal utility gained by consuming equal successive units of a good declines as the amount consumed increases. In other words, the number of utils gained by consuming the first unit of a good is greater than the number of utils gained by consuming the second unit (which is greater than the number gained by the third, which is greater than the number gained by the fourth, and so on).

The law of diminishing marginal utility is illustrated in Exhibit 1. The table in part (a) shows both the total utility of consuming a certain number of units of a good and the marginal utility of consuming additional units. The graph in part (b) shows the total utility curve for the data in part (a), and the graph in part (c) shows the marginal utility curve for the data in part (a). Notice how the graphs in (b) and (c) show that total utility can

Total Utility
The total satisfaction a person receives from consuming a particular quantity of a good.

Marginal Utility
The additional utility a person receives from consuming an additional unit of a good.

Law of Diminishing Marginal Utility
The marginal utility gained by consuming equal successive units of a good will decline as the amount consumed increases.

exhibit 1

Total Utility, Marginal Utility, and the Law of Diminishing Marginal Utility

TU = total utility and *MU* = marginal utility. (a) Both total utility and marginal utility are expressed in utils. Marginal utility is the change in total utility divided by the change in the quantity consumed of the good, $MU = \Delta TU/\Delta Q$. (b) Total utility curve. (c) Marginal utility curve. Together, (b) and (c) demonstrate that total utility can increase (b) as marginal utility decreases (c).

(1) Units of Good X	(2) Total Utility (utils)	(3) Marginal Utility (utils)
0	0	—
1	10	10
2	19	9
3	27	8
4	34	7
5	40	6

(a)

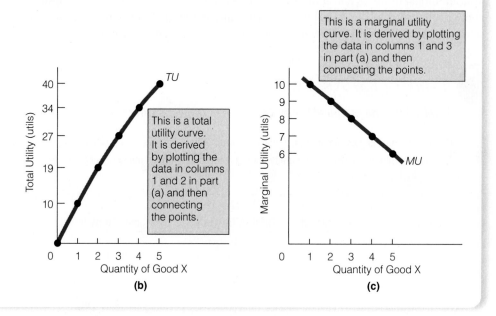

increase as marginal utility decreases. This relationship between total utility and marginal utility is important in unraveling the diamond-water paradox.

The law of diminishing marginal utility is based on the idea that if a good has a variety of uses but only 1 unit of the good is available, then the consumer will use the first unit to satisfy his or her most urgent want. If 2 units are available, the consumer will use the second unit to satisfy a less urgent want. Suppose that good X can be used to satisfy wants A through E, with A being the most urgent want and E being the least. Also, B is more urgent than C, C is more urgent than D, and D is more urgent than E. We can chart the wants as follows:

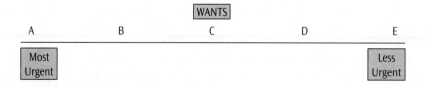

Suppose the first unit of good X can satisfy any one—but only one—of wants A through E. Which want does an individual choose to satisfy? The answer is the most urgent want: A. The individual chooses to satisfy A instead of B, C, D, or E because people ordinarily

WHO WOULD SPEND $16,000 FOR A PEANUT BUTTER AND JELLY SANDWICH?

How much is a peanut butter and jelly sandwich worth to you? Would you pay at least a dollar for one? What about two dollars? Would you pay $16,000? That is the amount Elvis Presley once paid for a peanut butter and jelly sandwich. He was in his hometown of Memphis one night when he got a craving for a particular peanut butter and jelly sandwich that he once had in Denver. So he and his buddies jumped on Elvis's private jet and flew to Denver to get one of those sandwiches.

© DANNY E HOOKS/SHUTTERSTOCK

What can we say about such behavior? A number of things come to mind. The first thing is that Elvis must have valued the peanut butter and jelly sandwich (in Denver) more than he valued the $16,000. In other words, the sandwich brought him greater utility than the money. Second, it is no doubt true for Elvis that money was subject to the diminishing law of diminishing marginal utility. Third—and not so obviously—Elvis didn't actually spend $16,000 for a peanut butter

sandwich or even for several peanut butter sandwiches (for him and his friends). Perhaps the peanut butter and jelly sandwich was only part of what Elvis was buying the night he flew from Memphis to Denver. Perhaps he was buying a good time with his buddies, or perhaps he was buying an event for his buddies that they would never forget. ("I was with Elvis this one time, and believe it or not, he flew all the way from Memphis to Denver for a peanut butter and jelly sandwich.") Fourth, because there is no record of Elvis ever flying halfway across the country a second, third, or fourth time for a peanut butter and jelly sandwich, we can assume that either (a) Elvis never again had a yearning for a peanut butter and jelly sandwich made in Denver or (b) if he did again have such a yearning, it wasn't worth as much. If the second possibility (b) is the case, then we can be fairly sure that the law of diminishing marginal utility holds for flying from Memphis to Denver for a peanut butter and jelly sandwich.

satisfy their most urgent want before all others. If you were dying of thirst in a desert (having gone without water for three days) and came across a quart of water, would you drink it or use it to wash your hands? You would drink it, of course, and satisfy your most urgent want first. Washing your hands in the water would give you less utility than drinking it.

 Finding ECONOMICS

When You're Studying

You sit down to study for your upcoming Biology test. One hour passes, then two, and finally three. You have a sense that your first hour of studying was the most productive, by which you mean that you learned the most in the first hour, less in the second, and even less in the third. Where is the economics here? Perhaps you are witnessing the law of diminishing marginal utility as applied to studying. You get greater utility (benefits, satisfaction) from studying the first hour, slightly less in the second, and even less in the third.

THE MILLIONAIRE AND THE PAUPER: WHAT THE LAW SAYS AND DOESN'T SAY Who gets more utility from one more dollar, a poor man or a millionaire? Most people would say that a poor man gets more utility from one more dollar because the poor man has so many fewer dollars than the millionaire. What's an extra dollar to a millionaire? Nothing. A millionaire has so many dollars, one more doesn't mean a thing.

Some people think the law of diminishing marginal utility substantiates the claim that a millionaire gets less utility from one more dollar than a poor man does. Unfortunately, though, this interpretation is a misreading of the law. The law says that for the millionaire or the poor man, an additional dollar is worth less than the dollar that preceded it. Let's say the millionaire has $2 million and the poor man has $1,000. We now give each of them one more dollar. The law of diminishing marginal utility says that (1) the additional dollar is worth less to the millionaire than her two-millionth dollar and (2) the additional dollar is worth less to the poor man than his one-thousandth dollar. That is all the law says. We do not and cannot know whether the additional dollar is worth more or less to the millionaire than it is to the poor man. In summary, the law says something about the millionaire and about the poor man (both persons value the last dollar less than the next-to-last dollar), but it does not say anything about the millionaire's utility compared to the poor man's utility.

To compare the utility the millionaire gets from the additional dollar with the utility the poor man gets from it is to fall into the trap of making an **interpersonal utility comparison**. The utility that one person gets cannot be scientifically or objectively compared with the utility that another person gets from the same thing because utility is subjective. Who knows for certain how much satisfaction (utility) the millionaire gets from the additional dollar, compared with that of the poor man? The poor man may care little for money; he may shun it, consider the love of it the root of all evil, and prefer to consume the things in life that do not require money. On the other hand, the millionaire may be interested only in amassing more money. We must not guess at the utility that someone obtains from consuming a certain item, compare it to our guess of the utility that another person obtains from consuming the same item, and then call our guesses scientific facts.

Interpersonal Utility Comparison

Comparing the utility one person receives from a good, service, or activity with the utility another person receives from the same good, service, or activity.

Thinking like AN ECONOMIST

Seeming Reasonable Is Not Enough

The economist knows that what looks true or seems true may not be true. Although assuming that the millionaire receives less utility from an additional dollar than a pauper may seem perfectly reasonable, the assumption does not make it so. At one time, believing that the world was flat seemed perfectly reasonable, but we know that the world is not flat.

The Solution to the Diamond-Water Paradox

Goods have both total utility and marginal utility. Water, for example, is extremely useful; we can't live without it. We would expect its total utility (its total usefulness) to be high, but its marginal utility to be low because water is relatively plentiful. As the law of diminishing marginal utility states, the utility of successive units of a good diminishes as its consumption increases. In short, water is immensely useful, but there is so much of it that individuals place relatively little value on another unit of it.

In contrast, diamonds are not as useful as water. We would expect the total utility of diamonds to be lower than that of water, but their marginal utility to be high. Because there are relatively few diamonds in the world, the consumption of diamonds (in contrast to water consumption) takes place at relatively high marginal utility. Diamonds, which are rare, are used only for their few valuable uses. Water, which is plentiful, gets used for its many valuable uses and for its not so valuable uses (e.g., spraying the car with the hose for two more minutes even though you are 99 percent sure that the soap is fully rinsed off).

So the total utility of water is high because water is extremely useful. The total utility of diamonds is comparatively low because diamonds are not as useful as water. The marginal utility of water is low because water is so plentiful that people consume it at low marginal utility. The marginal utility of diamonds is high because diamonds are so scarce that people consume them at high marginal utility.

Prices therefore reflect marginal utility, not total utility.

SELF-TEST

(Answers to Self-Test questions are in the Self-Test Appendix.)

1. State and solve the diamond-water paradox.

2. What does falling total utility imply for marginal utility? Give an arithmetical example to illustrate your answer.

3. When would a good's total utility and marginal utility be the same?

CONSUMER EQUILIBRIUM AND DEMAND

This section identifies the condition necessary for consumer equilibrium and then discusses the relationship between equilibrium and the law of demand. The analysis is based on the assumption that individuals seek to maximize utility.

Equating Marginal Utilities per Dollar

Suppose there are only two goods in the world: apples and oranges. At present, a consumer is spending his entire income consuming 10 apples and 10 oranges a week. We assume that for a particular week, the marginal utility (MU) and price (P) of each are as follows:[1]

$$MU_{oranges} = 30 \text{ utils}$$
$$MU_{apples} = 20 \text{ utils}$$
$$P_{oranges} = \$1$$
$$P_{apples} = \$1$$

So the consumer's marginal (last) dollar spent on apples returns 20 utils per dollar, and his marginal (last) dollar spent on oranges returns 30 utils per dollar. The ratio MU_O/P_O (O = oranges) is greater than the ratio MU_A/P_A (A = apples):

$$\frac{MU_O}{P_O} > \frac{MU_A}{P_A}$$

If the consumer found himself in this situation one week, he would redirect his purchases of apples and oranges the next week. He would think: "If I buy an orange, I receive more utility [30 utils] than if I buy an apple [20 utils]. It's better to buy 1 more orange with $1 and 1 less apple. I gain 30 utils from buying the orange, which is 10 utils more than if I buy the apple."

As the consumer buys 1 more orange and 1 less apple, however, the marginal utility of oranges falls (recall what the law of diminishing marginal utility says about consuming additional units of a good), and the marginal utility of apples rises (the consumer is

---

1. You may wonder where we get these marginal utility figures. They are points on hypothetical marginal utility curves, such as the one in Exhibit 1. The important point is that one number is greater than the other. We could easily have picked other numbers, such as 300 and 200.

consuming fewer apples). Because the consumer has bought 1 more orange and 1 less apple, he now has 11 oranges and 9 apples. At this new combination of goods,

$$MU_O = 25 \text{ utils}$$
$$MU_A = 25 \text{ utils}$$
$$P_O = \$1$$
$$P_A = \$1$$

Now, the ratio MU_O/P_O equals the ratio MU_A/P_A. The consumer is getting exactly the same amount of utility (25 utils) per dollar from each of the 2 goods. There is no way for the consumer to redirect his purchases (buy more of 1 good and less of another good) and have more utility. Thus the consumer is in equilibrium. In short, a consumer is in equilibrium when he or she derives the same marginal utility per dollar for all goods. The condition for **consumer equilibrium** is

$$\frac{MU_A}{P_A} = \frac{MU_B}{P_B} = \frac{MU_C}{P_C} = \cdots = \frac{MU_Z}{P_Z}$$

where the letters *A–Z* represent all the goods a person buys.[2]

A person in consumer equilibrium has *maximized his total utility*. By spending his dollars on goods that give him the greatest marginal utility and in the process bringing about the consumer equilibrium condition, he is adding as much to his total utility as he can possibly add.

Consumer Equilibrium
Equilibrium that occurs when the consumer has spent all income and the marginal utilities per dollar spent on each good purchased are equal: $MU_A/P_A = MU_B/P_B = \cdots = MU_Z/P_Z$, where the letters A–Z represent all the goods a person buys.

 Finding ECONOMICS

In Everyday Choices

You are standing in a store trying to decide whether you will buy another pair of shoes or one more sweater. What is the economics here? You might be seeking consumer equilibrium. Consumer equilibrium exists when the marginal utility-price ratios for all goods is the same, in this case, when the *MU/P* ratio for shoes is the same as the *MU/P* ratio for the sweater. When you are standing there trying to decide which to buy more of and which not to buy more of, you are deciding on how best you can spend that next dollar. If you feel that you will get more utility (or satisfaction) per dollar by buying one more pair of shoes instead of one more sweater, then you will buy one more pair of shoes. If you feel that you will get more utility per dollar buy buying one more sweater instead of one more pair of shoes, then you will buy one more sweater. Maybe, upon first reading about consumer equilibrium, you thought, "I never try to achieve consumer equilibrium." But that is exactly what you do if you have purchased one more unit of one good instead of one more unit of another good because you thought it was "worth it."

Maximizing Utility and the Law of Demand

Suppose a consumer is currently in equilibrium; that is,

$$\frac{MU_O}{P_O} = \frac{MU_A}{P_A}$$

When in equilibrium, the consumer is maximizing utility.

Now suppose the price of oranges falls. The situation now becomes this:

$$\frac{MU_O}{P_O} > \frac{MU_A}{P_A}$$

---

2. We are assuming that the consumer exhausts his or her income and that saving is treated as a good.

economics 24/7

HOW YOU PAY FOR GOOD WEATHER

Suppose two cities are alike in every way except one: the weather. One is called Good-Weather City (*GWC*) and the other Bad-Weather City (*BWC*). In *GWC*, temperatures are moderate all year (75 degrees) and the sky is always blue. In *BWC*, the winter brings snow and freezing rain, and the summer brings high humidity and high temperatures. *BWC* has all the forms of weather that people dislike. We assume that people get more utility from living in good weather than from living in bad weather and that the median price (*P*) of a home in the two cities is the same: $200,000. In terms of marginal utility and housing prices,

© BRAND X PICTURES/JUPITER IMAGES

$$\frac{MU_{GWC}}{P_{H,GWC}} > \frac{MU_{BWC}}{P_{H,BWC}}.$$

That is, the marginal utility of living in *GWC* (MU_{GWC}) divided by the price of a house in *GWC* ($P_{H,GWC}$) is greater than the marginal utility of living in *BWC* (MU_{BWC}) divided by the price of a house in *BWC* ($P_{H,BWC}$). In other words, there is greater utility per dollar in *GWC* than in *BWC*.

What will people do? At least some people will move from *BWC* to *GWC*. The people in *BWC* who want to move will put their houses up for sale. This will increase the supply of houses for sale and lower the price. As these people move to *GWC*, they increase the demand for houses, and house prices in *GWC* will begin to rise.

This process will continue until the price of a house in *GWC* has risen high enough, and the price of a house in *BWC* has fallen low enough, so that the *MU/P* ratios in the two cities are the same. In other words, the process continues until this condition is reached:

$$\frac{MU_{GWC}}{P_{H,GWC}} = \frac{MU_{BWC}}{P_{H,BWC}}.$$

Once this has occurred, a consumer receives the same utility per dollar in the two cities. In other words, the two cities are the same.

Now let's consider a young couple who have to choose between living in the two cities. Will the young couple necessarily choose *GWC* instead of *BWC* because *GWC* has a better climate? Not at all. *GWC* has a better climate than *BWC*, but *BWC* has lower housing prices. One partner says, "Let's live in *GWC*. Think of all that great weather we'll enjoy. We can go outside every day." The other partner says, "But if we live in *BWC*, we can have either a much bigger and better house for the money or more money to spend on things other than housing. Think of the better cars and clothes we'll be able to buy or the vacations we'll be able to take because we won't have to spend as much money to buy a house."

What has happened is that the initial greater satisfaction of living in *GWC* (the higher utility per dollar) has been eroded by people moving to *GWC*, thereby raising housing prices. *GWC* doesn't look as good as it once did.

On the other hand, *BWC* doesn't look as (relatively) bad as it once did. It still doesn't have the good climate that *GWC* has, but it has lower housing prices now. The utility per dollar of living in *BWC* has risen as a consequence of lowered housing prices.

As long as one city is better (in some way) than another, people will move to the relatively better city. In the process, they will change things just enough so that it is no longer relatively better. In the end, you have to pay for paradise.

The consumer will attempt to restore equilibrium by buying more oranges. This behavior—buying more oranges when the price of oranges falls—is consistent with the law of demand.

We conclude that the consumer's attempt to reach equilibrium—which is simply another way of saying that the consumer is seeking to maximize utility—is consistent with the law of demand. In short, utility maximization is consistent with the law of demand.

Common MISCONCEPTIONS

About Maximizing Utility

Alayperson says, "Economists say that individuals maximize utility, but I think they are wrong. I don't feel that I maximize utility." In way of retort, ask the person if his buying behavior is consistent with the law of demand. If he says yes, then it follows that he maximizes utility because utility maximization is consistent with the law of demand.

Or look at it this way: A person buys more clothes when they are lower in price. The same person argues that she doesn't maximize utility. The proof that she does is that her buying behavior is consistent with the law of demand, and the law of demand is consistent with utility maximization. Thus she maximizes utility.

Should the Government Provide the Necessities of Life for Free?

Some people argue that, because food and water are necessities of life and no one can live without them, it is wrong to charge for them. The government should provide them free to everyone. Similarly, others argue that medical care is a necessity for those who are sick. Without it, people will either die or experience an extremely low quality of life (you can't experience a high quality of life when you're sick). Making people pay for medical care is wrong. The government should provide it free to those who need it. Each statement labels something as a necessity of life (food and water, medical care) and then makes the policy proposal that government should provide the necessity for free.

Suppose government did give food, water, and medical care to everyone for free—at zero price (although not at zero taxes). At zero price, people would want to consume these goods up to the point of zero marginal utility for each good. They would do so because, if the marginal utility of the good (expressed in dollars) is greater than its price, people could derive more utility from purchasing the good than they would lose in parting with the dollar price of the good. That is, if the price of a good is $5, an individual will continue consuming the good as long as the marginal utility she derives from it is greater than $5. If the price is $0, she will continue to consume the good as long as the marginal utility she derives from it is greater than $0.

Resources must be used to produce every unit of a good consumed. If the government uses scarce resources to provide goods that have low marginal utility (which food, water, and medical care would have at zero price), then fewer resources are available to produce other goods. However, if some resources are withdrawn from producing these low-utility goods, total utility would fall very little. The resources could then be redirected to producing goods with a higher marginal utility, thereby raising total utility.

The people who argue that certain goods should be provided free implicitly assume that the not so valuable uses of food, water, and medical care are valuable enough to warrant a system of taxes to pay for the complete provision of these goods at zero price. It is questionable, however, whether the least valuable uses of food, water, and medical care are worth the sacrifices of other goods that would necessarily be forfeited if more of these goods were produced.

Think about the question this way: Currently, water is relatively cheap, and people use it to satisfy its valuable uses and its not so valuable uses. But suppose water was cheaper than it is; suppose it had a zero price. Would it be used to satisfy its more valuable uses, its not so valuable uses, and its absolutely least valuable use? If food had a zero price, would it be used to satisfy its more valuable uses, its not so valuable uses, and its absolutely least valuable use (food fights perhaps)?

Thinking like AN ECONOMIST

Yes, There Can Be Too Much of a Good Thing

As odd as it may sound to say so, there is such a thing as too much health care. The right amount of health care is the amount at which the marginal benefit or marginal utility (of an additional unit of health care) equals the marginal cost. Let's say that the marginal cost of health care is $40 but that, under the free-health-care-for-everyone system, no one directly pays even one cent for personal health care. All health care bills are paid by the federal government with tax monies. In such a case, an individual is likely to continue consuming health care until his marginal utility equals zero. In other words, he will consume, say, the one-hundredth unit of health care even though the one-hundredth unit comes with only $0.0000001 worth of benefits to him and a cost of $40 to society at large. Is this too much health care if individuals are getting not even a penny's worth of benefits from care that cost $40 to provide? The economist's answer is yes.

SELF-TEST

1. Alesandro purchases two goods, X and Y, and the utility gained for the last unit purchased of each is 16 utils and 23 utils, respectively. The prices of X and Y are $1 and $1.75, respectively. Is Alesandro in consumer equilibrium? Explain your answer.

2. In a two-good world, in which the goods are A and B, what does it mean to be in consumer disequilibrium?

BEHAVIORAL ECONOMICS

Economists are interested in how people behave. Economic theory predicts that, when the *MU/P* ratio for one good is greater than it is for another, individuals will buy more of the good with the higher *MU/P* ratio and less of the good with the lower *MU/P* ratio. In other words, individuals, seeking to maximize their utility, buy more of one good and less of another until the *MU/P* ratios for all goods are the same.

In traditional economic theories and models, individuals are assumed to be rational, self-interested, and consistent. For about the last 30 years, behavioral economists have challenged the traditional economic models. Behavioral economists argue that some human behavior does not fit neatly—at a minimum, easily—into the traditional economic framework. In this section, we describe some of the findings of behavioral economists.

Are People Willing to Reduce Others' Incomes?

Two economists, Daniel Zizzo and Andrew Oswald, set up a series of experiments with 4 groups, each with 4 people. Each person was given the same amount of money and asked to gamble with it. At the end of each act of gambling, 2 of the 4 persons in each group had won money and 2 had lost some. Then each of the 4 people in each group was given the opportunity to pay (or forfeit) some amount of money to reduce the take of the others in the group. To illustrate, in the group consisting of Smith, Matsui, Brown, and Riverra, Smith and Riverra had more money after gambling, and Matsui and Brown had less. All four were given the opportunity to reduce the amount of money held by the others in the group. For example, Brown could pay to reduce Smith's money, Matsui could pay to reduce Riverra's, and so on.

The expectation might be that no one will spend money to hurt someone else if it means leaving himself poorer. However, Zizzo and Oswald found that 62 percent of the participants did just that: They made themselves worse off to make someone else worse off.

WHICH IS BETTER: A TAX REBATE OR A TAX BONUS?[3]

In February 2008, then President George Bush and the Congress were talking about ways to stimulate the economy. The economy seemed to be heading into a recession, and the thinking was that the best way to stave off the recession (or at last to make it milder) was to get people to spend more money. With this in mind, the Congress and the president agreed on tax rebates. Simply put, the federal government would write out checks and send them to people; then the people would spend the money on various goods and services, stimulating the economy in the process. At the time, there was quite a bit of talk in the press about the tax rebates.

But if the objective was to get people to spend money, would it have been better to talk about a tax bonus instead of a tax rebate? According to Nicholas Epley, at the University of Chicago Graduate School of Business, it would have been. Here is Epley in his own words:

> Changing the way that identical income is described can significantly affect how people spend it. In an experiment I conducted at Harvard with my colleagues Dennis Mak and Lorraine Chen Idson, participants were given a $50 check. They were told that this money came from a faculty member's research budget, financed indirectly through tuition dollars. Roughly half of the participants had this money described as a "rebate," whereas the others had it described as a "bonus." When unexpectedly contacted one week later, participants who got a "rebate" reported spending less than half of what those who got a "bonus" reported spending ($9.55 versus $22.04, respectively).[4]

According to Epley, a rebate to most people is different from a bonus. A rebate is equated with returned income, whereas a bonus is equated with extra income. And his results show that people spend a greater percentage of extra income than they spend of returned income. He concludes that if the objective of the president and Congress was to get people to spend money (and to stimulate the economy), then it would have been much better to speak of tax bonuses than of tax rebates.

---

3. This feature is based on Nicholas Epley, "Rebate Psychology," *The New York Times*, January 31, 2008.
4. Ibid.

People behave this way possibly because they are more concerned with relative rank and status than with absolute well-being. Thus, the poorer of the two individuals doesn't mind paying, say, 25 cents if he can reduce the richer person's take by, say, $1. After the poorer person pays 25 cents, the gap between him and the richer person is smaller.

Some economists argue that such behavior is irrational and inconsistent with utility maximization. Other economists say it is no such thing. They argue that if people get utility from relative rank, then, in effect, they are buying a move up the relative rank ladder by reducing the size of the gap between themselves and others.

Is $1 Always $1?

Do people treat money differently depending on where it comes from? Traditional economics argues that they should not; after all, a dollar is a dollar is a dollar. Specifically, $1 that someone gives you as a gift is no different from $1 you earn or $1 you find on the street. When people treat some dollars differently from other dollars, they are *compartmentalizing*. They are saying that dollars in some compartments (of their minds) are valued differently from dollars in other compartments.

To illustrate, suppose you plan to see a Broadway play, the ticket for which costs $100. You buy the $100 ticket on Monday to see the play on Friday night. When Friday night arrives, you realize you have lost the ticket. Do you spend another $100 to buy another ticket (assuming another ticket can be purchased)?[5]

---

5. This example comes from Gary Belsky and Thomas Gilovich, *Why Smart People Make Big Money Mistakes and How to Correct Them* (New York: Simon & Schuster, 1999).

Now let's change the circumstances slightly. Suppose instead of buying the ticket on Monday, you plan to buy the ticket at the ticket window on Friday night. At the ticket window on Friday night, you realize you have lost $100 somewhere between home and the theater. Assuming you still have enough money to buy a $100 ticket to the play, do you buy it?

Regardless of how you answer each question, some economists argue that your answers should be consistent. If you say no to the first question, you should say no to the second question. If you say yes to the first, you should say yes to the second. The two questions, based on two slightly different settings, present you with essentially the same choice.

However, many people, when asked the two questions, say that they will not pay an additional $100 to buy a second ticket (having lost the first one) but will spend an additional $100 to buy a first ticket (having lost $100 in cash between home and the theater). Some people argue that spending an additional $100 on an additional ticket is the same as paying $200 to see the play—and that is just too much to pay. However, they don't see themselves as spending $200 to see the play when they lose $100 and pay $100 for a ticket. In either case, though, $200 is gone. Behavioral economists argue that people who answer the two questions differently (yes to one and no to the other) are compartmentalizing. They are treating two $100 amounts in two different ways—as if they come from two different compartments. For example, the person who says she will not buy a second $100 ticket (having lost the first $100 ticket) but will buy a first ticket (having lost $100 cash) is effectively saying by her behavior that $100 lost on a ticket is different from $100 lost in cash.

Let's consider another situation. Suppose you earn $1,000 by working hard at a job and also win $1,000 at the roulette table in Las Vegas. Would you feel freer to spend the $1,000 won in Las Vegas than to spend the $1,000 you earned? If the answer is yes, then you are treating money differently depending on where it came from and what you had to do to get it. Nothing is necessarily wrong or immoral about that, but it is interesting because $1,000 is $1,000 is $1,000—no matter where it came from and no matter what you had to do to get it.

Finally, let's look at an experiment conducted by two marketing professors. Drazen Prelec and Duncan Simester once organized a sealed-bid auction for tickets to a Boston Celtics basketball game. Half the participants in the auction were told that if they had the winning bid, they had to pay in cash. The other half of the participants were told that if they had the winning bid, they had to pay with a credit card.

One would think that the average bid from the people who had to pay cash would be the same as the average bid from the people who had to pay with a credit card, assuming that the two groups were divided randomly and that no group showed a stronger or weaker preference for seeing the Celtics game. But this didn't happen. The average bid of the people who had to pay with a credit card was higher than the average bid of the people who had to pay with cash. Using a credit card somehow caused people to bid higher dollar amounts than they would have bid if they had to pay cash. Money from the credit card compartment seemed to be more quickly or easily spent than money from the cash compartment.

Coffee Mugs and the Endowment Effect

In one economic experiment, coffee mugs were allocated randomly to half the people in a group. Each person with a mug was asked to state a price at which he would be willing to sell his mug. Each person without a mug was asked to state a price at which he would be willing to buy a mug.

Even though the mugs were allocated randomly (countering the idea that somehow the people who received mugs valued them more than those who did not receive them), the lowest price at which the owner would sell the mug was, on average, higher than the highest price at which a buyer would pay to buy a mug. It is as if sellers said they wouldn't sell the mugs for less than $15, and buyers said they wouldn't buy them for more than $10.

This outcome—called the *endowment effect*—is odd. Even though there is no reason to believe that the people who received the mugs valued them more than the people who didn't receive them, people place a higher value on something (like a mug) simply because they own it. In other words, people seem to show an inclination to hold on to what they have.

If this applies to you, think of what it means. When you go into a store to buy a sweater, you might determine that a sweater is worth no more to you than, say, $40 and that you are not willing to pay more than $40 for it. But if someone gave you the sweater as a gift and you were asked to sell it, you wouldn't be willing to sell it for less than, say, $50. Simply owning the sweater makes it more valuable to you.

Economist David Friedman says that such behavior is not limited to humans.[6] He points out that some species of animals exhibit territorial behavior—that is, they are more likely to fight to keep what they have than to fight to get what they don't have. As Friedman notes, "It is a familiar observation that a dog will fight harder to keep his own bone than to take another dog's bone."

Friedman argues that this type of behavior in humans makes perfect sense in a hunter-gatherer society. Here is what Friedman has to say:

> Now consider the same logic [found in the fact that a dog will fight harder to keep the bone he has than to take a bone from another dog] in a hunter-gatherer society—in which there are no external institutions to enforce property rights. Imagine that each individual considers every object in sight, decides how much each is worth to him, and then tries to appropriate it, with the outcome of the resulting Hobbesian struggle determined by some combination of how much each wants things and how strong each individual is. It does not look like a formula for a successful society, even on the scale of a hunter-gatherer band.
>
> There is an alternative solution, assuming that humans are at least as smart as dogs, robins, and fish. Some method, possibly as simple as physical possession, is used to define what "belongs to" whom. Each individual then commits himself to fight very hard to protect his "property"—much harder than he would be willing to fight in order to appropriate a similar object from someone else's possession—with the commitment made via some psychological mechanism presumably hardwired into humans. The result is both a considerably lower level of (risky) violence and a considerably more prosperous society.
>
> The fact that the result is attractive does not, of course, guarantee that it will occur—evolution selects for the reproductive interest of the individual, not the group. But in this case they are the same. To see that, imagine a population in which some individuals have adopted the commitment strategy [outlined above—that is, fighting for what you physically possess], and some have adopted different commitment strategies—for example, a strategy of fighting to the death for whatever they see as valuable. It should be fairly easy to see that individuals in the first group will, on average, do better for themselves—hence have (among other things) greater reproductive success—than those in the second group.
>
> How do I commit myself to fight very hard for something? One obvious way is some psychological quirk that makes that something appear very valuable to me. Hence the same behavior pattern that shows up as territorial behavior in fish and ferocious defense of bones in dogs shows up in Cornell students [who were given the coffee mugs] as an endowment effect. Just as in the earlier cases, behavior that was functional in the environment in which we evolved continues to be observed, even in an environment in which its function has largely disappeared.[7]

We value X more highly if we have it than if we do not have it because such behavior at one point in our evolution made possible a system of property rights in a world where the alternative was the Hobbesian jungle.

---

6. See his "Economics and Evolutionary Psychology" at his website, http://www.daviddfriedman.com/JLE/jie.htm.

7. Ibid., p. 10.

TO ACCEPT OR REJECT THE MONEY[8]

In the ultimatum game, there are two people and one pot of money. One person divides the money between himself and the other person. The other person can either accept his portion of the money or reject it. If he rejects it, then neither person gets any money. To illustrate, suppose Jack is going to divide $40 between himself and Bill. Jack gives himself $35 and he gives Bill $5. At this point, Bill can either accept or reject the $5 that Jack has apportioned to him. If he accepts it, then he gets the $5 and Jack gets the $35. But if he rejects it, neither he nor Jack get any money.

In Bill's position, what would you do? Would you accept the $5 or reject it? Often, your strategy may depend on whether this is a one-time deal or there are other rounds of play. For example, if there are other rounds of play, you might reject the initial offer of $5, so that you send a message to Jack: Either divide the money more nearly equal (closer to $20 each), or I will make sure you get nothing. If there are several rounds of play, this strategy may give you the most money overall.

But suppose it is a one-round deal? Does it make sense to reject the deal, no matter how Jack divides the money? For example, again suppose Jack gives himself $35 and you $5. If you reject the deal, you do not get the $5. If you accept the deal, you get at least the $5. When economists have experimented with the ultimatum game, they find that many participants reject the money offer if it is not close to half the money. In other words, they are likely to reject an offer of $35–$5 (where they receive the $5) or an offer of $30–$10. They are likely to accept, though, an offer of $20–$20.

What do such rejections show? Some economists reason that this shows people are more concerned with their relative income position than with their absolute income position. In other words, how much income one has does not seem to matter as much as how much income one has relative to others.

In one experiment, performed by economist Terence Burnham of Harvard University, the results showed that men with higher testosterone levels were more likely to reject unequal offers of money than those with lower testosterone levels. Five of seven men with the highest testosterone levels rejected an unequal offer, whereas only one of 19 men with lower testosterone rejected the same offer. Since high testosterone is highly correlated with social dominance (in many societies), one might conclude that the higher one's testosterone level is, the more relative (as opposed to the absolute) position seems to matter.

One way of looking at the results of the ultimatum game is to say that sometimes people are irrational. In other words, turning down, say, a $35–$5 offer is irrational, because it is better to have $5 than not to have $5. Of course, another perspective states that rejecting such an offer is not irrational at all for someone who is trying to maximize his or her relative position in society, not the number of dollars. In such a case, rejecting offers that lower one's relative position is not irrational.

---

8. This feature is based on "Money Isn't Everything" in *The Economist*, July 5, 2007.

Does the Endowment Effect Hold Only for New Traders?

The endowment effect has not gone untested. John List, an economist at the University of Maryland, wanted to know whether new traders were more likely to experience the endowment effect than experienced traders were. He went to a sports card exchange where people trade regularly. In one experiment, he took aside a group of card fans and gave them such things as sports autographs and sports badges. He then gave them the opportunity to trade. It turned out that the more experience traders had (at trading such items), the less prone they were to the endowment effect.

One criticism of this experiment was that novice traders were less likely to trade than experienced traders because novices were not sure of the value of the sports autographs. To meet this criticism, List conducted another experiment with chocolate and coffee mugs, where he was sure everyone did know the values of the items. Once again, there was some endowment effect, but it was not as strong as in the sports memorabilia case, and—more important—only newer traders demonstrated the effect. In other words, experience as a trader seems to make one less prone to the endowment effect.

"IS THERE AN INDIRECT WAY OF PROVING THE LAW OF DIMINISHING MARGINAL UTILITY?"

Student:

In class, you proved that the law of demand is consistent with utility maxization. This was an important proof for me because I had always accepted the law of demand as true, but I never really felt easy with the idea that indivduals seek to maximize utility. Your proof that the law of demand is consistent with utility maximization helps put this earlier uneasiness of mine to rest.

Having said that, is there any similar proof of the law of diminishing marginal utility? The law of diminishing marginal utility sounds true, but is there any way to prove that it is.

Instructor:

Yes, there is. To illustrate, let's start with something that we know is true because it is so obvious: People trade. Now it's not likely that they would trade if the law of diminishing marginal utility did not hold.

Student:

In other words, you're saying that the law of diminishing marginal utility is consistent with the fact that people trade.

Instructor:

Yes. To illustrate, consider two people, Smith and Jones. Smith has 100 apples and Jones has 100 oranges. As Smith consumes her apples, marginal utility declines. Her tenth apple doesn't give her as much utility as her ninth, and so on. The same is true for Jones with respect to oranges. In other words, as Smith and Jones consume successive units of what they have, marginal utility falls.

At some point, Smith's marginal utility of consuming another apple is likely less than her marginal utility of consuming something different—such as an orange. And at some point, Jones's marginal utility of consuming another orange is likely less than his marginal utility of consuming something different—say, an apple. When this point comes, Smith and Jones will trade. For Smith, the marginal utility of an apple will be less than the marginal utility of an orange, and she will gladly trade an apple for an orange. For Jones, the marginal utility of an orange will be less than the marginal utility of an apple, and he will gladly trade an orange for an apple.

Now suppose the law of diminishing marginal utility did not exist. Smith would have the same marignal utility when she consumed her first and her one-hundredth apple, and this marginal would always be greater than her marginal utility for an orange. The same would be

true for Jones with respect to oranges. In this case, Smith and Jones would not trade with each other. The law of diminishing marginal utility, at work on both apples and oranges, gets Smith and Jones eventually to trade with each other.

Points to Remember

1. The law of demand is consistent with utility maximization.
2. The law of diminishing marginal utility is consistent with the fact that individuals trade.

SELF-TEST

1. Brandon's grandmother is very cautious about spending money. Yesterday, she gave Brandon a gift of $100 for his birthday. Brandon also received a gift of $100 from his father, who isn't nearly as cautious about spending money as Brandon's grandmother. Brandon believes that it would some-how be wrong to spend his grandmother's gift on frivolous things, but it wouldn't be wrong to spend his father's gift on such things. Is Brandon compartmentalizing? Explain your answer.

2. Summarize David Friedman's explanation of the endowment effect.

a reader asks | Do People Really Equate Marginal Utility-Price Ratios?

Am I expected to believe that real people actually go around with marginal utility-price ratios in their heads and that they behave according to how these ratios change? After all, most people don't even know what marginal utility is.

We could answer that most people may not know the laws of physics, but their behavior is still consistent with such laws. But we present a different argument. Let's review how a person who equates *MU/P* ratios behaves in accordance with the law of demand. When the *MU/P* ratio for good A is equal to the *MU/P* ratio for good B, the person is in consumer equilibrium. Suppose the price of good A falls so that the *MU/P* ratio for good A is now greater than the *MU/P* ratio for B. What does the individual do? To maximize utility, we predict that the person will buy more of good A because she receives more utility per dollar buying A than she does buying B. Buying more A when the price of good A declines—to maximize utility—is consistent with the law of demand, which states that price and quantity demanded are inversely related, *ceteris paribus*. In other words, acting in accordance with the law of demand is consistent with equating *MU/P* ratios.

Now our real question is, can people act in a manner consistent with the law of demand, even though they don't know what the law of demand says? If the answer is yes, then they are acting *as if* they are equating *MU/P* ratios in their heads.

Instead of talking about people, let's talk about rats for a minute. Certainly, rats do not understand what marginal utility is. They cannot define it, compute it, or do anything else with it. But do they act *as if* they equate *MU/P* ratios? Do they observe the law of demand?

Consider an experiment conducted by economists at Texas A&M University, who undertook to study the "buying" behavior of two white rats. Each rat was put in a laboratory cage with two levers. By pushing one lever, a rat obtained root beer; by pushing the other lever, it obtained a nonalcoholic collins mix. Every day, each rat was given a so-called fixed income of 300 pushes. (When the combined total of pushes on the two levers reached 300, the levers could not be pushed down until the next day.) The prices of root beer and collins mix were both 20 pushes per milliliter of beverage. Given this income and the prices of root beer and collins mix, one rat settled in to consuming 11 milliliters of root beer and 4 milliliters of collins mix. The other rat settled in to consuming almost all root beer.

Then the prices of the two beverages were changed. The price of collins mix was halved while the price of root beer was doubled.[8] Using economic theory, we would predict that with these new prices, the consumption of collins mix would increase and the consumption of root beer would decrease. This is exactly what happened. Both rats began to consume more collins mix and less root beer. In short, both rats had downward-sloping demand curves for collins mix and root beer.

The point is that, if the behavior of rats is consistent with the law of demand and if the law of demand is consistent with equating *MU/P* ratios, then do you really have to know you are equating *MU/P* ratios before you can be doing it. Obviously not.

---

8. The researchers raised the price of root beer by reducing the quantity of root beer dispensed per push. This is the same as increasing the number of pushes necessary to obtain the original quantity of root beer.

Chapter Summary

THE LAW OF DIMINISHING MARGINAL UTILITY

- The law of diminishing marginal utility holds that as the amount of a good consumed increases, the marginal utility of the good decreases.

- The law of diminishing marginal utility should not be used to make interpersonal utility comparisons. For example, the law does not say that a millionaire receives less (or more) utility from an additional dollar than a poor man does. Instead, all it says is that for both the millionaire and the poor man, the last dollar has less value than the next-to-last dollar has.

THE DIAMOND-WATER PARADOX

- The diamond-water paradox states that what has great value in use sometimes has little value in exchange and that what has little value in use sometimes has great value in exchange. A knowledge of the difference between total utility and marginal utility is necessary to unravel the diamond-water paradox.

- A good can have high total utility and low marginal utility. For example, water's total utility is high, but because water is so plentiful, its marginal utility is low. In short, water is immensely useful, but it is so plentiful that individuals place relatively low value on another unit of it. In contrast, diamonds are not as useful as water, but because there are few diamonds in the world, the marginal utility of diamonds is high. In summary, a good can be extremely useful and have a low price if the good is in plentiful supply (high value in use, low value in exchange). On the other hand, a good can be of little use and have a high price if the good is in short supply (low value in use, high value in exchange).

CONSUMER EQUILIBRIUM

- Individuals seek to equate marginal utilities per dollar. For example, if a person receives more utility per dollar spent on good A than on good B, she will reorder her purchases and buy more A and less B. The tendency is to move away from the condition $MU_A/P_A > MU_B/P_B$ to the condition $MU_A/P_A = MU_B/P_B$. The latter condition represents consumer equilibrium (in a two-good world).

MARGINAL UTILITY ANALYSIS AND THE LAW OF DEMAND

- Marginal utility analysis can be used to illustrate the law of demand, which states that price and quantity demanded are inversely related, *ceteris paribus*. Starting from consumer equilibrium in a world in which there are only two goods, A and B, a fall in the price of A will cause MU_A/P_A to be greater than MU_B/P_B. As a result, the consumer will purchase more of good A to restore herself to equilibrium.

BEHAVIORAL ECONOMICS

- Behavioral economists argue that some human behavior does not fit neatly—at a minimum, easily—into the traditional economic framework.

- Behavioral economists believe they have identified human behaviors that are inconsistent with the model of men and women as rational, self-interested, and consistent. These behaviors include the following: (1) Individuals are willing to spend some money to lower the incomes of others even if doing so lowers their own incomes. (2) Individuals don't always treat $1 as $1; some dollars seem to be treated differently than others. (3) Individuals sometimes value X more if it is theirs than if it isn't theirs and they are seeking to acquire it.

Key Terms and Concepts

Diamond-Water Paradox	Util	Marginal Utility	Interpersonal Utility
Utility	Total Utility	Law of Diminishing	Comparison
		Marginal Utility	Consumer Equilibrium

Questions and Problems

1. Give a numerical example that illustrates total utility rising as marginal utility declines.

2. The law of diminishing marginal utility is consistent with the fact that people trade. Do you agree or disagree? Explain your answer.

3. "If we take $1 away from a rich person and give it to a poor person, the rich person loses less utility than the poor person gains." Comment.

4. Is it possible to get so much of a good that it turns into a bad? If so, give an example.

5. If a person consumes fewer units of a good, will marginal utility of the good increase as total utility decreases? Why or why not?

6. The marginal utility of good A is 4 utils and its price is $2, and the marginal utility of good B is 6 utils and its price is $1. Is the individual consumer maximizing (total) utility if

she spends a total of $3 by buying one unit of each good? If not, how can more utility be obtained?

7   Individuals who buy second homes usually spend less for them than they do for their first homes. Why is this the case?

8   Describe five everyday examples of you or someone else making an interpersonal utility comparison.

9   Is there a logical link between the law of demand and the assumption that individuals seek to maximize utility? (*Hint:* Think of how the condition for consumer equilibrium can be used to express the inverse relationship between price and quantity demanded.)

10   List five sets of two goods (each set is composed of two goods; e. g., diamonds and water are one set) where the good with the greater value in use has a lower value in exchange than does the good with the lower value in use.

11   Do you think people with high IQs are in consumer equilibrium (equating marginal utilities per dollar) more often than people with low IQs? Why or why not?

12   What is the endowment effect?

13   After each toss of the coin, one person has more money and one person has less. If the person with less money cares about relative rank and status, will he be willing to pay, say, $1 to reduce the other person's winnings by, say, 50 cents? Will he be willing to pay 25 cents to reduce the other person's winnings by $1? Explain your answers.

14   How is buying a house in a good school district like sending children to a private school?

15   Of two similar houses on a street, one faces the ocean and the other does not. How might we determine the price of an ocean view? Explain your answer.

Working with Numbers and Graphs

1   The marginal utility for the third unit of X is 60 utils, and the marginal utility for the fourth unit of X is 45 utils. If the law of diminishing marginal utility holds, what is the minimum total utility?

2   Fill in blanks A–D in the following table.

Units of Good Consumed	Total Utility (utils)	Marginal Utility (utils)
1	10	10
2	19	A
3	B	8
4	33	C
5	35	D

3   The total utilities of the first 5 units of good X are 10, 19, 26, 33, and 40 utils, respectively. In other words, the total utility of 1 unit is 10 utils, the total utility of 2 units is 19 utils, and so on. What is the marginal utility of the third unit?

Use the following table to answer Questions 4 and 5.

Units of Good X	*TU* of Good X (utils)	Units of Good Y	*TU* of Good Y (utils)
1	20	1	19
2	35	2	32
3	48	3	40
4	58	4	45
5	66	5	49

4   If George spends $5 (total) a week on good X and good Y, and if the price of each good is $1 per unit, then how many units of each good does he purchase to maximize utility?

5   Given the number of units of each good George purchases in question 4, what is his total utility?

6   Draw the marginal utility curve for a good that has constant marginal utility.

7   The marginal utility curve for units 3–5 of good X is below the horizontal axis. Draw the corresponding part of the total utility curve for good X.

BUDGET CONSTRAINT AND INDIFFERENCE CURVE ANALYSIS

This chapter uses marginal utility theory to discuss consumer choice. Sometimes budget constraint and indifference curve analysis are used instead, especially in upper-division economics courses. We examine this important topic in this appendix.

THE BUDGET CONSTRAINT

Budget Constraint
All the combinations or bundles of two goods a person can purchase, given a certain money income and prices for the two goods.

Societies have production possibilities frontiers, and individuals have **budget constraints**. The budget constraint is built on three constraints: two prices and the individual's income. To illustrate, consider O'Brien, who has a monthly income of $1,200. In a world of two goods, X and Y, O'Brien can spend his total income on X, he can spend his total income on Y, or he can spend part of his income on X and part on Y. Suppose the price of X is $100 and the price of Y is $80. If O'Brien spends his total income on X, he can purchase a maximum of 12 units; if he spends his total income on Y, he can purchase a maximum of 15 units. Locating these two points on a two-dimensional diagram and then drawing a line between them, as shown in Exhibit 1, gives us O'Brien's budget constraint. Any point on the budget constraint, as well as any point below it, represents a possible combination (a bundle) of the two goods available to O'Brien.

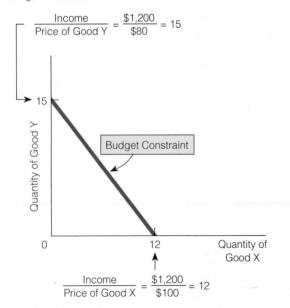
Slope of the Budget Constraint

The slope of the budget constraint has special significance. The absolute value of the slope represents the relative prices of the two goods, X and Y. In Exhibit 1, the slope, or P_X/P_Y, is equal to 1.25, indicating that the relative price of 1 unit of X is 1.25 units of Y.

What Will Change the Budget Constraint?

If any of the three variables changes—two prices and the individual's income—the budget constraint changes. Not all changes are alike, however. Consider a fall in the price of good X from $100 to $60. With this change, the maximum number of units of good X purchasable with an income of $1,200 rises from 12 to 20. The budget constraint revolves away from the origin, as shown in Exhibit 2(a). Notice that the number of O'Brien's possible combinations of the two goods increases; there are more bundles of the two goods available after the price decrease than before.

exhibit 2

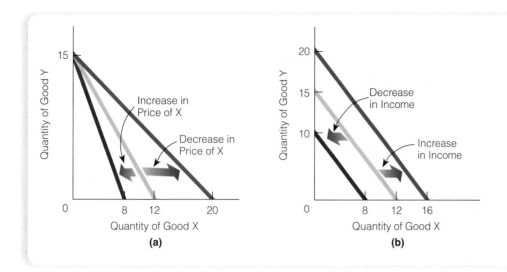

(a)

(b)

Changes in the Budget Constraint

(a) A change in the price of good X or good Y will change the slope of the budget constraint. (b) A change in income will change the position of the budget constraint while the slope remains constant. Whenever a budget constraint changes, the number of combinations (bundles) of the two goods available to the individual changes too.

Consider what happens to the budget constraint if the price of good X rises. If it goes from $100 to, say, $150, the maximum number of units of good X falls from 12 to 8. The budget constraint revolves toward the origin. As a consequence, the number of bundles available to O'Brien decreases. Therefore, a change in the price of either good changes the slope of the budget constraint, with the result that relative prices and the number of bundles available to the individual also change.

We turn now to a change in income. If O'Brien's income rises to $1,600, the maximum number of purchasable units of X rises to 16, and the maximum number of units of Y rises to 20. The budget constraint shifts rightward (away from the origin) and is parallel to the old budget constraint. As a consequence, the number of bundles available to O'Brien increases [Exhibit 2(b)]. If O'Brien's income falls from $1,200 to $800, the extreme end points on the budget constraint become 8 and 10 for X and Y, respectively. The budget constraint shifts leftward (toward the origin) and is parallel to the old budget constraint. As a consequence, the number of bundles available to O'Brien falls [Exhibit 2(b)].

INDIFFERENCE CURVES

An individual can, of course, choose any bundle of the two goods on or below the budget constraint. If she spends her total income and therefore chooses a point on the budget constraint, this action raises two important questions: (1) Which bundle of the many bundles of the two goods does the individual choose? (2) How does the individual's chosen combination of goods change, given a change in prices or income? Both questions can be answered by combining the budget constraint with the graphical expression of the individual's preferences: indifference curves.

CONSTRUCTING AN INDIFFERENCE CURVE

It is possible to be indifferent between two bundles of goods. Suppose that bundle A consists of 2 pairs of shoes and 6 shirts and that bundle B consists of 3 pairs of shoes and 4 shirts. A person who is indifferent between these two bundles is implicitly saying that one is as good as the other. She is likely to say this, though, only if she receives equal total utility from the two bundles. If not, she would prefer one bundle to the other.

exhibit 3

An Indifference Set and an Indifference Curve

An indifference set is a number of bundles of two goods in which each bundle yields the same total utility. An indifference curve represents an indifference set. In this exhibit, data from the indifference set (a) are used to derive an indifference curve (b).

An Indifference Set

Bundle	Milk (units)	Orange Juice (units)
A	8	3
B	5	4
C	3	5
D	2	6

(a)

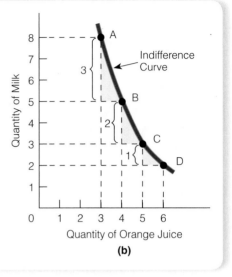

(b)

Indifference Set

Group of bundles of two goods that give an individual equal total utility.

Indifference Curve

The curve that represents an indifference set and that shows all the bundles of two goods giving an individual equal total utility.

If we tabulate all the different bundles from which the individual receives equal utility, we have an **indifference set**. We can then plot the data in the indifference set and draw an **indifference curve**. Consider the indifference set illustrated in Exhibit 3(a). Of the four bundles of goods, A–D, each bundle gives the same total utility as every other one. These equal-utility bundles are plotted in Exhibit 3(b). Connecting these bundles in a two-dimensional space gives us an indifference curve.

Characteristics of Indifference Curves

Indifference curves for goods have certain characteristics that are consistent with reasonable assumptions about consumer behavior.

1. *Indifference curves are downward sloping (from left to right).* The assumption that consumers always prefer more of a good to less requires that indifference curves slope downward left to right. Consider the alternatives to downward sloping: vertical, horizontal, and upward sloping (left to right). A horizontal or vertical curve would combine bundles of goods, some of which had more of one good and no less of another good than other bundles [Exhibit 4(a–b)]. (If bundle B contains more of one good and no less of another good than bundle A, an individual would not be indifferent between the two bundles. Individuals prefer more to less.) An upward-sloping curve would combine bundles of goods, some of which had more of both goods than other bundles [Exhibit 4(c)]. More simply, indifference curves are downward sloping because a person has to get more of one good in order to maintain a level of satisfaction (utility) when giving up some of another good.

2. *Indifference curves are convex to the origin.* As we move down and to the right along the indifference curve, it becomes flatter. For example, at 8 units of milk [point A in Exhibit 3(b)], the individual is willing to give up 3 units of milk to get an additional unit of orange juice (and thus move to point B). At point B, where she has 5 units of milk, she is willing to give up only 2 units of milk to get an additional unit of orange juice (and thus move to point C). Finally, at point C, with 3 units of milk, she is now willing to give up only 1 unit of milk to get an additional unit of orange juice. Therefore, the more of one good that an individual has, the more units he will give up to get an additional unit of another good; the less of one good that an individual has, the fewer units he will give up to get an additional unit of another good. This is

exhibit 4

Indifference Curves for Goods Do Not Look Like This

(a) Bundle B has more milk and no less orange juice than bundle A, so an individual would prefer B to A and not be indifferent between them. (b) Bundle B has more orange juice and no less milk than bundle A, so an individual would prefer B to A and not be indifferent between them. (c) Bundle B has more milk and more orange juice than bundle A, so an individual would prefer B to A and not be indifferent between them.

reasonable: Our observation is a reflection of diminishing marginal utility at work. As the quantity of a good consumed increases, the marginal utility of that good decreases; therefore, the more of one good an individual has, the more units he can (and will) sacrifice to get an additional unit of another good and still maintain total utility. Stated differently, if the law of diminishing marginal utility did not exist, it would not make sense to say that indifference curves of goods are convex to the origin.

An important peripheral point about marginal utilities is that *the absolute value of the slope of the indifference curve*—which is called the **marginal rate of substitution**—*represents the ratio of the marginal utility of the good on the horizontal axis to the marginal utility of the good on the vertical axis:*

$$\frac{MU_{\text{good on horizontal axis}}}{MU_{\text{good on vertical axis}}}$$

Let's look carefully at this assertion. First, the absolute value of the slope of the indifference curve is the marginal rate of substitution (*MRS*). The *MRS* is the amount of one good an individual is willing to give up to obtain an additional unit of another good and maintain equal total utility. For example, in Exhibit 3(b), we see that moving from point A to point B, the individual is willing to give up 3 units of milk to get an additional unit of orange juice, with total utility remaining constant (between points A and B). The marginal rate of substitution is therefore 3 units of milk for 1 unit of orange juice in the area between points A and B. Further, the absolute value of the slope of the indifference curve (the *MRS*) is equal to the ratio of the *MU* of the good on the horizontal axis to the *MU* of the good on the vertical axis. How can this be? If an individual giving up 3 units of milk and receiving 1 unit of orange juice maintains her total utility, then (in the area under consideration) the marginal utility of orange juice is approximately three times the marginal utility of milk. In general terms

Marginal Rate of Substitution
The amount of one good an individual is willing to give up to obtain an additional unit of another good and maintain equal total utility.

Absolute value of the slope of the indifference curve = Marginal rate of substitution

$$= \frac{MU_{\text{good on horizontal axis}}}{MU_{\text{good on vertical axis}}}$$

exhibit 5

An Indifference Map

A few of the many possible indifference curves are shown. Any point in the two-dimensional space is on an indifference curve. Indifference curves farther away from the origin represent greater total utility than those closer to the origin.

The farther away from the origin, the greater the total utility.

Indifference Curve Map
Represents a number of indifference curves for a given individual with reference to two goods.

Transitivity
The principle whereby if A is preferred to B, and B is preferred to C, then A is preferred to C.

exhibit 6

Crossing Indifference Curves Are Inconsistent with Transitive Preferences

Point A lies on both indifference curves I_1 and I_2. This means that the individual is indifferent between A and B and between A and C, which results in her

(supposedly) being indifferent between B and C. But individuals prefer more to less (when it comes to goods) and, thus, would prefer C to B. We cannot have transitive preferences and make sense of crossing indifference curves.

3. *Indifference curves that are farther from the origin are preferable because they represent larger bundles of goods.* Exhibit 3(b) shows only one indifference curve. However, different bundles of the two goods exist and have indifference curves passing through them. These bundles have less of both goods or more of both goods than those in Exhibit 3(b). Illustrating a number of indifference curves on the same diagram gives us an **indifference curve map**. Strictly speaking, an indifference curve map represents a number of indifference curves for a given individual with reference to two goods. A mapping is illustrated in Exhibit 5.

Although only five indifference curves have been drawn, many more could have been added. For example, there are many indifference curves between I_1 and I_2.

Also notice that the farther away from the origin an indifference curve is, the higher the total utility is that it represents. You can see this by comparing point A on I_1 and point B on I_2. At point B, there is the same amount of orange juice as at point A but more milk. Point B is therefore preferable to point A, and because B is on I_2 and A is on I_1, I_2 is preferable to I_1. The reason for this is simple: An individual receives more utility at any point on I_2 (because more goods are available) than at any point on I_1.

4. *Indifference curves do not cross (intersect).* Indifference curves do not cross because individuals' preferences exhibit **transitivity**. For example, if Kristin prefers Coca-Cola to Pepsi-Cola and she also prefers Pepsi-Cola to root beer, then it follows that she prefers Coca-Cola to root beer. If she preferred root beer to Coca-Cola, she would be contradicting her earlier preferences. To say that an individual has transitive preferences means that she maintains a logical order of preferences over a given time period. Consider what intersecting indifference curves would represent. In Exhibit 6, indifference curves I_1 and I_2 intersect at point A.

Notice that point A lies on both I_1 and I_2. Comparing A and B, we hold that the individual must be indifferent between them because they lie on the same indifference curve. The same holds for A and C. But if the individual is indifferent between A and B and between A and C, then she must be indifferent between B and C. But C has more of both goods than B, and thus the individual will not be indifferent between B and C; she will prefer C to B. We cannot have transitive preferences and make sense of crossing indifference curves. We can, however, have transitive preferences and make sense of noncrossing indifference curves. We go with the latter.

THE INDIFFERENCE MAP AND THE BUDGET CONSTRAINT COME TOGETHER

At this point, we bring the indifference map and the budget constraint together to illustrate consumer equilibrium. We have the following facts: (1) The individual has a budget constraint. (2) The absolute value of the slope of the budget constraint is the relative prices of the two goods under consideration, say, P_X/P_Y. (3) The individual has an indifference map. (4) The absolute value of the slope of the indifference curve at any point is the marginal rate of substitution, which is equal to the marginal utility of one good divided by the marginal utility of another good; for example, MU_X/MU_Y.

What is the necessary condition for consumer equilibrium? Obviously, the individual will try to reach a point on the highest indifference curve she can reach. This point will be where the slope of the budget constraint is equal to the slope of an indifference curve (or where the budget constraint is tangent to an indifference curve). At this point, consumer equilibrium is established and the following condition holds:

$$\frac{P_X}{P_Y} = \frac{MU_X}{MU_Y}$$

This condition is met in Exhibit 7 at point E. Note that this condition looks similar to the condition for consumer equilibrium earlier in this chapter. By rearranging the terms in the condition, we get[1]

$$\frac{MU_X}{P_X} = \frac{MU_Y}{P_Y}$$

FROM INDIFFERENCE CURVES TO A DEMAND CURVE

We can now derive a demand curve within a budget constraint–indifference curve framework. Exhibit 8(a) shows two budget constraints, one reflecting a $10 price for good X and the other reflecting a $5 price for good X. As the price of X falls, the consumer moves from point A to point B. At B, 35 units of X are consumed; at A, 30 units of

exhibit 7

Consumer Equilibrium

Consumer equilibrium exists at the point where the slope of the budget constraint is equal to the slope of an indifference curve, or where the budget constraint is tangent to an indifference curve. In the exhibit, this point is E. Here $P_X/P_Y = MU_X/MU_Y$; or, rearranging, $MU_X/P_X = MU_Y/P_Y$.

1. Start with $P_X/P_Y = MU_X/MU_Y$ and cross multiply. This gives $P_X MU_Y = P_Y MU_X$. Next, divide both sides by P_X. This gives $MU_Y = P_Y MU_X/P_X$. Finally, divide both sides by P_Y. This gives $MU_Y/P_Y = MU_X/P_X$.

exhibit 8

From Indifference Curves to a Demand Curve

(a) At a price of $10 for good X, consumer equilibrium is at point A with the individual consuming 30 units of X. As the price falls to $5, the budget constraint moves outward (away from the origin), and the consumer moves to point B and consumes 35 units of X. Plotting the price-quantity data for X gives a demand curve for X in (b).

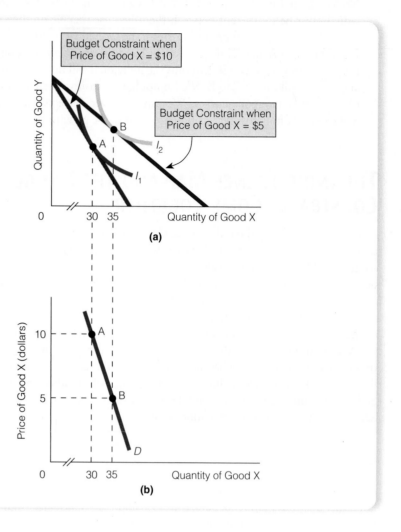

X were consumed. We conclude that a lower price for X results in greater consumption of X. By plotting the relevant price and quantity data, we derive a demand curve for good X in Exhibit 8(b).

Appendix Summary

- A budget constraint represents all combinations of bundles of two goods a person can purchase, given a certain money income and prices for the two goods.

- An indifference curve shows all the combinations or bundles of two goods that give an individual equal total utility.

- Indifference curves are downward sloping, convex to the origin, and do not cross. The farther away from the origin

an indifference curve is, the greater total utility it represents for the individual.

- Consumer equilibrium is at the point where the slope of the budget constraint equals the slope of the indifference curve.

- A demand curve can be derived within a budget constraint–indifference curve framework.

Questions and Problems

1   Diagram the following budget constraints:
    a. Income = \$4,000; P_X = \$50; P_Y = \$100.
    b. Income = \$3,000; P_X = \$25; P_Y = \$200.
    c. Income = \$2,000; P_X = \$40; P_Y = \$150.

2   Explain why indifference curves:
    a. Are downward sloping.
    b. Are convex to the origin.
    c. Do not cross.

3   Explain why consumer equilibrium is equivalent whether using marginal utility analysis or indifference curve analysis.

4   Derive a demand curve using indifference curve analysis.

CHAPTER 7

PRODUCTION AND COSTS

© DIGITAL VISION/GETTY IMAGES

Introduction Everyone deals with business firms on a daily basis. People buy goods from firms: cars, clothes, food, books, entertainment, and other products. And people work for firms as accountants, truck drivers, secretaries, vice presidents, and editors. Our lives are constantly intermingled with business firms, as buyers of goods and as sellers of our labor services. Even though we deal with business firms daily, most of us probably know little about them. Why do they exist? What do they try to maximize? How do they go about producing the goods they produce? What concepts must firms concern themselves with? In this chapter we answer many of these questions.

WHY FIRMS EXIST

A **business firm** is an entity that employs resources, or factors of production, to produce goods and services to be sold to consumers, other firms, or the government. To understand why firms exist, we must explain worker behavior, markets, and the questions a firm must answer.

The Market and the Firm: Invisible Hand Versus Visible Hand

Through the forces of supply and demand, the market guides and coordinates individuals' actions, and it does so in an impersonal manner. No one orders buyers to reduce quantity demanded when price increases; they just do it. No one orders sellers to increase quantity supplied when price increases; they just do it. No one orders more resources to be moved into the production of personal computers when the demand and price for personal computers increase. The market guides individuals from the production of one good into the production of another. It coordinates individuals' actions so that suppliers and demanders find mutual satisfaction at equilibrium. As economist Adam Smith observed, individuals in a market setting are "led by an invisible hand to promote an end which was no part of their intention."

Contrast the invisible hand of the market with the visible hand of a manager in a firm. The manager tells the employee on the assembly line to make more computer chips. The manager tells the employee to design a new engine, to paint the lamps green, to put steak and lobster on the menu. Thus, both the invisible hand of the market and the visible hand of the firm's manager guide and coordinate individuals' actions. There is, in other words, both **market coordination** and **managerial coordination**.

If the market is capable of guiding and coordinating individuals' actions, why did firms (and managers) arise in the first place? Why do firms exist?

The Alchian and Demsetz Answer

Economists Armen Alchian and Harold Demsetz suggest that firms are formed when benefits can be obtained from individuals working as a team.[1] Sometimes, the sum of what individuals can produce as a team is greater than the sum of what they can produce alone:

$$\text{Sum of team production} > \text{Sum of individual production}$$

Consider 11 individuals, all making shoe boxes. Each working alone produces 10 shoe boxes per day, for a total daily output of 110 shoe boxes. If they work as a team, however, the same 11 individuals can produce 140 shoe boxes. The added output (30 shoe boxes) may be reason enough for them to work together as a team and to create a firm.

Shirking in a Team

Although forming a firm can increase output, team production can have problems that do not occur in individual production. One problem of team production is **shirking**, which occurs when workers put forth less than the agreed-to effort. The amount of shirking increases in teams because the costs of shirking to individual team members are lower than when they work alone.

Consider five individuals, Alice, Bob, Carl, Denise, and Elizabeth, who form a team to produce light bulbs because they realize that the sum of their team production will be more than the sum of their individual production. They agree to team-produce light bulbs, sell them, and split the proceeds five equal ways. On an average day, they produce 140 light bulbs and sell each one for $2. Total revenue per day is $280, with each of the five team members receiving $56. Then Carl begins to shirk. Owing to his shirking, production falls to 135 light bulbs per day, and total revenue falls to $270 per day. Each person now receives $54. Notice that while Carl did all the shirking, Carl's reduction in pay was only $2, one-fifth of the $10 drop in total revenue.

In situations (such as team production) where one person receives all the benefits from shirking and pays only a part of the costs, economists predict there will be more shirking than when the person who shirks bears the full cost of shirking.

THE MONITOR (MANAGER): TAKING CARE OF SHIRKING The **monitor** (or manager) plays an important role in the firm. The monitor reduces the amount of shirking by firing shirkers and rewarding the productive members of the firm. In doing this, the monitor can preserve the benefits that often come with team production (increased output) and reduce, if not eliminate, the costs associated with team production (increased shirking). But then the question is who or what monitors the monitor? How can the monitor be kept from shirking?

Market Coordination
The process in which individuals perform tasks, such as producing certain quantities of goods, based on changes in market forces, such as supply, demand, and price.

Managerial Coordination
The process in which managers direct employees to perform certain tasks.

Shirking
The behavior of a worker who is putting forth less than the agreed-on effort.

Monitor
A person in a business firm who coordinates team production and reduces shirking.

---

1. Armen Alchian and Harold Demsetz, "Production, Information Costs, and Economic Organization," *American Economic Review* 62 (December 1972): 777–795.

Residual Claimants
Persons who share in the profits of a business firm.

One possibility is to give the monitor an incentive not to shirk by making him or her a **residual claimant** of the firm. A residual claimant receives the excess of revenues over costs (profits) as income. If the monitor shirks, then profits are likely to be lower (or even zero or negative), and therefore the monitor will receive less income.

Finding ECONOMICS

In a Classroom Project

Terry's sociology professor has broken her sociology class into teams of five persons each. Each team has to research a particular topic, write a 10-page paper, and then present the paper to the class. The grade that the paper and presentation receive will be the same grade that each member of the team receives for the assignment. Terry has been complaining recently that two of the members in particular don't make the team meetings regularly and are not doing their share of the assignment. Where is the economics here?

It sounds as though at least two team members are shirking. Shirking often happens in team environments where no one monitors the team or where there is no residual claimant. When the cost of shirking is spread over the entire team, instead of being incurred only by the person who shirks, there will be more shirking than when the shirker feels the full cost of his or her shirking.

Common MISCONCEPTIONS

About the Employee-Employer Relationship

Employees may often complain about their bosses. "He is a stickler when it comes to getting to work on time." "I am not sure she knows what she is doing. She fired someone the other day without having a good reason." Sometimes employees even suggest that they may be better off without a boss. They suggest running things democratically. But things may not turn out as they would like. Without a boss—without a monitor who is a residual claimant—shirking may rise to the degree that all team members are worse off than they would be with a boss.

Ronald Coase on Why Firms Exist

Ronald Coase, winner of the 1991 Nobel Prize in Economics, argued that "the main reason why it is profitable to establish a firm would seem to be that there is a cost of using the price mechanism."[2] Stated differently, firms exist either to economize on buying and selling everything or to reduce transaction costs.

For example, suppose it takes 20 different operations to produce good X. One way to produce good X, then, is to enter into a separate contract with everyone necessary to complete the 20 different operations. If we assume that one person completes one and only one operation, then we have 20 different contracts. Obviously, costs are associated with preparing and monitoring all these contracts. A firm is a recipe for reducing these costs, effectively replacing many contracts with one.

Here is what Coase had to say:

> *The costs of negotiating and concluding a separate contract for each exchange transaction which takes place on a market must also be taken into account. . . . It is true that contracts are not eliminated when there is a firm, but they are greatly reduced. A factor of production (or the owner thereof) does not have to make a series of contracts as would be necessary, of*

---

2. Ronald Coase, "The Nature of the Firm," *Economica,* November 1937.

course, if this co-operation were a direct result of the working of the price mechanism. For this series of contracts is substituted one. At this state, it is important to note the character of the contract into which a factor enters that is employed within a firm. The contract is one whereby the factor [the employee], for a certain remuneration (which may be fixed or fluctuating), agrees to obey the directions of an entrepreneur within certain limits.[3]

Markets: Outside and Inside the Firm

When we put the firm under the microeconomic microscope, basically we see a market of sorts at work. Economics is largely about trades or exchanges; it is about market transactions. In supply-and-demand analysis, the exchanges are between the buyers of goods and services and the sellers of goods and services. In the theory of the firm, the exchanges take place at two levels: (1) at the level of individuals coming together to form a team and (2) at the level of workers choosing a monitor.

Let's look at the theory of the firm in the context of exchange. Individuals initially come together because they realize that the sum of what they can produce as a team is greater than the sum of what they can produce as individuals. In essence, each individual trades working alone for working in a team. Later, after the team has been formed, the team members learn that shirking reduces the amount of the added output they came together to capture in the first place. Now the team members enter into another trade or market transaction. They trade some control over their daily behavior—specifically, they trade an environment in which the cost of shirking is low for an environment in which the cost of shirking is high—to receive a larger absolute amount of the potential benefits that drew them together. In this trade the monitor appears: Some individuals buy the monitoring services that other individuals sell.

As you continue your study of microeconomics, look for the markets that appear at different levels of analysis.

THE FIRM'S OBJECTIVE: MAXIMIZING PROFIT

Firms produce goods to sell them. Economists assume that a firm's objective in producing and selling goods is to maximize profit. **Profit** is the difference between total revenue and total cost.

Profit
The difference between total revenue and total cost.

$$\text{Profit} = \text{Total revenue} - \text{Total cost}$$

Total revenue is equal to the price of a good multiplied by the quantity of the good sold. For example, if a business firm sells 100 units of X at $10 per unit, its total revenue is $1,000. However, a disagreement sometimes arises as to what total cost should include. To illustrate, suppose Jill currently works as an attorney earning $80,000 a year. One day, dissatisfied with her career, Jill quits her job as an attorney and opens a pizzeria. After one year of operating the pizzeria, Jill sits down to compute her profit. She sold 20,000 pizzas at a price of $10 per pizza; so her total revenue (for the year) is $200,000. Jill computes her total costs by adding the dollar amounts she spent for everything she bought or rented to run the pizzeria. She spent $2,000 on plates, $3,000 on cheese, $4,000 on soda, $20,000 for rent in the mall where the pizzeria is located, $2,000 for electricity, and so on. The dollar payments Jill made for everything she bought or rented are called her *explicit costs*. An **explicit cost** is a cost that is incurred when an actual (monetary) payment is made. So Jill sums her explicit costs, which turn out to be $90,000. Then she computes her profit by subtracting $90,000 from $200,000, giving her a profit of $110,000.

Explicit Cost
A cost incurred when an actual (monetary) payment is made.

---

3. Ibid.

A few days pass before Jill tells her friend Marian that she earned a $110,000 profit her first year of running the pizzeria. Marian asks, "Are you sure your profit is $110,000?" Jill assures her that it is. "Did you count the salary you earned as an attorney as a cost?" Marian asks. Jill tells Marian that she did not count the $80,000 salary as a cost of running the pizzeria because the $80,000 is not something she paid out to run the pizzeria. "I wrote a check to my suppliers for the pizza ingredients, soda, dishes, and so on," Jill says, "but I didn't write a check to anyone for the $80,000."

Marian says that, although Jill did not pay out $80,000 in salary to run the pizzeria, still she forfeited $80,000 to run it. "What you could have earned but didn't is a cost to you of running the pizzeria," says Marian.

Jill's $80,000 salary is what economists call an *implicit cost*. An **implicit cost** is a cost that represents the value of resources used in production for which no actual (monetary) payment is made. It is a cost incurred as a result of a firm's using resources that it owns or that the owners of the firm contribute to it.

If total cost is computed as explicit costs plus implicit costs, then Jill's total cost of running the pizzeria is $90,000 plus $80,000, or $170,000. Subtracting $170,000 from a total revenue of $200,000 leaves a profit of $30,000.

Implicit Cost
A cost that represents the value of resources used in production for which no actual (monetary) payment is made.

Thinking like AN ECONOMIST

What Does the Person "Give Up"?

The economist wants to know what a person gives up when she goes into business for herself. What she gives up isn't only the money she pays for resources (to run the business), but also the job she would have had (and the income she would have earned) had she not gone into business for herself.

Accounting Profit Versus Economic Profit

Economists refer to the first profit that Jill calculated ($110,000) as *accounting profit*. **Accounting profit** is the difference between total revenue and total cost, where total cost equals explicit costs [see Exhibit 1(a)].

$$\text{Accounting profit} = \text{Total revenue} - \text{Total cost (Explicit costs)}$$

Economists refer to the second profit calculated ($30,000) as *economic profit*. **Economic profit** is the difference between total revenue and total cost, where total cost equals the sum of explicit and implicit costs [see Exhibit 1(b)].

$$\text{Economic profit} = \text{Total revenue} - \text{Total cost (Explicit costs + Implicit costs)}$$

To illustrate the difference between explicit and implicit costs, suppose a person has $100,000 in the bank, earning an interest rate of 5 percent a year. This amounts to $5,000 in interest a year. Now suppose the person takes the $100,000 out of the bank to start a business. The $5,000 in *lost interest* is included in the implicit costs of owning and operating the firm. To see why, let's change the example somewhat. Assume the person does not use her $100,000 in the bank to start a business but leaves it in the bank and instead takes out a $100,000 loan at an interest rate of 5 percent. The interest she has to pay on the loan—$5,000 a year—certainly would be an explicit cost and would take away from overall profit. It just makes sense, then, to count

Accounting Profit
The difference between total revenue and explicit costs.

Economic Profit
The difference between total revenue and total cost, including both explicit and implicit costs.

exhibit 1

Accounting and Economic Profit

Accounting profit equals total revenue minus explicit costs. Economic profit equals total revenue minus both explicit and implicit costs.

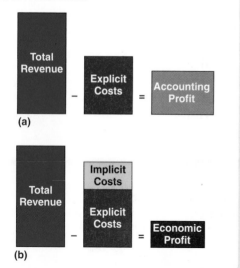

the $5,000 interest that the owner doesn't earn if she uses her own $100,000 to start the business (instead of taking out a loan) as a cost, albeit implicit.

Zero Economic Profit Is Not as Bad as It Sounds

Economic profit is usually lower (never higher) than accounting profit. Whereas economic profit is the difference between total revenue and total cost (where total cost is the sum of explicit and implicit costs), accounting profit is the difference between total revenue and only explicit costs. Thus, a firm could earn both a positive accounting profit and a zero economic profit. In economics, a firm that makes a zero economic profit is said to be earning a **normal profit**.

Normal profit = Zero economic profit

However, the owner of a firm should not be worried about making zero economic profit for the year just ending. A zero economic profit—as bad as it may sound—means the owner has generated total revenue sufficient to cover total cost—that is, *both explicit and implicit costs*. If, for example, the owner's implicit cost is a (forfeited) $100,000 salary working for someone else, then earning a zero economic profit means he has done as well as he could have done in his next best (alternative) line of employment.

When we realize that zero economic profit (or normal profit) means doing as well as could have been done, we understand that it isn't bad to make zero economic profit. Zero accounting profit, however, is altogether different; it implies that some part of total cost has not been covered by total revenue.

Normal Profit
Zero economic profit. A firm that earns normal profit is earning revenue equal to its total costs (explicit plus implicit costs). This is the level of profit necessary to keep resources employed in the firm.

Finding ECONOMICS

In a Sports Bar

Frank is sitting at the bar watching the game on the nearby television set. The bartender asks him whether he wants another drink, and he says yes. The bartender and Frank start talking, and Frank learns that the bartender owns the bar. In fact, he opened up the bar ten years ago. Is it more likely that, before the bartender opened up the bar, he was working at a high-paying job or at a medium-paying job? Is there any economics here?

Think implicit costs. There are benefits to the bartender of owning and operating a sports bar, but there are costs too. Some costs are explicit (rent for the bar, pretzels, TV sets, beer, etc.), and some are implicit (specifically, the salary he earned in the job he had before he was the owner and bartender). The higher those implicit costs are, the less likely it is that the bartender would have quit the job to open a sports bar.

SELF-TEST

(Answers to Self-Test questions are in the Self-Test Appendix.)

1. Will individuals form teams or firms in all settings?
2. Suppose everything about two people is the same except that currently one person earns a high salary and the other person earns a low salary. Which is more likely to start his or her own business and why?
3. Is accounting or economic profit larger? Why?
4. When can a business owner be earning a profit but not covering costs?

PRODUCTION

Production is a transformation of resources or inputs into goods and services. You may think of production as you might think of making a cake. It takes certain ingredients to make a cake—sugar, flour, and so on. Similarly, it takes certain resources, or inputs, to produce a computer, a haircut, a piece of furniture, or a house.

Economists often talk about two types of inputs in the production process: fixed and variable. A **fixed input** is an input whose quantity cannot be changed as output changes. To illustrate, suppose the McMahon and McGee Bookshelf Company has rented a factory under a six-month lease: McMahon and McGee, the owners of the company, have contracted to pay the $2,500 monthly rent for six months—no matter what. Whether McMahon and McGee produce one bookshelf or 7,000, the $2,500 rent for the factory must be paid. The factory is a fixed input in the production process of bookshelves.

A **variable input** is an input whose quantity can be changed as output changes. Examples of variable inputs for the McMahon and McGee Bookshelf Company include wood, paint, nails, and so on. These inputs can (and most likely will) change as the production of bookshelves changes. As they produce more bookshelves, McMahon and McGee purchase more of these inputs; as they produce fewer bookshelves, they purchase fewer of these inputs. Labor might also be a variable input for McMahon and McGee. As they produce more bookshelves, they might hire more employees; as they produce fewer bookshelves, they might lay off some.

If any of the inputs of a firm are fixed inputs, then it is said to be producing in the *short run*. In other words, the **short run** is a period of time in which some inputs are fixed.

If none of the inputs of a firm is a fixed input—if all inputs are variable—then the firm is said to be producing in the *long run*. In other words, the **long run** is a period of time in which all inputs can be varied (no inputs are fixed).

When firms produce goods and services and then sell them, they necessarily incur costs. In this section, we discuss the production activities of the firm in the short run, leading to the law of diminishing marginal returns and marginal costs. In the next section, we tie the production of the firm to all the costs of production in the short run. We then turn to an analysis of production in the long run.

Fixed Input
An input whose quantity cannot be changed as output changes.

Variable Input
An input whose quantity can be changed as output changes.

Short Run
A period of time in which some inputs in the production process are fixed.

Long Run
A period of time in which all inputs in the production process can be varied (no inputs are fixed).

Common MISCONCEPTIONS

About the Short Run and Long Run

Individuals naturally think that the long run is a longer period of time than the short run. For example, if the short run is 6 months, then the long run is, say, 10 months. But this is not the right way to differentiate the short run from the long run. Think of each as a period of time during which some condition exists. The short run is the period of time during which at least one input is fixed, and it could be a period of 6 months, 2 years, and so on. The long run is not necessarily longer in months and years than the short run. It is simply the period of time during which all inputs are variable (i.e., no input is fixed). In terms of days, weeks, and months, the short run could be a longer period of time than the long run.

Production in the Short Run

Suppose two inputs (or resources), labor and capital, are used to produce some good. Furthermore, suppose one of those inputs—capital—is fixed. Obviously, because an input is fixed, the firm is producing in the short run.

In Exhibit 2, column 1 shows the units of the fixed input, capital (fixed at 1 unit). Column 2 shows different units of the variable input, labor. Notice that we go from 0

exhibit 2

(1) Fixed Input, Capital (units)	(2) Variable Input, Labor (workers)	(3) Quantity of Output, Q (units)	(4) Marginal Physical Product of Variable Input (units) Δ(3)/Δ(2)
1	0	0	18
1	1	18	19
1	2	37	20
1	3	57	19
1	4	76	18
1	5	94	17
1	6	111	16
1	7	127	10
1	8	137	−4
1	9	133	−8
1	10	125	

Production in the Short Run and the Law of Diminishing Marginal Returns

In the short run, as additional units of a variable input are added to a fixed input, the marginal physical product of the variable input may increase at first. Eventually, the marginal physical product of the variable input decreases. The point at which marginal physical product decreases is the point at which diminishing marginal returns have set in.

(no workers) through 10 units (10 workers). Column 3 shows the quantities of output produced with 1 unit of capital and different amounts of labor. (The quantity of output is sometimes referred to as the *total physical product,* or *TPP.*) For example, 1 unit of capital and 0 units of labor produce 0 output; 1 unit of capital and 1 unit of labor produce 18 units of output; 1 unit of capital and 2 units of labor produce 37 units of output; 1 unit of capital and 3 units of labor produce 57 units of output; and so on.

Column 4 shows the marginal physical product of the variable input. The **marginal physical product (MPP)** of a variable input is equal to the change in output that results from changing the variable input by one unit, *holding all other inputs fixed.* Because in our example the variable input is labor, we are talking about the *MPP* of labor. Specifically, the *MPP* of labor is equal to the change in output, Q, that results from changing labor, L, by one unit, *holding all other inputs fixed.* Notice that the marginal physical product of labor first rises (from 18 to 19 to 20), then falls (from 20 to 19 to 18 to 17 to 16 to 10), and then becomes negative (−4 and −8). When the *MPP* is rising, we say there is increasing *MPP,* when it is falling, there is diminishing *MPP,* and when it is negative, there is negative *MPP.*

Focus on the point at which the *MPP* first begins to decline—with the addition of the fourth worker. The point at which the marginal physical product of labor first declines is the point at which diminishing marginal returns are said to have set in. Diminishing marginal returns are common in production—so common, in fact, that economists refer to the **law of diminishing marginal returns** (or the law of diminishing marginal product). The law of diminishing marginal returns states that *as ever larger amounts of a variable input are combined with fixed inputs, eventually the marginal physical product of the variable input will decline.*

The question is why the *MPP* of the variable input eventually declines. To answer this question, think of adding agricultural workers (variable input) to 10 acres of land (fixed input). The workers must clear the land, plant the crop, and then harvest the crop. In the early stages of adding labor to the land, perhaps the *MPP* rises or remains constant. But eventually, as we continue to add more workers to the land, it becomes overcrowded with workers. Workers are stepping around each other, stepping on the crops, and so on. Because of these problems, output growth begins to slow.

It may seem strange that the firm in Exhibit 2 would ever hire beyond the third worker. After all, the *MPP* of labor is at its highest (20) with the third worker. Why hire

Marginal Physical Product (MPP)

The change in output that results from changing the variable input by one unit, holding all other inputs fixed.

Law of Diminishing Marginal Returns

As ever larger amounts of a variable input are combined with fixed inputs, eventually the marginal physical product of the variable input will decline.

the fourth worker if the *MPP* of labor is going to fall to 19? The firm may hire the fourth worker because the worker adds output. It would be one thing if the quantity of output were 57 units with three workers and fell to 55 units with the addition of the fourth worker, but this isn't the case. With the addition of the fourth worker, output rises from 57 units to 76 units. The firm has to ask and answer two questions: (1) What can the additional 19 units of output be sold for? (2) What does it cost to hire the fourth worker? Suppose the additional 19 units can be sold for $100, and it costs the firm $70 to hire the fourth worker. In that case, hiring the fourth worker makes sense.

Thinking like AN ECONOMIST

Comparing One Thing to Another

In economics, when making decisions, you usually compare one thing to something else. To illustrate, suppose you need to decide how much time to devote to studying. Would you consider just the additional benefits of spending more time studying, or would you consider the additional costs of spending more time studying too? You would want to consider both.

Similarly, when a firm has to decide how many workers to hire, it wouldn't consider only the additional benefits of hiring more workers (as measured by their additional output times the price the additional output could be sold for). Instead, it would consider the additional benefits against the additional costs of hiring more workers.

Common MISCONCEPTIONS

Whose Marginal Productivity We Are Talking About

Look back at Exhibit 2, and note the data that follows the fourth worker. When the fourth worker is added, the quantity of output rises from 57 units to 76 units. Also, marginal productivity is 19 units. It is easy to fall into the trap of believing that 19 units is the marginal productivity of the fourth worker, but this is a misreading of the data. It's not as though the fourth worker walks through the door, and we attach the number "19" to him. Instead, 19 is the marginal productivity of labor when there are four workers working with the one (fixed) unit of capital. The number can be as easily attached to the first, second, or third worker as it can be to the fourth worker.

Marginal Physical Product and Marginal Cost

A firm's costs are tied to its production. Specifically, the *marginal cost* (*MC*) of producing a good is a reflection of the marginal physical product (*MPP*) of the variable input. Our objective in this section is to prove that this statement is true. Before doing so, we need to define and discuss some economic cost concepts.

SOME ECONOMIC COST CONCEPTS Certainly, a cost is incurred whenever a fixed input or variable input is employed in the production process. The costs associated with fixed inputs are called **fixed costs**. The costs associated with variable inputs are called **variable costs**.

Because the quantity of a fixed input does not change as output changes, neither do fixed costs. Payments for such things as fire insurance (the same amount every month), liability insurance, and the rental of a factory and machinery are usually considered fixed costs. Whether the business produces 1, 10, 100, or 1,000 units of output, the rent for its factory is not likely to change. The rent is whatever amount was agreed to with the owner of the factory for the duration of the rental agreement.

Fixed Costs
Costs that do not vary with output; the costs associated with fixed inputs.

Variable Costs
Costs that vary with output; the costs associated with variable inputs.

Because the quantity of a variable input changes with output, so do variable costs. For example, it takes labor, wood, and glue to produce wooden bookshelves. The quantity of all these inputs (labor, wood, and glue) changes as the number of wooden bookshelves produced changes.

The sum of fixed costs and variable costs is **total cost (TC)**. If total fixed costs (TFC) are $100 and total variable costs (TVC) are $300, then total cost ($TC$) is $400.

$$TC = TFC + TVC$$

Given total cost, we can formally define marginal cost. **Marginal cost (MC)** is the change in total cost, TC, that results from a change in output, Q.

$$MC = \frac{\Delta TC}{\Delta Q}$$

Total Cost (TC)
The sum of fixed costs and variable costs.

Marginal Cost (MC)
The change in total cost that results from a change in output: $MC = \Delta TC/\Delta Q$.

THE LINK BETWEEN MPP AND MC In Exhibit 3, we establish the link between the marginal physical product of a variable input and marginal cost. The first four columns present much of the same data first presented in Exhibit 2. Essentially, column 3 shows the different quantities of output produced by 1 unit of capital (fixed input) and various amounts of labor (variable input), and column 4 shows the MPP of labor. Exhibit 3(a)

exhibit 3

Marginal Physical Product and Marginal Cost

(a) The marginal physical product of labor curve. The curve is derived by plotting the data from columns 2 and 4 in the exhibit.
(b) The marginal cost curve. The curve is

derived by plotting the data from columns 3 and 8 in the exhibit. Notice that as the MPP curve rises, the MC curve falls; and as the MPP curve falls, the MC curve rises.

(1) Fixed Input, Capital (units)	(2) Variable Input, Labor (workers)	(3) Quantity of Output, Q (units)	(4) Marginal Physical Product of Variable Input (units) Δ(3)/Δ(2)	(5) Total Fixed Cost (dollars)	(6) Total Variable Cost (dollars)	(7) Total Cost (dollars) (5) + (6)	(8) Marginal cost (dollars) Δ(7)/Δ(3)
1	0	0	18	$40	$ 0	$ 40	$1.11
1	1	18	19	40	20	60	$1.05
1	2	37	20	40	40	80	$1.00
1	3	57	19	40	60	100	$1.05
1	4	76	18	40	80	120	$1.11
1	5	94	17	40	100	140	$1.17
1	6	111	16	40	120	160	$1.25
1	7	127		40	140	180	

(a)

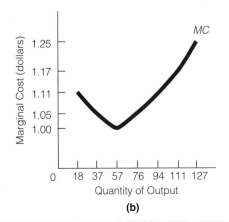

(b)

shows the *MPP* curve, which is based on the data in column 4. Notice that the *MPP* curve first rises and then falls.

In column 5, we have identified the total fixed cost (*TFC*) of production as $40. (Recall that fixed costs do not change as output changes.) For column 6, we have assumed that each worker is hired for $20; so when there is only 1 worker, total variable cost (*TVC*) is $20; when there are 2 workers, total variable cost is $40; and so on. Column 7 shows total cost at various output levels; the total cost figures in this column are simply the sum of the fixed costs in column 5 and the variable costs in column 6. Finally, in column 8, we compute marginal cost. Exhibit 3(b) shows the *MC* curve, which is based on the data in column 8.

Columns 4 and 8 show the *MPP* and *MC,* respectively. Notice that when the *MPP* is rising (from 18 to 19 to 20), marginal cost is decreasing (from $1.11 to $1.05 to $1.00), and when the *MPP* is falling (from 20 to 19, etc.), marginal cost is increasing (from $1.00 to $1.05, etc.). In other words, the *MPP* and *MC* move in opposite directions. You can also see this by comparing the *MPP* curve with the *MC* curve. When the *MPP* curve is going up, the *MC* curve is moving down, and when the *MPP* curve is going down, the *MC* curve is going up. Of course, all this is common sense: As marginal physical product rises—or, to put it differently, as the productivity of the variable input rises—we would expect costs to decline. And as the productivity of the variable input declines, we would expect costs to rise.

In conclusion, then, what the *MC* curve looks like depends on what the *MPP* curve looks like. Recall that the *MPP* curve must have a declining portion because of the law of diminishing marginal returns. So if the *MPP* curve first rises and then (when diminishing marginal returns set in) falls, the *MC* curve must first fall and then rise.

ANOTHER WAY TO LOOK AT THE RELATIONSHIP BETWEEN *MPP* AND *MC*

An easy way to see that marginal physical product and marginal cost move in *opposite directions* is to reexamine the definition of marginal cost (the change in total cost divided by the change in output). The change in total cost is the additional cost of an additional unit of the variable input (see Exhibit 3). The change in output is the marginal physical product of the variable input. Thus, marginal cost is equal to the additional cost of an additional unit of the variable input divided by the input's marginal physical product. In Exhibit 3, the variable input is labor; so $MC = W/MPP$, where MC = marginal cost, W = wage, and MPP = marginal physical product of labor. The following table reproduces column 4 from Exhibit 3, notes the wage, and computes MC using the equation $MC = W/MPP$.

MPP	Variable Cost (*W*)	*W/MPP = MC*
18 units	$20	$20/18 = $1.11
19	20	20/19 = 1.05
20	20	20/20 = 1.00
19	20	20/19 = 1.05
18	20	20/18 = 1.11
17	20	20/17 = 1.17
16	20	20/16 = 1.25

Now compare the marginal cost figures in the last column in the table with the marginal cost figures in column 8 of Exhibit 3. Whether marginal cost is defined as equal to $\Delta TC/\Delta Q$ or as equal to W/MPP, the result is the same. The latter way of defining marginal cost, however, explicitly shows that as *MPP* rises, *MC* falls and that as *MPP* falls, *MC* rises.

$$\frac{W}{MPP \uparrow} = MC \downarrow$$

$$\frac{W}{MPP \downarrow} = MC \uparrow$$

economics 24/7

HIGH SCHOOL STUDENTS, STAYING OUT LATE, AND MORE

Can marginal cost affect a person's behavior? Let's analyze two different situations in which it might.

High School Students and Staying Out Late

A 16-year-old high school student asks her parents if she can have the car tonight. She says she plans to go with some friends to a concert. Her parents ask what time she will get home. She says that she plans to be back by midnight.

The girl's parents tell her that she can have the car and that they expect her home by midnight. If she's late, she will lose her driving privileges for a week.

Later that night, it is midnight and the 16-year-old is 15 minutes away from home. When she realizes she can't get home until 12:15 a.m., will she continue on home? She may not. The marginal cost of staying out later is now zero. In short, whether she arrives home at 12:15, 1:15, or 2:25, the punishment is the same: She will lose her driving privileges for a week. There is no additional cost for staying out an additional minute or an additional hour. There may, however, be additional benefits. Her punishment places a zero marginal cost on staying out after midnight. Once midnight has come and gone, the additional cost of staying out later is zero.

No doubt her parents would prefer her to get home at, say, 12:01 rather than at 1:01 or even later. If this is the case, then they should not have made the marginal cost of staying out after midnight zero. They should have increased the marginal cost of staying out late for every minute (or 15-minute period) that the 16-year-old was late. In other words, one of the parents might have said, "For the first 15 minutes you're late, you'll lose 1 hour of driving privileges, for the second 15 minutes you're late, you'll lose 2 hours of driving privileges, and so on." This would have presented our teen with a rising marginal cost of staying out late. With a rising marginal cost, it is more likely she will get home close to midnight.

Crime

Suppose that the sentence for murder in the first degree is life imprisonment, that the sentence for burglary is 10 years, and that the burglary rate has skyrocketed in the past few months. Many of the city residents have become alarmed, calling on the police and other local and state officials to do something about the rising burglary rate.

Someone proposes that the way to lower the burglary rate is to increase the punishment for it. Instead of only 10 years in prison, make the punishment stiffer. In his zeal to reduce the burglary rate, a state legislator proposes that burglary carry the same punishment as first-degree murder: life in prison. That will certainly get the burglary rate down, he argues. After all, who will take the chance of committing a burglary knowing that if he gets caught and convicted, he will spend the rest of his days in prison?

Unfortunately, by making the punishment for burglary and murder the same, the marginal cost of murdering someone while burglarizing a home falls to zero. To illustrate, suppose Smith is burglarizing a home and the residents walk in on him. Realizing the residents can identify him as the burglar, Smith shoots and kills them. If he gets apprehended for burglary, the penalty is the same as it is for murder. Raising the cost of burglary from 10 years to life imprisonment may reduce the number of burglaries, but it may have the unintended effect of also raising the murder rate.

Average Productivity

When the press or laypersons use the word *productivity*, they are usually referring to *average physical product* instead of *marginal physical product*. To illustrate the difference, suppose 1 worker can produce 10 units of output a day and 2 workers can produce 18 units of output a day. Marginal physical product is 8 units (*MPP* of labor = $\Delta Q/\Delta L$). Average physical product, which is output divided by the quantity of labor, is equal to 9 units.

$$AP \text{ of labor} = \frac{Q}{L}$$

Usually, when the term *labor productivity* is used in the newspaper and in government documents, it refers to the average (physical) productivity of labor on an hourly basis. By computing the average productivity of labor for different countries and noting the annual percentage changes, we can compare labor productivity between and within countries.

Government statisticians have chosen 1992 as a benchmark year (a year against which we measure other years). They have also set a productivity index (a measure of productivity) for 1992 equal to 100. By computing a productivity index for other years and noting whether each index is above, below, or equal to 100, they know whether productivity is rising, falling, or remaining constant, respectively. Finally, by computing the percentage change in productivity indexes from one year to the next, they know the rate at which productivity is changing.

Suppose the productivity index for the United States is 120 in year 1 and 125 in year 2. Because the productivity index is higher in year 2 than in year 1, labor productivity increased over the year; that is, output produced increased per hour of labor expended.

SELF-TEST

1. If the short run is 6 months, does it follow that the long run is longer than 6 months? Explain your answer.

2. "As we add more capital to more labor, eventually the law of diminishing marginal returns will set in." What is wrong with this statement?

3. Suppose a marginal cost (*MC*) curve falls when output is in the range of 1 unit to 10 units. Then it flattens out and remains constant over an output range of 10 units to 20 units, and then rises over a range of 20 units to 30 units. What does this have to say about the marginal physical product (*MPP*) of the variable input?

exhibit 4

Total, Average, and Marginal Costs

TFC equals $100 (column 2) and *TVC* is as noted in column 4. From the data, we calculate *AFC, AVC, TC, ATC*, and *MC*. The curves associated with *TFC, AFC, TVC, AVC, TC, ATC*, and *MC* are shown in diagrams at the bottom of the corresponding columns. (Note: Scale is not the same for all diagrams.)

(1) Quantity of Output, Q (units)	(2) Total Fixed Cost (TFC)	(3) Average Fixed Cost (AFC) AFC = TFC/Q = (2)/(1)	(4) Total Variable Cost (TVC)	(5) Average Variable Cost (AVC) AVC = TVC/Q = (4)/(1)
0	$100	—	$ 0	—
1	100	$100.00	50	$50.00
2	100	50.00	80	40.00
3	100	33.33	100	33.33
4	100	25.00	110	27.50
5	100	20.00	130	26.00
6	100	16.67	160	26.67
7	100	14.28	200	28.57
8	100	12.50	250	31.25
9	100	11.11	310	34.44
10	100	10.00	380	38.00

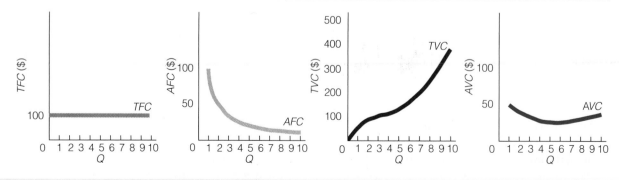

Costs of Production: Total, Average, Marginal

Continuing our discussion of the costs of production, the easiest way to see the relationships among the various costs is with the example in Exhibit 4.

Column 1 of Exhibit 4 shows the various quantities of output, ranging from 0 units to 10 units.

Column 2 shows the total fixed costs of production with *TFC* set at $100. Recall that fixed costs do not change as output changes. Therefore, *TFC* is $100 when output is 0 units, 1 unit, or 2 units, and so on. Because *TFC* does not change as *Q* changes, the *TFC* curve in the exhibit is a horizontal line at $100.

In column 3, we have computed **average fixed cost (AFC)**, which is total fixed cost divided by quantity of output.

$$AFC = \frac{TFC}{Q}$$

For example, look at the fourth entry in column 3. To get a dollar amount of $33. 33, we simply took *TFC* at 3 units of output, which is $100, and divided by 3. Notice that the *AFC* curve in the exhibit continually declines.

Average Fixed Cost (AFC)
Total fixed cost divided by quantity of output: AFC = TFC/Q.

exhibit 4

Continued

(6) Total Cost (TC) TC = TFC + TVC = (2) + (4)	(7) Average Total Cost (ATC) ATC = TC/Q = (6)/(1)	(8) Marginal Cost (MC) MC = ΔTC/ΔQ = Δ(6)/Δ(1)
$100.00	—	—
150.00	$150.00	$50.00
180.00	90.00	30.00
200.00	66.67	20.00
210.00	52.50	10.00
230.00	46.00	20.00
260.00	43.33	30.00
300.00	42.86	40.00
350.00	43.75	50.00
410.00	45.56	60.00
480.00	48.00	70.00

Average Variable Cost (AVC)
Total variable cost divided by quantity of output: $AVC = TVC/Q$.

In column 4, we have simply entered some hypothetical data for total variable cost (*TVC*). The *TVC* curve in the exhibit rises because variable costs are likely to increase as output increases.

In column 5, we have computed **average variable cost (AVC)**, which is total variable cost divided by quantity of output.

$$AVC = \frac{TVC}{Q}$$

For example, look at the third entry in column 5. To get a dollar amount of $40.00, we simply took *TVC* at 2 units of output, which is $80, and divided by 2. Notice that the *AVC* curve declines and then rises.

Column 6 shows total cost (*TC*). Total cost is the sum of total variable cost and total fixed cost. Notice that the *TC* curve does not start at zero because, even when output is zero, there are some fixed costs. In this example, total fixed cost (*TFC*) at zero output is $100. The total cost (*TC*) curve must start at $100 instead of at $0.

Average Total Cost (ATC), or Unit Cost
Total cost divided by quantity of output: $ATC = TC/Q$.

Column 7 shows **average total cost (ATC)**, which is total cost divided by quantity of output. Average total cost is sometimes called *unit cost*.

$$ATC = \frac{TC}{Q}$$

Alternatively, we can say that *ATC* equals the sum of *AFC* and *AVC*.

$$ATC = AFC + AVC$$

To understand why this makes sense, remember that $TC = TFC + TVC$. Thus, if we divide all total magnitudes by quantity of output (*Q*), we necessarily get $ATC = AFC + AVC$. Notice that the *ATC* curve falls and then rises.

Column 8 shows marginal cost (*MC*), which is the change in total cost divided by the change in output.

$$MC = \frac{\Delta TC}{\Delta Q}$$

The *MC* curve has a declining portion and a rising portion. When *MC* is declining, the *MPP* is rising. When *MC* is rising, the *MPP* of the variable input is falling. Obviously, the low point on the *MC* curve is when diminishing marginal returns set in.

Thinking like AN ECONOMIST

Deducing Things from What Is Known

E conomists often deduce things from what they know, as we just did when discussing *MPP* and *MC*. Here is what we know: *MPP* and *MC* are inversely related; as *MPP* rises, *MC* falls, and as *MPP* falls, *MC* rises. When diminishing marginal returns kick in, *MPP* begins to decline. We deduce, then, that when diminishing marginal returns kick in, *MC* begins to rise.

Average-Marginal Rule
When the marginal magnitude is above the average magnitude, the average magnitude rises; when the marginal magnitude is below the average magnitude, the average magnitude falls.

The *AVC* and *ATC* Curves in Relation to the *MC* Curve

What do the average total and average variable cost curves look like in relation to the marginal cost curve? To explain, we need to discuss the **average-marginal rule**, which is best defined with an example.

Suppose that 20 persons are in a room and that each person weighs 170 pounds. Your task is to calculate the average weight. This is accomplished by adding the individual weights and dividing by 20. Obviously, this average weight will be 170 pounds. Now an additional person enters the room. We will refer to this additional person as the marginal (additional) person, and, we will call the additional weight he brings into the room the marginal weight.

Let's suppose the weight of the marginal person is 275 pounds. The average weight based on the 21 persons now in the room is 175 pounds. The new average weight is greater than the old average weight. The average weight was pulled up by the weight of the additional person. In short, *when the marginal magnitude is above the average magnitude, the average magnitude rises.* This is one part of the average-marginal rule.

Suppose the weight of the marginal person is less than the average weight of 170 pounds, such as 65 pounds. Then the new average is 165 pounds. In this case, the average weight was pulled down by the weight of the additional person. Thus, *when the marginal magnitude is below the average magnitude, the average magnitude falls.* This is the other part of the average-marginal rule.

$$\text{Marginal} < \text{Average} \rightarrow \text{Average} \downarrow$$
$$\text{Marginal} > \text{Average} \rightarrow \text{Average} \uparrow$$

We can apply the average-marginal rule to find out what the average total and average variable cost curves look like in relation to the marginal cost curve. The following analysis holds for both the average total cost curve and the average variable cost curve.

We reason that

1. if marginal cost is below (less than) average variable cost, average variable cost is falling; and

2. if marginal cost is above (greater than) average variable cost, average variable cost is rising.

This reasoning implies that the relationship between the average variable cost curve and the marginal cost curve must look like that in Exhibit 5(a). In region 1 of (a), marginal

exhibit 5

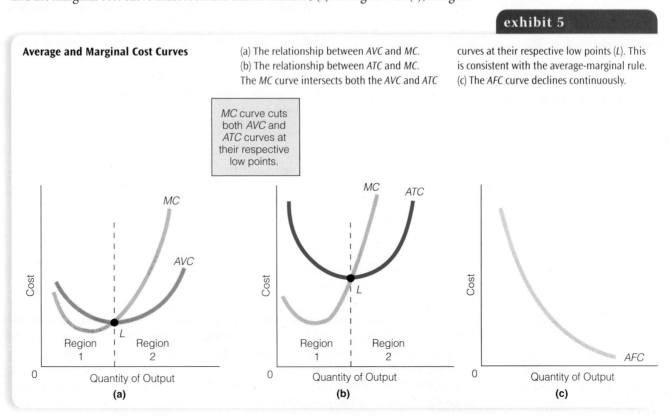

Average and Marginal Cost Curves

(a) The relationship between *AVC* and *MC*.
(b) The relationship between *ATC* and *MC*.
The *MC* curve intersects both the *AVC* and *ATC*

curves at their respective low points (*L*). This is consistent with the average-marginal rule.
(c) The *AFC* curve declines continuously.

MC curve cuts both *AVC* and *ATC* curves at their respective low points.

WHAT MATTERS TO GLOBAL COMPETITIVENESS?

What does a country need to do to be competitive in the global marketplace? The usual answer is that it needs to produce goods that people in other countries want to buy at prices they want to pay. For example, for the United States to be competitive in the global car and computer markets, U.S. firms must produce cars and computers at prices that people all over the world are willing and able to pay.

© IMAGE SOURCE/JUPITER IMAGES

Price is a major factor in the race to be competitive in the global market. If U.S. firms charge higher prices for their cars than German and Japanese firms charge for their similar-quality cars, then U.S. firms are unlikely to be competitive in the global car market. Therefore, if U.S. firms are to be competitive in the global market, they must keep their prices down, all other things equal.

But how do firms keep their prices down? One way is to keep their unit cost, or average total cost, down. Look at it this way:

Profit per unit = Price per unit − Unit cost (ATC)

The lower unit cost is, the lower price can go and still earn the producer/seller an acceptable profit per unit. That is, to be competitive on price, firms must be competitive on unit cost; they need to find ways to lower unit cost. This chapter shows how unit cost declines

when marginal cost (MC) is below unit cost (ATC). In other words, to lower ATC, marginal cost must fall and go below (current) average total cost.

But how do firms get MC to fall and eventually go below current ATC? This chapter also explains that, before MC can decline, marginal physical product (MPP) must rise.

To summarize, to be competitive in the global marketplace, U.S. firms must be competitive on price. To be competitive on price, firms must be competitive on unit cost (ATC). This requires firms to get their MC to decline and ultimately go below their current ATC. And the way to get MC to decline and go below current ATC is to raise the marginal productivity (MPP) of the inputs the firms use. To a large degree, the key to becoming or staying globally competitive is to find and implement ways to increase factor productivity.

How do you fit into the picture? Your education may affect the marginal physical product (MPP) of labor. As you learn more things and become more skilled (more productive)—and as many others do too—the MPP of labor in the United States rises. The rise in the MPP of labor, in turn, lowers firms' marginal cost, which ideally will decline enough to pull both average variable and average total costs down. As this happens, U.S. firms can become more competitive on price and still earn a profit.

---

cost is below average variable cost, and, consistent with the average-marginal rule, average variable cost is falling. In region 2 of (a), marginal cost is above average variable cost, and average variable cost is rising. In summary, the relationship between the average variable cost curve and the marginal cost curve in Exhibit 5(a) is consistent with the average-marginal rule.

In addition, because average variable cost is pulled down when marginal cost is below it and pulled up when marginal cost is above it, the marginal cost curve must intersect the average variable cost curve at the latter's lowest point. This lowest point is point L in Exhibit 5(a).

The same relationship that exists between the *MC* and *AVC* curves also exists between the *MC* and *ATC* curves, as shown in Exhibit 5(b). In region 1 of (b), marginal cost is below average total cost, and, consistent with the average-marginal rule, average total cost is falling. In region 2 of (b), marginal cost is above average total cost, and average total cost is rising. The marginal cost curve must therefore intersect the average total cost curve at the latter's lowest point.

There is no relationship between the average fixed cost curve and the marginal cost curve. We can indirectly see why by recalling that average fixed cost is simply total fixed cost (which is constant over output) divided by output ($AFC = TFC/Q$). As output (Q) increases and total fixed cost (TFC) remains constant, average fixed cost (TFC/Q) must decrease continuously [see Exhibit 5(c)].

Finding ECONOMICS

Why Doesn't Oliver Cheat?

Oliver is sitting in class taking a test, and his teacher is out of the class. He could easily look over at his neighbor's paper (which is uncovered) to see what the answer to question 25 is, but he doesn't. Why doesn't he cheat? Does it have anything to do with the average-marginal rule?

There may be a guilt cost to Oliver cheating, but let's ignore that reason for a moment. Even without a guilt cost and without the chance of being caught, Oliver may still not cheat for a reason that could have something to do with the average-marginal rule. People usually cheat by copying the work of someone they believe is smarter than they are. Suppose Oliver believes that his grade on the test will be 65 and that Ian (who is sitting next to him) will receive a grade of 60. Oliver's grade of 65 can be viewed as the average grade and Ian's as the marginal grade. Because the marginal grade is less than the average grade, the marginal will pull down the average. There's no need to cheat if copying someone else's work only lowers Oliver's grade. Oliver is more likely to cheat if he thinks cheating will raise his grade, but this can occur only if he cheats off a person whose grade is likely to be higher than his (when he doesn't cheat).

Tying Short-Run Production to Costs

To see how costs are tied to production, let's summarize some of our earlier discussions (see Exhibit 6). We assume production takes place in the short run; so there is at least one fixed input. Suppose we initially add units of a variable input to the fixed input, and the marginal physical product of the variable input (e.g., labor) rises. As a result of *MPP* rising, marginal cost (*MC*) falls. When *MC* has fallen enough to be below average variable cost (*AVC*), we know from the average-marginal rule that *AVC* will begin to decline. Also, when *MC* has fallen enough to be below average total cost (*ATC*), *ATC* will begin to decline.

exhibit 6

Tying Production to Costs

What happens in terms of production (*MPP* rising or falling) affects *MC*, which in turn eventually affects *AVC* and *ATC*.

Eventually, though, the law of diminishing marginal returns will set in. When this happens, the *MPP* of the variable input declines. As a result, *MC* rises. When *MC* has risen enough to be above *AVC*, *AVC* will rise. Also, when *MC* has risen enough to be above *ATC*, *ATC* will rise.

So what happens in terms of production (rising or falling *MPP*) affects *MC*, which in turn eventually affects *AVC* and *ATC*. In short, the cost of a good is tied to its production.

Thinking like AN ECONOMIST

Seeing How Things Came to Be

In economics, learning what comes before an event is important. To illustrate, suppose *ATC* is rising. Can you see the process that brought about this event (*ATC* rising) at this particular moment?

Let's take one step back at a time. *ATC* is rising because (one step back) *MC* rose to a level above *ATC*. But why did *MC* rise to a level above *ATC* or why is *MC* rising at all? *MC* is rising because *MPP* (one step back) is declining. But why is *MPP* declining? *MPP* is declining because (one step back) the law of diminishing marginal returns set in.

Looking at a tree, you see its branches and leaves. If you look back, though, you can see the seed that was planted and that grew into the tree. You can do the same in economics. When looking at rising *ATC*, most of us simply see rising *ATC*. But if you look far enough back, you can see the law of diminishing marginal returns growing into rising *ATC*.

One More Cost Concept: Sunk Cost

Sunk Cost
A cost incurred in the past that cannot be changed by current decisions and therefore cannot be recovered.

Sunk cost is a cost incurred in the past that cannot be changed by current decisions and therefore cannot be recovered. For example, suppose that a firm must purchase a $10,000 government license before it can legally produce and sell lamp poles and that the government will not buy back the license or allow it to be resold. The $10,000 the firm spends to purchase the license is a sunk cost. It is a cost that, after it has been incurred (the $10,000 was spent), cannot be changed by a current decision (the firm cannot go back into the past and undo what was done) and cannot be recovered (the government will neither buy back the license nor allow it to be resold).

Let's consider another example of a sunk cost. Suppose Jeremy buys a movie ticket, walks into the theater, and settles down to watch the movie. Thirty minutes into the movie, he realizes that he hates it. The money he paid for the ticket is a sunk cost. The cost was incurred in the past, it cannot be changed, and it cannot be recovered. (We are assuming that movie theaters do not give your money back if you dislike the movie.)

ECONOMISTS' ADVICE: IGNORE SUNK COSTS Economists advise individuals to ignore sunk costs. To illustrate, for Jeremy, who bought the movie ticket but dislikes the movie, the movie ticket is a sunk cost. Now suppose Jeremy says the following to himself as he is watching the movie:

I paid to watch this movie, but I really hate it. Should I get up and walk out or should I stay and watch the movie? I think I'll stay and watch the movie because if I leave, I'll lose the money I paid for the ticket.

The error that Jeremy is making is believing that if he walks out of the theater, he will lose the money he paid for the ticket. But he has already lost the money for the ticket. Whether he stays and watches the movie or leaves, the money is gone forever. It is a sunk cost.

An economist would advise Jeremy to ignore what has happened in the past and what can't be undone. In other words, ignore sunk costs. The question is not what have I already lost? Nothing can be done about what has already been lost. Instead, Jeremy should simply ask and answer these questions: What do I gain (what are my benefits) if I stay and watch the movie? What do I lose (what are my costs) if I stay and watch the movie? If what Jeremy expects to gain by staying and watching the movie is greater than what he expects to lose, he should stay and watch the movie. However, if what he expects to lose by staying and watching the movie is greater than what he expects to gain, he should leave.

To see this point more clearly, let's say that Jeremy has decided to stay and watch the movie because he doesn't want to lose the price of the movie ticket. Two minutes after he makes this decision, you walk up to him and offer him $200 to leave the theater. Do you think Jeremy will say, "I can't leave the movie theater because if I do, I will lose the price of the movie ticket"? Or do you think he is more likely to take the money and leave? Most people will say that Jeremy will take the $200 and leave the movie theater simply because if he doesn't leave, he loses the opportunity to receive $200.

However, wouldn't he have forfeited something—albeit not $200—if no one offered him $200 to leave? He might have given up at least $1 in benefits doing something else. In short, he must have had some opportunity cost of staying at the movie theater before the $200 was offered. The problem is that somehow, by letting sunk cost influence his decision, Jeremy was willing to ignore this opportunity cost of staying at the theater. The $200 offer only made this opportunity cost of staying at the movie theater obvious.

Consider another situation. Alicia purchases a pair of shoes on sale (no refunds), wears them for a few days, and then realizes they are uncomfortable. An economist would recommend that Alicia simply not wear the shoes. To an economist, the cost of the shoes is a sunk cost because it (1) was incurred in the past, (2) cannot be changed by a current decision, and (3) cannot be recovered. An economist would advise Alicia not to base her current decision as to whether to wear the shoes on what has happened and what cannot be changed. If Alicia lets what she has done and can't undo influence her present decision, she runs the risk of compounding her mistake.

To illustrate, if Alicia decides to wear the uncomfortable shoes because she thinks it is a waste of money not to, she may end up with an even bigger loss: certainly less comfort and possibly a trip to the podiatrist. The relevant question she must ask herself is not, "What did I give up by buying the shoes?" The right question is, "What will I give up by wearing the uncomfortable shoes?"

The message is that a present decision can affect only the future, never the past. Bygones are bygones; sunk costs are sunk costs.

BEHAVIORAL ECONOMICS AND SUNK COST In a real-life experiment, two researchers randomly distributed discounts to buyers of subscriptions to Ohio University's 1982–1983 theater season.[4] One group of ticket buyers paid the normal ticket price of $15 per ticket, a second group received $2 off per ticket, and a third group received $7 off per ticket. In short, some buyers paid lower ticket prices than others.

The researchers found that people who paid more for their tickets attended the theater performances more often than those who paid less. Some people argue that this is because the people who paid more for their tickets somehow wanted to attend the theater more than those who paid less. But this isn't likely because the discounts to buyers were distributed randomly. Instead, the case seems to be that the more someone paid for the ticket (and everyone paid for the ticket before the night of the performance), the greater the sunk

---

4. Hal Arkes and Catherine Blumer, "The Psychology of Sunk Cost," *Organizational Behavior and Human Decision Processes* 124 (1985).

"I HAVE TO BECOME AN ACCOUNTANT"

Hans: I don't like accounting, but I have to become an accountant.

Mike: Why?

Hans: Because I've spent four years in college studying accounting. I spent all that money and time on accounting; I have to get some benefits from it.

Mike: The money and time you spent on accounting are sunk costs. You can't get those back.

Hans: Sure I can. All I have to do is work as an accountant. I'll be earning a good income and making my college investment pay off.

Mike: It sounds to me as if you're letting your four years in college studying accounting determine what you will do for the rest of your working life. Why do that?

Hans: Because accounting is all I know how to do.

Mike: If you could do it over, what would you study and do?

Hans: I'd study English literature, and then I'd become a high school teacher.

Mike: Can't you still do that? You're only 24 years old.

Hans: Sure, but that would mean my last four years in college were completely wasted. I'm not going to waste them.

Mike: Again, you're letting your past determine what you do now and in the future.

Hans: It sounds like you're telling me to get out of accounting.

Mike: I'm not advising you to stay in or to get out of accounting. I'm simply saying that the time and money you spent getting a degree in accounting are sunk costs and that you shouldn't let sunk costs determine what you will do with your life.

Hans: It still seems as if you're advising me to get out of accounting.

Mike: But that's not true. I'm simply saying that you should look at the benefits and costs of being an accountant—starting at this moment in time. You shouldn't look over your shoulder and say that, just because you invested four years in accounting, you now have to become an accountant. Those four years are gone; you can never get them back. And you shouldn't try.

Hans: In other words, starting from this moment in time, I should ask myself what the costs and benefits are of becoming an accountant. If the costs are greater than the benefits, I should not become one, but if the benefits are greater than the costs, I should become one.

Mike: That's right. Let me put it to you this way. Suppose tomorrow the bottom fell out of the accounting market. Accountants couldn't earn even $100 a month. Would you still want to be an accountant?

cost was. And the greater the sunk cost, the more likely individuals were to attend the theater performance. In other words, at least some people were not ignoring sunk cost.

Thinking like AN ECONOMIST

Viewing Sunk Cost as a Constraint

Microeconomics emphasizes that all economic actors deal with objectives, constraints, and choices. Let's focus briefly on constraints. All economic actors would prefer to have fewer rather than more constraints and to have constraints that offer more rather than less latitude. For example, a firm would probably prefer to be constrained in having to buy its resources from five suppliers rather than from only one supplier. A consumer would rather have a budget constraint of $4,000 a month instead of $2,000 a month.

Person A considers sunk cost when she makes a decision, and person B ignores it when he makes a decision. Does one person face fewer constraints, *ceteris paribus*? The person who ignores sunk cost when making a decision, person B, faces fewer constraints. Person A acts as if a constraint is there—the constraint of sunk cost, the constraint of having to rectify a past decision—when it really exists only in person A's mind.

Hans: No way. It wouldn't make any sense. I couldn't earn enough income.

Mike: Well, if you wouldn't become an accountant because the benefits ($100 a month) are too low relative to the costs, doesn't it make sense not to become an accountant if the costs are too high relative to the benefits?

Hans: What do you mean?

Mike: Suppose the bottom does not fall out of the accounting market, and you can earn $4,000 a month working as an accountant. The question now is how much do you have to give up, say, in terms of less utility, to get the $4,000 a month? If you would be happy as an English literature teacher, although earning less than you would earn as an accountant, and unhappy as an accountant, then the cost of becoming an accountant and not a teacher may be more than $4,000 a month.

Hans: I agree that if I become an accountant, I will have to give up some happiness. But if I don't become an accountant and become a high school teacher instead, I will have to give up some income because I probably would earn less as a teacher than as an accountant. And by the way, income gives me some happiness.

Mike: I agree. But now you're at least looking at the choice you have to make without considering something in the past that you can't change—that is, studying accounting in college.

Hans: How so?

Mike: You're asking yourself what the benefits will be of becoming an accountant, and your answer seems to be the happiness or utility you'll receive from $4,000 a month. You're then asking yourself what the costs will be of becoming an accountant, and you seem to be saying that you'll have to forfeit some happiness. The question then becomes whether the $4,000 a month will provide you with enough utility to overcome the disutility you will feel because you're unhappy working as an accountant.

Hans: But by doing this, how am I ignoring sunk cost? All this seems to tell me is that economics is about utility, not money.

Mike: You're ignoring the sunk cost of obtaining an accounting degree because when you consider the costs of becoming an accountant, you're considering only what you will (in the future) give up if you become one. You're not considering what you already have (in the past) given up and that cannot be changed.

Hans: Are you suggesting that this is what I should do—consider only future costs, not sunk costs?

Mike: Yes, because you're better off not trying to change something that cannot be changed. You can't change the weather, and you shouldn't waste your time and energy trying. If you do try, you're forfeiting other things that you could be accomplishing.

Hans: In other words, I shouldn't try to get back the sunk costs I incurred getting an accounting degree because trying to do so means that I'll be forfeiting the opportunity to do other things. I'd be compounding an error. I'd be trying to get back something I can't get back and, in the process, losing important time, energy, and perhaps money that I could be using in a more utility productive way.

Mike: That's right.

In this sense, the fabricated constraint of sunk cost is very different from the real constraint of, say, scarcity. Whether a person believes it or not, scarcity exists. People are constrained by scarcity, just as they are by the force of gravity, whether they know it or not. But people are not constrained by sunk cost if they choose not to be. If you choose to let bygones be bygones, if you realize that sunk cost is a cost that has been incurred and cannot be changed, then it cannot constrain you when making a current decision.

Economists look at things this way: There are already enough constraints in the world. You are not made better off by behaving as if there is one more than there actually is.

SELF-TEST

1. Identify two ways to compute average total cost (*ATC*).
2. Would a business ever sell its product for less than cost? Explain your answer.
3. What happens to unit costs as marginal costs rise? Explain your answer.
4. Do changes in marginal physical product influence unit costs? Explain your answer.

Production and Costs in the Long Run

This section discusses production and long-run costs. As noted, in the long run, there are no fixed inputs and no fixed costs. Consequently, the firm has *greater flexibility* in the long run than in the short run. (Because we discuss both short-run and long-run average total cost curves, we distinguish between them with prefixes: *SR* for short run and *LR* for long run.)

Long-Run Average Total Cost Curve

In the short run, because there are fixed costs and variable costs, total cost is the sum of the two. But in the long run, there are no fixed costs; so variable costs *are* total costs. This section focuses on (1) the long-run average total cost (*LRATC*) curve and (2) what it looks like.

Consider the manager of a firm that produces bedroom furniture. When all inputs are variable, the manager must decide what the situation of the firm should be in the upcoming short-run period. For example, he might need to determine the size of the plant—small, medium, or large. Once this decision is made, the firm is locked into a specific plant size for the short run. Associated with each of the three different plant sizes is a short-run average total cost (*SRATC*) curve, as illustrated in Exhibit 7(a).

Suppose the manager of the firm wants to produce output level Q_1. Obviously, he will choose the plant size represented by $SRATC_1$. This gives a lower unit cost of producing Q_1 than the plant size represented by $SRATC_2$, which has a higher unit cost of producing Q_1 ($6 as opposed to $5).

exhibit 7

Long-Run Average Total Cost Curve (*LRATC*)

(a) There are three short-run average total cost curves for three different plant sizes. If these are the only plant sizes, the long-run average total cost curve is the heavily shaded, blue scalloped curve. (b) The long-run average total cost curve is the heavily shaded, blue smooth curve. The *LRATC* curve in (b) is not scalloped because it is assumed that there are so many plant sizes that the *LRATC* curve touches each *SRATC* curve at only one point.

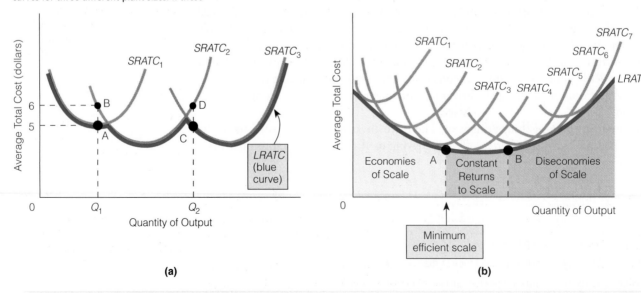

(a)

(b)

However, if the manager chooses to produce Q_2, he will choose the plant size represented by $SRATC_3$ because the unit cost of producing Q_2 is lower with that plant size than it is with the plant size represented by $SRATC_2$.

If we were to ask the same question for every (possible) output level, we would derive the **long-run average total cost (LRATC) curve.** The $LRATC$ curve shows the lowest unit cost at which the firm can produce any given level of output. In Exhibit 7(a), the $LRATC$ consists of the portions of the three $SRATC$ curves that are tangential to the blue curve; it is the scalloped blue curve.

Exhibit 7(b) shows a host of $SRATC$ curves and one $LRATC$ curve. In this case, the $LRATC$ curve is not scalloped, as in part (a). The $LRATC$ curve is smooth in part (b) because we assume there are many plant sizes in addition to the three represented in (a). In other words, although they have not been drawn, short-run average total cost curves representing different plant sizes exist in (b) between $SRATC_1$ and $SRATC_2$, between $SRATC_2$ and $SRATC_3$, and so on. In this case, the $LRATC$ curve is smooth and touches each $SRATC$ curve at one point.

Economies of Scale, Diseconomies of Scale, and Constant Returns to Scale

Suppose two inputs, labor and capital, are used together to produce a good. If inputs are increased by some percentage (say, 100 percent) and if output increases by a greater percentage (more than 100 percent), then unit costs fall and **economies of scale** are said to exist.

For example, suppose good X is made with two inputs, Y and Z, and it takes 20 Y and 10 Z to produce 5 units of X. The cost of each unit of input Y is $1, and the cost of each unit of input Z is $1. Thus, a total cost of $30 is required to produce 5 units of X. The unit cost (average total cost) of good X is $6 ($ATC = TC/Q$). Now consider a doubling of inputs Y and Z to 40 Y and 20 Z and a more than doubling in output, say, to 15 units of X. This means a total cost of $60 is required to produce 15 units of X, and the unit cost (average total cost) of good X is $4.

An increase in inputs can have two other results. If inputs are increased by some percentage and output increases by an equal percentage, then unit costs remain constant, and **constant returns to scale** are said to exist. If inputs are increased by some percentage and output increases by a smaller percentage, then unit costs rise, and **diseconomies of scale** are said to exist.

The three conditions can easily be seen in the $LRATC$ curve in Exhibit 7(b): If economies of scale are present, the $LRATC$ curve is falling; if constant returns to scale are present, the curve is flat; if diseconomies of scale are present, the curve is rising.

Economies of scale → *LRATC* is falling

Constant returns to scale → *LRATC* is constant

Diseconomies of scale → *LRATC* is rising

If, in the production of a good, economies of scale give way to constant returns to scale or to diseconomies of scale, as in Exhibit 7(b), the point at which this occurs is referred to as the minimum efficient scale. The **minimum efficient scale** is the lowest output level at which average total costs are minimized. Point A represents the minimum efficient scale in Exhibit 7(b).

The significance of the minimum efficient scale of output can be seen by looking at the long-run average total cost curve between points A and B in Exhibit 7(b). Between

Long-Run Average Total Cost (LRATC) Curve
A curve that shows the lowest (unit) cost at which the firm can produce any given level of output.

Economies of Scale
Economies that exist when inputs are increased by some percentage and output increases by a greater percentage, causing unit costs to fall.

Constant Returns to Scale
The condition when inputs are increased by some percentage and output increases by an equal percentage, causing unit costs to remain constant.

Diseconomies of Scale
The condition when inputs are increased by some percentage and output increases by a smaller percentage, causing unit costs to rise.

Minimum Efficient Scale
The lowest output level at which average total costs are minimized.

these points, there are constant returns to scale; the average total cost is the same over the various output levels between the two points. This means that larger firms (firms producing greater output levels) within this range do not have a cost advantage over smaller firms that operate at the minimum efficient scale.

Keep in mind that economies of scale, diseconomies of scale, and constant returns to scale are relevant only in the long run. Implicit in the definition of the terms and explicit in the example of economies of scale, all inputs necessary to the production of a good are changeable. Because no input is fixed, economies of scale, diseconomies of scale, and constant returns to scale must be relevant only in the long run.

Why Economies of Scale?

Up to a certain point, long-run unit costs of production fall as a firm grows for two main reasons: (1) Growing firms offer greater opportunities for employees to specialize. Individual workers can become highly proficient at narrowly defined tasks, often producing more output at lower unit costs. (2) Growing firms (especially large growing firms) can take advantage of highly efficient mass production techniques and equipment that ordinarily require large setup costs and thus are economical only if they can be spread over a large number of units. For example, assembly line techniques are usually relatively cheap when millions of units of a good are produced but are expensive when only a few thousand units are produced.

Why Diseconomies of Scale?

Diseconomies of scale usually arise at the point where a firm's size causes coordination, communication, and monitoring problems. In very large firms, managers often find it difficult to coordinate work activities, communicate their directives to the right persons in a timely way, and monitor personnel effectively. The business operation simply gets too big. There is, of course, a monetary incentive not to pass the point of operation where diseconomies of scale exist, and firms usually find ways to avoid them. They will reorganize, divide operations, hire new managers, and so on.

Minimum Efficient Scale and Number of Firms in an Industry

Some industries are composed of a smaller number of firms than other industries. Or we can say there is a different degree of concentration in different industries.

The minimum efficient scale (*MES*) as a percentage of U.S. consumption or total sales is not the same for all industries. For example, in industry X, *MES* as a percentage of total sales might be 6.6, and in industry Y, it might be 2.3. In other words, firms in industry X reach the minimum efficient scale of plant and thus exhaust economies of scale at an output level of 6.6 percent of total industry sales, whereas firms in industry Y experience economies of scale only up to an output level of 2.3 percent of total industry sales.

Clearly, we would expect to find fewer firms in industry X. By dividing the *MES* as a percentage of total sales into 100, we can estimate the number of efficient firms it takes to satisfy total consumption for a particular product. For the product produced by industry X, it takes 15 firms (100/6.6 = 15). For the product produced by industry Y, it takes 43 firms.

SHIFTS IN COST CURVES

In discussing the shape of short- and long-run cost curves, we assumed that certain factors remained constant. We discuss a few of these factors now and describe how changes in them can shift cost curves.

Taxes

Consider a tax on each unit of a good produced. Suppose company X has to pay a tax of $3 for each unit of X it produces. What effects will this have on the firm's cost curves? The tax won't affect the firm's fixed costs because the tax is paid only when output is produced, and fixed costs are present even if output is zero. (If the tax is a lump-sum tax—that is, the company pays a lump sum no matter how many units of X it produces—then the tax will affect fixed costs.) We conclude that the tax does not affect fixed costs and therefore cannot affect average fixed cost.

The tax will affect variable costs. As a consequence of the tax, the firm has to pay more for each unit of X it produces. Because variable costs rise, so does total cost. This means that average variable cost and average total cost rise and that the representative cost curves shift upward. Finally, because marginal cost is the change in total cost divided by the change in output, marginal cost rises and the marginal cost curve shifts upward.

Input Prices

A rise or fall in variable input prices causes a corresponding change in the firm's average total, average variable, and marginal cost curves. For example, if the price of steel rises, the variable costs of building skyscrapers rise, and so must average variable cost, average total cost, and marginal cost. The cost curves shift upward. If the price of steel falls, the opposite effects occur.

Technology

Technological changes often bring either (1) the capability of using fewer inputs to produce a good (e.g., the introduction of the personal computer reduced the hours necessary to key and edit a manuscript) or (2) lower input prices (e.g., technological improvements in transistors led to price reductions in the transistor components of calculators). In either case, technological changes of this variety lower variable costs and consequently lower average variable cost, average total cost, and marginal cost. The cost curves shift downward.

SELF-TEST

1. Give an arithmetical example to illustrate economies of scale.

2. What would the *LRATC* curve look like if there were always constant returns to scale? Explain your answer.

3. Firm A charged $4 per unit when it produced 100 units of good X, and it charged $3 per unit when it produced 200 units. Furthermore, the firm earned the same profit per unit in both cases. How can this happen?

"WHAT IS THE DIFFERENCE BETWEEN THE LAW OF DIMINISHING MARGINAL RETURNS AND DISECONOMIES OF SCALE?"

Student:

I'm not sure I understand the difference between the law of diminishing marginal returns and diseconomies of scale. They sound similar to me.

Instructor:

The law of diminishing marginal returns holds in the short run when at least one input is fixed. In our example in class, we held capital constant (at one unit) and changed the units of labor. Diseconomies of scale are relevant to the long run, which is a period when all inputs are variable. In other words, no input is fixed.

Student:

But don't both the law of diminishing marginal returns and diseconomies of scale have something to do with less output per unit of input?

Instructor:

Let's define each and see. The law of diminishing marginal returns says that as we add additional units of a variable input (such as labor) to a fixed input (such as capital), we get to a point where the marginal physical product of the variable input (the marginal physical product of labor) declines.

This has to do with less output per unit of input. Specifically, as we add additional units of the variable input to the fixed input, our output might rise, but it rises at a decreasing rate. To illustrate, adding the fourth worker to the production process might raise output from 100 units to 120 units (an addition of 20 units), but adding the fifth worker increases output from 120 units to 135 units (which is an addition of 15 units).

Student:

Okay, then, how is the law of diseconomies of scale different?

Instructor:

Here is an example of diseconomies of scale. The firm increases each of its inputs by, say, 10 percent, but its output rises by only 3 percent. In other words, its output rises less than the increase in its inputs.

Also, notice that we don't hold any input fixed. We have assumed that there are two inputs the firm uses, labor and capital, and that it increases its usage of each input by 10 percent.

Student:

Are we getting less output per unit of input, as we did with respect to the law of diminishing marginal returns?

Instructor:

Yes and no. We are getting less output per unit of input if we compare diseconomies of scale with, say, economies of scale. To illustrate, with economies of scale, we might increase each input by 10 percent and end up with 20 percent more output. With diseconomies of scale, we increase each input by 10 percent and end up with, say, 3 percent more output. Obviously, when diseconomies of scale exist we get less output for each percentage increase in inputs than when economies of scale exist.

Points to Remember

1. The law of diminishing returns holds in the short run when at least one input is fixed.

2. Diseconomies of scale are relevant to the long run, which is a period when all inputs are variable.

a reader asks | Will a Knowledge of Sunk Cost Help Prevent Me from Making a Mistake in the Stock Market?

I have a friend who bought some stock at $40 a share. Soon after she bought the stock, it fell to $30 a share. I asked my friend if she planned to sell. She said that she couldn't because if she did, she would take a $10 loss per share of stock. Is she looking at things correctly?

No. Your friend is letting a past decision (the purchase of stock at $40 a share) influence a present decision (whether or not to sell the stock).

Let's go back in time to when your friend was thinking about whether to buy the stock. Before she made the purchase, she must have asked herself, "Do I think the price of the stock will rise or fall?" She must have thought the price of the stock would rise, or else she wouldn't have

purchased it. Why, then, doesn't she ask herself the same question now that the price of the stock has fallen: "Do I think the price of the stock will rise or fall?" Isn't this the best question she can ask herself? If she thinks the price of the stock will rise, then she should not sell the stock. But if she thinks the price will fall, then she should sell the stock before it falls further in price.

Instead, she lets her past influence her present. She cannot change the past; she cannot change the fact that the price of her stock has fallen $10 per share. The $10 per share fall in price is a sunk cost. It is something that happened in the past and cannot be changed by a current decision. If she doesn't ignore sunk cost, she risks losing even more than she already has lost.

Chapter Summary

THE FIRM

- Armen Alchian and Harold Demsetz argue that firms are formed when individuals derive benefits from working as a team—specifically, when the sum of what individuals can produce as a team is greater than the sum of what individuals can produce alone: Sum of team production = Sum of individual production.

- Team production has its advantages and disadvantages. The chief advantage (in many cases) is the positive difference between the output produced by the team and the sum of the output produced by individuals working alone. The chief disadvantage is the increased shirking in teams. The role of the monitor (manager) in the firm is to preserve the increased output and to reduce or eliminate the increased shirking. The monitors have a monetary incentive not to shirk their monitoring duties when they are residual claimants.

- Ronald Coase argued that firms exist to reduce the "costs of negotiating and concluding a separate contract for each exchange transaction which takes place on a market." In short, firms exist to reduce transaction costs.

EXPLICIT COST AND IMPLICIT COST

- An explicit cost is incurred when an actual (monetary) payment is made. An implicit cost represents the value of resources used in production for which no actual (monetary) payment is made.

ECONOMIC PROFIT AND ACCOUNTING PROFIT

- Economic profit is the difference between total revenue and total cost, including both explicit and implicit costs. Accounting profit is the difference between total revenue and explicit costs. Economic profit is usually lower (never higher) than accounting profit. Economic profit (not accounting profit) motivates economic behavior.

PRODUCTION AND COSTS IN THE SHORT RUN

- The short run is a period in which some inputs are fixed. The long run is a period in which all inputs can be varied. The costs associated with fixed and variable inputs are referred to as fixed costs and variable costs, respectively.

- Marginal cost is the change in total cost that results from a change in output.

- The law of diminishing marginal returns states that as ever larger amounts of a variable input are combined with fixed inputs, eventually the marginal physical product of the variable input will decline. As this happens, marginal cost rises.

- The average-marginal rule states that if the marginal magnitude is above (below) the average magnitude, the average magnitude rises (falls).

- The marginal cost curve intersects the average variable cost curve at its lowest point. The marginal cost curve intersects the average total cost curve at its lowest point. There is no relationship between marginal cost and average fixed cost.

PRODUCTION AND COSTS IN THE LONG RUN

- In the long run, because there are no fixed costs, variable costs equal total costs.
- The long-run average total cost curve is the envelope of the short-run average total cost curves. It shows the lowest unit cost at which the firm can produce a given level of output.
- If inputs are increased by some percentage and output increases by a greater percentage, then unit costs fall and economies of scale exist. If inputs are increased by some percentage and output increases by an equal percentage, then unit costs remain constant and constant returns to scale exist. If inputs are increased by some percentage and output

increases by a smaller percentage, then unit costs rise and diseconomies of scale exist.

- The minimum efficient scale is the lowest output level at which average total costs are minimized.

SUNK COST

- Sunk cost is a cost incurred in the past that cannot be changed by current decisions and therefore cannot be recovered. A person or firm that wants to minimize losses will hold sunk costs to be irrelevant to present decisions.

SHIFTS IN COST CURVES

- A firm's cost curves will shift if there is a change in taxes, input prices, or technology.

Key Terms and Concepts

Business Firm	Accounting Profit	Law of Diminishing	Average Total Cost (ATC),
Market Coordination	Economic Profit	Marginal Returns	or Unit Cost
Managerial Coordination	Normal Profit	Fixed Costs	Average-Marginal Rule
Shirking	Fixed Input	Variable Costs	Sunk Cost
Monitor	Variable Input	Total Cost (TC)	Long-Run Average Total
Residual Claimant	Short Run	Marginal Cost (MC)	Cost ($LRATC$) Curve
Profit	Long Run	Average Fixed Cost	Economies of Scale
Explicit Cost	Marginal Physical Product	(AFC)	Constant Returns to Scale
Implicit Cost	(MPP)	Average Variable Cost	Diseconomies of Scale
		(AVC)	Minimum Efficient Scale

Questions and Problems

1 Explain the difference between managerial coordination and market coordination.

2 Is the managerial coordination that goes on within a business firm independent of market forces? Explain your answer.

3 Explain why even conscientious workers will shirk more when the cost of shirking falls.

4 Illustrate the average-marginal rule in a noncost setting.

5 "A firm that earns only normal profit is not covering all its costs." Do you agree or disagree? Explain your answer.

6 The average variable cost curve and the average total cost curve get closer to each other as output increases. What explains this?

7 Explain why earning zero economic profit is not as bad as it sounds.

8 Why does the *AFC* curve continually decline (and get closer and closer to the quantity axis)?

9 What is the difference between diseconomies of scale and the law of diminishing marginal returns?

10 When would total costs equal fixed costs?

11 Is studying for an economics exam subject to the law of diminishing marginal returns? If so, what is the fixed input? What is the variable input?

12 Some individuals decry the decline of the small family farm and its replacement with the huge corporate megafarm. Discuss the possibility that this is a consequence of economies of scale.

13 We know there is a link between productivity and costs. For example, recall the link between the marginal physical product of the variable input and marginal cost. With this in mind, what link might there be between productivity and prices?

14 Some people's everyday behavior suggests that they do not hold sunk costs irrelevant to present decisions. Give some examples different from those presented in this chapter.

15 Explain why a firm might want to produce its good even after diminishing marginal returns have set in and marginal cost is rising.

16 People often believe that large firms in an industry have cost advantages over small firms in the same industry. For example, they might think a big oil company has a cost advantage

over a small oil company. For this to be true, what condition must exist? Explain your answer.

17 The government says that firm X must pay $1,000 in taxes simply because it is in the business of producing a good. What cost curves, if any, does this tax affect?

18 Based on your answer to question 17, does *MC* change if *TC* changes?

19 Under what condition would Bill Gates be the richest person in the United States and earn zero economic profit?

Working with Numbers and Graphs

1 Determine the appropriate dollar amount for each lettered space.

(1) Quantity of Output, *Q* (units)	(2) Total Fixed Cost (dollars)	(3) Average Fixed Cost (*AFC*)	(4) Total Variable Cost (*TVC*)	(5) Average Variable Cost (*AVC*)	(6) Total Cost (*TC*)	(7) Average Total Cost (*ATC*)	(8) Marginal cost (*MC*)
0	$200	A	$0		V		
1	200	B	30	L	W	GG	QQ
2	200	C	50	M	X	HH	RR
3	200	D	60	N	Y	II	SS
4	200	E	65	O	Z	JJ	TT
5	200	F	75	P	AA	KK	UU
6	200	G	95	Q	BB	LL	VV
7	200	H	125	R	CC	MM	WW
8	200	I	165	S	DD	NN	XX
9	200	J	215	T	EE	OO	YY
10	200	K	275	U	FF	PP	ZZ

2 Give a numerical example to show that as marginal physical product (*MPP*) rises, marginal cost (*MC*) falls.

3 Price = $20, quantity = 400 units, unit cost = $15, implicit costs = $4,000. What does economic profit equal?

4 If economic profit equals accounting profit, what do implicit costs equal?

5 If accounting profit is $400,000 greater than economic profit, what do implicit costs equal?

6 If marginal physical product is continually declining, what does marginal cost look like? Explain your answer.

7 If the *ATC* curve is continually declining, what does this imply about the *MC* curve? Explain your answer.

CHAPTER 8

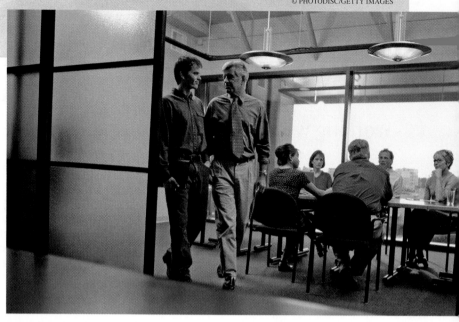

© PHOTODISC/GETTY IMAGES

PERFECT COMPETITION

Introduction Every firm shares two things with all other firms. First, every firm has to answer certain questions: (1) What price should the firm charge for the good it produces and sells? (2) How many units of the good should the firm produce? (3) How much of the resources that the firm needs to produce its good should it buy? Regardless of whether a firm sells shirts or cars, whether it is large or small, whether it is located in Georgia or Maine, it must answer all three of these questions. Period.

Second, every firm finds itself operating within a certain market structure. A **market structure** is a firm's environment or setting, the characteristics of which influence the firm's pricing and output decisions. Economists often discuss four different market structures: perfect competition, monopoly, monopolistic competition, and oligopoly. This chapter focuses on perfect competition.

Market Structure
The particular environment of a firm, the characteristics of which influence the firm's pricing and output decisions.

THE THEORY OF PERFECT COMPETITION

The theory of **perfect competition** is built on four assumptions:

Perfect Competition
A theory of market structure based on four assumptions: (1) There are many sellers and buyers, (2) sellers sell a homogeneous good, (3) buyers and sellers have all relevant information, and (4) entry into or exit from the market is easy.

1. *There are many sellers and many buyers, none of which is large in relation to total sales or purchases.* This assumption speaks to both demand (the number of buyers) and supply (the number of sellers). Because there are many buyers and sellers, each buyer and each seller may act independently of other buyers and sellers, respectively, and each is such a small a part of the market as to have no influence on price.

2. *Each firm produces and sells a homogeneous product.* Each firm sells a product that is indistinguishable from all other firms' products in a given industry. (For example, a buyer of wheat cannot distinguish between Farmer Stone's wheat and Farmer Gray's wheat.) As a consequence, buyers are indifferent to the sellers.

3. *Buyers and sellers have all relevant information about prices, product quality, sources of supply, and so forth.* Buyers and sellers know who is selling what, at what prices, at what

quality, and on what terms. In short, they know everything that relates to buying, producing, and selling the product.

4. *Firms have easy entry and exit.* New firms can enter the market easily, and existing firms can exit the market easily. There are no barriers to entry or exit.

Before discussing the perfectly competitive firm in the short and long run, we discuss some of the characteristics of the perfectly competitive firm that result from these four assumptions.

Thinking like An Economist

Think Theory

In Chapter 3, we briefly discussed what a theory is and why economists build theories. We are beginning to build a theory in this chapter: the theory of perfect competition. In every theory, assumptions are made. Do a theory's assumptions have to be perfectly realistic to be useful? Most economists think not. Economists judge the worthiness of theories not by how realistic its assumptions are, but by how well the theories predict real-world events. For example, the third assumption we made in the theory of perfect competition (buyers and sellers have all relevant information about prices, product quality, sources of supply, and so forth) may seem unrealistic. After all, buyers and sellers may not really have all relevant information. However, they may have enough of the relevant information (90 percent instead of 100 percent) so that things turn out as they would if they had all relevant information.

The point is simply this: Even though a theory's assumptions may not be 100 percent accurate, they may be, as economist Milton Friedman has noted, "sufficiently good approximations for the purpose at hand."

A Perfectly Competitive Firm Is a Price Taker

A perfectly competitive firm is a **price taker**. A price taker is a seller that does not have the ability to control the price of the product it sells; it takes the price determined in the market. For example, if Farmer Stone is a price taker, he can increase or decrease his output without significantly affecting the price of his product.

Why is a perfectly competitive firm a price taker? A firm is restrained from being anything but a price taker if it finds itself one among many firms where its supply is small relative to the total market supply (assumption 1 in the theory of perfect competition), and it sells a homogeneous product (assumption 2) in an environment where buyers and sellers have all relevant information (assumption 3).

Some people might suggest that the assumptions of the theory of perfect competition give economists what they want. Economists want the perfectly competitive firm to be a price taker, and so they choose the assumptions that make this so. But this isn't the case. Economists start out with certain assumptions and then logically conclude that the firm for which these assumptions hold—or that behaves as if these assumptions hold—is a price taker; that is, it has no control over price. Afterward, economists test the theory by observing whether it accurately predicts and explains the real-world behavior of some firms.

The Demand Curve for a Perfectly Competitive Firm Is Horizontal

In the perfectly competitive setting, there are many sellers and many buyers. Together, all buyers make up the market demand curve; together, all sellers make up the market supply curve. An equilibrium price is established at the intersection of the market demand and market supply curves [Exhibit 1(a)].

Price Taker
A seller that does not have the ability to control the price of the product it sells; the seller takes the price determined in the market.

exhibit 1

Market Demand Curve and Firm Demand Curve in Perfect Competition

(a) The market, composed of all buyers and sellers, establishes the equilibrium price. (b) A single perfectly competitive firm then faces a horizontal (flat, perfectly elastic) demand curve. We conclude that the firm is a price taker; it takes the equilibrium price established by the market and sells any and all quantities of output at this price. (The capital *D* represents the market demand curve; the lowercase *d* represents the single firm's demand curve.)

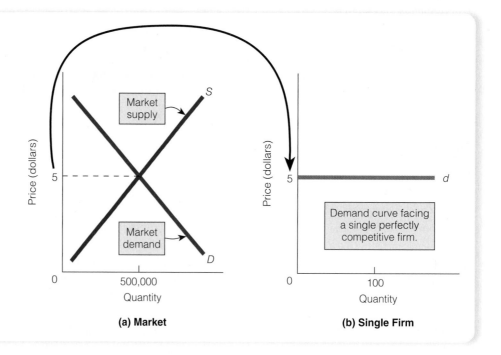

(a) Market **(b) Single Firm**

When the equilibrium price has been established, a single perfectly competitive firm faces a horizontal (flat, perfectly elastic) demand curve at the equilibrium price [Exhibit 1(b)]. In short, the firm takes the equilibrium price as given—hence the firm is a price taker—and sells all quantities of output at this price.[1]

WHY DOES A PERFECTLY COMPETITIVE FIRM SELL AT EQUILIBRIUM PRICE? If a perfectly competitive firm tries to charge a price higher than the market-established equilibrium price, it won't sell any of its product. This is because the firm sells a homogeneous product, its supply is small relative to the total market supply, and all buyers are informed about where they can obtain the product at the lower price.

If the firm wants to maximize profits, it does not offer to sell its good at a lower price than the equilibrium price. Why should it? It can sell all it wants at the market-established equilibrium price.

The equilibrium price is the only relevant price for the perfectly competitive firm.

Finding ECONOMICS

When Selling Shares of Stock

Roberta wakes up in the morning and turns on her computer. She checks the prices of the stocks she owns. The price of stock X is currently selling at $35 per share. She had bought 200 shares of the stock when the price was only $11 per share, and now she decides to sell. She places a sell order with her online broker and in a matter of minutes she has sold her 200 shares of stock. Where is the economics here? Does Roberta's sale of stock have anything to do with operating in a perfectly competitive market?

(continued)

---

1. The horizontal demand curve means *not* that the firm can sell an infinite amount at the equilibrium price, but that price will be virtually unaffected by the variations in output that the firm may find it practicable to make.

DO CHURCHES COMPETE?

Do religions compete in the same way that business firms do? Some economists think so; they go on to say that problems often arise when one religion tries to use government to prevent other religions from competing with it.

To illustrate, the United States has a rather open and free religious environment. The First Amendment of the U.S. Constitution states, "Congress shall make no law respecting an establishment of religion, or prohibiting the free exercise thereof." It would be unconstitutional, for example, for the U.S. government to say that only Christianity could be practiced in the United States. Doing so would be similar to saying that only Microsoft could sell software in the United States, that only NBC could broadcast television programs, or that only Harvard University could grant degrees of higher education.

When the Founding Fathers made it unconstitutional for government to favor one religion over another, they essentially made it impossible for any one religion to have a competition-free environment. Although Christianity is the major religion in the United States, someone can purchase, if you will, spirituality, codes of conduct, moral guides, and so on from any religion.

Because religions in the United States have to compete with other religions—for believers or, if we are to take the market analogy further, for customers—they serve people better. A religion that has to compete provides a higher-quality product than a religion that doesn't have to compete. Even within Christianity, different denominations compete. The Southern Baptist Church has to compete with the Methodist Church, and the Methodist Church competes with the Southern Baptists. Today, the competition among denominations and religions has provided the United States with a wide variety of religious experiences and institutions.

Contrast the United States with some Islamic countries, especially those where the Islamic clergy occupy high positions of state. In those counries, it is unlawful to openly practice other religions or even to conduct oneself in a way that is contrary to the clerics' interpretation of Islam. Government has effectively established one religion. The question is whether that one religion and the people in that country are better off because of government support. To economists, a single producer in a market, whether it's a software producer or a producer of religious doctrine, doesn't serve its customers or believers well. Competition drives producers to do better.

Finding Economics (continued)

If Roberta wants to sell her shares of stock X, she must sell at the current market price. Roberta, as a seller of stock, is a price taker. She cannot sell her shares of stock at $2 more per share than the current price; she will not sell below the market price. Why should she sell her shares of stock at 9 when she can sell them at the current market price of 11?

Common MISCONCEPTIONS

About Demand Curves

The law of demand posits an inverse relationship between price and quantity demanded. If a demand curve is to represent the law of demand graphically, it must be downward sloping. A common misconception, though, is to think that *all* demand curves have to be downward sloping. Why this is not true can be explained by distinguishing the market demand curve from the demand curve that a single firm faces.

As shown in Exhibit 1(a), the market demand curve is downward sloping, positing an inverse relationship between price and quantity demanded, *ceteris paribus*. The single perfectly competitive

(continued)

Common Misconceptions (continued)

firm's demand curve does not contradict this relationship; it simply represents the pricing situation in which the single perfectly competitive firm finds itself. Recall that the more substitutes there are for a good, the higher the price elasticity of demand. In the perfectly competitive market setting, there are many substitutes for the firm's product—so many, in fact, that the firm's demand curve is perfectly elastic.

The intuition is that a single perfectly competitive firm's supply is such a *small percentage* of the total market supply that the firm cannot perceptibly influence price by changing its quantity of output. To put it differently, the firm's supply is so small, compared with the total market supply, that the inverse relationship between price and quantity demanded, although present, cannot be observed on the firm's level, although it is observable on the market level.

The Marginal Revenue Curve of a Perfectly Competitive Firm Is the Same as Its Demand Curve

Total revenue is the price of a good multiplied by the quantity sold. If the equilibrium price is $5, as in Exhibit 2(a), and the perfectly competitive firm sells 3 units of its good, its total revenue is $15. Now suppose the firm sells an additional unit, bringing the total number of units sold to 4. Its total revenue is now $20.

A firm's **marginal revenue (MR)** is the change in total revenue (*TR*) that results from selling one additional unit of output (*Q*); that is,

Marginal Revenue (MR)
The change in total revenue that results from selling one additional unit of output.

$$MR = \frac{\Delta TR}{\Delta Q}$$

Column 4 in Exhibit 2(a) shows that the firm's marginal revenue ($5) at any output level is always equal to the equilibrium price ($5). For a perfectly competitive firm, therefore, price is equal to marginal revenue.

For a Perfectly Competitive Firm, $P = MR$

The Demand Curve and the Marginal Revenue Curve for a Perfectly Competitive Firm

(a) By computing marginal revenue, we find that it is equal to price. (b) By plotting columns 1 and 2, we obtain the firm's demand curve; by plotting columns 2 and 4, we obtain the firm's marginal revenue curve. The two curves are the same.

(1) Price	(2) Quantity	(3) Total Revenue = (1) × (2)	(4) Marginal Revenue = ΔTR/ΔQ = Δ(3)/Δ(2)
$5	1	$ 5	$5
5	2	10	5
5	3	15	5
5	4	20	5

(a)

Plotting columns 1 and 2 gives us the demand curve; plotting columns 2 and 4 gives us the marginal revenue curve.

(b)

If price is equal to marginal revenue, then *the marginal revenue curve for the perfectly competitive firm is the same as its demand curve.*

A demand curve plots price against quantity, whereas a marginal revenue curve plots marginal revenue against quantity. If price equals marginal revenue, then the demand curve and marginal revenue curve are the same [Exhibit 2(b)].

> For a Perfectly Competitive Firm, Demand curve = Marginal revenue curve

Theory and Real-World Markets

The theory of perfect competition describes how firms act in a market structure where (1) there are many buyers and sellers, none of whom is large in relation to total sales or purchases; (2) sellers sell a homogeneous product; (3) buyers and sellers have all relevant information; and (4) there is easy market entry and exit. These assumptions are closely met in some real-world markets, such as some agricultural markets and a small subset of the retail trade. The stock market, where there are hundreds of thousands of buyers and sellers of stock, is also sometimes cited as an example of perfect competition.

The four assumptions of the theory of perfect competition are also *approximated* in some real-world markets. In such markets, the number of sellers may not be large enough for every firm to be a price taker, but the firm's control over price may be negligible. The amount of control may be so negligible, in fact, that the firm acts *as if* it were a perfectly competitive firm.

Similarly, buyers may not have all relevant information concerning price and quality. However, they may still have a great deal of information, and the information they do not have may not matter. The products that the firms in the industry sell may not be homogeneous, but the differences may be inconsequential.

In short, a market that does not *exactly* meet the assumptions of perfect competition may nonetheless *approximate* the assumptions to a degree that it behaves *as if* it were a perfectly competitive market. If so, the theory of perfect competition can be used to predict the market's behavior.

SELF-TEST

(Answers to Self-Test questions are in the Self-Test Appendix.)

1. "If a firm is a price taker, it does not have the ability to control the price of the product it sells." What does this statement mean?

2. Why is a perfectly competitive firm a price taker?

3. The horizontal demand curve for the perfectly competitive firm signifies that it cannot sell any of its product for a price higher than the market equilibrium price. Why not?

4. Suppose the firms in a real-world market do not sell a homogeneous product. Does it necessarily follow that the market is not perfectly competitive?

PERFECT COMPETITION IN THE SHORT RUN

The perfectly competitive firm is a price taker. So for a perfectly competitive firm, price is equal to marginal revenue, $P = MR$, and therefore the firm's demand curve is the same as its marginal revenue curve. This section discusses the amount of output the firm will produce in the short run.

The Quantity of Output the Perfectly Competitive Firm Will Produce

The firm's demand curve is horizontal at the equilibrium price. Its demand curve is its marginal revenue curve. The firm produces that quantity of output at which $MR = MC$.

What Level of Output Does the Profit-Maximizing Firm Produce?

In Exhibit 3, the perfectly competitive firm's demand curve and marginal revenue curve (which are the same) are drawn at the equilibrium price of $5. The firm's marginal cost curve is also shown. On the basis of these curves, what quantity of output will the firm produce? The firm will continue to increase its quantity of output as long as marginal revenue is greater than marginal cost. It will not produce units of output for which marginal revenue is less than marginal cost. We conclude that the firm will stop increasing its quantity of output when marginal revenue and marginal cost are equal. The **profit maximization rule** for a firm says *produce the quantity of output at which $MR = MC$.*[2] In Exhibit 3, $MR = MC$ at 125 units of output.

For the perfectly competitive firm, the profit-maximization rule can be written as $P = MC$ because for the perfectly competitive firm, $P = MR$. In perfect competition, profit is maximized when

$$P = MR = MC$$

Profit-Maximization Rule

The rule that profit is maximized by producing the quantity of output at which $MR = MC$.

> **micro***theme* ➜ Firms have objectives, face constraints, and have to make choices. The perfectly competitive firm's objective is to maximize profit. It faces the constraint of having to sell its output at the market-determined price—and only at that price. It chooses to produce the quantity of output at which $MR = MC$.

 Common MISCONCEPTIONS

Over the Right Quantity to Produce

Some individuals jump to the conclusion that the firm should produce the quantity at which the biggest difference between marginal revenue (*MR*) and marginal (*MC*) exists. In Exhibit 3, this point comes at a quantity of 50 units. But this is the incorrect way to look at things. To see why, ask yourself what the firm would give up if it stopped producing at a quantity of 50 units. It wouldn't have produced (and sold) the 51st unit in Exhibit 3, but isn't the 51st unit worth producing because (as you can see from the exhibit) its marginal revenue is greater than its marginal cost? The same holds for the 52nd unit, and the 53rd unit, and so on. If the firm had stopped producing at a quantity of 50 units, it would have been like leaving money on the table. That money on the table is the positive dollar difference between marginal revenue and marginal cost (up until the 125th unit).

2. The profit-maximization rule is the same as the loss-minimization rule because it is impossible to maximize profits without minimizing losses. The profit-maximization rule holds for *all firms*, not just for perfectly competitive firms.

The Perfectly Competitive Firm and Resource Allocative Efficiency

Resources (or inputs) are used to produce goods and services; for example, wood may be used to produce a chair. To the buyers of the goods, the resources used in the production of goods have an exchange value that is approximated by the price that people pay for the good. For example, when buying a chair for $100, Smith values the resources used to produce the chair by at least $100. Wood that is used to produce chairs can't be used to produce desks. Hence, there is an opportunity cost of producing chairs that is best measured by its marginal cost.

Now suppose that 100 chairs are produced and that, at this quantity, price is greater than marginal cost; for example, price is $100 and marginal cost is $75. Obviously, buyers place a higher value on wood when it is used to produce chairs than when it is used to produce an alternative good.

Producing a good—any good—until price equals marginal cost ensures that all units of the good are produced that are of greater value to buyers than the alternative goods that might have been produced. Stated differently, a firm that produces the quantity of output at which price equals marginal cost ($P = MC$) is said to exhibit **resource allocative efficiency**.

Does the perfectly competitive firm exhibit resource allocative efficiency? We know two things about this type of firm: First, the perfectly competitive firm produces the quantity of output at which $MR = MC$, and, second, for this firm $P = MR$. If the perfectly competitive firm produces the output at which $MR = MC$ and if for this firm $P = MR$, then it follows that the firm produces the output at which $P = MC$. In short, the perfectly competitive firm *is* resource allocative efficient.

Also, for a perfectly competitive firm, profit maximization and resource allocative efficiency are not at odds. (Whether they might be for other market structures is discussed in the next two chapters.) The perfectly competitive firm seeks to maximize profit by producing the quantity of output at which $MR = MC$ and, because for the firm $P = MR$, it automatically accomplishes resource allocative efficiency ($P = MC$) when it maximizes profit ($MR = MC$).

> **Resource Allocative Efficiency**
> The situation when firms produce the quantity of output at which price equals marginal cost: $P = MC$.

Thinking like AN ECONOMIST

Profit Maximization Can Be Consistent with Consumer Welfare

Think of good X. With good X, as with all other goods, there is a right and a wrong quantity to produce. From the perspective of consumers, the right quantity is the efficient quantity. The consumer says to the manufacturers of X: "Keep producing X as long as its price is greater than its marginal cost. Stop when $P = MC$." Let's say that $P = MC$ when the quantity of X is 10,000 a month.

The question now is whether 10,000 units of X a month is what the manufacturers of X want to produce. The right quantity of X for manufacturers is the quantity at which $MR = MC$. In other words, X manufacturers will continue producing units of it as long as MR is greater than MC, and they will stop when $MR = MC$.

For a perfectly competitive firm, we know that $P = MR$; so it follows that what consumers want (produce until $P = MC$) is really the same thing that manufacturers want (produce until $MR = MC$). Simply put, when manufacturers do what is in their best interest—produce until $MR = MC$—they are automatically producing the efficient amount of the good, which is what consumers want. Who would have thought it?

To Produce or Not to Produce: That Is the Question

The following cases illustrate three applications of the profit-maximization (loss-minimization) rule by a perfectly competitive firm.

CASE 1: PRICE IS ABOVE AVERAGE TOTAL COST Exhibit 4(a) illustrates the perfectly competitive firm's demand and marginal revenue curves. If the firm follows the profit-maximization rule and produces the quantity of output at which marginal revenue equals marginal cost, it will produce 100 units of output. This will be the profit-maximizing quantity of output. Notice that at this quantity of output, price is above average total cost. Using the information in the exhibit, we can make the following calculations:

Case 1		
Equilibrium price (P)	=	$15
Quantity of output produced (Q)	=	100 units
Total revenue ($P \times Q = \$15 \times 100$)	=	$1,500
Total cost ($ATC \times Q = \$11 \times 100$)	=	$1,100
Total variable cost ($AVC \times Q = \$7 \times 100$)	=	$700
Total fixed cost ($TC - TVC = \$1,100 - \$700$)	=	$400
Profits ($TR - TC = \$1,500 - \$1,100$)	=	$400

exhibit 4

Profit Maximization and Loss Minimization for the Perfectly Competitive Firm: Three Cases

(a) In case 1, $TR > TC$ and the firm earns profits. It continues to produce in the short run.

(b) In case 2, $TR < TC$ and the firm takes a loss. It shuts down in the short run because it minimizes its losses by doing so; it is better to lose $400 in fixed costs than to take a loss of $450. (c) In case 3, $TR < TC$ and the firm takes

a loss. It continues to produce in the short run because it minimizes its losses by doing so; it is better to lose $80 by producing than to lose $400 in fixed costs.

(a) Case 1

(b) Case 2

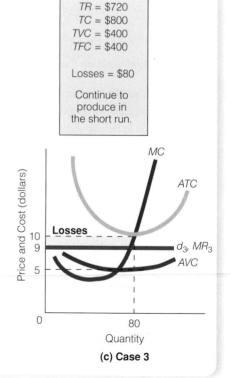

(c) Case 3

Therefore, if price is above the average total cost for the perfectly competitive firm, the firm maximizes profits by producing the quantity of output at which $MR = MC$.

CASE 2: PRICE IS BELOW AVERAGE VARIABLE COST

Exhibit 4(b) illustrates the case in which price is below average variable cost. The equilibrium price at which the perfectly competitive firm sells its good is $4. At this price, total revenue is less than both total cost and total variable cost, as the following calculations indicate. To minimize its loss, the firm should shut down.

Case 2		
Equilibrium price (P)	=	$4
Quantity of output produced (Q)	=	50 units
Total revenue ($P \times Q = \$4 \times 50$)	=	$200
Total cost ($ATC \times Q = \$13 \times 50$)	=	$650
Total variable cost ($AVC \times Q = \$5 \times 50$)	=	$250
Total fixed cost ($TC - TVC = \$650 - \$250$)	=	$400
Profits ($TR - TC = \$200 - \$650$)	=	$-\$450$

If the firm produces in the short run, it will take a loss of $450. If it shuts down, its loss will be less, losing its fixed costs, which amount to the difference between total cost and variable cost ($TFC + TVC = TC$, so $TC - TVC = TFC$). This is $400 ($650 − $250). So between the two options of producing in the short run or shutting down, the firm minimizes its losses by choosing to shut down ($Q = 0$). It will lose $400 by shutting down, whereas it will lose $450 by producing in the short run.

Therefore, if price is below the average variable cost, the perfectly competitive firm minimizes losses by choosing to shut down—that is, by not producing.

CASE 3: PRICE IS BELOW AVERAGE TOTAL COST BUT ABOVE AVERAGE VARIABLE COST

Exhibit 4(c) illustrates the case in which price is below average total cost but above average variable cost. Here the equilibrium price at which the perfectly competitive firm sells its good is $9. If the firm follows the profit-maximization rule, it will produce 80 units of output. At this price and quantity of output, total revenue is less than total cost (hence, there will be a loss), but total revenue is greater than total variable cost. The calculations are as follows:

Case 3		
Equilibrium price (P)	=	$9
Quantity of output produced (Q)	=	80 units
Total revenue ($P \times Q = \$9 \times 80$)	=	$720
Total cost ($ATC \times Q = \$10 \times 80$)	=	$800
Total variable cost ($AVC \times Q = \$5 \times 80$)	=	$400
Total fixed cost ($TC - TVC = \$800 - \$400$)	=	$400
Profits ($TR - TC = \$720 - \$800$)	=	$-\$80$

If the firm decides to produce in the short run, it will take a loss of $80. If it shuts down, it will lose its fixed costs, which, in this case, are $400 ($TC - TVC = \$800 - \$400$). It is better to continue to produce in the short run than to shut down. Losses are minimized by producing.

Therefore, if price is below average total cost but above average variable cost, the perfectly competitive firm minimizes its losses by continuing to produce in the short run instead of shutting down.

exhibit 5

What Should a Perfectly Competitive Firm Do in the Short Run?

The firm should produce in the short run as long as price (*P*) is above average variable cost (*AVC*). It should shut down in the short run if price is below average variable cost.

Common MISCONCEPTIONS

Over the Shut-Down Decision

Asked when a business firm should shut down (stop producing), the layperson is likely to say when the firm is no longer earning a profit. In economics, that is when price is lower than average total cost (*P* < *ATC*). But that is the wrong advice, as we have just shown. Even if price is below average total cost and a loss is being incurred, a firm should not necessarily shut down. Whether it should depends, in the short run, on whether the firm loses more by shutting down than by not shutting down. Even though price is below average total cost, it could still be above average variable cost, and, if it is, the firm minimizes its losses (in the short run) by continuing to produce rather than by shutting down.

Short-Run (Firm) Supply Curve
The portion of the firm's marginal cost curve that lies above the average variable cost curve.

SUMMARY OF CASES 1–3 *A perfectly competitive firm produces in the short run as long as price is above average variable cost (cases 1 and 3).*

$$P > AVC \rightarrow \text{Firm produces}$$

A perfectly competitive firm shuts down in the short run if price is less than average variable cost (case 2).

$$P < AVC \rightarrow \text{Firm shuts down}$$

We can summarize the same information in terms of total revenue and total variable costs. *A perfectly competitive firm produces in the short run as long as total revenue is greater than total variable costs (cases 1 and 3).*

$$TR > TVC \rightarrow \text{Firm produces}$$

A perfectly competitive firm shuts down in the short run if total revenue is less than total variable costs (case 2).

$$TR < TVC \rightarrow \text{Firm shuts down}$$

Exhibit 5 reviews some of the material discussed in this section.

The Perfectly Competitive Firm's Short-Run Supply Curve

The perfectly competitive firm produces (supplies output) in the short run if price is above average variable cost. It shuts down (does not supply output) if price is below average variable cost. Therefore, the **short-run supply curve** of the firm is the portion of its marginal cost curve that lies above the average variable cost curve. Only a price above average variable cost will induce the firm to supply output. The short-run supply curve of the perfectly competitive firm is illustrated in Exhibit 6.

exhibit 6

The Perfectly Competitive Firm's Short-Run Supply Curve

The short-run supply curve is that portion of the firm's marginal cost curve that lies above the average variable cost curve.

exhibit 7

Deriving the Market (Industry) Supply Curve for a Perfectly Competitive Market

In (a) we add (horizontally) the quantity supplied by each firm to derive the market supply curve. The market supply curve and the market demand curve are shown in (b). Together, they determine equilibrium price and quantity.

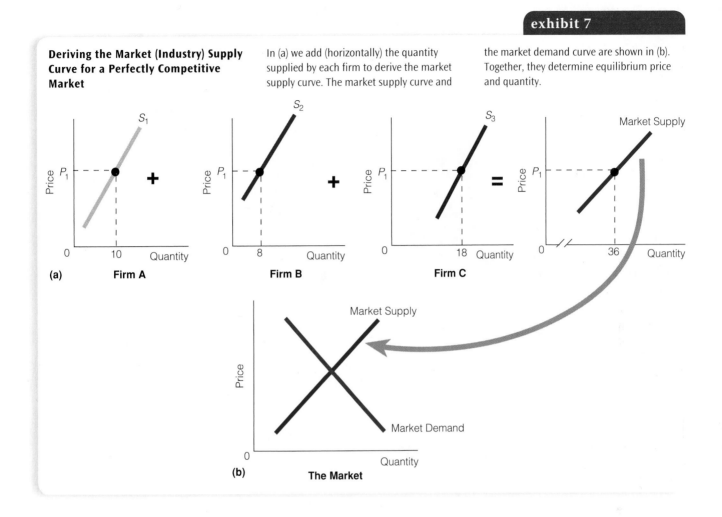

(a)   Firm A   Firm B   Firm C

(b)   The Market

From Firm to Market (Industry) Supply Curve

After we know that the perfectly competitive firm's short-run supply curve is the part of its marginal cost curve above its average variable cost curve, it is a simple matter to derive the **short-run market (industry) supply curve**.[3] We horizontally add the short-run supply curves for all firms in the perfectly competitive market or industry.

Consider, for simplicity, an industry made up of three firms: A, B, and C [see Exhibit 7(a)]. At a price of P_1, firm A supplies 10 units, firm B supplies 8 units, and firm C supplies 18 units. One point on the market supply curve thus corresponds to P_1 on the price axis and 36 units $(10 + 8 + 18 = 36)$ on the quantity axis.[4] If we follow this procedure for all prices, we have the short-run market supply curve. This market supply curve, shown in the market setting in part (b) of the exhibit, is used along with the market demand curve (derived in Chapter 3) to determine equilibrium price and quantity.

Short-Run Market (Industry) Supply Curve
The horizontal addition of all existing firms' short-run supply curves.

3. In discussing market structures, the words *industry* and *market* are often used interchangeably when a single-product industry is under consideration, which is the case here.

4. We add one qualification: Each firm's supply curve is drawn on the assumption that the prices of the variable input are constant.

FRANK SINATRA, SUGAR RAY ROBINSON, AND THE JAMESTOWN SETTLEMENT

Every year, the U.S. Postal Service issues commemorative stamps, which are stamps issued to honor or to commemorate a place, event, or person. In the past, commemorative stamps have been issued of Frank Sinatra, Sugar Ray Robinson, Hattie McDaniel, Benjamin Franklin, the settlement of Jamestown, flags of the nation, and so on.

© AP PHOTO/BILL KOSTROUN

Why does the U.S. Postal Service issue these special, commemorative stamps? To find out, let's analyze stamps from the point of view of the Postal Service.

Most people buy stamps to send letters or other items through the mail. When a stamp is placed on a letter, the Postal Service is required to deliver the letter to the address on the envelope. Suppose the unit variable cost (*AVC*) of producing a stamp is 7 cents, regardless of the likeness on the front, and the unit variable cost of delivering a letter with a stamp on it is 19 cents. The sum of the unit variable costs of producing the stamp and delivering the letter is 26 cents.

$$AVC \text{ stamp} = AVC \text{ producing the stamp} + AVC \text{ delivering the letter}$$

For simplicity, we assume *AFC* = 0; so *AVC* = *ATC*. In other words, the per-unit cost of the stamp is 26 cents. It follows, then, that if the price of a stamp is 42 cents, the U.S. Postal Service earns a per-unit profit of 16 cents per stamp issued and used.

Now suppose the U.S. Postal Service wants to increase its per-unit profit. One way to do so is to issue stamps that people wouldn't put on items to be mailed, that is, to issue stamps that people want to collect.

Hence the commemorative stamps that the U.S. Postal Service issues and sells. Many people buy these stamps not to mail letters, but to collect them. When the stamp is not used, the U.S. Postal Service doesn't incur the unit variable cost of delivering mail. Thus the average total cost of the commemorative stamp falls by the *AVC* of delivering the letter, which in turn means the *ATC* of the stamp falls to 7 cents (the *AVC* of producing the stamp). Consequently, the profit per unit for issuing collectors' stamps rises to 35 cents for a 42-cent stamp.

Why Is the Market Supply Curve Upward Sloping?

Recall that in Chapter 3, when the demand and supply curves were introduced, the supply curve was drawn upward sloping because of the law of diminishing marginal returns. To see this, consider the following questions and answers.

Question 1: Why do we draw market supply curves upward sloping?

Answer: Because market supply curves are the horizontal addition of firms' supply curves, and firms' supply curves are upward sloping.

Question 2: But why are firms' supply curves upward sloping?

Answer: Because the supply curve for each firm is that portion of its marginal cost (*MC*) curve that is *above* its average variable cost (*AVC*) curve—and this portion of the *MC* curve is upward sloping.

Question 3: But why do *MC* curves have an upward-sloping portion?

Answer: Because of the law of diminishing marginal returns. According to this law, the marginal physical product (*MPP*) of a variable input eventually declines. When this happens, the *MC* curve begins to rise. So, because of the law of diminishing marginal returns, *MC* curves are upward sloping, and because *MC* curves are upward sloping, so are market supply curves.

Finding ECONOMICS

In the Production of Air Conditioners

Peter is willing to produce more air conditioners if the price of a unit is $800 than if it is $600. Where is the economics here? We can detect the law of supply in Peter's behavior (he produces more at a higher price than at a lower price), and we know that his supply curve is upward sloping. But is there more? As already explained, supply curves are upward sloping because a producer's supply curve is the portion of his *MC* curve above the *AVC* curve, and that portion of the *MC* curve is upward sloping. Finally, at least a portion of an *MC* curve is upward sloping because of the law of diminishing marginal returns.

SELF-TEST

1. If a firm produces the quantity of output at which $MR = MC$, does it necessarily earn profits?

2. In the short run, if a firm finds that its price (*P*) is less than its average total cost (*ATC*), should it shut down its operation?

3. The layperson says that a firm maximizes profits when total revenue (*TR*) minus total cost (*TC*) is as large as possible and positive. The economist says that a firm maximizes profits when it produces the level of output at which $MR = MC$. Explain how the two ways of looking at profit maximization are consistent.

4. Why are market supply curves upward sloping?

PERFECT COMPETITION IN THE LONG RUN

The number of firms in a perfectly competitive market may not be the same in the short run as in the long run. For example, if the typical firm is making economic profits in the short run, new firms will be attracted to the industry, and the number of firms will increase. If the typical firm is sustaining losses, some existing firms will exit the industry, and the number of firms will decrease. This process is explained in greater detail later in this section. We begin by outlining the conditions of long-run competitive equilibrium.

The Conditions of Long-Run Competitive Equilibrium

The following conditions characterize **long-run competitive equilibrium**:

1. *Economic profit is zero: Price (P) is equal to short-run average total cost (SRATC).*

$$P = SRATC$$

The logic of this condition is clear when we analyze what will happen if price is above or below short-run average total cost. If it is above, positive economic profits will attract firms to the industry to obtain the profits. If price is below, losses will result, and some firms will want to exit the industry. Long-run competitive equilibrium cannot exist if firms have an incentive to enter or exit the industry in response to positive economic profits or losses, respectively. For long-run equilibrium to exist, there can be no incentive for firms to enter or exit the industry. This condition is brought about by zero economic profit (normal profit), which is a consequence of the equilibrium price being equal to short-run average total cost.

2. *Firms are producing the quantity of output at which price (P) is equal to marginal cost (MC).*

$$P = MC$$

Long-Run Competitive Equilibrium
The condition where $P = MC = SRATC = LRATC$. There are zero economic profits, firms are producing the quantity of output at which price is equal to marginal cost, and no firm has an incentive to change its plant size.

exhibit 8

Long-Run Competitive Equilibrium

(a) Equilibrium in the market.
(b) Equilibrium for the firm. In (b), $P = MC$ (the firm has no incentive to move away from the quantity of output at which this occurs, q_1); $P = SRATC$ (there is no incentive for firms to enter or exit the industry); and $SRATC = LRATC$ (there is no incentive for the firm to change its plant size).

(a) The Market

(b) The Firm

As previously noted, perfectly competitive firms naturally move toward the output level at which marginal revenue (or price because $MR = P$ for a perfectly competitive firm) equals marginal cost.

3. *No firm has an incentive to change its plant size to produce its current output; that is, SRATC = LRATC at the quantity of output at which P = MC.* To understand this condition, suppose $SRATC > LRATC$ at the quantity of output established in condition 2. If this is the case, the firm has an incentive to change plant size in the long run because it wants to produce its product with the plant size that will give it the lowest average total cost (unit cost). It will have no incentive to change plant size when it is producing the quantity of output at which price equals marginal cost and *SRATC* equals *LRATC*.

$$SRATC = LRATC$$

The three conditions necessary for long-run competitive equilibrium can be stated as (Exhibit 8):

Long-run competitive equilibrium exists when $P = MC = SRATC = LRATC$.

In conclusion, long-run competitive equilibrium exists when firms have no incentive to make any changes. Specifically, long-run competitive equilibrium exists when there is no incentive for firms to:

1. enter or exit the industry,
2. produce more or less output, and
3. change plant size.

Thinking like AN ECONOMIST

Equilibrium Is Where Things Are Headed

Perhaps as you have noticed by now, the concept of equilibrium is an important one in economics because equilibrium is where things are headed; in a way, it is the destination point. To illustrate, suppose that firms in a perfectly competitive market are currently earning positive economic

(continued)

Thinking Like An Economist (continued)

profit. At this point, there are, say, 100 firms in the market. But things are not likely to stay this way, and the number of firms is not likely to remain at 100. Firms are earning positive profits, and so firms not currently in the market will join the market, pushing the number of firms upward from 100. Only when all firms are earning normal profit (zero economic profit) will things remain the way they are. Only then will the market be in equilibrium.[5]

When you get on a train in, say, Los Angeles that is headed for New York City, you are fairly sure the trip is not over until you reach New York City. However, knowing when the trip is over in economics is not as easy. Theoretically, we know the trip is over when equilibrium has been reached. But then the economist has to define the conditions that specify equilibrium.

The Perfectly Competitive Firm and Productive Efficiency

A firm that produces its output at the lowest possible per-unit cost (lowest ATC) is said to exhibit **productive efficiency**. The perfectly competitive firm does this in long-run equilibrium, as shown in Exhibit 8. Productive efficiency is desirable from society's standpoint because it means that perfectly competitive firms are economizing on society's scarce resources and therefore not wasting them.

To illustrate, suppose the lowest unit cost at which good X can be produced is $3—the minimum ATC. If a firm produces 1,000 units of good X at this unit cost, its total cost is $3,000. Now suppose the firm produces good X not at its lowest unit cost of $3 but at a slightly higher unit cost of $3.50. Total cost now equals $3,500. Resources worth $500 were employed producing good X that could have been used to produce other goods, had the firm exhibited productive efficiency. Society could have been richer in goods and services, but now it is not.

Productive Efficiency
The situation that exists when a firm produces its output at the lowest possible per-unit cost (lowest *ATC*).

Industry Adjustment to an Increase in Demand

An increase in market demand for a product can throw an industry out of long-run competitive equilibrium. Suppose we start at long-run competitive equilibrium, where $P = MC = SRATC = LRATC$ (see Exhibit 9). Then market demand rises for the product produced by the firms in the industry, and equilibrium price rises. As a consequence, the demand curve faced by an individual firm (which is its marginal revenue curve) shifts upward.

Next, *existing firms* in the industry increase quantity of output because marginal revenue now intersects marginal cost at a higher quantity of output. In the long run, new firms begin to enter the industry because price is currently above average total cost, and there are positive economic profits.

As new firms enter the industry, the market (industry) supply curve shifts rightward. As a consequence, equilibrium price falls. It falls until long-run competitive equilibrium is reestablished—that is, until there is once again zero economic profit.

Look at the process again, from the initial increase in market demand to the reestablishment of long-run competitive equilibrium: Price increased in the short run (owing to the increase in demand) and then decreased in the long run (owing to the increase in supply). Also, profits increased (owing to the increase in demand and consequent increase in price) and then decreased (owing to the increase in supply and consequent decrease in price). They went from zero to some positive amount and then back to zero.

5. We are assuming that our other long-run equilibrium conditions hold, such as no firms want to change plant size and there is no incentive for any firm to produce any more or any less output.

exhibit 9

The Process of Moving from One Long-Run Competitive Equilibrium Position to Another

This exhibit describes what happens on both the market level and the firm level when demand rises and throws an industry out of long-run competitive equilibrium.

(1) The industry is in long-run competitive equilibrium. All firms earn zero economic profit.

(2) For some reason, the market demand curve rises and price rises.

(3) This raises the demand and marginal revenue curves for the firm, and it produces more output.

(4) At a higher price and demand curve, firms in the industry are now earning positive economic profits.

(5) Other firms (currently not in the industry) view the positive economic profits as an incentive to join the industry.

(6) As new firms join the industry, the market supply curve shifts to the right and price declines.

(7) This lowers the demand and marginal revenue curves for firms. Older firms, which made up the industry before market demand increased (back in box 2), cut back output.

(8) Eventually, all firms earn zero economic profit and are in long-run competitive equilibrium.

The *up-and-down* movements in both price and profits in response to an increase in demand are important to note. Too often people see only the primary upward movements in both price and profits, and they ignore or forget the secondary downward movements. However, the secondary effects in price and profits are as important as the primary effects.

The adjustment to an increase in demand brings up an important question: If price first rises owing to an increase in market demand and later falls owing to an increase in market supply, will the new equilibrium price be greater than, less than, or equal to the *original* equilibrium price? (In Exhibit 9, the new equilibrium is shown as equal to the original equilibrium price, but this need not be the case.)

exhibit 10

Long-Run Industry Supply Curves

LRS = Long-run industry supply. Each part illustrates the same scenario, but with different results depending on whether the industry has (a) constant costs, (b) increasing costs, or (c) decreasing costs. In each part, we start at long-run competitive equilibrium (point 1). Demand increases, price rises from P_1

to P_2, and there are positive economic profits. Consequently, existing firms increase output and new firms are attracted to the industry. In (a), input costs remain constant as output increases, so the firms' cost curves do not shift. Profits fall to zero through a decline in price. This implies that in a constant-cost industry, the supply curve shifts rightward by the same amount as the demand curve shifts rightward.

In (b), input costs increase as output increases. Profits are squeezed by a combination of rising costs and falling prices. The new equilibrium price (P_3) for an increasing-cost industry is higher than the old equilibrium price (P_1). In (c), input costs decrease as output increases. The new equilibrium price (P_3) for a decreasing-cost industry is lower than the old equilibrium price (P_1).

(a) Constant-Cost Industry

New equilibrium price (P_1) = Old equilibrium price (P_1)

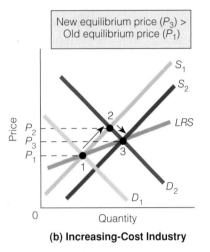

(b) Increasing-Cost Industry

New equilibrium price (P_3) > Old equilibrium price (P_1)

(c) Decreasing-Cost Industry

New equilibrium price (P_3) < Old equilibrium price (P_1)

For example, if the equilibrium price is $10 before the increase in market demand, will the new equilibrium price (after market and firm adjustments have taken place) be greater than, less than, or equal to $10? The answer depends on whether increasing cost, decreasing cost, or constant cost, respectively, describes the industry in which the increase in demand has taken place.

CONSTANT-COST INDUSTRY In a constant-cost industry, average total costs (unit costs) do not change as output increases or decreases when firms enter or exit the market or industry. If market demand increases for a good produced by firms in a constant-cost industry, price will initially rise and then will finally fall to its original level, as shown in Exhibit 10(a).

We start from a position of long-run competitive equilibrium where there are zero economic profits—at point 1. Then, demand increases and price rises from P_1 to P_2. At P_2, there are positive economic profits, which cause the firms currently in the industry to increase output. We move up the supply curve, S_1, from point 1 to point 2. Next, new firms, drawn by the profits, enter the industry, causing the supply curve to shift rightward.

For a constant-cost industry, output is increased without a change in the price of inputs. Because of this, the firms' cost curves do not shift. But if costs do not rise to reduce the profits in the industry, then price must fall. (Profits can be reduced in two ways: through a rise in costs or a fall in price.) Price must fall to its original level (P_1) before profits can be zero, implying that the supply curve shifts rightward by the same amount that the demand curve shifts rightward. In the exhibit, this is a shift from S_1 to S_2. The two long-run equilibrium points (1 and 3), where economic profits are zero, define the

Long-Run (Industry) Supply (LRS) Curve
Graphic representation of the quantities of output that the industry is prepared to supply at different prices after the entry and exit of firms are completed.

Constant-Cost Industry
An industry in which average total costs do not change as (industry) output increases or decreases when firms enter or exit the industry, respectively.

Increasing-Cost Industry
An industry in which average total costs increase as output increases and decrease as output decreases when firms enter and exit the industry, respectively.

Decreasing-Cost Industry
An industry in which average total costs decrease as output increases and increase as output decreases when firms enter and exit the industry, respectively.

long-run (industry) supply (*LRS*) curve. A **constant-cost industry** is thus characterized by a horizontal long-run supply curve.

INCREASING-COST INDUSTRY In an increasing-cost industry, average total costs (unit costs) increase as output increases and firms enter the industry, and they decrease as output decreases and firms exit the industry. If market demand increases for a good produced by firms in an increasing-cost industry, price will initially rise and then finally fall to a level above its original level.

In Exhibit 10(b), we start, as before, in long-run competitive equilibrium at point 1. Demand increases and price rises from P_1 to P_2. This shift brings about positive economic profits, which cause firms in the industry to increase output and new firms to enter the industry. So far, this is the same process as for a constant-cost industry. However, in an increasing-cost industry, as firms purchase more inputs to produce more output, some input prices rise and cost curves shift. In short, as industry output increases, profits are caught in a two-way squeeze: Price is coming down, and costs are rising. If costs are rising as price is falling, then it is not necessary for price to fall to its original level before zero economic profits rule once again. Price will not have to fall as far to restore long-run competitive equilibrium in an increasing-cost industry as in a constant-cost industry. We would expect, then, that when an increasing-cost industry experiences an increase in demand, the new equilibrium price will be higher than the old equilibrium price. This means the supply curve shifts rightward by less than the demand curve shifts rightward. An **increasing-cost industry** is characterized by an upward-sloping long-run supply curve.

DECREASING-COST INDUSTRY In a decreasing-cost industry, average total costs (unit costs) decrease as output increases as firms enter the industry, and they increase as output decreases and firms exit the industry. If market demand increases for a good produced by firms in a decreasing-cost industry, price will initially rise and then finally fall to a level below its original level. In Exhibit 10(c), price moves from P_1 to P_2 and then to P_3. In such an industry, average total costs decrease as new firms enter the industry; so price must fall below its original level to eliminate profits. A **decreasing-cost industry** is characterized by a downward-sloping long-run supply curve.

 Common MISCONCEPTIONS

About Profits

The layperson often views profits much the same way as the English teacher views a period. Profits come at the end of a production process, and a period comes at the end of a sentence. In reality, profit is more like a comma, in that something comes after it. Profit is more like an ongoing process, which we've just explained: Demand rises, causing price to rise, causing profits to rise. But things don't stop there. The higher profits call forth new firms into the market, causing the supply curve in the market to shift rightward, in turn causing price and profits to fall.

Think of how not knowing about the up-and-down movements in price and profits can lead to some unintended effects. The demand for a good rises, and with it both price and profits rise. Big profits are reported in the news. Politicians start talking about taxing those so-called high profits, but might taxing those high profits stop the price-profits story from continuing? Without the profits, new firms don't enter the market. Without the new firms, supply doesn't increase. In other words, to tax the profits might have the unintended effect of reducing the supply of goods from what it would be if the profits weren't taxed.

Finding ECONOMICS

In the Computer Industry and Elsewhere

Years ago, the prices of a personal computer, calculator, DVD recorder, and plasma television set were higher than they are today. Where is the economics here? Do higher prices have anything to do with what we have just discussed—prices and profits? The early introduction of these goods often came with (what in hindsight appears to be) high prices and high profits. The high profits called forth new firms into the market. The new firms ended up increasing supply and reducing prices and profits. (Other changes were occurring at the same time, such as changes in technology.)

Thinking like AN ECONOMIST

Easy Entry into a Market Matters

Once again demand rises, price rises, and profits go from zero to positive. As already explained, this is not the end of the story as long as new firms can enter the market. But suppose they can't. If something prevents firms from entering the market, will the end of the story be the same, with price moving down and profit returning to zero? Not at all. The different ending points out how important easy entry into the market is to the story. Without easy entry, the story is a different story altogether: prices are more likely to stay high and profits are more likely to stay positive.

Industry Adjustment to a Decrease in Demand

Demand can decrease as well as increase. For an increase in demand, we simply reverse the analysis to explain industry adjustment to a decrease in demand. Starting at long-run competitive equilibrium, market demand decreases. As a consequence, in the short run, the equilibrium price falls, effectively shifting the firm's demand curve (marginal revenue curve) downward. Following this, some firms in the industry decrease production because marginal revenue intersects marginal cost at a lower level of output, and some firms shut down.

In the long run, some firms will leave the industry because price is below the average total cost, and they are suffering continual losses. As firms leave the industry, the market supply curve shifts leftward. As a consequence, the equilibrium price rises and continues to rise until long-run competitive equilibrium is reestablished—that is, until there are, once again, zero economic profits (instead of negative economic profits). Whether the new equilibrium price is greater than, less than, or equal to the original equilibrium price depends on whether decreasing cost, increasing cost, or constant cost, respectively, describes the industry in which demand decreased.

Differences in Costs, Differences in Profits: Now You See It, Now You Don't

Suppose two farmers, Hancock and Cordero, produce wheat. Farmer Cordero grows his wheat on fertile land; farmer Hancock grows her wheat on poor soil. Both farmers sell their wheat for the same price, but because of the difference in the quality of their land, Cordero has lower average total costs than Hancock, as shown in Exhibit 11.

If we compare the initial situations of the two farmers (each farmer's ATC_1), we notice that Cordero is earning profits and Hancock is not. Cordero is earning profits because he pays lower average total costs than Hancock as a consequence of farming higher-quality land. But is this situation likely to continue? Is Cordero likely to continue earning profits? The answer is no.

Individuals will bid up the price of the fertile land that Cordero farms vis-à-vis the poor-quality land that Hancock farms. In other words, if Cordero is renting his farmland,

Differences in Costs, Differences in Profits: Now You See It, Now It's Gone

At ATC_1 for both farmers, Cordero earns profits and Hancock does not. Cordero earns profits because the land he farms is of higher quality (more productive) than Hancock's land. Eventually, this fact is taken into account, by Cordero either paying higher rent for the land or incurring implicit costs for it. This moves Cordero's ATC curve upward to the same level as Hancock's, and Cordero earns zero economic profits. The profits have gone as payment (implicit or explicit) for the higher quality, more productive land.

(a) Farmer Hancock

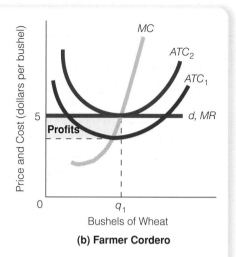

(b) Farmer Cordero

the rent he pays will increase to reflect the superior quality of the land. The rent will increase by an amount equal to the profits per time period—that is, an amount equal to the shaded portion in Exhibit 11(b). If Cordero owns the land, the superior quality of the land will have a higher implicit cost attached to it (Cordero can rent it for more than Hancock can rent her land, assuming Hancock owns her land). This process is reflected in the average total cost curve.

In Exhibit 11(b), ATC_2 reflects either the higher rent Cordero must pay for the superior land or the full implicit cost he incurs by farming land he owns. In either case, when the average total cost curve reflects all costs, Cordero will be in the same situation as Hancock; he, too, will be earning zero economic profits.

The profit has gone as payment for the higher-quality, more productive resource responsible for the lower average total costs in the first place. Consequently, average total costs are no longer relatively lower for the person or firm that employs the higher-quality, more productive resource or input.

Profit and Discrimination

A firm's discriminatory behavior can affect its profits in the context of the model of perfect competition. Let's start at the position of long-run competitive equilibrium, where firms are earning zero economic profits. Consider the owner of a firm who chooses not to hire an excellent worker (a worker who is above average, let's say) simply because of that worker's race, religion, or gender. If the owner of the firm discriminates in any way, what happens to his profits? If he chooses not to employ high-quality employees because of their race, religion, or gender, then his costs will rise above the costs of his competitors who hire the best employees—irrespective of race, religion, or gender. Because he is initially earning zero profit, where $TR = TC$, this act of discrimination will raise TC and push him into taking economic losses. If the owner in the example is a manager, he may lose his job because owners may decide to replace managers of firms earning subnormal profits. Thus, profit maximization by shareholders works to reduce discrimination.

Our conclusion is that if a firm is in a perfectly competitive market structure, it will pay penalties if it chooses to discriminate. This is to say not that discrimination will disappear, but only that discrimination comes with a price tag. And according to economic theory, the more something costs, the less of it there will be, *ceteris paribus.*

SELF·TEST

1. If firms in a perfectly competitive market are earning positive economic profits, what will happen?

2. If firms in a perfectly competitive market want to produce more output, is the market in long-run equilibrium?

3. If a perfectly competitive market in long-run equilibrium witnesses an increase in demand, what will happen to price?

4. Suppose two firms produce computer software. Firm A employs a software genius at the same salary that firm B employs a mediocre software engineer. Will the firm that employs the software genius earn higher profits than the other firm, *ceteris paribus*?

TOPICS FOR ANALYSIS WITHIN THE THEORY OF PERFECT COMPETITION

This section briefly analyzes three topics in the theory of perfect competition: higher costs and higher prices, advertising, and setting prices.

Do Higher Costs Mean Higher Prices?

Suppose that 600 firms are in an industry and that each firm sells the same product at the same price. Then one of these firms experiences a rise in its marginal costs of production. Someone immediately comments, "Higher costs for the firm today, higher prices for the consumer tomorrow," the assumption being that firms experiencing a rise in costs simply pass the higher costs on to consumers in the form of higher prices.

Will this occur in a perfectly competitive market structure? Remember that each firm in the industry is a price taker; furthermore, only one firm has experienced a rise in marginal costs. Because this firm supplies only a tiny percentage of the total market supply, the market supply curve is unlikely to undergo more than a negligible change. And if the market supply curve does not change, neither will equilibrium price. In short, a rise in costs incurred by one of many firms does not mean consumers will pay higher prices. Of course, if many of the firms in the industry experienced a rise in costs, the market supply curve would have been affected, along with price.

 Thinking like AN ECONOMIST

A Reasonable-Sounding Argument Is Not Enough

Sometimes, two or more explanations may seem equally reasonable. For example, observing that all firms in an industry sell their products for the same price, two explanations seem equally plausible: The firms collude on price. and the firms are price takers. But for the economist, a reasonable explanation is not sufficient; she wants the correct explanation. The economist is skeptical of any explanation that simply sounds reasonable. She needs evidence (often in the form of data) that supports the explanation.

Will the Perfectly Competitive Firm Advertise?

Individual farmers don't advertise. You've never seen an advertisement for, say, farmer Johnson's milk for a couple of reasons. First, farmer Johnson sells a homogeneous product; so advertising his milk is the same as advertising every dairy farmer's milk. Second, farmer

LOST SALARIES

We have to go back, Kate. We have to go back.
—Jack Shephard, "Through the Looking Glass," *Lost*, Season 3

In our discussion of Hancock and Cordero (two farmers who produce wheat), we found that Cordero was earning profits and Hancock was not because Cordero farmed higher-quality land than Hancock. In time, though, Cordero's higher profits ended up going into higher rent for the higher-quality land. The profit therefore went as payment for the higher-quality, more productive resource responsible for the lower average total costs in the first place.

Turn from farming to acting, in the second season of ABC's television show *Lost*, most cast members were earning in the range of $20,000 to $40,000 per episode. As *Lost* became an increasingly profitable show for ABC, the salaries of the cast members increased. In the third season of *Lost*, many of the cast members were earning $80,000

© TOUCHSTONE/ABC/THE KOBAL COLLECTION

per episode. One character in particular, Matthew Fox, who plays Jack Shephard on the program, received a bonus of $250,000 on top of his per-episode pay increase.

Thus the process that played out with our two farmers, Cordero and Hancock, plays out elsewhere, in this case in the television industry. In that industry, profits one day often get turned into salaries the next.

A secondary point is that market forces have much more to say about one's income than many of us might initially believe. Are the employees (the labor resources) of a firm at the mercy of the owners? Do they have to accept the salary that the owners want to pay, no matter how low? In the case of ABC and *Lost*, wouldn't ABC prefer paying cast members only $1,000 an episode instead of $80,000? And wouldn't a lower salary of $500 an episode be even better?

Johnson is in a perfectly competitive market; so he can sell all the milk he wants at the going price. Why should he advertise? From his viewpoint, advertising has costs and no benefits.

However, a perfectly competitive industry might advertise. For example, if farmer Johnson won't advertise his milk, the milk industry might advertise milk in general in the hope of shifting the market demand curve for milk to the right. This is actually what the milk industry hopes to do with its commercial message, "Got milk?"

Supplier-Set Price Versus Market-Determined Price: Collusion or Competition?

Suppose the only thing you know about a particular industry is that all the firms in it sell their products at the same price. To explain this, some people argue that the firms are colluding—that is, the firms come together, pick a price, and stick to it. This, of course, is one way all firms can arrive at the same price for their products, but it is not the only way. Another way, as described in this chapter, is that all firms are price takers; that is, the firms are in a perfectly competitive market structure. In this case, there is no collusion.

SELF-TEST

1. In a perfectly competitive market, do higher costs mean higher prices?
2. If you see a product advertised on television, does it follow that the product cannot be produced in a perfectly competitive market?

"DO YOU HAVE TO KNOW THE *MR = MC* CONDITION TO BE SUCCESSFUL IN BUSINESS?"

Student:

Here is what seems odd to me. I believe that some people are successful in business without their knowing any of the material in this chapter. Isn't it possible for a person to be successful in business without knowing the *MR = MC* condition, or the shutdown decision (shut down when *P* is less than *AVC*), and so on?

Instructor:

Yes, but keep in mind that just because someone doesn't have to know the *MR = MC* condition to try to put it into operation. Most people don't know the physics behind the operation of a car, but they drive a car as if they do know the physics.

Student:

Are you saying that it's possible to know and not know something at the same time? That sounds odd to me.

Instructor:

That's not exactly what I am saying. I'm saying it's possible to do something you don't know you're doing. Let me give you an example. Suppose Jack owns and operates his own business producing shoe boxes. He has never taken an economics course in his life, and he doesn't know the first thing about marginal revenue, marginal cost, average total cost, and so on. His not knowing these things doesn't mean he doesn't have to figure out how many shoe boxes to produce. So how does he do it without a knowledge of marginal revenue and marginal cost? All Jack has to know is that it is a good idea to keep producing shoe boxes when more money is coming in the front door (in additional revenue) than is going out the back door (in additional costs). That's it. That basic, very elemental idea is behind the *MR = MC* condition.

Student:

Does the same hold for the things like knowing when to continuing producing a good and knowing when to shut down?

Instructor:

Sure. The economist advises to shut down when *P < AVC*, but this is just a slightly more sophisticated way of expressing the idea that a firm should shut down when it would lose more from not shutting down. Consider Yvonne who, like Jack, owns her own business. She is currently wondering whether she should stop producing a good. She may not know the first thing about the relationship between price and average variable cost, but certainly she can put some numbers to paper and figure out how much money she loses if she shuts down and how much money she loses if she doesn't shut down.

Student:

I think I see what you are getting at. The economist seems only to be formalizing what people do if they are trying to maximize their profits or minimize their losses. The average Joe or Jane in business simply continues producing additional units of a good as long as more money comes into the firm by selling the additional unit than is going out by producing the additional unit. Then the economist simply says, "Produce as long as *MR* is greater than *MC*." Am I right?

Instructor:

Yes, you're right.

Student:

Looking at things this way makes the material in this chapter seem a little easier and a little more grounded in reality.

Points to Remember

1. Not knowing the *MR = MC* condition doesn't mean that a real-world businessperson doesn't abide by it.

2. Many of the rules or conditions in this chapter (produce until *MR = MC*, shut down when *P < AVC*) are simply formalized ways of expressing what individuals in business settings do when they seek to maximize profits or minimize losses.

a reader asks | Does Job Security Have Anything to Do with Fixed and Variable Costs?

What is the relationship among fixed, variable, and total costs, the firm's shutdown decision, and employee job security?

Consider the total fixed cost/total cost ratio (*TFC/TC*) for firms. The greater the ratio is—that is, the larger *TFC* is relative to *TC*—the more likely the firm is to operate in the short run; the smaller the ratio is, the less likely the firm is to operate in the short run. Therefore, the more likely the firm is to operate in the short run, the greater the job security will be for the employees of the firm; the less likely the firm is to operate in the short run, the less job security will be for the employees of the firm.

To illustrate, suppose two firms, X and Y, have the same following costs and ratios:

The two firms have the same total cost ($600), but the fixed and variable costs are different percentages of total cost. Firm X has a lower *TVC/TC* ratio and a higher *TFC/TC* ratio than firm Y has. If total revenue falls to, say, $499, firm Y will shut down because its total revenue will be less than its total variable cost (*TVC*), but firm X will continue to operate. For firm X, total revenue will have to fall below $400 before it will shut down. In other words, the firm with the higher *TFC/TC* ratio (firm X) stays operational longer than the firm with the lower *TFC/TC* ratio (firm Y). So, if everything else is equal between the two firms, an employee working for firm X is less likely to be laid off due to declining total revenue than an employee working for firm Y.

Firm X	Firm Y
$TC = \$600$	$TC = \$600$
$TVC = \$400$	$TVC = \$500$
$TFC = \$200$	$TFC = \$100$
$TVC/TC = \$400/\$600 = 0.66$	$TVC/TC = \$500/\$600 = 0.83$
$TFC/TC = \$200/\$600 = 0.33$	$TFC/TC = \$100/\$600 = 0.17$

Chapter Summary

THE THEORY OF PERFECT COMPETITION

- The theory of perfect competition is built on four assumptions: (1) There are many sellers and many buyers, none of whom is large in relation to total sales or purchases. (2) Each firm produces and sells a homogeneous product. (3) Buyers and sellers have all relevant information with respect to prices, product quality, sources of supply, and so on. (4) Entry into or exit from the industry is easy.

- The theory of perfect competition predicts the following: (1) Economic profits will be squeezed out of the industry in the long run by the entry of new firms; that is, zero economic profit exists in the long run. (2) In equilibrium, firms produce the quantity of output at which price equals marginal cost. (3) In the short run, firms will stay in business as long as price covers average variable costs. (4) In the long run, firms will stay in business as long as price covers average total costs. (5) In the short run, an increase in demand will lead to a rise in price; whether the price in the long run will be higher than, lower than, or equal to its original level depends on whether the firm is in an increasing-, decreasing-, or constant-cost industry.

THE PERFECTLY COMPETITIVE FIRM

- A perfectly competitive firm is a price taker. It sells its product only at the market-established equilibrium price.

- The perfectly competitive firm faces a horizontal (flat, perfectly elastic) demand curve. Its demand curve and its marginal revenue curve are the same.

- The perfectly competitive firm (as well as all other firms) maximizes profits (or minimizes losses) by producing the quantity of output at which $MR = MC$.

- For the perfectly competitive firm, price equals marginal revenue.

- A perfectly competitive firm is resource allocative efficient because it produces the quantity of output at which $P = MC$.

PRODUCTION IN THE SHORT RUN

- If $P > ATC$ ($> AVC$), the firm earns economic profits and will continue to operate in the short run.
- If $P < AVC$ ($< ATC$), the firm takes losses. It will shut down because the alternative (continuing to produce) increases the losses.
- If $ATC > P > AVC$, the firm takes losses. Nevertheless, it will continue to operate in the short run because the alternative (shutting down) increases the losses.
- The firm produces in the short run only when price is greater than the average variable cost. Therefore, the portion of its marginal cost curve that lies above the average variable cost curve is the firm's short-run supply curve.

CONDITIONS OF LONG-RUN COMPETITIVE EQUILIBRIUM

- Long-run competitive equilibrium exists when there is no incentive for firms (1) to enter or exit the industry, (2) to produce more or less output, and (3) to change plant size. We formalize these conditions as follows: (1) Economic profits are zero (that is, firms have no incentive to enter

or exit the industry). (2) Firms are producing the quantity of output at which price is equal to marginal cost. (Firms have no incentive to produce more or less output. After all, when $P = MC$, it follows that $MR = MC$ for the perfectly competitive firm, and thus the firm is maximizing profits.) (3) $SRATC = LRATC$ at the quantity of output at which $P = MC$ (that is, firms do not have an incentive to change plant size).

- A perfectly competitive firm exhibits productive efficiency because it produces its output in the long run at the lowest possible per-unit cost (lowest ATC).

INDUSTRY ADJUSTMENT TO A CHANGE IN DEMAND

- In a constant-cost industry, an increase in demand will result in a new equilibrium price equal to the original equilibrium price (before demand increased). In an increasing-cost industry, an increase in demand will result in a new equilibrium price higher than the original equilibrium price. In a decreasing-cost industry, an increase in demand will result in a new equilibrium price lower than the original equilibrium price.
- The long-run supply curve for a constant-cost industry is horizontal (flat, perfectly elastic). The long-run supply curve for an increasing-cost industry is upward sloping. The long-run supply curve for a decreasing-cost industry is downward sloping.

Key Terms and Concepts

Market Structure
Perfect Competition
Price Taker
Marginal Revenue (MR)
Profit-Maximization Rule

Resource Allocative Efficiency
Short-Run (Firm) Supply Curve
Short-Run Market (Industry) Supply Curve

Long-Run Competitive Equilibrium
Productive Efficiency
Constant-Cost Industry

Long-Run (Industry) Supply (LRS) Curve
Increasing-Cost Industry
Decreasing-Cost Industry

Questions and Problems

1 "The firm's entire marginal cost curve is its short-run supply curve." Is the statement true or false? Explain your answer.
2 "In a perfectly competitive market, firms always operate at the lowest per-unit cost." Is the statement true or false? Explain your answer.
3 "Firm A, one firm in a competitive industry, faces higher costs of production. As a result, consumers end up paying higher prices." Discuss.
4 Suppose all firms in a perfectly competitive market structure are in long-run equilibrium. Then demand for the firms' product increases. Initially, price and economic profits rise. Soon afterward, the government decides to tax most (but

not all) of the economic profits, arguing that the firms in the industry did not earn the profits. They were simply the result of an increase in demand. What effect, if any, will the tax have on market adjustment?
5 Explain why one firm sometimes appears to be earning higher profits than another but in reality is not.
6 For a perfectly competitive firm, profit maximization does not conflict with resource allocative efficiency. Do you agree? Explain your answer.
7 The perfectly competitive firm does not increase its quantity of output without limit even though it can sell all it wants at the going price. Why not?

8 Suppose you read in a business magazine that computer firms are reaping high profits. With the theory of perfect competition in mind, what do you expect to happen over time to the following: computer prices, the profits of computer firms, the number of computers on the market, the number of computer firms?

9 In your own words, explain resource allocative efficiency.

10 The term *price taker* can apply to buyers as well as sellers. A price-taking buyer is one who cannot influence price by changing the amount she buys. What goods do you buy for which you are a price taker? What goods do you buy for which you are not a price taker?

11 Why study the theory of perfect competition if no real-world market completely satisfies all of the theory's assumptions?

12 Explain why a perfectly competitive firm will shut down in the short run if price is lower than the average variable cost but will continue to produce if price is below the average total cost but above the average variable cost.

13 In long-run competitive equilibrium, $P = MC = SRATC = LRATC$. Because $P = MR$, we can write the condition as $P = MR = MC = SRATC = LRATC$. Now let's look at the condition as consisting of four parts: (a) $P = MR$, (b) $MR = MC$, (c) $P = SRATC$, and (d) $SRATC = LRATC$. To explain (b)—$MR = MC$—we say that this condition exists because the perfectly competitive firm attempts to maximize profits, and this is how it does it. What are the explanations for (a), (c), and (d)?

14 Suppose the government imposes a production tax on one perfectly competitive firm in an industry. For each unit the firm produces, it must pay $1 to the government. Will consumers in this market end up paying higher prices because of the tax? Why or why not?

15 Why is the marginal revenue curve for a perfectly competitive firm the same as its demand curve?

16 Many plumbers charge the same price for coming to your house to fix a kitchen sink. Is this because plumbers are colluding?

17 Do firms in a perfectly competitive market exhibit productive efficiency? Why or why not?

Working with Numbers and Graphs

1 Given the following information, state whether the perfectly competitive firm should shut down or continue to operate in the short run.

   a. $Q = 100; P = $10; AFC = $3; AVC = 4.

   b. $Q = 70; P = $5; AFC = $2; AVC = 7.

   c. $Q = 150; P = $7; AFC = $5; AVC = 6.

2 If total revenue increases at a constant rate, what does this imply about marginal revenue?

3 Using the following table, what quantity of output should the firm produce? Explain your answer.

Q	TR	TC
0	$0	$0
1	100	50
2	200	110
3	300	180
4	400	260
5	500	360
6	600	480

4 Is the firm in question 3 a perfectly competitive firm? Explain your answer.

5 Explain how a market supply curve is derived.

6 Draw the following:

   a. A perfectly competitive firm that earns profits.

   b. A perfectly competitive firm that incurs losses but that will continue operating in the short run.

   c. A perfectly competitive firm that incurs losses and that will shut down in the short run.

7 Why is the perfectly competitive firm's supply curve the portion of its marginal cost curve that is above its average variable cost curve?

8 In the following figure, what area(s) represent(s) the following at Q_1?

   a. Total cost

   b. Total variable cost

   c. Total revenue

   d. Loss (negative profit)

9 Why does the MC curve cut the ATC curve at the latter's lowest point?

10 Suppose all firms in a perfectly competitive market are in long-run equilibrium. Illustrate what a perfectly competitive firm will do if market demand rises.

© IOFOTO/SHUTTERSTOCK

CHAPTER 9

MONOPOLY

Introduction Monopoly is at the opposite end of the market structure spectrum from perfect competition, discussed in the last chapter. We begin our discussion of monopoly by outlining the assumptions on which the theory of monopoly is built. We move on to talk about the quantity of output the monopolist wants to produce and the price (per unit) at which it sells that output. Much of this chapter focuses on the differences between the perfectly competitive firm and the monopoly firm.

THE THEORY OF MONOPOLY

The theory of **monopoly** is built on three assumptions:

1. *There is one seller.* In effect, the firm is the industry. Contrast this situation with perfect competition, where many firms make up the industry.

2. *The single seller sells a product for which there are no close substitutes.* Because there are no close substitutes for its product, the single seller—the monopolist or monopoly firm—faces little, if any, competition.

3. *There are extremely high barriers to entry.* In the theory of perfect competition, it is easy for a firm to enter the industry. In the theory of monopoly, it is very hard (if not impossible) for a firm to enter the industry. Extremely high barriers keep out new firms.

Examples of monopoly include many public utilities (local public utilities such as electricity, water, and gas companies) and the U.S. Postal Service (in the delivery of first-class mail).

Barriers to Entry: A Key to Understanding Monopoly

If a firm is a single seller of a product, why don't other firms enter the market and produce the same product? Legal barriers, economies of scale, or one firm's exclusive

Monopoly
A theory of market structure based on three assumptions: There is one seller, it sells a product for which no close substitutes exist, and there are extremely high barriers to entry.

ownership of a scarce resource may make it difficult or impossible for new firms to enter the market.

LEGAL BARRIERS Legal barriers include public franchises, patents, and government licenses. A **public franchise** is a right that government grants to a firm and that permits the firm to provide a particular good or service and excludes all others from doing the same (thus eliminating potential competition by law). For example, the U.S. Postal Service has been granted the exclusive franchise to deliver first-class mail. Many public utilities operate under state and local franchises, as do food and gas suppliers along many state turnpikes.

In the United States, patents are granted to inventors of a product or process for a period of 20 years. During this time, the patent holder is shielded from competitors; no one else can legally produce and sell the patented product or process. The rationale behind patents is that they encourage innovation in an economy. It is argued that few people will waste their time and money trying to invent a new product if their competitors can immediately copy and sell it.

Entry into some industries and occupations requires a government-granted license. For example, radio and television stations cannot operate without a license from the Federal Communications Commission (FCC). In most states, a person needs to be licensed to join the ranks of physicians, dentists, architects, nurses, embalmers, barbers, veterinarians, and lawyers, among others.

Some cities also use licensing as a form of legal barrier. For example, the Taxi & Limousine Commission requires a person to have a taxi license, called a *taxi medallion,* to own and operate a taxi in New York City. The medallion is similar to a business license; a person needs it to lawfully operate a taxicab business. The number of taxi medallions (licenses) has been fixed at about 12,000 for many years. The price of a medallion changes according to changes in the demand for them. In 1976, a medallion was about $45,000; in 1988, it was $125,000; and in January 2008, it was $429,000. Obviously, many people find $429,000 a barrier to entering the taxi business. Thus, many economists believe that taxi medallions in New York City are a form of legal barrier.

ECONOMIES OF SCALE In some industries, low average total costs (low unit costs) are obtained only through large-scale production. Thus, if new entrants are to compete in the industry, they must enter it on a large scale. But having to produce on this scale is risky and costly, and it therefore acts as a barrier to entry. If economies of scale are so pronounced that only one firm can survive in the industry, the firm is called a **natural monopoly**. Often cited examples of natural monopoly include public utilities that provide gas, water, and electricity. A later chapter discusses government regulation of a natural monopoly.

EXCLUSIVE OWNERSHIP OF A NECESSARY RESOURCE Existing firms may be protected from the entry of new firms by the exclusive or nearly exclusive ownership of a resource needed to enter the industry. The classic example is the Aluminum Company of America (Alcoa), which for a time controlled almost all sources of bauxite in the United States. Alcoa was the sole producer of aluminum in the country from the late 19th century until the 1940s. Many people today view the De Beers Company of South Africa as a monopoly because it controls a large percentage of diamond production and sales. Strictly speaking, De Beers is more of a marketing cartel than a monopolist, although, as discussed in the next chapter, a successful cartel acts much like a monopolist.

Public Franchise
A right granted to a firm by government that permits the firm to provide a particular good or service and that excludes all others from doing the same.

Natural Monopoly
The condition where economies of scale are so pronounced that only one firm can survive.

MONOPOLY AND THE BOSTON TEA PARTY

The original meaning of the word *monopoly* was an exclusive right to sell something. At one time, kings and queens granted monopolies to people whom they favored. The monopoly entitled the person to be the sole producer or seller of a particular good. If anyone dared to compete, the crown could have the offender fined or imprisoned.

© BETTMANN/CORBIS

The issue of monopoly came up in the early history of America. In 1767, the British Parliament passed the Townsend Acts, which imposed taxes (or duties) on various products that were imported into the American colonies. The taxes were so hated in the colonies that they prompted protest and noncompliance, and the taxes were repealed in 1770, except for one: the tax on tea. Some historians state that the British Parliament left the tax on tea to show the colonists

that it had the right to raise tax revenue without seeking colonial approval. To get around the tax, the colonists started to buy tea from Dutch traders.

Then, in 1773, the British East India Company was in financial trouble. To help solve its financial problems, it sought a special privilege—a monopoly—from the British Parliament. In response, Parliament passed the Tea Act, which granted the company the sole right to export tea to the colonies—a monopoly. The combination of the tax and the monopoly right given to the British East India Company angered the colonists and is said to have led to the Boston Tea Party on December 16, 1773. The colonists who took part in the Boston Tea Party threw overboard 342 chests of tea owned by the monopoly-wielding British East India Company.

Finding ECONOMICS

At JFK Airport in New York City

Nathan has just picked up his luggage in the baggage terminal of JFK Airport. He is heading out of the terminal to find a taxi. His destination is the Sheraton Manhattan hotel in midtown Manhattan. As he walks out the doors of the baggage terminal, a man says to him, "Looking for a taxi?" Nathan says yes. The man says, "Walk with me. I'm over here." When Nathan gets to the man's car, he realizes he is not a yellow taxi driver but someone who does not have a license to operate a taxi in New York City but who is offering transportation services. Nathan mentions this fact to the man, who says he is still willing to drive Nathan to his destination for the same price a taxi service would charge. Nathan ends up not going with him. Where is the economics here?

What we *may* be witnessing is one of the effects of a legal barrier to entry. (We say "may" because we cannot be sure that the man who met Nathan really had Nathan's transportation interests in mind.) As explained earlier, a taxi medallion is needed to operate a taxi service in New York City. The limited number and expense of the medallions acts as a high barrier for individuals who want to enter the taxi business and who might have all the abilities necessary to operate a successful business. The man whom Nathan encountered was trying to bypass this legal barrier.

What Is the Difference Between a Government Monopoly and a Market Monopoly?

Sometimes high barriers to entry exist because competition is legally prohibited, and sometimes barriers exist independently. When high barriers take the form of public franchises, patents, or government licenses, competition is *legally* prohibited. When high barriers take the form of economies of scale or exclusive ownership of a resource, competition is not legally prohibited. In these latter cases, nothing legally prohibits rival firms from entering the market and competing, even though they may choose not to do so; there is no sign on the industry entrance that reads, "No competition allowed."

Some economists use the term *government monopoly* to refer to a monopoly that is legally protected from competition and the term *market monopoly* to refer to a monopoly that is not legally protected from competition. But these terms do not imply that one type is better or worse than the other.

SELF-TEST

(Answers to Self-Test questions are in the Self-Test Appendix.)

1. "There are always some close substitutes for the product any firm sells; therefore, the theory of monopoly (which assumes no close substitutes) cannot be useful." Comment.

2. How do economies of scale act as a barrier to entry?

3. How is a movie superstar like a monopolist?

MONOPOLY PRICING AND OUTPUT DECISIONS

Price Searcher

A seller that has the ability to control to some degree the price of the product it sells.

A monopolist is a **price searcher**, that is, a seller with the ability to control to some degree the price of the product it sells. In contrast to a price taker, a price searcher can raise its price and still sell its product—although not as many units as it could sell at the lower price. The pricing and output decisions of the price-searching monopolist are discussed in this section.

The Monopolist's Demand and Marginal Revenue

In the theory of monopoly, the monopoly firm is the industry, and the industry is the monopoly firm; they are one and the same. Thus the demand curve for the monopoly firm *is* the market demand curve, which is downward sloping. A downward-sloping demand curve posits an inverse relationship between price and quantity demanded: More is sold at lower prices than at higher prices, *ceteris paribus*. Unlike the perfectly competitive firm, the monopolist can raise its price and still sell its product (though not as much).

Because it faces a downward-sloping demand curve, to sell an additional unit of its product, the monopolist must necessarily lower price. For example, the monopoly seller originally planned to sell 2 units of X a day at $10 each and now wishes to sell 3 units a day. To sell more units, it must lower price to, say, $9.75. It sells the 3 units at $9.75 each.[1]

So to sell an additional unit, a monopoly firm must lower price on all previous units. Note that the terms *previous* and *additional* don't refer to an actual sequence of events. A firm doesn't sell 100 units of a good and then decide to sell one more unit. The firm is in an either-or situation. Either the firm sells 100 units over some period of time, or it sells 101 units over the same period of time. If the firm wants to sell 101 units, the price per unit must be lower than if it wants to sell 100 units.

A monopoly seller both gains and loses by lowering price. As Exhibit 1 shows, the monopolist in our example gains $9.75, the price of the additional unit sold, because price was lowered. It loses 50 cents: 25 cents on the first unit it used to sell at $10 plus 25 cents on the second unit it used to sell at $10.

---

1. This discussion is about the behavior of a single-price monopolist, which is a monopolist that sells all units of its product for the same price. Later, we discuss a price-discriminating monopolist.

exhibit 1

(1)	(2)	(3)	(4)
P	**Q**	**TR**	**MR**
$10.00	2	$20.00	
9.75	3	29.25	$9.25

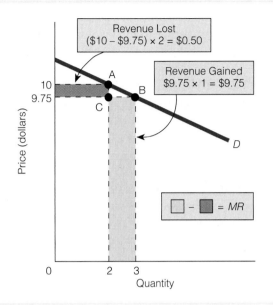

The Dual Effects of a Price Reduction on Total Revenue

To sell an additional unit of its good, a monopolist needs to lower price. This price reduction both gains revenue and loses revenue for the monopolist. In the exhibit, the revenue gained and revenue lost are shaded and labeled. Marginal revenue is equal to the larger shaded area minus the smaller shaded area.

Gains are greater than losses; the monopolist's net gain from selling the additional unit of output is $9.25 ($9.75 − $0.50 = $9.25). This is the monopolist's *marginal revenue*, the change in total revenue that results from selling one additional unit of output. (Total revenue is $20 when 2 units are sold at $10 each. Total revenue is $29.25 when 3 units are sold at $9.75 each. The change in total revenue that results from selling one additional unit of output is $9.25.)

Notice that the price of the good ($9.75) is greater than the marginal revenue ($9.25), $P > MR$. This is the case for a monopoly seller or any price searcher. (Recall that for the firm in perfect competition, $P = MR$.)

For a monopolist, $P > MR$

Common MISCONCEPTIONS

About Monopoly Pricing

Some individuals speak as if a monopoly firm is not constrained by its demand curve, saying, "A monopolist can charge anything it wants to charge." But this is wrong. The highest price a monopolist can charge is determined by the height of its demand curve. No monopoly firm can sell each unit of 100 units of output for, say, $1,000 per unit if the demand curve it faces limits the highest price it can charge to $100.

The Monopolist's Demand and Marginal Revenue Curves Are Not the Same

In perfect competition, the firm's demand curve *is* the same as its marginal revenue curve. In monopoly, the firm's demand curve is not the same as its marginal revenue curve but rather lies *above* its marginal revenue curve.

The demand curve plots price and quantity (P and Q); the marginal revenue curve plots marginal revenue and quantity (MR and Q). Because price is greater than marginal

For a monopolist, the marginal revenue curve lies below the demand curve.

revenue for a monopolist, its demand curve necessarily lies *above* its marginal revenue curve. (Note that price and marginal revenue are the same for the first unit of output; so the demand curve and the marginal revenue curve will share one point in common.) The relationship between a monopolist's demand and marginal revenue curves is illustrated in Exhibit 2.

Price and Output for a Profit-Maximizing Monopolist

The monopolist that seeks to maximize profit produces the quantity of output at which $MR = MC$ (as did the profit-maximizing perfectly competitive firm) and *charges the highest price per unit at which this quantity of output can be sold.*

In Exhibit 3, the highest price at which Q_1, the quantity at which $MR = MC$, can be sold is P_1. Notice that at Q_1, the monopolist charges a price that is greater than marginal cost, $P > MC$. Therefore, the monopolist is *not* resource allocative efficient.

Whether profits are earned depends on whether P_1 is greater or less than average total cost at Q_1. In short, the profit-maximizing price may be the loss-minimizing price. Monopoly profits and monopoly losses are illustrated in Exhibit 4.

Some people argue that suggesting that a monopolist can take a loss is unrealistic. If the monopolist is the only seller in the industry, they maintain that it is guaranteed a profit. But even when a firm is the only seller of a product, it may not earn profits. A monopolist cannot charge any price it wants for its good; it charges the highest price that the demand curve allows it to charge. In some instances, the highest price may be lower than the firm's average total costs (unit costs). If so, the monopolist incurs a loss, as shown in Exhibit 4(b).

If a Firm Maximizes Revenue, Does It Automatically Maximize Profit Too?

We assume that all firms, whether price searchers or price takers, seek to maximize profit. Many people easily fall into the trap of thinking that the price that maximizes total revenue is necessarily the price that maximizes profit. In other words, the higher the firm's total revenue (TR) is, the higher the firm's profit will be. But this is not necessarily the

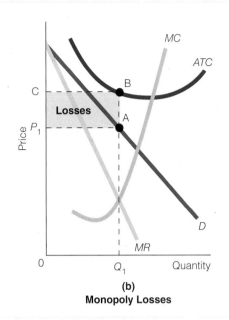

(a)
Monopoly Profits

(b)
Monopoly Losses

exhibit 4

Monopoly Profits and Losses

A monopoly seller is not guaranteed any profits. In (a), price is above average total cost at Q_1, the quantity of output at which $MR = MC$. Therefore, TR (the area $0P_1BQ_1$) is greater than TC (the area $0CAQ_1$), and profits equal the area CP_1BA. In (b), price is below average total cost at Q_1. Therefore, TR (the area $0P_1AQ_1$) is less than TC (the area $0CBQ_1$) and losses equal the area P_1CBA.

case. To illustrate, suppose $TR = \$100$, $TFC = \$40$, and $TVC = \$20$. Because $TC = TFC + TVC$, then $TC = \$60$. The firm's profit, which is $TR - TC$, is $\$40$.

Now suppose the firm can sell one more unit of a good and raise its TR to $\$105$. Whether it should sell one more unit depends, specifically, on how much more it costs to produce one more unit. Suppose producing one more unit raises the firm's TVC to $\$30$. Again, $TC = TFC + TVC$, and because TVC has risen to $\$30$, TC rises to $\$70$. The difference between TR and TC is now $\$35$ ($\$105 - \$70$). Thus, selling one more unit of the good raises TR from $\$100$ to $\$105$, but it lowers profit from $\$40$ to $\$35$. A firm seeks to maximize profit, not total revenue.

Under one condition, maximizing revenue will be the same as maximizing profit: when TC is constant. Of course, the only time TC is constant is when it is composed of only TFC, that is, when variable costs are zero. To illustrate, suppose $TR = \$100$, $TFC = \$40$, and $TVC = \$0$. Because $TVC = \$0$, it follows that $TC = TFC = \$40$.

Now again suppose that if the firm sells one more unit of a good, its TR will rise to $\$105$. Now obviously the firm should sell one more unit because, in this case, $TC = TFC$ (and TFC is constant), so TC remains at $\$40$. The firm increases its total revenue and its profit by $\$5$ if it sells an additional unit of the good.

Therefore, maximizing profit is not consistent with maximizing revenue when variable costs exist. But when variable costs do not exist (i.e., when variable costs are zero), maximizing profit is consistent with maximizing revenue.

Finding ECONOMICS

In the Price of the Songs

A musical artist is currently arguing with a few music company executives at BT Productions. The argument is over the price of her next CD. She wants the CD priced lower than the music executives want to price it. Where is the economics here?

(continued)

exhibit 5

The Music Company and the Musical Artist Opt for Different Prices

The artist faces zero costs of producing and selling the CD; BT Productions, the music company, faces positive (and we assume) constant marginal costs. Both the artist and the music company may want to equate marginal revenue and marginal cost, but they do not have the same marginal cost. The artist wants Q_A CDs produced and sold at a price of P_A; the music company wants Q_{BT} CDs produced and sold at a price of P_{BT}.

Finding Economics (continued)

To find the economics, first understand that the musical artist receives a royalty rate on total revenue: The bigger total revenue is, the more income she earns. (A royalty rate of 10 percent applied to a total revenue of $10 million is better than the same royalty rate applied to a total revenue of only $4 million.) In this setting, her objective is to choose a price that will maximize total revenue.

The situation is different for the music company. The company is not interested in maximizing revenue; it is interested in maximizing profit. Maximizing revenue and maximizing profit are not the same things as long as variable costs exist.

Exhibit 5 shows a demand curve and a marginal revenue curve for the CD. There are two marginal cost curves. The one for the music company (BT Productions) is positive and (we have assumed) constant. The other marginal cost curve is for the musical artist and is zero at all levels of output because we assume the artist does not incur any costs of actually producing and selling the CD (this is the music company's job). Because the musical artist receives a royalty rate based on total revenue, she wants to maximize total revenue, which happens when $MR = 0$. Think about this for a moment: If MR is positive, then total revenue is rising because MR is *additional* revenue. When $MR = 0$, there is no additional revenue.

Marginal revenue equals zero in Exhibit 5 at Q_A, which is also the point at which $MR = MC$ for the musical artist. The highest price (per unit) that this quantity can sell for is P_A. In other words, the musical artist wants to charge a price of P_A for her CD; this is the price that is best for her.

But the music company is better off producing Q_{BT}, where its MR equals its MC. The highest price (per unit) consistent with this quantity is P_{BT}. In other words, the best price for the music company is higher than the best price for the musical artist.

PERFECT COMPETITION AND MONOPOLY

Because perfect competition and monopoly are at opposite ends of the (market structure) spectrum, there are major differences between them. In this section, we discuss those differences.

Price, Marginal Revenue, and Marginal Cost

Here are two key differences between perfect competition and monopoly:

1. For the perfectly competitive firm, $P = MR$; for the monopolist, $P > MR$. The perfectly competitive firm's demand curve *is* its marginal revenue curve; the monopolist's demand curve lies *above* its marginal revenue curve.

2. The perfectly competitive firm charges a price equal to marginal cost; the monopolist charges a price greater than marginal cost.

$$\text{Perfect competition: } P = MR \text{ and } P = MC$$
$$\text{Monopoly: } P > MR \text{ and } P > MC$$

Monopoly, Perfect Competition, and Consumers' Surplus

A monopoly firm differs from a perfectly competitive firm in terms of how much consumers' surplus buyers receive. To illustrate, Exhibit 6 shows a downward-sloping market demand curve, a downward-sloping marginal revenue curve, and a horizontal marginal cost (MC) curve. Although you are used to seeing upward-sloping marginal cost curves, there is nothing to prevent marginal cost from being constant over some range of output. A horizontal MC curve simply means that marginal cost is constant. If the market in Exhibit 6 is perfectly competitive, the demand curve *is* the marginal revenue curve. Therefore, the profit-maximizing output is Q_{PC}.[2] The buyer will pay P_{PC} per unit of the good. Recall that consumers' surplus is the area under the demand curve and above the price. For the perfectly competitive firm, consumers' surplus is the area $P_{PC}AB$.

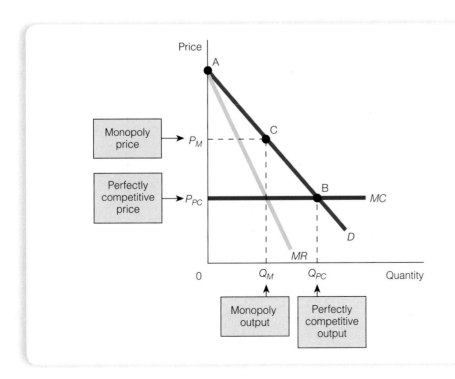

exhibit 6

Monopoly, Perfect Competition, and Consumers' Surplus

If the market in the exhibit is perfectly competitive, the demand curve is the marginal revenue curve. The profit-maximizing output is Q_{PC} and price is P_{PC}. Consumers' surplus is the area $P_{PC}AB$. If the market is a monopoly market, the profit-maximizing output is Q_M and price is P_M. In this case, consumers' surplus is the area P_MAC. Consumers' surplus is greater in perfect competition than in monopoly; it is greater by the area $P_{PC}P_MCB$.

---

2. The demand curve is downward sloping because we are looking at the market demand curve, not the firm's demand curve. All market demand curves are downward sloping.

Now suppose the market is a monopoly market. In this case, the demand curve and the marginal revenue curve are different. The profit-maximizing output is where the MR curve intersects the MC curve; thus, the profit-maximizing output is Q_M. The price the buyer pays is P_M. In the case of monopoly, consumers' surplus is $P_M AC$.

Obviously, consumers' surplus is greater in the perfectly competitive case than in the monopoly case by the area $P_{PC}P_M CB$. Stated differently, this is the loss in consumers' surplus due to monopolization.

Monopoly or Nothing?

Suppose you could push one of two buttons to determine the conditions under which a particular good is produced. If you push the first button, the good is produced under the conditions of perfect competition. If you push the second button, the good is produced under the conditions of monopoly. Which button would you push?

From a consumer's perspective, pushing the first button and producing the good under the conditions of perfect competition would seem to be the better choice. After all, perfect competition provides more output than monopoly and a lower price. In short, there is more consumers' surplus. Perfect competition would therefore seem to be superior to monopoly. But life doesn't always present a choice between perfect competition and monopoly. Sometimes it presents a choice between monopoly and nothing. To illustrate, Exhibit 7 shows the demand curve for a good, along with the relevant marginal revenue curve and two sets of MC and ATC curves. Let's assume that MC_1 and ATC_1 are the relevant cost curves. Because the MC_1 curve is so far above the MR curve, they do not intersect. In other words, there is no profit-maximizing quantity of output for a firm to produce. Simply put, although there is demand for the particular good, the costs of producing it are so high that no firm will produce it. Consumers therefore receive no consumers' surplus from the purchase and consumption of the good.

Now suppose a firm—a single firm—is able to lower costs to MC_2 and ATC_2. Now marginal cost is low enough for the firm to produce the good. The firm produces Q_M and charges a price of P_M. The area $P_M AB$ is equal to consumers' surplus.

No doubt the firm producing this good and charging a price of P_M is a monopoly firm. But are consumers better off having a monopoly firm produce the good than having

---

exhibit 7

Monopoly or Nothing?

We start with the demand and marginal revenue curves and with $MC_1 = ATC_1$. Because cost is "so high," no firm produces the good. Later, a single firm figures out how to lower cost to $MC_2 = ATC_2$. This firm produces Q_M and charges the monopoly price of P_M per unit. Is monopoly preferable to no firm producing the good? From a consumer's perspective, the answer is yes. Consumers' surplus is zero when no firm produces the good, and consumers' surplus is area $P_M AB$ when the monopoly firm produces the good.

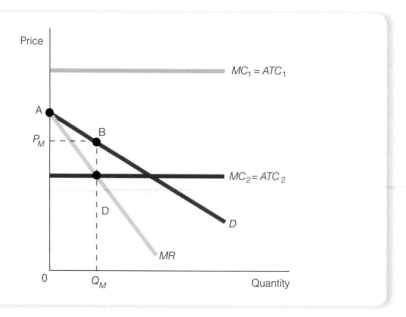

no firm produce it? If no firm produces the good (because costs are too high), consumers' surplus is zero. But when the monopoly firm produces the good, consumers' surplus is positive.

So under certain conditions, a monopoly may be created in a market because a firm figures out a way to lower the cost of producing a good enough to make producing it worthwhile. Of course, once the monopoly firm exists, consumers would prefer that the good be produced under perfect competition than under monopoly conditions. But that is not always the relevant choice. Sometimes, the choice is between monopoly and nothing, and, when this is the choice, the consumers' surplus is greater with monopoly than it is with nothing.

Thinking like An Economist

Comparing Real *Alternatives*

The economist tells us that it is better to compare real alternatives with other real alternatives, not with unreal alternatives. Thus it is better to compare (1) monopoly with nothing than to compare (2) monopoly with perfect competition when nothing is a real alternative and perfect competition is not. In short, we need to compare (1) what is with what is, and not (2) what is with what we wish it would be.

SELF-TEST

1. Why does the monopolist's demand curve lie above its marginal revenue curve?
2. Is a monopolist guaranteed to earn profits?
3. Is a monopolist resource allocative efficient? Why or why not?
4. Why do you think a monopolist is called a price searcher? What is it searching for?

THE CASE AGAINST MONOPOLY

Monopoly is often said to be inefficient in comparison with perfect competition. This section examines some of the shortcomings of monopoly.

The Deadweight Loss of Monopoly

Exhibit 8 shows demand, marginal revenue, marginal cost, and average total cost curves. We have made the simplifying assumption that the product is produced under constant cost conditions, so that marginal cost equals long-run average total cost. If the product is produced under perfect competition, output Q_{PC} is produced and is sold at a price of P_{PC}. At the competitive equilibrium output level, $P = MC$. If the product is produced under monopoly, output Q_M is produced and is sold at a price of P_M. At the monopoly equilibrium, $P > MC$.

Greater output is produced under perfect competition than under monopoly. The net value of the difference in these two output levels is said to be the **deadweight loss of monopoly**. In Exhibit 8, the value to buyers of increasing output from Q_M to Q_{PC} is equal to the maximum amount they would pay for this increase in output, designated by the area $Q_M CBQ_{PC}$. The costs that would have to be incurred to produce this additional output are designated by the area $Q_M DBQ_{PC}$. The difference between the two is the triangle DCB, *the amount buyers value the additional output over and above the costs of producing the additional output.* It is the loss attached to not producing the competitive quantity of output. The triangle DCB is referred to as the *deadweight loss triangle*.

Deadweight Loss of Monopoly
The net value (value to buyers over and above costs to suppliers) of the difference between the monopoly quantity of output (where $P > MC$) and the competitive quantity of output (where $P = MC$). The loss of not producing the competitive quantity of output.

exhibit 8

Deadweight Loss and Rent Seeking as Costs of Monopoly

The monopolist produces Q_M, and the perfectly competitive firm produces the higher output level Q_{PC}. The deadweight loss of monopoly is the triangle (DCB) between these two levels of output. Rent-seeking activity is directed to obtaining the monopoly profits, represented by the area $P_{PC}P_MCD$. Rent seeking is a socially wasteful activity because resources are expended to transfer income rather than to produce goods and services.

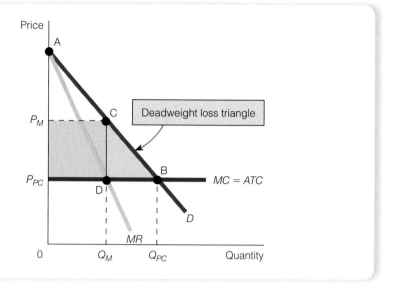

Therefore, monopoly produces a quantity of output that is too small in comparison to the quantity of output produced in perfect competition. This difference in output results in a welfare loss to society.

Arnold Harberger was the first economist who tried to determine the actual size of the deadweight loss cost of monopoly in the manufacturing sector of the U.S. economy. He estimated the deadweight loss to be a small percentage of the economy's total output. Additional empirical work by other economists puts the figure at approximately 1 percent of total output.

Rent Seeking

Sometimes, individuals and groups try to influence public policy in the hope of redistributing (transferring) income from others to themselves. To illustrate, look again at the perfectly competitive outcome in Exhibit 8: The market produces Q_{PC} output and charges a price of P_{PC}.

Suppose, however, that one of the, say, 100 firms currently producing some of Q_{PC} asks the government to grant it a monopoly; that is, firm A asks the government to prevent the 99 remaining firms from competing with it. Consider the benefit for firm A of becoming a monopolist (a single seller). Currently, it is earning zero economic profit because it is selling at a price that equals *ATC*. If it becomes a monopolist, though, it will earn profits equal to the area $P_{PC}P_MCD$ in Exhibit 8. These profits are the result of a *transfer* from buyers to the monopolist. To see this, consider what happens to consumers' surplus. If the market in Exhibit 8 is perfectly competitive, consumers' surplus is equal to the area $P_{PC}AB$; if the market is monopolized, consumers' surplus is equal to the area P_MAC. The difference is the area $P_{PC}P_MCB$, the area that represents the loss in consumers' surplus if the market is monopolized. Part of this area—$P_{PC}P_MCD$—is transferred to the monopolist in terms of profits. *In other words, if the market is monopolized, part of the consumers' surplus that is lost to buyers becomes profits for the monopolist.* (The other part is the deadweight loss of monopoly, identified by the deadweight loss triangle.)

If firm A tries to get the government to transfer income in the form of consumers' surplus from buyers to itself, it is undertaking a *transfer-seeking activity.* In economics, these transfer-seeking activities are usually called **rent seeking**. In other words, firm A is rent seeking.[3]

Economist Gordon Tullock has made the point that rent-seeking behavior is individually rational but socially wasteful. To see why, let's say the profits in Exhibit 8 (the area $P_{PC}P_M$CD) are equal to $10 million. Firm A wants the $10 million in profits; so it asks the government for a monopoly because it wants the government to prevent 99 firms from competing with it.

Firm A will not get its monopoly privilege simply by asking for it. The firm will have to spend money and time to convince government officials that it should be given this monopoly privilege. It will have to hire lobbyists, take politicians and other government officials to dinner, and perhaps give donations to some of them. Firm A will have to spend resources to get what it wants, and all the resources firm A uses to try to bring about a transfer from buyers to itself are wasted, says Tullock. The reason is that the resources used to bring about a transfer can't be used to produce shoes, computers, television sets, and many other things that people would like to buy. The resources are used to try to transfer income from one party to another, not to produce more goods and services.

What would society look like if no one produced anything but only invested time and money in rent seeking? Jones would try to get what is Matsui's, Matsui would try to get what is Kahn's, and Kahn would try to get what is Patel's. No one would produce anything; everyone would simply spend time and money trying to get what currently belongs to someone else. In this world, who would produce the food, the computers, and the cars? The answer is no one.

Tullock makes the point that the resource cost of rent seeking should be added to the deadweight loss of monopoly. This addition, according to Tullock, makes the overall cost of monopoly to society higher than anyone initially thought.

 Thinking like AN ECONOMIST

No $10 Bills

Here is a joke that tells us something about how economists think: Two economists are walking down the street. One sees a $10 bill lying on the sidewalk and asks the other, "Isn't that a $10 bill?" "Obviously not," says the other. "If it were, someone would have already picked it up." Specifically, economists believe that if the opportunity for gain exists, it won't last long because someone will grab it—quickly. By the time you come along, it's gone.

Apply this thinking to what Gordon Tullock says about monopoly. As a seller, being a monopolist is better than being a competitive firm. Like a $10 bill lying on the sidewalk, a monopoly position is worth something. Just as people will pick up a $10 bill on the sidewalk, they'll try to become monopolists.

In terms of rent seeking, to which Tullock first called our attention, just as people will bend down to pick up the $10 bill, so will they invest resources to capture the monopoly rents. No opportunity for gain is likely to be ignored.

Rent Seeking
Actions of individuals and groups who spend resources to influence public policy in the hope of redistributing (transferring) income to themselves from others.

3. The word *rent* (used in this context) often confuses people. In everyday life, *rent* refers to the payment for an apartment. In economics, rent, or more formally, economic rent, is a payment in excess of opportunity cost. The term *rent seeking* was introduced by economist Anne Krueger in her article "The Political Economy of the Rent-Seeking Society," *American Economic Review* 64 (June 1974): 291–303.

X-Inefficiency

Economist Harvey Leibenstein maintains that the monopolist is not under pressure to produce its good at the lowest possible cost; it can produce its good above the lowest possible unit cost and still survive. Certainly, the monopolist benefits if it can and does lower its costs, but it doesn't have to in order to survive (with the proviso that average total costs cannot rise so high as to be higher than price). When the monopolist operates at a cost that is higher than the lowest possible, Leibenstein refers to the organizational slack that is directly tied to this as **X-inefficiency**.

Obtaining accurate estimates of X-inefficiency is difficult, but, whatever its magnitude, forces are at work to mitigate it. For example, if a market monopoly is being run inefficiently, other people realizing this may attempt to buy the monopoly and, if successful, lower costs to make higher profits.

X-Inefficiency

The increase in costs and organizational slack in a monopoly resulting from the lack of competitive pressure to push costs down to their lowest possible level.

PRICE DISCRIMINATION

We have assumed that the monopoly seller sells all units of its product for the same price (it is a single-price monopolist). However, under certain conditions, a monopolist could practice **price discrimination**. This occurs when the seller charges different prices for the product it sells and the price differences do not reflect cost differences.

Types of Price Discrimination

There are three types of price discrimination: perfect price discrimination, second-degree price discrimination, and third-degree price discrimination.

Suppose a monopolist produces and sells 1,000 units of good X. It sells each unit separately, charging the highest price that each consumer would be willing to pay for the product rather than go without it. In this case, the monopolist is said to practice **perfect price discrimination**, sometimes called *discrimination among units*.

If it charges a uniform price per unit for one specific quantity, a lower price for an additional quantity, and so on, the monopolist practices **second-degree price discrimination**, sometimes called *discrimination among quantities*. For example, the monopolist might sell the first 10 units for $10 each, the next 20 units for $9 each, and so on.

If it charges different prices in different markets or charges different prices to different segments of the buying population, the monopolist practices **third-degree price discrimination**, sometimes called *discrimination among buyers*. For example, if your local pharmacy charges senior citizens lower prices for medicine than it charges nonsenior citizens, it practices third-degree price discrimination.

Why a Monopolist Wants to Price Discriminate

Suppose these are the maximum prices at which the following units of a product can be sold: first unit, $10; second unit, $9; third unit, $8; fourth unit, $7. If the monopolist wants to sell 4 units, and it charges the same price for each unit (it is a single-price monopolist), its total revenue is $28 ($7 × 4). Now suppose the monopolist can and does practice perfect price discrimination. It charges $10 for the first unit, $9 for the second unit, $8 for the third unit, and $7 for the fourth unit. Its total revenue is $34 ($10 + $9 + $8 + $7). A comparison of total revenues with and without price discrimination explains why the monopolist would want to price discriminate. A perfectly price-discriminating monopolist receives the maximum price for each unit of the good it sells; a single-price monopolist does not.

For the monopolist who practices perfect price discrimination, price equals marginal revenue, $P = MR$. To illustrate, when the monopolist sells its second unit for $9 (having

Price Discrimination

A price structure in which the seller charges different prices for the product it sells and the price differences do not reflect cost differences.

Perfect Price Discrimination

A price structure in which the seller charges the highest price that each consumer is willing to pay for the product rather than go without it.

Second-Degree Price Discrimination

A price structure in which the seller charges a uniform price per unit for one specific quantity, a lower price for an additional quantity, and so on.

Third-Degree Price Discrimination

A price structure in which the seller charges different prices in different markets or charges a different price to different segments of the buying population.

economics 24/7

AMAZON AND PRICE DISCRIMINATION[4]

Not too long ago, Amazon, the online retailer, charged different customers different prices for DVDs. For example, it charged some customers $74.99 for the movie *Planet of the Apes,* whereas it charged other customers $64.99 for the same movie. Amazon charged the higher price to persons who used Internet Explorer as a browser, and it charged the lower price to persons who used Netscape Navigator. At other times, Amazon charged different customers different prices depending on whether they were repeat buyers or first-time buyers and depending on what Internet service provider they used.

How does Amazon know which customers are willing to pay a higher price for a DVD and which customers are not? An Amazon spokesperson said that the price differences on certain DVDs were the result of tests that the company performs to reevaluate various aspects of its website, such as the navigation system, what the home page looks

like, overall site design, and product pricing. Some economists speculated that it had much to do with maximizing profits.

As stated in this chapter, one condition of price discrimination is that sellers must be able to distinguish among buyers who would be willing to pay different prices. For example, book publishers price discriminate through their sales of hardcover and paperback books. Most books are first offered in hardcover, and the people who are least price sensitive buy the hardcover version. Later, the book is released as a paperback, and the most price-sensitive persons buy the paperback.

The Internet makes such market segmentation as that used by book publishers seem rather crude. Online sellers often ask for (and receive) market information from their customers. Sellers can analyze and categorize this information to get an idea of the likelihood of a particular customer paying a higher price for a particular good. For example, customers who live in a certain zip code area or state (a high-income state or area as opposed to a low-income state or area) may be more likely to pay a higher price for a good than customers who live in a different zip code area or state.

4. This feature is based on Paul Krugman, "Reckonings: What Price Fairness?" *New York Times*, October 4, 2000.

---

sold the first unit for $10), its total revenue is $19—or its marginal revenue is $9, which is equal to price.

Conditions of Price Discrimination

Why the monopolist would want to price discriminate is obvious. However, to price discriminate, the following conditions must hold:

1. The seller must exercise some control over price; that is, it must be a price searcher.

2. The seller must be able to distinguish among buyers who would be willing to pay different prices.

3. It must be impossible or too costly for one buyer to resell the good to other buyers. **Arbitrage**, or buying low and selling high, must not be possible.

If the seller is not a price searcher (if it is a price taker), it has no control over price and therefore cannot sell a good at different prices to different buyers. Also, unless the seller can distinguish among buyers who would pay different prices, it cannot price discriminate. After all, how would it know whom to charge the higher (lower) prices? Finally, if a buyer can resell the good, price discrimination is not possible because buyers of the good at a lower price will simply resell it to other buyers for a price lower than the original seller's higher price. In time, no one will pay the higher price.

Arbitrage
Buying a good at a low price and selling it for a higher price.

Common Misconceptions

About Price Discrimination

Some people argue that if a firm charges one person $40 for its product and charges another person only $33, the first person is paying a higher price so that the second person can pay a lower price. But this is not the case. Suppose the maximum price O'Neill will pay for good X is $40, and the maximum price Stevens will pay is $33. If a monopolist can and does perfectly price discriminate, it charges O'Neill $40 and charges Stevens $33.

Is O'Neill somehow paying the higher price so that Stevens can pay the lower price? It is easy to see that O'Neill is not by considering whether the monopolist would have charged O'Neill a price under $40 if Stevens's maximum price had been $39 instead of $33. Probably it wouldn't. Why should it when it could have received O'Neill's maximum price of $40?

The point is that the perfectly price-discriminating monopolist tries to get the highest price from each customer, irrespective of what other customers pay. In short, the price O'Neill is charged is independent of the price Stevens pays.

Moving to $P = MC$ Through Price Discrimination

We learned in the last chapter that the perfectly competitive firm exhibits resource allocative efficiency; it produces the quantity of output at which $P = MC$. We learned earlier in this chapter that the single-price monopolist produces the quantity of output at which $P > MC$, that is, it produces an inefficient level of output. But does the monopolist, which can and does practice perfect price discrimination, also produce an inefficient level of output?

The answer is no. A perfectly price-discriminating monopolist does not lower price on all previous units to sell an additional unit of its product. For it, $P = MR$ (as is the case for the perfectly competitive firm). Naturally, when the perfectly price-discriminating monopolist produces the quantity of output at which $MR = MC$, it automatically produces the quantity where $P = MC$. In short, the perfectly price-discriminating monopolist and the perfectly competitive firm both exhibit resource allocative efficiency.

Exhibit 9 illustrates some important points. In part (a), the perfectly competitive firm produces where $P = MC$. In part (b), the single-price monopolist produces where $P > MC$. In part (c), the perfectly price-discriminating monopolist produces where $P = MC$. There is one important difference between the perfectly competitive firm and the perfectly price-discriminating monopolist. Although both produce where $P = MC$, the perfectly competitive firm charges the same price for each unit of the good it sells, and the perfectly price-discriminating monopolist charges a different price for each unit of the good it sells.

You Can Have the Comics, Just Give Me the Coupons

Third-degree price discrimination, or discrimination among buyers, is sometimes employed through the use of cents-off coupons. (Remember that third-degree price discrimination exists if a seller sells the same product at different prices to different segments of the population.)

One of the conditions of price discrimination is that the seller has to be able to distinguish among customers who are willing to pay different prices. For example, some sellers think that people who value their time highly are willing to pay a higher price for a product than people who do not. Sellers argue that people who place a high value on their time want to economize on the shopping time connected with the purchase. If sellers want to price discriminate between these two types of customers—charging more to

economics 24/7

WHY DO DISTRICT ATTORNEYS PLEA-BARGAIN?

On the television series *Law & Order,* the assistant district attorney often offers the accused a chance to plead to a lesser charge in return for providing information about a crime or for agreeing to testify against someone. In short, the assistant district attorneys on *Law & Order* are willing to plea-bargain.

To some people, a district attorney who plea-bargains is similar to a seller who price discriminates. To see whether this comparison is valid, suppose two people, Smith and Jones, have committed the same crime. The district attorney has the same type and amount of evidence against each person, and the chance of a successful prosecution is approximately the same in each case. A successful prosecution will end in a prison sentence of 25 years.

The district attorney offers Smith a plea bargain. In exchange for Smith's testimony against Brown, who is someone the DA's office has been after for a long time, Smith will be charged with a lesser crime and will have to serve only 5 years in prison. Thus, Smith can pay a smaller price for his crime than Jones must pay. In other words, each person commits the same crime, and each has an equal chance of being successfully prosecuted for that crime, but Smith (if he accepts the plea bargain) will serve 5 years in prison and Jones will serve 25 years.

Do district attorneys want to plea-bargain for a reason analogous to why sellers want to price discriminate?[5] A seller wants to price discriminate because it raises total revenue without affecting costs. In the example in the text, $10 is the highest price at which the first unit of a good can be sold, $9 is the highest price for the second unit, $8 is the highest price for the third unit, and $7 is the highest price for the

fourth unit. A single-price monopolist that wants to sell 4 units of the good charges a price of $7 per unit and earns total revenue of $28. But a perfectly price-discriminating monopolist charges the highest price per unit and gains total revenue of $34. In other words, price discrimination leads to higher total revenue.

District attorneys do not want to maximize total revenue, but they may want to maximize the number of successfully prosecuted crimes given certain budget constraints. Just as price discrimination leads to higher total revenue, plea bargaining may lead to more successfully prosecuted crimes. Smith and Jones committed the same crime, and, without a plea bargain, they both go to prison for 25 years. But if the DA offers Smith 5 years, and in return Smith helps the DA send Brown to prison, then, because of the plea bargain, three crimes are successfully prosecuted: the crimes committed by Smith, Jones, and Brown.

Finally, just as certain conditions have to be met before a seller can price discriminate, certain conditions have to be satisfied before district attorneys can plea-bargain successfully. To price discriminate, a seller must exercise some control over the price of the product sold. To plea-bargain, a district attorney has to exercise some control over the sentence for the accused. In reality, district attorneys do exercise some control over sentences because they largely control the charges they bring. If they reduce the charges (say, from murder to manslaughter), they automatically affect the sentence.

A seller who price discriminates has to be able to distinguish among customers who are willing to pay different prices for the good sold. Similarly, a district attorney has to be able to distinguish among accused persons who do and do not have something to sell to the authorities. District attorneys seem to be able to do this. In many cases, the accused person who has something to sell will say so.

Finally, for price discrimination to exist, arbitrage has to be impossible or too costly. Obviously, reselling a plea bargain is not possible.

---

5. Be careful: We are not saying that a plea bargain is an act of price discrimination, broadly defined. We are saying that there are similarities between why sellers want to price discriminate and why district attorneys want to plea-bargain. Later in the feature, we explain that just as certain conditions need to be met to price discriminate, certain conditions need to be met for district attorneys to offer plea bargains and that there seems to be a rough similarity between the two sets of conditions.

customers who value time more and charging less to customers who value time less—they must determine the category into which each of their customers falls.

If you were a seller, how would you go about this? Many real-world sellers place cents-off coupons in newspapers and magazines. They hypothesize that people who place a relatively low value on their time are willing to spend it clipping and sorting coupons. People who place a relatively high value on their time are not. In effect, price discrimination

exhibit 9

Comparison of a Perfectly Competitive Firm, Single-Price Monopolist, and Perfectly Price-Discriminating Monopolist

For both the perfectly competitive firm and the perfectly price-discriminating monopolist, $P = MR$ and the demand curve is the marginal revenue curve. Both produce where $P = MC$. The single-price monopolist, however, produces where $P > MC$ because for it, $P > MR$ and its demand curve lies above its marginal revenue curve. One difference between the perfectly competitive firm and the perfectly price-discriminating monopolist is that the former charges the same price for each unit of the good it sells and the latter charges a different price for each unit of the good it sells.

(a)
Perfectly
Competitive Firm

(b)
Single-Price
Monopolist

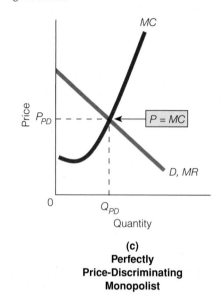

(c)
Perfectly
Price-Discriminating
Monopolist

works much like the following in, say, a grocery store:

1. The posted price for all products is the same for all customers.

2. Both Linda and Josh put product X in their shopping carts.

3. When Linda gets to the checkout counter, the clerk asks, "Do you have any coupons today?" Linda says no. She is therefore charged the posted price for all products, including X.

4. When Josh gets to the checkout counter, the clerk asks, "Do you have any coupons today?" Josh says yes and gives the clerk a coupon for product X. Josh pays a lower price for product X than Linda pays.

Thus, one of the uses of the cents-off coupon is to make it possible for the seller to charge a higher price to one group of customers than to another group. (We say one of the uses because cents-off coupons are also used to induce customers to try a product.)

microtheme → In an earlier chapter, we explained that microeconomics is about objectives, constraints, and choices. We have talked about three types of firms so far: the perfectly competitive firm, the single-price monopolist, and the perfectly price-discriminating monopolist. All three firms have the same *objective*: to maximize profit. All three firms face *constraints*, although not always the same constraints. For example, the single-price monopolist is constrained to selling its good for the same price to each customer, whereas the price-discriminating monopolist is not. Finally, all three firms make *choices* such as choosing the quantity of output to produce, the price to charge, and so on.

IF I WANT ESPN, WHY AM I BUYING MSNBC TOO?

Cable companies often bundle television and cable networks; that is, they include a number of different television and cable networks in a package and offer them as a package. The basic cable package, for example, includes a number of different networks—such as NBC, CBS, ABC, ESPN, MSNBC, Fox News, QVC, Bravo, Lifetime, and so on. Some people have asked, "Why do I have to pay for something I don't want? Why can't I buy only the channels I want to watch?" That's a good question, and it doesn't come up in all contexts. For example, in the grocery store you don't find that milk, cereal, and raisins are packaged together (bundled). So why does bundling appear in some market settings but not in all of them?

© VICKI BEAVER

One answer is that bundling is more likely when the marginal costs of delivering a good or service are small. It doesn't cost the cable company much in additional (marginal) cost to provide a new customer with a channel that many other customers already receive. Stated differently, once a customer has selected one cable channel to receive, it doesn't cost the cable company much to add other channels. Therefore we expect bundling to be more common when the things being bundled have low marginal cost.

To understand why a company would want to bundle, suppose we have two cable customers, Hannah and Mia. Hannah places a value of $8 (a month) on having the ESPN channel and a value of $3 on having MSNBC. Mia places a value of $7 on having MSNBC and only $4 on ESPN. If the cable company sells each channel separately, and charges the same price per channel per customer, it will likely charge $7 for ESPN (the highest price Mia is willing to pay) and $3 for MSNBC (the highest price Hannah is willing to pay). At these prices, both Hannah and Mia will buy both channels ($10 per person), and the cable company will receive a total revenue of $20 for the two customers.

Or the cable company can bundle the two channels and charge a price that makes it worthwhile for the two customers to buy the bundle. This price is $10.99 because $10.99 is less than the $11 value that each customer places on having the two channels. Now total revenue for the cable company is $21.98. In other words, bundling brings about a higher total revenue for the cable company (and not much more in total costs, if any at all). In the end, the cable company's profits rise.

One last point: Often the customer's intuition is that companies bundle in order to force customers to buy something they don't want to buy. Economist George Stigler questions that intuition. He argues that if a customer did not want one of the bundled goods, it would be cheaper for the company to leave out the unwanted good from the bundle. To illustrate, suppose a customer values good A at $10 and good B at $0. The highest price the company can get for bundled goods A and B is $10 because the customer won't pay more than $10 just because a worthless good was added to the bundle. Why, then, add good B to the bundle, especially if there is any marginal cost to producing and delivering an additional unit of good B? It is better to simply charge $10 for good A.

Finding ECONOMICS

At a Car Dealership and in a TV Show

Blake is shopping for a new car. At every dealership he has visited, the salesperson asked him what he does for a living. Where is the economics here?

Think price discrimination. One of the conditions for price discrimination is that the seller must be able to distinguish among buyers who are willing to pay different prices. Willingness to pay is, of course, not the same as ability to pay, but the difference might not prevent the salesperson from

(continued)

"DOES THE SINGLE-PRICE MONOPOLIST LOWER PRICE ONLY ON THE ADDITIONAL UNIT?"

Student:

You said that a single-price monopolist has to lower its price to sell an additional unit of the good it produces. Does this mean that it can sell the first unit of a good for, say, $20, but that, if it wants to sell a second unit, it has to lower the price to, say, $19?

Instructor:

I would say things a little differently. If the monopoly firm wants to sell one unit, it charges $20, but if it wants to sell two units, it must charge $19 for each of the two units.

Student:

How is what you said different from what I said?

Instructor:

I spoke of two units instead of the second unit.

Student:

I don't see the critical difference.

Instructor:

The way you said things made it sound as if the monopolist earned $20 on the first unit and $19 on the second unit, but this is not how things work for a single-price monopolist. A single-price monopolist has to charge the same price for every unit of the good it sells. In other words, if it sells 100 units, it sells each of the 100 units for the same price. It doesn't sell the first unit for $20 and the second unit for $19 and so on.

Student:

But I'm still confused. We know that a monopoly firm has to lower its price to sell an additional unit; so why can't we just say that it has to lower price to sell the *second* unit?

Instructor:

Because it has to lower price on the previous (the first) unit too if it wants to sell two units. To illustrate, suppose the price of a good is $20 and at this price quantity demand is 1 unit. At a price of $19, quantity demanded rises to 2 units. What you said implied that the firm would sell the first unit for $20. Then, with that transaction done, it now considers whether it wants to sell an additional unit (the second unit). If it does, it charges $19 for it.

That's not the way things happen. The firm—from the beginning, before any units of the good have been sold—has to decide whether it wants to sell 1 unit or 2. If it wants to sell only 1 unit, it charges $20. If it wants to sell 2 units, it sells each unit for $19.

Student:

I think I understand now. That's what you must have meant in class when you said that the word *additional* does not refer to a sequence of events, as in sell the first unit, then sell the additional unit (the second unit), and so on. Instead, it is sell 1 unit at $4 *or* sell two units at $3 each, *or* sell three units at $2 each, and so on.

Instructor:

Yes, that's correct.

Points to Remember

1. A single-price monopolist must lower its price to sell an additional unit of the good it produces.

2. The lower price (necessary to sell an additional unit) applies to the additional unit and *to all units that preceded it.*

Finding Economics (continued)

thinking that the two are strongly correlated. The salespersons might be asking Blake what he does for a living in order to get some idea of what the prospect can afford to pay for a car.

All this is reminiscent of an episode of *The Cosby Show*. Dr. Huxtable (played by Bill Cosby) was thinking of buying a new car. He went to the new car dealership showroom with a friend. Dr. Huxtable made sure to dress down because he didn't want the car salesperson to think he earned a high income. Dr. Huxtable is negotiating the price when all of a sudden his friend, who is on the other side of the showroom, yells, "Dr. Huxtable . . . !" The doctor grimaces because he now knows the cat is out of the bag.

SELF-TEST

1. What are some of the costs, or shortcomings, of monopoly?
2. What is the deadweight loss of monopoly?
3. Why must a seller be a price searcher (among other things) before he can price discriminate?

a reader asks | Do Colleges and Universities Price Discriminate?

At the university I attend, scholarships are given to students with low incomes, excellent grades, or athletic ability. Are these scholarships a form of price discrimination?

Let's rephrase the question: Do scholarships to these types of students (low income, high academic ability, high athletic ability) satisfy the definition of price discrimination? The low-income student might not come to the university unless he or she pays a lower tuition price (than other students pay). The university price discriminates because the scholarship, in effect, reduces the tuition for the low-income student. The excellent student and the athlete have numerous universities competing for them. In other words, both have a high elasticity of demand for education at a given university because they have so many substitutes (other universities) from which to choose. Consequently, a university has to offer them a lower tuition price to secure them as students. The university price discriminates by means of an academic scholarship for the excellent student and an athletic scholarship for the athlete.

Even so, let's consider whether the university meets the criteria of a price discriminator. First, it is a price searcher. Not all universities are alike, nor do they sell a homogeneous good, as they would in the case of perfect competition (price taker).

Second, the university can distinguish among students (customers) who would be willing to pay different prices. For example, the student with few universities seeking him would probably be willing to pay more than the student with many options. Third, the service being purchased cannot be resold to someone else. For example, reselling an economics lecture is difficult. You could, of course, tell someone what was covered in the lecture, perhaps for a small payment or a promise to do the same for you at a later time, but this is like telling someone about a movie. It is often difficult or impossible to resell something that is consumed on the premises.

Chapter Summary

THE THEORY OF MONOPOLY

- The theory of monopoly is built on three assumptions: (1) There is one seller. (2) The single seller sells a product for which there are no close substitutes. (3) There are extremely high barriers to entry into the industry.

- High barriers to entry may take the form of legal barriers (public franchise, patent, government license), economies of scale, or exclusive ownership of a scarce resource.

MONOPOLY PRICING AND OUTPUT

- The profit-maximizing monopolist produces the quantity of output at which $MR = MC$ and charges the highest price per unit at which this quantity of output can be sold.

- For the single-price monopolist, $P > MR$; therefore, its demand curve lies above its marginal revenue curve.

- The single-price monopolist sells its output at a price higher than its marginal cost, $P > MC$, and therefore is *not* resource allocative efficient.

- Consider a perfectly competitive market and a monopoly market, each with the same demand and marginal cost curves. Consumers' surplus is greater in the perfectly competitive market.

RENT SEEKING

- Activity directed at competing for and obtaining transfers is referred to as rent seeking. From society's perspective, rent seeking is a socially wasteful activity. People use resources to bring about a transfer of income from others to themselves instead of producing goods and services.

PRICE DISCRIMINATION

- Price discrimination occurs when a seller charges different prices for its product and the price differences are not due to cost differences.

- Before a seller can price discriminate, certain conditions must hold: (1) The seller must be a price searcher. (2) The seller must be able to distinguish among customers who are willing to pay different prices. (3) It must be impossible or too costly for a buyer to resell the good to others.

- A seller that practices perfect price discrimination (charges the maximum price for each unit of product sold) sells the quantity of output at which $P = MC$. It exhibits resource allocative efficiency.

- The single-price monopolist is said to produce too little output because it produces less than would be produced under perfect competition. This is not the case for a perfectly price-discriminating monopolist.

Key Terms and Concepts

Monopoly
Public Franchise
Natural Monopoly
Price Searcher

Deadweight Loss of
  Monopoly
Rent Seeking
X-Inefficiency

Price Discrimination
Perfect Price Discrimination
Second-Degree Price
  Discrimination

Third-Degree Price
  Discrimination
Arbitrage

Questions and Problems

1 The perfectly competitive firm exhibits resource allocative efficiency ($P = MC$), but the single-price monopolist does not. What is the reason for this difference?

2 Because the monopolist is a single seller of a product with no close substitutes, is it able to obtain any price for its good that it wants? Why or why not?

3 When a single-price monopolist maximizes profits, price is greater than marginal cost. In other words, buyers are willing to pay more for additional units of output than the units cost to produce. Given this, why doesn't the monopolist produce more?

4 Is there a deadweight loss if a firm produces the quantity of output at which price equals marginal cost? Explain.

5 Under what condition will a monopoly firm earn losses?

6 A perfectly competitive firm will produce more output and charge a lower (per-unit) price than a single-price monopoly firm. Do you agree or disagree with this statement? Explain your answer.

7 Rent seeking is individually rational but socially wasteful. Explain.

8 Occasionally, students accuse their instructors, rightly or wrongly, of practicing grade discrimination. These students claim that the instructor "charges" some students a higher price for a given grade than he or she charges other students (by requiring some students to do more or better work). Unlike price discrimination, grade discrimination involves

no money. Discuss the similarities and differences between the two types of discrimination. Which do you prefer less or perhaps dislike more? Why?

9 Make a list of real-world price discrimination practices. Do they meet the conditions posited for price discrimination?

10 For many years in California, car washes would advertise Ladies' Day. On one day during the week, a woman could have her car washed for a price lower than what a man would pay. Some people argued that this was a form of sexual discrimination. A California court accepted the argument and ruled that car washes could no longer have a Ladies' Day. Do you think this was a case of sexual discrimination or price discrimination? Explain your answer.

11 Make a list of market monopolies and a list of government monopolies. Which list is longer? Why do you think this is so?

12 Fast-food stores often charge higher prices for their products in high-crime areas than they charge in low-crime areas. Is this an act of price discrimination? Why or why not?

13 In general, coupons are more common on small-ticket items than they are on big-ticket items. Explain why.

14 A firm maximizes its total revenue. Does it automatically maximize its profit too? Why or why not?

Working with Numbers and Graphs

1 Draw a graph that shows a monopoly firm incurring losses.

2 A monopoly firm is currently earning positive economic profit, and the owner decides to sell it. He asks for a price that takes into account the economic profit. Explain and diagrammatically show what this does to the average total cost (ATC) curve of the firm.

3 Suppose a single-price monopolist sells its output (Q_1) at P_1. Then it raises its price to P_2 and its output falls to Q_2. In terms of Ps and Qs, what does marginal revenue equal?

Use the following figure to answer questions 4–6.

4 If the market is perfectly competitive, what does profit equal?

5 If the market is a monopoly market, what does profit equal?

6 Redraw the figure and label consumers' surplus when the market is perfectly competitive and when it is monopolized.

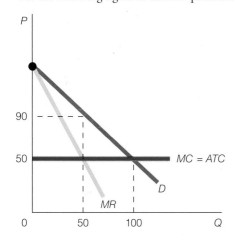

CHAPTER *10*

MONOPOLISTIC COMPETITION, OLIGOPOLY, AND GAME THEORY

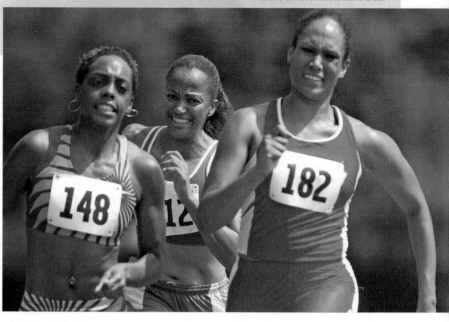

Introduction How do firms in a market act toward each other? Are they fiercely competitive, much as runners in a race to the finish line where only one can be the winner? Or do firms act like people strolling in a park on a warm spring day, without a care in the world and certainly without competition on their minds? As you read this chapter, keep these two images in your mind. Also keep two words in mind: competition and collusion. This chapter is about both.

THE THEORY OF MONOPOLISTIC COMPETITION

Monopolistic Competition
A theory of market structure based on three assumptions: many sellers and buyers, firms producing and selling slightly differentiated products, and easy entry and exit.

The theory of **monopolistic competition** is built on three assumptions:

1. *There are many sellers and buyers.* This assumption holds for perfect competition too. For this reason, you might think the monopolistic competitor should be a price taker, but this is not the case. It is a price searcher, basically because of the next assumption.

2. *Each firm (in the industry) produces and sells a slightly differentiated product.* Differences among the products may be due to brand names, packaging, location, credit terms connected with the sale of the product, the friendliness of the salespeople, and so forth. Product differentiation may be real or imagined. For example, aspirin may be aspirin, but if some people view a name brand aspirin (such as Bayer) as better than a generic brand, product differentiation exists.

3. *There is easy entry and exit.* Monopolistic competition resembles perfect competition in this respect. There are no barriers to entry and exit, legal or otherwise.

Examples of monopolistic competition include retail clothing, computer software, restaurants, and service stations.

The Monopolistic Competitor's Demand Curve

The perfectly competitive firm has many rivals, all producing the same good, and so there are an endless number of substitutes for the good it produces. The elasticity of demand for its product is extremely high—so high, in fact, that the demand curve it faces is horizontal (for all practical purposes).

The monopoly firm has practically no rivals, and it produces a good for which there are no substitutes. The elasticity of demand for its product is low, as reflected by its downward-sloping demand curve.

What is the situation for the monopolistic competitor? Like the perfectly competitive firm, it has many rivals. But unlike the perfectly competitive firm, its rivals don't sell exactly the same product the monopolistic competitor sells. Because there are substitutes for its product, but not perfect substitutes, the elasticity of demand for its product is not as great as that of the perfectly competitive firm. Nor does its demand curve look like the demand curve faced by the perfectly competitive firm. The monopolistic competitor's demand curve is not horizontal; it is downward sloping.

The Relationship Between Price and Marginal Revenue for a Monopolistic Competitor

Because a monopolistic competitor faces a downward-sloping demand curve, it has to lower price to sell an additional unit of the good it produces. (It is a price searcher.) For example, let's say that it can sell 3 units at $10 each but that it has to lower its price to $9 to sell 4 units. Its marginal revenue is therefore $6 (total revenue at 3 units is $30 and total revenue at 4 units is $36), which is below its price of $9. Thus, for the monopolistic competitor $P > MR$.

exhibit 1

The Monopolistic Competitive Firm's Output and Price

The monopolistic competitor produces that quantity of output for which $MR = MC$. This is q_1 in the exhibit. It charges the highest price consistent with this quantity, which is P_1.

At q_1, $P > MC$

Output, Price, and Marginal Cost for the Monopolistic Competitor

The monopolistic competitive firm is the same as both the perfectly competitive firm and the monopoly firm in one regard: It produces the quantity of output at which $MR = MC$. We see this in Exhibit 1, where the firm produces q_1. What price does the monopolistic competitor charge for this quantity? Answer: The highest price it can charge. This is P_1 in the exhibit.

For the monopolistic competitor, $P > MR$. Because the monopolistic competitor produces the quantity of output at which $MR = MC$, it must produce a level of output at which price is greater than marginal cost, $P > MC$. This is obvious in Exhibit 1.

> micro*theme* ➜ We have studied various firms in the last three chapters. A firm faces either (1) a horizontal demand curve or (2) a downward-sloping demand curve. Another way of putting this is to say that a firm is either (1) a price taker or a (2) price searcher. If it faces a horizontal demand curve (which means it can sell its good only at the market equilibrium price), then it is a price taker. If it faces a downward-sloping demand curve (which means it can sell some of its good at different prices, albeit less at higher prices), then it is a price searcher. In other words, the firms you encounter in the real world are either price takers or price searchers.

Will There Be Profits in the Long Run?

If the firms in a monopolistic competitive market are currently earning profits, such as the firm in Exhibit 1, will they continue to earn profits in the long run? Most likely they

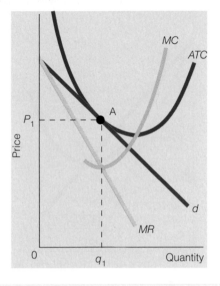

exhibit 2

Monopolistic Competition in the Long Run

Because of easy entry into the industry, there are likely to be zero economic profits in the long run for a monopolistic competitor. In other words, $P = ATC$.

won't. The assumption of easy entry and exit precludes this possibility. If firms in the industry are earning profits, new firms will enter the industry and reduce the demand that each firm faces. In other words, the demand curve for each firm may shift to the left. Eventually, competition will reduce economic profits to zero in the long run, as shown for the monopolistic competitive firm in Exhibit 2.

Note, however, that the answer to the question of whether firms will continue to earn profits in the long run was most likely they won't, instead of no. In monopolistic competition, new firms usually produce a *close substitute* for the product produced by existing firms rather than the *identical* product. Is this difference enough to upset the zero economic profit condition in the long run? In some instances, it may be. An existing firm may differentiate its product sufficiently in the minds of buyers such that it continues to earn profits, even though new firms enter the industry and compete with it.

Firms that try to differentiate their products from those of other sellers in ways other than price are said to be engaged in *nonprice competition.* This type of competition may take the form of advertising or of trying to establish a well respected brand name, among other efforts. For example, soft drink companies' advertising often tries to stress the uniqueness of their product. In the past, Dr. Pepper has been advertised as "the unusual one," 7-Up as "the uncola," Wheaties as the "breakfast of champions," and Budweiser as the "king of beers." Apple has a well respected name in personal computers, Bayer in aspirin, Marriott in hotels. Such well respected names sometimes sufficiently differentiate products in the minds of buyers so that short-run profits are not easily, or completely, eliminated by the entry of new firms into the industry.

 Finding ECONOMICS

On an Online Radio Service

Abbie just found an online radio station that plays the songs and artists she wants to hear. She types in the title of the song or the name of the artist she would like to hear, then the online radio service creates a virtual radio station just for her. Where is the economics here?

Firms can compete in terms of price or things other than price (price competition versus nonprice competition). With respect to free radio (radio you do not pay to hear), radio stations cannot compete on price, and so they must turn to nonprice competition. Customizing a radio station for a listener is a nonprice way of competing for listeners.

Excess Capacity: What Is It, and Is It "Good" or "Bad"?

The theory of monopolistic competition makes a major prediction, which is generally referred to as the **excess capacity theorem**. The theorem states that in equilibrium, a monopolistic competitor will produce an output smaller than the one that would minimize its unit costs of production.

To illustrate, look at point A in Exhibit 3(a). At this point, the monopolistic competitor is in long-run equilibrium because profits are zero ($P = ATC$). Notice that point A is *not* the lowest point on the average total cost curve. The lowest point on the ATC curve is point L. Therefore, in long-run equilibrium, when the monopolistic competitor earns zero economic profits, it is not producing the quantity of output at which average

Excess Capacity Theorem

Theorem that a monopolistic competitor in equilibrium produces an output smaller than the one that would minimize its costs of production.

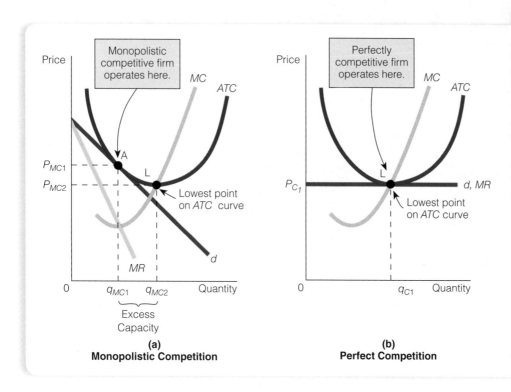

exhibit 3

A Comparison of Perfect Competition and Monopolistic Competition: The Issue of Excess Capacity

The perfectly competitive firm produces a quantity of output consistent with lowest unit costs. The monopolistic competitor does not. If it did, it would produce q_{MC2} instead of q_{MC1}. The monopolistic competitor is said to underutilize its plant size or to have excess capacity.

total costs (unit costs) are minimized for the given scale of plant. Exhibit 3 contrasts the perfectly competitive firm and the monopolistic competitor in long-run equilibrium. In part (b), the perfectly competitive firm is earning zero economic profits, and price (P_{C1}) equals average total cost (ATC). Furthermore, the point at which price equals average total cost (point L) is the lowest point on the ATC curve. In long-run equilibrium, the perfectly competitive firm produces the quantity of output at which unit costs are minimized.

Now look back at part (a). The monopolistic competitor is earning zero economic profits, and price (P_{MC1}) equals average total cost. As previously noted, the monopolistic competitor does not produce the quantity of output at which unit costs are minimized. If it did, it would produce q_{MC2}. For this reason, it has been argued that the monopolistic competitor produces too little output (q_{MC1} instead of q_{MC2}) and charges too high a price (P_{MC1} instead of P_{MC2}). With respect to the former, too little output translates into the monopolistic competitor's underutilizing its present plant size; it is said to have *excess capacity*. In part (a), the excess capacity is equal to the difference between q_{MC2} and q_{MC1}.

It is sometimes argued that the monopolistic competitor operates at excess capacity because it faces a downward-sloping demand curve. In Exhibit 3(a), the only way the firm would not operate at excess capacity is if its demand curve were tangent to the ATC curve at point L—the lowest point on the ATC curve. But for this to occur, the demand curve *would have to be horizontal*, which would require homogeneous products. A downward-sloping demand curve cannot be tangent to the ATC curve at point L.

In short, *the monopolistic competitor operates at excess capacity as a consequence of its downward-sloping demand curve,* and its downward-sloping demand curve is a consequence of differentiated products. A question that many economists ask but do not all answer in the same way is this: *If excess capacity is the price we pay for differentiated products (more choice), is it too high a price?*

THE PEOPLE WEAR PRADA

Suppose you own a business that is considered a monopolistic competitive firm. Your business is one of many sellers, you sell a product slightly differentiated from the products of your competitors, and there is easy entry into and exit from the industry. Would you rather your business were a monopoly firm? Wouldn't it be better for you to be the only seller of a product than to be one of many? Most business owners would say that it is better to be a monopoly firm than a monopolistic competitive firm. This being the case, we consider how monopolistic competitors may try to become monopolists.

One possibility is through a designer label. If a monopolistic competitor can, through the use of a designer label, persuade the buying public that her product is *more than just slightly differentiated* from those of her competitors, she stands a better chance of becoming a

© AP PHOTO/KEVORK DIANSEZIAN

monopolist. (Remember that a monopolist produces a good for which there are no close substitutes.)

For example, many firms produce women's jeans, and, to many people, the jeans produced by these firms look very much alike. How, then, does any one firm differentiate its product from the pack? It could add a designer label to the jeans to suggest uniqueness—that they are the only *Tag Jeans*, for example. For added impact, it could try to persuade the buying public through advertising that its jeans are "the" jeans worn by the most famous, best looking people.

Think of a list of firms that have gone with a designer label to try to outcompete their competitors: Gucci, Tommy Hilfiger, Perry Ellis, Liz Claiborne, Armani, Versace, Dolce & Gabbana, Prada, Valentino, Chanel, L.L. Bean, Da-Nang, Primp, and many others.

The Monopolistic Competitor and Two Types of Efficiency

An earlier chapter explained that a firm is resource allocative efficient if it charges a price that is equal to marginal cost, $P = MC$. Because the monopolistic competitive firm charges a price that is greater than marginal cost ($P > MC$), it is not resource allocative efficient.

An earlier chapter also explained that a firm is productive efficient if it charges a price that is equal to its lowest ATC. Because the monopolistic competitor operates at excess capacity, it is not productive efficient.

SELF-TEST

(Answers to Self-Test questions are in the Self-Test Appendix.)

1. How is a monopolistic competitor like a monopolist? How is it like a perfect competitor?
2. Why do monopolistic competitors operate at excess capacity?

Oligopoly
A theory of market structure based on three assumptions: few sellers and many buyers, firms producing either homogeneous or differentiated products, and significant barriers to entry.

OLIGOPOLY: ASSUMPTIONS AND REAL-WORLD BEHAVIOR

Unlike perfect competition, monopoly, and monopolistic competition, there is no one theory of **oligopoly**. However, the different theories of oligopoly have the following common assumptions:

1. *There are few sellers and many buyers.* The assumption is usually that the few firms of an oligopoly are interdependent; each one is aware that its actions influence the other firms and that the actions of the other firms affect it. This interdependence among firms is a key characteristic of oligopoly.

2. *Firms produce and sell either homogeneous or differentiated products.* Aluminum is a homogeneous product produced in an oligopolistic market; cars are a differentiated product produced in an oligopolistic market.

3. *There are significant barriers to entry.* Economies of scale are perhaps the most significant barrier to entry in oligopoly theory, but patent rights, exclusive control of an essential resource, and legal barriers also act as barriers to entry.

The oligopolist is a price searcher. Like all other firms, it produces the quantity of output at which $MR = MC$.

The Concentration Ratio

Which industries today are dominated by a small number of firms, that is, are oligopolistic? Economists have developed the *concentration ratio* to help answer this question. The **concentration ratio** is the percentage of industry sales (or assets, output, labor force, or some other factor) accounted for by *x* number of firms in the industry. The *x* number in the definition is usually four or eight, but it can be any number (although it is usually small).

> *Four-firm concentration ratio:* CR_4 = Percentage of industry sales accounted for by four largest firms
>
> *Eight-firm concentration ratio:* CR_8 = Percentage of industry sales accounted for by eight largest firms

Concentration Ratio
The percentage of industry sales (or assets, output, labor force, or some other factor) accounted for by *x* number of firms in the industry.

A high concentration ratio implies that few sellers make up the industry; a low concentration ratio implies that more than a few sellers make up the industry.

Suppose we calculate a four-firm concentration ratio for industry Z. Total industry sales for a given year are $5 million, and the four largest firms in the industry account for $4.5 million in sales. The four-firm concentration ratio is 0.90, or 90 percent ($4.5 million is 0.90 of $5 million). Industries with high four- and eight-firm concentration ratios in recent years include cigarettes, cars, tires, cereal breakfast foods, farm machinery, and soap and other detergents, to name a few.

Although concentration ratios are often used to determine the extent (or degree) of oligopoly, they are not perfect guides to industry concentration. Most important, they do not take into account foreign competition and competition from substitute domestic goods. For example, the U.S. automobile industry is concentrated, but it still faces stiff competition from abroad. A more relevant concentration ratio for this particular industry might be one computed on a worldwide basis.

PRICE AND OUTPUT UNDER THREE OLIGOPOLY THEORIES

There is not just one theory of oligopoly; there are many. We present three in this section: the cartel theory, the kinked demand curve theory, and the price leadership theory.

The Cartel Theory

The key behavioral assumption of the **cartel theory** is that oligopolists in an industry act as if there were only one firm in the industry. In short, they form a cartel to capture the benefits that would exist for a monopolist. A **cartel** is an organization of firms that reduces output and increases price in an effort to increase joint profits.

Cartel Theory
In this theory of oligopoly, oligopolistic firms act as if there were only one firm in the industry.

Cartel
An organization of firms that reduces output and increases price in an effort to increase joint profits.

exhibit 4

The Benefits of a Cartel (to Cartel Members)

We assume the industry is in long-run competitive equilibrium, producing Q_1 and charging P_1. There are no profits. A reduction in output to Q_c through the formation of a cartel raises prices to P_c and brings profits of CP_cAB. (Note:

In an earlier chapter, a horizontal demand curve faces the *firm*. Here a downward-sloping demand curve faces the *industry*. Don't be misled by this difference. No matter what type of demand curve we use, long-run competitive equilibrium is where $P = MC = SRATC = LRATC$.)

Forming and maintaining a cartel has its benefits. Exhibit 4 shows an industry in long-run competitive equilibrium. Price is P_1 and quantity of output is Q_1. The industry is producing the output at which price equals marginal cost, and there are zero economic profits. Now suppose the firms making up the industry form a cartel and reduce output to Q_c. The new price is P_c (cartel price), and there are profits equal to the area CP_cAB, which can be shared among the members of the cartel. With no cartel, there are no profits; with a cartel, profits are earned. Thus, the firms have an incentive to form a cartel and to behave cooperatively rather than competitively.

However, firms may not be able to form a cartel, even though they have a profit incentive to do so. Also, even if they are able to form the cartel, the firms may not be able to maintain it. Firms that wish to form and maintain a cartel will encounter several problems, in addition to the fact that legislation prohibits certain types of cartels in the United States. Organizing and forming a cartel involves costs as well as benefits.[1]

THE PROBLEM OF FORMING THE CARTEL Even if it were legal, getting the sellers of an industry together to form a cartel can be costly, even when the number of sellers is small. Each potential cartel member may resist incurring the costs of forming the cartel because it stands to benefit more if other firms do the work. In other words, each potential member has an incentive to be a free rider—to stand by and take a free ride on the actions of others.

THE PROBLEM OF FORMULATING CARTEL POLICY Even if prospective firms form a cartel, next is the problem of formulating policy. For example, firm A might propose that each cartel member reduce output by 10 percent, and firm B advocates that all bigger cartel members reduce output by 15 percent and all smaller members reduce output by 5 percent. In fact, there may be as many policy proposals as there are cartel members. Reaching agreement may be difficult. Such disagreements become harder to resolve as the differences among cartel members in costs, size, and so forth grow.

THE PROBLEM OF ENTRY INTO THE INDUSTRY Even if the cartel members manage to agree on a policy that generates high profits, those high profits will provide an incentive for firms outside the industry to join the industry. If current cartel members cannot keep new suppliers from entering, the cartel is likely to break up.

THE PROBLEM OF CHEATING As paradoxical as it first appears, after the cartel agreement is made, members have an incentive to cheat on it. Exhibit 5 shows three

---

1. Sometimes, economists discuss the benefits and costs of organizing a cartel without specifying the market structure. We have followed suit here by broadening our discussion of cartel theory to include market structures other than oligopoly. This will be noticeable in places. For example, even though there are few sellers in oligopoly, we discuss cartel theory in the context of both few and many sellers.

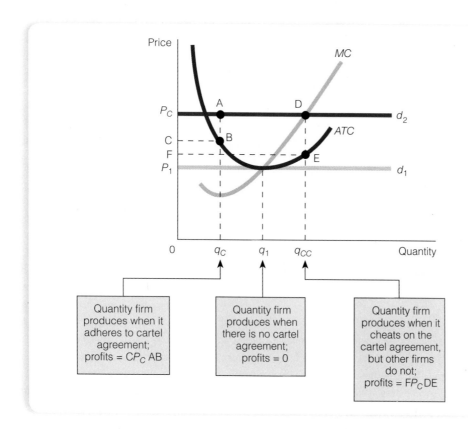

exhibit 5

The Benefits of Cheating on the Cartel Agreement

The situation for a representative firm of a cartel: in long-run competitive equilibrium, it produces q_1 and charges P_1, earning zero economic profits. As a consequence of the cartel agreement, it reduces output to q_C and charges P_C. Its profits are the area CP_CAB. If it cheats on the cartel agreement and others do not, the firm will increase output to q_{CC} and reap profits of FP_CDE. Note, however, that if this firm can cheat on the cartel agreement, so can others. Given the monetary benefits gained by cheating, it is likely that the cartel will exist for only a short time.

situations for a *representative firm* of the cartel: (1) the situation before the cartel is formed, (2) the situation after the cartel is formed when all members adhere to the cartel price, and (3) the situation if the firm cheats on the cartel agreement, but the other cartel members do not.

Before the cartel is formed, the firm is in long-run competitive equilibrium; it produces output q_1 and charges price P_1. It earns zero economic profits. Next, it reduces its output to q_C as directed by the cartel (the cartel has set a quota for each member), and it charges the cartel price of P_C. Now the firm earns profits equal to the area CP_CAB.

What happens if the firm cheats on the cartel agreement and produces q_{CC} instead of the stipulated q_C? As long as other firms do not cheat, this firm views its demand curve as horizontal at the cartel price (P_C). The reason is simple: Because it is one of a number of firms, it cannot affect price by changing output. Therefore, it can produce and sell additional units of output without lowering price. We conclude that if the firm cheats on the cartel agreement and other firms do not, then the cheating firm can increase its profits from the smaller amount CP_CAB to the larger amount FP_CDE. Of course, if all firms cheat, the cartel members are back where they started—with no cartel agreement and at price P_1.

This analysis illustrates a major theme of cartels: Firms have an incentive to form a cartel, but once it is formed, they have an incentive to cheat. As a result, some economists have concluded that even if cartels are formed successfully, they are not likely to be effective for long.

HOW IS A NEW YEAR'S RESOLUTION LIKE A CARTEL AGREEMENT?

In a cartel, one firm makes an agreement with another firm or other firms. In a New Year's resolution, you essentially make an agreement with yourself. So both cases—the cartel and the resolution—involve an agreement.

Both cases also raise the possibility of cheating on the agreement. Suppose your New Year's resolution is to exercise more, take better notes in class, and read one good book a month. You might set such objectives for yourself because you know you will be better off in the long run if you do these things. Then the short run enters into the picture. You have to decide between exercising today or plopping down in your favorite chair and watching television. You have to decide between starting to read *Moby Dick* or catching up on the latest entertainment news in *People* magazine. The part of you that wants to hold to the resolution is at odds with the part of you that wants to watch television or read *People*. Often, the television-watching, *People*-reading part wins out. Breaking a New Year's resolution—as you probably already know—is just too easy.

So is breaking a cartel agreement. For the firm that has entered into the agreement, the lure of higher profits is often too strong to resist.

© SUPERSTOCK/JUPITER IMAGES

In addition, the firm is concerned that if it doesn't break the agreement (and cheat), some other firm might, and then it will have lost out completely.

In short, both resolutions and cartel agreements take a lot of willpower to hold them together. And willpower, it seems, is in particularly short supply. Something is needed to take the place of willpower. Both a resolution and a cartel agreement need something else in order to endure. Something or someone has to exact a penalty from the party who breaks the resolution or cartel agreement. Government sometimes plays this role for firms. Family members and friends occasionally play this role for individuals by reminding or reprimanding them if they fail to live up to their resolutions. (Usually, though, family members and friends are not successful.)

We therefore conclude: First, an agreement is at the heart of both a New Year's resolution and a cartel. Second, both the resolution and the cartel are subject to cheating behavior. Third, if the resolution and the cartel are to have a long life, they often need someone or something to prevent each party from breaking the agreement.

 Thinking like AN ECONOMIST

The Target Sometimes Moves

In economics, there are moving targets. Consider the target of higher profits for the firms in an oligopolistic industry. After the firms form a cartel to capture the higher profits, the target of higher profits moves—to where a cartel member must cheat on the cartel to hit it. But if all cartel members take aim at the target's new position, the target moves back to its original position—to where cartel members must agree to stop cheating.

The layperson may think that an economic objective, or economic target, is stationary. All that an economic actor has to do to hit it is to take careful aim. But the economist knows that sometimes the target moves, and a careful aim is not always enough.

The Kinked Demand Curve Theory

The behavioral assumption in the **kinked demand curve theory** is that if a single firm lowers price, other firms will do likewise, but if a single firm raises price, other firms will not follow suit. Suppose there are five firms in an industry: A, B, C, D, and E. If firm A raises its price, the other firms maintain their prices. If firm A cuts its price, the other firms match the price cut.

The kinked demand curve theory, developed in the 1930s by Paul Sweezy, is best explained using the example in Exhibit 6. The current price charged by the firm is $25. If the firm raises its price to $27, other firms will not match it, and therefore the firm's sales will drop (from 20 to 10). In short, the demand curve for the firm above $25 is highly elastic. However, if the firm lowers its price to, say, $23, other firms will match the price cut, and therefore the firm's sales will not increase by much (only from 20 to 22). Demand is much less elastic below $25 than above it. Thus there is a kink in the firm's demand curve at the current price (point K in Exhibit 6). The kink signifies that other firms respond radically differently to a single firm's price hikes than they do to its price cuts.

Actually, the kinked demand curve theory involves two demand curves and two marginal revenue curves, as shown in the window in Exhibit 6. Only the thicker portions of the curves in the window are relevant, however, and thus they appear in the main diagram. To illustrate, starting at a price of $25, the firm believes price cuts will be matched but price hikes will not. So when considering a price cut, the firm believes it faces the more inelastic of the two demand curves, d_2, and the corresponding marginal revenue curve, MR_2. But when considering a price hike, the firm believes it faces the more elastic of the two demand curves, d_1, and the corresponding marginal revenue curve, MR_1. Therefore, the firm's demand curve includes part of d_1 and part of d_2; the firm's marginal revenue curve includes part of MR_1 and part of MR_2. This occurs because the theory assumes the market reacts one way to a price cut and in a different way to a price hike.

PRICE RIGIDITY Look at the marginal revenue curve for the oligopolist in the main diagram of Exhibit 6. Directly below the kink, it drops sharply. In fact, the marginal

Kinked Demand Curve Theory
A theory of oligopoly that assumes that if a single firm in the industry cuts prices, other firms will likewise, but if it raises price, other firms will not follow suit. The theory predicts price stickiness or rigidity.

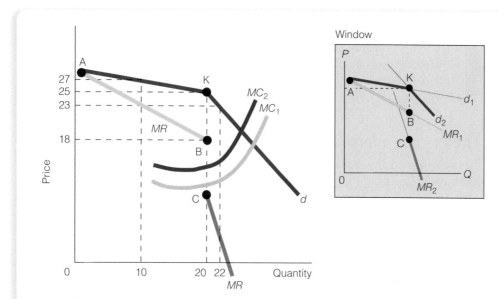

exhibit 6

Kinked Demand Curve Theory

The key behavioral assumption of the theory is that rival firms will not match a price hike but will match a price cut. The theory predicts that changes in marginal costs between B and C will not cause changes in price or output. The window in the exhibit shows two demand curves and two marginal revenue curves. The firm believes it faces d_2, the more inelastic demand curve, if it cuts price; the firm believes it faces d_1, the more elastic demand curve, when it raises price. The relevant portions of each demand curve are indicated by heavy lines. Only the relevant parts of the demand and marginal revenue curves are shown in the main diagram.

revenue curve can be viewed as three segments: a line from point A to point B, which corresponds to the upper part of the demand curve; a gap between points B and C directly below the kink in the demand curve; and a line from point C onward, which corresponds to the lower part of the demand curve (from point K onward).

The gap between points B and C represents the sharp change in marginal revenue that occurs when price is lowered below the kink on the demand curve. The gap helps explain why prices might be less flexible (more rigid) in oligopoly than in other market structures.

Recall that the oligopolistic firm produces the output at which $MR = MC$. For the firm in Exhibit 6, though, marginal cost (MC) can change between points B and C, and the firm will continue to produce the same quantity of output and charge the same price. For example, an increase in marginal cost from MC_1 to MC_2 will not lead to a change in production levels or price.

To put it differently, prices are "sticky" if oligopolistic firms face kinked demand curves. Costs can change within certain limits, and such firms will not change their prices because they expect that none of their competitors will follow their price hikes, but all will match their price cuts.

CRITICISMS OF THE KINKED DEMAND CURVE THEORY The kinked demand curve (and resulting MR curve) posits that prices in oligopoly will be less flexible (or more rigid) than in other market structures. The theory has been criticized on both theoretical and empirical grounds.

On a theoretical level (see Exhibit 6), the theory fails to explain how the original price of $25 came about, that is, why the kink comes at $25. The theory is better at explaining things after the kink (the current price) has been identified than at explaining the placement of the kink. On empirical grounds, the theory has been challenged as a general theory of oligopoly. For example, economist George Stigler found no evidence that the oligopolists he examined were more reluctant to match price increases than price cuts, which calls into question the behavioral assumption behind the theory.

> micro*theme* → All firms have to make choices—how much to produce, how much to charge, and so on. When the perfectly competitive firm makes such choices, it does not strategize. It doesn't say, "I will do W if my competitors do X, but I will do Y if my competitors do Z." However, there is strategizing in oligopoly. For example, one oligopolistic firm in a given market might lower price if other oligopolistic firms in the market lower price, but it won't raise price if other firms raise price. In other words, compared with a perfectly competitive market, in an oligopolistic market one firm's behavior depends to a greater degree on the behavior of other firms.

The Price Leadership Theory

Price Leadership Theory
In this theory of oligopoly, the dominant firm in the industry determines price, and all other firms take their price as given.

The key behavioral assumption in the **price leadership theory** is that one firm in the industry—called the dominant firm—determines price and that all other firms take this price as given. Suppose that there are ten firms in an industry, A–J, that firm A is the dominant firm, and that firm A is much larger than its rival firms. (The dominant firm need not be the largest firm in the industry; it could be the lowest-cost firm.) The dominant firm sets the price that maximizes its profits, and all other firms take this price as given. All other firms, then, are seen as price takers; thus, they equate price with their respective marginal costs.

The price leadership explanation suggests that the dominant firm acts without regard to the other firms in the industry and simply forces the other firms to adapt. This

exhibit 7

Price Leadership Theory

There is one dominant firm and a number of fringe firms. (a) The horizontal sum of the marginal cost curves of the fringe firms is their supply curve. At P_1, the fringe firms supply the entire market. (b) The dominant firm derives its demand curve by computing the difference between market demand, D, and MC_F at each price below P_1. It then produces q_{DN} (where $MR_{DN} = MC_{DN}$) and charges P_{DN}. P_{DN} becomes the price that the fringe firms take. They equate price and marginal cost and produce q_F in (a). The remainder of the output—the difference between Q_2 and q_F—is produced by the dominant firm.

assumption is not quite correct. The dominant firm sets the price based on information it has about the other firms in the industry, as shown in Exhibit 7.

Part (a) shows the market demand curve and the horizontal sum of the marginal cost curves of the fringe firms (all firms other than the dominant firm). Because these fringe firms are price takers, the marginal cost curve in (a) is their supply curve. The dominant firm observes that at a price of P_1, the fringe firms alone can supply the entire market. They will supply Q_1. In short, P_1 and Q_1 define the situation in the industry or market that excludes the dominant firm.

Now add the dominant firm. It derives its demand curve, D_{DN}, by noting how much is left for it to supply at each given price. For example, at a price of P_1, the fringe firms would supply the entire market, and nothing would be left for the dominant firm to supply. So a price of P_1 and an output of zero is one point on the dominant firm's demand curve, as shown in part (b). (Sometimes the dominant firm's demand curve is referred to as the *residual demand curve* for obvious reasons.) The dominant firm continues to locate other points on its demand curve by noting the difference between the market demand curve (D) and MC_F at each price below P_1.

After the dominant firm calculates its residual demand curve, it produces the quantity of output at which its marginal revenue equals its marginal cost. This level is q_{DN} in Exhibit 7(b). It charges the highest price for this quantity of output, which is P_{DN}. This is the price that the dominant firm sets and that the fringe firms take. Because they act as price takers, the fringe firms equate P_{DN} with marginal cost and produce q_F, as shown in part (a). The remainder of the total output produced by the industry—the difference between Q_2 and q_F—is produced by the dominant firm. Therefore, the distance from the origin to q_{DN} in (b) is equal to the difference between Q_2 and q_F in (a).

At one time or another, the following firms have been price leaders in their industries: R. J. Reynolds (cigarettes), General Motors (autos), Kellogg's (breakfast cereals), and Goodyear Tire and Rubber (tires).

SELF·TEST

1. "Firms have an incentive to form a cartel, but once it is formed, they have an incentive to cheat." What is the specific incentive to form the cartel, and what is the incentive to cheat on the cartel?

2. What explains the kink in the kinked demand curve theory of oligopoly?

3. According to the price leadership theory of oligopoly, how does the dominant firm determine the price to charge?

GAME THEORY, OLIGOPOLY, AND CONTESTABLE MARKETS

Of the four market structures (perfect competition, monopoly, monopolistic competition, and oligopoly), oligopoly is often described as the most difficult to analyze. Analysis is difficult because of the interdependence among firms in such a market. Economists often use game theory to get a workable understanding of the interdependence of oligopoly firms. **Game theory** is a mathematical technique used to analyze the behavior of decision makers who (1) try to reach an optimal position through game playing or the use of strategic behavior, (2) are fully aware of the interactive nature of the process at hand, and (3) anticipate the moves of other decision makers.

In this section, we describe a famous game in game theory and then use it to discuss oligopoly behavior. We also discuss the issue of contestable markets.

Game Theory

A mathematical technique used to analyze the behavior of decision makers who try to reach an optimal position for themselves through game playing or the use of strategic behavior, who are fully aware of the interactive nature of the process at hand, and who anticipate the moves of other decision makers.

Prisoner's Dilemma

A well-known game in game theory, called *prisoner's dilemma,* illustrates a case in which individually rational behavior leads to a jointly inefficient outcome. The lesson of the game has been described this way: "You do what is best for you, I'll do what is best for me, and somehow we end up in a situation that is not best for either of us." Here is how the game is played.

THE FACTS Two men, Bob and Nathan, are arrested and charged with jointly committing a crime. They are put into separate cells so that they cannot communicate with each other. The district attorney goes to each man separately and says the following:

- If you confess to the crime and agree to turn state's evidence and if your accomplice does not confess, I will let you off with a $500 fine.

- If your accomplice confesses to the crime and agrees to turn state's evidence and if you do not confess, I will fine you $5,000.

- If both you and your accomplice remain silent and refuse to confess to the crime, I will charge you with a lesser crime, which I can prove you committed, and both you and your accomplice will pay fines of $2,000.

- If both you and your accomplice confess, I will fine each of you $3,000.

THE OPTIONS AND CONSEQUENCES Each man has two choices: confess or not confess, as shown in the grid in Exhibit 8. According to the possibilities laid out by the district attorney:

- Box 1: If both men do not confess, each pays a fine of $2,000.

- Box 2: If Nathan confesses and Bob does not, then Nathan gets off with the light fine of $500 and Bob pays the stiff penalty of $5,000.

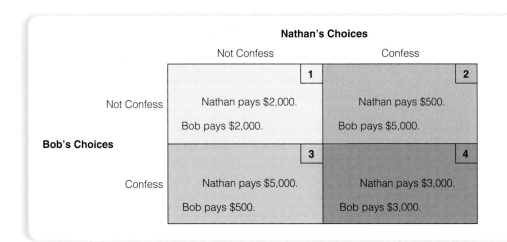

exhibit 8

Prisoner's Dilemma

Nathan and Bob each have two choices: confess or not confess. No matter what Bob does, it is always better for Nathan to confess. No matter what Nathan does, it is always better for Bob to confess. Both Nathan and Bob confess and end up in box 4 where each pays a $3,000 fine. Both men would have been better off had they not confessed. That way they would have ended up in box 1 paying a $2,000 fine.

- Box 3: If Nathan does not confess and Bob confesses, then Nathan pays the stiff penalty of $5,000 and Bob pays the light fine of $500.
- Box 4: Finally, if both men confess, each pays $3,000.

WHAT NATHAN THINKS Nathan considers his choices and their possible outcomes. He reasons to himself, "I have two options, confess or not confess, and Bob has the same two options. Let me ask myself two questions:

- *"If Bob chooses not to confess, what is the best thing for me to do?* The answer is to confess because if I do not confess, I will end up in box 1 paying $2,000, but if I confess I will end up in box 2 paying only $500. No doubt about it, if Bob chooses not to confess, I should confess.
- *"If Bob chooses to confess, what is the best thing for me to do?* The answer is to confess because if I do not confess, I will end up in box 3 paying $5,000, but if I confess I will pay $3,000. No doubt about it, if Bob chooses to confess, I should confess."

NATHAN'S CONCLUSION Nathan concludes that no matter what Bob chooses to do—not confess or confess—he is always better off if he confesses. Nathan decides to confess to the crime.

THE SITUATION IS THE SAME FOR BOB Bob goes through the same mental process that Nathan does. Asking himself the same two questions Nathan asked himself, Bob gets the same answers and draws the same conclusion. Bob decides to confess to the crime.

THE OUTCOME The DA goes to each man and asks what he has decided. Both Nathan and Bob say, "I confess." The outcome is shown in box 4, with each man paying a fine of $3,000.

LOOK WHERE THEY COULD BE There is an outcome, represented by one of the four boxes, that is better for both Nathan and Bob than the outcome where each pays $3,000. In box 1, both Nathan and Bob pay $2,000. To get to box 1, all the two men had to do was keep silent and not confess.

CHANGING THE GAME What would happen if the DA gave Nathan and Bob another chance? Suppose she tells them that she will not accept their confessions. Instead, she wants them to talk it over together for ten minutes, after which time she will come back, place each man in a separate room, and ask for his decision. The second time, she will accept each man's decision, no matter what.

Will a second chance change the outcome? Most people will say yes, arguing that Nathan and Bob will now see that their better choice is to remain silent so that each ends up with a $2,000 fine instead of a $3,000 fine. Let's assume this happens, and Nathan and Bob enter into an agreement to remain silent.

NATHAN'S THOUGHTS ON THE WAY TO HIS ROOM The DA returns and takes Nathan to a separate room. On the way, Nathan thinks to himself, "I'm not sure I can trust Bob. Suppose he goes back on our agreement and confesses. If I hold to the agreement and he doesn't, he'll end up with a $500 fine and I'll end up paying $5,000. Of course, if I break the agreement and confess and he holds to the agreement, then I'll reduce my fine to $500. Maybe the best thing for me to do is break the agreement and confess, hoping that he doesn't and I'll pay only $500. If I'm not so lucky, at least I'll protect myself from paying $5,000."

Once in the room, the DA asks Nathan what his decision is. He says, "I confess."

THE SITUATION IS THE SAME FOR BOB Bob sees the situation the same way Nathan does and again chooses to confess.

THE OUTCOME AGAIN Both men end up confessing a second time. Each pays $3,000, realizing that if they had been silent and kept to their agreement, their fine would be only $2,000 each.

 Finding ECONOMICS

In a Water Shortage

During a water shortage, the water authority has asked people to conserve, but most people do not comply. Where is the economics here?

The people are in a prisoner's dilemma setting. Specifically, each person might agree (with all others) that conserving water is a good thing to do, but then each person realizes that he is better off if everyone conserves except him. Everyone can think the same way, of course. In the end, we are likely to find few people conserving.

Oligopoly Firms' Cartels and the Prisoner's Dilemma

When oligopoly firms enter into a cartel agreement, do they create a prisoner's dilemma? Most economists answer yes. To illustrate, two firms, A and B, produce and sell the same product and are in stiff competition with each other. Currently, the competition between them is so stiff that each earns only $10,000 profits. Soon the two firms decide to enter into a cartel agreement in which each agrees to raise prices and, after prices are raised, not to undercut the other. If they hold to the agreement, each firm will earn profits of $50,000. But if one firm holds to the cartel agreement and the other does not, the one that does not will earn profits of $100,000 and the one that does will earn $5,000 profits. Of course, if neither holds to the agreement, then both will be back where they started—earning $10,000 profits. The choices for the two firms and the possible outcomes are outlined in Exhibit 9.

Each firm is likely to behave as the two prisoners did in the prisoner's dilemma game. Each firm will see the chance to earn $100,000 by breaking the agreement (instead of

exhibit 9

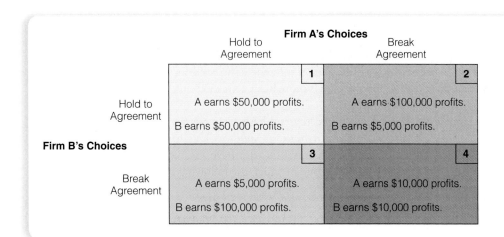

Cartels and Prisoner's Dilemma

Many economists suggest that firms trying to form a cartel are in a prisoner's dilemma situation. Both firms A and B earn higher profits holding to a (cartel) agreement than not, but each will earn even higher profits it it breaks the agreement while the other firm holds to it. If cartel formation is a prisoner's dilemma situation, we predict that cartels will be short-lived.

$50,000 by holding to it); each will also realize that if it does not break the agreement and the other firm does, it will be in a worse situation than before entering into the cartel. Most economists predict that the two firms will end up in box 4 in Exhibit 9, earning the profits they did before they entered into the agreement. In summary, they will cheat on the cartel agreement and again be in competition—the very situation they wanted to escape.

The only way out of the prisoner's dilemma for the two firms is to have some entity actually enforce the cartel agreement so that the two firms do not cheat. As odd as it may sound, sometimes government has played this role. Normally we think of government as trying to break up cartel agreements because, after all, such agreements are illegal. Nevertheless, sometimes government acts as the enforcer, not the eliminator, of the cartel agreement.

Consider the Civil Aeronautics Board (CAB) in the days of airline regulation. The CAB was created to protect the airlines from so-called cutthroat competition. It had the power to set airfares, allocate air routes, and prevent the entry of new carriers into the airline industry. In the days before deregulation, the federal government's General Accounting Office estimated that airline fares would have been, on average, as much as 52 percent lower if the CAB had not been regulating them. Clearly, the CAB was doing for the airlines what an airline cartel would have done: prevent price competition, allocate routes, and prevent new entries into the industry.

In a similar vein, Judge Richard Posner has observed that "the railroads supported the enactment of the first Interstate Commerce Act, which was designed to prevent railroads from price discrimination, because discrimination was undermining the railroad's cartels."[2]

Common MISCONCEPTIONS

About the Role Government Plays

Some say that government is on the side of competition and against cartels. "There is no way," they say, "that government is going to provide the glue to hold a cartel together that could not exist without it." But that is a misconception about how government sometimes operates. Knowingly or unknowingly, government sometimes does more to stifle competition than to promote it.

2. Richard A. Posner, "Theories of Regulation," *Bell Journal of Economics and Management Science* 5 (Autumn): 337.

Are Markets Contestable?

Market structures, from perfect competition to oligopoly, have been defined by the *number of sellers*. In perfect competition, there are many sellers; in monopoly, there is only one; in monopolistic competition, there are many; in oligopoly, there are few. The message is that the number of sellers in a market influences the behavior of the sellers in the market. For example, the monopoly seller is more likely to restrict output and charge higher prices than is the perfect competitor.

Some economists have shifted the emphasis from the number of sellers in a market to the issue of *entry into and exit from an industry*. This focus is a result of the work of William Baumol and other economists who have put forth the idea of contestable markets. A **contestable market** is one in which the following conditions are met:

Contestable Market
A market in which entry is easy and exit is costless, new firms can produce the product at the same cost as current firms, and exiting firms can easily dispose of their fixed assets by selling them.

1. *There is easy entry into the market and costless exit from the market.*

2. *New firms entering the market can produce the product at the same cost as current firms.*

3. *Firms exiting the market can easily dispose of their fixed assets by selling them elsewhere* (less depreciation; thus, fixed costs are not sunk but recoverable).

To illustrate, suppose that eight firms are in an industry and that all of them are earning profits. Firms outside the industry notice this and decide to enter the industry (nothing prevents entry). They acquire the necessary equipment and produce the product at the same cost as current producers do. Time passes, and the firms that entered the industry decide to exit it. They can either switch their machinery into another line of production or sell their equipment for what they paid for it, less depreciation.

Perhaps the most important element of a contestable market is so-called hit-and-run entry and exit. New entrants can enter (hit), produce the product and take profits from current firms, and then exit costlessly (run).

The theory of contestable markets has been criticized because of its assumptions—in particular, the assumption that there is extremely free entry into and costless exit from the industry. However, even though this theory, like most theories, does not perfectly describe the real world, it has its usefulness.

At a minimum, contestable markets theory has rattled orthodox market structure theory. Here are a few of its conclusions:

1. Even if an industry is composed of a small number of firms or even just one firm, this is not evidence that the firms perform in a noncompetitive way. They might be extremely competitive if the market they are in is contestable.

2. Profits can be zero in an industry even if the number of sellers in the industry is small.

3. If a market is contestable, inefficient producers cannot survive. Cost inefficiencies invite lower cost producers into the market, driving price down to minimum *ATC* and forcing inefficient firms to change their ways or exit the industry.

4. If, as the previous conclusion suggests, a contestable market encourages firms to produce at their lowest possible average total cost and charge $P = ATC$, then they will also sell at a price equal to marginal cost. (Recall that the marginal cost curve intersects the average total cost curve at its minimum point.)

The theory of contestable markets has also led to a shift in policy perspectives. To some (but certainly not all) economists, the theory suggests a new way to encourage firms to act as perfect competitors. Rather than direct interference in the behavioral patterns of firms, efforts should perhaps be directed at lowering entry and exit costs.

exhibit 10

Characteristics and Consequences of Market Structures

Market Structure	Number of Sellers	Type of Product	Barriers to Entry	Long-Run Market Tendency of Price and *ATC*
Perfect competition	Many	Homogeneous	No	$P = ATC$ (zero economic profits)
Monopoly	One	Unique	Yes	$P > ATC$ (positive economic profits)[a, c]
Monopolistic competition	Many	Slightly differentiated	No	$P = ATC$ (zero economic profits)[b]
Oligopoly	Few	Homogeneous or differentiated	Yes	$P > ATC$ (positive economic profits)[a, c]

a. It is possible for positive profits to turn to zero profits through the capitalization of profits or rent-seeking activities.
b. It is possible for the firm to earn positive profits in the long run if it can differentiate its product sufficiently in the minds of the buying public.
c. It is possible for positive profits to turn to zero profits if the market is contestable.

A REVIEW OF MARKET STRUCTURES

Exhibit 10 reviews some of the characteristics and consequences of the four different market structures: perfect competition, monopoly, monopolistic competition, and oligopoly. The first four columns of the exhibit summarize the characteristics. The last column notes the long-run market tendencies of price and average total cost. The relationship between price and *ATC* indicates whether long-run profits are possible.

Note that three of the four market structures (monopoly, monopolistic competition, and oligopoly) have superscript letters beside the possible profits. These letters refer to notes that describe alternative market tendencies given different conditions. For example, the market tendency in oligopoly is for $P > ATC$ and for profits to exist in the long run. Because there are significant barriers to entry in oligopoly, short-run profits cannot be reduced by competition from new firms entering the industry. However, the market tendency of price and average total cost may be different if the particular oligopolistic market is contestable.

APPLICATIONS OF GAME THEORY

Game theory, especially prisoner's dilemma, is applicable in a number of real-world situations. In this section, we discuss a few of these applications.

Grades and Partying

Your economics professor announces in class one day that on the next test, she will give the top 10 percent of the students in the class As, the next 15 percent Bs, and so on. You realize it takes less time studying to get, say, a 60 than a 90 on the test, so you hope everyone studies only a little. That way, you can study only a little and earn a high letter grade. But, of course, everyone in the class is thinking the same thing.

Envision yourself entering into an agreement with your fellow students. You say the following to them one day:

There are 30 students in our class. Each of us can choose to study either 2 hours or 4 hours for the test. Our relative standing in the class will be the same whether we all study for 2 hours or all study for 4 hours. So why don't we all agree to study for only 2 hours. That way, we have 2 extra hours to do other things. I'd rather receive my B by studying only 2 hours instead of by studying 4 hours.

Everyone agrees with the logic of the argument and agrees to study only 2 hours. Of course, once everyone has agreed to this, there is an incentive to cheat on the agreement and study more. If everyone else in your class agrees to study 2 hours and you study 4 hours, you increase your relative standing in the class. You go from, say, a B to an A.

exhibit 11

Studying and Grades

Suppose your letter grade in class depends on how well you do relative to others. In this setting, you and the other students are in a prisoner's dilemma, which is shown here. If both you and Jill (a representative other student) each study 4 hours, each of you earns a point grade of 85, which is a B (box 4). If each of study 2 hours, each of you earn a point grade of 65, which is a B (box 1). Box 1 is preferred over box 4 because you get the same letter grade in each box, but you study less in box 1 than in box 4.

If you study 4 hours while Jill studies 2 hours, your point grade rises to 85 and Jill's point grade remains at 65. In this case, 85 is an A and 65 is a C (box 2). You are better off and Jill is worse off.

If you study 2 hours while Jill studies 4 hours, Jill's point grade rises to 85 and your point grade remains at 65. Jill earns a letter grade of A, and you earn a letter grade of C.

No matter what Jill decides to do—study 2 or 4 hours—it is always better for you to study 4 hours (assuming the costs of studying additional hours are less than the benefits of studying additional hours). The same holds for Jill. Our outcome, then, is box 4, where both you and Jill study 4 hours.

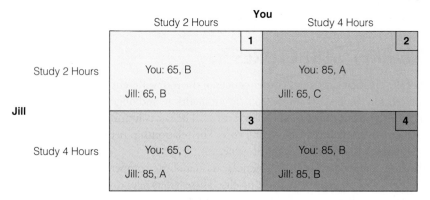

You and the other students in your class are in a prisoner's dilemma. Exhibit 11 shows the payoffs for you and for Jill, a representative other student. If both you and Jill study 4 hours, each receives an 85, which is a B (box 4). With your professor's new relative grading plan, if you study 2 hours and Jill studies 2 hours, the grade for each of you falls to 65, but now 65 is a B (box 1). In other words, in comparison with box 4, box 1 is better because you receive the same letter grade (B) in both cases but spend less time studying.

Of course, once you and Jill agree to lower your study time from 4 hours to 2 hours, each of you has an incentive to cheat on the agreement. If you study 4 hours and Jill studies 2 hours, then you raise your grade to an 85, which is now an A, while Jill's grade is 65, which now becomes a C (box 2). Of course, if Jill studies 4 hours and you study 2 hours, then Jill raises her grade to an 85, which is now an A, and your grade is 65, which is now a C (box 3).

No matter what you think Jill is going to do, the best thing for you to do is study 4 hours.[3] The same holds for Jill with respect to whatever you choose to do. The outcome then is box 4, where both of you study 4 hours.

Ideally, what you need (and Jill needs too) is a way to enforce your agreement not to study more than 2 hours. How might students do this? One way is to party. (That's right: party.) If you can get all the students in your class together and party, you can be fairly sure that no one is studying.

In general, students in the same class understand (1) that some professors set aside some percentage of As for the top students in the class (no matter how low the top is) and (2) that they are in a prisoner's dilemma. They realize it would be better for them

---

3. We are assuming that the cost of studying 2 additional hours is lower than the benefits you receive by raising your grade one letter.

to cooperate and study less than to compete and study more. Instead of actually entering into an agreement to study less (sign on the dotted line), they think up ways to keep the studying time down. One way to keep the studying time down—one way to enforce the implicit and unspoken agreement not to study too much—is to do things with others that do not entail studying. One such institution that satisfies all requirements is partying: Everyone is together, not studying.

The Arms Race

During much of the Cold War, the United States and the Soviet Union engaged in an arms race. Each country was producing armaments that were directed at the other. Occasionally, representatives of the two countries would meet and try to slow down the race. The United States would agree to cut armaments production if the Soviet Union did, and vice versa. Many arms analysts generally agreed that the arms agreements between the United States and the Soviet Union were unsuccessful. In other words, representatives of the two countries would meet and enter into an agreement not to compete so heavily, but then the countries would just keep competing on arms production.

The two countries were in a prisoner's dilemma. Look at Exhibit 12. When both the United States and the Soviet Union were competing on arms production, they were in box 4, each receiving a utility level of 7. Their collective objective was to move from box 4 to box 1, where each cooperated with the other and reduced its armaments production. In box 1, each country received a utility level of 10. The arms agreements that the United States and the Soviet Union entered into were attempts to get to box 1.

Of course, after the agreement was signed, each country had an incentive to cheat. Certainly, the United States would be better off if it increased its armaments production while the Soviet Union cut back its production. Then the United States could establish clear military superiority over the Soviet Union. The same held for the Soviet Union with respect to the United States.

exhibit 12

An Arms Race

In the days of the Cold War, the United States and the Soviet Union were said to be in an arms race. Actually, the arms race was a result of the two countries being in a prisoner's dilemma. Start with each country racing to produce more military goods than the other country; that is, each country is in box 4. In their attempt to move to box 1, they enter into an arms agreement (to reduce the rate at which they produce arms). But no matter what the Soviet Union does (hold to the arms agreement or break it), it is always better for the United States to break the agreement. The same holds for the Soviet Union with respect to the United States. The two countries end up in box 4. (Note: In the exhibit, the higher the number, the better the position for the country.)

United States

Soviet Union	Hold to Arms Agreement	Break Arms Agreement
Hold to Arms Agreement	**1** United States, 10 / Soviet Union, 10	**2** United States, 15 / Soviet Union, 5
Break Arms Agreement	**3** United States, 5 / Soviet Union, 15	**4** United States, 7 / Soviet Union, 7

economics 24/7

GRADE INFLATION AT COLLEGE

At Harvard in 1966, 22 percent of all grades were As. By 2002, that percentage had risen to 46 percent.

Were the students at Harvard in 2002 a lot smarter than the students in 1966? Were the professors at Harvard in 2002 much better teachers than the professors in 1966? If neither smarter students nor better professors can explain the growing percentage of As at Harvard overtime, then what does?

Many suggest it is grade inflation. Student performance on tests, exams, and papers that once received a grade of C today receives a grade of B; what once received a grade of B now receives a grade of A.

Harvard is not unusual when it comes to grade inflation. It exists on many other college campuses. College professors often acknowledge it

("Years ago this would be a C paper instead of a B paper"), and some complain about it. Some even go so far as wanting to change it—to end grade inflation. So, then, why don't they?

College professors might be in a prisoner's dilemma setting. To illustrate, suppose college professors (on a particular college campus) enter into an agreement with other college professors to stop inflating grades. Each professor now has the choice of holding to the agreement or breaking it (continuing to inflate grades). If a professor wants to raise the grades of his students relative to other students, he may choose to inflate grades—thinking that other professors are not inflating grades. The result? All (or almost all) professors will end up inflating grades.

The payoff matrix in Exhibit 12 makes it is easy to see that the best strategy for the United States or the Soviet Union was to compete. So the two countries ended up in box 4, racing to outproduce the other in arms.

Speed Limit Laws

Envision a world with no law against speeding. In this world, you and everyone else speeds. With everyone speeding, a good number of accidents occur each day, some of which may involve you. In time, everyone decides that something has to be done about the speeding. It is just too dangerous, everyone admits, to let it continue.

Someone offers a proposal: "Let's agree that we will post signs on the road that state the maximum speed. Furthermore, let's agree here and now that we will all obey the speed limits." The proposal sounds like a good one, and so everyone agrees to it.

Of course, as we know by now, once the agreement not to speed is made, we have a prisoner's dilemma. Each person will be better off if he (and he alone) speeds while everyone else obeys the speed limit. In the beginning, everyone agrees to the speed limit; in the end, however, everyone breaks it.

What is missing, of course, is an effective enforcement mechanism. To move the speeders out of the classic prisoner's dilemma box (box 4 in our earlier examples) to box 1, someone or something has to punish people who do not cooperate. A law against speeding—backed up by the police and the court system—solves the prisoner's dilemma. The law, the police, and the court system change the payoff for cheating on the agreement.

The Fear of Guilt as an Enforcement Mechanism

Might there be a social purpose—a good reason—for feeling guilty? Consider the following scenario. John and Mary decide to get married. As part of their wedding vows, they promise to remain faithful to each other. In other words, each promises the other that he or she will not cheat. Of course, once an agreement is made between two parties, often each party will be better off if one party cheats and the other does not. In the case of John and Mary, John may think, "I can gain utility by cheating on Mary." Of course, Mary can think the same thing with respect to John. Their utility payoffs are shown in Exhibit 13.

Notice in part (a) that both Mary and John receive a utility level of 15 when one cheats but the other does not. Possibly, if each person felt some guilt over cheating, the utility level would be something lower than 15. In some sense, both Mary and John might prefer to feel guilty when cheating. After all, both would prefer to be in box 1, where neither is cheating, than in box 4, where both are cheating. In short, given that box 1 is better than box 4 for both Mary and John, we would expect that both would opt for some enforcement mechanism that prevented them from moving away from box 1. Didn't the speeders want a law against speeding, enforced by the police and courts?

Of course, there is no outside enforcement mechanism for John and Mary, but an internal sense of guilt over cheating might be a good substitute for such a mechanism.

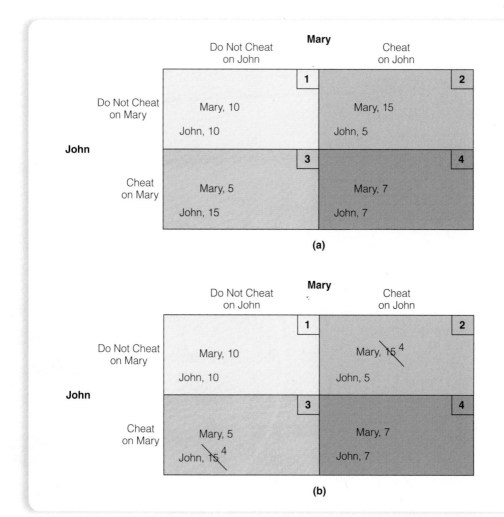

(a)

(b)

exhibit 13

Cheating and Guilt

Does guilt sometimes serve a useful social purpose? John and Mary are married and may be in a prisoner's dilemma. If Mary cheats on John, but John doesn't cheat on Mary, Mary may be better off and therefore moves from box 1 to box 2 in part (a). If John cheats on Mary, but Mary doesn't cheat on John, John may be better off and therefore moves from box 1 to box 3 in (a). Of course, if both cheat, they both end up in box 4, which is inferior for both to box 1. A sense of guilt for each person may change the payoffs in part (a). If each person feels guilty about cheating, then the payoff from cheating is lowered. Look at the new payoffs for each person in part (b). The payoff for cheating goes from 15 to 4 for both Mary and John. With the new, lower payoffs (resulting from a sense of guilt over cheating), both Mary and John remove themselves from a prisoner's dilemma and therefore are more likely to end up in box 1, a box that is better for both.

"ARE FIRMS (AS SELLERS) PRICE TAKERS OR PRICE SEARCHERS?"

Student:

Now that I have studied four different market structures, I want to see if I have some things correct. First, am I correct that all firms—no matter the market structure—will seek to produce that quantity of output at which $MR = MC$?

Instructor:

Yes, that's correct.

Student:

And is it correct that a firm either faces a horizontal demand curve and is a price taker or faces a downward-sloping demand curve and is a price searcher? In other words, is it true that a firm is either one or two things: a price taker or a price searcher? To put it differently, (1) perfectly competitive firms are price takers and (2) monopoly, monopolistic competitive, and oligopolistic firms are price searchers.

Instructor:

Yes, that's correct. To be more specific, if a firm is a price taker, it does not have to lower its price to sell additional units of a good. It can sell 100 units at $4 per unit, and it can sell 200 units at $4 a unit. But for a price searcher, the only way it can sell additional units of a good is to lower price. In other words, it can sell 100 units at $4 per unit, but if it wants to sell 101 units, it has to charge less than $4 per unit.

Student:

As to the issue of resource allocative efficiency ($P = MC$), am I right that a price taker is resource allocative efficient but a price searcher is not?

Instructor:

Yes, that's correct.

Points to Remember

1. All firms seek to produce the quantity of output at which $MR = MC$.

2. A firm faces either a horizontal demand curve or a downward-sloping demand curve; that is, a firm is either a price taker or a price searcher, respectively.

3. Perfectly competitive firms are price takers, and monopoly, monopolistic competitive, and oligopolistic firms are price searchers.

4. A price taker is resource allocative efficient, and a price searcher is not.

Instead of the police and the court system putting John and Mary in prison for cheating, each one's sense of guilt will put him or her in a personal jail. Isn't this idea implied when someone says, "I can't do that; I would feel too guilty." In other words, many people want to prevent themselves from suffering the pangs of guilt in much the same way they don't want to suffer the pain of prison. Both guilt pangs and prison are *bads*. Both come with disutility.

Suppose, as shown in Exhibit 13(b), a sense of guilt would change Mary's utility level in box 2 from 15 to 4 and would change John's utility level in box 3 from 15 to 4. Then neither Mary nor John would find it advantageous to cheat on the other if the spouse did not cheat.[4]

In the end, the question is, when is guilt good? One answer is that guilt is good when the fear of it motivates two people to remove themselves from a setting they would prefer not to be in to a better setting. If the fear of guilt moves Mary and John from box 4 to box 1 (which is what they want), then the fear of guilt is good.

a reader asks | Are Some Prisoner's Dilemmas Good and Others Bad?

Are we sometimes glad that people are in a prisoner's dilemma and not glad at other times? In other words, do we actually want people to end up in box 4 instead of box 1 in some settings, and do we want people to end up in box 1 instead of box 4 in other settings?

Let's look again at two of the prisoner's dilemma settings in the chapter: the cartel and the arms race.

In the cartel setting, two competing sellers enter into an agreement to reduce or eliminate the competition between them. If the cartel agreement is successful, sellers are better off and consumers are worse off. If the cartel agreement is unsuccessful (if one or both of the sellers break the cartel agreement), then sellers are worse off and consumers are better off.

The sellers, as you know, are in a prisoner's dilemma. Each seller agrees to cooperate with the other (to reduce or eliminate cooperation) but also has an incentive to cheat. The incentive to cheat (and to make oneself better off at the other's expense) is what gets each seller to break the cartel agreement. The outcome is that competition between sellers means benefits for consumers.

Consumers should be glad that sellers are in a prisoner's dilemma and therefore end up in box 4 competing with each other for consumers' business. In other words, if the sellers weren't in a prisoner's dilemma, consumers would want to put them in one.

Now consider our discussion about the arms race between the United States and the Soviet Union. Just like our two sellers, the two countries are in a prisoner's dilemma. Each country agrees to cooperate with the other (to slow the arms race between them) but also has an incentive to cheat on any agreement. The incentive to cheat (and to establish clear military superiority over the other country) is what gets each country to break the arms agreement. The outcome is a continuing arms race.

Not so clear in this case is whether there are any beneficiaries (other than perhaps armament producers) of the two countries being stuck in a prisoner's dilemma and ending up in box 4, engaged in an arms race. So this might be an example of a prisoner's dilemma that almost everyone would have preferred did not exist.

4. Of course, the way we have structured the payoff matrix, each finds it advantageous to cheat on the other if the other cheats. If Mary does not cheat on John, then John is better off not cheating than cheating, but if Mary cheats on John, and John knows that Mary is cheating on him, then he is better off cheating than not cheating.

Chapter Summary

MONOPOLISTIC COMPETITION

- The theory of monopolistic competition is built on three assumptions: (1) There are many sellers and buyers. (2) Each firm in the industry produces and sells a slightly differentiated product. (3) There is easy entry and exit.

- The monopolistic competitor is a price searcher.

- For the monopolistic competitor, $P > MR$, and the marginal revenue curve lies below the demand curve.

- The monopolistic competitor produces the quantity of output at which $MR = MC$. It charges the highest price per unit for this output.

- Unlike the perfectly competitive firm, the monopolistic competitor does not exhibit resource allocative efficiency.

- The monopolistic competitive firm does not earn profits in the long run (because of easy entry into the industry) unless it can successfully differentiate its product (e.g., by brand name) in the minds of buyers.

EXCESS CAPACITY THEOREM

- The excess capacity theorem states that a monopolistic competitor will, in equilibrium, produce an output smaller than that at which average total costs (unit costs) are minimized. Thus, the monopolistic competitor is not productive efficient.

OLIGOPOLY ASSUMPTIONS

- All of the many different oligopoly theories are built on the following assumptions: (1) There are few sellers and many buyers. (2) Firms produce and sell either homogeneous or differentiated products. (3) There are significant barriers to entry.

- One of the key characteristics of oligopolistic firms is their interdependence.

OLIGOPOLY THEORIES

- The cartel theory assumes that firms in an oligopolistic industry act in a manner consistent with there being only one firm in the industry.

- Four problems are associated with cartels: (1) the problem of forming the cartel, (2) the problem of formulating policy, (3) the problem of entry into the industry, and (4) the problem of cheating.

- Firms that enter into a cartel agreement are in a prisoner's dilemma situation, where individually rational behavior leads to a jointly inefficient outcome.

- The kinked demand curve theory assumes that if a single firm lowers price, other firms will do likewise but that if a single firm raises price, other firms will not follow suit.

- The kinked demand curve theory predicts that an oligopolistic firm will experience price stickiness or rigidity. This characteristic results from a gap in its marginal revenue curve in which the firm's marginal cost can rise or fall and the firm will still produce the same quantity of output and charge the same price. The evidence in some empirical tests rejects the theory.

- The price leadership theory assumes that the dominant firm in the industry determines price and all other firms take this price as given.

THE THEORY OF CONTESTABLE MARKETS

- The conditions for a contestable market are as follows: (1) There is easy entry into the market and costless exit from it. (2) New firms entering the market can produce the product at the same cost as current firms. (3) Firms exiting the market can easily dispose of their fixed assets by selling them elsewhere (less depreciation).

- Compared to orthodox market structure theories, the theory of contestable markets places more emphasis on the issue of entry into and exit from an industry and less emphasis on the number of sellers in an industry.

GAME THEORY

- Game theory is a mathematical technique used to analyze the behavior of decision makers who (1) try to reach an optimal position through game playing or the use of strategic behavior, (2) are fully aware of the interactive nature of the process at hand, and (3) anticipate the moves of other decision makers.

- The prisoner's dilemma game illustrates individually rational behavior leading to a jointly inefficient outcome.

Key Terms and Concepts

Monopolistic Competition	Cartel Theory	Game Theory
Excess Capacity Theorem	Cartel	Contestable Market
Oligopoly	Kinked Demand Curve Theory	
Concentration Ratio	Price Leadership Theory	

Questions and Problems

1 What, if anything, do all firms in all four market structures have in common?

2 What causes the unusual appearance of the marginal revenue curve in the kinked demand curve theory?

3 "Excess capacity is the price we pay for production differentiation." Evaluate this statement in terms of monopolistic competition.

4 Why might a producer use a designer label to differentiate her product from that of another producer?

5 Will there be profits in the long run in a monopolistic competitive market? Explain your answer.

6 Would you expect cartel formation to be more likely in industries comprised of a few firms or in those that include many firms? Explain your answer.

7 Does the theory of contestable markets shed any light on oligopoly pricing theories? Explain your answer.

8 There are 60 types or varieties of product X on the market. Is product X made in a monopolistic competitive market? Explain your answer.

9 Why does the interdependence of firms play a major role in oligopoly but not in perfect competition or monopolistic competition?

10 Concentration ratios have often been used to note the tightness of an oligopoly market. A high concentration ratio indicates a tight oligopoly market, and a low concentration ratio indicates a loose oligopoly market. Would you expect firms in tight markets to reap higher profits, on average, than firms in loose markets? Would it matter if the markets were contestable? Explain your answers.

11 Market theories are said to have the happy consequence of getting individuals to think in more focused and analytical ways. Is this true for you? Give examples to illustrate.

12 Give an example of a prisoner's dilemma situation other than the ones mentioned in this chapter.

13 How are oligopoly and monopolistic competition alike? How are they different?

14 Explain the price leadership theory of oligopoly.

Working with Numbers and Graphs

1 Diagrammatically identify the quantity of output a monopolistic competitor produces and the price it charges.

2 Diagrammatically identify a monopolistic competitor that is incurring losses.

3 In Exhibit 6, what is the highest dollar amount to which marginal cost can rise without changing price?

4 Total industry sales are $105 million. The top four firms account for sales of $10 million, $9 million, $8 million, and $5 million, respectively. What is the four-firm concentration ratio?

5 According to the kinked demand curve theory, if the firm is considering a price hike, which demand curve in the following figure does it believe it faces and why?

6 Refer to the following figure. Because of a cartel agreement, the firm has been assigned a production quota of q_2 units. The cartel price is P_2. What do the firm's profits equal if it adheres to the cartel agreement? What do the firm's profits equal if it breaks the cartel agreement and produces q_3?

CHAPTER *11*

GOVERNMENT AND PRODUCT MARKETS: ANTITRUST AND REGULATION

© GLOW IMAGES/ALAMY

Introduction In Washington, D.C., you may see the building that houses the Department of Justice. One of the many duties of the Justice Department is the enforcement of the country's antitrust laws, whose stated purpose is to control monopoly and to preserve and promote competition. Does it matter to your life whether the Justice Department does a good, bad, or mediocre job of controlling monopoly and preserving and promoting competition? Does it matter how the Justice Department does its job? It matters in more ways than you can possibly imagine.

ANTITRUST

A monopoly (1) produces a smaller output than is produced by a perfectly competitive firm with the same revenue and cost considerations, (2) charges a higher price, and (3) causes a deadweight loss. Some economists argue that, based on these facts, government should place restrictions on monopolies. In addition, government should restrict the activities of cartels because the objective of a cartel is to behave as if it were a monopoly.

Other economists argue that monopolies do not have as much market power as some people think: Witness the competition some monopolies face from broadly defined substitutes and imports. As for cartels, they usually contain the seeds of their own destruction; so it is only a matter of (a usually short) time before they crumble naturally.

We are not concerned with the debate about whether to restrict monopoly power, but with how government deals with it, specifically through its antitrust laws and regulation. We examine antitrust law in this section and regulation in the next.

Antitrust law is legislation passed for the stated purpose of controlling monopoly power and preserving and promoting competition. Let's look at the uses and effects of a few of the major antitrust acts.

Antitrust Law
Legislation passed for the stated purpose of controlling monopoly power and preserving and promoting competition.

Antitrust Acts

A few key acts that constitute U.S. antitrust policy are the Sherman Act (1890), the Clayton Act (1914), the Federal Trade Commission Act (1914), the Robinson-Patman Act (1936), the Wheeler-Lea Act (1938), and the Celler-Kefauver Antimerger Act (1950).

THE SHERMAN ACT (1890) The Sherman Act was passed when mergers of companies were common. (A merger occurs when two companies combine under single ownership of control.) At that time, the organization that companies formed by combining was called a **trust**; this in turn gave us the word *antitrust.*

Trust
A combination of firms that come together to act as a monopolist.

The Sherman Act contains two major provisions:

1. "Every contract, combination in the form of trust or otherwise, or conspiracy, in restraint of trade or commerce among the several states, or with foreign nations, is hereby declared to be illegal."

2. "Every person who shall monopolize, or attempt to monopolize, or combine or conspire with any other person or persons to monopolize any part of the trade or commerce . . . shall be guilty of a misdemeanor."

Some people have argued that the provisions of the Sherman Act are vague. For example, the act never explains which specific acts constitute a restraint of trade, although it declares such acts illegal.

THE CLAYTON ACT (1914) The Clayton Act makes the following business practices illegal when their effects "may be to substantially lessen competition or tend to create a monopoly":

1. *Price discrimination*—charging different customers different prices for the same product when the price differences are not related to cost differences.

2. *Exclusive dealing*—selling to a retailer on the condition that the retailer not carry any rival products.

3. *Tying contracts*—arrangements whereby the sale of one product is dependent on the purchase of some other product or products.

4. *The acquisition of competing companies' stock if the acquisition reduces competition.* (Some say a major loophole of the act is that it does not ban the acquisition of competing companies' physical assets and therefore does not prevent anticompetitive mergers from doing what they are intended to do.)

5. *Interlocking directorates*—an arrangement whereby the directors of one company sit on the board of another company in the same industry. These were made illegal, irrespective of their effects (i.e., interlocking directorates are illegal at all times, not just when their effects "may be to substantially lessen competition . . .").

THE FEDERAL TRADE COMMISSION ACT (1914) The Federal Trade Commission Act contains the broadest and most general language of any antitrust act. It declares illegal "unfair methods of competition in commerce." In essence, it declares illegal acts that are judged to be "too aggressive" in competition. The problem is how to decide what is fair and what is unfair, what is aggressive but not too aggressive. This act also set up the Federal Trade Commission (FTC) to deal with "unfair methods of competition."

THE ROBINSON-PATMAN ACT (1936) The Robinson-Patman Act was passed in an attempt to decrease the failure rate of small businesses by protecting them from the competition of large and growing chain stores. The large chain stores were receiving price discounts from suppliers and, in turn, passing the discounts on to their customers. As

THOMAS EDISON AND HOLLYWOOD

© CRAIG AURNESS/CORBIS

Thomas Alva Edison was born in 1847 and died in 1931. In his 84 years of life, Edison was granted 1,093 patents. Almost everyone knows the role Edison played in the development of electric light and power, but not everyone knows the role he played in indirectly and unwittingly making Hollywood the film capital of the world.

Our story begins with an Edison invention—a machine called the kinetophonograph, which showed a moving picture that was synchronized with a phonograph record. Later, Edison invented the kinetoscope, which was a device that allowed users to deposit a coin and watch a short motion picture through a small hole.

After inventing the kinetophonograph and kinetoscope, Edison went on to construct the first building that was used solely to make movies. A hole in the ceiling of the building allowed the sun to shine through and illuminate the stage. The entire building was on a set of tracks so that it could be moved around to follow the sun. The first film that Edison produced was a 15-minute movie called *The Great Train Robbery*. Over the years, he produced more than 2,000 short films.

There is some evidence that Edison and a few other people tried to gain complete control over the movie industry in its early days. Edison played a critical role in putting together the Movie Trust, sometimes called the Edison Trust, a group of ten film producers and distributors. The Movie Trust reportedly tried to eliminate its competition. First, the Movie Trust entered into a contract with Eastman Kodak Company, which manufactured film, to sell film only to it. Second, the Movie Trust refused to lease or sell equipment to certain filmmakers and theater owners. One of the independent movie producers whom the Movie Trust tried to run out of the industry was Carl Laemmie. Laemmie and some other movie producers decided to leave the East Coast, where the Movie Trust had the greatest control over the industry, and went to the West Coast, specifically to southern California. Others soon followed. The rush of independent filmmakers to southern California set the stage for the development of Hollywood as the film capital of the world. In 1917, the Movie Trust was dissolved by court order, but by then the movie industry had a new home. Laemmie, for example, founded Universal Studios in Hollywood in 1912.

It is doubtful that Hollywood would be the film capital of the world had it not been for the Movie Trust. Without the exclusionary and anticompetitive tactics of the Movie Trust, the film capital of the world would probably be on the East Coast of the United States, very likely in or near New York City.

a result, small businesses had a difficult time competing, and many of them failed. The Robinson-Patman Act prohibits suppliers from offering special discounts to large chain stores unless they also offer the discounts to everyone else. Many economists believe that, rather than preserving and strengthening competition, the Robinson-Patman Act limits it. The act seems to be more concerned about a certain group of competitors than about the process of competition and the buying public as a whole.

THE WHEELER-LEA ACT (1938) The Wheeler-Lea Act empowers the Federal Trade Commission to deal with false and deceptive acts or practices. Major moves in this area have been against advertising that the FTC has deemed false and deceptive.

THE CELLER-KEFAUVER ANTIMERGER ACT (1950) The Celler-Kefauver Act was designed to close the merger loophole in the Clayton Act (see point 4 of the Clayton Act). It bans anticompetitive mergers that occur as a result of one company's acquiring the physical assets of another company.

Unsettled Points in Antitrust Policy

Not always clear is where the lines should be drawn in implementing antitrust policy: Which firms should be allowed to enter into a merger and which prohibited? What constitutes restraint of trade? Which firms should be treated as monopolists and broken into smaller firms, and which firms should be left alone?

As you might guess, not everyone answers these questions the same way. In short, some points of antitrust policy are still unsettled.

DOES THE DEFINITION OF THE MARKET MATTER? How a market is defined—broadly or narrowly—helps determine whether a firm is considered a monopoly. For example, in an important antitrust suit in 1945, a court ruled that Alcoa (Aluminum Company of America) was a monopoly because it had 90 percent of the virgin aluminum ingot market. If Alcoa's market had been broadened to include stainless steel, copper, tin, nickel, and zinc (some of the goods competing with aluminum), it is unlikely that Alcoa would have been ruled a monopoly.

Later court rulings have tended to define markets broadly rather than narrowly. For instance, in the DuPont case in 1956, the market relevant to DuPont was ruled to be the flexible wrapping materials market rather than the narrower cellophane market.

CONCENTRATION RATIOS Concentration ratios have often been used to gauge the amount of competition in an industry, but, as pointed out in the last chapter, their use presents two major problems. First, concentration ratios do not address the issue of foreign competition. For example, the four-firm concentration ratio may be very high, but the four firms that make up the concentration ratio may still face stiff competition from abroad. Second, a four-firm concentration ratio can remain stable over time even though there is competition among the four major firms in the industry.

In 1982, the Justice Department replaced the four- and eight-firm concentration ratios with the Herfindahl index, although it too is subject to some of the same criticisms as the concentration ratios. The **Herfindahl index**, which measures the degree of concentration in an industry, is equal to the sum of the squares of the market shares of each firm in the industry:

$$\text{Herfindahl index} = (S_1)^2 + (S_2)^2 + \ldots + (S_n)^2$$

where S_1 through S_n are the market shares of firms 1 through n. For example, if there are 10 firms in an industry and if each firm has a 10 percent market share, the Herfindahl index is 1,000 ($10^2 + 10^2 + 10^2 + 10^2 + 10^2 + 10^2 + 10^2 + 10^2 + 10^2 + 10^2 = 1,000$).

Exhibit 1 compares the Herfindahl index and the four-firm concentration ratio. When the four-firm concentration ratio is used, the top four firms, A-B-C-D, have a 48 percent market share, which generally is thought to describe a concentrated industry. A merger between any of the top four firms and any other firm (e.g., between firm B and firm G in Exhibit 1) would give the newly merged firm a greater market share than any existing firm and usually would incur frowns at the Justice Department.

The Herfindahl index for the industry is 932, however, and the Justice Department generally considers any number less than 1,000 representative of an unconcentrated (or competitive) industry. An index between 1,000 and 1,800 is considered representative of a moderately concentrated industry, and an index greater than 1,800 is representative of a concentrated industry.

When is the Justice Department likely to take antitrust actions? According to the statement made at the website of the Antitrust Division of the Justice Department "transactions that increase the HHI by more than 100 points in concentrated

Herfindahl Index
Index that measures the degree of concentration in an industry, equal to the sum of the squares of the market shares of each firm in the industry.

A Comparison of the Four-Firm Concentration Ratio and the Herfindahl Index

Using the old method (in this case, the four-firm concentration ratio), the top four firms in the industry have a 48 percent market share. The Justice Department would likely frown on a proposed merger between any of the top four firms and any other firm. However, the Herfindahl index of 932 is representative of an unconcentrated industry.

Firms	Market Share
A	15%
B	12
C	11
D	10
E	8
F	7
G	7
H	6
I	6
J	6
K	6
L	6

OLD METHOD: FOUR-FIRM CONCENTRATION RATIO
15% + 12% + 11% + 10% = 48%

NEW METHOD: HERFINDAHL INDEX
Square the market share of each firm and then add:
$(15)^2 + (12)^2 + (11)^2 + (10)^2 + (8)^2 + (7)^2 + (7)^2 + (6)^2 + (6)^2 + (6)^2 + (6)^2 + (6)^2 = 932$

markets [markets with an index greater than 1,800] presumptively raise antitrust concerns. . . ."[1]

To illustrate, suppose 8 firms are in an industry. Two of the firms, A and B, want to merge. The market share of firm A is 30 percent, and the market share of firm B is 22 percent. We assume that market shares for the other six firms in the industry are 15 percent, 10 percent, 10 percent, 5 percent, 5 percent, and 3 percent. The Herfindahl index in this industry currently is 1,868 $(30^2 + 22^2 + 15^2 + 10^2 + 10^2 + 5^2 + 5^2 + 3^2)$.

If the merger is approved, there will be 7, not 8, firms. Moreover, the market share of the merged firm (A and B now form one firm) will be 52 percent. The Herfindahl index after the merger will be 3,188. In other words, there will be an increase of 1,320 points if the firms merge. With this substantial increase in the index, the proposed merger is likely to be blocked.

INNOVATION AND CONCENTRATION RATIOS According to the 1999 *Economic Report of the President,* more than half of all productivity gains in the U.S. economy in the previous 50 years, as measured by output per labor hour, came from innovation and technical change. Because innovation and technical change are so important to our economic well-being, some economists argue that concentration ratios should not play so large a role in determining a merger's approval. The merger's effect on innovation should also be taken into account. There is some evidence that antitrust authorities are beginning to accept this line of thinking.

It used to be thought that small firms in highly competitive markets with many rivals had a stronger incentive to innovate than firms in markets where only a few firms existed and where each firm had sizable market power. Increasingly, however, it is thought that these small competitive firms often face a greater risk of innovation than firms with substantial market power and that therefore they innovate less.

To illustrate, consider a market with 100 firms, each of which supplies one-hundredth of the market. Suppose one of these firms invests heavily in research and develops a new product or process. It has to worry about any of its 99 rivals soon developing a similar innovation and therefore reducing the value of its innovation. On the other hand, if a firm is one of four firms and has substantial market power, it doesn't face as much so-called innovative risk. It has only three, not 99, rivals to worry about. And, of course, the less likely it is that competitors can make one's own innovations less valuable, the higher the expected return from innovating will be.

---

1. See http://www.usdoj.gov/atr/public/testimony/hhi.htm.

Today, antitrust authorities say that they consider the benefits of both competition and innovation when ruling on proposed mergers. On the one hand, increased competition lowers prices for consumers. On the other hand, monopoly power may yield more innovation. If it does, then the lower prices brought about through increased competition have to be weighed against the increased innovation that may come about through greater market concentration and monopoly power.

Thinking like An Economist

Different Roads to the Same Destination

If a firm has a large share of the market, the economist will ask, "Is there only one possible explanation for this, or are there many?" If there are many, then the economist will try to find out which is the correct explanation. As an analogy, suppose someone gets the highest grade in three of three courses. There may well be more than one explanation: The person could be studying more than anyone else. Or the person could be innately smarter than anyone else. Or the person could be cheating. The economist knows that usually different roads end up at the same destination. Trying to figure out which road was taken to the destination is part of the task economists set for themselves.

Antitrust and Mergers

There are three basic types of mergers.

1. A **horizontal merger** is a merger between firms that are selling similar products in the same market. For example, suppose both companies A and B produce cars. If the two companies combine under single ownership of control, it is a horizontal merger.

2. A **vertical merger** is a merger between companies in the same industry but at different stages of the production process. Stated differently, a vertical merger occurs between companies where one buys (or sells) something from (or to) the other. For example, suppose company C, which produces cars, buys tires from company D. If the two companies combine under single ownership of control, it is a vertical merger.

3. A **conglomerate merger** is a merger between companies in different industries. For example, if company E, in the car industry, and company F, in the pharmaceutical industry, combine under single ownership of control, it is a conglomerate merger.

Of the three types of mergers—vertical, horizontal, and conglomerate—the federal government looks most carefully at proposed horizontal mergers. These mergers are more likely (than vertical or conglomerate mergers) to change the degree of concentration, or competition, in an industry. For example, if General Motors (cars) and Ford Motor Company (cars) horizontally merge, competition in the car industry is likely to decrease by more than if General Motors (cars) and BF Goodrich (tires) vertically merge. In the latter case, the competition among car companies and among tire companies is likely to be the same after the merger as it was before. This is not necessarily the case, however, and the government does not always approve vertical mergers; in some notable examples, it has not.

Seven Antitrust Cases and Actions

Most people agree that the stated purpose of the antitrust laws—promoting and strengthening competition—is a worthwhile goal. Often, however, the stated purpose or objective of a policy turns out to be quite different from its effects. Some economists have argued that the antitrust laws have not, in all instances, accomplished their stated objective.

Horizontal Merger
A merger between firms that are selling similar products in the same market.

Vertical Merger
A merger between companies in the same industry but at different stages of the production process.

Conglomerate Merger
A merger between companies in different industries.

The following cases and actions illustrate some of the ways that courts and government policy makers have approached antitrust cases over the years.

CASE 1: VON'S GROCERY In 1966, the U.S. Supreme Court ruled on the legality of a merger between Von's Grocery Co. and Shopping Bag Food Stores, both of Los Angeles. Together, the two grocery chains had a little more than 7 percent of the grocery market in the Los Angeles area. However, the Supreme Court ruled that a merger between the two companies violated the Clayton Act. The Court based its ruling largely on the fact that, between 1950 and the early 1960s, the number of small grocery stores in Los Angeles had declined sharply. The Court took this as an indication of increased concentration in the industry.

Economists are quick to point out that the number of firms in an industry might be falling due to technological changes and that, when this happens, the average size of an existing firm rises. Justice Potter Stewart, in a dissenting opinion to the 1966 decision, argued that the Court had erroneously assumed that the "degree of competition is invariably proportional to the number of competitors."

CASE 2: UTAH PIE In 1967, the Utah Pie Company, which was based in Salt Lake City, charged that three of its competitors in Los Angeles were practicing price discrimination. Utah Pie charged that these companies were selling pies in Salt Lake City for lower prices than they were selling pies near their plants of operation. The Supreme Court ruled in favor of Utah Pie.

Some economists note, though, that Utah Pie charged lower prices for its pies than did its competitors and that it continued to increase its sales volume and make a profit during the time that its competitors were supposedly exhibiting anticompetitive behavior. They suggest that Utah Pie was using the antitrust laws to hinder its competition.

CASE 3: CONTINENTAL AIRLINES In 1978, Continental Airlines set out to acquire National Airlines. The Justice Department opposed the merger of the two companies on the grounds that the merged company would dominate the New Orleans air traffic market. The Civil Aeronautics Board (CAB) did not oppose the merger because it believed the market under consideration was contestable. Recall that firms in a contestable market that operate inefficiently or that consistently earn positive economic profits will be joined by competing firms. By refusing to oppose the merger, the CAB implied that it believed that statistical measures, such as concentration ratios, mean less than whether the market is contestable.

CASE 4: IBM In 1969, the Justice Department filed antitrust charges against IBM, saying that it had monopolized the "general-purpose computer and peripheral-equipment" industry. IBM argued that the antitrust authorities had interpreted its market too narrowly.

After 13 years of litigation against IBM, the government decided to drop the suit. During the years of litigation, the computer market had changed, and new competitors entered the broadly defined computer market. Although IBM might have once dominated the mainframe computer industry, there was little evidence that it dominated the minicomputer, word processor, or computer services markets.

CASE 5: UNIVERSITIES For many years, the upper level administrators of some of the country's top universities—Brown, Columbia, Cornell, Dartmouth, Harvard, MIT, Princeton, the University of Pennsylvania, and Yale—met to discuss such things as tuition, faculty salaries, and financial aid. There seemed to be evidence that these meetings occurred because the universities were trying to align tuition, faculty raises, and financial aid. For example, one of the universities once wanted to raise faculty salaries by more than the others wanted and was persuaded not to do so. At these meetings, the administrators also compared lists of applicants to find the names of students who had applied to more than one of their schools (e.g., someone who might have applied to Harvard, Yale, and MIT). Then the administrators adjusted their financial aid packages for that student so that no university was offering more than another.

The Justice Department charged the universities with a conspiracy to fix prices. Eight of the universities settled the case by agreeing to sign a consent decree to cease colluding on tuition, salaries, and financial aid. MIT did not agree to sign the consent decree and pursued the case to the Supreme Court. In 1992, the Supreme Court ruled against MIT, saying that it had violated antitrust laws.

CASE 6: LOCKHEED MARTIN AND NORTHROP GRUMMAN In 1997, Lockheed Martin Corporation proposed to acquire Northrop Grumman Corporation. Both Lockheed and Northrop were leading suppliers of aircraft and electronics systems to the U.S. military. The Justice Department challenged the acquisition, saying that it would give Lockheed a monopoly in fiber optic–towed decoys and in systems for airborne early warning radar. In this case, the issue of innovation played a major role. The Justice Department noted that both Lockheed and Northrop had invested heavily in the research and development of advanced airborne early warning radar systems. If the two companies merged, research and development activities would decline, and innovation would be hampered. The Justice Department blocked the acquisition.

CASE 7: BOEING AND MCDONNELL DOUGLAS In 1997, the Federal Trade Commission approved the merger of Boeing Co. and McDonnell Douglas Corp., the two largest commercial aircraft manufacturers in the United States. Innovation was an issue in the Boeing-McDonnell Douglas case, just as it was in the Lockheed Martin-Northrop Grumman case, but it played a different role: The FTC approved the merger to increase innovation. The FTC's analysis showed that McDonnell Douglas had fallen behind technologically and was no longer applying competitive innovative pressure on Boeing. The FTC felt that because McDonnell Douglas was not stimulating innovation in the aircraft manufacturing market, nothing in the way of innovation would be lost in allowing the two firms to merge. In fact, something might be gained. McDonnell Douglas's assets might be put to better use by a technologically advanced company like Boeing.

Common MISCONCEPTIONS

About Antitrust Policy

Some people mistakenly believe that all the big issues in antitrust policy have been settled. Not true.

For example, predatory pricing practices—or selling a good for a low price to eliminate competitors—are deemed illegal. But difficult questions arise: How low must a price be before it is deemed predatory? How long must the low price persist before it is deemed predatory?

Also, in a monopoly case, the relevant market is not always obvious. For example, is the relevant market for soft drinks the soft drink market, or is it the beverage market, or is it the anything-to-drink market (which includes water, juices, coffee, tea, and so on)?

Finally, mergers and tying arrangements are deemed illegal if they "substantially reduce competition," but how much competition has to be reduced before it is substantial?

Network Monopolies

A network connects things. For example, a telephone network connects telephones, the Internet (which is a network of networks) connects computers, and a bank network may connect automated teller machines (ATMs). A **network good** is a good whose value increases as the expected number of units sold increases. A telephone is a network good; you buy a telephone to network with other people. It has little value to you if you expect only 100 people to buy telephones, but its value increases if you expect thousands of people to buy telephones. Software is also a network good in the sense that if Smith and Jones both buy software X, they can then easily exchange documents. As new buyers buy a network good, the present owners of the good receive greater benefits because the network connects them to more people. For example, if Brown and Thompson also buy software X, Smith and Jones will receive greater benefits because they can exchange documents with two more people.

The production and sales of a network good can lead to monopoly. Suppose three companies (A, B, and C) make some version of network good X. Company A makes the most popular version; so its good is said to have the greatest network worthiness. Consequently, people who are thinking of buying good X buy it from company A. As more people purchase good X from company A, the network worthiness increases, prompting even more people to buy good X from company A rather than buying it from the other two companies. Eventually, the customers of companies B and C may switch to company A, and at some point almost everyone buys good X from company A. Company A is a network monopoly.

ANTITRUST POLICY FOR NETWORK MONOPOLIES Currently, the antitrust authorities move against a network monopoly based on how it behaves, not because of what it is. For example, the authorities would not issue a complaint against company A in our example unless it undertook predatory or exclusionary practices to *maintain* its monopoly position.

INNOVATION IN NETWORK MONOPOLIES Recall that economists are undecided as to whether market share assists or detracts from innovation. For example, it was argued that one firm among four firms may have less innovative risk than one firm among 100 firms. Therefore, the firm with a larger market share would innovate more, *ceteris paribus.* Presumably, a network monopoly will have a large market share and therefore should be a major innovator.

Actually, the situation may be different for network monopolies because high switching costs sometimes accompany a network monopoly. To illustrate, suppose firm A produces network good A. Network good A begins to sell quite well, and because it is a network good, its robust sales increase its value to potential customers. Potential customers turn into actual customers, and before long good A has set the market, or industry, standard.

Because network good A is now the industry standard and because network goods (especially those related to the high-tech industries) are sometimes difficult to learn, it may have a lock on the market. Specifically, a **lock-in effect** increases the costs of switching from good A to another good. Because of the (relatively) high switching costs, good A has some staying power in the market. Firm A, the producer of good A, thus has staying power too, possibly causing firm A to rest on its laurels. Instead of innovating, instead of trying to outcompete its existing and future rivals with better production processes or better products, it may do very little. Firm A will realize that the high switching costs keep customers from changing to a different network good. Some economists suggest that in this environment, the network monopoly may have little reason to innovate.

Network Good
A good whose value increases as the expected number of units sold increases.

Lock-In Effect
The situation when a particular product or technology becomes the standard and is difficult or impossible to dislodge as the standard.

economics 24/7

HIGH-PRICED INK CARTRIDGES AND EXPENSIVE MINIBARS

Shopping for a printer for your computer, you see one priced at $69. That's a good price, you think; so you buy it. Later, you learn that you have to pay $33 for an ink cartridge. The printer wasn't so well-priced after all.

You spend the night at a hotel. Once in your room, you look in the minibar and decide to eat a small bag of almonds. You learn later, after looking at your bill, that the small bag of almonds came with the big price of $6.

You sign up with a cell phone company, decide on a plan, and get a free cell phone. Later, you learn that for every minute you go over your allotted monthly number of minutes, you pay 33 cents.

Because of such everyday occurrences, some economists today are talking about the hidden fee economy—an economy in which many main items for sale (a printer, a hotel room, cell phone service) come with high hidden fees—fees you did not expect when you purchased the main item.

According to two economists, David Laibson and Xavier Gabaix, firms reap certain benefits through hidden fees. (There are certain costs, too, but sometimes the benefits are greater than the costs.) For example,[2] there are two similar hotels, X and Y. Hotel X rents its rooms for $80 a night and has some hidden fees: $12 for parking, $6 for a small bag of almonds from the minibar, and $3 for a local call. Hotel Y rents its rooms for $95 a night, and it has no high hidden fees. It does not charge for parking or for a local call, and the small bag of almonds comes at the same price one could buy it at a grocery store. What are the major differences between the two hotels? On the basis of just the price of a room, hotel X is cheaper than hotel Y. Add in hidden and unexpectedly high fees, and hotel X is a culprit and hotel Y is not.

The natural question is why doesn't hotel Y simply advertise the fact that its competitor, hotel X, is trying to dupe its customers by charging high hidden fees? (The ad might read, "Sure, hotel X has cheaper rooms, but what about all the hidden fees?") According to Laibon and Gabaix, that strategy could backfire because of one of the two types of customers that frequent hotel X.

One type of customer is unaware of the hidden fees and initially responds to the lower room rate of hotel X. With this customer, the strategy of pointing out the hidden fees of hotel X will be successful. Another type of customer is sophisticated when it comes to sellers' tactics. This customer realizes that if she doesn't park at hotel X, doesn't purchase anything from the minibar, and makes calls on her cell phone instead of on the hotel telephone, she can then get a lower-priced room at hotel X. The ad by hotel Y simply notifies the sophisticated customer that she can get a good deal at the hotel with the hidden fees—assuming she doesn't purchase the goods or services that come with the high hidden fees.

So hotel Y gains and loses with its ad pointing out the high hidden fees of hotel X. It gains the clueless customers ("thanks for telling me about those hidden fees"), but it may lose some sophisticated customers ("thanks for telling me about the lower-priced rooms your competitor is offering"). If it thinks it will lose more sophisticated customers than it will gain clueless customers, it will not run the ad. Instead, it may simply join the ranks of hotels like hotel X and lower its room rate and increase the use of high hidden fees.

But there is something else to consider. Barry Nalebuff, a professor of business strategy, has noted that there is a cost to a firm that charges hidden fees. That cost comes in the form of customers getting angry at the hidden fees, and angry customers, Nalebuff says, often turn their backs on sellers they are angry with. In other words, they seek out other (perhaps more up front and straightforward) sellers to buy from.

In the end, it becomes a matter of a seller having to consider both the benefits and the costs of a hidden fees strategy. Perhaps initially the benefits outweigh the costs, but there is no guarantee that in time the costs won't rise above the benefits.

---

2. The source of the material in this feature (and the example) is Christopher Shea, "The Hidden Economy," *The Boston Globe*, June 27, 2006.

Civil Action No. 98-1232

On May 18, 1998, the U.S. Department of Justice joined with 20 states and issued a civil action complaint against Microsoft, Inc. The action claimed basis in Sections 1 and 2 of the Sherman Act. Claiming that Microsoft possessed monopoly power in the market for personal computer operating systems, the complaint stated that (1) Microsoft Windows is used on more than 80 percent of Intel-based PCs and (2) there are high barriers to entry in the market for PC operating systems essentially because Microsoft Windows is a network good that is the industry standard.

The Justice Department claimed that Microsoft:

- Was using its dominance in the personal computer operating systems market not only to maintain monopoly power but also to gain dominance in the Internet browser market.

- Packaged its Internet browser with Windows and required computer manufacturers to agree, as a condition for receiving licenses, to install Windows on their products, not to remove Microsoft's browser, and not to allow a more prominent display of a rival browser.

- Refused to display the icons of Internet service providers (ISPs) on the main Windows screen unless the ISPs would first agree to withhold information from their customers about non-Microsoft browsers.

In the antitrust case, Microsoft argued that it did not have a monopoly in the operating systems market and that it was part of a cutthroat software industry where today's industry leaders could go out of business tomorrow. It essentially maintained that none of its business practices hurt any consumers and that all were necessary to its survival. Microsoft claimed that if it was guilty of anything, it was guilty of charging prices that were too low. It charged nothing, for example, for its Internet browser. Furthermore, Microsoft said that the addition of its browser to Windows was not an attempt to monopolize anything; it was an attempt to provide the buying public with a better product. In short, the browser was simply a new feature of Windows, not an illegal tie-in that violated a consent degree that Microsoft had signed in 1995.

Some economists contended that Microsoft's low pricing strategy made sense and that it approximated marginal cost pricing. After all, software, once written, costs very little for each additional copy. Also, low prices are simply a way to sell a lot of copies. And what's wrong with that?

Critics contended that the low prices to gain customers worked to Microsoft's advantage because its operating system was a network good. Low prices mean more customers, and more customers mean Microsoft would eventually become the industry standard. Once the standard, it would wield its market power to maintain its current position and would try to establish itself as a monopolist in other markets (such as the browser market).

On Friday, November 4, 1999, Judge Thomas Penfield Jackson, the judge who heard the case against Microsoft, issued his findings of fact, which simply present the facts of the case as the judge sees them and which do not constitute a ruling. (The ruling came later.) In his findings of fact, Judge Jackson essentially agreed with the case the Justice Department made against Microsoft. He said that Microsoft is not only a monopolist in the operating systems market but also that it used its monopoly power to thwart competition. Specifically, it tied its operating system (Windows) together with its browser (Internet Explorer) not for purposes of efficiency and not to satisfy consumers but to establish a monopoly position in the browser market and to preserve its monopoly position in the operating systems market.

Before issuing his final judgment in the case, Judge Jackson appointed Judge Richard Posner, chief of the 7th U.S. Circuit of Appeals, to try to mediate a settlement between the government and Microsoft. After a few months, mediation talks broke down, and there was to be no settlement between the two parties.

On Monday, April 3, 2000, Judge Jackson issued a ruling in the case: Microsoft had violated the Sherman Act. The judge wrote that Microsoft was guilty of "unlawfully

MACS, PCS, AND PEOPLE WHO ARE DIFFERENT

Tracey currently works on a Windows-based PC but is thinking of switching to a Mac: "I have heard good things about a Mac, and part of me would like to switch to a Mac, but I have some problems. First, many more people use a PC than a Mac. Second, I am not sure how long it will take me to get up to speed on a Mac. I don't think the learning curve is that steep, but it is something to consider."

What Tracey is noticing is that her Windows-based PC is a network good (a good whose value increases as the expected number of units sold increases). In other words, Tracey might stick with a PC partly because so many other people use PCs. This is not to say that a PC is not a good product. It's just that, despite how good a product it is, people either initially choose a PC instead of a Mac or stay with a PC instead of switching to a Mac partly because so many more millions of people use PCs than Macs.

Next, as Tracey has pointed out, she will have to learn how to do things if she switches from a PC to a Mac; that is, there are switching costs. The greater the switching costs are, the more likely Tracey will feel locked in to a PC. So thinking about switching from a PC to a Mac involves considering network goods and lock-in effects.

Let's apply the concepts of a netwook good and lock-in effect to something else. All of us were born into a certain world, where certain people were around us, speaking a certain language, listening to certain kinds of music, abiding by certain rules and customs, and so on. Might our immediate environment and the people, language, and customs we deal with in that environment be a network good of sorts? Specifically, consider the language we learned as a child. We learn a language—any language—partly because other people speak the language. There is no reason to learn Italian, English, or Spanish if only a few people speak these languages.

Of course, when we learned a language as children, we didn't choose the language we would learn; we learned the language that the people around us spoke. Still, ask yourself what language you would have chosen to learn if you could (as an infant) so choose. It is very likely that you would have chosen the language that your parents and relatives were speaking.

Now, of course, that you have learned a language, there are costs to learning another language, which is analogous to the situation of a person who has learned how to operate a PC and is learning how to operate a Mac. In other words, there are switching costs involved in learning a new language. To a degree, these costs might keep many people locked in to their native language.

Let's extend this thinking. Just as it might be costly to learn a new language, it might be costly to learn how to deal with people who are different from you: people raised in a different culture, people who like different music than you, people who eat different foods, and so on. The PC-Mac issue might simply be presenting itself in a different guise. Speaking English, listening to rock 'n' roll, eating steak, and watching sports might be the network good in much the same way that the Windows-based PC was the network good. The switching costs of learning to speak Italian, listening to opera, eating different-tasting foods, and watching soccer might come with (what you deem to be) unusually high switching costs. To a degree, you might feel (and be) locked in to who you are and what you do (and perhaps even what you think) because the switching costs are as high as they are.

tying its Web browser" to Windows. He continued by saying that "Microsoft's anti-competitive actions trammeled the competitive process through which the computer software industry generally stimulates innovation."

On July 7, 2000, Judge Jackson issued his final ruling in the case. He ordered that Microsoft be split into two companies: one for operating systems and one for applications. Bill Gates said that Microsoft would appeal the ruling to a higher court.

The U.S. Court of Appeals heard the case months later. On June 28, 2001, the U.S. Court of Appeals reversed Judge Jackson's order to break up Microsoft, but it agreed with some of the judge's findings—specifically, that Microsoft had broken federal antitrust law. The appeals court sent the Microsoft case back to a lower court, this time to a different judge.

The new judge, U.S. District Judge Colleen Kollar-Kotelly, ordered both Microsoft and the Justice Department to set out the key issues in the case and determine how it might proceed. Before Judge Kollar-Kotelly issued a decision in the case, Microsoft and the Justice Department announced on November 2, 2001, that they had reached a settlement that would end the case. Under the settlement, Microsoft would make portions of its Windows software code available to competitors and allow computer manufacturers to choose the products they would load onto their machines without the threat of any retaliation from Microsoft. As of this writing, the plaintiffs in the case and the defendant (Microsoft) periodically file joint status reports on Microsoft's compliance with the final judgment. These reports can be found at the U.S. Department of Justice website (http://www.usdoj.gov).

SELF-TEST

(Answers to Self-Test questions are in the Self-Test Appendix.)

1. Why does it matter whether a market is defined broadly or narrowly for purposes of antitrust policy?

2. Suppose that 20 firms are in an industry and that each firm has a 5 percent market share. What is the four-firm concentration ratio for this industry? What is the Herfindahl index?

3. What is the advantage of the Herfindahl index over the four- and eight-firm concentration ratios? Explain your answer.

---

exhibit 2

The Natural Monopoly Situation

The only existing firm produces Q_1 at an average total cost of ATC_1. (Q_1 is the output at which $MR = MC$; to simplify the diagram, the MR curve is not shown.) Resource allocative efficiency exists at Q_2. There are two ways to obtain this output level: (1) The only existing firm can increase its production to Q_2, or (2) a new firm can enter the market and produce Q_3, which is the difference between Q_2 and Q_1. The first way minimizes total cost; the second way does not. This, then, is a natural monopoly situation: One firm can supply the entire output demanded at a lower cost than two or more firms can.

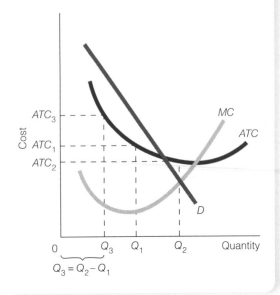

REGULATION

This section examines the types of regulation, theories of regulation, the stated objectives of regulatory agencies, and the effects of regulation on natural and other monopolies.

The Case of Natural Monopoly

In an earlier chapter, we saw that if economies of scale are so pronounced or large in an industry that only one firm can survive, that firm is a *natural monopoly*. Firms that supply local electricity, gas, and water service are usually considered natural monopolies.

In Exhibit 2, there is one firm in the market, and it produces Q_1 units of output at an average total cost of ATC_1. (Q_1 is the output at which $MR = MC$; to simplify the diagram, the MR curve is not shown.) At Q_1, there is an inefficient allocation of resources. Resource allocative efficiency exists when the marginal benefit to demanders of the resources used in the goods they buy equals the marginal cost to suppliers of the resources used in the production of the goods they sell. In Exhibit 2, resource allocative efficiency exists at Q_2, corresponding to the point where the demand curve intersects the MC curve.

There are two ways to reach the higher, efficient quantity of output, Q_2: (1) The firm currently producing Q_1 could increase its output to Q_2. (2) Another firm could enter the market and produce Q_3—the difference between Q_2 and Q_1. Each way has its associated costs. If the firm currently in the market increases its production to Q_2, it incurs average total costs of ATC_2. If, instead, a new firm enters the market and produces Q_3, it incurs an average total cost of ATC_3. In this way, both firms together produce Q_2, but the new firm incurs average total costs of ATC_3, whereas the existing firm incurs average total costs of ATC_1.

As long as the objective is to increase output to the level of resource allocative efficiency, it is cheaper (total costs are lower) to have the firm currently in the market increase its output to Q_2 than to have two firms together produce Q_2. So the situation in Exhibit 2 describes a natural monopoly situation. *Natural monopoly* exists when one firm can supply the entire output demanded at lower cost than two or more firms can. It is a natural monopoly because a monopoly situation will naturally evolve over time as the low-cost producer undercuts its competitors.

Some economists say that the natural monopolist will charge the monopoly price. In Exhibit 3, the natural monopoly firm produces Q_1, at which marginal revenue equals marginal cost, and charges price P_1, which is the highest price per unit consistent with the output it produces.

Because it charges the monopoly price, some people argue that the natural monopoly firm should be regulated. The form that the regulation should take is a question addressed in the next section.

exhibit 3

The Profit-Maximizing Natural Monopoly

The natural monopoly that seeks to maximize profits will produce the quantity of output at which $MR = MC$ and charge the (monopoly) price, P_1.

Profit-maximizing natural monopoly will:

1. Produce Q_1 where $MR = MC$
2. Charge monopoly price, P_1

Regulating the Natural Monopoly

The natural monopoly may be regulated through price, profit, or output regulation.

1. *Price regulation.* Marginal cost pricing is one form of price regulation. The objective is to set a price for the natural monopoly firm that equals its marginal cost at the quantity of output at which demand intersects marginal cost. In Exhibit 4, this price is P_1. At this price, the natural monopoly takes a loss. At Q_1, average total cost

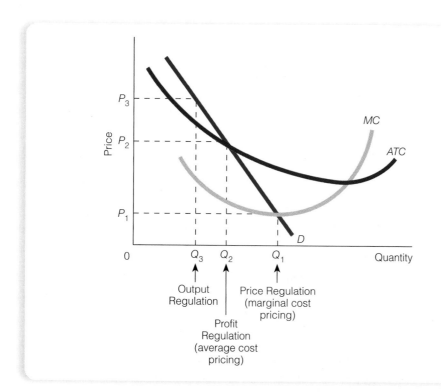

exhibit 4

Regulating a Natural Monopoly

The government can regulate a natural monopoly through (1) price regulation, (2) profit regulation, or (3) output regulation. Price regulation usually means marginal cost pricing, and profit regulation usually means average cost pricing.

is greater than price, and thus, total cost is greater than total revenue.[3] Obviously, the natural monopoly would rather go out of business than be subject to this type of regulation unless it receives a subsidy for its operation.

2. *Profit regulation.* Government may want the natural monopoly to earn only zero economic profits. If so, government will require the natural monopoly to charge a price of P_2 (because $P_2 = ATC$) and to supply the quantity demanded at that price (Q_2). This form of regulation is often called *average cost pricing.* Theoretically, this may seem like a good way to proceed, but in practice it often turns out differently. The problem is that if the natural monopoly is always held to zero economic profits—and is not allowed to fall below or rise above this level—then it has an incentive to let costs rise. Higher costs—in the form of higher salaries or more luxurious offices—simply mean higher prices to cover the higher costs. In this case, it is unlikely that average cost pricing is an efficient way to proceed.

3. *Output regulation.* Government can mandate a quantity of output it wants the natural monopoly to produce. Suppose this is Q_3 in Exhibit 4, where there are positive economic profits because price is above average total cost at Q_3. However, the natural monopoly could want even higher profits, and, at a fixed quantity of output, higher profits can be obtained by lowering costs. The natural monopolist might lower costs by reducing the quality of the good or service it sells, knowing that it faces no direct competition and that it is protected (by government) from competitors.

Government regulation of a natural monopoly does not always turn out the way it was intended. Regulation—whether it takes the form of price, profit, or output regulation—can distort the incentives of those who operate the natural monopoly. For example, if profit is regulated to the extent that zero economic profits are guaranteed, then the natural monopoly has little incentive to hold costs down. Furthermore, the owners of the natural monopoly have an incentive to try to influence the government officials or other persons who are regulating the firm.

In addition, each of the three types of regulation requires information. For example, if the government wishes to set price equal to marginal cost or average total cost for the natural monopoly, it must know the cost conditions of the firm.

Three problems arise in gathering information: (1) The cost information is not easy to determine, even for the natural monopoly itself. (2) The cost information can be rigged (to a degree) by the natural monopoly, and therefore the regulators will not get a true picture of the firm. (3) The regulators have little incentive to obtain accurate information because they are likely to keep their jobs and prestige even if they work with less than accurate information. (This raises the question: who will ensure that the regulators do a good job?)

Regulatory Lag
The time period between when a natural monopoly's costs change and when the regulatory agency adjusts prices for it.

Finally, the issue of *regulatory lag* is indirectly related to information. **Regulatory lag** is the time period between when a natural monopoly's costs change and when the regulatory agency adjusts prices for the natural monopoly. For example, suppose the local gas company rates are regulated. The gas company's costs rise, and it seeks a rate hike through the local regulatory body. The rate hike is not likely to be approved quickly. The gas company will probably have to submit an application for a rate hike, document its case, have a date set for a hearing, argue its case at the hearing, and then wait for the regulatory agency to decide on the merits of the application. Many months may pass between the beginning of the process and the end. During that time, the regulated firm is operating in ways and under conditions that both the firm and the regulatory body might not have desired.

---

3. Remember that $TC = ATC \times Q$ and $TR = P \times Q$. Here $ATC > P$; so it follows that $TC > TR$.

economics 24/7

WHY AM I ALWAYS FLYING TO DALLAS?

Although the shortest distance between two points is a straight line, some say that the airline industry doesn't care much about straight lines (or obviously about short distances). It cares about hubs and spokes. If you want to go from Phoenix to New York City, the shortest route is the direct route: Phoenix directly to New York. Very likely, however, you won't be able to get a direct flight. Often (but not always), you will be routed through Dallas or Chicago. In other words, you will get on the plane in Phoenix, get off the plane in Dallas, get on another plane in Dallas, fly to New York, and finally get off the plane in New York. This process is referred to as the hub-and-spoke delivery system. The hub represents the center of an airline network; the spokes (much like the spokes on a bicycle wheel) represent origin and destination cities and are always linked through the hub.

The hub-and-spoke system has been used more often since airline deregulation. In several instances, airline departures from major hubs (e.g., Dallas and Chicago) have doubled. Most economists believe the increased use of the hub-and-spoke system, which makes average travel time longer, is the result of increased price competition brought on by deregulation.

© STEVE HAMBLN/ALAMY

After deregulation, airlines were under greater pressure to compete on price; thus, cutting costs became more important. One way to cut costs is to use bigger planes because bigger planes cost less to operate per seat mile—but it takes more people to fill the bigger planes. To accomplish both objectives—flying bigger, fully occupied planes—the airlines began to gather passengers at one spot. Then at the hub, they could put more passengers on one plane and fly them to the same destination. For example, instead of flying people in Phoenix and people in Albuquerque directly but separately to New York, both groups of people are flown first to Dallas, and then the combined group is flown to New York.

This system may have benefits that offset the costs of inconvenience and longer travel time. Some people think it is better to pay lower airline ticket prices and reach one's destination a little later than to pay higher prices and get there sooner. They also maintain that the increased use of the hub-and-spoke system has given passengers more options to travel on different airlines (in Dallas, numerous airlines can fly you to New York) and at more convenient times (numerous flights leave Dallas every hour).

Thinking like AN ECONOMIST

Something Is Not Always Better Than Nothing

The public is perhaps naturally inclined to think that a solution (e.g., regulation) to a problem (e.g., monopoly) is better than no solution at all—that something is better than nothing. The economist has learned, though, that a so-called solution can do one of three things: (1) solve a problem, (2) not solve a problem but do no damage, or (3) make the problem worse. Thinking through the entire range of possibilities is natural for an economist, who, after all, understands that solutions come with both costs and benefits.

Regulating Industries That Are Not Natural Monopolies

Some firms are regulated even though they are not natural monopolies. For instance, in the past, government has regulated both the airline and trucking industries. In the trucking industry, the Interstate Commerce Commission (ICC) fixed routes, set minimum freight rates, and erected barriers to entry. In the airline industry, the Civil Aeronautics

Board (CAB) did much the same thing. Some economists view the regulation of competitive industries as unnecessary. They see it as evidence that the firms being regulated are, in turn, controlling the regulation to reduce their competition.

Theories of Regulation

The **capture theory of regulation** holds that no matter what the motive is for the initial regulation and the establishment of the regulatory agency, eventually the agency will be captured (controlled) by the special interests of the industry being regulated. The following are a few of the interrelated points that have been put forth to support this theory:

1. In many cases, persons who have been in the industry are asked to regulate the industry because they know the most about it. Such regulators are likely to feel a bond with people in the industry, to see their side of the story more often than not, and thus to be inclined to cater to them.

2. At regulatory hearings, members of the industry attend in greater force than do taxpayers and consumers. The industry turns out in force because the regulatory hearing can affect it substantially and directly. In contrast, the effect on individual taxpayers and consumers is usually small and indirect (the effect is spread over millions of people). Thus, regulators are much more likely to hear and respond to the industry's side of the story.

3. Members of the regulated industry make a point of getting to know the members of the regulatory agency. They may talk frequently about business matters; perhaps they socialize. The bond between the two groups grows stronger over time, possibly having an impact on regulatory measures.

4. After they either retire or quit their jobs, regulators often go to work for the industries they once regulated.

The capture theory is markedly different from what has come to be called the **public interest theory of regulation**. This theory holds that regulators are seeking to do—and will do through regulation—what is in the best interest of the public or society at large.

An alternative to both theories is the **public choice theory of regulation**. This theory suggests that to understand the decisions of regulatory bodies, we must first understand how the decisions affect the regulators themselves. For example, a regulation that increases the power, size, and budget of the regulatory agency should not be viewed the same way as a regulation that decreases the agency's power and size. The theory predicts that the outcomes of the regulatory process will tend to favor the regulators instead of either business interests or the public.

These are three interesting, different, and, at first sight, believable theories of regulation, and economists have directed much effort to testing them. There is no clear consensus yet, but in the area of business regulation, the adherents of the capture and public choice theories have been increasing.

The Costs and Benefits of Regulation

Suppose a business firm is polluting the air with smoke from its factories. The government passes an environmental regulation requiring such firms to purchase antipollution devices that reduce the smoke emitted into the air.

What are the benefits of this kind of regulation? The obvious benefit is cleaner air, but cleaner air can lead to other benefits. For example, people may have fewer medical problems in the future. In some parts of the country, pollution from cars and factories causes people to cough, feel tired, and experience eye discomfort. More important, some people have chronic medical problems from constantly breathing dirty air. Government regulation that reduces the amount of pollution in the air clearly helps these people.

However, regulation usually comes with costs as well as with benefits. For example, when a business firm incurs the cost of antipollution devices, its overall costs of production rise. Simply put, it is costlier for the business firm to produce its product after the regulation is imposed. As a result, the business firm may produce fewer units of its product, raising its product price and causing some workers to lose their jobs.

If you are a worker who loses your job, you may view the government's insistence on antipollution devices differently than if, say, you are a person suffering from chronic lung disease. If you have asthma, less pollution may be the difference between feeling well and feeling sick. If you are a worker for the business firm, less pollution may cost you your job. Ideally, you prefer a little less pollution in your neighborhood, but perhaps not at the cost of losing your job.

Economists are neither for nor against such government regulation. The job of the economist is to make the point that regulation involves both benefits and costs. To the person who sees only the costs, the economist asks, what about the benefits? And to the person who sees only the benefits, the economist asks, what about the costs? Then, the economist goes on to outline the benefits and the costs as best she can.

Finding ECONOMICS

In an Irish Pub

One person in an Irish pub says to a second person, "Remember the days when we could smoke in the pub?" The second person says, "I miss those days." Where is the economics?

What we see is regulation: At one time it was permissible to smoke in Irish pubs; today it is not. When regulation is under discussion, the question is often who has the right to regulate what? Critics of the Irish nonsmoking regulation argue that the pub owner should be the person who decides whether smoking will be allowed in the pub. Others argue differently, saying that people should not have to breathe in cigarette or cigar smoke if they don't want to. In other words, smoking is fine as long as others are not bothered by the smoke.

Some Effects of Regulation Are Unintended

Besides outlining the benefits and costs of regulation, the economist tries to point out the unintended effects that can occur with regulation. To illustrate, consider fuel standards. Suppose the government requires new cars to get an average of 40 miles per gallon of gasoline instead of, say, 30 miles per gallon. Many people will say that this is a good thing, reasoning that if car companies are made to produce cars that get better mileage, people will not need to buy and burn as much gasoline. Burning less gasoline means less air pollution.

There is no guarantee the regulation will have this effect, though. The effects could be quite different. If cars are more fuel efficient, people will buy less gasoline to drive from one place to another—say, from home to college. So the dollar cost per mile of driving will fall, and, as a result, people might drive more. Leisure driving on the weekend might become more common, people might begin to drive farther on vacations, and so on. If people begin to drive more, then the gasoline saving that resulted from the higher fuel economy standards might be offset or even outweighed. Higher gasoline consumption due to more driving will mean burning more gasoline and sending more pollutants into the air.

Thus a regulation requiring automakers to produce cars that get better fuel mileage may have an unintended effect. The net result might be that people purchase and burn more gasoline and thus produce more air pollution, not less as the government intended.

Deregulation

In the early 1970s, many economists, basing their arguments on the capture and public choice theories of regulation, argued that regulation was actually promoting and protecting market power instead of reducing it. They argued for deregulation. Since the late 1970s, many industries have been deregulated, including airlines, trucking, long-distance telephone service, and others.

Consider a few details that relate to the deregulation of the airline industry. The Civil Aeronautics Act, which was passed in 1938, gave the Civil Aeronautics Authority (CAA) the authority to regulate airfares, the number of carriers on interstate routes, and the pattern of routes. The CAA's successor, the Civil Aeronautics Board (CAB), regulated fares in such a way that major air carriers could meet their average costs. An effect of this policy was that fares were raised so that high-cost, inefficient air carriers could survive. In addition, the CAB did not allow price competition between air carriers. As a result, air carriers usually competed in a nonprice dimension: They offered more scheduled flights, better meals, more popular in-flight movies, and so forth.

In 1978, under CAB Chairman Alfred Kahn, an economist, the airline industry was deregulated. With deregulation, airlines can compete on fares, initiate service along a new route, or discontinue a route. Empirical research after deregulation showed that passenger miles increased and fares decreased. For example, in 1978, fares fell 20 percent, and between 1979 and 1984 fares fell approximately 14 percent.

Deregulation has also led to a decline in costs in various industries. For example, a study by Clifford Winston of the Brookings Institution shows that since deregulation, costs in the airline industry have fallen 24 percent (per unit of output); in trucking, operating costs have fallen 30–35 percent per mile; in railroads, there has been a 50 percent decline in costs per ton-mile and a 141 percent increase in productivity; and in natural gas, there has been a 35 percent decline in operating and maintenance expenses.

SELF-TEST

1. What is a criticism of average cost pricing?
2. State the essence of the capture theory of regulation.
3. What is the difference between the capture theory and the public choice theory of regulation?
4. Are economists for or against regulation?

office hours

"WHAT IS THE ADVANTAGE OF THE HERFINDAHL INDEX?"

Student:
In the last chapter we learned about the four- and eight- firm concentration ratios. These ratios were used to compute the percentage of industry sales accounted for by the largest four or eight firms in the industry, respectively. In other words, the ratios were used to measure concentration in an industry. In this chapter we learned about the Herfindahl index, which also measures concentration in an industry. Is the Herfindahl index better at measuring concentration than the two ratios we learned about in the last chapter?

Instructor:
Many economists think so. The Herfindahl index provides some information that the four- and eight- firm concentration ratios do not. To illustrate, consider two settings: (1) Four firms together have a 50 percent market share, and there are only five other firms in the industry; (2) four firms together have a 50 percent market share, and there are 50 other firms in the industry. The four-firm concentration ratio is the same in both settings, but the Herfindahl index is not.

Student:
In other words, the four-firm concentration ratio is 50 percent in both settings, but the Herfindahl index in the first setting would be different from the Herfindahl index in the second setting because of how the Herfindahl index is calculcated. Is that correct?

Instructor:
Yes, that's correct.

Student:
This has me thinking. Something about the concentration ratios and Herfindahl index make me a little uneasy. In the past, I haven't been able to figure out what it is, but now I think I can. It seems to me that a little too much emphasis and importance is being put on a single number. Is a high number for the Herfindahl index (say, above 1,800) always bad? It just seems to me that a high number doesn't always have to signify the same thing.

Instructor:
Others have made the point. In fact, both the four- and eight-firm concentration ratios, as well as the Herfindal index, have been criticized for implicitly arguing from firm size and industry concentration to market power. Both assume firms with large market shares have market power that they are likely to be abusing, but that may not be the case. Size could be a function of efficiency, and a firm with a large market share could be serving the buying public well.

Student:
Yes, that is what I was getting at. It seems to me the process of how a firm got to be big matters.

Instructor:
I should say that the terms *process* and *behavior* have come to mean more in recent years, particularly with economists and with the Antitrust Division of the U.S. Justice Department. With respect to behavior, more emphasis these days is placed on how the firm behaves—no matter its size and market power. To illustrate, two firms of equal size relative to other firms in their respective industries could behave differently. One firm reduces output and charges higher prices, and the other firm increases output and charges lower prices.

Points to Remember

1. In the two settings (four firms have 50 percent market share but the number of remaining firms in the industry is different), the four-firm concentration ratio is the same, but the Herfindahl index is not. The Herfindahl index supplies more information than either the four- or eight-firm concentration ratios; specifically, it provides information about the dispersion of firm size in an industry.

2. In recent years, process (how did the firm get to be big?) and behavior (how does the firm act?) have come to mean more when evaluating firms.

a reader asks | Do Some Companies Engage in Price Fixing?

Not too long ago, I read that the two major auction houses, Sotheby's and Christie's, were engaged in price fixing. What were the details?

Sotheby's (founded in 1744) and Christie's (founded in 1766) are the two biggest auction houses in the world. In 1983, A. Alfred Taubman, a Michigan shopping mall magnate, bought Sotheby's (some say for his wife as a wedding present). In 1994, Taubman appointed Diana Brooks president and CEO of Sotheby's. In 1997, the U.S. Justice Department began investigating possible collusion between Sotheby's and Christie's to fix the prices people paid to have their items auctioned.

Under American law, accused conspirators are encouraged to confess and to name others involved in the conspiracy. In fact, the first party to do this is given leniency. Christopher Davidge, the president and CEO of Christie's, came forth and turned over papers describing the price-fixing arrangement with Sotheby's.

According to Diana Brooks, who pleaded guilty to the charge, she had been ordered by Taubman to enter into the illegal collusive agreement with Christie's. Taubman claimed that Brooks was lying. Taubman's spokesman declared, "We believe that Mrs. Brooks is lying to save her skin and that she has a clear motivation for doing so."

On April 23, 2002, A. Alfred Taubman was sentenced to a year and a day in prison and fined $7.5 million for leading a 6-year price-fixing scheme with Sotheby's chief competitor, Christie's, that is said to have swindled more than $100 million from their customers. In handing down the sentence, the judge said, "Price fixing is a crime whether it's committed in the grocery store or the halls of a great auction house."

Chapter Summary

DEALING WITH MONOPOLY POWER

- A monopoly produces less than a perfectly competitive firm produces (assuming the same revenue and cost conditions), charges a higher price, and causes a deadweight loss. This is the monopoly power problem, and solving it is usually put forth as a reason for antitrust laws and/or government regulatory actions. Some economists note, though, that government antitrust and regulatory actions do not always have the intended effect. In addition, such actions are sometimes implemented when there is no monopoly power problem to solve.

ANTITRUST LAWS

- Two major criticisms have been directed at the antitrust acts. First, some argue that the language in the laws is vague; for example, even though the words "restraint of trade" are used in the Sherman Act, the act does not clearly explain what actions constitute a restraint of trade. Second, it has been argued that some antitrust acts appear to hinder, rather than promote, competition; an example is the Robinson-Patman Act.

- There are a few unsettled points in antitrust policy. One centers on the proper definition of a market—whether it should be defined narrowly or broadly. How this question is answered will have an impact on which firms are considered monopolies. In addition, the use of concentration ratios for identifying monopolies or deciding whether to allow two firms to enter into a merger has been called into question. Recently, concentration ratios have been largely replaced (for purposes of implementing antitrust policy) with the Herfindahl index. This index is subject to some of the same criticisms as the concentration ratios. Antitrust authorities are also beginning to consider the benefits of innovation in ruling on proposed mergers.

REGULATION

- Even if we assume that the intent of regulation is to serve the public interest, it does not follow that this will be accomplished. To work as desired, regulation must be based on complete information (e.g., the regulatory body must know the cost conditions of the regulated firm), and it must not distort incentives (e.g., to keep costs down). Many economists are quick to point out that neither condition is likely to be fully met. In itself, this outcome does not mean that regulation should not be implemented but only that regulation may not have the expected effects.

- Government uses three basic types of regulation to regulate natural monopolies: price, profit, or output regulation. Price regulation usually means marginal cost price regulation—that is, setting $P = MC$. Profit regulation usually means zero economic profits. Output regulation specifies a particular quantity of output that the natural monopoly must produce.

- The capture theory of regulation holds that no matter what the motive is for the initial regulation and the establishment of the regulatory agency, eventually, the agency will be captured (controlled) by the special interests of the industry being regulated. The public interest theory holds that regulators are seeking to do—and will do through regulation— what is in the best interest of the public or society at large. The public choice theory holds that regulators are seeking to do—and will do through regulation—what is in their best interest (specifically, to enhance their own power, size, and budget).

Key Terms and Concepts

Antitrust Law	Vertical Merger	Regulatory Lag
Trust	Conglomerate Merger	Capture Theory of Regulation
Herfindahl Index	Network Good	Public Interest Theory of Regulation
Horizontal Merger	Lock-In Effect	Public Choice Theory of Regulation

Questions and Problems

1 Why was the Robinson-Patman Act passed? The Wheeler-Lea Act? The Celler-Kefauver Antimerger Act?

2 Explain why defining a market narrowly or broadly can make a difference in how antitrust policy is implemented.

3 What is one difference between the four-firm concentration ratio and the Herfindahl index?

4 How does a vertical merger differ from a horizontal merger? Why would the government look more carefully at one than at the other?

5 What is the implication of saying that regulation is likely to affect incentives?

6 Explain price regulation, profit regulation, and output regulation.

7 Why might profit regulation lead to rising costs for the regulated firm?

8 What is the major difference between the capture theory of regulation and the public interest theory of regulation?

9 George Stigler and Claire Friedland studied both unregulated and regulated electric utilities and found no difference in the rates they charged. One could draw the conclusion that regulation is ineffective when it comes to utility rates. What ideas or hypotheses presented in this chapter might have predicted this result?

10 The courts have ruled that it is a reasonable restraint of trade (and therefore permissible) for the owner of a business to sell his business and sign a contract with the new owner saying he will not compete with her within a vicinity of, say, 100 miles, for a period of, say, 5 years. If this is a reasonable restraint of trade, can you give an example of what you would consider an unreasonable restraint of trade? Explain how you decide what is a reasonable restraint of trade and what isn't.

11 In your opinion, what is the best way to deal with the monopoly power problem? Do you advocate antitrust laws, regulation, or something not discussed in the chapter? Give reasons for your answer.

12 It is usually asserted that public utilities such as electric companies and gas companies are natural monopolies, but an assertion is not proof. How would you go about trying to prove (or disprove) that electric companies and the like are (or are not) natural monopolies? (Hint: Consider comparing the average total cost of a public utility that serves many customers with the average total cost of a public utility that serves relatively few customers.)

13 Discuss the advantages and disadvantages of regulation (as you see it).

14 Explain how the lock-in effect might make it less likely for the firm (that benefits from the lock-in effect) to innovate.

Working with Numbers and Graphs

1   Calculate the Herfindahl index and the four-firm concentration ratio for the following industry:

Firms	Market Share
A	17%
B	15
C	14
D	14
E	12
F	10
G	9
H	9

Use the following figure to answer questions 2–4.

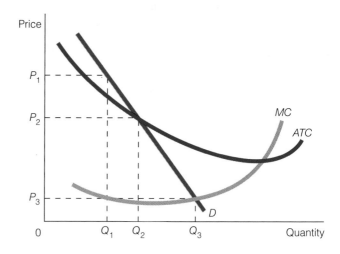

2   Is the firm in the figure a natural monopoly? Explain your answer.

3   Will the firm in the figure earn profits if it produces Q_3 and charges P_3? Explain your answer.

4   Which quantity in the figure is consistent with profit regulation? With price regulation? Explain your answers.

CHAPTER 12

FACTOR MARKETS: WITH EMPHASIS ON THE LABOR MARKET

Introduction Employees want to know why their salaries can't be higher; they would like to have more income for spending and saving. Employees might wonder, "Why am I not getting paid $10,000 more? Why not $20,000 more?" Of course, employers look at salaries differently; they would like to pay lower salaries. Employers may look at a salary and wonder, "Why couldn't I have paid $10,000 less? Why not $20,000 less?" Salaries are determined by economic forces. This chapter identifies the factors and the process affecting your pay. Is this chapter relevant to you? Without a doubt.

FACTOR MARKETS

Just as there is a demand for and supply of a product, there is a demand for and a supply of a factor, or resource, such as labor.

The Demand for a Factor

All firms purchase factors to make products to sell, whether they are perfectly competitive firms, oligopolistic firms, or whatever. For example, farmers buy tractors and fertilizer to produce crops to sell. General Motors buys steel to build cars to sell.

The demand for factors is a **derived demand**. It is derived from and directly related to the demand for the product that the resources go to produce. If the demand for the product rises, so does the demand for the factors used to produce the product. If the demand for the product falls, so does the demand for the factors used to produce the product. For example, if the demand for a university education falls, so does the demand for university professors. If the demand for computers rises, so does the demand for skilled computer workers.

When the demand for a seller's product rises, the seller needs to decide how much more of a factor to buy. Marginal revenue product and marginal factor cost are relevant to this decision.

Derived Demand
Demand that is the result of some other demand. For example, factor demand is the result of the demand for the products that the factors go to produce.

Finding ECONOMICS

In a Restaurant

Frank is sitting in a restaurant giving his order to the server. Where is the economics here? It is to be found in the server. The demand for servers is a derived demand—derived from the demand for eating out at restaurants. If the demand for eating out falls, we can expect the demand for servers to fall; if the demand for eating out rises, we can expect the demand for servers to rise.

Marginal Revenue Product: Two Ways to Calculate It

Marginal Revenue Product (*MRP*)

The additional revenue generated by employing an additional factor unit.

Marginal revenue product (*MRP*) is the additional revenue generated by employing an additional factor unit. For example, if a firm employs one more unit of a factor and its total revenue rises by \$20, the *MRP* of the factor equals \$20. Marginal revenue product can be calculated in two ways:

$$MRP = \frac{\Delta TR}{\Delta \text{Quantity of the factor}}$$

or

$$MRP = MR \times MPP$$

where *TR* = total revenue, *MR* = marginal revenue, and *MPP* = marginal physical product. Exhibit 1 presents data for a hypothetical firm to show the two methods for calculating *MRP*.

METHOD 1: *MRP* = Δ*TR*/Δ QUANTITY OF THE FACTOR Look at Exhibit 1(a).

- Column 1 shows the different quantities of factor X. Column 2 shows the quantity of output produced at the different quantities of factor X.

- Column 3 lists the price and the marginal revenue of the product that the factor goes to produce. Notice that we have assumed that the price of the product (*P*) equals the product's marginal revenue (*MR*). So we have assumed the seller in Exhibit 1 is a perfectly competitive firm. Recall that for a perfectly competitive firm, *P* = *MR*.

- In column 4, we calculate the total revenue, or price multiplied by quantity.

- In column 5, we calculate the marginal revenue product (*MRP*) by dividing the change in total revenue (from column 4) by the change in the quantity of the factor.

METHOD 2: *MRP* = *MR* × *MPP* Now look at Exhibit 1(b). Columns 1 and 2 are the same as in Exhibit 1(a).

- In column 3, we calculate the marginal physical product (*MPP*) of factor X. Recall that *MPP* is the change in the quantity of output divided by the change in the quantity of the factor.

exhibit 1

Calculating Marginal Revenue Product (MRP) There are two methods of calculating MRP. Part (a) shows one method (MRP = ΔTR/ΔQuantity of the factor), and (b) shows the other (MRP = MR × MPP).

(1) Quantity of Factor X	(2) Quantity of Output, Q	(3) Product Price, Marginal Revenue (P = MR)	(4) Total Revenue TR = P × Q = (3) × (2)	(5) Marginal Revenue Product of Factor X MRP = ΔTR/ΔQuantity of factor X = Δ(4)/Δ(1)
0	10*	$5	$ 50	—
1	19	5	95	$45
2	27	5	135	40
3	34	5	170	35
4	40	5	200	30
5	45	5	225	25

(a)

(1) Quantity of Factor X	(2) Quantity of Output, Q	(3) Marginal Physical Product MPP = Δ(2)/Δ(1)	(4) Product Price, Marginal Revenue (P = MR)	(5) Marginal Revenue Product of Factor X MRP = MR × MPP = (4) × (3)
0	10*	—	$5	—
1	19	9	5	$45
2	27	8	5	40
3	34	7	5	35
4	40	6	5	30
5	45	5	5	25

(b)

*Because the quantity of output is 10 at 0 units of factor X, other factors (not shown in the exhibit) must also be used to product the good.

- Column 4 lists the price and marginal revenue of the product. Column 4 is the same as column 3 in part (a).

- In column 5, we calculate the MRP by multiplying the marginal revenue (in column 4) by MPP (in column 3). The MRP figures in column 5 of (b) are the same as the MRP figures in column 5 of (a), showing that MRP can be calculated in two ways.

The MRP Curve Is the Firm's Factor Demand Curve

Look again at column 5 in Exhibit 1, which shows the MRP for factor X. By plotting the data in column 5 against the quantity of the factor (shown in column 1), we derive the MRP curve for factor X. This curve is the same as the firm's demand curve for factor X (or simply the firm's factor demand curve) (see Exhibit 2).

MRP curve = Factor demand curve

Notice that the MRP curve in Exhibit 2 is downward sloping. You can understand why when you recall that MRP can be calculated as MRP = MR × MPP. With regard to

exhibit 2

The *MRP* Curve Is the Firm's Factor Demand Curve

The data in columns (1) and (5) in Exhibit 1 are plotted to derive the *MRP* curve. The *MRP* curve shows the various quantities of the factor the firm is willing to buy at different prices, which is what a demand curve shows. The *MRP* curve is the firm's factor demand curve.

MPP, the marginal physical product of a factor, you know that, according to the law of diminishing marginal returns, eventually the *MPP* of a factor will diminish. Because *MRP* is equal to *MR* × *MPP* and because *MPP* will eventually decline, *MRP* will eventually decline too.

Value Marginal Product

Value marginal product (*VMP*) is equal to the price of the product multiplied by the marginal physical product of the factor:

$$VMP = P \times MPP$$

For example, if $P = \$10$ and $MPP = 9$ units, then $VMP = \$90$. Think of *VMP* as a measure of the value that each factor unit adds to the firm's product. Or you can think of it simply as *MPP* measured in dollars.

A firm wants to know the *VMP* of a factor because it helps in deciding how many units of the factor to hire. To illustrate, put yourself in the shoes of the owner of a firm that produces computers. One of the factors you need to produce computers is labor, and currently you are thinking of hiring an additional worker. Whether you actually hire the additional worker will depend on (1) how much better off you are—in dollars and cents—with the additional worker and (2) what you have to pay to hire the worker. Simply put, you want to know what the worker will do for you and what you will have to pay the worker. The *VMP* of a factor is a dollar measure of how much an additional unit of the factor will do for you.

Value Marginal Product (*VMP*)
The price of the good multiplied by the marginal physical product of the factor: *VMP* = *P* × *MPP*.

 Common MISCONCEPTIONS

About Hiring Employees

The instructor in class says that, when the first employee is hired, *VMP* is $40. When the second employee is hired, *VMP* falls to $30. When the third employee is hired, it falls to $20. Then the instructor asks, should the firm hire the third employee? Often the answer is a resounding yes: As long as *VMP* is positive, the next employee should be hired. But this answer overlooks something. More than *VMP* matters. What also matters is how much the firm must pay for the next employee.

An Important Question: Is *MRP* = *VMP*?

In the computations of *MRP* in Exhibit 1, price (*P*) was equal to marginal revenue (*MR*) because we assumed the firm was perfectly competitive. Because $P = MR$ for a perfectly competitive firm, then for a perfectly competitive firm $MRP = VMP$. Given that

$$MRP = MR \times MPP$$

and

$$VMP = P \times MPP$$

then, because $P = MR$ for a perfectly competitive firm,

$$MRP = VMP \text{ for a perfectly competitive firm}$$

See Exhibit 3(a).

exhibit 3

MRP and VMP Curves

$MRP = MR \times MPP$ and $VMP = P \times MPP$.
(a) The *MRP* (factor demand) curve and *VMP*

curve. These are the same for a price taker, or perfectly competitive firm, because $P = MR$.
(b) The *MRP* (factor demand) curve and *VMP* curve for a firm that is a price searcher

(monopolist, monopolistic competitor, oligopolist). The *MRP* curve lies below the *VMP* curve because for these firms, $P > MR$.

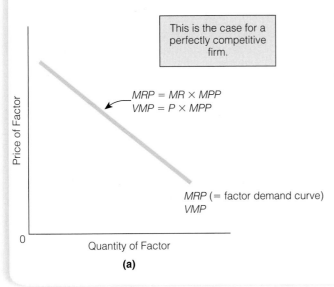

This is the case for a perfectly competitive firm.

$MRP = MR \times MPP$
$VMP = P \times MPP$

MRP (= factor demand curve)
VMP

(a)

This is the case for a monopolist, a monopolistic competitor, and an oligopolist.

$MRP = MR \times MPP$

$VMP = P \times MPP$

VMP

MRP (= factor demand curve)

(b)

Although $MRP = VMP$ for perfectly competitive firms, this is not the case for firms that are price searchers: monopolist, monopolistic competitive, and oligopolistic firms. All these firms face downward-sloping demand curves for their products. For all of these firms, $P > MR$, and so VMP (which is $P \times MPP$) is greater than MRP (which is $MR \times MPP$).[1] See Exhibit 3(b).

Marginal Factor Cost: The Firm's Factor Supply Curve

Marginal factor cost (*MFC*) is the additional cost incurred by employing an additional factor unit. It is calculated as

$$MFC = \frac{\Delta TC}{\Delta \text{Quantity of the factor}}$$

where TC = total costs.

Let's suppose a firm is a **factor price taker:** It can buy all it wants of a factor at the equilibrium price. For example, suppose the equilibrium price for factor X is $5. If a firm is a factor price taker, it can buy any quantity of factor X at $5 per factor unit [see Exhibit 4(a)].

For this kind of firm, the marginal factor cost (*MFC*) curve (the firm's factor supply curve) would be horizontal (flat, or perfectly elastic), as shown in Exhibit 4(b).[2]

Marginal Factor Cost (*MFC*)
The additional cost incurred by employing an additional factor unit.

Factor Price Taker
A firm that can buy all of a factor it wants at the equilibrium price. It faces a horizontal (flat, perfectly elastic) supply curve of factors.

1. An exception is the perfectly price-discriminating monopoly firm. For this firm, $P = MR$.

2. Although the *MFC* (factor supply curve) for the single factor price taker is horizontal, the market supply curve is upward sloping. This is similar to the situation for the perfectly competitive firm where the firm's demand curve is horizontal but the market (or industry) demand curve is downward sloping. In factor markets, we are simply talking about the supply side of the market instead of the demand side. The firm's supply curve is flat because it can buy additional factor units without driving up the price of the factor; it buys a relatively small portion of the factor. For the industry, however, higher factor prices must be offered to entice factors (e.g., workers) from other industries. The difference in the two supply curves—the firm's and the industry's—is basically a reflection of the different sizes of the firm and the industry.

Calculating *MFC* and Deriving the *MFC* Curve (the Firm's Factor Supply Curve)

In (a), *MFC* is calculated in column 4. Notice that the firm is a factor price taker because it can buy a quantity of factor X at a given price ($5, as shown in column 2). In (b), the data from columns (1) and (4) are plotted to derive the *MFC* curve, which is the firm's factor supply curve.

(1) Quantity of Factor X	(2) Price of Factor X	(3) Total cost $TC = (2) \times (1)$	(4) $MFC = \Delta TC/\Delta Quantity$ of the factor $= \Delta(3)/\Delta(1)$
0	$5	$ 0	—
1	5	5	$5
2	5	10	5
3	5	15	5
4	5	20	5
5	5	25	5
6	5	30	5

(a)

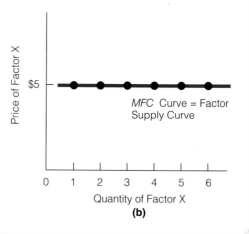

(b)

How Many Units of a Factor Should a Firm Buy?

Suppose you graduate with a BA in economics and go to work for a business firm. The first day on the job, you are involved in a discussion about factor X. Your employer asks you, "How many units of this factor should we buy?" What would you say?

Recall that economists often make use of marginal analysis. An economist is likely to answer this question by saying, "Continue buying additional units of the factor until the additional revenue generated by employing an additional factor unit is equal to the additional cost incurred by employing an additional factor unit." Simply stated, keep buying additional units of the factor until $MRP = MFC$. In Exhibit 5, MRP equals MFC at a factor quantity of Q_1.

Equating *MRP* and *MFC*

The firm continues to purchase a factor as long as the factor's *MRP* exceeds its *MFC*. In the exhibit, the firm purchases Q_1.

Thinking like AN ECONOMIST

Comparing One Thing to Another

As already stated, when decisions need to be made, one thing is compared to another. The decision before the firm is how much of a factor or resource should it buy or hire? When making this decision, the firm will want to look at the additional benefits of hiring or buying one more unit of the factor against the additional costs of hiring or buying one more unit of the factor.

Thinking like AN ECONOMIST

Different Markets, Same Principles

In the product market, a firm produces that quantity of output at which marginal revenue equals marginal cost, *MR* = *MC*. In the factor market, a firm buys the factor quantity at which marginal revenue product equals marginal factor cost, *MRP* = *MFC*. The economic principle of equating additional benefits with additional costs holds in both markets.

When There Is More Than One Factor, How Much of Each Factor Should the Firm Buy?

Until now, we have discussed only the purchase of one factor. Now suppose a firm requires two factors, labor (*L*) and capital (*K*), to produce its product. How does it combine these two factors to minimize costs? Does it combine, say, 20 units of labor with 5 units of capital or perhaps 15 units of labor with 8 units of capital?

The firm purchases the two factors until the ratio of *MPP* to price for one factor equals the ratio of *MPP* to price for the other factor. In other words,

$$\frac{MPP_L}{P_L} = \frac{MPP_K}{P_K}$$

This is the **least-cost rule**. To understand the logic behind it, consider an example. Suppose for a firm that (1) the price of labor is $5, (2) the price of capital is $10, (3) an extra unit of labor results in an increase in output of 25 units, and (4) an extra unit of capital results in an increase in output of 25 units. Notice that MPP_L/P_L is greater than MPP_K/P_K: 25/$5 > 25/$10. Thus, for this firm, $1 spent on labor is more effective at raising output than $1 spent on capital. In fact, it is twice as effective.

Now suppose the firm currently spends an extra $5 on labor and an extra $10 on capital. With this purchase of the two factors, the firm *is not* minimizing costs. It spends an additional $15 and produces 50 additional units of output. If, instead, it spends an additional $10 on labor and $0 on capital, it can still produce the 50 additional units of output and save $5.

To minimize costs, the firm will rearrange its purchases of factors until the least-cost rule is met. To illustrate, if $MPP_L/P_L > MPP_K/P_K$, the firm buys more labor and less capital. As a result, the *MPP* of labor falls and the *MPP* of capital rises, bringing the two ratios closer in line. The firm continues to buy more of the factor whose *MPP*-to-price ratio is larger. It stops when the two ratios are equal.

Least-Cost Rule
Rule that specifies the combination of factors that minimizes costs. This requires that the following condition be met: $MPP_1/P_1 = MPP_2/P_2 = \ldots = MPP_N/P_N$, where the numbers stand for the different factors.

Thinking like AN ECONOMIST

Two Different Settings, Same Principles

We can compare a firm's least-cost rule with how buyers allocate their consumption dollars. A buyer of goods in the product market chooses combinations of goods so that the marginal utility of good A divided by the price of good A is equal to the marginal utility of good B divided by the price of good B; that is, $MU_A/P_A = MU_B/P_B$.

A firm buying factors in the factor market chooses combinations of factors so that the marginal physical product of, say, labor divided by the price of labor (the wage rate) is equal to the marginal physical product of capital divided by the price of capital; that is, $MPP_L/P_L = MPP_K/P_K$.

Consumers buy goods the same way firms buy factors. This similarity points out something that you may have already sensed: Economic principles are few, but they sometimes seem numerous because we find them in so many different settings.

The same economic principle lies behind equating the MU/P ratio for different goods in the product market and equating the MPP/P ratio for different resources in the resource market. In short, only one economic principle is at work in the two markets—not two different ones. That principle simply says that economic actors will, in their attempt to meet their objectives, arrange their purchases in such a way that they receive equal additional benefits per dollar of expenditure.

Seeing how a few economic principles operate in many different settings is part of the economic way of thinking.

SELF·TEST

(Answers to Self-Test questions are in the Self-Test Appendix.)

1. When a perfectly competitive firm employs one worker, it produces 20 units of output, and when it employs two workers, it produces 39 units of output. The firm sells its product for $10 per unit. What is the marginal revenue product connected with hiring the second worker?

2. What is the difference between marginal revenue product (*MRP*) and value marginal product (*VMP*)?

3. What is the distinguishing characteristic of a factor price taker?

4. How much labor should a firm purchase?

THE LABOR MARKET

Labor is a factor of special interest because, at one time or another, most people find themselves in the labor market. This section discusses first the demand for labor, then the supply of labor, and finally the two together. The section focuses on the firm that is a price taker in the product market (i.e., a perfectly competitive firm) and in the factor market.[3] In this setting, the demand for and supply of labor determine wage rates.

Shifts in a Firm's *MRP*, or Factor Demand, Curve

As already explained, a firm's *MRP* curve is its factor demand curve, and marginal revenue product equals marginal revenue multiplied by marginal physical product:

$$MRP = MR \times MPP \tag{1}$$

---

3. Keep in mind that, in the labor market here, neither buyers nor sellers have any control over wage rates. Consequently, supply and demand are our analytical tools. In the next chapter, we modify this analysis.

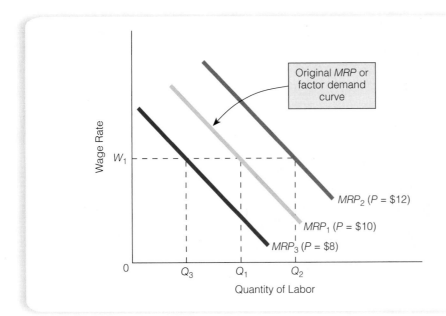

exhibit 6

Shifts in the Firm's *MRP*, or Factor Demand, Curve

It is always the case that *MRP* = *MR* × *MPP*. For a perfectly competitive firm, where *P* = *MR*, it follows that *MRP* = *P* × *MPP*. If *P* changes, *MRP* will change. For example, if product price rises, *MRP* rises, and the firm's *MRP* curve (factor demand curve) shifts rightward. If product price falls, *MRP* falls, and the firm's *MRP* curve (factor demand curve) shifts leftward. If *MPP* rises (reflected in a shift in the *MPP* curve), *MRP* rises and the firm's *MRP* curve shifts rightward. If *MPP* falls, *MRP* falls and the firm's *MRP* curve shifts leftward.

For a perfectly competitive firm, where $P = MR$, we can write equation (1) as

$$MRP = P \times MPP \qquad\qquad (2)$$

Now consider the demand for a specific factor input, labor. What will happen to the factor demand (*MRP*) curve for labor as the price of the product that the labor produces changes? In Exhibit 6, we start with a product price of $10 and factor demand curve MRP_1. At the wage rate of W_1, the firm hires Q_1 labor. Suppose product price rises to $12. As we can see from equation (2), *MRP* rises. At each wage rate, the firm wants to hire more labor. For example, at W_1, it wants to hire Q_2 labor instead of Q_1. In short, a rise in product price shifts the firm's *MRP*, or factor demand, curve rightward. If product price falls from $10 to $8, *MRP* falls. At each wage rate, the firm wants to hire less labor. For example, at W_1, it wants to hire Q_3 labor instead of Q_1. In short, a fall in product price shifts the firm's *MRP*, or factor demand, curve leftward.

Changes in the *MPP* of the factor—reflected in a shift in the *MPP* curve—also change the firm's *MRP* curve. As we can see from equation (2), an increase in, say, the *MPP* of labor will increase *MRP* and shift the *MRP*, or factor demand, curve rightward. A decrease in *MPP* will decrease *MRP* and shift the *MRP*, or factor demand, curve leftward.[4]

micro*theme* ➔ An ongoing theme in microeconomics is this one: (1) Derive a particular curve and then (2) explain what factors will shift it. We first encountered this theme back in Chapter 3 when discussing supply and demand. We derived a demand curve (from a demand schedule) and then discussed the factors that could shift the curve. We are playing that theme again here. We have just derived the firm's demand curve for a factor. Then we identified factors (e.g., a change in the price of the good the factor goes to produce and a change in *MPP*) that could shift the curve.

4. We are talking about a change in *MPP* that is reflected in a *shift* in the *MPP* curve; we are not talking about a *movement* along a given *MPP* curve.

economics 24/7

WHY JOBS DON'T ALWAYS MOVE TO THE LOW-WAGE COUNTRY

Some people think that tariffs are needed to protect U.S. workers. They argue that without tariffs, U.S. companies will relocate to countries where wages are lower. They will produce their products there and then transport the products to the United States to sell them. Tariffs will make this scenario less likely because the gains the companies receive in lower wages will be offset by the tariffs imposed on their goods.

© AP PHOTO/EDUARDO VERDUGO

What this argument overlooks is that U.S. companies are interested not only in what they pay workers, but also in the marginal productivity of the workers. For example, suppose a U.S. worker earns $10 an hour and a Mexican worker earns $4 an hour. Also suppose the marginal physical product (*MPP*) of the U.S. worker is 10 units of good X and the *MPP* of the Mexican worker is 2 units of good X. Thus, we have lower wages in Mexico and higher productivity in the United States. Where will the company produce?

To answer this question, compare the output produced per $1 of cost in the two countries.

$$\text{Output produced per \$1 of cost} = \frac{MPP \text{ of the factor}}{\text{Cost of the factor}}$$

In the United States, at an *MPP* of 10 units of good X and a wage rate of $10, workers produce 1 unit of good X for every $1 they are paid:

$$\frac{MPP \text{ of U.S. labor}}{\text{Wage rate of U.S. labor}} = \frac{10 \text{ units of good X}}{\$10}$$
$$= 1 \text{ unit of good X per \$1}$$

In Mexico, at an *MPP* of 2 units and a wage rate of $4, workers produce half a unit of good X for every $1 they are paid:

$$\frac{MPP \text{ of Mexican labor}}{\text{Wage rate of Mexican labor}}$$
$$= \frac{2 \text{ units of good X}}{\$4}$$
$$= 1/2 \text{ unit of good X per \$1}$$

Thus, the company gets more output per $1 of cost by using U.S. labor and will produce good X in the United States. It is cheaper to produce the good in the United States than it is in Mexico—even though wages are lower in Mexico.

In other words, U.S. companies look at the following ratios:

(1)	(2)
$\dfrac{MPP \text{ of labor in U.S.}}{\text{Wage rate in U.S.}}$	$\dfrac{MPP \text{ of labor in country X}}{\text{Wage rate in country X}}$

If ratio (1) is greater than ratio (2), U.S. companies will hire labor in the United States. As they do so, the *MPP* of labor in the United States will decline. (Remember the law of diminishing marginal returns.) Companies will continue to hire labor in the United States until ratio (1) is equal to ratio (2).

Market Demand for Labor

We would expect the market demand curve for labor to be the horizontal addition of the firm's demand curves (*MRP* curves) for labor. However, this is not the case, as Exhibit 7 illustrates. Two firms, A and B, make up the buying side of the factor market, and the product price for both firms is P_1. Parts (a) and (b) in the exhibit show the *MRP* curves for the two firms based on this product price.

At a wage rate of W_1, firm A purchases 100 units of labor, the amount of labor at which its marginal revenue product equals marginal factor cost (or the wage). At this same wage rate, firm B purchases 150 units of labor. If we horizontally add the *MRP* curves of firms A and B, we get the *MRP* curve in (c), where the two firms together purchase 250 units of labor at W_1.

Now assume the wage rate increases to W_2. In (c), firms A and B move up the given MRP_{A+B} curve and purchase 180 units of labor. This may seem to be the end of the

exhibit 7

The Derivation of the Market Demand Curve for Labor Units

Two firms, A and B, make up the buying side of the market for labor. At a wage rate of W_1, firm A purchases 100 units of labor and firm B purchases 150 units. Together, they purchase

250 units, as illustrated in (c). The wage rate rises to W_2, and the amount of labor purchased by both firms initially falls to 180 units, as shown in (c). Higher wage rates translate into higher costs, a fall in product supply, and a rise in product price from P_1 to P_2. Finally, an

increased price raises MRP and each firm has a new MRP curve. The horizontal "addition" of the new MRP curves shows they purchase 210 units of labor. Connecting the units of labor purchased by both firms at W_1 and W_2 gives the market demand curve.

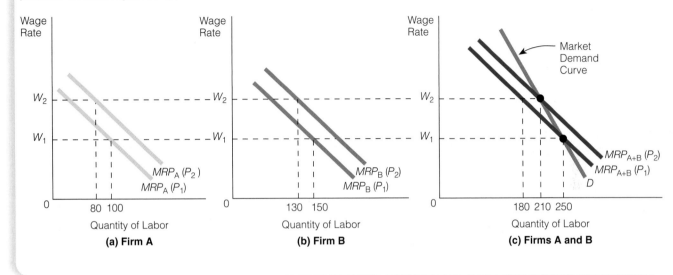

(a) Firm A

(b) Firm B

(c) Firms A and B

process, but of course it is not because a higher wage rate increases each firm's costs and thus shifts its supply curve leftward. This, in turn, leads to an increase in product price to P_2.

Recall that the firm's marginal revenue product is equal to marginal revenue (or price, when the firm is perfectly competitive) times marginal physical product: $MRP = MR \times MPP = P \times MPP$. So if price rises (which it has), so does MRP, and therefore each firm faces a new MRP curve at the wage rate W_2. Parts (a) and (b) in Exhibit 7 illustrate these new MRP curves for firms A and B, and (c) shows the horizontal addition of the *new MRP* curves. The firms together now purchase 210 units of labor at W_2.

After all adjustments have been made, connecting the units of labor purchased by both firms at W_1 and W_2 gives the market demand curve in (c).

The Elasticity of Demand for Labor

If the wage rate rises, firms will cut back on the labor they hire, but how much they cut back depends on the elasticity of demand for labor. The **elasticity of demand for labor** is the percentage change in the quantity demanded of labor divided by the percentage change in the price of labor (the wage rate).

$$E_L = \frac{\text{Percentage change in quantity demanded of labor}}{\text{Percentage change in wage rage}}$$

Elasticity of Demand for Labor
The percentage change in the quantity demanded of labor divided by the percentage change in the wage rate.

where E_L = coefficient of elasticity of demand for labor, or simply elasticity coefficient.

For example, suppose when the wage rate changes by 20 percent, the quantity demanded of a particular type of labor changes by 40 percent. Then the elasticity of demand for this type of labor is 2 (40 percent ÷ 20 percent), and the demand between the old wage rate and the new wage rate is elastic. There are three main determinants of elasticity of demand for labor.

ELASTICITY OF DEMAND FOR THE PRODUCT THAT LABOR PRODUCES If the demand for the product that labor produces is highly elastic, a small percentage increase in price (e.g., owing to a wage increase that shifts the supply curve for the product leftward) will decrease quantity demanded of the product by a relatively large percentage. In turn, this will greatly reduce the quantity of labor needed to produce the product, implying that the demand for labor is highly elastic too.

The relationship between the elasticity of demand for the product and the elasticity of demand for labor is as follows:

> *The higher the elasticity of demand is for the product, the higher the elasticity of demand is for the labor that produces the product; the lower the elasticity of demand for the product, the lower the elasticity of demand for the labor that produces the product.*

RATIO OF LABOR COSTS TO TOTAL COSTS Labor costs are a part of total costs. Consider two situations: In one, labor costs are 90 percent of total costs, and in the other, labor costs are only 5 percent of total costs. Now suppose wages increase by $2 per hour. Total costs are affected more when labor costs are 90 percent of total costs (the $2-per-hour wage increase is being applied to 90 percent of all costs) than when labor costs are only 5 percent of total costs. Thus, price rises by more when labor costs are a larger percentage of total costs. And, of course, the more price rises, the more the quantity demanded of the product falls. Therefore, labor, being a derived demand, is affected more. In short, for a $2-per-hour wage increase, the decline in the quantity demanded of labor is greater when labor costs are 90 percent of total costs than when labor costs are 5 percent of total costs.

The relationship between the ratio of labor cost to total cost and the elasticity of demand for labor is as follows:

> *The higher the ratio of labor cost to total cost is, the higher the elasticity of demand is for labor (the greater the cutback in labor for any given wage increase); the lower the ratio of labor cost to total cost, the lower the elasticity of demand for labor (the less the cutback in labor for any given wage increase).*

NUMBER OF SUBSTITUTE FACTORS The more substitutes there are for labor, the more sensitive buyers of labor will be to a change in the price of labor. This principle was established in the discussion of price elasticity of demand. The more possibilities there are for substituting other factors for labor, the more likely it is that firms will cut back on their use of labor if the price of labor rises.

> *The more substitutes there are for labor, the higher the elasticity of demand is for labor; the fewer substitutes for labor, the lower the elasticity of demand for labor.*

Market Supply of Labor

As the wage rate rises, the quantity supplied of labor rises, *ceteris paribus.* The upward-sloping labor supply curve in Exhibit 8 illustrates this. At a wage rate of W_1, individuals are willing to supply 100 labor units. At the higher wage rate of W_2, individuals are willing to supply 200 labor units. Some individuals who were not willing to work at a wage rate of W_1 are willing to work at a wage rate of W_2, and some individuals who were working at W_1 will be willing to supply more labor units at W_2. At the even higher wage rate of W_3, individuals are willing to supply 280 labor units.

exhibit 8

The Market Supply of Labor

A direct relationship exists between the wage rate and the quantity of labor supplied.

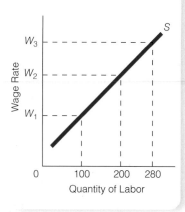

HOW CRIME, OUTSOURCING, AND MULTITASKING MIGHT BE RELATED

Consider three seemingly unrelated images of life in the United States in recent years:

1. A lower crime rate. For example, violent crime, property crime, and homicides were all down in the late 1990s and early 2000s.
2. Increasingly more professional people outsourcing their routine tasks. They are hiring people to run errands, buy groceries, plan parties, drop off dry cleaning, take pets to the vet, and do other chores.
3. More people choosing to multitask—that is, to work on more than one task at a time. If you drive a car at the same time as you talk to your office on your cell phone, you are multitasking.

Could all three images be the result of the same thing—higher real wages?[5] How might higher real wages affect crime, multitasking, and outsourcing?

Let's consider crime first. Committing a crime has both costs and benefits. As long as the benefits are greater than the costs, crimes will be committed; increase the costs of crime relative to the benefits, and the crime rate will decline. Suppose part of the cost of crime is equal to the probability of being sentenced to jail multiplied by the real wage that would be earned if the person were not in jail.

Part of the cost of crime = Probability of jail sentence × Real wage

If this is the case, then, as the real wage rises, the overall cost of crime rises and fewer crimes will be committed.

To illustrate how does the real wage relate to individuals outsourcing their routine tasks, suppose John and Mary are married and have two daughters. Mary works as a physician, and John works part-time as an accountant. Because John has chosen to work part-time, he takes care of many of the routine household tasks: buying the groceries, running the errands, and so on. If the real wage rises for accountants, John may rethink his part-time work. An increase in the real wage is the same as an increase in the reward from working, and so John may choose to work more. In fact, it may be cheaper for him to work full-time and pay someone else to run the errands, buy the groceries, and so on.

Finally, what about multitasking? As the real wage rises, one's time becomes more valuable. And as time becomes more valuable, people want to economize on using it. One way to economize on time is to do several things simultaneously. Instead of spending 20 minutes driving to work and another 10 minutes talking on the phone, you kill two birds with one stone and talk on the phone while driving to work. You save 10 minutes this way. Of course, there is a downside. (Economists are quick to point out that most activities come with both benefits and costs.) Talking on a cell phone while driving is not only illegal in some states, but it probably makes you and others around you less safe while driving.

If higher real wages can affect the crime rate, the amount of outsourcing, and how much people multitask, knowing what can cause real wages to rise becomes important. One way real wages can rise is through a technological advance that increases the quality of the capital goods used by labor. To illustrate, consider a technological advance that makes it possible for computers to complete more tasks in less time than before. As a result, the productivity of labor rises and the demand curve for labor shifts to the right. Higher demand for labor increases the nominal wage rate and, as long as the price level doesn't rise by more than the nominal wage rate, the real wage rises too.

Can a technological advance indirectly lead to a lower crime rate, more outsourcing, and greater multitasking? We think so.

---

5. Nominal wages are dollar wages—such as $30 an hour. Real wages are nominal wages adjusted for price changes. Stated differently, real wages measure what nominal wages can actually buy in terms of goods and services. So when real wages rise, people can buy more goods and services.

An Individual's Supply of Labor

Exhibit 8 shows an upward-sloping *market* supply curve of labor. Let's consider an individual's supply curve of labor—specifically, whether John's supply curve of labor is upward sloping. The answer depends on the relative strengths of the substitution and income effects.

John currently earns $10 an hour and works 40 hours a week. If John's wage rate rises to, say, $15 an hour, he will feel two effects, each pulling him in opposite directions.

1. *Substitution effect.* As his wage rate rises, John recognizes that the monetary reward from working has increased. As a result, John will want to work more—say, 45 hours a week instead of 40 hours (an additional 5 hours).

2. *Income effect.* As his wage rate rises, John knows that he can earn $600 a week (40 hours at $15 an hour) instead of $400 a week (40 hours at $10 an hour). If leisure is a normal good (the demand for which increases as income increases), then John will want to consume more leisure as his income rises. But the only way to consume more leisure is to work fewer hours. Let's say John wants to decrease his work hours per week from 40 to 37 hours (3 fewer hours).

The substitution effect pulls John in one direction (toward working 5 more hours), and the income effect pulls John in the opposite direction (toward working 3 fewer hours). Which effect is stronger? In our numerical example, the substitution effect is stronger; so, on net, John wants to work 2 more hours a week as his wage rate rises. This means that John's supply curve of labor is upward sloping between a wage rate of $10 and $15.

Finding ECONOMICS

In the Number of Hours a Person Works

Larry works at a job where it is easy to get overtime hours. He has been earning $20 an hour for the last year, and most weeks he works 45 hours. He recently got a raise to $23 an hour. Since getting his $3-an-hour raise, he has been working about 40 hours a week. Where is the economics?

The economics can be found in the substitution and income effects. As a result of the higher wage, part of Larry wants to work more; this is the substitution effect at work. But part of Larry wants to work less; this is the income effect at work. In the end, Larry works fewer hours (40 instead of 45 hours), which means his income effect was stronger than his substitution effect.

Shifts in the Labor Supply Curve

Changes in the wage rate change the quantity supplied of labor units; that is, they cause a *movement* along a given supply curve. But what *shifts* the entire labor supply curve? Two factors of major importance are wage rates in other labor markets and the nonmoney, or nonpecuniary, aspects of a job.

WAGE RATES IN OTHER LABOR MARKETS   Deborah works as a technician in a television manufacturing plant, but she has skills suitable for a number of jobs. One day, she learns that the computer manufacturing plant on the other side of town is offering 33 percent more pay per hour. Deborah is also trained to work as a computer operator; so she decides to leave her current job and apply for work at the computer manufacturing plant. In short, the wage rate offered in other labor markets can bring about a shift of the supply curve in a particular labor market.

NONMONEY, OR NONPECUNIARY, ASPECTS OF A JOB   Other things held constant, people prefer to avoid dirty, heavy, dangerous work in cold climates. An increase in the overall unpleasantness of a job (e.g., an increased probability of contracting lung cancer working in a coal mine) will cause a decrease in the supply of labor to that firm or industry and a leftward shift in its labor supply curve. An increase in the overall pleasantness of a job (e.g., employees are now entitled to a longer lunch break and use of the company gym) will cause an increase in the supply of labor to that firm or industry and a rightward shift in its labor supply curve.

Putting Supply and Demand Together

Exhibit 9 illustrates a labor market. The equilibrium wage rate and quantity of labor are established by the forces of supply and demand. At a wage rate of W_2, there is a surplus of labor. Some people who want to work at this wage rate will not be able to find jobs, and a subset of this group will begin to offer their services for a lower wage rate. The wage rate will move down until it reaches W_1.

At a wage rate of W_3, there is a shortage of labor. Some demanders of labor will begin to bid up the wage rate until it reaches W_1. At the equilibrium wage rate, W_1, the quantity supplied of labor equals the quantity demanded of labor.

Why Do Wage Rates Differ?

To discover why wage rates differ, we must determine what conditions are necessary for everyone to receive the same pay. Assume the following conditions hold:

1. The demand for every type of labor is the same. (Throughout our analysis, any wage differentials caused by demand are short-run differentials.)

2. There are no special nonpecuniary aspects to any job.

3. All labor is ultimately homogeneous and can costlessly be trained for different types of employment.

4. All labor is mobile at zero cost.

Given these conditions, there would be no difference in wage rates in the long run. Exhibit 10 shows two labor markets, A and B. Initially, the supply conditions are different, with a greater supply of workers in labor market B (S_B) than in labor market A (S_A). Because of the different supply conditions, more labor is employed in labor market B

Equilibrium in a Particular Labor Market

The forces of supply and demand bring about the equilibrium wage rate and quantity of labor. At the equilibrium wage rate, the quantity demanded of labor equals the quantity supplied. At any other wage rate, there is either a surplus or a shortage of labor.

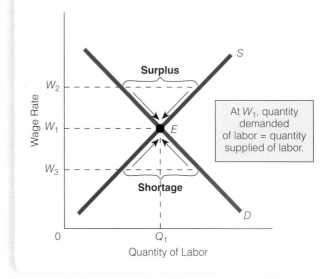

At W_1, quantity demanded of labor = quantity supplied of labor.

Wage Rate Equalization Across Labor Markets

Given the four necessary conditions (noted in the text), there will be no wage rate differences across labor markets. We start with a wage rate of $30 in labor market A and a wage rate of $10 in labor market B. Soon some individuals in B relocate to A. This increases the supply in one market (A), driving down the wage rate, and decreases the supply in the other market (B), driving up the wage rate. Equilibrium comes when the same wage rate is paid in both labor markets. This outcome critically depends on the necessary conditions holding.

(a) Labor Market A

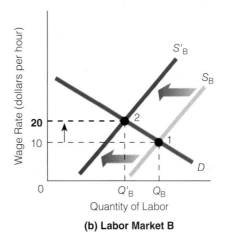

(b) Labor Market B

(Q_B) than in labor market A (Q_A), and the equilibrium wage rate in labor market B ($10) is lower than the equilibrium wage rate in labor market A ($30).

The differences in the wage rates between the two labor markets will not last. We have assumed (1) labor can move costlessly from one labor market to another (so labor moves from the lower-paying job to the higher-paying job), (2) there are no special nonpecuniary aspects to any job (no nonpecuniary reason for not moving), (3) labor is ultimately homogeneous (workers who work in labor market B can work in labor market A), and (4) if workers need training to make a move from one labor market to another, they not only are capable of being trained but also can acquire the training costlessly.

As a result, some workers in labor market B will relocate to labor market A, decreasing the supply of workers to S'_B in labor market B and increasing the supply to S'_A in market A. The relocation of workers ends when the equilibrium wage rate in both markets is the same at $20. Therefore, wage rates will not differ in the long run if our four conditions hold.

Because we know the conditions under which wage rates will not differ, we now know why wage rates do differ. Obviously, they differ because demand conditions are not the same in all labor markets (important to explain short-run wage differentials only) and because supply conditions are not the same in all markets: There *are* nonpecuniary aspects to different jobs, labor is *not* homogeneous, labor *cannot* be retrained without cost, and labor is *not* costlessly mobile.

Why Demand and Supply Differ Among Labor Markets

If wage rates differ because demand and supply conditions differ from one market to another, the next question is why. Let's consider the factors that affect the demand for and supply of labor.

DEMAND FOR LABOR The market demand curve for labor is based on the *MRP* curves for labor of the individual firms in the market. So we need to look at what affects the components of *MRP*, namely, *MR* and *MPP*.

Marginal revenue, *MR*, is indirectly affected by product supply and demand conditions because these conditions determine price ($MR = \Delta TR/\Delta Q$ and $TR = P \times Q$). Thus, product demand and supply conditions affect factor demand. In short, because the supply and demand conditions in product markets are different, the demand for labor in labor markets will be different too.

The second factor, the marginal physical product of labor, is affected by individual workers' *own abilities and skills* (both innate and learned), the *degree of effort* they put forth on the job, and the *other factors of production* available to them. With respect to the latter, American workers are more productive than workers in many other countries because they work with many more capital goods and much more technical know-how. If all individuals had the same innate and learned skills and abilities, applied the same degree of effort on the job, and worked with the same amount and quality of other factors of production, wages would differ less than they currently do.

SUPPLY OF LABOR As already noted, the supply conditions in labor markets are different. First, jobs have *different nonpecuniary qualities.* Working as a coal miner in West Virginia is not as attractive a job as working as a tour guide at a lush resort in Hawaii. We would expect this fact to be reflected in the supply of coal miners and tour guides.

Second, supply is also a reflection of the *number of persons who can actually do a job.* Williamson may want to be a nuclear physicist but may not have the ability in science and mathematics to become one. Johnson may want to be a basketball player but may not have the ability to become one.

exhibit 11

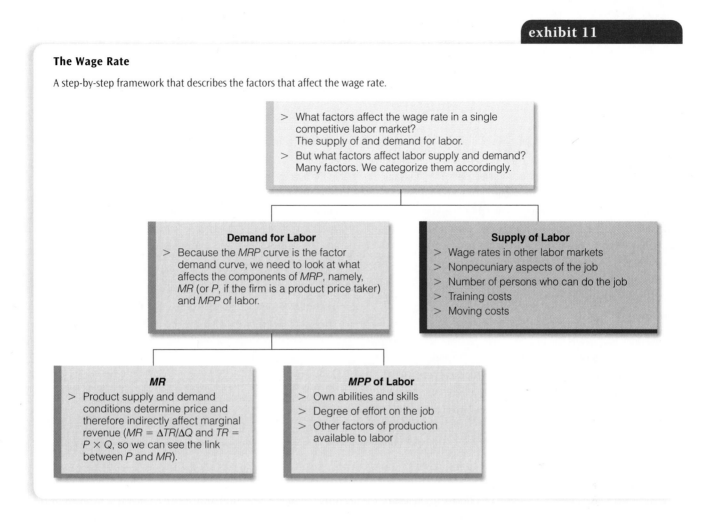

The Wage Rate

A step-by-step framework that describes the factors that affect the wage rate.

> What factors affect the wage rate in a single competitive labor market?
> The supply of and demand for labor.
> But what factors affect labor supply and demand?
> Many factors. We categorize them accordingly.

Demand for Labor
> Because the *MRP* curve is the factor demand curve, we need to look at what affects the components of *MRP*, namely, *MR* (or *P*, if the firm is a product price taker) and *MPP* of labor.

Supply of Labor
> Wage rates in other labor markets
> Nonpecuniary aspects of the job
> Number of persons who can do the job
> Training costs
> Moving costs

MR
> Product supply and demand conditions determine price and therefore indirectly affect marginal revenue ($MR = \Delta TR/\Delta Q$ and $TR = P \times Q$, so we can see the link between P and MR).

MPP of Labor
> Own abilities and skills
> Degree of effort on the job
> Other factors of production available to labor

Third, even if individuals have the ability to work at a certain job, they may perceive the *training costs as too high* (relative to the perceived benefits) to train for it. Tyler may have the ability to be a brain surgeon but views the years of schooling required to be too high a price to pay.

Fourth, sometimes supply in different labor markets reflects a difference in the *cost of moving* across markets. Wage rates might be higher in Alaska than in Alabama for comparable labor because the workers in Alabama find the cost of relocating to Alaska too high relative to the benefits of receiving a higher wage.

In conclusion, because the wage rate is determined by supply-and-demand forces, the factors that affect these forces indirectly affect wage rates. Exhibit 11 summarizes these factors.

Why Did You Choose Your Major?

What happens in the labor market sometimes influences our lives. Consider a college student who is trying to decide whether to major in accounting or English. The student believes that English is more fun and interesting but that accounting, on average, will earn her enough additional income to compensate for the lack of fun in accounting. Specifically, at a $55,000 annual salary for accounting and a $39,000 annual salary for teaching English, the student is indifferent between accounting and English. But at a

economics 24/7

THE WAGE RATE FOR A STREET-LEVEL PUSHER IN A DRUG GANG

Gangs that deal drugs exist in almost every large city in the United States. It is not uncommon to see a 16- or 17-year-old gang member selling or delivering drugs in Los Angeles, New York, Chicago, Houston, or other big cities. In the public debate about drug dealing in these cities, one argument goes like this: "No wonder these kids sell drugs; it's the best job they can get. When your alternatives are working at McDonald's earning the minimum wage or selling drugs for big money, you sell drugs. If we want to get kids off the streets and out of gangs and if we want to stop them from selling drugs, we need to have something better for them than the minimum wage."

One question, however, is whether the young gang members who sell and deliver drugs really earn big money. Economics would predict that they don't. After all, one would think that the supply of people who can sell or deliver drugs is rather large. In fact, a recent study found that low-level foot soldiers in a drug gang actually earned very low wages.

Steven Levitt, an economist, and Sudhir Venkatesh, a sociologist, analyzed the data set of a drug-selling street gang.[6] They estimated that the average hourly wage rate in the gang was $6 at the time they started the study and $11 at the time they finished.[7] They also noted that the distribution of wages was extremely skewed. Actual street-level dealers (foot soldiers) appeared to earn less than the minimum wage. According to Levitt and Venkatesh,

> While these wages are almost too low to be believable, there are both theoretical arguments and corroborating empirical evidence in support of these numbers. From a theoretical perspective, it is hardly surprising that foot-soldier wages would be low given the minimal skill requirements for the job and the presence of a 'reserve army' of potential replacements among the rank and file.

6. Steven Levitt and Sudhir Venkatesh, *An Economic Analysis of a Drug-Selling Gang's Finances*, NBER Working Paper No. W6592 (Cambridge, MA: National Bureau of Economic Research, 1998).

7. Wage rates are in 1995 dollars.

$56,000 annual salary for accounting and a $39,000 annual salary for teaching English, accounting moves ahead.

Of course, what accounting pays is determined by the demand for and supply of accountants. When we realize this, we see that other people influenced the person's decision to become an accountant. To illustrate, suppose Congress passes more intricate tax laws that require more accountants to figure them out. This increases the demand for accountants, which in turn raises the wage rate for them. And an increase in the wage rate for accountants increases the probability that more people—perhaps you—will major in accounting, not in English, philosophy, or history.

As you can see, economics—in which markets play a major role—helps explain why part of your life is the way it is.

Marginal Productivity Theory

An analysis of some of the things we know from this chapter leads us the following conclusions:

1. If a firm is a factor price taker, marginal factor cost is constant and equal to factor price, $MFC = P$. Suppose the factor price taker hires labor. For the firm, $MFC = W$, where W is the wage rate.

2. Firms hire the factor quantity at which $MRP = MFC$.

3. Given points 1 and 2 together, a factor price taker pays labor a wage equal to its marginal revenue product: $W = MRP$. Because $MFC = W$ (point 1) and $MRP = MFC$ (point 2), then $W = MRP$.

economics 24/7

IT'S A PARTY EVERY NIGHT[8]

Workers who portray Disney characters at Disneyland and Disney World earn as little as $7.60 an hour. They can also suffer from certain injuries, many of which are the result of having to wear heavy costumes.

But even though the wages are low and the possibility of injury is high, Disney doesn't seem to suffer from a lack of job applicants. More importantly, the people who work at the Disney parks (in all capacities) seem rather happy with their jobs. According to one employee, "It's a party every night."

© AP PHOTO/NICK UT

Perhaps it's a party every night because many of the employees who play Disney characters are young (college student age), from various countries, who live near each other in Disney-provided apartments. In other words, $7.60 an hour gets you work, plus certain social amenities—such as being able to get together with other people who are your age and single.

There may be something else, too. Disney calls the people who work for the company not employees or workers, but cast members. And to become a cast member, one does not apply for a job; one auditions.

This background relates to the nonpecuniary aspects of a job. Earlier in the chapter we said that, other things held constant, people prefer to avoid dirty, heavy, dangerous work in cold climates. An increase in a job's overall unpleasantness (e.g., an increased probability of contracting lung cancer working in a coal mine) will cause a decrease in the supply of labor to that firm or industry and a leftward shift in its labor supply curve. An increase in the overall pleasantness (e.g., a longer lunch break and use of the company gym) will cause an increase in the supply of labor to that firm or industry and a rightward shift in its labor supply curve.

Working as a Disney character seems to come with both the pleasant and the unpleasant. Wearing a heavy costume is unpleasant. Sustaining certain injuries (from wearing a heavy costume) is unpleasant. On the other hand, if you are young and single, socializing with other young and single persons is pleasant. Being called a cast member is pleasant. And even getting to party every night could be considered pleasant by some people.

On net, given that Disney doesn't have a difficult time finding cast members and that the wages for Disney characters are relatively low, the pleasantness of the job seems to outweigh its unpleasantness by a good amount. And it probably doesn't hurt that Disney advertises many of its jobs on a website called Yummy Jobs (yummyjobs.com).

---

8. This feature is adapted from "The Myth and Magic of Mickey Mouse," *Economist*, March 30, 2007.

---

4. If a firm is perfectly competitive, $MRP = VMP$.

5. If a firm is both perfectly competitive (a product price taker) and a factor price taker, it pays labor a wage equal to its value marginal product: $W = VMP$. Because $W = MRP$ (point 3) and $MRP = VMP$ (point 4), then $W = VMP$.

This is the **marginal productivity theory**, which states that if a firm sells its product and purchases its factors in competitive or perfect markets (i.e., it is a perfectly competitive firm and a factor price taker), it pays its factors their MRP or VMP (the two are equal for a product price taker).

The theory holds that under the competitive conditions specified, if a factor unit is withdrawn from the productive process and the amount of all other factors remains the same, then the decrease in the value of the product produced equals the factor payment

Marginal Productivity Theory
Theory stating that firms in competitive or perfect product and factor markets pay factors their marginal revenue products.

received by the factor unit. To illustrate, suppose Wilson works for a perfectly competitive firm (firm X) producing good X. One day, he quits his job (but nothing else relevant to the firm changes). As a result, the total revenue of the firm falls by $100. If Wilson was paid $100, then he received his *MRP*. He was paid a wage equal to his contribution to the productive process.[9]

Finding ECONOMICS

In a Salary of $27,708,525

Alex Rodriguez, who plays third base for the New York Yankees, earned a salary of $27,708,525 in 2007. Where is the economics here?

The economics deals with Alex Rodriguez's *MRP*. Many people, when they read about the salaries of some sports, movie, and TV stars, say, "No one is worth that much money." With reference to Alex Rodriguez, we can ask whether he is worth $27 million a year. The answer is that he is worth this amount if his *MRP* is greater than $27 million a year. In other words, if his *MRP* is, say, $28 million a year, and the Yankees organization pays him $27 million a year, then he is certainly worth the $27 million he earns. Of course, if his *MRP* is $20 million a year and the Yankees pay him $27 million, the Yankees organization has made a mistake becaue Rodriguez isn't worth as much as he is being paid. In short, without knowing Alex Rodriguez's *MRP*, we can't say for sure whether he is worth his salary. However, we can say that the Yankees organization management would not have paid Rodriguez $27 million unless they thought he was worth this amount.

SELF-TEST

1. The demand for labor is a derived demand. What could cause the firm's demand curve for labor to shift rightward?
2. Suppose the coefficient of elasticity of demand for labor is 3. What does this mean?
3. Why are wage rates higher in one competitive labor market than in another? In short, why do wage rates differ?
4. Workers in labor market X do the same work as workers in labor market Y, but they earn $10 less per hour. Why?

LABOR MARKETS AND INFORMATION

This section looks at job hiring, employment practices, employment discrimination, and how information or the lack of it affects these processes.

Screening Potential Employees

Employers typically do not know exactly how productive a prospective employee will be. What the employer wants but lacks is complete information about the employee's future job performance. This need raises two questions: Why would an employer want complete information about a potential employee's future job performance? What does the employer do in the absence of such complete information?

---

9. Recall that there are two ways to calculate *MRP*: $MRP = \Delta TR / \Delta$Quantity of the factor, and $MRP = MR \times MPP$. In this example, we use the first method. When Wilson quits his job, the change in the denominator is 1 factor unit. If, as a result, *TR* falls by $100, then the change in the numerator must be $100.

The answer to the first question is obvious. Employers have a strong monetary incentive to hire good, stable, quick-learning, responsible, hardworking, punctual employees. One study found that corporate spending on training employees reached $40 billion annually. Obviously, corporations want to see the highest return possible for their training expenditures; so they try to hire employees who will make the training worthwhile. This is where screening comes in.

Screening is the process employers use to increase the probability of choosing good employees based on certain criteria. For example, an employer might ask a young college graduate searching for a job what his or her GPA was in college. This is a screening mechanism. The employer might know from past experience that persons with high GPAs turn out to be better employees, on average, than persons with low GPAs. Screening is one thing an employer does in the absence of complete information.

Screening
The process employers use to increase the probability of choosing good employees based on certain criteria.

Promoting from Within

Sometimes, employers promote from within the company because they have more information about present employees than about prospective employees.

Suppose the executive vice president in charge of sales is retiring from Trideck, Inc. The president of the company could hire an outsider to replace the vice president, but often she will select an insider whom she knows well. What may look like discrimination to outsiders—"That company discriminates against persons not working for it"—may simply be a reflection of the difference in costs to the employer of acquiring relevant information about employees inside and outside the company.

Discrimination or an Information Problem?

Suppose the world is made up of just two kinds of people: those with characteristic X and those with characteristic Y—X people and Y people. Over time, we observe that most employers are X people and that they tend to hire and promote proportionally more X than Y people. Are the Y people being discriminated against?

They could be. Nothing we have said so far rules this out. But another explanation is that, over time, X employers have learned that Y people, on average, do not perform as well as X people. So in this example, we simply state that X people are not discriminating against Y people. Instead, Y people are not being hired and promoted as often as X people because, for whatever reason, Y people, on average, are not as productive as X people.

Suppose in this environment, an extremely productive Y person applies for a job with an X employer. The problem is that the X employer does not know—she lacks complete information about—the full abilities of the Y person. Furthermore, acquiring complete information is costly. She bases her decision to reject the Y person's job application on what she knows about Y people, which is that, on average, they are not as productive as X people. She makes this decision not because she has something against Y people but because acquiring complete information on every potential employee—X or Y—is simply too costly.

Not everything that looks like discrimination is only a problem of the high cost of information. Nonetheless, sometimes what looks like discrimination ("he doesn't like me; I'm a Y person") is a consequence of living in a world where acquiring complete information is too costly.

Legislation mandating equal employment opportunities requires employers to absorb some information costs to open labor markets to all. All but the smallest of firms are required to search for qualified Y persons who can perform the job even if the employer believes that the average Y person cannot. Requiring employers to forgo the use of a screening mechanism typically increases firm costs and raises prices to consumers, but the premise of the legislation is that the social benefits of having more Y persons in the mainstream of society more than outweigh such costs.

"WHY DO ECONOMISTS THINK IN TWOS?"

Student:

Before I read this chapter, I had thought that U.S. firms would rather pay low wages in other countries than to pay high wages in the United States. Now I realize that wages aren't the only thing that matters to a firm. The productivity of labor matters too.

Instructor:

Does this ring a bell?

Student:

What do you mean?

Instructor:

Well, one of the things emphasized in the "Thinking Like an Economist" feature in various chapters is that economists often compare one thing to another when trying to determine what economic actors will do. To illustrate, when a firm decides where to hire labor, it compares wage rates in various countries to productivity in various countries. The firm compares marginal revenue to marginal cost when it decides how much of a good to produce. Marginal revenue product is compared to marginal factor cost when a firm decides how much of a factor to hire or buy. A consumer who decides to buy more or less of various goods compares marginal utility to price.

Student:

What's the lesson here? Why do economists seem to think in twos?

Instructor:

The lesson goes back to something explained in Chapter 1: Usually there are costs and benefits to our activities. There is a cost to producing goods in the United States (paying high wages), but there is a benefit too (high productivity). There is a cost to producing an additional unit of a good (*MC*), but there is an additional benefit too (*MR*). There is a cost to hiring an additional unit of labor (the wage rate), but there is a benefit too (*VMP* or *MRP*). In the end, what matters is not the costs alone, nor the benefits alone, but the benefits relative to the costs.

Points to Remember

1. When firms are trying to decide where to hire workers (the United States or Mexico), wages are not the only factor that matters. Productivity matters too.
2. Economists often think in twos. They often compare the benefits and costs of doing X, where X can stand for various actions (e.g., hiring workers in various countries, producing an additional unit of a good, etc.).

a reader asks | "Does Education Matter to Income?"

The greater the demand is for my labor and the smaller the supply is, the higher my wage will be. One thing that can shift the factor demand curve for my labor to the right (and thus bring me a higher wage) is a rise in my *MPP*. So, does more education lead to a higher *MPP* and higher wages?

Certainly, some people with little education earn high salaries, but generally more education seems to raise one's productivity, and, as a result, it tends to raise one's pay. For example, in 2001, a person with a high school diploma had average annual earnings of $26,795; a person with a bachelor's degree, $50,623; and a person with a master's degree, $63,592.

Consider Charles, who is 22 years old and has just completed his associate's degree. He is trying to decide whether to continue his education. In 2001, a person with an associate's degree (as the highest degree) had average annual earnings of $34,744.

Let's look at Charles's lifetime earnings in two cases. On the one hand, if Charles stops his education with an associate's degree and works until he is 65 years old, he will earn $34,744 each year for 43 years,[10]

_____
10. We are not adjusting in our example for annual percentage increases in earnings.

for a total of $1,493,992. If, on the other hand, Charles goes on to get a master's degree and we assume it takes him 6 more years of schooling to do so, then he will earn $63,592 each year for the next 37 years, for a total of $2,352,904. The difference in lifetime earnings for a person with an associate's degree and a person with a master's degree is $858,912. Stated differently, Charles's lifetime earnings will be approximately 57 percent higher with a master's degree than with an associate's degree (as the highest degree).

The difference in lifetime earnings is even greater for a person with a doctorate. (In 2001, a person with a doctorate had average annual earnings of $85,675.) If we assume a doctorate requires 2 years of additional schooling beyond a master's degree, then the total lifetime earnings with a doctorate will be $2,998,625. The difference in lifetime earnings between an associate's degree and a doctorate is $1,504,633, more than 100 percent more lifetime earnings.

Or we can think of it this way. If going from an associate's degree to a doctorate more than doubles Charles's lifetime earnings, it is as if he produces a clone of his associate-degree self during his 8 more years of schooling. (What do you produce in school? Nothing is the wrong answer. You produce clones of yourself.)

Chapter Summary

DERIVED DEMAND

- The demand for a factor is derived; hence, it is called a *derived demand*. Specifically, it is derived from and directly related to the demand for the product that the factor goes to produce; for example, the demand for auto workers is derived from the demand for autos.

MRP, MFC, VMP

- Marginal revenue product (*MRP*) is the additional revenue generated by employing an additional factor unit. Marginal factor cost (*MFC*) is the additional cost incurred by employing an additional factor unit. The profit-maximizing firm buys the factor quantity at which $MRP = MFC$.

- The *MRP* curve is the firm's factor demand curve; it shows how much of a factor the firm buys at different prices.

- Value marginal product (*VMP*) is a measure of the value that each factor unit adds to the firm's product. Whereas $MRP = MR \times MPP$, $VMP = P \times MPP$. For a perfectly competitive firm, $P = MR$, so $MRP = VMP$. For a monopolist, a monopolistic competitor, or an oligopolist, $P > MR$; so $VMP > MRP$.

THE LEAST-COST RULE

- A firm minimizes costs by buying factors in the combination at which the *MPP*-to-price ratio for each factor is the same. For example, if there are two factors, labor (*L*) and capital (*K*), the least-cost rule reads $MPP_L/P_L = MPP_K/P_K$.

LABOR AND WAGES

- A change in the price of the product that labor produces or a change in the marginal physical product of labor (reflected in a shift in the *MPP* curve) will shift the demand curve for labor.

- The higher (lower) the elasticity of demand is for the product that labor produces, the higher (lower) the elasticity of demand is for labor. The higher (lower) the ratio is of labor cost to total cost, the higher (lower) the elasticity of demand is for labor. The more (fewer) substitutes there are for labor, the higher (lower) the elasticity of demand is for labor.

- As the wage rate rises, the quantity supplied of labor rises, *ceteris paribus*.

- At the equilibrium wage rate, the quantity supplied of labor equals the quantity demanded of labor.

DEMAND FOR AND SUPPLY OF LABOR

- The demand for labor is affected by (1) marginal revenue and (2) marginal physical product. The supply of labor is affected by (1) wage rates in other labor markets, (2) the nonpecuniary aspects of the job, (3) the number of persons who can do the job, (4) training costs, and (5) moving costs.

MARGINAL PRODUCTIVITY THEORY

- Marginal productivity theory states that firms in competitive or perfect product and factor markets pay their factors their marginal revenue products.

Key Terms and Concepts

Derived Demand	Marginal Factor Cost (*MFC*)	Elasticity of Demand for Labor
Marginal Revenue Product (*MRP*)	Factor Price Taker	Marginal Productivity Theory
Value Marginal Product (*VMP*)	Least-Cost Rule	Screening

Questions and Problems

1 What does it mean to say that the demand for a factor is a derived demand?

2 Why is the *MRP* curve a firm's factor demand curve?

3 "*VMP* = *MRP* for a price taker but not for a price searcher." Do you agree or disagree with this statement? Explain your answer.

4 Compare the firm's least-cost rule to how buyers allocate their consumption dollars.

5 The supply curve is horizontal for a factor price taker; however, the industry supply curve is upward sloping. Explain why this occurs.

6 What forces and factors determine the wage rate for a particular type of labor?

7 What is the relationship between labor productivity and wage rates?

8 What might be one effect of government legislating wage rates?

9 Using the theory developed in this chapter, explain the following:

   a. Why a worker in Ethiopia is likely to earn much less than a worker in Japan.

   b. Why the army expects recruitment to rise during economic recessions.

   c. Why basketball stars earn relatively large incomes.

   d. Why jobs that carry a health risk offer higher pay than jobs that do not, *ceteris paribus*.

10 Discuss the factors that might prevent the equalization of wage rates for identical or comparable jobs across labor markets.

11 Prepare a list of questions that an interviewer is likely to ask an interviewee in a job interview. Try to identify which of the questions are part of the interviewer's screening process.

12 Explain why the market demand curve for labor is not simply the horizontal addition of the firms' demand curves for labor.

13 Discuss the firm's objective, its constraints, and how it makes choices in its role as a buyer of resources.

14 Explain the relationship between each of the following pairs of concepts:

   a. The elasticity of demand for a product and the elasticity of demand for the labor that produces the product.

   b. The ratio of labor cost to total cost and the elasticity of demand for labor.

   c. The number of substitutes for labor and the elasticity of demand for labor.

15 How might you go about determining whether a person is worth the salary he or she is paid?

16 What do substitution and income effects have to do with the supply curve of labor?

Working with Numbers and Graphs

1   Determine the appropriate numbers for the lettered spaces.

(1) Units of Factor X	(2) Quantity of Output	(3) Marginal Physical Product of X (MPP_x)	(4) Product Price, Marginal Revenue $(P = MR)$	(5) Total Revenue	(6) Marginal Revenue Product of X (MRP_x)
0	15	0	$8	F	L
1	24	A	8	G	M
2	32	B	8	H	N
3	39	C	8	I	O
4	45	D	8	J	P
5	50	E	8	K	Q

2   If the price of a factor is constant at $48, how many units of the factor will the firm buy?

3   In one diagram, draw the *VMP* curve and the *MRP* curve for an oligopolist. Explain why the curves look the way you drew them.

4   Explain why the factor supply curve is horizontal for a factor price taker.

5   Look at the two factor demand curves in the following figure. Is the price of the product that labor goes to produce higher for MRP_2 than for MRP_1? Explain your answer.

CHAPTER 13

WAGES, UNIONS, AND LABOR

© JIM WEST/ALAMY

Introduction Certain organizations seem to engender controversy. Labor unions are such organizations. Some people are strongly prounion; others are strongly antiunion. And many millions of people between these extremes don't have a strong opinion on labor unions. In this chapter, we discuss labor unions in as objective, unbiased a way as possible. The topics include the objectives, practices, and effects of unions.

THE FACTS AND FIGURES OF LABOR UNIONS

This section discusses the different types of labor unions and presents some statistics that show the place of unions within the overall labor force.

Types of Unions

Craft (Trade) Union
A union whose membership is made up of individuals who practice the same craft or trade.

Industrial Union
A union whose membership is made up of individuals who work in the same firm or industry but do not all practice the same craft or trade.

Public Employee Union
A union whose membership is made up of individuals who work for the local, state, or federal government.

Economists often speak of three different types of labor unions: craft (trade) unions, industrial unions, and public employee unions. A **craft** or **trade union** is a union whose membership is made up of individuals who practice the same craft or trade. Examples are the plumbers', electricians', and musicians' unions.

An **industrial union** is a union whose membership is made up of workers who work in the same firm or industry but who do not all practice the same craft or trade. Examples are the autoworkers' and the steelworkers' unions. For an industrial union to be successful, it must unionize all firms in an industry. If it does not, union firms will face competition from (possibly lower cost) nonunion firms, which may lead to a decrease in the number of union firms and workers.

A **public employee union** is a union whose membership is made up of workers who work for the local, state, or federal government. Examples include teachers', police, and firefighters' unions.

Besides these three types of unions, some economists hold that employee associations, such as the American Medical Association (AMA), the American Association of University Professors (AAUP), and the American Bar Association (ABA), constitute a type of union. An **employee association** is an organization whose members belong to a particular profession. Many people would probably not place professional employee associations in the union category. Some economists argue, however, that employee associations often have the same objectives and implement the same practices to meet those objectives as craft, industrial, and public employee unions; consequently, these associations should be considered unions.

Employee Association
An organization whose members belong to a particular profession.

Union Membership: The United States and Abroad

Union membership as a percentage of the U.S. labor force (total number of union members divided by total work force) was 5.6 percent in 1910, rising to about 12 percent in 1920. By 1930, it was down to about 7.4 percent, and in 1934 it fell to approximately 5 percent. From the late 1930s until the mid-1950s, union membership as a percentage of the labor force grew. It reached its peak of 25 percent in the mid-1950s. In recent years, union membership has declined. In 1983, it was 20.1 percent; in 1998, it was 13.9 percent; and in 2006, it was 12 percent.

Union membership as a percentage of the labor force is much higher in some countries than it is in the United States. For example, it is 41 percent in Belgium, 30 percent in Finland, 26 percent in Norway, and 53 percent in Italy.

OBJECTIVES OF LABOR UNIONS

Labor unions usually seek one of three objectives: (1) to employ all their members, (2) to maximize the total wage bill, or (3) to maximize income for a limited number of union members.

Employment for All Members

To illustrate the objective of employment for all of a union's members, suppose the demand curve in Exhibit 1 represents the demand for labor in a given union. Also assume

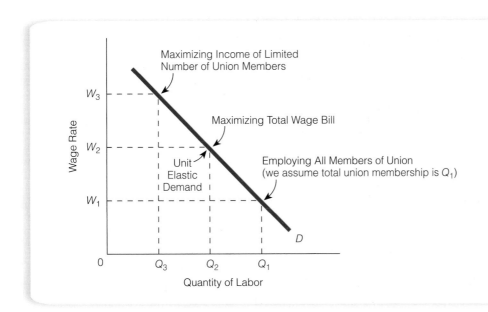

exhibit 1

Labor Union Objectives

If total membership in the union is Q_1, and the union's objective is employment for all its members, it chooses W_1. If the objective is to maximize the total wage bill, it chooses W_2, where the elasticity of demand for labor equals 1. If the union's objective is to maximize the income of a limited number of union workers (represented by Q_3), it chooses W_3.

the total membership of the union is Q_1. If the objective of the union is to have its total membership employed, then the wage rate that must exist in the market is W_1. At W_1, firms want to hire the total union membership.

Maximizing the Total Wage Bill

The total wage bill received by the membership of a union is equal to the wage rate multiplied by the number of labor hours worked. A possible objective of a labor union is to maximize this dollar amount, that is, to maximize the number of dollars coming *from* the employer *to* union members.

In Exhibit 1, the wage rate that maximizes the total wage bill is W_2. At W_2, the quantity of labor is Q_2 and the elasticity of demand for labor is equal to 1. Recall that total revenue (or total expenditure) is maximized when price elasticity of demand is equal to 1, or demand has unit elasticity. It follows that the total wage bill is maximized at that point where the demand for labor is unit elastic. However, less union labor is working at W_2 than at W_1, indicating that there is a trade-off between higher wages and the employment of union members.

Maximizing Income for a Limited Number of Union Members

Some economists have suggested that a labor union might want neither total employment of its membership nor maximization of the total wage bill. Instead, it might prefer to maximize income for a *limited number* of union members, perhaps those with the most influence or seniority in the union. Suppose this group is represented by Q_3 in Exhibit 1. The highest wage at which this group can be employed is W_3; thus, the union might seek this wage rate instead of any lower rate.

microtheme ➜ In an earlier chapter, we said that economic agents (firms, individuals, etc.) have objectives. Once we know their objectives, we can predict their behavior. To illustrate, if the firm's objective is to maximize profit, then it will produce the quantity of output at which $MR = MC$. We also know that different behavior is a result of different objectives. For example, the firm will behave differently if it wants to maximize profit than if it wants to maximize sales. The same idea holds with respect to labor unions. If the objective of the labor union is to, say, employ all the workers in the union, then it will behave differently from when its objective is to maximize the income for a limited number of individuals. In the first case, the wage rate that the union seeks will be lower than in the second case.

Wage-Employment Trade-Off

Exhibit 1 suggests that a union can get higher wage rates, but some of the union members will lose their jobs in the process. Hence, there is a wage-employment trade-off that depends on the *elasticity of demand for labor*.

To illustrate, consider the demand for labor in two unions, A and B, in Exhibit 2. Suppose both unions bargain for a wage increase from W_1 to W_2. The quantity of labor drops much more in union B, where demand for labor is elastic between the two wage rates, than in union A, where the demand for labor is inelastic between the two wage rates. We would expect union B to be less likely than union A to push for higher wages, *ceteris paribus*. The reason is that the wage-employment trade-off is more pronounced for union B than for union A. It is simply costlier (in terms of union members' jobs) for union B to push for higher wages than it is for union A.

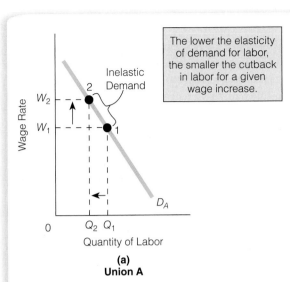

The lower the elasticity of demand for labor, the smaller the cutback in labor for a given wage increase.

(a)
Union A

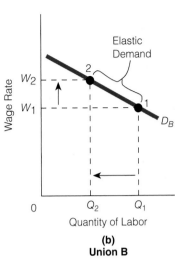

(b)
Union B

exhibit 2

The Wage-Employment Tradeoff: Two Cases

For union A, which has an inelastic demand for its labor between W_1 and W_2, a higher wage rate brings about a smaller cutback in the quantity of labor than for union B, which has an elastic demand for its labor between W_1 and W_2. We predict that union B will be less likely to push for higher wages than union A because its wage-employment tradeoff is more pronounced.

 Finding ECONOMICS

In a Union Roundtable Discussion

The leaders of a union are sitting around the table discussing what to do in the current situation. One person argues for a 7 percent wage increase. Another person argues for a 10 percent wage increase, saying, "I don't think a 10 percent wage increase will cost us many jobs—if any." Where is the economics?

The economics appears in the statement about the 10 percent wage increase. Believing that few jobs will be lost, if any, tells us she believes either that the wage-employment trade-off is small or that the demand for union labor is highly inelastic (maybe even perfectly inelastic if there will be *no loss* of jobs).

PRACTICES OF LABOR UNIONS

This section explains how labor unions try to meet their objectives by influencing one or more of the following factors: the elasticity of demand for labor, the demand for labor, and the supply of labor. We also discuss how unions can directly affect wages.

Affecting Elasticity of Demand for Union Labor

Exhibit 2 shows that the lower the elasticity of demand for labor, the smaller the cutback in labor for any given wage increase. Obviously, the smaller the cutback in labor for a given wage increase, the better it is from the viewpoint of the labor union. Given a choice between losing either 200 jobs or 50 jobs because of a wage rate increase of $2, the labor union prefers to lose the smaller number of jobs. Thus, a labor union looks for ways to lower the elasticity of demand for its labor. It does this mainly by attempting to reduce the availability of substitutes.

AVAILABILITY OF SUBSTITUTE PRODUCTS Consider the autoworkers' union, whose members produce American automobiles. We know that the lower the elasticity of demand for American automobiles, the lower the elasticity of demand for the labor that produces automobiles. We would expect, then, that unions would attempt to reduce the availability of substitutes for the products they produce through such means as import restrictions.

AVAILABILITY OF SUBSTITUTE FACTORS The fewer the substitute factors for union labor, the lower the elasticity of demand for union labor. There are two general substitutes for union labor: nonunion labor and certain types of machines. For example, a musical synthesizer (which can sound like many different instruments) is a substitute for a group of musicians playing different instruments. Labor unions have often attempted to reduce the availability of substitute factors—both the nonunion labor variety and the nonhuman variety. Thus, labor unions commonly oppose the relaxation of immigration laws, they usually favor the repatriation of illegal aliens, they generally are in favor of a high minimum wage (which increases the relative price of nonunion labor vis-à-vis union labor), and they usually oppose machines that can be substituted for their labor. Also, in the area of construction, unions usually specify that certain jobs are done by, say, electricians only (thus prohibiting substitute factors from being employed on certain jobs).

Affecting the Demand for Union Labor

Labor unions can try to meet their objectives by increasing the demand for union labor. All other things held constant, this leads to higher wage rates and more union labor employed. How can labor unions increase the demand for their labor? Consider the following possibilities.

INCREASING PRODUCT DEMAND Unions occasionally urge the buying public to buy the products produced by union labor. Union advertisements urge people to "look for the union label" or to look for the label that reads "Made in the U.S.A." As already mentioned, unions sometimes also support legislation that either keeps out imports altogether or that makes them more expensive.

INCREASING SUBSTITUTE FACTOR PRICES If union action leads to a rise in the relative price of factors that are substitutes for union labor, the demand for union labor rises. (Recall that if X and Y are substitutes and the price of X rises, so does the demand for Y.) For this reason, unions have often lobbied for an increase in the minimum wage—the wage received mostly by unskilled labor, which is a substitute for skilled union labor. The first minimum wage legislation was passed in 1938 when many companies were moving from the unionized North to the nonunionized South. The minimum wage made the nonunionized, relatively unskilled labor in the South more expensive and is said to have slowed the movement of companies to the South.

INCREASING MARGINAL PHYSICAL PRODUCT If unions can increase the productivity of their members, the demand for their labor will rise. With this in mind, unions prefer to add skilled labor to their ranks, and they sometimes undertake training programs for new entrants.

Finding ECONOMICS

In a Friend's Remark

Smith, who lives in Michigan, is currently speaking with a friend who is a member of a labor union and works for General Motors. Smith's friend knows that Smith recently bought a car made in Germany. The friend says to Smith, "You know, you really should buy American cars." Where is the economics?

(continued)

Finding Economics (continued)

Most likely, Smith is witnessing his friend's attempt to increase the demand for American cars. Perhaps because his friend knows that the demand for his services (in the American auto industry) is dependent on (derived from) the demand for American cars.

Affecting the Supply of Union Labor

Labor unions try to meet their objectives also by decreasing the supply of labor because a decreased supply translates into higher wage rates. How might the labor union decrease the supply of labor from what it might be if the labor union did not exist? One way is to control the supply of labor in a market.

Craft unions, in particular, have been moderately successful in getting employers to hire only union labor. In the past, they were successful at turning some businesses into closed shops. A **closed shop** is an organization in which an employee must belong to the union before being able to work. (In contrast, in an *open shop,* an employer may hire union or nonunion workers.) When unions can determine, or at least control in some way, the supply of labor in a given market, they can decrease it from what it would be otherwise. They can do this by restricting membership, by requiring long apprenticeships, or by rigid certification requirements. The closed shop was prohibited in 1947 by the Taft-Hartley Act.

The union shop, however, is legal in many states today. A **union shop** is an organization that does not require individuals to be union members to be hired but does require them to join the union within a certain period of time after becoming employed.

Today, unions typically argue for union shops, against open shops, and against the prohibition of closed shops. They also typically argue against state right-to-work laws (which some, but not all, states have), which make it illegal to require union membership for purposes of employment. (The Taft-Hartley Act allowed states to pass right-to-work laws and thus to override federal legislation that legalized union shops.) In short, the union shop is illegal in right-to-work states.

Affecting Wages Directly: Collective Bargaining

Besides increasing wage rates indirectly by influencing the demand for and supply of their labor, unions can directly affect wage rates through collective bargaining. **Collective bargaining** is the process whereby wage rates are determined by union's bargaining with management on behalf of all its members. In collective bargaining, union members act together as a single unit to increase their bargaining power with management. On the other side of the market, the employers of labor may also band together and act as one unit, with the same objective: to increase their bargaining power.

From the viewpoint of the labor union, collective bargaining is unlikely to be successful unless the union can strike. A **strike** occurs when unionized employees refuse to work at a certain wage or under certain conditions. Exhibit 3 illustrates the effects of successful union collective bargaining. Suppose the initial wage rate that exists in the labor market is the competitive wage rate W_1. This is the wage rate that would exist if

Closed Shop
An organization in which an employee must belong to the union before he or she can be hired.

Union Shop
An organization in which a worker is not required to be a member of the union to be hired but must become a member within a certain period of time after being employed.

Collective Bargaining
The process whereby wage rates and other issues are determined by a union bargaining with management on behalf of all union members.

exhibit 3

Successful Collective Bargaining by the Union

We start at a wage rate of W_1. The union's objective is to increase the wage rate to W_2. This means the union holds that the new supply curve of labor is $S'S$—the heavy supply curve. To convince management that the new supply curve looks as the union says it does, the union will have to either threaten a strike or call one. We assume that the union is successful at raising the wage rate to W_2. As a consequence, the quantity of labor employed is less than it would have been at W_1.

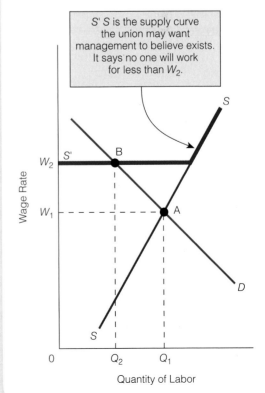

S' S is the supply curve the union may want management to believe exists. It says no one will work for less than W_2.

Strike
The situation in which union employees refuse to work at a certain wage or under certain conditions.

each employee were to bargain separately with management. The equilibrium quantity of labor is Q_1.

Management and the union (which represents all labor in this market) now sit down at a collective bargaining session. The union specifies that it wants a wage rate of W_2 and says that *none of its members will work at a lower wage rate.* Thus the union holds that the new supply curve is $S'S$—the heavy supply curve in Exhibit 3. In effect, the union is telling management that it cannot hire anyone for a wage rate lower than W_2.

Whether the union can bring about this higher wage rate (W_2) depends on whether it can prevent labor from working at less than this wage. That is, if management does not initially agree to W_2, the union will have to call a strike and show management that it cannot hire any labor for a wage rate lower than W_2. It has to convince management that the new supply curve looks the way the union says it looks. We assume in Exhibit 3 that the strike threat, or actual strike, is successful for the union and that management agrees to the higher wage rate of W_2. As a result, the quantity of labor employed, Q_2, is less than it would have been at W_1. The new equilibrium is at point B instead of point A.

Strikes

The purpose of a strike is to convince management that the supply curve is what the union says it is. Often, this depends on the ability of striking union employees to prevent nonstriking and nonunion employees from working for management at a lower wage rate than the union is seeking through collective bargaining. For example, if management can easily hire individuals at a wage rate lower than W_2 in Exhibit 3, it will not be convinced that the heavy supply curve is the relevant supply curve.

Common MISCONCEPTIONS

About Higher Wages and the Firm's Labor Costs

A common belief is that, if a striking labor union receives higher wages, the firm that employs the union workers will incur higher labor costs. For example, if a company employs 100 workers, each at $100 a day, its daily wage bill is $10,000. If the employees strike for and receive, say, $120 a day, then the daily wage bill rises to $12,000. But, of course, labor costs will increase only if the demand for labor is perfectly inelastic (i.e., the same number of workers are employed no matter what the wage rate is). If the demand for labor is downward sloping, then fewer persons will be employed at a higher wage than at a lower wage.

What matters to the daily wage bill is the elasticity of demand for labor—whether demand is elastic or inelastic. To illustrate, suppose the demand for labor is elastic and the wage rises 20 percent from $100 to $120. As a result, the quantity demanded of labor declines by something more than 20 percent. Let's say it declines by 30 percent (from 100 workers to 70 workers). Multiplying 70 workers receiving $120 a day gives us a daily wage bill of $8,400.

SELF-TEST

(Answers to Self-Test questions are in the Self-Test Appendix.)

1. What will lower the demand for union labor?
2. What is the difference between a closed shop and a union shop?
3. What is the objective of a strike?

TECHNOLOGY, THE PRICE OF COMPETING FACTORS, AND DISPLACED WORKERS[1]

For most of the 18th century in England, spinners and weavers worked on hand-operated spinning wheels and looms. Then in the 1770s, a mechanical spinner was invented that required steam or water power, and so yarn-spinning factories were set up near water mills. The factory workers, working with mechanical spinners, could produce 100 times more yarn in a day than they could using hand-operated spinners.

Because of the increased supply of yarn, the price fell and the quantity demanded of yarn increased substantially. In turn, this increased the demand for weavers, who continued to use hand-operated looms. As a result of the increased demand for weavers, their wages increased. In reaction to the higher wages for weavers, entrepreneurs and inventors

began to experiment with different kinds of weaving machines. Their experiments began to pay off; in 1787, the power loom was invented, although it was not perfected until the 1820s. By the 1830s, two workers using a power loom could produce in one day 20 times what a weaver could produce on a hand-operated loom.

Soon, the weavers who used hand-operated looms found themselves without jobs, displaced by the power loom. Some of the displaced workers showed their frustration and anger at their predicament by burning power looms and factories.

The story of spinners and weavers in 18th-century England helps us realize two important points about technology. First, as long as there are advancements in technology, some workers will be temporarily displaced. Second, an advance in technology often has an identifiable cause; it doesn't simply fall out of the sky. If it had not been for the higher weavers' wages, the power loom might not have been invented.

1. This feature is based on Elizabeth Hoffman, "How Can Displaced Workers Find Better Jobs?" in *Second Thoughts: Myths and Morals of U.S. Economic History*, ed. by Donald McCloskey (Oxford: Oxford University Press, 1993).

EFFECTS OF LABOR UNIONS

What are the effects of labor unions on wage rates? Are the effects the same in all labor markets? This section addresses these two questions.

The Case of Monopsony

A single buyer in a factor market is known as a **monopsony**. Some economists refer to a monopsony as a buyer's monopoly. Whereas a monopoly is a single seller of a product, a monopsony is a single buyer.

For example, if a firm in a small town is the only buyer of labor because there are no other firms for miles around, the firm would be a monopsony. Because it is a monopsony, it cannot buy additional units of a factor without increasing the price it pays for it (in much the same way that a monopolist in the product market cannot sell an additional unit of its good without lowering price). The reason is that the supply of labor it faces is the market supply of labor.

For the monopsonist, marginal factor cost increases as it buys additional units of a factor, and the supply curve of the factor *is not the same* as the monopsonist's marginal factor cost curve. In the last chapter, we saw that for a price taker in the factor market, marginal factor cost was constant, and the *MFC* curve was the same as the supply curve for the factor. A monopsonist is not a price taker in the factor market: Marginal factor cost rises as it buys additional units of a factor, and its *MFC* curve and supply curve (for the factor) are not the same.

Monopsony
A single buyer in a factor market.

327

economics 24/7

COLLEGE PROFESSORS' OBJECTIVES

Labor unions try to meet their objectives by influencing the elasticity of demand and the demand itself for labor. To influence these factors, they try to (1) reduce the availability of substitute products, (2) reduce the availability of substitute factors, (3) increase demand for the product they produce, (4) increase substitute factor prices, and (5) increase the MPP of their members. Labor unions try to do (1) and (2) because they want the elasticity of demand for their labor to be low (so that any wage increase only slightly reduces the quantity demanded of union labor). They try to do (3), (4), and (5) because they want the demand for their labor to be high (so that they will receive high wages). Thus, labor unions have as overall objectives to reduce the wage-employment trade-off and to raise their wages. Unionized workers are not the only group of people with these overall objectives.

Do classroom college professors do some of the same things that labor unions do, that is, reduce their wage-employment trade-off and raise their wages? Some anecdotal evidence that they do is often found by listening to how college professors discuss college education. Let's examine the behavior of college professors in terms of three of the five factors mentioned with respect to labor unions: (1) reduce the availability of substitute services, (2) reduce

© COMSTOCK IMAGES/JUPITER IMAGES

the availability of substitute factors, and (3) increase demand for what they sell.

Reduce the Availability of Substitute Services

Classroom college professors often argue that the college classroom is the best setting in which to learn. In a classroom, lectures can be given, discussions carried out, questions asked and answered, and so on.[2]

Alternatives, such as courses on the Internet, correspondence courses, and other educational settings, cannot take the place of the college classroom experience. The implication is that the classroom experience is unique and that, if it is unique, it has no substitutes.

Recall that the fewer substitutes there are for a good or service, the lower the price elasticity of demand is for the good or service, *ceteris paribus*. And, of course, as the elasticity of demand for the service of college professors decreases, the wage-employment trade-off diminishes for the professors.

Are college professors simply acting selfishly when they argue this way, or are they stating the truth? The answer to both questions could

---

2. The author of the text is a college professor and often finds he argues this way. He is not saying anything about college professors in this feature that may not hold for him too.

As shown in Exhibit 4, marginal factor cost increases as additional units of the factor are purchased. Notice in part (a) that as workers are added, the wage rate rises. For example, for the monopsonist to employ two workers, the wage rate must rise from $6.00 per hour to $6.05. To employ three workers, the monopsonist must offer to pay $6.10. Comparing column 2 with column 4, we notice that the marginal factor cost for a monopsonist is greater than the wage rate (in the same way that for a monopolist in a product market, price is greater than marginal revenue). Plotting columns 1 and 2 gives the supply curve for the monopsonist [see Exhibit 4(b)]; plotting columns 1 and 4 gives the monopsonist's *MFC* curve. Because *MFC* is greater than the wage rate, the supply curve lies below the *MFC* curve.

Exhibit 4(b) shows that the monopsonist chooses to purchase Q_1 units of labor (where $MRP = MFC$) and that it pays a wage rate of W_1 (the wage rate necessary to get Q_1 workers to offer their services).

If the monopsonist were to pay workers what their services were worth to it (as represented by the *MRP* curve), it would pay a higher wage. Some persons contend be yes. The college classroom may be the best setting in which to learn, and it may also be in the best interest of college professors to make sure that students (customers) understand this.

Reduce the Availability of Substitute Factors

College professors often argue against large classes (90 students or more), asserting that students can get a better education when classes are smaller—ideally, about 30 students. In a smaller class, the professor can give students more individual attention, can discuss things with them that are impossible to discuss in large lecture halls, can give them more writing assignments, which are important to their education, and so on.

All the rationales sound reasonable, and they may be true. But arguing against large classes is also a way of trying to reduce the availability of substitute factors. To illustrate, suppose that 10 economics professors are at one college, that each professor teaches 3 classes a semester, and that classes are limited to 30 students each. Thus, 30 economics classes are offered each semester. Furthermore, suppose students may enroll in any of the 30 economics classes. In this setting, Professor Polidor teaches, say, 3 classes, and 9 professors are substitutes for him (who teach a total of 27 substitute courses for his courses).

Then one day, 1 of the 10 economics professors retires from the college. The college mandates that the new professor who replaces her must teach 3 classes each semester and that each class must have 90 students. Thus, the new professor teaches 3 times as many students each semester as every other professor. By raising class size for the new professor, is the university adding only 1 professor or the equivalent of 3 professors?

From Professor Polidor's point of view, he still teaches three classes a semester, and there are still only nine professors who are substitutes for him. But under the old standard, where one class equals 30 students, the new professor is doing her job and the job of two other professors. It is as if the new professor brought two other (shadow) professors with

her; she walked into the college as three people, not as a single person. So instead of Professor Polidor having 9 other professors who are substitutes for him (together teaching 27 substitute classes), he effectively has 11 other professors who are substitutes for him (together teaching 33 substitute classes). In conclusion, when Professor Polidor argues against big classes, he effectively argues against substitutes for himself.

Increase Demand for What Professors Sell

Most college professors argue in favor of subsidies for higher education.[3] Occasionally, a university professor may say that all higher education should be privatized and that government shouldn't use tax dollars to subsidize a person's college education, but this is a rare event. Most college professors are in favor of subsidies for college education, and many of them would like to see the subsidies increased. We do not mean to imply that professors' arguments for subsidizing higher education are fallacious; we state only that they make these arguments. Certainly, however, subsidies for higher education cause the demand for a college education to be higher than it would be otherwise. And if the demand for a college education is higher, so is the demand for college professors because the demand for college professors is a derived demand.

Conclusion

Many college professors argue that the college classroom is the best setting in which to learn. They also argue against large classes and in favor of subsidies for higher education. They may be sincere in their arguments, and, moreover, their arguments may be solid and true. Still, these positions, if realized, have the effect of reducing the college professor wage-employment trade-off and increasing college professors' salaries.

---

3. For our purposes here, think of the subsidy as a dollar rebate for each unit of education purchased. This has the effect of shifting the demand curve upward vertically by a distance equal to the subsidy.

that labor unions and collective bargaining are necessary in such situations where labor is paid less than its marginal revenue product. Furthermore, they argue that successful collective bargaining on the part of the labor union in this setting will not be subject to the wage-employment trade-off it encounters in other settings, as illustrated in Exhibit 4(c).

In Exhibit 4(c), successful collective bargaining by the labor union moves the wage rate from W_1 to W_2. The labor union is essentially saying to the monopsonist that it cannot hire any labor below W_2. This changes the monopsonist's marginal factor cost curve from MFC to MFC', which corresponds to the new supply curve the monopsonist faces, $S'S$. The monopsonist once again purchases the quantity of labor at which marginal revenue product equals marginal factor cost. But now, because the marginal factor cost curve is MFC', equality is at Q_2 workers and a wage rate of W_2. Therefore, over a range, there is no wage-employment trade-off for the labor union when it faces a monopsonist. It can raise both the wage rate and the number of workers employed.

exhibit 4

The Labor Union and the Monopsonist

(a) For the monopsonist, *MFC* > wage rate. This implies that the supply curve the monopsonist faces lies below its *MFC* curve. (b) The monopsonist purchases Q_1 quantity of labor and pays a wage rate of W_1, which is less than *MRP* (labor is being paid less than its *MRP*). (c) If the labor union succeeds in increasing the wage rate from W_1 to W_2 through collective bargaining, then the firm will also hire more labor (Q_2 instead of Q_1). We conclude that in the case of monopsony, higher wage rates (over a range) do not imply fewer persons working.

(1) Workers	(2) Wage Rate	(3) Total Labor Cost (1) × (2)	(4) Marginal Factor Cost $\frac{\Delta(3)}{\Delta(1)}$
0	—	—	—
1	$6.00	$6.00	$6.00
2	6.05	12.10	6.10
3	6.10	18.30	6.20
4	6.15	24.60	6.30
5	6.20	31.00	6.40

(a)

(b)

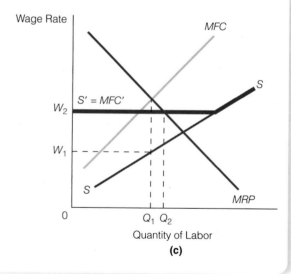

(c)

micro*theme* → All actors have to make certain decisions. An individual consumer has to decide which combination of goods to buy (how much of good X and how much of good Y); a firm has to decide which quantity of output to produce. A firm that is a monopsonist in a factor market also has to make a decision: how much of a factor (e.g., labor) to hire. It decides to buy the quantity of a factor at which *MRP* = *MFC*.

Unions' Effects on Wages

Most studies show that some unions have increased their members' wages substantially, whereas other unions have not increased their members' wages at all. Work by H. Gregg Lewis concludes that during the period 1920–1979, the average wage of union members was 10 to 15 percent higher than that of comparable nonunion labor. (Keep in mind, though, that the union-nonunion wage differential can differ quite a bit in different years and between industries.) For data on this subject, see Exhibit 5.

exhibit 5

Median Weekly Earnings in the Union and Nonunion Sectors, Selected Industries, 2006

In four of the five (selected) industries shown, union workers earned a higher weekly salary in 2006 than did nonunion workers. Overall in 2006, the median weekly salary was $827 for a union worker and $642 for a nonunion worker (not shown).

Source: Statistical Abstract of the United States, 2007.

Median Weekly Earnings of Persons Represented by Unions

Median Weekly Earnings of Persons Not Represented by Unions

Construction: $956 / $610
Manufacturing: $753 / $692
Wholesale and Retail Trade: $632 / $575
Finance, Insurance, and Real Estate: $651 / $759
Services: $794 / $550

THE UNION-NONUNION WAGE GAP Exhibit 6 illustrates the theoretical basis of the observation that higher union wages lead to lower nonunion wages or to a union-nonunion wage gap. Two sectors of the labor market are shown: the unionized sector in part (a) and the nonunionized sector in part (b). We assume that labor is homogeneous and that the wage rate is $15 an hour in both sectors.

exhibit 6

The Effect of Labor Unions on Union and Nonunion Wages

We begin at a wage rate of $15 in both the unionized sector, (a), and the nonunion-ized sector, (b). Next, the union manages to increase its wage rate to $18 either through collective bargaining or by decreasing the supply of labor in the unionized sector (shown). Fewer persons now work in the unionized sector, and we assume that those persons who lose their jobs move to the nonunionized sector. The supply of labor in the nonunionized sector rises, and the wage rate falls.

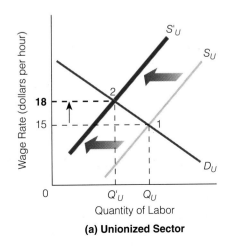

Changes in supply conditions and wage rates in the unionized sector can cause changes in supply and wage rates in the nonunionized sector.

(a) Unionized Sector

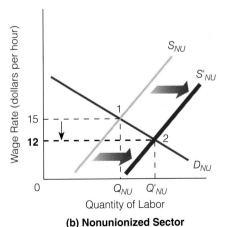

(b) Nonunionized Sector

The labor union either collectively bargains to a higher wage rate of $18 an hour or manages to reduce supply so that the higher wage rate comes about (the exhibit shows a decrease in supply). As a consequence, less labor is employed in the unionized sector. If the persons who now are not working in the unionized sector can work in the nonunionized sector, then the supply of labor in the nonunionized sector increases from S_{NU} to S'_{NU} and the wage rate in the nonunionized sector falls to $12 an hour. Therefore, there are theoretical and empirical reasons for believing that labor unions increase the wages of union employees and decrease the wages of nonunion employees.

However, the higher wages that union employees receive through unionization do not seem to outweigh the lower wages that nonunion employees receive in terms of the percentage of the national income that goes to labor. The percentage of the national income that goes to labor (union plus nonunion labor) has been fairly constant over time. In fact, it was approximately the same when unions were weak and union membership was relatively low as when unions were strong and union membership was relatively high.

WHY DON'T EMPLOYERS PAY? The layperson's view of labor unions is that they obtain higher wages for their members *at the expense of the owners of the firms,* not at the expense of other workers. The preceding section suggests that this may not be true—that the higher wages going to union employees do not come out of profits.

To explain why, we need to differentiate between the short run and the long run. In the theory of perfect competition, when there are short-run profits, new firms enter the industry, the industry supply curve shifts rightward, prices fall, and profits are competed away. Conversely, when there are short-run losses, firms exit the industry, the industry supply curve shifts leftward, prices increase, and losses finally disappear. So in the long run, there is zero economic profit in the perfectly competitive market.

In this market structure, consider a labor union that manages to obtain higher wages for its members. In the short run, these higher wages can diminish profits—the way any cost increase would diminish profits, *ceteris paribus*—but in the long run, there will be adjustments as firms exit the industry, supply curves shift, and prices change. In the long run, zero economic profit will exist. Therefore, in the short run, higher wages may come out of profits, but in the long run this isn't likely.

Thinking like AN ECONOMIST

Primary and Secondary Effects

E conomists make the important distinction between primary and secondary effects, that is, between what happens in the short run and what happens in the long run. For example, higher wages for union workers may initially come at the expense of profits, but as time passes this may not continue to be the case.

Unions' Effects on Prices

One effect of labor unions is that union wages are relatively higher and nonunion wages are relatively lower. The higher union wages mean higher costs for the firms that employ union labor, and higher costs affect supply curves, which in turn affect product prices. Therefore, higher union wages will cause higher prices for the products that the union labor produces. Conversely, lower nonunion wages mean lower costs for the firms that employ nonunion labor and thus lower prices for the products produced by nonunion labor.

economics 24/7

ARE YOU READY FOR SOME FOOTBALL?

Sometimes, firms that sell a similar good try to form a cartel so that they can act as a monopoly. Can firms that buy a factor do the same, that is, form a cartel so that they can act as a monopsony? Students know such a "firm." Many universities and colleges have banded together to buy the services of college-bound athletes. In other words, they have entered into a cartel agreement to reduce the monetary competition among themselves for college-bound athletes. The National Collegiate Athletic Association (NCAA) is the cartel or monopsony enforcer.

© PAN AMERICA/JUPITER IMAGES

Here's how it works. The NCAA sets certain rules and regulations by which its member universities and colleges must abide or else face punishment and fines. For example, universities and colleges are prohibited from offering salaries to athletes to play on their teams. They are prohibited from making work for them at the university or paying them relatively high wage rates for a job that usually pays much less—for example, paying athletes $30 an hour to reshelve books in the university library. Universities and colleges are also prohibited from offering inducements such as cars, clothes, and trips to attract athletes.

The stated objectives of these NCAA regulations are to maintain the amateur standing of college athletes, to prevent the rich schools from getting all the good players, and to enhance the competitiveness of college sports. Some economists suggest that some schools may have other objectives. They note that college athletics can be a revenue-raising activity for schools and that these institutions would rather

pay college athletes less than their marginal revenue products (the way a monopsony does) to play sports. Currently, universities and colleges openly compete for athletes by offering scholarships, free room and board, and school jobs. They also compete in terms of their academic reputations and the reputations of their sports programs (obviously, some find it easier to do this than others).

Although the practice is prohibited, some universities and colleges compete for athletes in ways not sanctioned by the NCAA; that is, they compete, as it is said, under the table. Such practices are evidence, some economists maintain, that certain schools are cheating on the cartel agreement. Such cheating usually benefits the college athletes, who receive a payment for their athletic abilities that is closer to their marginal revenue products. For example, some college athletes, many of whom come from families of modest means, drive flashy, expensive cars, which often come from community friends of the university or boosters of its sports program. Such payments to college athletes may be prohibited by the NCAA, but, as we have seen, members of cartels (of the monopoly or monopsony variety) usually find ways of evading the rules.

Not all economists agree that the NCAA is a cartel. Some economists argue that paying college athletes would diminish the reputation of college athletics, thus decreasing the public demand for college sports programs. They conclude that the NCAA imposes its rules and regulations—one of which is that college athletes should not be paid to play sports—to keep college sports nonprofessional and in relatively high demand, not to suppress players' wages.

Unions' Effects on Productivity and Efficiency: Two Views

There are two major views of the effects that labor unions have on productivity and efficiency.

THE TRADITIONAL (OR ORTHODOX) VIEW The traditional view holds that labor unions have a negative impact on productivity and efficiency. Its proponents make the following arguments: (1) Labor unions often have unnecessary staffing requirements and insist that only certain persons be allowed to do certain jobs. Because of this, the economy operates below its potential—that is, inefficiently. (2) Strikes disrupt production and prevent the economy from realizing its productive potential. (3) Labor unions drive an artificial wedge between the wages of comparable labor in the union and nonunion sectors of the labor market.

This last point warrants elaboration. In Exhibit 6, labor is homogeneous, and the wage rate is the same in both sectors of the labor market. Union efforts increase the wage rate in the union sector and decrease the wage rate in the nonunion sector.

At this point, the marginal revenue product of persons who work in the union sector is higher than the marginal revenue product of individuals who work in the nonunion sector. [We are farther up the factor demand curve (*MRP* curve) in the union than in the nonunion sector.] If labor could move from the nonunionized sector to the unionized sector, it would be moving from where it is worth less to where it is worth more, but it cannot do so because of the supply-restraining efforts of the union. Economists call this a misallocation of labor; not all labor is employed where it is most valuable.

A NEW VIEW: THE LABOR UNION AS A COLLECTIVE VOICE There is evidence that, in some industries, union firms have a higher rate of productivity than nonunion firms. Some economists believe this is a result of the labor union's role as a collective voice mechanism for its members. Without a labor union, workers who are disgruntled with their jobs, who feel taken advantage of by their employers, or who feel unsafe in their work will leave their jobs and seek work elsewhere. This job-exiting phenomenon comes at a cost: It raises the turnover rate, results in lengthy job searches during which individuals are not producing goods and services, and raises training costs. Such costs can be reduced, it is argued, when a labor union acts as a collective voice for its members. Instead of individual employees having individually to discuss ticklish employment matters with their employer, the labor union does so for them. Overall, the labor union makes employees feel more confident, less intimidated, and more secure in their work. Such positive feelings usually mean happier, more productive employees. Some proponents of this view also hold that employees are less likely to quit their jobs. In fact, there is evidence that unionism does indeed reduce job quits.

Critics have contended, though, that the reduced job quits are less a function of the labor union as a collective voice mechanism than of the labor union as an institution capable of increasing its members' wages. Also, the productivity-increasing aspects of the labor union, which are linked to its role as a collective voice mechanism, are independent of the productivity-decreasing aspects of the labor union in its role as a monopolizer of labor.

SELF-TEST

1. What is a major difference between a monopsonist and a factor price taker?
2. Under what conditions will the minimum wage increase the number of people working?
3. How could a collectively bargained higher wage rate in the unionized sector of the economy lead to a lower wage rate in the nonunionized sector of the economy?

"DON'T HIGHER WAGES REDUCE PROFITS?"

Student:

I'm beginning to find that many things in economics are counterintuitive. Things I expected to be true turn out to be false, and things that I thought were false turn out to be true.

Instructor:

Are you thinking of something in particular?

Student:

I had thought that labor unions obtained higher wages at the expense of the firm's owners (by reducing the owners' profits). Now I know that this is not necessarily true in the long run, especially in a perfectly competitive market.

Instructor:

Any thoughts on why economics is full of the counterintuitive?

Student:

I'm not sure.

Instructor:

Well, part of the answer might have to do with how far we take the analysis. To illustrate, consider your example dealing with the labor union and profits. You had thought that the labor union obtained higher wages at the expense of the firm's owners. That can be true in the short run. In other words, your intuition was correct for the short run. But when we extended the analysis beyond the immediate effects of higher wages, things began to turn out differently than you thought.

Student:

So, is there a lesson here?

Instructor:

Don't stop analyzing things too soon. The problem, though, is that we don't always know that we're stopping too soon.

Student:

In other words, I saw the story this way: Wages for members of labor unions rise, which causes profits to fall for owners of firms. But I should have seen it this way: Wages for members of labor unions rise, profits fall for owners of firms, some firms leave the industry, the market supply curve shifts leftward, and price rises.

Of course, my problem, as you imply, was that I didn't know I should have gone beyond steps (1) and (2). I didn't know steps (3) through (5) were there. So I guess my question now is how do you get to those steps if you don't know they exist?

Instructor:

That's a good question. What you need is a device to use that can propel you onward. That device comes in the form of the question, is there anything else? To illustrate, go back to the way you initially saw the story: Wages for members of labor unions rise, which causes profits to fall for owners of firms.

Now, instead of putting a period at the end of that, ask a question: If profits fall for the owners of firms, what, if anything, will falling profits lead to? This question—a form of the *is there anything else* question—propels you forward and reduces the probability that you will stop before you have tried to figure out the full story.

Points to Remember

1. Do higher wages lead to lower profits—end of story? Our answer depends on how far we take the analysis.

2. To propel our analysis forward, we often need to ask whether there is anything else.

a reader asks | What Are the Facts of Labor Unions?

If 12 percent of the U.S. labor force is comprised of union workers, in what state is union membership the largest percentage of the work force? Is union membership greater in some industries than in others? Is the private sector more or less unionized than the public sector?

Some of the following information about labor unions, which is from 2006, will answer your questions.

- The five states with the highest union membership rates (percentage of workers in unions) were Hawaii, Alaska, New York, New Jersey, and Washington. Union membership in these states is between 19.8 percent and 24.7 percent. The two states with the lowest membership rates are North Carolina (3.3) and South Carolina (3.3).
- Six states—California, New York, Illinois, Michigan, Ohio, and New Jersey—account for approximately 50 percent of all union members.
- Workers in the public sector had unionization rates that are five times higher than their counterparts in the private sector.
- The unionization rate of government workers was about 36.2 percent, compared with 7.5 percent among private sector employees.

- Local government workers—a group that includes police officers and firefighters—had the highest unionization rate (41.9 percent) among all occupations.
- The nonagricultural industry with the lowest unionization rate (2.3 percent) was financial activities.
- Union membership rates of government employees have held steady since 1983, whereas those of private nonagricultural employees have declined.
- Unionization membership rates were higher among men (13 percent) than among women (10.9 percent).
- African Americans have the highest rate of union membership among all major worker groups.
- Workers aged 45 to 64 were more likely to be unionized than either their younger or their older counterparts.
- Full-time workers were more than twice as likely as part-time workers to be members of a union.
- Approximately 1.6 million workers who were not union members were represented by unions at their place of work.
- About 15.4 million workers in the United States were members of a labor union.

Chapter Summary

TYPES OF UNIONS

- There are three different types of labor unions: craft (or trade) unions, industrial unions, and public employee unions. Some economists hold that employee associations are also a type of union.

OBJECTIVES OF A UNION

- Objectives of a union include (1) employment for all its members, (2) maximization of the total wage bill, and (3) maximization of the income for a limited number of union members. A labor union faces a wage-employment trade-off; higher wage rates mean lower labor union employment. An exception is when a labor union faces a monopsonist; it is possible then for the union to raise both wage rates and employment of its members (over a range). Exhibit 4(c) illustrates this.

PRACTICES OF A LABOR UNION

- To soften the wage-employment trade-off, a labor union seeks to lower the elasticity of demand for its labor. Ways of doing this are (1) reducing the availability of substitute products and (2) reducing the availability of substitute factors for labor.
- Union wage rates can be increased indirectly by increasing the demand for union labor or by reducing the supply of union labor, or they can be increased directly by collective bargaining. To increase demand for its labor, a union might try to increase (1) the demand for the good it produces, (2) substitute factor prices, or (3) its marginal physical product. To decrease the supply of its labor, a union might argue for closed and union shops and against right-to-work laws.
- In a way, successful collective bargaining on the part of a labor union changes the supply curve of labor that the employer faces. The labor union is successful if, through

its collective bargaining efforts, it can prevent the employer from hiring labor at a wage rate below a union-determined level. In this case, the supply curve of labor becomes horizontal at this wage rate (see Exhibit 3).

MONOPSONY

- For a monopsonist, marginal factor cost rises as it buys additional units of a factor and its supply curve lies below its marginal factor cost curve. The monopsonist buys the factor quantity at which $MRP = MFC$. The price of the factor is less than the monopsonist's marginal factor cost; so the monopsonist pays the factor less than its marginal revenue product.

EFFECTS OF UNIONS

- There is evidence that labor unions generally have the effect of increasing their members' wage rates (over what they would be without the union) and lowering the wage rates of nonunion labor.

- The traditional view of labor unions holds that unions negatively affect productivity and efficiency by (1) arguing for and often obtaining unnecessary staffing requirements, (2) calling strikes that disrupt production, and (3) driving an artificial wedge between the wages of comparable labor in the union and nonunion sectors.

- The new view of labor unions holds that labor unions act as a collective voice mechanism for individual union employees and cause them to feel more confident in their jobs and less intimidated by their employers. This effort leads to more productive employees, who are less likely to quit.

Key Terms and Concepts

Craft (Trade) Union	Employee Association	Collective Bargaining
Industrial Union	Closed Shop	Strike
Public Employee Union	Union Shop	Monopsony

Questions and Problems

1 What is the difference between a craft (trade) union and an industrial union?

2 Will a union behave differently if it wants to employ all members instead of maximizing the total wage bill? Explain your answer.

3 What does the elasticity of demand for labor have to do with the wage-employment trade-off?

4 Identify one practice of labor unions consistent with:

a. Affecting the elasticity of demand for union labor.

b. Increasing the demand for union labor.

c. Decreasing the supply of labor union workers.

5 What view is a labor union likely to hold on each of the following issues?

a. Easing of the immigration laws.

b. A quota on imported products.

c. Free trade.

d. A decrease in the minimum wage.

6 Most actions or practices of labor unions are attempts to affect one of three factors. What are these three factors?

7 Explain why the monopsonist pays labor a wage rate less than labor's marginal revenue product.

8 Organizing labor unions may be easier in some industries than in others. What industry characteristics make unionization easier?

9 What is the effect of labor unions on nonunion wage rates?

10 Some persons argue that a monopsony firm exploits its workers if it pays them less than their marginal revenue products. Others disagree. They say that as long as the firm pays the workers their opportunity costs (which must be the case or the workers would not stay with the firm), the workers are not being exploited. This view suggests that there are two definitions of exploitation.

a. Paying workers below their marginal revenue products (even if wages equal the workers' opportunity costs).

b. Paying workers below their opportunity costs.

Keeping in mind that this may be a subjective judgment, which definition of exploitation do you think is more descriptive of the process and why?

11 A discussion of labor unions usually evokes strong feelings. Some people argue vigorously against labor unions; others argue with equal vigor for them. Some people see labor unions as the reason workers in this country enjoy as high a standard of living as they do; others see labor unions as the reason the country is not so well off economically as it

might be. Speculate on why the topic of labor unions generates such strong feelings and emotions—and often such little analysis.

12 What forces may lead to the breakup of an employer (monopsony) cartel?

13 Unions can affect (a) a firm's profits, (b) the price consumers pay for a good, and (c) the wages received by nonunion workers. Do you agree or disagree? Explain your answer.

14 Contrast the traditional (or orthodox) and new view of labor unions.

Working with Numbers and Graphs

1 Determine the appropriate numbers for the lettered spaces.

(1) Workers	(2) Wage Rate	(3) Total Labor Cost	(4) Marginal Factor Cost
1	A	$12.00	$12.00
2	$12.10	24.20	E
3	12.20	C	F
4	B	D	12.60

2 Which demand curve for labor in the following figure exhibits the most pronounced wage-employment trade-off? Explain your answer.

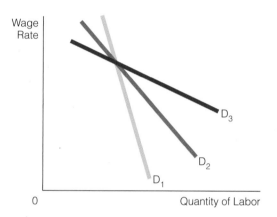

3 Diagrammatically explain how changes in supply conditions and wage rates in the unionized sector can cause changes in supply and wage rates in the nonunionized sector.

CHAPTER 14

THE DISTRIBUTION OF INCOME AND POVERTY

Introduction A random sample of people from the general population will have various incomes. Some people will be in the top 20 percent of income earners, some in the lowest 20 percent, and many others between these two extremes. In other words, some people earn high incomes, some earn low incomes, and many earn middle incomes. What factors influence the amount of income a person earns? Why are some people more likely than others to be poor? Why are some people more likely to be rich? You'll find the answers to these questions and many other questions about the distribution of income and poverty in this chapter.

SOME FACTS ABOUT INCOME DISTRIBUTION

In discussing public policy issues, people sometimes talk about a single fact when they should talk about a collection of facts. A single fact is usually not as informative as a collection of facts, in much the same way that a single snapshot does not tell as much of a story as a moving picture—a succession of snapshots. This section presents a few facts about the distribution of income.

Who Are the Rich and How Rich Are They?

By many interpretations, the lowest fifth (the lowest quintile) of households in the United States is considered poor, the top fifth is considered rich, and the middle three-fifths are considered middle income.[1]

---

1. A household consists of all people who occupy a housing unit. It includes the related family members and all unrelated people.

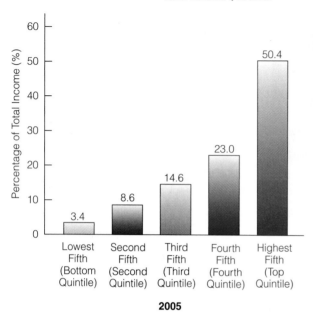

exhibit 1

Distribution of Household Income Shares, 2005

The annual income shares for different quintiles of households is shown here.

Source: U.S. Bureau of the Census.

2005

In 2005, the lowest fifth (the poor) in the United States received 3.4 percent of the total money income, the second fifth received 8.6 percent, the third fifth received 14.6 percent, the fourth fifth received 23.0 percent, and the top fifth (the rich) received 50.4 percent (see Exhibit 1).[2]

Has the income distribution become more or less equal over time? Exhibit 2 shows the income shares of households in 1967 and 2005. In 1967, the highest fifth (top) of households accounted for 43.8 percent of all income; in 2005, the percentage had risen to 50.4 percent.

At the other end of the income spectrum, in 1967, the lowest fifth received 4.0 percent of all income; in 2005, the percentage had fallen to 3.4 percent. The middle groups—the three-fifths of income recipients between the lowest fifth and the highest fifth—accounted for 52.3 percent of all income in 1967 and 46.2 percent in 2005.

Keep in mind as you look at the data that most persons implicitly assume that the quintiles (the fifths) in income distributions contain equal shares of the population. But the official income quintiles of the Bureau of the Census do not contain equal shares of the population. The Census Bureau quintiles are unequal in size because they are based on a count of households rather than persons. In the United States, high-income households tend to be married couples with many members and earners. Low-income households tend to be single persons with little or no earnings. The average household in the top quintile contains 3.2 persons, and the average household in the bottom quintile contains 1.8 persons.

Some economists have argued that the unequal quintile populations skew the Census's measure of the income distribution. For example, in 2002, the top quintile contained 24.6 percent of the population, and the bottom quintile contained 14.3 percent of the population. Stated differently, 69.4 million persons were in the highest fifth, and 40.3 million persons were in the lowest fifth.

If we adjust the income distribution so that each quintile actually contains 20 percent of the population, we get different results. In 2002, the income share of the lowest fifth rises from 3.5 percent to 9.4 percent, and the income share of the highest fifth falls from 49.7 percent to 39.6 percent.

Sometimes economists make further adjustments to income distribution. For example, the persons in each fifth do not all work the same number of hours. In 2002, individuals in the lowest fifth performed 4.3 percent of all work in the U.S. economy, and those in the highest fifth performed 33.9 percent. To be fair, the low levels of paid employment in the lowest fifth reflect the low numbers of working-age population in this group. In 2002, the lowest fifth contained only 11.2 percent of all working-age adults, and the highest fifth contained 27.6 percent. However, when we compare working-age adults in the lowest fifth with working-age adults in the highest fifth, we learn that the average working-age adult in the lowest fifth worked about half as many hours a year as the working-age adult in the highest fifth.

---

2. Percentages in this chapter do not always equal 100 due to rounding.

exhibit 2

Income Distribution, 1967 and 2005

Note that income shares have not been adjusted for such things as taxes and in-kind transfer payments, which are transfer payments made in terms of a specific good or service rather than in cash.

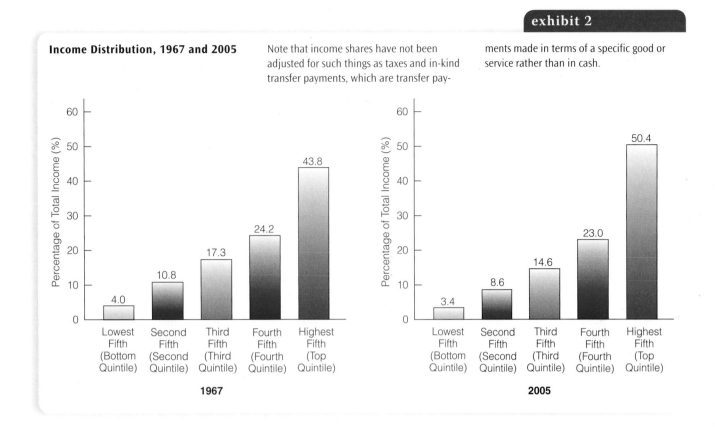

1967

2005

The Effect of Age on the Income Distribution

In analyzing the income distribution, we have to distinguish between people who are poor for long periods of time (sometimes their entire lives) and people who are poor temporarily. Consider Sherri Holmer, who attends college and works part-time as a waitress at a nearby restaurant. Currently, her income is so low that she falls into the lowest quintile of income earners, but she isn't likely always to be in this quintile. After she graduates from college, Sherri's income will probably rise. If she is like most people, her income will rise during her twenties, thirties, and forties. In her late forties or early fifties, her income will take a slight downturn and then level off.

Possibly—in fact very likely—a person in her late twenties, thirties, or forties will have a higher income than a person in his early twenties or a person in her sixties, even though their total lifetime incomes will be identical. If we view each person over time, income equality is greater than if we view each person at a particular point in time (say, when one person is 58 years old and the other is 68).

To illustrate, look at Exhibit 3, which shows the incomes of John and Stephanie in different years. In 2000, John is 18 years old and earning $10,000 per year, and Stephanie is 28 years old and earning $30,000 a year. The income distribution between John and Stephanie is unequal in 2000. Ten years later, the income distribution is still unequal, with Stephanie earning $45,000 and John earning $35,000. In fact, the income distribution is unequal in every year shown in the exhibit. However, the total income earned by each person is $236,000, giving a perfectly equal income distribution over time.

In the United States, there seems to be quite a bit of upward income mobility over time. The University of Michigan's Panel Survey on Dynamics tracked 50,000 Americans

exhibit 3

Income Distribution at One Point in Time and Over Time

In each year, the income distribution between John and Stephanie is unequal, with Stephanie earning more than John in 2000, 2010, 2020, and 2030 and John earning more than Stephanie in 2040. In the five years specified, however, both John and Stephanie earned the same total income of $236,000, giving a perfectly equal income distribution over time.

Year	John's Age	John's Income	Stephanie's Age	Stephanie's Income
2000	18 years	$10,000	28 years	$30,000
2010	28	35,000	38	45,000
2020	38	52,000	48	60,000
2030	48	64,000	58	75,000
2040	58	75,000	68	26,000
Total		$236,000		$236,000

for 17 years. Of the people in the lowest fifth of the income distribution in 1975, only 5.1 percent were still there in 1991—and 29 percent of them were in the highest fifth.

Common MISCONCEPTIONS

About the Poor

Some people seem to think that there is little to no mobility between income groups. This is not true. According to the Bureau of the Census, of households that were in the lowest quintile in 1996, 38 percent were in a higher quintile in 1999. Of households that were in the highest quintile in 1996, 34 percent were in a lower quintile in 1999. Also, 49.5 percent of persons living in poverty in 1996 were not in poverty in 1999.

Thinking like AN ECONOMIST

Why Poor?

Many people believe that poor is poor, but not the economist, who wants to know why the person is poor. Is he poor because he is young and just starting out in life? Would he be poor if we were to consider the **in-kind transfer payments** or in-kind benefits he receives? Some people argue that when someone is poor, you don't ask questions, you simply try to help him. But the economist knows that not everyone is in the same situation for the same reason. The reason may determine whether you proceed with help and, if you do proceed, how to do so. Both the elderly person with a disability and the young, smart college student may earn the same low income, but you may feel more obliged to help the elderly person with a disability than the college student.

In-Kind Transfer Payments
Transfer payments, such as food stamps, medical assistance, and subsidized housing, that are made in a specific good or service rather than in cash.

A Simple Equation

We need to identify the factors that determine a person's income. The following simple equation combines four of these factors:

Individual income = Labor income + Asset income + Transfer payments − Taxes

STATISTICS CAN MISLEAD IF YOU DON'T KNOW HOW THEY ARE MADE

If you read that U.S. household income has not grown in the last 20 years, would you conclude that incomes in the United States are stagnant? Many people might think so, but it may not be true. A household consists of all the people who occupy a housing unit. Individual incomes can rise while household incomes remain unchanged if, in fact, households become smaller over time.

To illustrate, suppose there are 10 households with four persons in each. Each person in each household earns $30,000 a year. So each household earns an income of $120,000 a year.

Some years pass, each person's income (in each household) rises to $60,000, but two of every four persons in each household leave to set up a new household. In other words, we now have 20 households with two persons in each, and the total income of each of the 20 households is still $120,000.

On an individual basis, certainly all 40 persons are better off earning $60,000 each than earning $30,000 each. But on the basis of household income, we get a very different picture.

Lesson: It is possible for individual income to rise as household income remains unchanged because households could be getting smaller as individual incomes rise.

Now consider another assertion: "The middle class in this country is getting smaller and smaller." On the surface, this statement sounds fairly ominous. Where is the middle class going? Is it disappearing and becoming poorer? Or is it disappearing and becoming richer?

The problem is that if we have a fixed definition of the middle class—say, persons who earn between $40,000 and $50,000 a year—then a changing income distribution can cause the number of persons in that (middle-class) income range to fall. To illustrate, suppose that, of 10 people, the lowest-earning person earns $10,000 a year, the next-lowest-earning person earns $20,000 a year, and so on up to the highest-earning person, who earns $100,000 a year.

Incomes for various persons (in thousands of dollars)

10, 20, 30, 40, 50, 60, 70, 80, 90, 100

Now let's say that the middle class consists of persons in the middle of the income distribution who earn between $40,000 and $70,000. In other words, the middle class consists of four persons. We have enclosed these four persons' incomes in brackets.

10, 20, 30, [40, 50, 60, 70], 80, 90, 100

Years pass, and now everyone earns $50,000 more than she earned before. So now the lowest-earning person earns $60,000 a year and the highest-earning person earns $150,000.

Incomes for various persons (in thousands of dollars)

60, 70, 80, 90, 100, 110, 120, 130, 140, 150

The income distribution has become skewed toward higher incomes. The middle class has been cut in half if we continue to define it as persons earning between $40,000 and $70,000 a year. Now only two persons fall within this category: the person who once earned $10,000 and now earns $60,000 and the person who once earned $20,000 and now earns $70,000.

Lesson: As individuals income rise, the middle class can get smaller (and disappear altogether) if the middle class is defined as being in a fixed income range. Contrary to what some people believe, a disappearing middle class does not necessarily connote a world of only the rich and the poor.

Labor income is equal to the wage rate an individual receives multiplied by the number of hours he or she works. *Asset income* consists of such things as the return to saving, the return to capital investment, and the return to land. **Transfer payments** are payments to persons that are not made in return for goods and services currently supplied (e.g., Social Security payments and cash welfare assistance are government transfer payments). Finally, from the sum of labor income, asset income, and transfer payments, we subtract *taxes* to see what an individual is left with (i.e., individual income).

This equation provides a quick way of focusing on the direct and indirect factors affecting an individual's income and the degree of income inequality. The next section examines the conventional ways that income inequality is measured.

Transfer Payments
Payments to persons that are not made in return for goods and services currently supplied.

SELF-TEST

(Answers to Self-Test questions are in the Self-Test Appendix.)

1. How can government change the distribution of income?

2. "Income inequality at one point in time is sometimes consistent with income equality over time." Comment.

3. Smith and Jones have the same income this year: $40,000. Does it follow that their income came from the same sources? Explain your answer.

MEASURING INCOME EQUALITY

Two commonly used measures of income inequality are the Lorenz curve and the Gini coefficient.

The Lorenz Curve

Lorenz Curve

A graph of the income distribution that expresses the relationship between the cumulative percentage of households and the cumulative percentage of income.

The **Lorenz curve** represents the distribution of income; it expresses the relationship between cumulative percentage of households and *cumulative percentage of income*. Exhibit 4 shows a hypothetical Lorenz curve.

The data in part (a) are used to plot the Lorenz curve in part (b). According to (a), the lowest fifth of households has an income share of 10 percent, the second fifth has an income share of 15 percent, and so on. The Lorenz curve in (b) is derived by plotting five points. Point A represents the cumulative income share of the lowest fifth of households (10 percent of income goes to the lowest fifth of households). Point B represents

---

exhibit 4

A Hypothetical Lorenz Curve

The data in (a) were used to derive the Lorenz curve in (b). The Lorenz curve shows the cumulative percentage of income earned by

the cumulative percentage of households. If all households received the same percentage of total income, the Lorenz curve would be the line of perfect income equality. The

bowed Lorenz curve shows an unequal distribution of income. The more bowed the Lorenz curve is, the more unequal the distribution of income.

Quintile	Income Share (percent)	Cumulative Income Share (percent)
Lowest fifth	10%	10%
Second fifth	15	25
Third fifth	20	45
Fourth fifth	25	70
Highest fifth	30	100

(a)

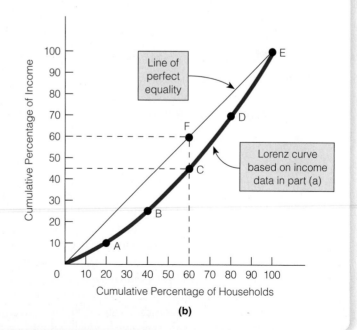

(b)

the cumulative income share of the lowest fifth plus the second fifth (25 percent of income goes to two-fifths, or 40 percent, of the income recipients). Point C represents the cumulative income share of the lowest fifth plus the second fifth plus the third fifth (45 percent of income goes to three-fifths, or 60 percent, of the income recipients). The same procedure is used for points D and E. Connecting these points gives the Lorenz curve that represents the data in (a); the Lorenz curve is another way of depicting the income distribution in (a). Exhibit 5 illustrates the Lorenz curve for the United States based on the (money) income shares in Exhibit 1.

What would the Lorenz curve look like if there were perfect income equality among different households? In this case, every household would receive exactly the same percentage of total income, and the Lorenz curve would be the line of perfect income equality illustrated in Exhibit 4(b). At any point on this 45-degree line, the cumulative percentage of income (on the vertical axis) equals the cumulative percentage of households (on the horizontal axis). For example, at point F, 60 percent of the households receive 60 percent of the total income.

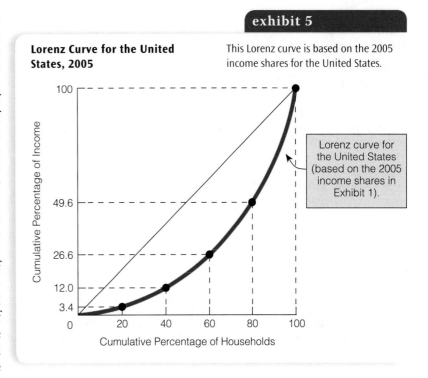

exhibit 5

Lorenz Curve for the United States, 2005

This Lorenz curve is based on the 2005 income shares for the United States.

Lorenz curve for the United States (based on the 2005 income shares in Exhibit 1).

Cumulative Percentage of Income

Cumulative Percentage of Households

The Gini Coefficient

The **Gini coefficient** is a measure of the degree of inequality in the income distribution and is used in conjunction with the Lorenz curve. It is equal to the area between the line of perfect income equality (or 45-degree line) and the actual Lorenz curve, divided by the entire triangular area under the line of perfect income equality.

Gini Coefficient
A measure of the degree of inequality in the income distribution.

$$\text{Gini coefficient} = \frac{\text{Area between the line of perfect income equality and actual Lorenz curve}}{\text{Entire triangular area under the line of perfect income equality}}$$

Exhibit 6 illustrates both the line of perfect income equality and an actual Lorenz curve. The Gini coefficient is computed by dividing the shaded area (the area between the line of perfect income equality and the actual Lorenz curve) by the area 0AB (the entire triangular area under the line of perfect income equality).

The Gini coefficient is a number between 0 and 1. At one extreme, the Gini coefficient equals 0 if the numerator in the equation is 0. A numerator of 0 means there is no area between the line of perfect income equality and the actual Lorenz curve, implying that they are the same. Thus a Gini coefficient of 0 means perfect income equality.

At the other extreme, the Gini coefficient equals 1 if the numerator in the equation is equal to the denominator. If this is the case, the actual Lorenz curve is as far away from the line of perfect income equality as is possible. Thus a Gini coefficient of 1 means complete income inequality. (In this situation, in terms of the actual Lorenz curve, one person would have all the total income, and no one else would have any income. In Exhibit 4, a Lorenz curve representing complete income inequality would lie along the horizontal axis from 0 to A and then move from A to B.)

exhibit 6

The Gini Coefficient

The Gini coefficient is a measure of the degree of income inequality. It is equal to the area between the line of perfect income equality and the actual Lorenz curve divided by the entire triangular area under the line of perfect income equality. In the diagram, this is equal to the shaded portion divided by the triangular area 0AB. A Gini coefficient of 0 means perfect income equality; a Gini coefficient of 1 means complete income inequality. The larger the Gini coefficient, the greater the income inequality; the smaller the Gini coefficient, the lower the income inequality

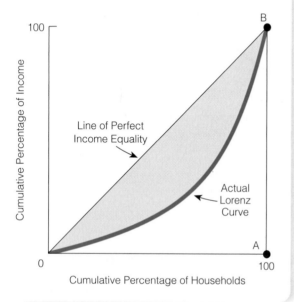

If a Gini coefficient of 0 represents perfect income equality and a Gini coefficient of 1 represents complete income inequality, then the larger the Gini coefficient is, the higher the degree of income inequality there will be. Conversely, the smaller the Gini coefficient is, the lower the degree of income inequality. In 2005, the Gini coefficient in the United States was 0.450; in 1947, it was 0.376. As a point of comparison, here are the Gini coefficients for some other countries: Russia, 0.413 (2007), Argentina, 0.49 (2006), Mexico, 0.509 (2005), United Kingdom, 0.34 (2005), Spain, 0.32 (2005), Sweden, 0.23 (2005).

A Limitation of the Gini Coefficient

Although we can learn the degree of inequality in the income distribution from the Gini coefficient, we have to be careful not to misinterpret it. For example, if the Gini coefficient is 0.33 in country 1 and 0.25 in country 2, we know that the income distribution is more equal in country 2 than in country 1. But in which country does the lowest fifth of households receive the larger percentage of income? The natural inclination is to answer in the country with the more equal income distribution—country 2. However, this may not be true.

Exhibit 7 shows two Lorenz curves. Overall, Lorenz curve 2 is closer to the line of perfect income equality than Lorenz curve 1; thus, the Gini coefficient is smaller for Lorenz curve 2 than for Lorenz curve 1. But the lowest 20 percent of households have a smaller percentage of total income with Lorenz curve 2 than with Lorenz curve 1.

Therefore, the Gini coefficient cannot tell us what is happening in different quintiles. We should not jump to the conclusion that because the Gini coefficient is lower in country 2 than in country 1, the lowest fifth of households has a greater percentage of total income in country 2 compared to country 1.

exhibit 7

Limitation of the Gini Coefficient

By itself, the Gini coefficient cannot tell us anything about the income share of a particular quintile. Although there is a tendency to believe that the bottom quintile receives a larger percentage of total income the lower the Gini coefficient, this need not be the case. In the diagram, the Gini coefficient for Lorenz curve 2 is lower than the Gini coefficient for Lorenz curve 1. But, the bottom 20 percent of households obtains a smaller percentage of total income in the lower Gini coefficient case.

Common Misconceptions

About Income Inequality

Some people suggest that, in a country where income inequality is rising, individuals cannot become better off. To see whether this is correct, consider the following example. A society is made up of five individuals, A–E. The yearly income for each individual is as follows: A earns $20,000, B earns $10,000, C earns $5,000, D earns $2,500, and E earns $1,250. The total yearly income in this society is $38,750, and the distribution of income is certainly unequal. A earns 51.61 percent of the income, B earns 25.81 percent, C earns 12.90 percent, D earns 6.45 percent, and E earns only 3.23 percent.

Now each person earns additional real income. A earns $10,000 more real income for a total of $30,000, B earns $3,000 more real income for a total of $13,000, C earns $2,000 more real income for a total of $7,000, D earns $1,000 more real income for a total of $3,500, and E earns $200 more real income for a total of $1,450. In terms of real income, each of the five persons is better off, but the income distribution has become even more unequal. For example, A (at the top fifth of income earners) now receives 54.60 percent of all income instead of 51.61 percent, and E (at the bottom fifth of income earners) now receives 2.64 percent instead of 3.22 percent. A newspaper headline might read, "The rich get richer as the poor get poorer." People reading this headline might naturally think that the poor in society are now worse off. But we know they are not worse off in terms of the goods and services they can purchase. They now have more real income than they had when the income distribution was less unequal. In short, everyone can be better off even if the income distribution becomes more unequal.

SELF-TEST

1. Starting with the top fifth of income earners and proceeding to the lowest fifth, suppose the income share of each group is 40 percent, 30 percent, 20 percent, 10 percent, and 5 percent. Can these percentages be right?

2. Country A has a Gini coefficient of 0.45. What does this mean?

WHY INCOME INEQUALITY EXISTS

The question of why income inequality exists can be answered by focusing on our simple equation:

Individual income = Labor income + Asset income + Transfer payments − Taxes

Generally, income inequality exists because people do not receive the same labor income, asset income, and transfer payments, and/or because they do not pay the same taxes. This section discusses some of the specific reasons that people don't receive, say, the same labor income and asset income by focusing on factors that often contribute to differences. The next section looks at some of the proposed standards of income distribution.

Factors Contributing to Income Inequality

Six factors that contribute to income inequality are innate abilities and attributes, work and leisure, education and other training, risk taking, luck, and wage discrimination.

INNATE ABILITIES AND ATTRIBUTES Individuals are not all born with the same innate abilities and attributes. People vary in their degrees of intelligence, appearances, and creativity. Some individuals have more marketable innate abilities and attributes than others. For example, the man or woman born with exceptionally good looks, the natural athlete, or the person who is musically gifted or mathematically adept is more likely to earn a higher income than someone with lesser abilities or attributes.

WORK AND LEISURE There is a trade-off between work and leisure: More work means less leisure, and less work means more leisure. Some individuals will choose to work more hours (or take a second job) and thus have less leisure, and this choice will be reflected in their labor income. They will earn a larger income than persons who choose not to work more, *ceteris paribus.*

EDUCATION AND OTHER TRAINING Economists usually refer to schooling and other types of training as an investment in human capital. To buy a capital good or to invest in one, a person has to give up present consumption and does so in the hope that the capital good will increase future consumption.

Schooling can be looked on as capital. First, one must give up present consumption to obtain it. Second, by providing individuals with certain skills and knowledge, schooling can increase their future consumption over what it would be without the schooling. Schooling, then, is human capital. In general, **human capital** includes education, the development of skills, and anything else that is particular to the individual and increases productivity.

Contrast a person who has obtained an education with a person who has not. The educated person is likely to have certain skills, abilities, and knowledge that the uneducated person lacks. Consequently, the educated person is likely to be worth more to an employer. Most college students know this; it is part of the reason they attend college.

RISK TAKING Individuals have different attitudes toward risk. Some individuals are more willing to take on risk than others. Some of the individuals who are willing to take on risk will do well and rise to the top of the income distribution, and others will fall to the bottom. Individuals who prefer to play it safe aren't as likely to reach the top of the income distribution or to hit the bottom.

LUCK When individuals can't explain why something has happened to them, they often say it was the result of good or bad luck. At times, the good or bad luck explanation makes sense; at other times, it is more of a rationalization than an explanation.

Good and bad luck may influence incomes. For example, the college student who studies biology only to find out in her senior year that the bottom has fallen out of the biology market has experienced bad luck. The farmer who hits oil while digging a well has experienced good luck. An automobile worker who is unemployed owing to a recession he had no part in causing is experiencing bad luck. A person who trains for a profession in which there is an unexpected increase in demand experiences good luck.

Although luck can and does influence incomes, it is not likely to have (on average) a great or long-run effect. The person who experiences good luck today and whose income reflects this fact isn't likely to experience luck-boosting income increases time after time. In the long run, such factors as innate ability and attributes, education, and personal decisions (how much work, how much leisure?) are more likely to have a greater, more sustained effect than luck on income.

WAGE DISCRIMINATION **Wage discrimination** exists when an employer pays different wages to individuals of equal ability and productivity, as measured by their marginal

Human Capital
Education, development of skills, and anything else that is particular to the individual and that increases personal productivity.

Wage Discrimination
The situation that exists when individuals of equal ability and productivity (as measured by their contribution to output) are paid different wage rates.

revenue products. For example, in the period as a whole since World War II, the median income of African Americans has been approximately 60 percent that of whites, and, since the late 1950s, females working full-time have earned approximately 60–70 percent of the male median income. These differences between white and black incomes and between male and female incomes are not due wholly to discrimination. Most empirical studies show that approximately half the differences are due to variations in education, productivity, and job training (although one may ask if discrimination has anything to do with the education, productivity, and job training differences). The remainder of the wage differential is due to other factors, one of which is hypothesized to be discrimination.

Most people agree that discrimination exists, although they differ on how much they think it affects income. Also, discrimination is not always directed at employees by employers. For example, consumers may practice discrimination—some white consumers may wish to deal only with white physicians and lawyers; some Asian Americans may wish to deal only with Asian American physicians and lawyers.

Income Differences: Some Are Voluntary, Some Are Not

Even in a world with no discrimination, differences in income would still exist due to other factors, as noted. Some individuals would have more marketable skills than others, some individuals would decide to work harder and longer hours than others, some individuals would take on more risk than others, and some individuals would undertake more schooling and training than others. Thus, some degree of income inequality occurs because individuals are innately different and make different choices. However, some degree of income inequality is also due to factors unrelated to innate ability or choices—such as discrimination or luck.

In an ongoing and interesting debate on the topic of discrimination-based income inequality, the opposing sides weight various factors differently. Some people argue that wage discrimination would be reduced if markets were allowed to be more competitive, more open, and freer. They believe that in an open and competitive market with few barriers to entry and with no government protection of privileged groups, discrimination would have a high price. Firms that didn't hire the best and the brightest—regardless of a person's race, religion, or gender—would suffer. They would ultimately pay for their act of discrimination by having higher labor costs and lower profits. Individuals holding this view usually propose that government deregulate, reduce legal barriers to entry, and in general not hamper the workings of the free market mechanism.

Others contend that even if the government were to follow this script, much wage discrimination would still exist. They think government should play an active legislative role in reducing both wage discrimination and other types of discrimination that they believe ultimately result in wage discrimination, such as discrimination in education and discrimination in on-the-job training. Proponents of an active role for government usually believe that such policy programs as affirmative action, equal pay for equal work, and comparable worth (equal pay for comparable work) are beneficial in reducing both the amount of wage discrimination in the economy and the degree of income inequality.

SELF-TEST

1. Jack and Harry work for the same company, but Jack earns more than Harry. Is this evidence of wage discrimination? Explain your answer.

2. A person decides to assume a lot of risk in earning an income. How could this affect her income?

WINNER-TAKE-ALL MARKETS[3]

Two economists, Robert Frank and Philip Cook, published a book in 1995 titled *The Winner-Take-All Society*. A winner-take-all market is one in which the top producer or performer in the market earns appreciably more than others in the market. In fact, the top producers earn so much more than others that it is as if they "take it all."

For example, in making major movies, the producer, director, and leading actor may earn much more than anyone else involved in the movie. In the sports market, the sports stars earn more than their fellow players. For example, the last year that Michael Jordan played basketball with the Chicago Bulls, he earned 121 times the salary of the lowest paid player.

In their book, Frank and Cook argue that there are more winner-take-all markets today than in the past. They state that there is nothing new about winner-take-all markets in sports and entertainment. What is new,

© 20TH CENTURY FOX/CLINICA ESTETICO/THE KOBAL COLLECTION

they argue, is that winner-take-all is becoming a common feature of other markets. Winner-take-all is becoming increasingly more descriptive in such fields as law, journalism, design, and medicine.

The data seem to support what Frank and Cook are saying. Recent statistics show that so-called within-group income inequality has been rising. In other words, the winnings, as it were, have come to be concentrated in the hands of a smaller percentage of people in an industry. To illustrate, in 1980, major U.S. chief executive officers (CEOs) earned an average of 42 times the amount an average American production worker earned; by 2003, this multiple had jumped to 301.[4] Other examples illustrate the same phenomenon, prompting Frank and Cook to comment that we are increasingly coming to live in a winner-take-all society.

---

3. This feature is based on Robert H. Frank, "Talent and the Winner-Take-All Society," in the *American Prospect*, no. 17 (Spring 1994): 97–107.

4. The 2003 multiple is from *BusinessWeek's* 54th Annual Executive Compensation Survey, April 2004.

NORMATIVE STANDARDS OF INCOME DISTRIBUTION

For hundreds of years, economists, political philosophers, and political scientists, among others, have debated what constitutes a proper, just, or fair distribution of income and have proposed various normative standards. This section discusses three of the better-known normative standards of income distribution: the marginal productivity normative standard, the absolute (complete) income equality normative standard, and the Rawlsian normative standard.

The Marginal Productivity Normative Standard

The marginal productivity theory of factor prices states that in a competitive setting, people tend to be paid their marginal revenue products.[5] The marginal productivity normative standard of income distribution holds that people *should* be paid their marginal revenue products.

---

5. Recall that in a competitive setting, value marginal product (*VMP*) equals marginal revenue product (*MRP*). Thus, the marginal productivity theory holds that in a competitive setting, people tend to be paid their *VMP*, or *MRP*.

To explain what has happened in recent years to bring about more winner-take-all markets and greater within-group income inequality, Frank and Cook identify two things: (1) developments in communications, manufacturing technology, and transportation costs that let top performers serve broader markets (a global marketplace) and (2) implicit and explicit rules that have led to more competition for top performers.

Developments in Communications, Manufacturing Technology, and Transportation Costs

In a winner-take-all market, the demand for goods and services is focused on a small number of suppliers. This is not, as some may think, because government is limiting our choices. According to Frank and Cook, we are simply focusing on "the best" suppliers to a greater degree than before because of changes in technology, communications, and transportation costs.

For example, consumers today do not have to settle for buying tires, cars, clothes, books, or much of anything else from regional or national producers of these items. They can buy these items from the best producers in the world. As Frank notes, whereas once a firm that produced a good tire in northern Ohio could be assured of selling tires in its regional market, today it cannot. Consumers buy tires from a handful of the best tire producers in the world.

Consider another example, in which technological development plays an important part. Before there were records, tapes, or CDs, a person had to go to a concert to hear music. After the technology was developed for producing records, tapes, and CDs, concertgoing was no longer necessary. The best singers and bands in the world could simply put their music on a record, tape, or CD, and anyone in the world could listen to it. A person living in a small town no longer had to go to a local concert to hear music performed by what may have been a very mediocre musician. Now, that person could listen to music performed by the best musicians in the world. His demand for music, as well as that of others, became focused on a smaller pool of musicians. As a consequence, these top musicians began to witness large increases in their earnings.

Within-Group Income Inequality

Frank and Cook argue that greater competition for top performers can be the result of a legal change. For example, consider the deregulation in airline, trucking, banking, brokerage, and other industries. Deregulation may have increased the salary competition for top performers, thus driving up their wages.

Deregulation can have such an effect because, in a deregulated environment, market competition comes to play a bigger role in determining outcomes—both good and bad. Specifically, in a deregulated environment, the potential for both profits and losses is greater than in a regulated (less competitive) environment. To capture the higher potential profits and to guard against the increased likelihood of losses, talented professionals become more valuable to a firm.

Also, perhaps as a result of a less regulated, more fiercely competitive product market, the once widely accepted practice of companies promoting from within is today falling by the wayside. Increasingly, companies search for the top talent in other firms and industries, not just the top talent in their company pool. Although at one time a top performer in a soft-drink company could expect only soft-drink companies to compete for his or her services, that employee can now expect to receive offers from soft-drink companies, computer companies, insurance companies, and other types of firms.

This idea is illustrated in Exhibit 8(a). The first income pie in (a) represents the actual income shares of eight individuals, A–H, who work in a competitive setting and are paid their respective *MRP*s. The income distribution is unequal because the eight persons do not contribute equally to the productive process; some are more productive than others.

The second income pie in (a), which is the same as the first, is the income distribution proposed by the marginal productivity normative standard adherents. In short, individuals should be paid their marginal revenue products. Proponents of this position argue that it is just for individuals to receive their contribution (high, low, or somewhere in between) to the productive process, no more and no less. In addition, paying people according to their productivity gives them an incentive to become more productive. For example, individuals have an incentive to learn more and to become better trained if they know they will be paid more as a consequence. According to this argument, without such incentives, work effort would decrease, laziness would increase, and in time the entire society would feel the harmful effects. Critics respond that some persons are innately more productive than others and that rewarding them for innate qualities is unfair.

exhibit 8

Different Normative Standards of Income Distribution

(a) The marginal productivity, (b) the absolute, and (c) the Rawlsian normative

standards of income distribution. Note that the income pies do not change as income distribution changes. In reality, the size of the income pies might depend on the income distribution. We are not concerned

with this point here, but only with illustrating what different income distributions, based on different normative standards, look like at one point in time.

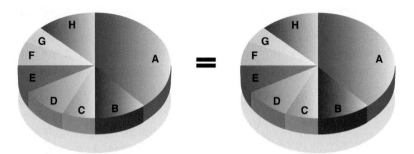

Income Distribution That Is = Income Distribution That Should Be

(a) Marginal Productivity Normative Standard

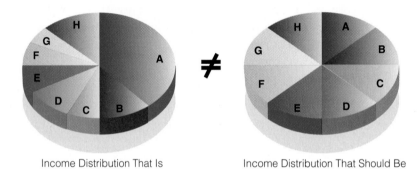

Income Distribution That Is ≠ Income Distribution That Should Be

(b) Absolute Income Equality Normative Standard

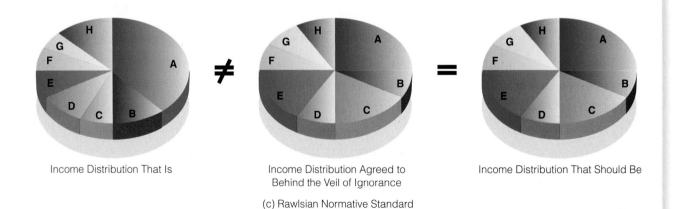

Income Distribution That Is ≠ Income Distribution Agreed to Behind the Veil of Ignorance = Income Distribution That Should Be

(c) Rawlsian Normative Standard

Keep in mind that this discussion assumes a competitive setting where people are paid their *MRP*s. Even if a person is in a monopsony setting and is not being paid his *MRP*, the proponents of the marginal productivity normative standard argue that he should be. Those who propose normative standards think the marginal productivity standard should be applied regardless of the setting. In other words, you can be a proponent of the marginal productivity normative standard whether or not you believe people are currently being paid their marginal revenue products.

The Absolute Income Equality Normative Standard

Exhibit 8(b) illustrates the viewpoint of persons who advocate the absolute income equality normative standard. The first income pie represents the income distribution that exists—in which there is income inequality. The second income pie represents the would-be income distribution proposed by those who argue for absolute income equality. Each individual receives an equal percentage of the income pie; no one has any more or any less than anyone else.

Proponents of this position hold that an equal distribution of income will lead to the maximization of total utility in society. The argument is as follows: (1) Individuals are alike when it comes to how much satisfaction they receive from an added increase in income. (2) Receiving additional income is subject to the law of diminishing marginal utility; that is, each additional dollar is worth less to the recipient than the preceding dollar. (3) Therefore, redistributing income from the rich to the poor will raise total utility. The rich will not lose as much utility from the redistribution as the poor will gain. Overall, the total utility (of society) will rise through the redistribution of income from the rich to the poor. Total utility will be maximized when all persons receive the same income.

Opponents of this position hold that knowing whether all individuals receive equal utility from an added dollar of income is impossible and that a rich person may receive far more utility from an added dollar of income than a poor person receives. If so, then redistributing income until it is equalized would not maximize total utility.

The Rawlsian Normative Standard

In *A Theory of Justice,* philosopher John Rawls states that individuals are less likely to argue for a different income distribution if they know what their position is in the current income distribution than if they don't know what their position is.[6]

To illustrate, Patricia Jevons is thought to be a rich person. With income of $500,000 per year, she is in the top 5 percent of income earners. Furthermore, the income distribution in which she occupies this position is largely unequal. There are few rich people and many poor people. Given that Patricia knows her position in the income distribution and considers it a comfortable position to occupy, she is less likely to argue for a more equal income distribution (and the high taxes that will be needed to bring it about) than if she were placed behind John Rawls's fictional *veil of ignorance.*

The **veil of ignorance** is the imaginary veil, or curtain, that prevents a person from knowing her position in the income distribution; that is, a person does not know whether she will be rich or poor when the veil is removed. Rawls argues that the average person would be more likely to vote for a more equal income distribution behind the veil than she would vote for without the veil.

The full power of Rawls's veil of ignorance idea and its impact on income distribution can be seen in the following scenario. On Monday, everyone knows his position in the income distribution. Some people are arguing for more income equality, but a sizable group does not want this. They are satisfied with the status quo income distribution.

On Tuesday, everyone is somehow magically transported behind Rawls's veil of ignorance. Behind it, no one knows his position—whether he is rich or poor, innately talented or not, lucky or unlucky. As a group, the persons behind the veil must decide on

Veil of Ignorance
The imaginary veil or curtain behind which a person does not know his or her position in the income distribution.

---

6. John Rawls, *A Theory of Justice* (Cambridge: Harvard University Press, 1971).

the income distribution they wish to have when the veil is removed. Rawls believes that individuals are largely risk avoiders and will not take the chance that, when the veil is removed, they will be poor. They will opt for an income distribution that will assure them that if they are (relatively) poor, their standard of living is not too low.

The Rawlsian normative standard is illustrated in Exhibit 8(c), which shows three income pies. The first represents the income distribution that currently exists. The second represents the income distribution that individuals would accept while behind the veil of ignorance. The third and last income pie, which is the same as the second, represents the income distribution that Rawls holds should exist because it was agreed to in an environment where individuals were, in a sense, equal: No one knew how he or she would fare when the veil was removed.

Critics of the Rawlsian position argue that individuals behind the veil of ignorance might not reach a consensus on the income distribution that should exist and that they might not be risk avoiders to the degree that Rawls assumes they will be.

Furthermore, the individuals behind the veil of ignorance will consider the trade-off between less income inequality and more output. In a world where the income distribution is likely to be unequal due to unequal individual productivities (sharply different marginal revenue products), reducing income inequality requires higher taxes and a lower reward for productive effort. In the end, this will lead to less productive effort and less output for consumption. In short, the size of the income pie might change, given different income distributions. Some of Rawls's critics maintain that individuals are likely to consider this information to a greater degree than Rawls assumes they will.

Thinking like AN ECONOMIST

One Moment in Time Versus Changes over Time

The income pies in Exhibit 8 are drawn so that their sizes don't change no matter what the income distribution is. To an economist, however, the size of the pie is likely to change over time, and how much it changes may be related to income distribution. To illustrate, suppose government is determined to make all incomes the same, no matter how much income growth there is in a country. Given this aim, we would expect that the size of the income pie would not grow much at all. After all, individuals may not work as hard if they know that government is determined to make all incomes the same.

POVERTY

This section presents some facts about poverty and examines its causes.

What Is Poverty?

There are principally two views on poverty. One view holds that poverty should be defined in absolute terms; the other holds that poverty should be defined in relative terms.

In absolute terms, poverty might be defined as follows: Poverty exists when the income of a family of four is less than $10,000 per year. In relative terms, poverty might be defined as follows: Poverty exists when the income of a family of four places it in the lowest 10 percent of income recipients.

Viewing poverty in relative terms means that poverty will always exist—unless, of course, there is absolute income equality. Given any unequal income distribution, some individuals will always occupy the bottom rung of the income ladder; thus, there will always be poverty. This holds no matter how high the absolute standard of living is of the members of the society. For example, in a society of 10 persons where 9 earn $1 million per year and 1 earns $400,000 per year, the person earning $400,000 per year is in the bottom 10 percent of the income distribution. If poverty is defined in relative terms, this person is considered to be living in poverty.

The U.S. government defines poverty in absolute terms. The absolute poverty measure was developed in 1964 by the Social Security Administration based on findings of the Department of Agriculture. Called the **poverty income threshold** or **poverty line**, this measure refers to the income below which people are considered to be living in poverty. Individuals or families with incomes below the poverty income threshold, or poverty line, are considered poor.

The poverty threshold is updated yearly to reflect changes in the consumer price index. In 2006, the poverty income threshold was $20,416 for a family of four. It was $10,488 for an individual under 65 years old. For an individual 65 years and older, it was $9,669. Also in that year, 36.4 million people (in the United States), or 12.3 percent of the entire population, were living below the poverty line.

Poverty Income Threshold (Poverty Line)
Income level below which people are considered to be living in poverty.

Limitations of the Official Poverty Income Statistics

The official poverty income statistics have certain limitations and shortcomings.

- First, the poverty figures are based solely on money incomes. Many money-poor persons receive in-kind benefits. For example, a family of four with a money income of $20,416 in 2006 was defined as poor, although it might have received in-kind benefits worth, say, $4,000. If the poverty figures are adjusted for in-kind benefits, the percentage of persons living in poverty drops.

- Second, poverty figures are not adjusted for unreported income, leading to an overestimate of poverty.

- Third, poverty figures are not adjusted for regional differences in the cost of living, leading to both overestimates and underestimates of poverty.

- Finally, government counters are unable to find some poor persons—such as some of the homeless—which leads to an underestimate of poverty.

Who Are the Poor?

Although the poor are persons of all religions, colors, genders, ages, and ethnic backgrounds, some groups are represented much more prominently in the poverty figures than others. For example, a greater percentage of African Americans and Hispanics than whites are poor. In 2005, 24.9 percent of African Americans, 21.8 percent of Hispanics, and 10.6 percent of whites lived below the poverty line.

A greater percentage of families headed by females than families headed by males are poor, and families with seven or more persons are much more likely to be poor than are families with fewer than seven. In addition, a greater percentage of young persons than other age groups are poor, and the uneducated and poorly educated are more likely to be poor than are the educated. Overall, a disproportionate percentage of the poor are African American or Hispanic, and they live in large families headed by a female who is young and has little education.

If we look at poverty in terms of absolute numbers instead of percentages, then most poor persons are white, largely because more whites are in the total population than other groups. In 2005, 24.8 million whites, 9.1 million African Americans, and 9.3 million Hispanics lived below the poverty line.

economics 24/7

Q&A: POVERTY AND INCOME

Question: What is the poverty rate for people in a family headed by a female with no husband present?

Answer: In 2006, it was 30.5 percent.

Question: What is the poverty rate for people under the age of 18? Over 18 years old?

Answer: For under 18 years old, it was 14.4 percent in 2006. For over 18 years old (or 18–64), it was 10.8 percent.

Question: Is the poverty rate higher for men or for women?

Answer: Generally it is higher for women. In 2006, the poverty rate for men was 11 percent; for women it was 13.6 percent.

Question: In what region of the country is the poverty rate the highest?

Answer: In 2006, it was in the South. The poverty rate for various regions of the country is South (13.8 percent), Midwest (11.2 percent), Northeast (11.5 percent), and West (11.6 percent).

Question: What percentages of the poor are made up by different age groups?

Answer: In 2006, people 65 or over accounted for 9.3 percent of the poor. Children under 18 years old made up 35.2 of the poor, and people in the age group 18–64 accounted for 55.5 percent.

Question: What percentage of the poor are made up of full-time workers?

Answer: In 2006, it was 11.7 percent. If we add persons who worked but who did not work full-time or during a full year, the percentage jumps to 36.9 percent.

Question: What state has the highest poverty rate? The lowest?

Answer: In 2006, Mississippi had the highest poverty rate (20.6 percent) and New Hampshire had the lowest (5.4 percent).

Question: What is the median (total money household) income?

Answer: In 2006, it was $48,201.

Question: Does the median (total money household) income differ among groups?

Answer: Yes. In 2006 in the United States, it was $52,423 for whites, $31,969 for African Americans, $63,900 for Asians, and $37,781 for Hispanics.

Question: Is the poverty rate in the United States the same for the native-born population as it is for the foreign-born population?

Answer: No. Among the native-born population, 11.9 percent were in poverty in 2006. Among the foreign-born population, 15.2 percent were in poverty in 2006.

Question: What percentage of the U.S. households fall into different income categories? For example, what percentage earn over $100,000 a year?

Answer: In 2005, 17.2 percent of households earned $100,000 or more. Here is the 2005 percentage breakdown for all income ranges:

Income Range	Percentage of Households (%)
Under $15,000	14.7
$15,000–$24,999	12.4
$25,000–$34,999	11.4
$35,000–$49,999	14.9
$50,000–$74,999	18.4
$75,000–$99,999	11.1
$100,000 and over	17.2

Question: How many millionaires (people with a net worth of a million dollars or more) are there in the United States?

Answer: According to the *Statistical Abstract of the United States*, there were 3,510,000 millionaires in the United States in 2001. The state with the most millionaires that year was California (572,000); the state with the fewest was Vermont (3,000).

What Is the Justification for Government Redistributing Income?

Some individuals say there is no justification for government welfare assistance—that is, redistributing income. In their view, playing Robin Hood is not a proper role of government. Persons who make this argument say they are not against helping the poor (e.g., they are usually in favor of private charitable organizations), but they are against government using its powers to take from some to give to others.

Others who believe in government welfare assistance usually present the *public good–free rider* justification or the *social-insurance* justification. Proponents of the public good–free rider position make the following arguments:

1. Most individuals in society would feel better if there were little or no poverty. It is distressing to view the signs of poverty, such as slums, hungry and poorly clothed people, and the homeless. Therefore, there is a demand for reducing or eliminating poverty.

2. The reduction or elimination of poverty is a *(nonexcludable) public good*—a good that, if consumed by one person, can be consumed by other persons to the same degree and the consumption of which cannot be denied to anyone. That is, when poverty is reduced or eliminated, everyone will benefit from no longer viewing the ugly and upsetting sights of poverty, and no one can be excluded from such benefits.

3. If no one can be excluded from experiencing the benefits of poverty reduction, then individuals will not have any incentive to pay for what they can get for free. Thus, they will become free riders. Economist Milton Friedman sums up the force of the argument this way:

> *I am distressed by the sight of poverty. I am benefited by its alleviation; but I am benefited equally whether I or someone else pays for its alleviation; the benefits of other people's charity therefore partly accrue to me. To put it differently, we might all of us be willing to contribute to the relief of poverty, provided everyone else did it. We might not be willing to contribute the same amount without such assurance.[7]*

Accepting the public good–free rider argument means that government is justified in taxing all persons to pay for the welfare assistance of some.

The social-insurance justification is a different type of justification for government welfare assistance. It holds that individuals currently not receiving welfare think they might one day need welfare assistance and thus are willing to take out a form of insurance for themselves by supporting welfare programs (with their tax dollars and votes).

SELF-TEST

1. "Poor people will always exist." Comment.

2. What percentage of the U.S. population was living in poverty in 2006?

3. What is the general description of a disproportionate percentage of the poor?

---

7. Milton Friedman, *Capitalism and Freedom* (Chicago: University of Chicago Press, 1962), p. 191.

office hours

"ARE THE NUMBER OF PERSONS IN EACH FIFTH THE SAME?"

Student:

Earlier you said that in 2005, the lowest fifth of household income earners in the United States received 3.4 percent of the total money income, the second fifth received 8.6 percent, the third fifth received 14.6 percent, the fourth fifth received 23.0 percent, and the top fifth (the rich) received 50.4 percent. Am I right that each fifth contains the same number of individuals? In other words, if there are 100 individuals in the lowest fifth, it follows that there are 100 individuals in the top fifth too.

Instructor:

No, you are not right. The quintiles (the fifths) are unequal in size because they are based on a count of households rather than persons, and not every household has the same number of persons it. For example, one household can have 2 persons in it, and another has 4.

Student:

Well, then, are there more persons in the top fifth of income earners than in the lowest fifth of income earners?

Instructor:

Yes. For example, in 2002, the top fifth contained 24.6 percent of the population, whereas the lowest fifth contained 14.3 percent of the population. Stated differently, the top fifth contained 69.4 million persons, and the lowest fifth contained 40.3 million persons.[8]

Student:

What happens to the income distribution if we adjust each fifth so that it has an equal number of persons in it? In other words, what happens if we adjust every fifth so that it contains 20 percent of the population?

Instructor:

The income distribution becomes less unequal. To illustrate, if you look at the data for 2002 and deal with households instead of persons, you'd conclude that the lowest fifth received 3.5 percent of the total money income and the top fifth received 49.7 percent. Now if you adjust the fifths so that each fifth has 20 percent of the population, the lowest fifth received 9.4 percent (instead of 3.5 percent) of the total money income and the top fifth received 39.6 percent (instead of 49.7 percent).

---

8. The adjusted income distributions in this feature come from Census Bureau data and a publication by Robert Rector and Rea Hederman, Jr., *Two Americas: One Rich, One Poor? Understanding Income Inequality in the United States* (August 24, 2004) at http://www.heritage.org/Research/Taxes/bg1791.cfm.

Student:

Can income distribution be adjusted for other things?

Instructor:

Yes. For example, persons in each fifth do not all work the same number of hours. For example, in 2002, individuals in the lowest fifth performed 4.3 percent of all work in the U.S. economy, and those in the highest fifth performed 33.9 percent. To be fair, though, the low levels of paid employment in the lowest fifth reflect the low numbers of working-age population in this group. In 2002, the lowest fifth contained only 11.2 percent of all working-age adults, whereas the highest fifth contained 27.6 percent. However, when we compare working-age adults in the lowest fifth with working-age adults in the highest fifth, we learn that the average working-age adult in the lowest fifth worked about half as many hours a year as the working-age adult in the highest fifth.

Now if we adjust the income distribution to show us what it would look like if average working-age adult in the lowest fifth worked as many hours as the average working-age adult in the top fifth, the income distribution becomes less unequal. In 2002, the lowest fifth would receive 12.3 percent (instead of 3.5 percent) of the total money income, and the top fifth would receive 35.8 percent (instead of 49.7 percent).

Student:

The income distribution seems as though it can be portrayed in different ways. We can adjust for taxes and transfer payments or choose not to; we can choose to adjust for number of persons or choose not to; we can choose to adjust for number of hours worked or choose not to.

Instructor:

You are right about that. And that is part of the reason for such heated debate over the income distribution. Person A might think it better to view the income distribution after having adjusted for something (such as taxes, transfer payments, the number of persons, etc.), and Person B might think it better to view the income distribution before adjusting.

Points to Remember

1. The bottom fifth of household income earners does not contain the same number of persons as the top fifth of household income earners. For example, in 2002, the top fifth contained 69.4 million persons while the lowest fifth contained 40.3 million persons.

2. The income distribution (or distribution of income) can be adjusted for various factors. Such adjustments often change the degree of income equality/inequality of the income distribution.

a reader asks | Are There Degrees of Poverty?

For a family of four, the poverty threshold or poverty line was $20,416 in 2006. So if a family of four earned less than $20,416 in 2006, it was living in poverty. But setting a dollar figure below which someone is said to be living in poverty doesn't seem to capture the severity or depth of poverty. After all, couldn't two four-person families have earned less than $20,416 in 2006, but still one family have earned much less than the other?

To focus in on the severity or depth of poverty, economists sometimes talk about the ratio of income to poverty.

$$\text{Ratio of income to poverty} = \frac{\text{Family's income}}{\text{Family's poverty income threshold}}$$

For example, consider two four-person families, A and B. In 2006, family A earned $16,000 and family B earned $9,000. The ratio of income to poverty for family A is:

$$\frac{\$16,000}{\$20,416} = 0.78$$

The ratio of income to poverty for family B is

$$\frac{\$9,000}{\$20,416} = 0.44$$

In other words, both families are poor, but family B is poorer than family A. The depth or severity of family B's poverty is greater than family A's poverty.

Now suppose we consider family C, another four-person family, whose income was, say, $22,000 in 2006. The ratio of income to poverty for family C is:

$$\frac{\$22,000}{\$20,416} = 1.08$$

Any time the ratio of income to poverty is greater than 1.00, a family is not considered to be living in poverty. However, if the ratio of income to poverty is between 1.00 and 1.25, the family is considered to be nearly poor. Family C, therefore, is nearly poor.

Chapter Summary

THE DISTRIBUTION OF INCOME

- In 2005, the lowest fifth of households received 3.4 percent of the total money income, the second fifth received 8.6 percent, the third fifth received 14.6 percent, the fourth fifth received 23.0 percent, the top fifth received 50.4 percent.

- The government can change the distribution of income through taxes and transfer payments. Individual income = Labor income + Asset income + Transfer payments − Taxes. Government directly affects transfer payments and taxes.

- The Lorenz curve represents the income distribution. The Gini coefficient is a measure of the degree of inequality in the distribution of income. A Gini coefficient of 0 means perfect income equality; a Gini coefficient of 1 means complete income inequality.

- Income inequality exists because individuals differ in their innate abilities and attributes, their choices of work and leisure, their education and other training, their attitudes about risk taking, the luck they experience, and the amount of wage discrimination directed against them. Some income inequality is the result of voluntary choices, and some is not.

- There are three major normative standards of income distribution: (1) The marginal productivity normative standard holds that the income distribution should be based on workers being paid their marginal revenue products. (2) The absolute income equality normative standard holds that there should be absolute or complete income equality. (3) The Rawlsian normative standard holds that the income distribution decided on behind the veil of ignorance (where individuals are equal) should exist in the real world.

POVERTY

- The income poverty threshold, or poverty line, is the income level below which a family or person is considered poor and living in poverty.

- It is important to be aware of the limitations of poverty income statistics. The statistics are usually not adjusted for (1) in-kind benefits, (2) unreported and illegal income, and (3) regional differences in the cost of living. Furthermore, the statistics do not count the poor who exist but who are out of sight, such as some of the homeless.

- People who believe government should redistribute income from the rich to the poor usually base their argument on the public good–free rider justification or the social-insurance justification. The public good–free rider justification holds that many people are in favor of redistributing income from the rich to the poor and that the elimination of poverty is a public good. Unfortunately, individuals cannot produce public goods because of the incentive everyone has to free-ride on the contributions of others. Consequently, government is justified in taxing all persons to pay for the welfare assistance of some. The social-insurance justification holds that individuals not currently receiving redistributed monies may one day find themselves in a position where they will need to; so they are willing to take out a form of insurance. In essence, they are willing to support redistribution programs today so that the programs exist if they should need them in the future.

Key Terms and Concepts

In-Kind Transfer Payments
Transfer Payments
Lorenz Curve

Gini Coefficient
Human Capital
Wage Discrimination

Veil of Ignorance
Poverty Income Threshold (Poverty Line)

Questions and Problems

1 What percentage of total money income did the lowest fifth of households receive in 2005? The fourth fifth?

2 "The Gini coefficient for country A is 0.35, and for country B it is 0.22. Therefore, the bottom 10 percent of income recipients in country B have a greater percentage of the total income than the bottom 10 percent of the income recipients in country A." Do you agree or disagree? Why?

3 Would you expect greater income inequality in country A, where there is great disparity in age, or in country B, where there is little disparity in age? Explain your answer.

4 Has U.S. income inequality increased or decreased (if we compare the income distribution in 1967 with the income distribution in 2005)? What percentage of total money income did the top fifth of U.S. households receive in 2005?

5 What role might each of the following play in contributing to income inequality?

   a. Risk taking.

   b. Education.

   c. Innate abilities and attributes.

6 What is a major criticism of the absolute income equality normative standard?

7 In what ways does the Rawlsian technique of hypothesizing individuals behind a veil of ignorance help or not help us decide whether we should have a 65-mile-per-hour speed limit or a higher one, a larger or smaller welfare system, and higher or lower taxes imposed on the rich?

8 Welfare recipients would rather receive cash benefits than in-kind benefits, but much of the welfare system provides in-kind benefits. Is there any reason for not giving recipients their welfare benefits the way they want to receive them? Would it be better to move to a welfare system that provides benefits only in cash?

9 What is the effect of age on income distribution?

10 Can more people live in poverty at the same time that a smaller percentage of people live in poverty? Explain your answer.

11 How would you determine whether the wage difference between two individuals is due to wage discrimination?

Working with Numbers and Graphs

1 The lowest fifth of income earners have a 10 percent income share, the second fifth a 17 percent income share, the third fifth a 22 percent income share, the fourth fifth a 24 percent income share, and the highest fifth a 27 percent income share. Draw the Lorenz curve.

2 In Exhibit 7, using Lorenz curve 2, approximately what percentage of income goes to the second-highest 20 percent of households?

3 Is it possible for everyone's real income to rise even though the income distribution in a society has become more unequal? Prove your answer with a numerical example.

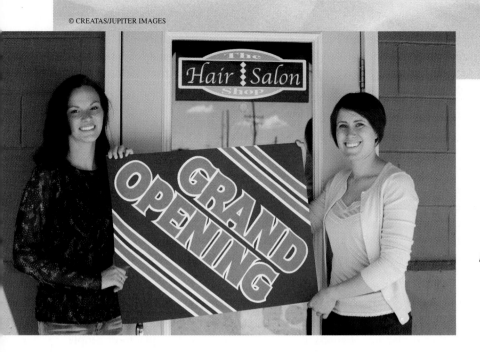

© CREATAS/JUPITER IMAGES

CHAPTER 15

INTEREST, RENT, AND PROFIT

Introduction From the time individuals decide to start a business until the day they open their door for the first time can seem like forever. Starting up a business involves decisions and payments. Most likely, the entrepreneurs will need to obtain a loan, on which they will pay interest. They will need to find a suitable location and may need to pay rent on a piece of land. Finally, the grand opening day arrives, and the new owners can look forward to earning profit.

Interest, rent, and profit are the payments to capital, land, and entrepreneurship. A knowledge of these three payments is critical to understanding how markets operate and how economies function.

INTEREST

The word *interest* is used in two ways in economics. Sometimes, it refers to the price for credit or **loanable funds**. For example, Lars borrows $100 from Rebecca and a year later pays her back $110. The interest is $10.

Interest can also refer to the return that capital earns as an input in the production process. A person who buys a machine (a capital good) for $1,000 and earns $100 a year by using the productive services of the machine is said to earn $100 interest, or a 10 percent interest rate, on the capital.

Economists refer to both the price for loanable funds and the return on capital goods as interest because the two tend to become equal, as discussed later in this section.

Loanable Funds: Demand and Supply

The equilibrium interest rate, or the price for loanable funds (or credit), is determined by the demand for and supply of loanable funds (or credit). The demand for loanable funds is composed of the demand for consumption loans, the demand for investment loans, and government's demand for loanable funds [the U. S. Treasury may need to finance budget

Loanable Funds
Funds that someone borrows and another person lends, for which the borrower pays an interest rate to the lender.

deficits by borrowing (demanding) loanable funds in the loanable funds market]. This chapter focuses on the demand for consumption loans and the demand for investment loans. The supply of loanable funds comes from people's saving and from newly created money. This chapter discusses only people's saving.

Therefore, in our discussion in this chapter, the demand for loanable funds is composed of (1) the demand for consumption loans and (2) the demand for investment loans. The supply of loanable funds is composed of people's saving.

THE SUPPLY OF LOANABLE FUNDS Savers are people who consume less than their current income. Without savers, there would be no supply of loanable funds. Savers receive an interest rate for the use of their funds, and the amount of funds saved and loaned is directly related to the interest rate.[1] Specifically, the supply curve of loanable funds is upward sloping: The higher the interest rate is, the greater the quantity supplied of loanable funds will be; the lower the interest rate, the less the quantity supplied of loanable funds.

THE DEMAND FOR LOANABLE FUNDS: CONSUMPTION LOANS Consumers demand loanable funds because they have a **positive rate of time preference**; that is, consumers prefer earlier availability of goods to later availability. For example, most people would prefer to have a car today than to have one five years from today.

Positive Rate of Time Preference

Preference for earlier over later availability of goods.

There is nothing irrational about a positive rate of time preference; most, if not all, people have it. People differ, though, as to the *degree* of their preference for earlier, compared with later, availability. Some people have a high rate of time preference, signifying that they greatly prefer present to future consumption ("I must have that new car today"). Other people have a low rate, signifying that they prefer present to future consumption only slightly. People with a high rate of time preference are less likely to postpone consumption than people with a low rate. People with a high rate of time preference feel they need to have things now.

Because consumers have a positive rate of time preference, there is a demand for consumption loans. Consumers borrow today to buy today; they will pay back the borrowed amount plus interest tomorrow. The interest payment is the price consumers/borrowers pay for the earlier availability of goods.

THE DEMAND FOR LOANABLE: INVESTMENT LOANS Investors (or firms) demand loanable funds (or credit) so that they can invest in capital goods and finance roundabout methods of production. A firm using a **roundabout method of production** first directs its efforts to producing capital goods and then uses those goods to produce consumer goods.

Roundabout Method of Production

The production of capital goods that enhance productive capabilities to ultimately bring about increased consumption.

Let's consider the direct method and the roundabout method for catching fish. In the direct method, a person uses his hands to catch fish. In the roundabout method, the person weaves a net (which is a capital good) and then uses the net to catch fish. Let's suppose that by using the direct method, Charlie can catch 4 fish per day. Using the roundabout method, he can catch 10 fish per day. Further suppose that it takes Charlie 10 days to weave a net. If Charlie does not weave a net and instead catches fish by hand, he can catch 1,460 fish per year (4 fish per day times 365 days). If, however, Charlie spends 10 days weaving a net (during which time he catches no fish), he can catch 3,550 fish the first year (10 fish per day times 355 days). Thus, the capital-intensive roundabout method of production is highly productive.

---

1. Because a higher interest rate may have both a substitution effect and an income effect, many economists argue that a higher interest rate can lead to either more saving or less saving depending on which effect is stronger. We ignore these complications at this level of analysis and hold that the supply curve of loanable funds (from savers) is upward sloping.

Because roundabout methods of production are so productive, investors are willing to borrow funds to finance them. For example, Charlie might reason, "I'm more productive if I use a fishing net, but I'll need to take 10 days off from catching fish and devote all my energies to weaving a net. What will I eat during the 10 days? Perhaps I can borrow some fish from my neighbor. I'll need to borrow 40 fish for the next 10 days. But I must make it worthwhile for my neighbor to enter into this arrangement, so I will promise to pay her back 50 fish at the end of the year. Thus, my neighbor will lend me 40 fish today in exchange for 50 fish at the end of the year. I realize I'm paying an interest rate of 25 percent [the interest payment of 10 fish is 25 percent of the number of fish borrowed, 40], but still it will be worth it." The highly productive nature of the capital-intensive roundabout method of production is what makes it worthwhile.

The reasoning in our fish example is repeated whenever a firm makes a capital investment. Producing computers on an assembly line is a roundabout method of production compared with producing them one by one by hand. Making copies on a copying machine is a roundabout method of production compared with copying by hand. In both cases, firms are willing to borrow now, use the borrowed funds to invest in capital goods to finance roundabout methods of production, and pay back the loan with interest later. If roundabout methods of production were not productive, firms would not be willing to do this.

THE LOANABLE FUNDS MARKET The sum of the demand for consumption loans and the demand for investment loans is the total demand for loanable funds. The demand curve for loanable funds is downward sloping. As interest rates rise, consumers' cost of earlier availability of goods rises, and they curtail their borrowing. Also, as interest rates rise, some investment projects that would be profitable at a lower interest rate will no longer be profitable. Therefore, the interest rate and the quantity demanded of loanable funds are inversely related.

Exhibit 1 illustrates the demand for and supply of loanable funds. The equilibrium interest rate occurs where the quantity demanded of loanable funds equals the quantity supplied of loanable funds.

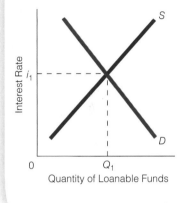

exhibit 1

Loanable Funds Market

The demand curve shows the different quantities of loanable funds demanded at different interest rates. The supply curve shows the different quantities of loanable funds supplied at different interest rates. Through the forces of supply and demand, the equilibrium interest rate and the quantity of loanable funds at that rate are established as i_1 and Q_1.

Common MISCONCEPTIONS

About Interest

Today, when you make the interest payments on a loan, you make them in money. Because interest payments are made in money, some people believe that interest would not exist in a moneyless or barter economy, but this isn't true. Interest will exist any time people have a positive rate of time preference, which is the case in both a money and a barter economy. In a money economy, interest payments are made in money. In a barter economy, interest payments are made in goods ("I borrowed 7 apples from you last month and today I am repaying you 8 apples").

Finding ECONOMICS

In Buying a Car

Annabelle takes out a car loan to buy a car. Where is the economics here? By taking out a loan, Annabelle is expressing a positive rate of time preference. She prefers having the car now to having the car later.

The Price for Loanable Funds and the Return on Capital Goods Tend to Equality

As already explained, both the *price for loanable funds* and the *return on capital* are referred to as interest because they tend to equality. To illustrate, suppose the return on capital is 10 percent and the price for loanable funds is 8 percent. In this setting, firms will borrow in the loanable funds market and invest in capital goods. As they do so, the quantity of capital increases, and its return falls (capital is subject to diminishing marginal returns). In short, the return on capital and the price for loanable funds begin to approach each other.

Suppose, instead, that the percentages are reversed, and the price for loanable funds is 10 percent and the return on capital is 8 percent. In this situation, no one will borrow loanable funds at 10 percent to invest at 8 percent. Over time, the capital stock will decrease (capital depreciates over time; it doesn't last forever), its marginal physical product will rise, and the return on capital and the price for loanable funds will eventually equal each other.

Why Do Interest Rates Differ?

The supply-and-demand analysis in Exhibit 1 suggests that there is only one interest rate in the economy. In reality, there are many. For example, a major business is not likely to pay the same interest rate for an investment loan to purchase new machinery as the person next door pays for a consumption loan to buy a car. Some of the factors that affect interest rates are discussed next. In each case, the *ceteris paribus* condition holds.

RISK Any time a lender makes a loan, there is a possibility that the borrower will not repay it. Some borrowers are better credit risks than others. A major corporation with a long and established history is probably a better credit risk than a person who has been unemployed three times in the last seven years. The more risk there is associated with a loan, the higher the interest rate will be; the less risk associated with a loan, the lower the interest rate.

TERM OF THE LOAN In general, the longer the term of the loan is, the higher the interest rate will be; the shorter the term of the loan, the lower the interest rate. Borrowers are usually more willing to pay higher interest rates for long-term loans because this gives them greater flexibility. Lenders require higher interest rates to part with their funds for extended periods.

COST OF MAKING THE LOAN A loan for $1,000 and a loan for $100,000 may require the same amount of record keeping, making the larger loan cheaper (per dollar) to process than the smaller loan. In addition, some loans require frequent payments (e.g., payments for a car loan), whereas others do not. This difference is likely to be reflected in higher administrative costs for loans with more frequent payments. Therefore, loans that cost more to process and administer will have higher interest rates than loans that cost less to process and administer.

 Thinking like AN ECONOMIST

Tending to Equality

In economics, factors typically converge. For example, in supply-and-demand analysis, the quantity demanded and the quantity supplied of a good tend to equality (through the equilibrating process). In consumer theory, the marginal utility-price ratios for different goods tend to equality. And, as just discussed, the price of loanable funds and the return on capital tend to equality.

(continued)

Thinking Like An Economist (continued)

In economics, many things tend to equality because equality is often representative of equilibrium. When quantity demanded equals quantity supplied, a market is said to be in equilibrium. When the marginal utility-price ratio for all goods is the same, the consumer is said to be in equilibrium. Inequality therefore often signifies disequilibrium. When the price of loanable funds is greater than the return on capital, there is disequilibrium.

The economist, knowing that equality often signifies equilibrium, looks for inequalities and then asks, "So what happens now?"

Nominal and Real Interest Rates

The **nominal interest rate** is the interest rate determined by the forces of supply and demand in the loanable funds market. It is the interest rate in current dollars. The nominal interest rate will change if the demand for or supply of loanable funds changes. Individuals' expectations of inflation are one of the factors that can change both the demand for and supply of loanable funds. Inflation occurs when the money prices of goods, on average, increase over time.

Exhibit 2 shows how inflation can affect the nominal interest rate. We start with an interest rate of 8 percent and an actual and expected inflation rate of zero (actual inflation rate = expected inflation rate = 0 percent). Later, both the demanders and suppliers of loanable funds expect a 4 percent inflation rate. In anticipation of a 4 percent inflation rate borrowers (demanders of loanable funds) will be willing to pay 4 percent more interest for their loans because they expect to be paying back the loans with dollars that have 4 percent less buying power than the dollars they are being lent. (Another way of looking at this is to say that if they wait to buy goods, the prices of the goods they want will have risen by 4 percent. To beat the price increase, they are willing to pay up to 4 percent more to borrow and purchase the goods now.) In effect, the demand for loanable funds curve shifts rightward, so that at Q_1 borrowers are willing to pay a 4 percent higher interest rate.

At the same time, the lenders (suppliers of loanable funds) require a 4 percent higher interest rate (i.e., 12 percent) to compensate them for the 4 percent less valuable dollars in which the loan will be repaid. In effect, the supply of loanable funds curve shifts leftward, so that at Q_1 lenders will receive an interest rate of 12 percent.

Thus, an expected inflation rate of 4 percent increases the demand for loanable funds and decreases the supply of loanable funds, so that the interest rate is 4 percent higher than it was when the expected inflation rate was zero. In this example, 12 percent is the nominal interest rate. It is the interest rate in current dollars, and it includes the expected inflation rate.

If we adjust for the expected inflation rate, we have the **real interest rate**. The real interest rate is the nominal interest rate adjusted for the expected inflation rate; that is, it is the nominal interest rate minus the expected inflation rate. In our example, the real interest rate is 8 percent (real interest rate = nominal interest rate – expected inflation rate).

The real interest rate, not the nominal interest rate, matters to borrowers and lenders. Consider a lender who grants a $1,000 loan to a borrower at a 20 percent nominal interest rate at a time when the actual inflation rate is 15 percent. The amount repaid to the lender is $1,200, but $1,200

Nominal Interest Rate
The interest rate determined by the forces of supply and demand in the loanable funds market.

Real Interest Rate
The nominal interest rate adjusted for expected inflation—that is, the nominal interest rate minus the expected inflation rate.

exhibit 2

Expected Inflation and Interest Rates

We start at an 8 percent interest rate and an actual and expected inflation rate of 0 percent. Later, both borrowers and lenders expect an inflation rate of 4 percent. Borrowers are willing to pay a higher interest rate because they will be paying off their loans with cheaper dollars. Lenders require a higher interest rate because they will be paid back in cheaper dollars. The demand and supply curves shift such that at Q_1, borrowers are willing to pay and lenders require a 4 percent higher interest rate. The nominal interest rate is now 12 percent. The real interest rate is 8 percent (the real interest rate = nominal interest rate − expected inflation rate).

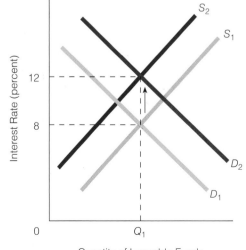

Quantity of Loanable Funds

with a 15 percent inflation rate does not have the buying power that $1,200 with a zero inflation rate has. The 15 percent inflation rate wipes out much of the gain, and the lender's real return on the loan is not 20 percent, but rather only 5 percent. Thus, the rate lenders receive and borrowers pay (and therefore the rate they care about) is the real interest rate.

Common MISCONCEPTIONS

About Interest Rates

A lender charges one borrower a higher interest rate than he charges another borrower. This is not necessarily some form of price discrimination. Price discrimination entails charging one customer a higher price than another customer when there is no difference in the cost of providing the good. In this case, a lender charges a higher interest rate to one borrower than to another because the risk of one borrower paying back the loan is higher than the risk of the other borrower paying back the loan.

Present Value: What Is Something Tomorrow Worth Today?

Present Value
The current worth of some future dollar amount of income or receipts.

Because of people's positive rate of time preference, $100 today is worth more than $100 a year from now. (Don't you prefer $100 today to $100 in a year?) Thus, $100 a year from now must be worth less than $100 today. The question is *how much* $100 a year from now is worth today. This question introduces the concept of *present value*. **Present value** is the current worth of some future dollar amount (of receipts or income). In our example, present value refers to what $100 a year from now is worth today.

Present value (*PV*) is computed by using the formula:

$$PV = \frac{A_n}{(1 + i)^n}$$

where A_n is the actual amount of income or receipts in a particular year in the future, i is the interest rate (expressed as a decimal), and n is the number of years in the future. The present value of $100 one year in the future at a 10 percent interest rate is $90.91:

$$PV = \frac{\$100}{(1 + 0.10)^1}$$
$$= \$90.91$$

Thus the right to receive $100 a year from now is worth $90.91 today. Another way to look at this is to realize that if $90.91 is put in a savings account paying a 10 percent interest rate, it would equal $100 in a year.

Now suppose we wanted to know what a particular future income stream was worth today. That is, instead of finding out what a particular future dollar amount is worth today, our objective is to find out what a series of future dollar amounts are worth today. The general formula is:

$$PV = \frac{\Sigma A_n}{(1 + i)^n}$$

where the Greek letter Σ stands for sum of.

Suppose a firm buys a machine that will earn $100 a year for the next 3 years. What is this future income stream, at $100 per year for 3 years, worth today? What is its present value? At a 10 percent interest rate, this income stream has a present value of $248.68:

IS THE CAR WORTH BUYING?

Business firms often compute present values when trying to decide whether to buy capital goods. Should consumers do the same when they are thinking about buying a durable good (a good that will last for a few years), such as a car?

Suppose you're thinking about buying a car. The market price of the car is $15,500, and you anticipate that you will receive $2,000 worth of services from the car each year for the next 10 years, after which time the car will have to be scrapped and will have no scrap value.

What is the question you should ask yourself? Ask the same question that the business firm asks when it considers buying a capital good. In your case ask: Is the present value of the car more than, less than, or equal to the present market price of the car?

What is the present value of the car? A car that yields $2,000 worth of benefits each year for 10 years at a 4 percent interest rate has a present value of approximately $16,223:

© MONKEYBUSINESS IMAGES/SHUTTERSTOCK

$$PV = \frac{\$2,000}{(1 + 0.04)^1} + \frac{\$2,000}{(1 + 0.04)^2}$$
$$+ \frac{\$2,000}{(1 + 0.04)^{10}} = \$16,223$$

(approximately)

The market price of the car ($15,500) is less than its present value ($16,223); so it is worthwhile to purchase the car.

You should be attentive to the interest rate. All other things remaining constant, an increase in the interest rate will lower the present value of the car. For example, at a 7 percent interest rate, the present value of the car is approximately $15,377. Now, the market price of the car ($15,500) is greater than the present value of the car ($15,377); it is not worthwhile to purchase this car. We would expect fewer cars to be sold when the interest rate rises and more cars to be sold when the interest rate falls because a change in the interest rate changes the present value of cars.

$$PV = \frac{A_1}{(1 + 0.10)^1} + \frac{A_2}{(1 + 0.10)^2} + \frac{A_3}{(1 + 0.10)^3}$$
$$= \frac{\$100}{1.10} + \frac{\$100}{1.21} + \frac{\$100}{1.331}$$
$$= \$90.91 + \$82.64 + \$75.13 = \$248.68$$

Deciding Whether or Not to Purchase a Capital Good

Business firms often compute present values when trying to decide whether to buy a capital good. Let's look again at the machine that will earn $100 a year for the next 3 years. Suppose, after the 3-year period, the machine must be scrapped and will have no scrap value. The firm will compare the present value of the future income generated by the machine ($248.68) with its cost, which is, say, $250. The firm will decide not to buy it because the cost of the machine is greater than the present value of the income stream the machine will generate.

If, however, the interest rate had been 4 percent instead of 10 percent, the business firm would be more likely to buy the machine. The present value of $100 a year for 3 years at 4 percent interest is $278. Comparing this amount with the cost of the machine ($250), we see that the firm is likely to buy the machine. Therefore, as interest rates decrease, present values increase, and firms will buy more capital goods; as interest rates increase, present values decrease, and firms will buy fewer capital goods, all other things held constant.

LOANS FOR THE POOREST OF THE POOR

The Norwegian Nobel Committee decided to award the Nobel Peace Prize for 2006, divided into two equal parts, to Muhammad Yunus and Grameen Bank for their efforts to create economic and social development from below, which also serves to advance democracy and human rights. Lasting peace cannot be achieved unless large population groups find ways to break out of poverty. Microcredit is one such means.

—October 13, 2006

On October 13, 2006, Muhammad Yunus and the bank that he founded, Grameen Bank, were jointly awarded the Nobel Peace Prize. Yunus, an economist, thought that giving loans to the poorest of the poor—even if they did not have any collateral—would not only help them, but could be a successful business too. (The Grameen Bank has been profitable in all but three years since it came into existence.) Giving loans to the poorest of the poor goes by different names: microfinance, microcredit, microloans. Here is how Yunus describes microfinance in an October 14, 2006, article he wrote for *The Wall Street Journal*.

> The basic philosophy behind micro-finance is that the poor, although spurned by traditional banks because they can't provide collateral, are actually a great investment: No one works harder than someone who is striving to achieve life's basic necessities, particularly a woman with children to support.[2]

Back in 1974, when Muhammad Yunus was a young economics professor at Chittagong University in Bangladesh, he started a conversation with a 21-year-old woman making bamboo stools in a small Bangladeshi village. It turned out that she had borrowed approximately 9 cents to buy the materials she needed to make the stools. After she paid back the lender, she would earn only a few cents for her work. Yunus found 43 others in the same situation as the young woman; in total they had borrowed $27. Yunus promised the people he would give them the $27 to pay off their loan if they assumed mutual responsibility (for the $27 loan) and pledged to guarantee repayment. They did, and in a year they had paid back the money. If it worked one time, why not again, Yunus must have thought. Today, the Grameen Bank gives loans to those who might want to start a business, buy a cow or a rickshaw, or buy materials such as cloth or pottery.

One of the interesting things about the repayment plan for the loans is that every person who receives a microloan from the Grameen Bank must be part of a five-member group of borrowers. The first two borrowers in the group must begin repaying the loan over a set period of time before the other members of the group can take out loans. Thus, peer pressure gives borrowers an incentive to repay their loans.

According to Yunus, since the Grameen Bank officially opened, it has given out $5.7 billion in loans (97 percent of the loans have gone to women). The average loan is about $100 and the recovery rate on the loans is approximately 99 percent. In many cases, the microloans have made the difference between people living in poverty and getting out of poverty. As Muhammad Yunus has stated ". . . very poor people need only a little money to set up a business that can make a dramatic difference in the quality of their lives."[3]

---

2. "A Hand Up Doesn't Always Require a Handout," *The Wall Street Journal*, October 14, 2006: A6.

3. Ibid.

 Finding ECONOMICS

In Living Longer

Suppose that because of an advancement in medical science, people start living longer. Can living longer affect the price of antique cars, famous paintings, and fine jewelry? Where is the economics here?

It can be found in the concept of present value. Suppose that you are considering the purchase of a painting and that you would receive $2,000 worth of benefits a year from owning and viewing it. The dollar price you would be willing to pay for the painting is partly based on the present value of the benefits over the number of years you plan to enjoy the painting. The number of years could be a higher number because you expect to live longer. At a given interest rate, the longer you expect to live, the greater will be the present value of the benefits you receive from the painting, and the more you would be willing to pay for the painting.

SELF-TEST

(Answers to Self-Test questions are in the Self-Test Appendix.)

1. Why does the price for loanable funds tend to equal the return on capital goods?

2. Why does the real interest rate, and not the nominal interest rate, matter to borrowers and lenders?

3. What is the present value of $1,000 two years from today if the interest rate is 5 percent?

4. A business firm is thinking of buying a capital good, which will earn $2,000 a year for the next 4 years and cost $7,000. The interest rate is 8 percent. Should the firm buy the capital good? Explain your answer.

RENT

Mention the word *rent*, and people naturally think of someone living in an apartment and making monthly payments to a landlord. This is not the type of rent discussed here. To an economist, rent means **economic rent**, that is, a payment in excess of opportunity costs. (We discussed economic rent in the chapter on monopoly.) A subset of economic rent, called **pure economic rent**, is a payment in excess of opportunity costs when opportunity costs are zero. Historically, the term *pure economic rent* was first used to describe the payment to the factor land, which is perfectly inelastic in supply.

In Exhibit 3, the total supply of land is fixed at Q_1 acres; there can be no more and no less than this amount of land. The payment for land is determined by the forces of supply and demand; this payment turns out to be R_1. Notice that R_1 is more than sufficient to bring Q_1 acres into supply. In fact, by reason of the fixed supply of land (the supply curve is perfectly inelastic), Q_1 acres would have been forthcoming at a payment of $0. In short, this land has zero opportunity costs. Therefore, the full payment—all of R_1—is referred to as pure economic rent.

David Ricardo, the Price of Grain, and Land Rent

In 19th-century England, people were concerned about the rising price of grains, which were a staple in many English diets. Some argued that grain prices were rising because land rents were going up rapidly. People began pointing fingers at the landowners, maintaining that the high rents the landowners received for their land made it more and more costly for farmers to raise grains. These higher costs, in turn, were passed on to consumers in the form of higher prices. According to this argument, the solution was to lower rents, which would lead to lower costs for farmers and eventually to lower prices for consumers.

English economist David Ricardo thought this reasoning was faulty. He contended that grain prices weren't high because rents were high (as most individuals thought) but rather that rents were high because grain prices were high. In current economic terminology, his argument was as follows: Land is a factor of production; therefore, the demand for it is derived. Land is also in fixed supply; therefore, the only thing that will change the payment made to land is a change in the demand for land. (The supply curve isn't going to shift, and thus the only thing that can change price is a shift in the demand curve.) Landowners have no control over the demand for land, which comes from other persons who want to use it.

In 19th-century England, the demand came from farmers who were raising grains and other foodstuffs. Landowners could not have pushed up land rents because they had no control over the demand for their land. Therefore, rents were high because the demand for land was high, and the demand for land was high because grain prices were high. Economists put it this way: *Land rents are price determined, not price determining.*

Economic Rent
Payment in excess of opportunity costs.

Pure Economic Rent
A category of economic rent where the payment is to a factor that is in fixed supply, implying that it has zero opportunity costs.

exhibit 3

Pure Economic Rent and the Total Supply of Land

The total supply of land is fixed at Q_1. The payment for the services of this land is determined by the forces of supply and demand. Because the payment is for a factor in fixed supply, it is referred to as pure economic rent.

Finding ECONOMICS

In a Sandwich and a Soft Drink in New York City

Rachel is visiting New York City. She recently ordered a sandwich and soft drink for lunch in a restaurant. Her bill was $21. She complained to a friend later in the day, saying, "I don't know why everything is so expensive in New York. I paid $21 for a sandwich and drink today." Her friend replied, "Sandwich prices are high because the owner of the restaurant has to pay such high rent for his place." Where is the economics?

Here is the same misperception about rents and prices that Ricardo found in the 19th century. Many people today complain that prices in stores, hotels, and restaurants in New York City are high. When they notice that land rents are also high, they reason that prices are high because land rents are high. But, as Ricardo pointed out, the reverse is true: Land rents are high because prices are high. If the demand for living, visiting, and shopping in New York City was not as high as it is, prices for goods would not be as high. In turn, the demand for land would not be as high, and therefore the payments to land would not be as high.

The Supply Curve of Land Can Be Upward Sloping

Exhibit 3 depicts the supply of land as fixed—the case when the total supply of land is in question. For example, this country has only so many acres of land, and that amount is not likely to change.

Most subparcels of land, however, have competing uses. Consider 25 acres of land on the periphery of a major city. It can be used for farmland, a shopping mall, or a road. If a parcel of land (as opposed to all land, or the total supply of land) has competing uses (the land can be used one way or another), the parcel has opportunity costs. Land that is used for farming could have been used for a shopping mall. To reflect the opportunity cost of that land, the supply curve is upward sloping. The upward slope implies that if individuals want more land for a specific purpose—say, for a shopping mall—they must bid high enough to attract existing land away from other uses (e.g., farming). Exhibit 4 illustrates this phenomenon, where the equilibrium payment to land is R_1. The shaded area indicates the economic rent.

Economic Rent and Other Factors of Production

The concept of economic rent applies to economic factors besides land. For example, it applies to labor. Suppose Hanson works for company X and is paid $60,000 a year. Further suppose that in his next best alternative job, he would be earning $57,000. Hanson is receiving economic rent working for company X in that he is receiving a payment in excess of his opportunity costs; thus, he is receiving economic rent.

Or consider the local McDonald's that hires teenagers. It pays all its beginning employees the same wage, but not all beginning employees have the same opportunity cost. Suppose two teenagers, Tracy and Paul, sign on to work at McDonald's for $8.00 an hour. Tracy's next best alternative wage is $8.00 an hour working for her mother's business, and Paul's next best alternative wage is $7.25 an hour. Tracy receives no economic rent in her McDonald's job, but Paul receives 75 cents an hour economic rent in the same job.

Over time, teenagers and other beginning employees usually find that their opportunity costs rise (owing to continued schooling and job experience) and that the McDonald's wage no longer covers their opportunity costs. When this happens, they quit.

exhibit 4

Economic Rent and the Supply of Land (Competing Uses)

A particular parcel of land, as opposed to the total supply of land, has competing uses, or positive opportunity costs. For example, to obtain land to build a shopping mall, the developers must bid high enough to attract existing land away from competing uses. The supply curve is upward-sloping. At a payment of R_1, economic rent is identified as the payment in excess of (positive) opportunity costs.

Economic Rent and Baseball Players: The Perspective from Which the Factor Is Viewed Matters

Economic rent differs depending on the perspective from which the factor is viewed. Suppose that, if a baseball star who earns $1 million a year playing baseball weren't playing baseball, he would be a coach at a high school. Therefore, the difference between what he is currently paid ($1 million a year) and what he would earn as a coach (say, $40,000 a year) is economic rent. This amounts to $960,000. Thus economic rent is determined by identifying the alternative to the baseball star's playing baseball.

However, a different alternative would be identified by asking, what is the alternative to the baseball star's playing baseball for his present team? The answer is that he probably can play for another team. For example, if he weren't playing for the Boston Red Sox, he might be playing for the Pittsburgh Pirates and earning $950,000 a year. His economic rent in this instance is only $50,000. So the player's economic rent as *a player for the Boston Red Sox* is $50,000 a year (his next best alternative is playing for the Pittsburgh Pirates earning $950,000 a year). But his economic rent as *a baseball player* is $960,000 (his next best alternative is being a high school coach earning $40,000 a year).

Competing for Artificial and Real Rents

Individuals and firms compete for both *artificial rents* and *real rents*. An artificial rent is an economic rent that is artificially contrived by government; that is, it would not exist without government. Suppose government decides to award a monopoly right to one firm to produce good X. In so doing, it legally prohibits all other firms from producing good X. If the firm with the monopoly right receives a price for good X in excess of its opportunity costs, it receives a rent or monopoly profit because of government's supply restraint. Firms that compete for the monopoly right to produce good X expend resources in a socially wasteful manner.[4] They use resources to lobby politicians in the hope of getting the monopoly, and those resources (from society's perspective) could be better used to produce goods and services.

Competing for real rents is different, however. If the rent is real (not artificially created) and if there are no barriers to competing for it, resources are used in a way that is socially productive. For example, suppose firm Z currently receives economic rent in the production of good Z. Government does not prohibit other firms from competing with firm Z; so some do. These other firms also produce good Z, thus increasing its supply and lowering its price. The lower price reduces the rent firm Z receives in its production of good Z. In the end, firm Z has less rent, and society has more of good Z and pays a lower price for it.

Do People Overestimate Their Worth to Others, or Are They Simply Seeking Economic Rent?

Johnson is an accountant with seven years of experience who is currently earning $95,000 annually. One day, he walks into his employer's office and asks for a raise in salary to $105,000. His employer asks him why he thinks he deserves the $10,000 raise. Johnson says that he is sure he is worth that much. (If he is, he can leave his current company and receive an offer of $105,000 from another company. We don't know whether he can do this.)

His employer believes that Johnson is overestimating his worth to others. She thinks, "There is no way Johnson is worth $10,000 more a year. He is simply overestimating his worth."

---

4. This may sound familiar. The process described, where individuals expend resources lobbying government for a special privilege, was described as rent seeking in the chapter about monopoly.

However, Johnson is not necessarily overestimating his worth to others. He could believe his worth to others is $95,000—in other words, $95,000 is his opportunity cost—but he could be attempting to receive economic rent ($10,000 more than his opportunity cost) by getting his employer to believe his opportunity cost is really $105,000. Thus, a person who may appear to others to be overestimating his worth may be attempting to obtain economic rent.

SELF·TEST

1. Give an example to illustrate that economic rent differs depending on the perspective from which the factor is viewed.

2. Nick's salary is pure economic rent. What does this imply about Nick's next best alternative salary?

3. What are the social consequences of firms competing for artificial rents, as opposed to competing for real rents (where there are no barriers to competing for real rents)?

PROFIT

The so-called profits that appear in newspaper headlines are *accounting profits,* not economic profits. Economic profit is the difference between total revenue and total cost, where both explicit and implicit costs are included in total cost. Economists emphasize economic profit over accounting profit because economic profit determines entry into and exit from an industry. For the most part, this is how economic profit figured in the discussion of market structures in previous chapters.

In this section, we discuss profit as the payment to a resource. Recall that economists talk about four resources, or factors of production: land, labor, capital, and entrepreneurship. Firms make payments to each of these resources: Wages are the payment to labor, interest is the payment to capital, rent is the payment to land, and profit is the payment to entrepreneurship. A discussion of the source of profits enables us to find out why economic profit exists.

Theories of Profit

Several different theories address the question of where profit comes from, or the source of profit. One theory holds that profit would not exist in a world of certainty; hence, uncertainty is the source of profit. Another theory holds that profit is the return for alertness to broadly defined arbitrage opportunities. A third theory holds that profit is the return to the entrepreneur as innovator.

PROFIT AND UNCERTAINTY Uncertainty exists when a potential occurrence is so unpredictable that a probability cannot be estimated. (For example, what is the probability that the United States will enter a world war in 2020?) Risk, which many people mistake for uncertainty, exists when the probability of a given event can be estimated. (For example, a coin toss has a 50-50 chance coming up heads.) Therefore, risks can be insured against, but uncertainties cannot.

Anything that can be insured against can be treated as just another cost of doing business, and thus insurance coverage is an input in the production process. Only uncertain events can cause a firm's revenues to diverge from costs (including insurance costs). The investor/decision maker who is adept at making business decisions under conditions of uncertainty earns a profit. For example, based on experience and some insights, an entrepreneur may believe that 75 percent of college students will buy personal computers next year. This assessment, followed by investing in a chain of retail computer stores near college campuses, will ultimately prove to be right or wrong. The essential point is that the entrepreneur's judgment cannot be insured against. If correct, the entrepreneur will earn a profit; if incorrect, a loss.

PROFIT AND ARBITRAGE OPPORTUNITIES The way to make a profit, the advice goes, is to buy low and sell high (usually the same item). For example, someone might buy an ounce of gold in New York for $750 and sell the same ounce of gold in London for $770. We might say that the person is alert to where she can buy low and sell high, thereby earning a profit. She is alert to what is called an arbitrage opportunity.

Sometimes, buying low and selling high does not refer to the same item. The opportunity can refer to buying factors in one set of markets at the lowest possible prices, combining the factors into a finished product, and then selling the product in another market for the highest possible price. An example of this is buying oranges and sugar (in the oranges and sugar markets), combining the two, and selling an orange soft drink (in the soft drink market). If doing this results in profit, the person who undertook the act is considered alert to a (broadly defined) arbitrage opportunity. He saw that oranges and sugar together, in the form of an orange soft drink, would fetch more than the sum of oranges and sugar separately.

PROFIT AND INNOVATION In this theory, profit is the return to the entrepreneur as innovator—the person who creates new profit opportunities by devising a new product, production process, or marketing strategy. Viewed this way, profit is the return to innovative genius. People such as Thomas Edison, Henry Ford, and Richard Sears and Alvah Roebuck are said to have had innovative genius.

Thinking like AN ECONOMIST

About Interest, Land Rent, and Profits

Throughout history, interest, land rent, and profits have often been attacked. For example, Henry George (1839–1897), who wrote the influential book *Progress and Poverty*, believed that all land rents were pure economic rents and should be heavily taxed. Landowners benefited simply because they had the good fortune to own land. In George's view, landowners did nothing productive. He maintained that the early owners of land in the American West reaped high land rents not because they had made their land more productive but because individuals from the East began to move West, driving up the price of land. In arguing for a heavy tax on land rents, George said there would be no supply response in land owing to the tax because land was in fixed supply.

Profits have also frequently come under attack. High profits are somehow thought to be evidence of corruption or manipulation. Those who earn profits are sometimes considered no better than thieves.

The economist thinks of interest, land rent, and profits differently from many laypersons. The economist understands that all are returns to resources, or factors of production. Most people find it easy to understand that labor is a factor of production and that wages are the return to this factor. But understanding that land, capital, and entrepreneurship are also genuine factors of production, with returns that flow to them, seems more difficult.

Another overlooked point is that interest exists largely because individuals naturally have a positive rate of time preference. Those who dislike interest are in fact criticizing a natural characteristic of individuals. If the critics could change this natural trait and make individuals stop weighting present consumption higher than future consumption, interest would diminish.

A similar point can be made about profit. Some say profit is the consequence of living in a world of uncertainty. If those who do not like profit could make the world less uncertain, or bring certainty to it, then profit would disappear.

INSURING ONESELF AGAINST TERRORISM[5]

Meet Abbas Shaheed al-Taiee, an executive at the Iraq Insurance Company in Baghdad, Iraq. Mr. Shaheed is an innovator who came up with the idea of selling the Iraqi people something he thought they had a demand for: terrorism insurance.

Mr. Shaheed says terrorism insurance is his gift to the Iraqi people: "We have expanded the principles of life insurance to cover everything that happens in Iraq." The ter-

© PATRICK BAZ/AFP/GETTY IMAGES

rorism insurance policy looks much like an ordinary life insurance policy, except for a one-page rider that insures a person against (1) explosions caused by weapons of war and car bombs, (2) assassinations, and (3) terrorist attacks. According to Mr. Shaheed, it doesn't matter who fires the shots or sets off the bombs. The policy pays off no matter who is at fault.

The cost of the policy depends on your occupation. If it is one of the safer occupations, the cost is $45 for about $3,500 worth of coverage (which is what an Iraqi police officer earns a year). If you have a relatively unsafe profession (e.g., a police officer or translator for a Western company), the cost is $90 for about $3,500 worth of coverage.

5. This feature is based on Robert F. Worth, "New Business Blooms in Iraq: Terror Insurance," *The New York Times*, March 21, 2006.

What Is Entrepreneurship?

We have defined entrepreneurship as the talent of some people for organizing the resources of land, labor, and capital to produce goods, seek new business opportunities, and develop new ways of doing things. Taking the three profit theories together, we can define entrepreneurship more narrowly: *An entrepreneur bears uncertainty, is alert to arbitrage opportunities, and exhibits innovative behavior.* Most entrepreneurs probably exhibit different degrees of each. For example, Thomas Edison may have been more the innovator entrepreneur than the arbitrager entrepreneur.

Notice that entrepreneurship is not like the other factors of production (land, labor, capital) in that it cannot be measured. There are no entrepreneurial units as there are for labor, capital, and land units. Furthermore, an entrepreneur receives profit as a residual after the other factors of production have been paid. Thus, the actual dollar amount of profit depends on the payments to the other three factors of production.

What a Microwave Oven and an Errand Runner Have in Common

A microwave oven and an errand runner both economize on your time. Many people today complain that they don't have enough time to do all they want to do. Where these people see a problem, the entrepreneur sees a business opportunity. If people do not have enough time to do what they want, she reasons, then perhaps they will be willing to pay for a product or service that economizes on their time and frees time for other uses. The microwave oven, for example, reduces the time it takes to cook a meal, thus freeing time for other activities such as reading a book, working, sleeping, and so on.

Stanley Richards is another example. He recently started a business that economizes on people's time. Richards started a company called Stan's Mobile Car Service. For $29.95 plus tax, he drives to a customer's car, whether it is at home or at work, and changes the oil, lubricates the chassis, and checks the engine. He says that he expects to do 90 jobs a day after his three vans are in operation.

Or consider the professional errand runner, who will pick up the laundry, manage the house, feed the cat, pick up food for a party, and do other such things. In some large cities around the country, professional errand runners will do the things that two-earner families or working single men and women would rather pay someone to do than take the time to do themselves.

Profit and Loss as Signals

Although profit and loss are often viewed in terms of the benefit or hurt they bring to persons, they also signal how a market may be changing. When a firm earns a profit, entrepreneurs in other industries view the profit as a signal that the firm is producing and selling a good that buyers value more than the factors that go to make the good. (The firm would not earn a profit unless its product had more value than the total of the payments to the other three factors of production.) The profit causes entrepreneurs to move resources into the production of the profit-linked good. In short, resources follow profit.

On the other hand, if a firm is taking a loss, the loss is a signal to the entrepreneur that the firm is producing and selling a good that buyers value less than the factors that go to make the good. The loss causes resources to move out of the production of the loss-linked good. Resources turn away from losses.

SELF-TEST

1. What is the difference between risk and uncertainty?
2. Why does profit exist?
3. "Profit is not simply a dollar amount; it is a signal." Comment.

"HOW IS PRESENT VALUE USED IN THE COURTROOM?"

Student:

I've heard that present value is sometimes used in law cases. Is this true? And if so, how is it used?

Instructor:

Yes, it is true. It could be used in a divorce case. For example, suppose Jack and Carol are getting a divorce. Carol worked during the time Jack went to medical school. In the divorce, Carol and Jack agree to split the assets they own together: the house, the paintings, the jewelry, the cars, and so on. Carol claims that the Jack's medical degree is an asset that she should have part of. "After all," she says, "I helped pay for Jack's medical education."

Student:

So is the objective now to find out what the medical degree is worth?

Instructor:

Yes. And this is where present value comes in. Suppose Jack will earn $100,000 more each year for the next 25 years because he went to medical school. Carol's attorney needs to find the present value of this dollar amount, which turns out to be approximately $1.57 million. Now the court has to decide whether the medical degree is an asset whose proceeds should be divided between Carol and Jack.

Student:

Does present value come up in any other cases?

Instructor:

Yes. Present value is sometimes used in injury cases. For example, suppose Yvonne gets hit by a drunk driver and can't work any longer. She might ask to be compensated for the injury plus the loss in her earning power. Her lawyer will need to find the present value of her lost earnings (over, say, the next 10 years).

Points to Remember

1. Present value can be used to determine today's worth of a medical education.
2. Present value can be used to determine today's worth of a loss in earning power.

a reader asks | Are There Calculators to Help Me Plan My Life?

Present value is discussed in this chapter, and I know that the World Wide Web has calculators available for finding present value. Are other calculators available—especially ones that will help me plan my life?

People often have questions about the financial aspects of their lives. For example, you might want to know how much you have to save each month (beginning now) to have $1 million by the time you retire. Or you might want to know what your mortgage payments will be if you put a $50,000 down payment on a house that sells for $200,000. Or you want to know what $1 million will be worth 10 years from now if the annual inflation rate over this time period is 4 percent.

Here are some typical questions (yours may be similar) and their answers, along with the location of the online calculators we used.

1. I plan on taking out a $200,000 mortgage loan to buy a house. The term of the loan will be 30 years, and the interest rate will be 7 percent. What will my monthly mortgage payment be? Answer: $1,330.60.

    Go to http://www.bloomberg.com/analysis/calculators/mortgage.html and fill in the information for loan amount, number of years, and interest rate.

2. If I save $200 a month at 5 percent interest (compounded monthly), how much will I have in savings in 30 years? Answer: $166,451.

    Go to http://www.planningtips.com/cgi-bin/savings.pl and click Simple Savings Calculator. Fill in the information requested. By the way, just adding another $100 a month increases the total to approximately $250,000.

3. I am 20 years old and plan to retire when I am 65. I currently have $5,000 in my savings account. If I reap an annual return of 6 percent, how much do I need to save each year to retire with $1 million? Answer: $4,377.

    Go to http://www.bloomberg.com/invest/calculators/retire.html and fill in the information.

4. I have a young child who will start college in the year 2020. The college I would like her to attend currently charges $20,000 tuition per year. If tuition inflation is 2 percent, a 5 percent return on savings is reasonable, and I am paying a 28 percent marginal tax rate, what dollar amount must I save each week to pay my child's tuition in the future? Answer: $80.93.

    Go to http://www.bloomberg.com/invest/calculators/mortgage.html and fill in the information.

5. I currently have a $200,000 mortgage loan (30 years) at 8 percent. My monthly payment is $1,467. If I want to pay off the loan in half the time (15 years), what should I increase my monthly mortgage payment to? Answer: $1,916.

    Go to http://www.hughchou.org/calc/duration.cgi and fill in the information.

    If you voluntarily increase your payment by $449 a month, you will pay off your loan 15 years earlier and save approximately $185,195 in interest.

Chapter Summary

INTEREST

-   Interest refers to (1) the price paid by borrowers for loanable funds and (2) the return on capital in the production process. There is a tendency for these two to become equal.

-   The equilibrium interest rate (in terms of the price for loanable funds) is determined by the demand for and supply of loanable funds. The supply of loanable funds comes from savers, people who consume less than their current incomes. The demand for loanable funds comes from the demand for consumption and investment loans.

-   Consumers demand loanable funds because they have a positive rate of time preference; they prefer earlier rather than later availability of goods. Investors (or firms) demand loanable funds so that they can finance roundabout methods of production.

-   The nominal interest rate is the interest rate determined by the forces of supply and demand in the loanable funds market; it is the interest rate in current dollars. The real interest rate is the nominal interest rate adjusted for expected inflation. Specifically, real interest rate = nominal interest rate – expected inflation rate (which means nominal interest rate = real interest rate + expected inflation rate).

RENT

- Economic rent is a payment in excess of opportunity costs. A subset of this is pure economic rent, which is a payment in excess of opportunity costs when opportunity costs are zero. Historically, the term *pure economic rent* was used to describe the payment to the factor land because land (in total) was assumed to be fixed in supply (perfectly inelastic). Today, the terms *economic rent* and *pure economic rent* are also used when speaking about economic factors other than land.

- David Ricardo argued that high land rents were an effect of high grain prices, not a cause of them (in contrast to many of his contemporaries who thought high rents caused the high grain prices). Land rents are price determined, not price determining.

- The amount of economic rent a factor receives depends on the perspective from which the factor is viewed. For example, a university librarian earning $50,000 a year receives $2,000 economic rent if his next best alternative income at another university is $48,000. The economic rent is $10,000 if his next best alternative is in a nonuniversity (nonlibrarian) position that pays $40,000.

PROFIT

- Several different theories of profit address the question of the source of profit. One theory holds that profit would not exist in a world of certainty; hence, uncertainty is the source of profit. Another theory holds that profit is the return for alertness to arbitrage opportunities. A third holds that profit is the return to the entrepreneur as innovator.

- Taking the three profit theories together, we can say that profit is the return to entrepreneurship, where entrepreneurship entails bearing uncertainty, being alert to arbitrage opportunities, and being innovative.

Key Terms and Concepts

Loanable Funds	Nominal Interest Rate	Economic Rent
Positive Rate of Time Preference	Real Interest Rate	Pure Economic Rent
Roundabout Method of Production	Present Value	

Questions and Problems

1 What does it mean to say that an individual has a positive rate of time preference?

2 What does having a positive rate of time preference have to do with positive interest rates?

3 How would the interest rate change as a result of the following?

   a. A rise in the demand for consumption loans.

   b. A decline in the supply of loanable funds.

   c. A rise in the demand for investment loans.

4 The interest rate on loan X is higher than the interest rate on loan Y. What might explain the difference in interest rates between the two loans?

5 The real interest rate can remain unchanged as the nominal interest rate rises. Do you agree or disagree with this statement? Explain your answer.

6 What type of person is most willing to pay high interest rates?

7 Some people have argued that in a moneyless (or barter) economy, interest would not exist. Is this true? Explain your answer.

8 In what ways are a baseball star who can do nothing but play baseball and a parcel of land similar?

9 What does it mean to say that land rent is price determined, not price determining?

10 What is the link between profit and uncertainty?

11 What is the overall economic function of profits?

12 "The more economic rent a person receives in his job, the less likely he is to leave the job and the more content he will be on the job." Do you agree or disagree? Explain your answer.

13 It has been said that a society with a high savings rate is a society with a high standard of living. What is the link (if any) between saving and a relatively high standard of living?

14 Make an attempt to calculate the present value of your future income.

15 Describe the effect of each of the following events on individuals' rate of time preference and thus on interest rates:

   a. A technological advance that increases longevity.

   b. An increased threat of war.

   c. Growing older.

16 "As the interest rate falls, firms are more inclined to buy capital goods." Do you agree or disagree? Explain your answer.

Working with Numbers and Graphs

1 Compute the following:
   a. The present value of $25,000 each year for 4 years at a 7 percent interest rate.
   b. The present value of $152,000 each year for 5 years at a 6 percent interest rate.
   c. The present value of $60,000 each year for 10 years at a 6.5 percent interest rate.

2 Bobby is a baseball player who earns $1 million a year playing for team X. If he weren't playing baseball for team X, he would be playing baseball for team Y and earning $800,000 a year. If he weren't playing baseball at all, he would be working as an accountant earning $120,000 a year. What is his economic rent as a baseball player playing for team X? What is his economic rent as a baseball player?

3 Diagrammatically represent pure economic rent.

CHAPTER *16*

MARKET FAILURE: EXTERNALITIES, PUBLIC GOODS, AND ASYMMETRIC INFORMATION

© CREATAS/JUPITER IMAGES

Introduction Markets are a major topic in this book. We have analyzed how markets work, beginning with the simple supply-and-demand model, as well as various market structures: perfect competition, monopoly, and others. Goods and services are produced in markets. For example, cars are produced in car markets, houses are produced in housing markets, and computers are produced in computer markets. We now ask do these markets produce the right amount (the optimal or ideal amount) of these various goods? What is the right amount? For example, what is the ideal or optimal amount of houses to produce, and does the housing market actually produce this amount?

When a market produces more or less than the ideal or optimal amount of a particular good, economists say there is **market failure**. Economists want to know under what conditions market failure may occur. This chapter presents three topics in which market failure is a prominent part of the discussion: externalities, public goods, and asymmetric information.

Market Failure
A situation in which the market does not provide the ideal or optimal amount of a good.

EXTERNALITIES

Externality
A side effect of an action that affects the well-being of third parties.

Sometimes, when goods are produced and consumed, side effects (spillover or third-party effects) are felt by people who are not directly involved in the market exchanges. In general, these side effects are called **externalities** because the costs or benefits are external to the persons who caused them. In this section, we discuss the various costs and benefits of different activities and describe how and when activities cause externalities. We then explain graphically how externalities can result in market failure.

Costs and Benefits of Activities

Most activities in life have both costs and benefits. For example, when Jim sits down to read a book, reading has some benefits for Jim and some costs. These benefits and costs are private to him—they affect only him—hence, we call them *private benefits* and *private costs.*

Jim can also undertake an activity that has benefits and costs not only for him but also for others. Suppose he decides to smoke a cigarette in the general vicinity of Angelica. For Jim, smoking the cigarette has both benefits and costs—his private benefits and costs. But Jim's smoking might also affect Angelica in some way if, for example, she reacts to cigarette smoke by coughing. In this case, Jim's smoking might impose a cost on Angelica. Because the cost Jim imposes on her is external to him, we call it an *external cost.* We might say that Jim's activity imposes a *negative externality* on Angelica, for which she incurs an external cost. A **negative externality** exists when a person's or group's actions cause a cost (or adverse side effect) to be felt by others.

In a slightly different example, suppose Jim lives across the street from Yvonne and beautifies his front yard (which Yvonne can clearly see from her house) by planting trees, flowers, and a new lawn. Obviously, Jim receives some benefits and costs by beautifying his yard, but Yvonne enjoys some benefits too. Not only does she have a pretty yard to gaze at (in much the same way that someone might benefit by gazing at a beautiful painting), but Jim's beautification efforts may also raise the market value of Yvonne's property.

Because the benefit that Jim generates for Yvonne is external to him, we call it an *external benefit.* We might say that Jim's activity generates a *positive externality* for Yvonne, for which she receives an external benefit. A **positive externality** exists when a person's or group's actions cause a benefit (or beneficial side effect) to be felt by others.

> **Negative Externality**
> The condition that exists when a person's or group's actions cause a cost (adverse side effect) to be felt by others.

> **Positive Externality**
> The condition that exists when a person's or group's actions cause a benefit (beneficial side effect) to be felt by others.

Finding ECONOMICS

Students Talking in Class

Blake sits near the back of the room in his biology class. Two students who sit near Blake often talk to each other while the class is in session. They usually whisper, but still their talking disturbs Blake. Where is the economics? As far as Blake is concerned, the two talking students are doing something (talking during the class) that adversely affects him. For Blake, their talking is a negative externality.

Marginal Costs and Benefits of Activities

When considering activities for which there are different degrees or amounts of costs and benefits (does Jim smoke one cigarette an hour or two? does he plant three trees or four?), it makes sense to speak in terms of marginal benefits and costs. More specifically, for Jim, various activities have marginal private benefits (*MPB*) and marginal private costs (*MPC*). If Jim's activities generate external benefits or costs for others, then it makes sense to speak in terms of marginal external benefits (*MEB*) and marginal external costs (*MEC*).

To analyze the effects of an activity, we need to know the total marginal costs and benefits. So we sum them.

The sum of marginal private costs (*MPC*) and marginal external costs (*MEC*) is **marginal social costs (MSC)**.

$$MSC = MPC + MEC$$

> **Marginal Social Costs (MSC)**
> The sum of marginal private costs (*MPC*) and marginal external costs (*MEC*): *MSC* = *MPC* + *MEC*.

In our example of Jim smoking a cigarette and imposing an external cost on Angelica, suppose Jim's MPC of smoking a cigarette is $1, and Angelica's MEC of Jim's smoking a cigarette is $2. Therefore, the MSC of Jim smoking a cigarette (taking into account both Jim's private costs and Angelica's external costs) is $3.

The sum of marginal private benefits (MPB) and marginal external benefits (MEB) is **marginal social benefits (MSB)**.

Marginal Social Benefits (MSB)
The sum of marginal private benefits (MPB) and marginal external benefits (MEB): $MSB = MPB + MEB$.

$$MSB = MPB + MEB$$

In our example of Jim beautifying his yard and causing an external benefit for Yvonne, suppose Jim's MPB of beautifying his yard is $5, and Yvonne's MEB is $3. The MSB of Jim's beautifying his yard (at a given level of beautification) is therefore $8.

Social Optimality, or Efficiency, Conditions

Socially Optimal Amount (Output)
An amount that takes into account and adjusts for all benefits (external and private) and all costs (external and private). The socially optimal amount is the amount at which $MSB = MSC$. Sometimes, the socially optimal amount is referred to as the efficient amount.

For an economist, there is always a right amount of something. There is a right amount of time to study for a test, a right amount of exercise, and a right number of cars to be produced. The right amount, for an economist, is the **socially optimal amount (output)**, or the efficient amount (output). This is the amount at which a particular condition is met: $MSB = MSC$. In other words, the right amount of anything is the amount at which the MSB (of that thing) equals the MSC (of that thing). Later in this section, we illustrate this condition graphically.

Three Categories of Activities

For the person who engages in an activity (whether producing a computer or studying for an exam), the activity almost always brings benefits and costs. It is hard to think of any activities in life in which private benefits and private costs do not exist.

It is not so hard, however, to think of activities in life in which external benefits and external costs do not exist. For example, when reading a book, a person incurs benefits and costs, but probably no one else does. We can characterize this effect in the following way: $MPB > 0$, $MPC > 0$, $MEB = 0$, $MEC = 0$. Marginal private benefits and costs are both positive (greater than zero), but there are no marginal external benefits or costs. In other words, the activity has no positive or negative externalities.

Therefore, activities may be categorized according to whether negative or positive externalities exist, as shown in the following table:[1]

Category	Definition	Meaning in Terms of Marginal Benefits and Costs
1	No negative or positive externality	$MEC = 0$ and $MEB = 0$; it follows that $MSC = MPC$ and $MSB = MPB$
2	Negative externality but no positive externality	$MEC > 0$ and $MEB = 0$; it follows that $MSC > MPC$ and $MSB = MPB$
3	Positive externality but no negative externality	$MEB > 0$ and $MEC = 0$; it follows that $MSB > MPB$ and $MSC = MPC$

---

1. Theoretically, there is a fourth category—where both a positive externality and a negative externality exist—but one would reasonably assume that this category has little, if any, practical relevance. For example, suppose Jim smokes a cigarette, and cigarette smoke is a negative externality for Angelica but a positive externality for Bobby. It is possible that what is a bad for Angelica is a good for Bobby, but little is added to the discussion (at this time) by reviewing such cases.

economics 24/7

SWITCHING COSTS AND MARKET FAILURE (MAYBE)

Some economists believe that a series of events are occurring today. A company produces a good, say, software X, and it finds that its major costs of producing the software are up front—at the research and development stage. After it has produced one copy of the software program, producing each additional copy is relatively cheap. The company sells software X at a price that is likely to generate a large number of sales. As some people buy the software program, additional people find it worth buying because the good is important in terms of networking with others. (For example, if many of the people you know use the spreadsheet Excel, you may choose Excel as your spreadsheet.) Because of its network externalities, good X becomes widely used in the industry. At some point, the good simply dominates the market with, say, 90 percent of market sales.

Some economists then ask whether good X is the best product or inferior to the substitutes that exist for it. For example, if software programs Y and Z are substitutes for X, is X superior to both Y and Z or is either Y or Z superior to X? A real-world example illustrates our point. Both Beta and VHS formats for VCRs came out at about the same time. VHS initially sold better than Beta, although Beta was a strong competitor. At some point, the higher percentage of VHS users in the market (relative to Beta users) seemed to matter to people who were considering buying a VCR. The VHS format seemed more common; so sharing videotapes with more people should be easier. At this point, the sales of VHS began to explode, and before long very few people were buying Beta. Some of the initial buyers of the Beta format even switched over to the VHS format. In the race between VHS and Beta,

VHS won, not necessarily because it is superior to Beta, but simply because it had an early lead in the race. If network externalities are present, the early lead may be the only lead that is necessary to win the race for customers' dollars.

Some economists conclude that if only the early lead counts and not the quality of the product, then an inferior product that gets an early lead could outsell a superior product that comes to market later. So, if X outcompetes Y and Z not because it is superior but because it gets an early lead in the software market, then the market might have chosen the inferior product. Stated differently, there is market failure in the sense that the market has failed to choose a superior product over an inferior product.

But not all economists agree. Some say that choosing an inferior product over a superior product is not sufficient to constitute market failure. There must also be net benefits to switching (from the inferior to the superior product) that market participants are not acting on. To illustrate, suppose the market has chosen good X, that it is inferior to good Y, and that the benefits of switching from X to Y are $30 and the costs of switching are $45. In this case, even if the market stays with good X, there is no market failure because switching to the superior product is not worthwhile. The market fails, argue these economists, only if the benefits of switching are, say, $30 and the costs are $10 (and therefore there are net benefits to switching), yet the market doesn't switch. In short, when the benefits and costs of switching are considered, what may initially look like a market failure may turn out not to be.

Externalities in Consumption and in Production

Externalities can arise because someone *consumes* something that has an external benefit or cost for others or because someone *produces* something that has an external benefit or cost for others. Consider two examples. Suppose Barbara plays the radio in her car loudly, adversely affecting drivers around her at the stoplight. In this situation, Barbara is consuming music and creating a negative externality for others. Now consider John, who produces cars in his factory. As a result of the production process, he emits pollution into the air that adversely affects some people who live downwind from the factory. In this situation, we have a negative externality that is the result of John's producing a good.

exhibit 1

The Negative Externality Case

Because of a negative externality, marginal social costs (*MSC*) are greater than marginal private costs (*MPC*) and the market output is greater than the socially optimal output. The market is said to fail in that it overproduces the good.

Diagram of a Negative Externality

Exhibit 1 shows the downward-sloping demand curve, *D*, for some good. Because the demand curve represents the marginal private benefits received by the buyers of the good, it is the same as the *MPB* curve. Because there are no positive externalities in this case, *MPB* = *MSB*. So the demand curve is also the *MSB* curve.

The supply curve, *S*, represents the marginal private costs (*MPC*) of the producers of the good. Equilibrium in this market setting is at E_1; Q_1 is the output—specifically, the market output.

Now assume negative externalities arise as a result of the production of the good. For example, suppose the good happens to be cars whose production in a factory causes the emission of some air pollution. Due to the negative externalities, external costs associated with the production of the good are not taken into account at the market output. The marginal external costs linked to the negative externalities are taken into account by adding them (as best we can) to the marginal private costs. The result is the marginal social cost (*MSC*) curve shown in Exhibit 1. If all costs are taken into account (both external costs and private costs), equilibrium is at E_2, where *MSB* = *MSC*. The quantity produced at E_2 (Q_2) is the socially optimal output, or efficient output.

Notice that the market output (Q_1) is greater than the socially optimal output (Q_2) when negative externalities exist. The market is said to fail (hence market failure) because it *overproduces* the good connected with the negative externality. The triangle in Exhibit 1 is the visible manifestation of the market failure. It represents the net social cost of producing the market output (Q_1) instead of the socially optimal output (Q_2), or of moving from the socially optimal output to the market output.

To understand exactly how the triangle in Exhibit 1 represents the net social cost of moving from the socially optimal output to the market output, look at Exhibit 2, where, as in Exhibit 1, Q_2 is the socially optimal output and Q_1 is the market output. If society moves from Q_2 to Q_1, who specifically benefits and how do we represent these benefits? Buyers benefit (they are a part of society) because they will be able to buy more output at prices they are willing to pay. Thus, the area under the demand curve between Q_2 and Q_1 represents the benefits to society of moving from Q_2 to Q_1 (see the shaded area in window 1 of Exhibit 2).

Next, if society moves from Q_2 to Q_1, how can we illustrate the costs that are incurred? Both sellers and third parties incur costs. Sellers incur private costs, and third parties incur external costs. The area under *S* (the *MPC* curve) takes into account only part of society—sellers—and ignores third parties. The area under the *MSC* curve between Q_2 and Q_1 represents the full costs to society of moving from Q_2 to Q_1 (see the shaded area in window 2).

The shaded area in window 2 is larger than the shaded area in window 1; so the costs to sellers and third parties of moving from Q_2 to Q_1 outweigh the benefits to buyers of moving from Q_2 to Q_1. The difference between the shaded areas is the triangle shown in

Window 1
Benefits of moving from Q_2 to Q_1

Window 2
Costs of moving from Q_2 to Q_1

exhibit 2

The Triangle

Q_2 is the socially optimal output; Q_1 is the market output. If society moves from Q_2 to Q_1, buyers benefit by an amount represented by the shaded area in window 1, but sellers and third parties together incur greater costs, represented by the shaded area in window 2. The triangle (the difference between the two shaded areas) represents the net social cost to society of moving from Q_2 to Q_1, or of producing Q_1 instead of Q_2.

the main diagram. Thus, the costs to society outweigh the benefits to society by the triangle. In short, the triangle in this example represents the net social cost of moving from Q_2 to Q_1, or of producing Q_1 instead of Q_2.

 Thinking like AN ECONOMIST

The Complete Picture

Economists prefer to look at the complete picture instead of only part of it. If there are both private and external costs, economists will consider both, not just one or the other. Similarly, if there are both private and external benefits, economists will consider both.

Diagram of a Positive Externality

Exhibit 3 shows the downward-sloping demand curve, D, for some good. This curve represents the marginal private benefits received by the buyers of the good, and so it is the same as the MPB curve.

The supply curve, S, represents the marginal private costs (MPC) of the producers of the good. The marginal social costs (MSC) are the same as the marginal private costs—$MPC = MSC$—because there are no negative externalities in this case. Equilibrium in this market setting is at E_1; Q_1 is the output—specifically, the market output.

Now assume positive externalities arise as a result of the production of the good. For example, suppose Erica is a beekeeper who produces honey. The hives are near an apple

The Positive Externality Case

Because of a positive externality, marginal social benefits (*MSB*) are greater than marginal private benefits (*MPB*) and the market output is less than the socially optimal output. The market is said to fail in that it underproduces the good.

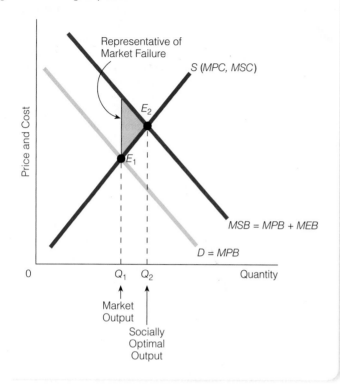

Representative of Market Failure

S (*MPC, MSC*)

E_2

E_1

MSB = MPB + MEB

$D = MPB$

Quantity

Q_1 Q_2

Price and Cost

0

Market Output

Socially Optimal Output

orchard, and her bees occasionally fly over to the orchard and pollinate the blossoms, in the process making the orchard more productive. The orchard owner thus benefits from Erica's bees.

Because positive externalities exist, production of the good has external benefits that are not taken into account at the market output. The marginal external benefits linked to the positive externalities are taken into account by adding them (as best we can) to the marginal private benefits. The result is the marginal social benefit (*MSB*) curve shown in Exhibit 3. If all benefits are taken into account (both external benefits and private benefits), equilibrium is at E_2, where $MSB = MSC$. The quantity produced at E_2 (Q_2) is the socially optimal output, or efficient output.

Notice that the market output (Q_1) is less than the socially optimal output (Q_2) when positive externalities exist (just the opposite of when negative externalities exist). The market is said to fail (hence market failure) because it *underproduces* the good connected with the positive externality. The triangle in Exhibit 3 is the visible manifestation of the market failure. It represents the net social benefit *that is lost* by producing the market output (Q_1) instead of the socially optimal output (Q_2). Stated differently, at the socially optimal output (Q_2), society realizes greater benefits than at the market output (Q_1). So by being at Q_1, society loses out on some net benefits it could obtain if it were at Q_2.

Thinking like AN ECONOMIST

The Benefits and the Costs of Making the Move

From what we have said so far, it may seem that the economist prefers the socially optimal output (where all benefits and costs are taken into account) to the market output (where only private benefits and costs are taken into account). But this is not necessarily true. An economist prefers the socially optimal output to the market output (assuming they are different) only when the benefits of moving from the market output to the socially optimal output are greater than the costs. To illustrate, suppose $400 in benefits exists if we move from the market output to the socially optimal output, but the costs of making the move are $1,000. According to an economist, it wouldn't be worthwhile trying to make the adjustment.

SELF-TEST

(Answers to Self-Test questions are in the Self-Test Appendix.)

1. What is the major difference between the market output and the socially optimal output?

2. For an economist, is the socially optimal output preferred to the market output?

WANT TO LEASE A RAINFOREST FOR $1.6 MILLION PER YEAR?[2]

Suppose you read in the newspaper that a rainforest in Cameroon (in central and western Africa) may be leased out to timber company. If the timber company gets the lease, it will certainly cut down many trees. Underneath your breath, you mutter, "That is a horrible thing to happen."

In February 2008, Joseph Matta, the forestry minister of Cameroon, was searching for charities like Conservation International to lease 830,000 hectares of a rainforest called Ngoyla-Mintom. The price tag was $1.6 million a year or $1.93 a hectare. Joseph Matta preferred a conservationist tenant (like Conservation International) over a timber company, but since 2001 no conservationist group had come forward to lease the forest. Joseph Matta said that if a conservationist group did not step forward soon, he would be forced to lease the land to a timber company.

There are two ways to look at what is happening. One is to say that conservationists don't seem to be putting their money where their mouths are. In other words, they talk about conservation (and saving the environment), but they don't really care enough to pay for what it is they say they want. Actions speak louder than words.

Another, very different, perspective is that a free-rider problem is involved. The conservationists of the world might value the rainforest

© ANNE KITZMAN/SHUTTERSTOCK

more than any timber company, but they can't get the total amount of money (at which they value the rainforest) together. To illustrate, suppose the conservationists value the rainforest at $2 million a year and the timber company values it at $1.8 million a year. Given this, the conservationists would seem to be the likely ones to lease the forest. But what if each of the many conservationists sees his or her contribution to the conservationist fund as negligible ("What does my $5 matter?")? In this case, each conservationist might end up not contributing; therefore the total value of the rainforest to the conservationists (as a whole) cannot be expressed.

Postscript: Today, if you want to help save that rainforest, you can do so. If you go the website of Conservation International (http://www.conservation.org/Pages/default.aspx), a private charity and team of conservationists, you can make a donation that might help save the rainforest. Back in 2000, Conservation International came up with the idea of bidding for the same natural resources that the timber companies were bidding for. Currently it has leased forests in Guyana—where it has 80,000 hectares of Upper Essequibo—and in Peru, Sierra Leone, Papua New Guinea, Fiji, and Mexico.

---

2. This feature is adapted from "The Unkindest Cut," *Economist*, February 14, 2008.

INTERNALIZING EXTERNALITIES

An externality is **internalized** if the persons or group generating the externality incorporate into their own private or *internal* cost-benefit calculations the external benefits (in the case of a positive externality) or the external costs (in the case of a negative externality) that third parties bear. Simply put, internalizing externalities is the same as adjusting for externalities. An externality has been internalized, or adjusted for, *completely* if, as a result, the socially optimal output emerges. A few of the numerous ways to adjust for, or internalize, externalities are presented in this section.

Persuasion

Many negative externalities arise partly because persons or groups do not consider other individuals when they decide to undertake an action, like the person who plays his CD player loudly at 3 o'clock in the morning. Perhaps if he considered the external cost of his action to his neighbors, he either would not play the CD player at all or tune it down.

Internalizing Externalities
An externality is internalized if the persons or group that generated the externality incorporate into their own private or internal cost-benefit calculations the external benefits (in the case of a positive externality) or the external costs (in the case of a negative externality) that third parties bear.

387

exhibit 4

A Corrective Tax Gone Wrong

Government may miscalculate external costs and impose a tax that moves the supply curve from S_1 to S_3 instead of from S_1 to S_2. As a result, the output level will be farther away from the socially optimal output than before the "corrective" tax was applied. Q_3 is farther away from Q_2 than Q_1 is from Q_2.

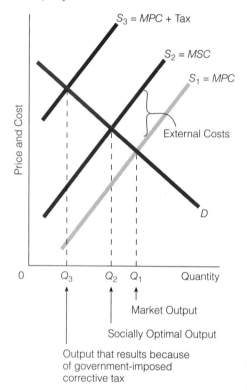

Trying to persuade those who impose external costs on us to take these costs into account is one way to make the imposers adjust for—or internalize—externalities. In today's world, such slogans as "Don't Drink and Drive" and "Don't Litter" are attempts to persuade individuals to take into account the fact that their actions affect others. The golden rule of ethical conduct, "Do unto others as you would have them do unto you," makes the same point.

Taxes and Subsidies

Taxes and subsidies are sometimes used as corrective devices for a market failure. A tax adjusts for a negative externality; a subsidy adjusts for a positive externality.

Consider the negative externality case in Exhibit 1. The objective of a corrective tax is to move the supply curve from S to the MSC curve (recall that a tax can shift a supply curve) and therefore move from the market determined output, Q_1, to the socially optimal output, Q_2.

In the case of a positive externality, illustrated in Exhibit 3, the objective is to subsidize the demand side of the market so that the demand curve moves from D to the MSB curve and output moves from Q_1 to the socially optimal output, Q_2.

However, taxes and subsidies also involve costs and consequences. For example, suppose, as illustrated in Exhibit 4, government misjudges the external costs when it imposes a tax on the supplier of a good. Instead of the supply curve moving from S_1 to S_2 (the MSC curve), it moves from S_1 to S_3. As a result, the output level will be farther away from the socially optimal output than it was before the corrective tax was applied.

Assigning Property Rights

Consider the idea that air pollution and ocean pollution—both of which are examples of negative externalities—are the result of the air and oceans being unowned. No one owns the air, no one owns the oceans, and because no one does, many individuals feel free to emit wastes into them. If private property, or ownership, rights in air and oceans could be established, the negative externalities would likely decrease. If someone owns a resource, then actions that damage it have a price; namely, the resource owner can sue for damages.

For example, in the early West, when grazing lands were open and unowned (common property), many cattle ranchers allowed their herds to overgraze. The reason was simple. No one owned the land, so no one could stop the overgrazing to preserve the value of the land. Even if one rancher decided not to allow his herd to graze, all he did was leave more grazing land for other ranchers. As a consequence of overgrazing, a future generation inherited barren, wasted land. From the point of view of future generations, the cattle ranchers who allowed their herds to overgraze were generating negative externalities.

If the Western lands had been privately owned, overgrazing would not have occurred because the monetary interests of the landowner would not have permitted it. The landowner would have charged ranchers a fee to graze their cattle, and more grazing would have entailed additional fees. There would have been less grazing at a positive fee than at a zero fee (the case when the lands were open and unowned). The externalities would have been internalized.

Voluntary Agreements

Externalities can sometimes be internalized through individual voluntary agreements. Suppose Pete and Sean live alone on a tiny island. They have agreed, between themselves, that Pete owns the northern part of the island and Sean owns the southern part. Pete occasionally plays his drums in the morning, and the sound awakens Sean, causing a negative externality problem. Pete wants to be free to play his drums in the morning, and Sean would like to sleep.

Suppose Sean values his sleep in the morning by a maximum of 6 oranges; that is, he would give up 6 oranges to be able to sleep without Pete playing his drums. On the other hand, Pete values drum playing in the morning by 3 oranges. He would give up a maximum of 3 oranges to be able to play his drums in the morning. Because Sean values his sleep by more than Pete values playing his drums, they have an opportunity to strike a deal. Sean can offer Pete some number of oranges greater than 3, but fewer than 6, to refrain from playing his drums in the morning. The deal will make both Pete and Sean better off.

In this example, the negative externality problem is successfully addressed through the individuals' voluntarily entering into an agreement. The condition for this output is that the *transaction costs,* or costs associated with making and reaching the agreement, must be low relative to the expected benefits of the agreement.

Combining Property Rights Assignments and Voluntary Agreements

The last two ways of internalizing externalities—property rights assignments and voluntary agreements—can be combined, as in the following example.[3] Suppose a rancher's cattle occasionally stray onto the adjacent farm and damage or eat some of the farmer's crops. The court assigns liability to the cattle rancher and orders him to prevent his cattle from straying; thus a property rights assignment solves the externality problem. As a result, the rancher puts up a strong fence to prevent his cattle from damaging his neighbor's crops.

But the court's property rights assignment may be undone by the farmer and the cattle rancher if they find it in their mutual interest to do so. Suppose the rancher is willing to pay $100 a month to the farmer for permission to allow his cattle to stray onto the farmer's land, and the farmer is willing to give permission for $70 a month. Assuming trivial or zero transaction costs, the farmer and the rancher will undo the court's property rights assignment. For a payment of $70 or more a month, the farmer will allow the rancher's cattle to stray onto his land.

COASE THEOREM Suppose in our example that the court, instead of assigning liability to the cattle rancher, had given him the property right to allow his cattle to stray. What would the resource allocative outcome have been in this case? With the opposite property rights assignment, the cattle would have been allowed to stray (which was exactly the outcome of the previous property rights assignment after the cattle rancher and farmer voluntarily agreed to undo it). Therefore, *in the case of trivial or zero transaction costs, the property rights assignment does not matter to the resource allocative outcome.* In a nutshell, this is the **Coase theorem**.

Coase Theorem
In the case of trivial or zero transaction costs, the property rights assignment does not matter to the resource allocative outcome.

3. See Ronald Coase, "The Problem of Social Cost," *Journal of Law and Economics,* 3 (October 1960): 1–44.

The Coase theorem can be expressed in other ways, two of which are as follows: (1) In the case of trivial or zero transaction costs, a property rights assignment will be undone (exchanged) if it benefits the relevant parties to undo it. (2) In the case of trivial or zero transaction costs, the resource allocative outcome will be the same no matter who is assigned the property right.

The Coase theorem is significant for two reasons: (1) It shows that under certain conditions, the market can internalize externalities. (2) It provides a benchmark for analyzing externality problems; that is, it shows what will happen if transaction costs are trivial or zero.

PIGOU VERSUS COASE The first editor of the *Journal of Law and Economics* was Aaron Director. In 1959, Director published an article by Ronald Coase entitled "The Federal Communications Commission." In the article, Coase took issue with economist A. C. Pigou, a trailblazer in the area of externalities and market failure, who had argued that government should use taxes and subsidies to adjust for negative and positive externalities, respectively. Coase argued that in the case of negative externalities, it is not clear that the state should tax the person imposing the negative externality. First, Coase stressed the reciprocal nature of externalities, pointing out that it takes two to make a negative externality (who is harming whom is not always clear). Second, Coase proposed a market solution to externality problems that was not implicit in Pigou's work.

Aaron Director and others believed that Coase was wrong and Pigou was right. Coase, who was teaching at the University of Virginia at the time, was invited to discuss his thesis with Director and a handful of well-known economists. The group included Martin Bailey, Milton Friedman, Arnold Harberger, Reuben Kessel, Gregg Lewis, John McGee, Lloyd Mints, George Stigler, and, of course, Director.

The group met at Aaron Director's house one night. Before Coase began to outline his thesis, the group took a vote and found that everyone (with the exception of Coase) sided with Pigou. Then the sparks began to fly, Friedman, it is reported, opening fire on Coase. Coase answered the intellectual attacks of his colleagues, and, at the end of the debate, another vote was taken. Everyone sided with Coase against Pigou. It is reported that as the members of the group left Director's home that night, they said to one another that they had witnessed history in the making. The Coase theorem had taken hold in economics.

Beyond Internalizing: Setting Regulations

One way to deal with externalities, in particular with negative externalities, is for government to apply regulations directly to the activities that generate the externalities. For example, factories producing goods also produce smoke, which is often seen as a negative externality. Government may decide that the factory must install pollution-reducing equipment, that it can emit only a certain amount of smoke into the air per day, or that it must be moved to a less populated area.

Critics of this approach often note that regulations, once instituted, are difficult to remove even if conditions warrant removal. Also, regulations are often applied across the board when individual circumstances dictate otherwise. For example, factories in relatively pollution-free cities might be required to install the same pollution control equipment as factories in smoggy, pollution-ridden cities.

Finally, regulation entails costs. If government imposes regulations, there must be regulators (whose salaries must be paid), offices (to house the regulators), word processors (to produce the regulations), and more. As previously noted, dealing with externalities successfully may offer benefits, but the costs need to be considered as well.

TELEMARKETERS, WHERE ARE YOU?

Effective October 1, 2003, the Federal Trade Commission (FTC) amended its Telemarketing Sales Rule (TSR). The amended rule created a National Do Not Call Registry. Anyone could add his telephone number to the registry if he chose not to be called by telemarketers.

Essentially, the change in rules entails two property rights assignments: Before October 1, 2003, telemarketers had the right to call you on the phone. After October 1, 2003, they did not.

To determine whether the change in the property rights assignment was consistent with efficiency, think of what was happening before October 1, 2003. Surely, some people who were being called by telemarketers valued not being called more than the telemarketers valued calling them. For example, suppose that Smith valued not being called at $10 a month and that collectively the telemarketers valued calling him at $8 a month. If Smith were called, a net loss would arise. Perhaps this is why so many individuals got angry over being called by telemarketers (especially around dinner time). It is likely, though, that some individuals place a lower value on not being called than others. Therefore, calling these persons could have been efficient.

The Do Not Call Registry acts as a means for individuals to register how much they value not being called. Those who value not being called quite a bit will likely place their phone numbers on the registry. Those who do not place a high value on not being called will not. With the Do Not Call Registry, we are closer to achieving efficiency than we were without it. Telemarketers will call people who place a low value on not being called, and they will not call people who place a high value on not being called.

Some economists have proposed that an even better system to achieve efficiency exists. Instead of simply allowing individuals to register their phone numbers with the Do Not Call Registry, allow them the added advantage of stating the dollar price they value not being called. For example, Smith is willing to pay $1 not to be called by telemarketers. She registers her phone number with the Do Not Call Registry along with the $1 she is willing to pay not to be called by telemarketers. A telemarketer notices that Smith's phone number is registered and calls her only if he is willing to pay something more than $1 to Smith.

So telemarketers will call persons who value not being called less than the telemarketer values calling. They will not call persons who value not being called more than the telemarketer values calling.

SELF-TEST

1. What does it mean to internalize an externality?

2. Are the transaction costs of buying a house higher or lower than those of buying a hamburger at a fast-food restaurant? Explain your answer.

3. Does the property rights assignment a court makes matter to the resource allocative outcome?

4. What condition must be satisfied for a tax to correctly adjust for a negative externality?

DEALING WITH A NEGATIVE EXTERNALITY IN THE ENVIRONMENT

The environment has become a major economic, political, and social issue. Environmental problems are manifold and include acid rain, the greenhouse effect, deforestation (including the destruction of the rain forests), solid waste (garbage) disposal, water pollution, air pollution, and many more. This section discusses mainly air pollution.

Economists make three principal points about pollution. First, it is a negative externality. Second, and perhaps counterintuitively, no pollution is sometimes worse than some pollution. Third, the market can be used to deal with the problem of pollution. In this section, we discuss the last two points.

Is No Pollution Worse Than Some Pollution?

Some pollution might be preferred to no pollution when all other things are not held constant—in short, most of the time. Certainly, if all other things are held constant, less pollution is preferred to more pollution, and therefore no pollution is preferred to some pollution.

But the world would be different with no pollution—not only because it would have cleaner air, rivers, and oceans. Pollution is a by-product of the production of many goods and services. For example, steel probably could not be produced without some pollution as a by-product. Given the current state of pollution technology, less pollution from steel production means less steel and fewer products made from steel.

Pollution is also a by-product of many of the goods we use daily, including our cars. We could certainly end the pollution caused by cars tomorrow, but to do so we would have to give up driving cars. As long as driving cars has any benefits, we won't choose zero pollution. In short, zero pollution is not preferable to some positive amount of pollution when we realize that goods and services must be forfeited to have less pollution.

The same conclusion can be reached through Coasian-type analysis. Suppose there are two groups: polluters and nonpolluters. For certain units of pollution, the value of polluting to polluters might be greater than the value of a less polluted environment to nonpolluters. In the presence of trivial or zero transaction costs, a deal will be struck. The outcome will be characterized by some positive amount of pollution.

Two Methods to Reduce Air Pollution

Let's consider two methods of reducing pollution. In method 1, the government sets pollution standards. In method 2, the government allocates pollution permits and allows them to be traded.

METHOD 1: GOVERNMENT SETS POLLUTION STANDARD Suppose three firms, X, Y, and Z, are located in the same area. Currently, each firm is spewing 3 units of pollution into the area under consideration, for a total of 9 pollution units. The government wants to reduce the total pollution in the area to 3 units and, to accomplish this objective, sets pollution standards (or regulations) stating that each firm must reduce its pollution by 2 units.

Exhibit 5 shows the respective cost of eliminating each unit of pollution for the three firms. The costs are different because eliminating pollution is more difficult for some kinds of firms than it is for others. For example, the air pollution that an automobile

---

exhibit 5

The Cost of Reducing Pollution for Three Firms

These are hypothetical data showing the cost of reducing pollution for three firms. The text shows that it is cheaper to reduce pollution through market environmentalism than through government standards or regulations.

Cost of Eliminating:	Firm X	Firm Y	Firm Z
First unit of pollution	$ 50	$ 70	$ 500
Second unit of pollution	75	85	1,000
Third unit of pollution	100	200	2,000

manufacturer produces might be more costly to eliminate than the air pollution from a clothing manufacturer. Stated differently, we assume that the three firms eliminate pollution by installing antipollution devices in their factories, and the cost of the antipollution devices may be much higher for an automobile manufacturer than for a clothing manufacturer.

The cost to firm X of eliminating its first 2 units is $125 ($50 + $75 = $125); the cost to firm Y of eliminating its first 2 units is $155; and the cost to firm Z of eliminating its first 2 units is $1,500. Thus, the total cost of eliminating 6 units of pollution is $1,780 ($125 + $155 + $1,500).

METHOD 2: MARKET ENVIRONMENTALISM AT WORK: GOVERNMENT ALLOCATES POLLUTION PERMITS AND THEN ALLOWS THEM TO BE BOUGHT AND SOLD The objective of the government is still to reduce the pollution in the area of firms X, Y, and Z from 9 units to 3 units, but this time, the government issues one pollution permit (sometimes these permits are called allowances or credits) to each firm. The government tells each firm that it can emit 1 unit of pollution for each permit it has in its possession. Furthermore, the firms are allowed to buy and sell the permits.

Look at the situation from the perspective of firm X. It has one pollution permit in its possession; so it can emit 1 unit of pollution and must eliminate the other 2. But firm X does not have to keep its pollution permit and emit 1 unit of pollution. Instead, it can sell its permit, but then it can emit no pollution. Might firm X be better off selling the permit and eliminating all 3 units of pollution?

Firm Y is in the same situation as firm X. This firm also has only one permit and must therefore eliminate 2 units of pollution. Firm Y also wonders whether it might be better off selling the permit and eliminating 3 units of pollution.

Firm Z is in a different situation. Exhibit 5 shows that this firm has to pay $500 to eliminate its first unit of pollution and $1,000 to eliminate its second unit. Firm Z wonders whether it might be better off buying the two other permits from firms X and Y and not eliminating any pollution at all.

So the owners of the three firms get together. The owner of firm Z says to the owners of the other firms, "I have to spend $500 to eliminate my first unit of pollution and $1,000 to eliminate my second unit. If either of you is willing to sell me your pollution permit for less than $500, I'm willing to buy it." The owners of the three firms agree on a price of $330 for a permit, and both firms X and Y sell their permits to firm Z. This exchange benefits all three parties. Firm X receives $330 for its permit and then spends $100 to eliminate its third unit of pollution. Firm Y receives $330 for its permit and then spends $200 to eliminate its third unit of pollution. Firm Z spends $660 for the two pollution permits instead of spending $1,500 to eliminate its first 2 units of pollution.

Under this scheme, firms X and Y eliminate all their pollution (neither firm has a pollution permit). Firm X spends $225 ($50 + $75 + $100) to eliminate all 3 units of its pollution, and firm Y spends $355 to do the same. The two firms together spend $580 ($225 + $355) to eliminate 6 units of pollution. The total cost of eliminating 6 units of pollution through market environmentalism is therefore only $580.

This cost is lower than the cost incurred by the three firms when government standards simply ordered each to eliminate 2 units of pollution (or 6 units for all three firms). The cost in that case was $1,780. In both cases, however, 6 pollution units were eliminated. Therefore, it is less costly for firms to eliminate pollution when the government allocates pollution permits that can be bought and sold than when it simply directs each firm to eliminate so many units of pollution.

Common MISCONCEPTIONS

About the $660

The total cost of eliminating 6 units of pollution using pollution permits was $580. Some argue that this dollar figure should be adjusted for the $660 that firm Z paid to buy the two pollution permits, but that is not correct. Although the $660 is a real cost of doing business for firm Z, *it is not a cost to society of eliminating pollution*. The $660 was not actually used to eliminate pollution. It was simply a transfer from firm Z to firms X and Y. The distinction is between a resource cost, which signifies an expenditure of resources, and a transfer, which does not.

SELF-TEST

1. The layperson finds it odd that economists often prefer some pollution to no pollution. Explain how the economist reaches this conclusion.

2. Why does reducing pollution cost less by using market environmentalism than by setting standards?

3. Under market environmentalism, the dollar amount firm Z has to pay to buy the pollution permits from firms X and Y is not counted as a cost to society. Why not?

PUBLIC GOODS: EXCLUDABLE AND NONEXCLUDABLE GOODS

Many economists maintain that the market fails to produce nonexcludable public goods. In this section, we discuss public goods in general and nonexcludable public goods in particular.

Goods

Economists talk about two kinds of goods: private goods and public goods. A *private good* is a good whose consumption by one person reduces its consumption for another person. For example, a sweater, an apple, and a computer are all private goods. If one person is wearing a sweater, another person cannot wear (consume) it. If one person takes a bite of an apple, there is less apple for someone else to consume. If someone is using a computer, someone else can't use it. A private good is said to be **rivalrous in consumption**.

A **public good**, in contrast, is a good whose consumption by one person does not reduce its consumption by another person. For example, a movie in a movie theater is a public good. If there are 200 seats in the theater, then 200 people can see the movie at the same time, and no one person's viewing of the movie detracts from another's. An economics lecture is also a public good. If there are 30 seats in the classroom, then 30 people can consume the economics lecture at the same time, and one person's consumption does not detract from any other's. The chief characteristic of a public good is that it is **nonrivalrous in consumption**, which means that its consumption by one person does not reduce its consumption by others.

All public goods are nonrivalrous in consumption, but they are not all the same. Some public goods are excludable and some are nonexcludable. A public good is **excludable** if it is possible, or not prohibitively costly, to exclude someone from obtaining the benefits of the good after it has been produced. For example, a movie in a movie theater is excludable in that persons who do not pay to see the movie can be excluded from seeing it. The same holds for an economics lecture. Someone who does not pay the tuition to obtain

Rivalrous in Consumption
A good is rivalrous in consumption if its consumption by one person reduces its consumption by others.

Public Good
A good the consumption of which by one person does not reduce the consumption by another person—that is, a public good is characterized by nonrivalry in consumption. There are both excludable and nonexcludable public goods. An excludable public good, while nonrivalrous in consumption, can be denied to a person who does not pay for it. A nonexcludable public good is nonrivalrous in consumption and cannot be denied to a person who does not pay for it.

Nonrivalrous in Consumption
A good is nonrivalrous in consumption if its consumption by one person does not reduce its consumption by others.

Excludable
A characteristic of a good whereby it is possible, or not prohibitively costly, to exclude someone from receiving the benefits of the good after it has been produced.

the lecture can be excluded from consuming it. So both movies in movie theaters and economics lectures in classrooms are *excludable public goods.*

A public good is **nonexcludable** if it is impossible, or prohibitively costly, to exclude someone from obtaining the benefits of the good after it has been produced. Consider national defense. First, national defense is a public good in that it is nonrivalrous in consumption. For example, if the U.S. national defense system is protecting people in New Jersey from incoming missiles, then it is automatically protecting people in New York as well. And just as important, protecting people in New Jersey does not reduce the degree of protection for the people in New York. Second, once national defense has been produced, excluding someone from consuming its services is impossible (or prohibitively costly). Thus, national defense is a *nonexcludable public good.* The same holds for flood control or large-scale pest control. After the dam has been built or the pest spray has been sprayed, excluding persons from benefiting from it is impossible.

Nonexcludable
A characteristic of a good whereby it is impossible, or prohibitively costly, to exclude someone from receiving the benefits of the good after it has been produced.

The Free Rider

When a good is excludable (whether private or public), individuals can obtain the benefits of it only if they pay for it. For example, no one can consume an apple (a private good) or a movie in a movie theater (a public good) without first paying for it. This is not the case with a nonexcludable public good, though. Individuals can obtain the benefits of a nonexcludable public good without paying for it. Persons who do so are referred to as **free riders**. Because of the so-called *free-rider problem,* most economists hold that the market will fail to produce nonexcludable public goods or at least fail to produce them at a desired level.

Free Rider
Anyone who receives the benefits of a good without paying for it.

To illustrate, consider someone contemplating the production of nonexcludable public good X, which, because it is a public good, is also nonrivalrous in consumption. After good X has been produced and provided to one person, others have no incentive to pay for it (even if they demand it) because they can receive all of its benefits without paying. No one is likely to supply a good that people can consume without paying for it. The market, it is argued, will not produce nonexcludable public goods. The door then is opened to government involvement in the production of nonexcludable public goods. It is often stated that if the market will not produce nonexcludable public goods, although they are demanded, then the government must.

The free-rider argument is the basis for accepting government's (the public's or taxpayers') provision of nonexcludable public goods. We need to remind ourselves, though, that a nonexcludable public good is not the same as a government-provided good. A nonexcludable public good is a good that is nonrivalrous in consumption and nonexcludable. A government-provided good is self-defined: a good that government provides. In some instances, a government-provided good is a nonexcludable public good, such as when the government furnishes national defense, but it need not be. The government furnishes mail delivery and education, two goods that are also provided privately and are excludable and thus not subject to free riding.

Nonexcludable Versus Nonrivalrous

The market fails to produce a demanded good only when the good is nonexcludable because the free-rider problem arises only if the good is nonexcludable. The rivalry versus nonrivalry issue is not relevant to the issue of market failure; that is, a good can be rivalrous in consumption or nonrivalrous in consumption and still be produced by the market. For example, a movie may be nonrivalrous in consumption but be excludable too. And the market has no problem producing movies and movie theaters. The free-rider problem occurs only with goods that are nonexcludable.

The lighthouse metaphor in economics is relevant to this discussion. For a long time, a lighthouse was thought to have the two characteristics of a nonexcludable public good:

economics 24/7

THE RIGHT AMOUNT OF NATIONAL DEFENSE

Because of free riders, the market is unlikely to produce nonexcludable public goods. This is the basis for accepting the government's provision of nonexcludable public goods.

Let's say the particular nonexcludable public good that government will now provide is national defense. A thorny issue immediately arises: What quantity and quality of national defense will government provide? Will it produce a large national defense with many technologically advanced weapons systems? Will it produce a small national defense with very few technologically advanced weapons systems but with a relatively large number of soldiers?

Providing a good is one thing; providing the precise number of units of the good and the exact quality of the good that most people demand is quite another.

Some Americans want a national defense that consists of U.S. armed forces present in many different countries around the world. They argue that the U.S. needs to have a presence in countries such as Saudi Arabia, Iraq, Germany, and other parts of the world because it is in the best interests of the safety and security of the United States.

Other Americans vehemently disagree, demanding the type of national defense where U.S. armed forces stay home until and unless the United States is provoked in some way—for example, by an attack on U.S. citizens residing in the United States.

The point is simple: Once nonexcludable public goods are provided, people are likely to argue over how much of it is provided and what quality it is. Things are noticeably different with private goods. People can consume the particular type of a private good they demand. There are a wide variety of private goods to choose from. For example, if one person wants brown shoes and another person wants black shoes, the person who wants brown shoes buys brown and the person who wants black buys black.

But there is usually only one nonexcludable public good for everyone to consume. There is only one U.S. national defense and national defense policy, and everyone in the United States, no matter what his or her individual preferences, consumes that same national defense and national defense policy. As a result, people often argue over, and try to change, the one nonexcludable public good they all have to consume in a way that comes closer to matching their personal preferences.

(1) It is nonrivalrous in consumption; any ship can use the light from the lighthouse, and one ship's use of the light does not detract from another's. (2) It is nonexcludable; it is difficult to exclude any nonpaying ships from using the light. The lighthouse seemed to be a perfect good for government provision.

However, economist Ronald Coase found that in the 18th and early 19th centuries, many lighthouses were privately owned, which meant that the market had not failed to provide lighthouses. Economists were left to conclude either that the market could provide nonexcludable public goods or that the lighthouse wasn't a nonexcludable public good, as had been thought. Closer examination showed that although the lighthouse was nonrivalrous in consumption (it was a public good), the costs of excluding others from using it were fairly low (so it was an excludable public good). Lighthouse owners knew that usually only one ship was near the lighthouse at a time and that they could turn off the light if a ship did not exhibit the flag of a paying vessel.

SELF-TEST

1. Why does the market fail to produce nonexcludable public goods?
2. Identify each of the following goods as a nonexcludable public good, an excludable public good, or a private good:
   a. Composition notebook used for writing.
   b. Shakespearean play performed in a summer theater.
   c. An apple.

d. Telephone service.

e. Sunshine.

3. Give an example, other than a movie in a movie theater or a play in a theater, of a good that is nonrivalrous and excludable.

ASYMMETRIC INFORMATION

Market failure is a situation in which the market does not provide the efficient or optimal amount of a good. This chapter has shown that both externalities and nonexcludable public goods can lead to market failure. Specifically, in the presence of externalities, the market output is different from the socially optimal output. In the case of negative externalities, the market produces too much; in the case of positive externalities, the market produces too little. In the case of nonexcludable public goods, some economists maintain that the market produces zero output. Assuming that there is a demand for the nonexcludable public good, this is definitely too little.

This section looks at another possible cause of market failure: asymmetric information. **Asymmetric information** exists when either the buyer or the seller in a market exchange has some information that the other does not have. In other words, some information is hidden. For example, the seller of a house may have information about the house that the buyer does not have, such as that the roof leaks during a heavy rainfall.

The analysis of the effects of asymmetric information is similar to the analysis of externalities—with one important difference. The discussion of externalities considers buyers, sellers, and third parties; this discussion considers only buyers and sellers.

Asymmetric Information in a Product Market

In the discussion of externalities, the demand for a good represents marginal private benefits, and the supply of a good represents marginal private costs. This is also the case for the asymmetric information situation shown in Exhibit 6; that is, the demand curve, D_1, represents marginal private benefits (MPB) and the supply curve, S_1, represents marginal private costs (MPC). In Exhibit 6, D_1 and S_1 are the relevant curves when the seller has

> **Asymmetric Information**
> Information that either the buyer or the seller in a market exchange has and that the other does not have.

---

exhibit 6

Asymmetric Information in a Product Market

Initially, the seller has some information that the buyer does not have; there is asymmetric information. As a result, D_1 represents the demand for the good and Q_1 is the equilibrium quantity. Then the buyer acquires the information that she did not have earlier, and there is symmetric information. The information causes the buyer to lower her demand for the good so that now D_2 is the relevant demand curve and Q_2 is the equilibrium quantity. Conclusion: Fewer units of the good are bought and sold when there is symmetric information than when there is asymmetric information.

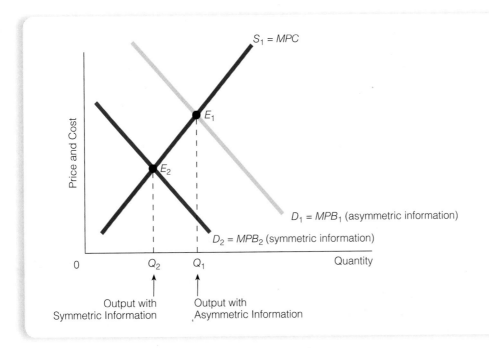

exhibit 7

Asymmetric Information in a Factor Market

Initially, the buyer (of the factor labor), or the firm, has some information that the seller (of the factor) does not have; there is asymmetric information. Consequently, S_1 is the relevant supply curve, W_1 is the equilibrium wage, and Q_1 is the equilibrium quantity of labor. Then sellers acquire information that they did not have earlier, and there is symmetric information. The information causes the sellers to reduce their supply of the factor so that now S_2 is the relevant supply curve, W_2 is the equilibrium wage, and Q_2 is the equilibrium quantity of labor. Conclusion: Fewer factor units are bought and sold and wages are higher when there is symmetric information than when there is asymmetric information.

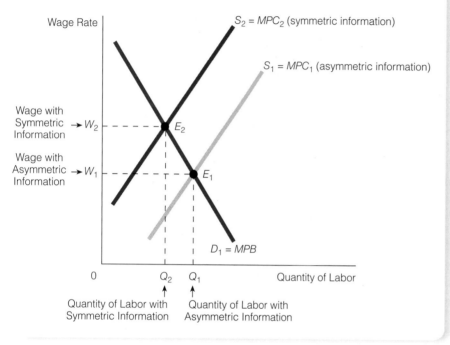

some information that the buyer does not have. It follows that Q_1 is the market output when there is asymmetric information.

Now suppose the buyer acquires the information she previously did not have (but which the seller did have). With the new information, buying this particular good does not seem as appealing. The acquired information causes the buyer to lower her demand for the good. The relevant demand curve is now D_2. With symmetric information, the market output will be Q_2, which is less than Q_1.

As an example, the suppliers of cigarettes know that cigarette consumption can cause cancer but do not release this information to potential buyers. Under this condition, suppliers of cigarettes have certain information about cigarettes that buyers don't have; there is asymmetric information. Without this information, the demand for cigarettes may be higher than it would be if buyers had the information. In Exhibit 6, demand is D_1 instead of D_2. It follows, then, that more cigarettes will be purchased and consumed (Q_1) when there is asymmetric information than when there is symmetric information (Q_2).

Asymmetric Information in a Factor Market

Now consider a resource or factor market, such as the labor market shown in Exhibit 7. In this case, the buyer has information that the seller does not have. Suppose a firm knows that its workers will be using a possibly toxic substance that may cause health problems in 20 to 30 years. Further, the company does not release this information to workers, but hides it from them. Without this information, the supply curve of labor is represented by S_1, and the quantity of labor will be Q_1 at a wage rate of W_1. With the information, though, not as many people will be willing to work at the firm at the current wage. The supply curve of labor shifts left to S_2. The new equilibrium position shows that the quantity of labor falls to Q_2, and the wage rate rises to W_2.

Is There Market Failure?

Does asymmetric information cause markets to fail? That is, does it create a situation in which the market does not provide the optimal output of a particular good? Certainly, in our examples, the output level of a good and the quantity of labor were lower when there was symmetric information than when there was asymmetric information. Stated differently, asymmetric information seemingly resulted in too much or too many of something—either too much of a good being consumed or too many workers for a particular firm.

Some people argue that asymmetric information exists in nearly all exchanges. Rarely do buyers and sellers have the same information; each usually knows something the other doesn't. However, this argument misses the point, which is whether the asymmetric information fundamentally changes the outcome from what it would be if there were symmetric information. For example, a seller may know something that a buyer doesn't know, but even if the buyer knew what the seller knows, it may not change the outcome.

To illustrate, suppose a person buys a medication to relieve a severe headache. The person does not know that one side effect of the medication is sleepiness. Asymmetric information may not matter. Possibly the buyer would not have changed her behavior even if she had known the medication caused sleepiness. So there is asymmetric information, but it may not change the outcome.

Of course, in another setting, the result may be different. Suppose the seller of a used car knows the car is a lemon, but the buyer doesn't know this. The person buys the car because he doesn't have the information the seller has. Asymmetric information matters in the outcome if the buyer would not have bought the car—or would not have bought the car at a given price—had he known what the seller knew. In this setting, asymmetric information changes the outcome.

Therefore, the presence of asymmetric information does not guarantee that the market fails. What matters is whether the asymmetric information brings about a different outcome than what would happen if there were symmetric information. If this occurs, then the case for market failure can be made.

Adverse Selection

Some economists argue that under certain conditions, information problems can eliminate markets (i.e., create *missing markets*) or change the composition of markets (i.e., bring about *incomplete markets*). In the used car market of our example,[4] sellers know more than buyers about the cars they are offering to sell; there is asymmetric information. For example, a seller knows whether the car requires a lot of maintenance. Because it is difficult for most buyers to tell the difference between good used cars and lemons, a single used car price will emerge for a given model-make-year car that is a reflection of both lemons and good cars.

Suppose this price is $10,000. A lemon owner will think this is a good price because she will receive an average price for a below-average car. On the other hand, a person who owns an above-average car will find this price too low; he won't want to sell his above-average car for an average price. As a result of lemon owners' liking the price and good car owners' not liking it, lemon owners will offer their cars for sale (the price is great), and the owners of good used cars will not (the price is too low).

This situation is called the problem of adverse selection. **Adverse selection** exists when the parties on one side of the market, who have information not known to others, self-select in a way that adversely affects the parties on the other side of the market. In the example, the owners of lemons offer their cars for sale—they select to sell their cars—because they know (and only they know) that the average price they are being offered for their below-average cars is a good deal.

Through adverse selection, the supply of lemons on the market will rise, and the supply of high-quality, or good, used cars will fall. The relatively greater number of lemons will lower the average quality of a used car. As a result, for a given make-model-year used car, a new average price will emerge that is lower than it was before. Let's say this new price is $8,000. The process repeats: People with above-average cars will think the average

Adverse Selection
A phenomenon that occurs when the parties on one side of the market, who have information not known to others, self-select in a way that adversely affects the parties on the other side of the market.

---

4. This material is based on the classic article by George Akerlof, "The Market for Lemons," *Quarterly Journal of Economics* (August 1970): 488–500.

ARRIVING LATE TO CLASS, GRADING ON A CURVE, AND STUDYING TOGETHER FOR THE MIDTERM

A series of young children's books titled *Where's Waldo?* present the character Waldo drawn among hundreds of people and things. Although the objective, finding Waldo, may seem easy, finding Waldo is roughly similar to finding a needle in a haystack. If you look long and hard, you'll eventually find him; if you simply glance at the page, you won't.

Finding economics is similar to finding Waldo. If you simply glance at your daily life, you'll miss the economics; if you look long and hard, you'll often find it. With this in mind, consider your life as a college student. On a typical day, you walk into a college classroom, sit down, listen to a lecture and take notes, enter into discussions, ask questions, answer questions, and then leave. Can you find the economics in this daily experience? Here are some places you might find economics lurking.

Arriving Late to Class

Class started five minutes ago. You are sitting at your desk, listening to the professor, and taking notes. The professor is discussing an unusually challenging topic today, and you are listening attentively. Then the classroom door opens. You turn at the sound and see two of your classmates arriving late to class. For a few seconds, your attention is diverted from the lecture. When you refocus your attention on the professor, you realize that you have missed an essential point, and you become mildly frustrated.

The scenario described is a negative externality. Your two classmates undertook an action—arriving at class late—and you incurred a cost because of their action. Your two classmates considered only their private benefits and costs of arriving to class late. They did not consider your cost—the external cost—of their action.

price of $8,000 is too low, and people with below-average cars will think this is a good price. The people with above-average cars will drop out of the used car market, leaving only those with below-average used cars. Again, this will lead to a decline in the average quality of a used car, and eventually the average price of a used car will drop.

Thus, asymmetric information leads to adverse selection, which in the used car market example, brings about a steady decline in the quality of used cars offered for sale. Theoretically, the adverse selection problem could lead to the total elimination of the good used car market. In other words, the lemons will drive all the good cars out of the market.

There are several possible reasons that the ultimate adverse selection would not happen in the used car market. For example, a buyer could hire his own mechanic to check the car he is thinking about buying. By doing this, he would acquire almost as much, if not as much, information about the car as the seller has. Thus, there would no longer be asymmetric information. Or the seller of a high-quality used car could offer a warranty on her car. Essentially, she could offer to fix any problems with the used car for a period of time after she sells it. The warranty offer would likely increase both the demand for the car and its price. (Lemon owners would not be likely to offer warranties; so their cars would sell for less than cars with warranties.)

In some cases, government has played a role in dealing with adverse selection problems. State governments can pass, and in some situations have passed, lemon laws, stating that car dealers must take back any defective cars. In addition, many states now require car dealers to openly state on used cars whether a car is offered with a warranty or as is.

Moral Hazard

In the used car example illustrating adverse selection, asymmetric information existed *prior* to an exchange. That is, before dollars changed hands, the seller of the used car had information about the car that the potential buyer did not have.

To get students to internalize the cost to others of their being late, the professor could try to persuade students not to be late. She could say that lateness imposes a cost on those who arrive at class on time and are attentively listening to the lecture. Alternatively, the professor could impose a corrective tax on tardy students. In other words, she could set a tax equal to the external cost, perhaps taking one-half to one point off a student's test grade for each lateness.

Grading on a Curve

Alex is currently taking a sociology course. Ideally, he would like to get an A or a B in the class, but believes he is likely to receive a C or a D. Alex's situation is similar to that of a person who would like to be healthy every day for the rest of his life but knows that he probably won't be.

When a person knows he probably won't be healthy for his entire life, he buys health insurance. And as explained in this chapter, after a person purchases health insurance, a moral hazard problem may arise. The person may not have so strong an incentive to remain healthy when he has health insurance as when he doesn't.

Would Alex react the same way if he could buy grade insurance? Suppose his sociology professor promises Alex that she will grade on a curve and that no one in the class will receive a grade lower than a C. With this assurance from his professor, will Alex have as strong an incentive to work hard to learn sociology? Does a moral hazard now arise? An economist is likely to answer the first question no and the second question yes.

Studying Together for the Midterm

Students usually study together if they think doing so will be mutually beneficial. That is, when two people agree to study together (say, for a midterm), they are usually entering into an exchange: "I will help you learn more of the material so that you can get a better grade if you do the same for me."

Consider two types of colleges: (1) a dormitory-based college in which many of the students live on campus in dormitories and (2) a commuter college in which the entire student body lives off campus.

Students study together more commonly on dormitory-based campuses than on commuter campuses because the transaction costs of studying together—of entering into the exchange—are lower on a dormitory-based campus. If you live in a dormitory on campus, you incur relatively low transaction costs by studying with someone who also lives on campus (maybe a person living down the hall from you). But if everyone lives off campus, you incur relatively high transaction costs by studying with a fellow student. One of you has to drive to the other's house or apartment, or you have to meet at a local coffee bar.

Asymmetric information can also exist *after* a transaction has been made. If it does, it can cause a moral hazard problem. **Moral hazard** occurs when one party to a transaction changes his behavior in a way that is hidden from and costly to the other party. For example, suppose Smith buys a health insurance policy. After she has the insurance, she may be less careful to maintain good health because the cost to her of future health problems is not as high as it would have been without the insurance. Smith doesn't set out to make herself ill so that she can collect on the insurance, but her incentive to be as careful about her health and physical well-being is not as strong as it once was. As another example, a person with automobile collision insurance may be more likely to drive on an icy road in December in Minneapolis than if he didn't have the insurance. Or a person who has earthquake insurance may be more likely to forget to do a few things that will minimize damage during an earthquake, such as attaching bookcases to the walls. In these examples, the moral hazard problem causes people to take too few precautionary actions.

Insurance companies try to control for moral hazard in different ways. One way is by specifying certain precautions that an insured person must take. For example, a company that insures your house from fire may require you to have smoke detectors and a fire extinguisher. The insurance company may also set a deductible so that you must pay part of the loss in case of a fire. This increases your cost of a fire and provides you with an added incentive to be careful.

Moral Hazard
A condition that exists when one party to a transaction changes his or her behavior in a way that is hidden from and costly to the other party.

SELF-TEST

1. Give an example that illustrates how asymmetric information can lead to more of a good being consumed than if there is symmetric information.

2. Adverse selection has the potential to eliminate some markets. How is this possible?

3. Give an example that is not discussed in the text and that illustrates moral hazard.

"IT SEEMS WRONG TO LET SOME BUSINESS FIRMS PAY TO POLLUTE"

Student:

In our discussion, I know that pollution permits proved to be less costly at reducing pollution than setting pollution standards, but it seems wrong to me to let a business firm get away with polluting if it can pay enough money. It seems as if it is paying to do something wrong.

Instructor:

There is a different way to look at things. The firm is not paying to pollute; it is paying to have some other business firm reduce its pollution. Suppose firm A can eliminate its pollution at a lower cost than firm B. Firm B now pays firm A to eliminate its own (firm A's) pollution. Instead of saying that firm B is "paying to pollute," why not say that "firm B is paying firm A not to pollute."

Student:

Putting it that way makes firm B sound like the good guy—the firm that pays other firms not to pollute.

Instructor:

My point is that you cast firm B as the bad guy—the firm that pays to pollute. What I did was simply bring out another aspect of what is happening. Firm B *pays firm A not to pollute* (that is my part of the story) so that in turn *it can pollute* (that is your part of the story). Also keep in mind that at the end of process, there is less, not more, pollution. Instead of having the pollution from firms A and B, we have less (or no) pollution from firm A and perhaps the same amount of pollution from firm B.

Student:

I see your point, but wouldn't it still be fairer if no money changed hands and both firms A and B were told that they had to eliminate *x* amount of pollution? In other words, wouldn't it be fairer to treat each firm the same way?

Instructor:

Let's divide the world up into the two firms, A and B, and everyone else. Now as far as A and B are concerned, each of these two firms would prefer a system of pollution permits to a system of standards. We know this because a pollution permits program can always be turned into a standards program if doing so is preferable to buying and selling permits. To illustrate, suppose firms A and B are each emitting 3 units of pollution. The government now gives each firm 1 pollution permit, allowing it to emit 1 unit of pollution. If neither firm buys or

sells its 1 permit, then what we essentially have is a standards system for eliminating (some) pollution. Each firm reduces its pollution from 3 units to 1 unit. End of story. But if the two firms start trading permits for money, we can conclude that each firm is better off with a pollution permits system than with a standards system. And this is what we usually see: firms buying and selling permits.

Student:

So the point is that firms A and B prefer a pollution permits system to a standards system?

Instructor:

Yes. But now we are left with everyone else. Is everyone else better off with a pollution permits system than with a standards system? The answer is yes because it is less costly to eliminate a given amount of pollution with a pollution permits system than with standards. "Less costly" here means "fewer resources used." If fewer resources are used to eliminate pollution, then more resources are left over for other things. As a member of the Everyone Else Group, I am better off with more resources left over than with fewer resources to produce things that I want to buy.

So let's now return to your original question: Wouldn't it be fairer if no money changed hands and both firms A and B were told that they had to eliminate *x* amount of pollution? To whom would that be fairer? It's not fairer to firms A and B because they prefer pollution permits to standards. And it's not really fairer to everyone else, because we suspect that everyone else prefers to have more instead of fewer resources left over after *x* amount of pollution has been emitted.

Points to Remember

1. Saying that "firms are paying to pollute" leaves out some of what is happening with a pollution permits system. Some firms are paying other firms not to pollute so that they can pollute. Firm B is paying firm A to not to pollute so that it (firm B) can pollute.

2. Pollution permits (that can be bought and sold) can eliminate a given amount of pollution with a lower resource cost than can a standards system.

a reader asks | Are Houses and Shopping Centers a Sign of Progress?

I live in an area that used to have many trees, large parcels of empty land, creeks, and so on, but in the past two years, more and more houses, apartment buildings, and shopping centers have been built. What was once a nice place to live has become filled with people; the natural beauty of the place and the quality of life have suffered. Would an economist call what has happened progress?

The economist doesn't have a preconceived notion of how the world should look—whether an area should have creeks, trees, and birds or houses and shopping centers. The economist wants resources to be allocated in a welfare-maximizing way.

To illustrate, let's discuss the area you live in. To keep things simple, suppose we are talking about an area of five square miles that we will call area X. It sounds like you (and perhaps others) preferred area X the way it was. Let's say that you and others with similar preferences constitute group A. Perhaps other persons prefer area X the way it has become; let's call them group B. In some sense, then, we are talking about two groups of people—A and B—who want to do different things with area X.

Group A wants to keep area X the way it is: an area with few houses and shopping centers and with many trees, empty parcels of land, and natural features. Group B wants the right to change area X the way it wants: an area with many houses and shopping centers and with few trees, empty parcels of land, and such characteristics.

Which group should get to do what it wants? Suppose group A values area X at a maximum of $40 million, and group B values it at a maximum of $50 million. If group A owned area X, it would sell it to group B. If group B offered $45 million for area X, group A would sell it because area X is only worth a maximum of $40 million to group A. (If the dollar amounts were reversed, group A wouldn't sell area X.)

However, how much group A values area X the way it was is hard to determine. Group A may certainly value area X more than group B did, but perhaps the transaction costs of individuals in this group getting together and bidding the land away from group B were just too high to overcome. In this case, area X may have ended up in the hands of people who value it less than others do.

It may also be that, because certain things were not priced, group B was able to buy area X for something less than a price that accounts for full costs. To illustrate, suppose some of the members of group B are developers who bought parcels of area X to put up houses. In building the houses, they create noise and congestion (on the roads) for the nearby residents. As far as the nearby residents are concerned, the noise and congestion are negative externalities. If the price of the land the developers purchased (for building houses) did not fully reflect the external costs incurred by nearby residents, then possibly more houses were built in area X than was socially optimal or efficient.

Chapter Summary

EXTERNALITIES

- An externality is a side effect of an action that affects the well-being of third parties. There are two types of externalities: negative and positive. A negative externality exists when an individual's or group's actions cause a cost (an adverse side effect) to be felt by others. A positive externality exists when an individual's or group's actions cause a benefit (a beneficial side effect) to be felt by others.

- When either negative or positive externalities exist, the market output is different from the socially optimal output. In the case of a negative externality, the market is said to overproduce the good connected with the negative externality (the socially optimal output is less than the market output). In the case of a positive externality, the market is said to underproduce the good connected with the positive externality (the socially optimal output is greater than the market output). See Exhibits 1 and 3.

- Negative and positive externalities can be internalized or adjusted for in a number of different ways, including persuasion, the assignment of property rights, voluntary agreements, and taxes and subsidies. Also, regulations may be used to adjust for externalities directly.

THE COASE THEOREM

- The Coase theorem holds that when transaction costs are trivial or zero, the property rights assignment does not matter to the resource allocative outcome. To put it differently, a property rights assignment will be undone if it benefits the relevant parties to undo it. The Coase theorem is significant for two reasons: (1) It shows that under certain conditions, the market can internalize externalities. (2) It provides a benchmark for analyzing externality problems; that is, it shows what would happen if transaction costs are trivial or zero.

THE ENVIRONMENT

- Some pollution is likely to be a better situation than no pollution because people derive utility from things that cause pollution, such as cars to drive.

- There is more than one way to tackle environmental problems. For example, both setting standards and selling pollution permits can be employed to deal with pollution. The economist is interested in finding the cheapest way to solve environmental problems. Often, this tends to be through some measure of market environmentalism.

PUBLIC GOODS

- A public good is a good characterized by nonrivalry in consumption. A public good can be excludable or nonex-

cludable. Excludable public goods are goods that, while nonrivalrous in consumption, can be denied to people if they do not pay for them. Nonexcludable public goods are goods that are nonrivalrous in consumption and cannot be denied to people who do not pay for them. The market is said to fail in the provision of nonexcludable public goods because of the free-rider problem; that is, a supplier of the good is not able to extract payment for the good because its benefits can be received without making payment.

ASYMMETRIC INFORMATION

- Asymmetric information exists when either the buyer or the seller in a market exchange has some information that the other does not have. Outcomes based on asymmetric information may be different from outcomes based on symmetric information.

- Adverse selection exists when the parties on one side of the market, who have information not known to others, self-select in a way that adversely affects the parties on the other side of the market. Adverse selection can lead to missing or incomplete markets.

- Moral hazard occurs when one party to a transaction changes his or her behavior in a way that is hidden from and costly to the other party.

Key Terms and Concepts

Market Failure	Socially Optimal Amount (Output)	Excludable
Externality	Internalizing Externalities	Nonexcludable
Negative Externality	Coase Theorem	Free Rider
Positive Externality	Rivalrous in Consumption	Asymmetric Information
Marginal Social Costs (*MSC*)	Public Good	Adverse Selection
Marginal Social Benefits (*MSB*)	Nonrivalrous in Consumption	Moral Hazard

Questions and Problems

1 Under what condition will $MSC = MPC$? When will $MSB = MPB$?

2 Suppose there is a negative externality. If a tax is used to correct for the negative externality, what condition must be satisfied? (What must the tax equal?)

3 In Exhibit 3, explain why the shaded triangle is representative of a market failure.

4 When will asymmetric information in a product market not cause market failure?

5 Give an example that illustrates the difference between private costs and social costs.

6 Consider two types of divorce laws. Law A allows either the husband or the wife to obtain a divorce without the other person's consent. Law B permits a divorce only if both parties agree to the divorce. Will there be more divorces under law A or law B, or will there be the same number of divorces under both laws? Why?

7 People have a demand for sweaters, and the market provides sweaters. There is evidence that people also have a demand for national defense, but the market does not provide national defense. Why doesn't the market provide national defense? Is it because government is providing national defense, and therefore there is no need for the market to

do so? Or is it because the market can't provide national defense?

8 Identify three activities that generate negative externalities and three activities that generate positive externalities. Explain why each activity you identified generates the type of externality you specified.

9 Give an example of each of the following:

   a. A good rivalrous in consumption and excludable.

   b. A good nonrivalrous in consumption and excludable.

   c. A good rivalrous in consumption and nonexcludable.

   d. A good nonrivalrous in consumption and nonexcludable.

10 Some individuals argue that with increased population growth, negative externalities will become more common, and there will be more instances of market failure and more need for government to solve externality problems. Other individuals believe that as time passes, technological advances will be used to solve negative externality problems. They conclude that over time there will be fewer instances of market failure and less need for government to deal with externality problems. What do you believe will happen? Give reasons to support your position.

11 Name at least five government-provided goods that are not nonexcludable public goods.

12 One view is that life is one big externality: Just about everything someone does affects someone else either positively or negatively. To permit government to deal with externality problems is to permit government to tamper with everything in life. No clear line divides externalities in which government should become involved from those it should not. Do you support this position? Why or why not?

13 Economists sometimes shock noneconomists by stating that they do not favor the complete elimination of pollution. Explain the rationale for this position.

14 Why is it cheaper to reduce, say, air pollution through market environmentalism than through government standards and regulations?

15 Identify each of the following as an adverse selection or a moral hazard problem:

   a. A person with car insurance fails to lock his car doors when he shops at a mall.

   b. A person with a family history of cancer purchases the most complete health coverage available.

   c. A person with health insurance takes more risks on the ski slopes of Aspen than he would otherwise.

   d. A college professor receives tenure (assurance of permanent employment) from her employer.

   e. A patient pays his surgeon before she performs the surgery.

Working with Numbers and Graphs

1 Graphically portray:

   a. A negative externality.

   b. A positive externality.

2 Graphically represent:

   a. A corrective tax that achieves the socially optimal output.

   b. One that moves the market output farther away from the socially optimal output than was the case before the tax was applied.

3 Using the following data, prove that pollution permits that can be bought and sold can reduce pollution from 12 units to 6 units at lower cost than a regulation that specifies each of the three firms must cut its pollution in half.

	Firm X	Firm Y	Firm Z
Cost of eliminating:			
First unit of pollution	$200	$500	$1,000
Second unit of pollution	300	700	2,000
Third unit of pollution	400	800	2,900
Fourth unit of pollution	500	900	3,400

CHAPTER *17*

PUBLIC CHOICE: ECONOMIC THEORY APPLIED TO POLITICS

Public Choice
The branch of economics that deals with the application of economic principles and tools to public sector decision making.

Introduction Economics is a powerful analytical tool. As you have seen, it can be used to analyze how markets and the economy work. In this chapter, we use economics to analyze the behavior of politicians, voters, members of special interest groups, and bureaucrats. Specifically, we analyze **public choice**, the branch of economics that deals with the application of economic principles and tools to public sector decision making. Public choice is, in a sense, economics applied to politics.

PUBLIC CHOICE THEORY

Public choice theorists reject the notion that people are like Dr. Jekyll and Mr. Hyde: exhibiting greed and selfishness by their transactions in the private (market) sector and altruism and public spirit by their actions in the public sector. The same people who are the employers, employees, and consumers in the market sector are the politicians, bureaucrats, members of special interest groups, and voters in the public sector. According to public choice theorists, people in the market sector and people in the public sector behave differently not because they have different motives (or are different types of people) but because the two sectors have different institutional arrangements.

As a simple example, Erin Bloom works for a private, profit-seeking firm that makes radio components. Erin is cost conscious, does her work on time, and generally works hard. She knows that she must exhibit this type of work behavior if she wants to keep her job, get a raise, and be promoted. In time, Erin leaves her job at the radio components company and takes a job with the Department of Health and Human Services (HHS) in Washington, D.C. Is Erin a different person (with different motives) working for HHS than she was when she worked for the radio components company? Public choice economists would say no. She is the same person.

However, even though Erin is the same person in and out of government, she will not necessarily exhibit the same work behavior. The costs and benefits of certain actions may be substantially different at HHS than at the radio components company. For example, perhaps the cost of being late for work is less in Erin's new job at HHS than it was at her old job. In her former job, she had to work overtime if she came in late; in her new job, her boss doesn't say anything. We predict that Erin is more likely to be late in her new job than she was in her old one. She is simply responding to costs and benefits as they exist in her new work environment.

 Common MISCONCEPTIONS

About How Government Works

Some people talk as if government is made up exclusively of good and giving people who have only the public good in mind. Others speak as if government is made up exclusively of bad and grabbing people who have only their own welfare at stake. According to public choice economists, both are caricatures of the real people who work in government. One of the founders of public choice, James Buchanan, said, "If men should cease and desist from their talk about and their search for evil men [and his sentiments include "purely good men" too] and commence to look instead at the institutions manned by ordinary people, wide avenues for genuine social reform might appear."

THE POLITICAL MARKET

Economists who practice positive economics want to understand their world. They want to understand not only the production and pricing of goods, unemployment, inflation, and the firm, but also political outcomes and political behavior. This section is an introduction to the political market.

Moving Toward the Middle: The Median Voter Model

During political elections, voters often complain that the candidates for office are too much alike. Some find the similarities frustrating, saying they would prefer to have more choice. However, as the following discussion illustrates, two candidates running for the same office often sound alike because they are competing for votes.

In Exhibit 1, parts (a), (b), and (c) all show a distribution of voters in which the political spectrum goes from the Far Left to the Far Right. Relatively few voters hold positions

exhibit 1

The Move Toward the Middle

Political candidates tend to move toward the middle of the political spectrum. Starting with (a), the Republican receives more votes than the Democrat and would win the election if it were held today. To offset this, as shown in (b), the Democrat moves inward toward the middle of the political spectrum. The Republican tries to offset the Democrat's movement inward by also moving inward. As a result, both candidates move toward the political middle, getting closer to each other over time.

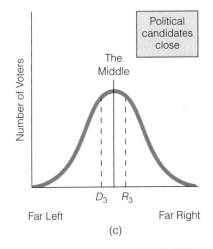

in either of the two extreme wings. Assuming that voters will vote for the candidate who comes closest to matching their ideological or political views, then people whose views are in the Far Left of the political spectrum will vote for the candidate closest to the Far Left and so on.

Our election process begins with two candidates, a Democrat and a Republican, occupying the positions D_1 and R_1 in part (a), respectively. If the election were held today, the Republican would receive more votes than his Democratic opponent. The Republican would receive all the votes of the voters who position themselves to the right of R_1, the Democrat would receive all the votes of the voters who position themselves to the left of D_1, and the voters between R_1 and D_1 would divide their votes between the two candidates. The Republican would receive more votes than the Democrat.

If, however, the election were not held today, the Democrat would likely notice (through polls and the like) that her opponent was doing better than she was. To offset this, she would move toward the center, or middle, of the political spectrum to pick up some votes. Part (b) in Exhibit 1 illustrates this move by the Democrat. Relative to her position in part (a), the Democrat is closer to the middle of the political spectrum, and as a result she picks up votes. Voters to the left of D_2 would vote for the Democrat, voters to the right of R_2 would vote for the Republican, and the voters between the two positions would divide their votes between the two candidates. If the election were held now, the Democrat would win.

In part (c), each candidate, in an attempt to get more votes than the opponent, has moved closer to The Middle (D_3 and R_3). At election time, the two candidates are likely to be positioned side by side at the political center, or middle. In part (c), both candidates have become middle-of-the-roaders in their attempt to pick up votes.

The tendency of political candidates to move to a position at the center of the voter distribution—captured in the **median voter model**—is what causes many voters to complain that there is not much difference between candidates.

What Does the Theory Predict?

The median voter model explains why politicians running for the same office often sound alike, but what does the model predict? Here are a few of the theory's predictions:

1. *Candidates will label their opponent as being either too far to the right or too far to the left.* The candidates know that whoever is closer to the middle of the political spectrum (in a two-person race) will win more votes and thus the election. To win, they will move toward the political middle, at the same time saying that their opponent is a member of the political fringe (i.e., a person far from the center). A Democrat may argue that his Republican opponent is too conservative; a Republican may argue that her Democrat opponent is too liberal.

2. *Candidates will call themselves middle-of-the-roaders, not right- or left-wingers.* In their move toward the political middle, candidates will try to portray themselves as moderates. In their speeches, they will assert that they represent the majority of voters and that they are practical, not ideological. They will not be likely to refer to themselves as ultraliberal or ultraconservative or as right- or left-wingers because to do so would send the wrong message to the voters.

3. *Candidates will take polls, and, if they are not doing well in the polls and their opponents are, they will modify their positions to become more like their opponents.* Polls tell candidates who the likely winner of the election will be. A candidate who finds out that she will lose the election (she is down in the polls) is not likely to sit back and do nothing. The candidate will change her positions. Often, this means becoming more like the winner of the poll—that is, becoming more like her opponent in the political race.

Median Voter Model

A model suggesting that candidates in a two-person political race will move toward matching the preferences of the median voter (i.e., the person whose preferences are at the center, or in the middle, of the political spectrum).

A SIMPLE MAJORITY VOTING RULE: THE CASE OF THE STATUE IN THE PUBLIC SQUARE

Public questions are often decided by the simple majority decision rule. Although most people think this is the fair and democratic way to do things, in certain instances a simple majority vote leads to undertaking a project whose costs are greater than its benefits.

Consider a community of 10 people. The names of the individuals in the community are listed in column 1 of Exhibit 2. The community is considering whether to purchase a statue to put in the center of the public square. The cost of the statue is $1,000, and the community has previously agreed that if the statue is purchased, the 10 individuals will share the cost equally—that is, each will pay $100 in taxes (see column 3).

Column 2 shows the dollar value of the benefits that each individual will receive from the statue. For example, Applebaum places a dollar value of $150 on the statue, Browning places a dollar value of $140 on the statue, and so on. Column 4 notes the net benefit (+) or net cost (−) of the statue to each individual. There is a net benefit for an individual if the dollar value he or she places on the statue is greater than the tax (cost) incurred. There is a net cost if the reverse holds true.

Finally, column 5 indicates how each member of the community would vote. An individual who believes the statue has a net benefit will vote for it, and an individual who believes the statue has a net cost will vote against it. Six individuals vote for the statue, and four individuals vote against it. The majority rules, and the statue is purchased and placed in the center of the public square.

However, the total dollar value of benefits to the community ($812) is less than the total tax cost to the community ($1,000). Using the simple majority decision rule has resulted in the purchase of the statue even though the benefits of the statue to the community are less than its costs to the community.

This outcome is not surprising when you understand that the simple majority decision rule does not take into account the intensity of individuals' preferences. No matter how strongly a person feels about the issue, he or she registers only one vote. For example, even though Emerson places a net benefit of $1 on the statue and Isley places a net cost of $90 on the statue, each individual has only one vote. Isley has no way to register that he does not want the statue more than Emerson wants it.

exhibit 2

Simple Majority Voting and Inefficiency

The simple majority decision rule sometimes generates inefficient results. Here the statue is purchased even though the total dollar value of the benefits of the statue is less than the total dollar costs.

(1) Individuals	(2) Dollar Value of Benefits to Individual	(3) Tax Levied on Individual	(4) Net Benefit (+) or Net Cost (−)	(5) Vote For or Against
Applebaum	$150	$ 100	+$50	For
Browning	140	100	+ 40	For
Carson	130	100	+ 30	For
Davidson	110	100	+ 10	For
Emerson	101	100	+ 1	For
Finley	101	100	+ 1	For
Gunter	50	100	− 50	Against
Harris	10	100	− 90	Against
Isley	10	100	− 90	Against
Janowitz	10	100	− 90	Against
Total	$812	$1,000		

4. *Candidates will speak in general, instead of specific, terms.* Voters agree more on ends than on the means of accomplishing those ends. For example, voters of the left, right, and middle believe that a strong economy is better than a weak economy. However, they do not all agree on the best way to make the economy strong. The person on the right might advocate less government intervention as one way, whereas the person on the left might advocate more government intervention. Most political candidates soon learn that addressing the issues specifically requires them to discuss means and that doing so increases the probability they will have an extreme-wing label attached to them.

For example, a candidate who advocates less government intervention in the economy is more likely to be labeled a right-winger than a candidate who simply calls for a stronger national economy without discussing any specific means. In the candidate's desire to be perceived as a middle-of-the-roader, he is much more likely to talk about ends, on which voters agree, than about means, on which voters disagree.

Finding ECONOMICS

In a Presidential Election Debate

During a presidential election debate, one presidential candidate is asked what his plan is for health care in the country. He says that his plan would make health care more affordable and responsive to people's needs. He then goes on to say that health care has been a problem in the United States for a long time and that it is about time for a solution for the problem to be put forth. Where is the economics?

The median voter model predicts that candidates will speak in general, not specific, terms. This is what we have just heard one of the candidates do. He did not get into any specifics about his plan. For example, he probably will not specifically address how much the health care plan will cost, and so on.

Thinking like AN ECONOMIST

Testing Theories

An economist thinks about theories and then tests them. She is not content to have a theory—such as the one that says candidates in a two-person political race will gravitate toward the center of the political distribution—simply sound right. The economist asks, "If the theory is right, what should I expect to see in the real world? If the theory is wrong, what should I expect to see in the real world?" Such questions direct the economist to look at effects to see whether the theory has explanatory and predictive power. If we actually see the four predictions of the median voter theory occurring in the real world—candidates labeling themselves one way, speaking in general terms, and so on—then we can conclude that the evidence supports the theory. But if we see that candidates en masse do not behave as the model predicts, then we would know to reject the theory.

VOTERS AND RATIONAL IGNORANCE

The preceding section explains something about the behavior of politicians, especially near or at election time. We turn now to voters.

The Costs and Benefits of Voting

Political commentators often remark that the voter turnout for this or that election was low. They might say, "Only 54 percent of registered voters actually voted." Are voter turnouts low because Americans are apathetic or because they do not care who wins an election? Are they uninterested in political issues?

Public choice economists often explain low voter turnouts in terms of the costs and benefits of voting. As an example, Mark Quincy is thinking about voting in a presidential election. Mark may receive many benefits from voting: He may feel more involved in public affairs or think that he has met his civic responsibility. He may see himself as patriotic, or he may believe he has a greater right to criticize government if he takes an active part in it. In short, he may benefit from seeing himself as a doer instead of a talker. Ultimately, however, he will weigh these positive benefits against the costs of voting, which include driving to the polls, standing in line, and so on. If, in the end, Mark perceives the benefits of voting as greater than the costs, he will vote.

But suppose Mark believes he receives only one benefit from voting—that his vote will have an impact on the election outcome. His benefits-of-voting equation may look like this:

$$\text{Mark's benefits of voting} = \text{Probability of Mark's vote affecting the outcome} \times \text{Additional benefits Mark receives if his candidate wins}$$

Suppose two candidates, A and B, are running for office. If Mark votes, he will vote for A because he estimates that he benefits $100 if A is elected but only $40 if B is elected. The difference, $60, represents the additional benefits Mark receives if his candidate wins.

However, the probability of Mark's vote affecting the outcome is questionable. With many potential voters, such as in a presidential election, the probability that one person's vote will affect the outcome is close to 0. To recognize this fact on an intuitive level, suppose A and B are the two major candidates in a presidential campaign. If you, as an individual voter, vote for A, the outcome of the election is likely to be the same as if you had voted for B or as if you had not voted at all. In other words, whether you do not vote, vote for A, or vote for B, the outcome is likely to be the same. In short, when there are many potential voters, the probability of one person's vote changing the outcome of an election is close to 0. In Mark's benefits-of-voting equation, $60 is multiplied by a probability so small that it might as well be 0. So $60 times 0 is 0. In short, Mark receives no benefits from voting.

But Mark may face certain costs. His costs-of-voting equation may look like this:

$$\text{Mark's cost of voting} = \text{Cost of driving to the polls} + \text{Cost of standing in line} + \text{Cost of filling out the ballot}$$

Obviously, Mark faces some positive costs of voting. Because his benefits of voting are 0 and his costs of voting are positive, Mark makes the rational choice if he decides not to vote.

Clearly, not everyone behaves this way—that is, chooses not to vote. Many people do vote in elections. Probably what separates the Marks in the world from the people who vote is that the people who vote receive some benefits from voting that Mark does not. They might receive benefits simply from being part of the excitement of election day, from doing what they perceive as their civic duty, or from some other reason.

The point that public choice economists make is that if many individual voters vote only if they perceive their vote as making a difference, then they probably will not vote

ARE YOU RATIONALLY IGNORANT?

Rational ignorance is usually easier to see in others than in ourselves. We understand that most people are not well informed about politics and government, but we often fail to put ourselves in the same category, even when we deserve to be there. We can take a giant leap forward in understanding rational ignorance and special interest legislation if we see ourselves more clearly. With this in mind, try to answer the following questions about politics or government.

1. What is the name of your most recently elected U.S. senator, and what party does he or she belong to?
2. How has your congressional representative voted in any of the last 20 votes in Congress?
3. What is the approximate dollar amount of federal government spending? What is the approximate dollar amount of federal government tax revenues?
4. Which political party controls the House of Representatives?
5. What is the name of your representative in the state legislature?
6. Name just one special interest group and note how much it received in federal monies (within a broad range) in the last federal budget.
7. Explain an issue in the most recent local political controversy that did not have to do with someone's personality or personal life.
8. Approximately how many persons sit in your state's legislature?
9. What political positions (if any) did the governor of your state hold before becoming governor?
10. In what month and year will the next congressional elections in your state be held?

If you know the answers to only a few of the questions, then consider yourself rationally ignorant about politics and government. This is what public choice analysis would predict.

Now ask yourself why you don't know the answers. Are the questions too hard (or impossible) to answer, or have you just not been interested in answering them?

Finally, ask yourself whether you will now take the time to find the answers. If you do not know the answer to question 6, for example, are you going to take the time to get it? We think not. If so, then you should now understand rational ignorance—on a personal level.

because their vote is unlikely to make a difference. The low turnouts that appear to be a result of voter apathy may instead be a result of cost-benefit calculations.

Rational Ignorance

How often have you heard something like this? "Democracy would be better served if voters would take more of an interest in and become better informed about politics and government. Voters don't know much about the issues."

The problem is not that voters are too stupid to learn about the issues. Many voter-citizens who know little about politics and government are quite capable of learning about both, but they choose not to make the effort. The reason is perhaps predictable: The benefits of becoming informed are often outweighed by the costs. In short, many persons believe that becoming informed is simply not worth the effort. Hence, on an individual basis, it makes sense to be uninformed about politics and government, that is, to be in a state of **rational ignorance**.

As an example, Shonia Tyler has many things she can do with her leisure time. She could read a good novel, watch a television program, go out with friends, or become better informed about the candidates and the issues in the upcoming U.S. Senate race. Becoming informed, however, has costs. If Shonia stays home and reads about the issues, she can't go out with her friends. If she stays up late to watch a news program, she might be too tired to work efficiently the next day. These costs have to be weighed against the

Rational Ignorance
The state of not acquiring information because the costs of acquiring it are greater than the benefits.

ECONOMIC ILLITERACY AND DEMOCRACY

Citizens can vote even if they have no idea what they are doing. If enough voters fit that description, democratic governments are bound to make foolish decisions.
—Bryan Caplan, *Straight Talk About Economic Literacy*

Economist Bryan Caplan argues that a large percentage of the American public is economically illiterate. The result? A lot of foolishness gets turned into national economic policy.[1]

Although it might be easy to determine whether someone is illiterate, it is not so easy to determine whether someone is economically illiterate. To determine illiteracy, you can just ask people to read or write something. If they can read and write, they are not illiterate. If they can't read and write, they are illiterate.

Unfortunately, there is not as simple a test to determine economically illiteracy. Instead Caplan points to a survey that compared the responses of average Americans (1,510 of them) and professional economists (250 of them) to the same set of questions concerning economics and the economy. Here is one question from the survey: "Which do you think is more responsible for the recent increase in gasoline prices: the normal law of supply and demand, oil companies trying to increase profits, both, or neither?" Although only 8 percent of economists said recent increases in gas prices were due to oil companies trying to increase profits, 78 percent of the noneconomists polled explained high gas prices this way. The explanation for high gas prices chosen by 83 percent of economists was supply and demand.

Indirectly, Caplan uses the economists' overwhelming response to the question as a benchmark by which to measure the economic illiteracy of the public. The closer the public responses are to the economists' responses, the less economically illiterate the public is; the farther away the public responses are from the economists' responses, the more economically illiterate the public is.

According to Caplan, looking at responses to numerous questions, the American public is largely economically illiterate. Caplan argues that such a great degree of economic illiteracy has to do with the price one pays to be economically illiterate. Simply put, the price is rather low; so you would expect a higher degree of economic illiteracy when the price is low than when it is high. In a phrase: False beliefs about economics are cheap. According to Caplan, if you underestimate the costs of excessive drinking, you can ruin your life. But if you underestimate the economic benefits of, say, free international trade, nothing really bad happens to you. The same thing happens to you that would have happened if you didn't underestimate the economic benefits of free international trade. In other words, when there is really no cost to being wrong, a lot of people will be wrong—especially if one receives a personal psychological lift from holding an erroneous belief or position. Caplan puts it succinctly: "In a sense, then, there is a method to the average voter's madness. Even when his views are completely wrong, he gets the psychological benefit of emotionally appealing political beliefs at a bargain price. No wonder he buys in bulk."[2] In other words, *X* might be the wrong answer to the question, but if *X* is emotionally appealing to the respondent, and if having the wrong answer doesn't adversely affect the respondent, then *X* it is.

But if many people choose *X*, perhaps at a national level *X* gets turned into policy. In other words, if the majority of voting Americans believe that placing tariffs on foreign imports is desirable (when economists largely disagree), then it is likely, in a political system where politicians compete for votes, that the public's erroneous belief will find its way into international trade policy.

If one person's erroneous belief adversely affects only him, that is one thing. But it is quite another thing, Caplan argues, when the erroneous beliefs of many people adversely affect those who do not hold that belief. Yet this is what we often get in a representative democracy. Economically erroneous beliefs, chosen on an individual level because they are cheap to choose, often add up to democracies' choosing bad economic policies.

1. See Bryan Caplan's book, *The Myth of the Rational Voter: Why Democracies Choose Bad Policies* (Princeton, NJ: Princeton University Press, 2007).

2. See "The Myth of the Rational Voter," in *Cato Unbound*, November 6, 2006, at http://www.cato-unboundorg/2006/11/06/bryan-caplan-the-myth-of-the-rational-voter/.

benefits of becoming better informed about the candidates and the issues. For Shonia, as for many people, the benefits are unlikely to be greater than the costs.

Many people see little personal benefit to becoming more knowledgeable about political candidates and issues. As with voting, the decision to remain uninformed may be linked to the small impact any single individual can have in a large-numbers setting.

Common MISCONCEPTIONS

About Being Uninformed

A college professor once told his class of students that they were apathetic because they didn't know more about political issues. But maybe apathy is not what the students feel—not the reason they don't know more about political issues. The reason could simply be that they are rationally ignorant. Currently for them the costs of becoming informed (on various political issues) are greater than the benefits.

SELF-TEST

(Answers to Self-Test questions are in the Self-Test Appendix.)

1. If a politician running for office does not speak in general terms, does not try to move to the middle of the political spectrum, and does not take polls, does it follow that the median voter model is wrong?

2. Voters often criticize politicians running for office who do not speak in specific terms (tell them what spending programs will be cut, whose taxes will be raised, etc.). If voters want politicians running for office to speak in specific terms, why don't politicians do so?

3. Would bad weather be something that could affect the voter turnout? Explain your answer.

MORE ABOUT VOTING

Voting is often the method used to make decisions in the public sector. In this section, we discuss two examples to describe some of the effects (some might say problems) of voting as a decision-making method.

Example 1: Voting for a Nonexcludable Public Good

Suppose a community of 7 persons, A–G, wants to produce or purchase nonexcludable public good X. Each person in the community wants a different number of units of X, as shown in the following table:

Person	Number of Units of X Desired
A	1
B	2
C	3
D	4
E	5
F	6
G	7

If the community of 7 persons holds a simple majority vote, then all 7 will vote to produce or purchase at least 1 unit of X. Six people (B–G) will vote for at least 2 units. Five people (C–G) will vote for at least 3 units. Four people (D–G) will vote for at least 4 units. Three people (E–G) will vote for at least 5 units. Two people (F–G) will vote for at least 6 units. Only one person (G) will vote for 7 units.

The largest number of units that receives a simple majority vote (half the total number of voters plus 1, or 4 votes) is 4 units. In other words, the community will vote to produce or purchase 4 units of X. What is interesting is that 4 units is the most preferred outcome of only one of the seven members of the community, person D, who is the median voter. Half the voters (A, B, and C) prefer fewer than 4 units, and half the voters (E, F, and G) prefer more than 4 units. Thus, our voting process has resulted in only the median voter obtaining his most preferred outcome.

The outcome would have been the same even if the numbers had looked as they do in the following table:

Person	Number of Units of X Desired
A	0
B	0
C	0
D	4
E	7
F	7
G	7

In this case, 4 people (D–G) would have voted for at least 4 units and only 3 people would have voted for anything less than 4 units. Again, 4 units would have been the outcome of the vote, and only the median voter would have obtained his most preferred outcome.

Example 2: Voting and Efficiency

Suppose three individuals have the marginal private benefits (*MPB*) shown in the following table for various units of nonexcludable public good Y.

Person	MPB of First Unit of Y	MPB of Second Unit of Y	MPB of Third Unit of Y
A	$400	$380	$190
B	150	110	90
C	100	90	80

If the cost of providing a unit of good Y is $360, what is the socially optimal, or efficient, amount of good Y? To answer this question, we need to review a few of the relationships from the last chapter:

1. The socially optimal, or efficient, amount of anything is the amount at which the marginal social benefits (*MSB*) equal the marginal social costs (*MSC*).

2. The sum of the marginal private benefits and the marginal external benefits equals the marginal social benefits: $MPB + MEB = MSB$.

3. The sum of the marginal private costs and the marginal external costs equals the marginal social costs: $MPC + MEC = MSC$.

In our example, the *MSC* for each unit is given as $360. We calculate the *MSB* for each unit by summing its *MPB*. For the first unit, the *MSB* is $650 ($400 + $150 + $100); for the second unit, it is $580; and for the third unit, it is $360. The socially optimal, or efficient, amount of good Y is 3 units because this is the amount at which $MSB = MSC$.

Whether voting will give us efficiency largely depends on what tax each person, A–C, expects to pay. Suppose each person must pay an equal share of the price of a unit of good Y. In other words, the tax for each person is $120 ($360 per unit ÷ 3 persons = $120 per person per unit).

Person A will vote for 3 units because his *MPB* for each unit is greater than his tax of $120 per unit. Person B will vote for only 1 unit because his *MPB* for the first unit is greater than his tax of $120 per unit, but his *MPB* is not greater for the second or third unit. Person *C* will not vote for any units because his *MPB* for each unit is less than his tax of $120 per unit. The outcome, using a simple majority vote, is only 1 unit. A process of voting where each voter pays an equal tax results in an inefficient outcome.

Now suppose, instead of paying an equal tax (of $120), each person pays a tax equal to his *MPB* at the socially optimal, or efficient, outcome. The socially optimal, or efficient, outcome is 3 units of good Y, so person A would pay a tax of $190 (his *MPB* for the third unit is $190). Person B would pay a tax of $90, and person C would pay a tax of $80. (The sum of the taxes paid is equal to the cost of the unit, or $360.)

With this different tax structure, will voting generate efficiency? If each person casts a truthful vote, the answer is yes. Each person will vote for 3 units.[3] In other words, if everyone casts a truthful vote and everyone pays a tax equal to his or her *MPB* at the efficient outcome, then voting will generate efficiency.

Comparing the two tax structures—one where each person pays an equal tax and one where each person pays a tax equal to his *MPB*—we see that the tax structure makes the difference. In the case of equal tax shares, voting did not lead to efficiency; in the case of unequal tax shares, it did.

SELF-TEST

1. If the *MSC* in Example 2 had been $580 instead of $360, what would the socially optimal, or efficient, outcome have been?

2. In Example 2 with equal taxes, did the outcome of the vote make anyone worse off? If so, who and by how much?

SPECIAL INTEREST GROUPS

Special Interest Groups
Subsets of the general population that hold (usually) intense preferences for or against a particular government service, activity, or policy. Often, special interest groups gain from public policies that may not be in accord with the interests of the general public.

Special interest groups are subsets of the general population that hold (usually) intense preferences for or against a particular government service, activity, or policy. Often, special interest groups gain from public policies that may not be in accord with the interests of the general public. In recent decades, they have played a major role in government.

Information and Lobbying Efforts

Although the general voter is usually uninformed about issues, members of a special interest group are very well informed. For example, teachers are likely to know a lot about government education policies, farmers about government farm policies, and union members about government union policies. When it comes to their issues of interest, the special interest group members know much more than the general voter. The reason is simple: The more directly and intensely issues affect them, the greater the incentive is for individuals to become informed about them.

Given an electorate composed of uninformed general voters and informed members of a special interest group, the special interest group is often able to sway politicians in its direction. This occurs even when the general public is made worse off by such actions (which, of course, is not always the case).

Suppose special interest group A, composed of 5,000 individuals, favors a policy that will result in the redistribution of $50 million from 100 million general taxpayers to the group.

---

3. Look at the situation for person A: His *MPB* for the first unit is $400 and his tax is $190; so he votes for the first unit. His *MPB* for the second unit is $380 and his tax is $190; so he votes for the second unit. His *MPB* for the third unit is $190 and his tax is $190; so he votes for the third unit. With respect to the last unit for person A, we are assuming that if his *MPB* is equal to the tax, he will vote in favor of the unit. The same holds for the analysis of voting for persons B and C.

The dollar benefit for each member of the special interest group is $10,000. Given this substantial dollar amount, members of the special interest group are likely to (1) have sponsored or proposed the legislation and (2) lobby the politicians who will decide the issue.

And the politicians will probably not hear from the general voter (general taxpayer)? The general voter/taxpayer will be less informed about the legislation than the members of the special interest group, and, even if adequately informed, each person would have to calculate the benefits and the costs of lobbying against the proposed legislation. If the legislation passes, the average taxpayer will pay approximately 50 cents, and the benefits of lobbying against the legislation are probably not greater than 50 cents. Therefore, even if informed about the legislation, the general taxpayer would not be likely to argue against it. The benefits just wouldn't be worth the time and effort. We predict that special interest bills have a good chance of being passed in our legislatures.

Congressional Districts as Special Interest Groups

Most people do not ordinarily think of congressional districts as special interest groups. Special interest groups are commonly thought to include the ranks of public school teachers, steel manufacturers, automobile manufacturers, farmers, environmentalists, bankers, truck drivers, doctors, and the like. For some issues, however, a particular congressional district may be a special interest group.

Suppose an air force base is located in a Texas congressional district. Then a Pentagon study determines that the base is not needed and that Congress should close it down. The Pentagon study demonstrates that the cost to the taxpayers of keeping the base open is greater than the benefits to the country of maintaining it. But closing the air force base will hurt the pocketbooks of the people in the congressional district that houses the base. Their congressional representative not only knows as much, but also that if she can't keep the base open, she isn't as likely to be reelected to office.

Therefore, she speaks to other members of Congress about the proposed closing. In a way, she is a lobbyist for her congressional district. Most members of Congress are probably willing to go along with the Texas representative, even though they know that their constituents will be paying more in taxes than the Pentagon has said is necessary to ensure the national security of the country. If they don't go along with her, when they need a vote on one of their own special interest (sometimes the term *pork barrel* is used) projects, the representative from Texas may not be as cooperative. In short, members of Congress sometimes trade votes: my vote on your air force base for your vote on subsidies to dairy farmers in my district. This type of vote trading—the exchange of votes to gain support for legislation—is commonly referred to as **logrolling**.

Public Interest Talk, Special Interest Legislation

Special interest groups lobbying for special interest legislation usually don't use that name, but rather something like "legislation in the best interest of the general public." A number of examples, both past and present, come to mind.

In the early 19th century, the British Parliament passed the Factory Acts, which put restrictions on women and children working. Those who lobbied for the restrictions said they did so for humanitarian reasons, such as to protect young children and women from difficult and hazardous work in the cotton mills. There is evidence, however, that the men working in the factories were the main lobbyists for the Factory Acts and that a reduced supply of women and children directly benefited them by raising their wages. The male factory workers appealed to individuals' higher sensibilities instead of letting it be known that they would benefit at the expense of others.

Today, people calling for, say, economic protection from foreign competitors or greater federal subsidies rarely explain that they favor the measure because it will make

Logrolling
The exchange of votes to gain support for legislation.

them better off while someone else pays the bill. Instead, they usually voice the public interest argument. Economic protectionism isn't necessary to protect industry X, but it is necessary to protect American jobs and the domestic economy. The special interest message often is, "Help yourself by helping us."

Sometimes this message holds true, but other times it does not. Nevertheless, it is likely to be as forcefully voiced in either case.

Special Interest Groups and Rent Seeking

Special interest groups often engage in rent-seeking behavior, which has consequences for society as a whole. We review rent seeking here and describe how it relates to special interest groups.

RENT VERSUS PROFIT The term *rent seeking* was first used by Anne Krueger in an article in 1974, but the theory behind rent seeking had already been put forth by Gordon Tullock in a 1969 article. Strictly speaking, the term *rent* refers to the part of the payment to an owner of resources over and above the amount those resources could command in any alternative use. In other words, rent is payment over and above opportunity cost. Everyone would like to receive payment in excess of opportunity cost; so the motive to seek rent is strong.

When rent is the result of entrepreneurial activity designed either to satisfy a new demand or to rearrange resources in an increasingly valuable way, then rent is usually called profit. To illustrate, suppose Jack finds a way to rearrange resources X, Y, and Z to produce a new good, A. If Jack receives a price for A that is greater than the cost of the resources, he receives a payment in excess of opportunity cost. Thus, Jack receives some rent; but in this setting, the rent is called profit.

Rent is not referred to as profit *in a setting where no new demand is satisfied or no additional value is created.* To illustrate, Vernon lives and works as a taxi driver in a city in the Midwest. The city council licenses taxi drivers as long as they meet certain minimum requirements, such as having a valid driver's license and so on. Currently, Vernon receives a monthly income that is equal to his opportunity cost. In other words, he does not receive any rent. Then, one day, Vernon and the other taxi drivers in the city lobby the city council to stop issuing taxi licenses, and the city council grants this request. Over time, the demand for taxis is likely to rise, but the supply of taxis will not. As a result, the dollar price for a taxi ride will rise. In time, Vernon can earn an income over and above his opportunity cost. In other words, he will receive some rent.

In this setting, Vernon and the other taxi drivers have neither satisfied a new demand nor rearranged resources in a way that increases value. They have simply lobbied the city government to bring about a change that results in their receiving higher taxi fares and higher incomes at the expense of the customers who must pay the higher fares. There has been a transfer of income from taxi riders to taxi drivers. However, this transfer of income has a cost. Vernon and the other taxi drivers expended resources to bring about this pure transfer, which is referred to as rent seeking. In short, *rent seeking is the expenditure of scarce resources to capture a pure transfer.*

RENT SEEKING IS SOCIALLY WASTEFUL From society's perspective, the resources used in rent seeking are wasted and make society (but not necessarily all individuals in society) poorer as a result. To illustrate, suppose only two people are in a society, Smith and Brown. The total amount of resources in this society, or the total income, is $10,000. We could (1) give all of the income to Smith, (2) give all of it to Brown, or (3) give some amount to each. Exhibit 3 shows a line, I_1, that represents the possible combinations of income the two persons may receive. Currently, Smith and Brown are located at point A on I_1, where each receives some income.[4]

Smith would prefer to be located at point B, where he would receive more income than he currently does at point A. To this end, Smith lobbies legislators to pass a law that effectively redistributes income from Brown to him. Smith is successful in his lobbying efforts, and the law passes. But Brown and Smith don't move from point A to point B as a result. This movement doesn't adjust for the resources that were used by Smith when he was rent seeking. If we take these resources into account, there is now less total income for Smith and Brown to share. If Smith expended $1,000 worth of resources in effecting the transfer, income is now $9,000 instead of $10,000. Therefore, I_1 is no longer relevant; I_2 is. The result of Smith's rent seeking is that he and Brown move from point A to point C. At point C, Smith receives more income than he did at point A and Brown receives less.

One effect of Smith's rent seeking is that he is made better off and Brown is made worse off. The other effect is that society as a whole (i.e., the sum of Smith and Brown) is poorer than it was when there was no rent seeking. In short, rent seeking may be rational from an individual's perspective (after all, Smith does make himself better off through rent seeking), but it is harmful to society.

Now consider a slight modification. Suppose Brown is aware that Smith is lobbying legislators in an attempt to transfer income from her to him. Brown may try to lobby defensively—that is, to lobby against Smith. Brown's lobbying efforts are not costless; resources are expended in trying to defend the status quo in income distribution. Brown may not be seeking rent, but she is using resources to prevent someone else from doing so. The resources she uses are wasted as far as society is concerned because they do not go to build bridges, educate children, or do any number of other things. These resources are used to prevent a pure transfer. In other words, because of Brown's defensive lobbying efforts, society may move from I_1 to I_2. If Brown is successful at preventing Smith from effecting a pure transfer, then Brown and Smith may end up moving from point A to point D. The relative income shares of the two individuals may not be any different at point D than at point A, but both Brown and Smith receive less income at point D than at point A. The combination of offensive lobbying (for rent) by Smith and defensive lobbying (to prevent Smith from getting rent) by Brown results in both individuals being made worse off.

---

exhibit 3

Rent Seeking

Brown and Smith are the only two people in a society in which the total amount of resources, or the total income, is $10,000. Currently, Brown and Smith are located at point A on I_1, where each receives some of the $10,000. Smith wants to move to point B, where he would receive more income than he does at point A. To try to bring this outcome about, he lobbies legislators to pass a law that will transfer income away from Brown to him. In other words, he is rent seeking. Because rent-seeking activity uses resources in a socially unproductive way, there are fewer resources, or less total income, to divide between Brown and Smith. Still, Smith may not mind this if he has moved from point A on I_1 to point C on I_2 as a result of his rent-seeking activities. Overall, Brown and Smith are worse off (sharing $9,000 instead of $10,000), but Smith is better off at point C than at point A.

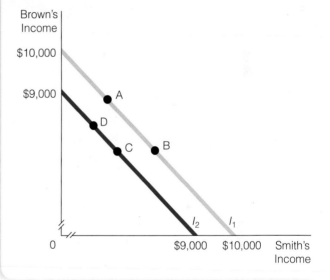

---

4. This analysis is based on Chapter 18, "The Rent Seeking Society," in Richard McKenzie and Gordon Tullock, *The New World of Economics* (New York: McGraw-Hill, 1994).

INHERITANCE, HEIRS, AND WHY THE FIRSTBORN BECAME KING OR QUEEN

Some economists have said that rent-seeking activity often goes on within families, especially when an inheritance is involved. We present their argument in the form of a short story.

An elderly widow with three children has an estate worth $10 million, which she will leave to her children upon her death. But, of course, there are different ways to leave $10 million to three adult children. She can split the $10 million into three equal parts, leaving $3.333 million to each. Or she can divide the $10 million unequally, perhaps leaving $9 million to A, $500,000 to B, and $500,000 to C. Furthermore, she can either tell each child how much he or she will inherit, or she can keep the dollar amount secret (until after her death). In other words, the elderly

© YALE CENTER FOR BRITISH ART, PAUL MELLON COLLECTION, USA/THE BRIDGEMAN ART LIBRARY

woman has two major decisions to make: how much money she will give each child and whether to tell them what they will receive upon her death.

If the woman is the type of person who craves attention and wants her children to fawn over her, she can use her inheritance to bring this about. All she has to do is tell her children (1) that she will not divide her estate equally among the three of them and (2) that she hasn't yet decided on the amount each will receive. If she promises unequal inheritances that are yet to be determined, she almost guarantees that her children will engage in a rent-seeking battle for the bulk of her inheritance. The resultant battle is likely to take the form of each child fawning over the mother to curry favor.

SELF-TEST

1. The average farmer is likely to be better informed about federal agricultural policy than the average food consumer is. Why?

2. Consider special interest legislation that will transfer $40 million from group A to group B, where group B includes 10,000 persons. Is this special interest legislation more likely to pass (a) when group A includes 10,000 persons or (b) when group A includes 10 million persons? Explain your answer.

3. Give an example of public interest talk spoken by a special interest group.

4. Why is rent-seeking activity socially wasteful?

GOVERNMENT BUREAUCRACY

A discussion of politics and government is not complete without mention of the government bureau and bureaucrat. A **government bureaucrat** is an unelected person who works in a government bureau and is assigned a special task that relates to a law or program passed by the legislature.

Let's consider a few facts about government bureaus:

1. A government bureau receives its funding from the legislature. Often, its funding in future years depends on how much it spends in carrying out its specified duties in the current year.

2. A government bureau does not maximize profits.

Government Bureaucrat
An unelected person who works in a government bureau and who is assigned a special task relating to a law or program passed by the legislature.

From the perspective of any one child, say A, he knows that there is a fixed inheritance, $10 million, and that what goes to one of his siblings will not go to him. For example, if $3 million goes to sibling B or C, there is $3 million less for him. The widow has effectively put her three children in a situation in which they will invest resources (fawn over her) to effect a pure transfer. This is rent seeking.

The situation is different if the woman tells her children what she plans to leave each and then guarantees that under no circumstances will she change her mind. For example, if she tells child A that he will receive $2 million, child B that she will receive $7 million, and child C that he will receive $1 million, then there is no reason for any of the children to invest resources in rent seeking. The $10 million has already been split up.

Alternatively, the mother can simply tell her children that she plans to divide her inheritance equally and nothing on earth can get her to do differently. Once again, if the children know how things are guaranteed to turn out and that any resources they use to change the results will be wasted, they will decide against trying to change the outcome. No child will seek rents, in other words.

Rent seeking used to be common in a slightly different context. In the days when kings and queens ruled, the firstborn of a king or queen usually inherited the throne. But why the first child? The third child could be a more capable king or queen than the first. Surely not every first child was more capable of being king or queen than every second, third, or fourth child.

Consider what might have happened if the firstborn was not predetermined to inherit the throne. The king's or queen's children would have engaged in a rent-seeking battle for the throne. In and of itself, the queen or king may not have had anything against this, and, in fact, they may have liked it.

But they wouldn't have liked it if their children engaged in such an intense rent-seeking battle that they tried to kill each other. From the child's perspective, there would be two ways to get the throne: (1) have the queen or king choose you from among all your brothers and sisters to ascend to the throne; (2) kill your brothers and sisters so that you were the only one left. One way to cut down on sibling killings was to simply have a rule stating that the firstborn would become king or queen. This rule didn't eliminate sibling murders completely—the second child might try to kill the first and therefore inherit the throne—but it certainly kept the number of sibling murders lower than what it might have been if any of the many children could ascend to the throne.

3. There are no transferable ownership rights in a government bureau. There are no stockholders in a government bureau.

4. Many government bureaus provide services for which there is no competition. For example, if a person wants a driver's license, there is usually only one place to go: the Department of Motor Vehicles.

5. If the legislation that established the government bureau in the first place is repealed, there is little or no need for the government bureau.

These five facts about government bureaus have corresponding consequences. Many economists see these consequences as follows:

1. Government bureaus are not likely to end the current year with surplus funds. If they do, their funding for the following year is likely to be less than it was for the current year. Their motto is, "Spend the money, or lose it."

2. Because a government bureau does not attempt to maximize profits, as a private firm would, it does not watch its costs as carefully. Given points 1 and 2, government bureau costs are likely to remain constant or rise but are not likely to fall.

3. No one has a monetary incentive to monitor the government bureau because no one owns the government bureau and no one can sell an ownership right in it. Stockholders in private firms have a monetary incentive to ensure that the managers of the firms do an efficient job. Because there is no analog to stockholders in a government bureau, there is no one to ensure that the bureau manager operates the bureau efficiently.

4. Government bureaus and bureaucrats are not as likely to try to please the customer as private firms are because (in most cases) they have no competition and are not threatened by any in the future. If the lines are long at the Department of Motor Vehicles, the bureaucrats do not care. Customers cannot go anywhere else to get what they need.

5. Government bureaucrats are likely to lobby for the continued existence and expansion of the programs they administer. To behave differently would go against their best interests. To argue for the repeal of a program, for example, is to argue for the abolition of their jobs.

A VIEW OF GOVERNMENT

The view of government presented in this chapter is perhaps much different from the view presented by your elementary school social studies teacher. Politicians and bureaucrats were kind, charitable, altruistic, generous, and above all, dedicated to serving the public good. Voters willingly performed their civic responsibility.

No doubt some will say that the view of government in this chapter is cynical and exaggerated. It may very well be. But it is based on a theory, and most theories are not descriptively accurate. The real question is whether the theory of public sector decision making presented here meets the test that any theory must meet. It must explain and predict real-world events. Numerous economists and political scientists have concluded that it does.

"DOESN'T PUBLIC CHOICE PAINT A BLEAK PICTURE OF POLITICS AND GOVERNMENT?"

Student:
In a way, public choice paints a rather bleak picture of politics and government.

Instructor:
How so?

Student:
Politicians don't seem to care about what is right or wrong. They just move to the middle of the voter distribution. People don't always vote because it is sometimes too costly to vote. People aren't always well informed on issues because it is too costly to be well informed. And to top it off, special interests are engaged in rent seeking. Doesn't all this sound dismal to you?

Instructor:
It sounds as if you may have wanted things to turn out differently. Unfortunately, we don't always get the results we want.

Student:
I have to confess that I did. I wanted politicians to do the right thing, and I wanted people to be informed on issues and to cast intelligent votes.

Instructor:
Probably many people want the same thing. My guess is that public choice economists want the same thing. But we can't let what we want color how we see the world.

Student:
But who is to say that public choice economists analyze the world the right way? Maybe they are an overly cynical bunch of economists.

Instructor:
What they are doesn't matter. What matters is what they say and what they predict. We don't judge a economic theory by how it sounds to us or by how we feel about it; we judge it by how well it explains and predicts what we see in the world. If politicians move to the center of the voter distribution, if people are rationally ignorant, and if special interests sometimes engage in rent seeking, then that is the way things are whether we like it or not.

Student:
But aren't economists supposed to be trying to make the world better?

Instructor:
Let's assume that they are. Then isn't a good understanding of the world critical to doing this? For example, if the world is X, and I think it is Y, then I might make mistakes when I try to make the world a better place. Basing what I do on how things are has to be better than basing them on how I might want them to be.

Student:
I can see your point. It's sort of like a doctor who wants to know your true condition before she prescribes any therapy. She may not like the fact that you have a particular disease, but it's important that she know about it so that she can prescribe the right medicine.

Instructor:
I think that captures the spirit of what I'm talking about.

Student:
Does it follow, then, that everything in public choice theory is right?

Instructor:
No, it doesn't follow. Public choice theory—just like any theory in economics—has to be judged on how well it explains and predicts.

Points to Remember

1. Theories should be judged on how well they explain and predict (not how they sound or feel).
2. Good economics seeks to know what exists, no matter how pleasant or unpleasant that is.

a reader asks | What Is the Significance of Public Choice?

Public choice hits on some interesting topics—such as the median voter model, special interests, and rational ignorance—but why is it studied in economics? Why isn't it studied in political science?

According to public choice economists, public choice fills a gap that existed in economics. They often say that before public choice came along, too many economists simply assumed that if markets failed, government would and could step up and fix the problem. For example, if a negative externality caused the market to fail—and the market overproduced a good—then government officials could be relied on to set the right tax and correct the problem. If individuals demanded a nonexcludable public good and the market didn't provide it, then government would. In the area of macroeconomics, if the self-regulating properties of the economy were not working and the unemployment rate rose too high, then government would step forward and stimulate the economy in just the right way to reduce the unemployment rate to an acceptable level.

What was assumed, say public choice economists, is that government would work flawlessly to correct the failures of the market. Public choice theory questions whether government works as flawlessly and as unselfishly as was assumed. Just as there is market failure, say public choice economists, there is government failure, or political failure.

Here is what James Buchanan, one of the founders of public choice, has to say about the subject:

> Lest we forget, it is useful to remind ourselves in the 1990s that the predominant emphasis of the theoretical welfare economics of the 1950s and 1960s was placed on the identification of "market failure," with the accompanying normative argument for politicized correction. In retrospect, it seems naïve in the extreme to advance institutional comparisons between the workings of an observed and idealized alternative. Despite Wicksell's early criticism, however, economists continued to assume, implicitly, that politics would work ideally in the corrective adjustments to market failures that analysis enabled them to identify.
>
> The lasting contribution of public choice theory has been to correct this obvious imbalance in analysis. Any institutional comparison that is worthy of serious considerations must compare relevant alternatives; if market organization is to be replaced by politicized order, or vice versa, the two institutional structures must be evaluated on the basis of predictions as to how they will actually work. Political failure, as well as market failure, must become central to the comprehensive analysis that precedes normative judgment.[5]

5. James M. Buchanan, *Better Than Plowing and Other Personal Essays* (Chicago: University of Chicago Press, 1992), p. 99.

Chapter Summary

POLITICIANS AND THE MIDDLE: THE MEDIAN VOTER MODEL

- In a two-person race, candidates for the same office will gravitate toward the middle of the political spectrum to pick up votes. If a candidate does not do this and her opponent does, the opponent will win the election.

- Candidates do a number of things during campaigns that indicate they understand where they are headed—toward the middle. For example, candidates attempt to label their opponents as either too far right or too far left.

- Candidates usually pick labels for themselves that represent the middle of the political spectrum, they speak in general terms, and they take polls and adjust their positions accordingly.

VOTING AND RATIONAL IGNORANCE

- Voting has both costs and benefits. Many potential voters will not vote because the costs of voting—in terms of time spent going to the polls and so on—outweigh the benefits of voting, measured as the probability of their single vote affecting the election outcome.

- There is a difference between being unable to learn certain information and choosing not to learn it. Most voters choose not to be informed about political and government issues because the costs of becoming informed outweigh the benefits of becoming informed. They choose to be rationally ignorant.

MORE ABOUT VOTING

- In a simple majority vote, where there are several options to choose from, the voting outcome is the same as the most preferred outcome of the median voter.

- Simple majority voting and equal tax shares can generate a different result than simple majority voting and unequal tax shares.

SPECIAL INTEREST GROUPS

- Special interest groups are usually well informed about their issues. Individuals have a greater incentive to become informed about issues that directly and intensely affect them.

- Legislation that concentrates the benefits on a few and disperses the costs over many is likely to pass because the beneficiaries will have an incentive to lobby for it, whereas those who pay the bill will not lobby against it because each of them pays such a small part of the bill.

- Special interest groups often engage in rent seeking, which is the expenditure of scarce resources to capture a pure transfer. Rent seeking is a socially wasteful activity because the resources used to effect transfers are not used to produce goods and services.

BUREAUCRACY

- Public choice economists do not believe government bureaucrats are bad people set on taking advantage of the general public. They believe bureaucrats are ordinary people (just like our friends and neighbors) who behave in predictable ways in a government bureau that is funded by the legislature, does not maximize profits, has no analog to private sector stockholders, has little (if any) competition, and depends on the continuance of certain legislation for its existence.

Key Terms and Concepts

Public Choice
Median Voter Model

Rational Ignorance
Special Interest Groups

Logrolling

Government Bureaucrat

Questions and Problems

1 Some observers maintain that not all politicians move toward the middle of the political spectrum to obtain votes. They often cite Barry Goldwater in the 1964 presidential election and George McGovern in the 1972 presidential election as examples. Goldwater was viewed as occupying the right end of the political spectrum and McGovern the left end. Would this necessarily be evidence that does not support the median voter model? Are the exceptions to the theory explained in this chapter?

2 James Buchanan said that, "If men should cease and desist from their talk about and their search for evil men and commence to look instead at the institutions manned by ordinary people, wide avenues for genuine social reform might appear." What did he mean?

3 Would voters have a greater incentive to vote in an election in which there were only a few registered voters or in one in which there were many? Why? Why might a Republican label her opponent too far left and a Democrat label his opponent too far right?

4 Many individuals learn more about the car they are thinking of buying than about the candidates running for president of the United States. Explain why.

5 If the model of politics and government presented in this chapter is true, what are some of the things we would expect to see?

6 It has often been remarked that Democratic candidates are more liberal in Democratic primaries and Republican candidates are more conservative in Republican primaries than either is in the general election, respectively. Explain why.

7 What are some ways of reducing the cost of voting to voters?

8 Provide a numerical example that shows simple majority voting may be consistent with efficiency. Next, provide a numerical example that shows simple majority voting may be inconsistent with efficiency.

9 John chooses not to vote in the presidential election. Does it follow that he is apathetic when it comes to presidential politics? Explain your answer.

10 What are some ways of making government bureaucrats and bureaus more cost conscious?

11 Some individuals see national defense spending as benefiting special interests—in particular, the defense industry. Others see it as directly benefiting not only the defense industry but the general public as well. Does this same difference in view exist for issues other than national defense? Name a few.

12 Evaluate each of the following proposals for reform in terms of the material discussed in this chapter:

a. Linking all spending programs to visible tax hikes.

b. A balanced budget amendment stipulating that Congress cannot spend more than total tax revenues.

c. A budgetary referenda process whereby the voters actually vote on the distribution of federal dollars to the different categories of spending (X percentage to agriculture, Y percentage to national defense, etc.) instead of letting elected representatives decide.

13 Rent seeking may be rational from the individual's perspective, but it is not rational from society's perspective. Do you agree or disagree? Explain your answer.

Working with Numbers and Graphs

1 Suppose that three major candidates, A, B, and C, are running for president of the United States and that the distribution of voters is the same as shown in Exhibit 1. Two of the candidates, A and B, are currently viewed as right of the median, and C is viewed as left of the median. Is it possible to predict which candidate is the most likely to win?

2 Look back at Exhibit 2. Suppose that the net benefits and net costs for each person are known a week before election day and that it is legal to buy and sell votes. Furthermore,

suppose there is no conscience cost to either buying or selling votes. Would the outcome of the election be the same? Explain your answer.

3 In part (a) of the following figure, the distribution of voters is skewed to the left; in part (b), the distribution of voters is skewed neither left nor right; and in part (c), the distribution of voters is skewed right. Assuming a two-person race for each distribution, will the candidate who wins the election in (a) hold different positions from the candidates who win the elections in (b) and (c)? Explain your answer.

(a)

(b)

(c)

CHAPTER 18

INTERNATIONAL TRADE

Introduction Economics is about trade, and trade crosses boundaries. People trade not only with people who live in their city, state, or country, but also with people in other countries. Many of the goods you consume are undoubtedly produced in other countries. This chapter examines international trade and the prohibitions sometimes placed on it.

INTERNATIONAL TRADE THEORY

International trade takes place for the same reasons that trade at any level exists. Individuals trade to make themselves better off. Pat and Zach, both of whom live in Cincinnati, Ohio, trade because they both value something the other has more than they value some of their own possessions. On an international scale, Elaine in the United States trades with Cho in China because Cho has something that Elaine wants and Elaine has something that Cho wants.

Obviously, the countries of the world have different terrains, climates, resources, worker skills, and so on. Therefore, some countries will be able to produce goods that other countries cannot produce or can produce only at extremely high costs. For example, Hong Kong has no oil, and Saudi Arabia has a large supply of it. Bananas do not grow easily in the United States, but they flourish in Honduras. Americans could grow bananas if they used hothouses, but it is cheaper for Americans to buy bananas from Hondurans than to produce bananas themselves.

Major U.S. exports include automobiles, computers, aircraft, corn, wheat, soybeans, scientific instruments, coal, and plastic materials. Major imports include petroleum, automobiles, clothing, iron and steel, office machines, footwear, fish, coffee, and diamonds. Some of the countries of the world that are major exporters are the United States, Germany, Japan, France, and the United Kingdom. These same countries are also some of the major importers in the world.

How Countries Know What to Trade

Recall the concept of *comparative advantage,* an economic concept first discussed in Chapter 2. In this section, we discuss comparative advantage in terms of countries rather than in terms of individuals.

COMPARATIVE ADVANTAGE Assume a two-country–two-good world. The countries are the United States and Japan, and the goods are food and clothing. Both countries can produce the two goods in the four different combinations listed in Exhibit 1. For example, the United States can produce 90 units of food and 0 units of clothing, 60 units of food and 10 units of clothing, or other combinations. Japan can produce 15 units of food and 0 units of clothing, 10 units of food and 5 units of clothing, or other combinations.

Suppose the United States is producing and consuming the two goods in the combination represented by point B on its production possibilities frontier, and Japan is producing and consuming the combination of the two goods represented by point F on its production possibilities frontier. In this case, neither of the two countries is specializing in the production of one of the two goods, nor are the two countries trading with each other. We call this the *no specialization–no trade (NS-NT) case* (see column 1 in Exhibit 2).

Now suppose the United States and Japan decide to specialize in the production of a specific good and to trade with each other, in what is called the *specialization-trade (S-T) case.* Whether the two countries will be better off through specialization and trade is best explained by means of a numerical example, but first we need to find the answers to two other questions: What good should the United States specialize in producing? What good should Japan specialize in producing? The general answer to both questions is the same:

exhibit 1

Production Possibilities in Two Countries

The United States and Japan can produce the two goods in the combinations shown. Initially, the United States is at point B on its PPF and Japan is at point F on its PPF. Both countries can be made better off by specializing in and trading the good in which each has a comparative advantage.

United States			Japan		
Points on Production Possibilities Frontier	Food	Clothing	Points on Production Possibilities Frontier	Food	Clothing
A	90	0	E	15	0
B	60	10	F	10	5
C	30	20	G	5	10
D	0	30	H	0	15

Both Countries Gain from Specialization and Trade

Column 1: Both the United States and Japan operate independently of each other. The United States produces and consumes 60 units of food and 10 units of clothing. Japan produces and consumes 10 units of food and 5 units of clothing. Column 2: The United States specializes in the production of food; Japan specializes in the production of clothing. Column 3: The United States and Japan agree to the terms of trade of 2 units of food for 1 unit of clothing. They actually trade 20 units of food for 10 units of clothing. Column 4: Overall, the [...] consumes 70 units of food and 1[...] of clothing. Japan consumes 20 units of food and 5 units of clothing. Column 5: Consumption levels are higher for both the United States and Japan in the S-T case than in the NS-NT case.

	No Specialization-No Trade (NS-NT) Case	Specialization-Trade (S-T) Case			
Country	**(1)** Production and Consumption in the NS-NT Case	**(2)** Production in the S-T Case	**(3)** Exports (−) Imports (+) Terms of Trade Are 2F = 1C	**(4)** Consumption in the S-T Case (2) + (3)	**(5)** Gains from Specialization and Trade (4) − (1)
United States					
Food	60 ⎫ Point B in	90 ⎫ Point A in	−20	70	10
Clothing	10 ⎭ Exhibit 1	0 ⎭ Exhibit 1	+10	10	0
Japan					
Food	10 ⎫ Point F in	0 ⎫ Point H in	+20	20	10
Clothing	5 ⎭ Exhibit 1	15 ⎭ Exhibit 1	−10	5	0

Countries specialize in the production of the good in which they have a comparative advantage. A country has a **comparative advantage** in the production of a good when it can produce the good at lower opportunity cost than another country can.

Comparative Advantage
The situation when a country can produce a good at lower opportunity cost than another country can.

For example, in the United States, the opportunity cost of producing 1 unit of clothing (C) is 3 units of food (F); for every 10 units of clothing it produces, it forfeits 30 units of food. So the opportunity cost of producing 1 unit of food is 1/3 unit of clothing. In Japan, the opportunity cost of producing 1 unit of clothing is 1 unit of food (for every 5 units of clothing it produces, it forfeits 5 units of food). To recap, in the United States, the situation is 1 C = 3 F, or 1 F = 1/3 C; in Japan the situation is 1 C = 1 F, or 1 F = 1 C. The United States can produce food at a lower opportunity cost (1/3 C, as opposed to 1 C in Japan), whereas Japan can produce clothing at a lower opportunity cost (1 F, as opposed to 3 F in the United States). Thus, the United States has a comparative advantage in food, and Japan has a comparative advantage in clothing.

Suppose the two countries specialize in the production of the goods in which they have a comparative advantage. That is, the United States specializes in the production of food (producing 90 units), and Japan specializes in the production of clothing (producing 15 units). In Exhibit 1, the United States locates at point A on its PPF, and Japan locates at point H on its PPF (see column 2 in Exhibit 2).

SETTLING ON THE TERMS OF TRADE After they have determined the goods to specialize in producing, the two countries must settle on the terms of trade—that is, how much food to trade for how much clothing. The United States faces the following situation: For every 30 units of food it does not produce, it can produce 10 units of clothing, as shown in Exhibit 1. Thus, 3 units of food have an opportunity cost of 1 unit of clothing (3 F = 1 C), or 1 unit of food has a cost of 1/3 unit of clothing (1 F = 1/3 C). Japan faces the following situation: For every 5 units of food it does not produce, it can produce 5 units of clothing. Thus, 1 unit of food has an opportunity cost of 1 unit of clothing (1 F = 1 C). For the United States, 3 F = 1 C, and for Japan, 1 F = 1 C.

With these cost ratios, both countries should be able to agree on terms of trade that specify 2 F = 1 C. The United States would benefit by giving up 2 units of food instead of 3 units for 1 unit of clothing, whereas Japan would benefit by getting 2 units of food instead of only 1 unit for 1 unit of clothing. Suppose the two countries agree to the terms of trade of 2 F = 1 C and trade, in absolute amounts, 20 units of food for 10 units of clothing (see column 3 in Exhibit 2). Will they make themselves better off? We'll soon see that they do.

RESULTS OF THE SPECIALIZATION-TRADE (S-T) CASE Now the United States produces 90 units of food and trades 20 units to Japan, receiving 10 units of clothing in exchange. It consumes 70 units of food and 10 units of clothing. Japan produces 15 units of clothing and trades 10 to the United States, receiving 20 units of food in exchange. It consumes 5 units of clothing and 20 units of food (see column 4 in Exhibit 2).

Comparing the consumption levels in both countries in the two cases, the United States and Japan each consume 10 more units of food and no less clothing in the specialization-trade case than in the no specialization–no trade case (column 5 in Exhibit 2). We conclude that a country gains by specializing in producing and trading the good in which it has a comparative advantage.

 Common MISCONCEPTIONS

About How Much We Can Consume

No country can consume beyond its PPF if it doesn't specialize and trade with other countries. But, as we have just seen, it can do so when there is specialization and trade. Look at the PPF for the United States in Exhibit 1. In the NS-NT case, the United States consumes 60 units of food and 10 units of clothing; that is, the United States consumes at point B on its PPF. In the S-T case, however, it consumes 70 units of food and 10 units of clothing. A point that represents this combination of the two goods is beyond the country's PPF.

How Countries Know when They Have a Comparative Advantage

Government officials of a country do not analyze pages of cost data to determine what their country should specialize in producing and then trade. Bureaucrats do not plot production possibilities frontiers on graph paper or calculate opportunity costs. Instead, the individual's desire to earn a dollar, a peso, or a euro determines the pattern of international trade. The desire to earn a profit determines what a country specializes in and trades.

To illustrate, Henri, an enterprising Frenchman, visits the United States and observes that beef is relatively cheap (compared with the price in France) and that perfume is relatively expensive. Noticing the price differences for beef and perfume between his country and the United States, he decides to buy some perfume in France, bring it to the United States, and sell it for the relatively higher U.S. price. With his profits from the perfume transaction, he buys beef in the United States, ships it to France, and sells it for the relatively higher French price. Obviously, Henri is buying low and selling high. He buys a good in the country where it is cheap and sells it in the country where it is expensive.

Henri's activities have a couple of consequences. First, he is earning a profit. The larger the price differences are between the two countries and the more he shuffles goods between countries, the more profit Henri earns.

Second, Henri's activities are moving each country toward its comparative advantage. The United States ends up exporting beef to France, and France ends up

DIVIDING THE WORK

John and Veronica, husband and wife, have divided their household tasks: John usually does all the lawn work, fixes the cars, and does the dinner dishes, and Veronica cleans the house, cooks the meals, and does the laundry. Some sociologists might suggest that John and Veronica divided the household tasks along gender lines: Men have for years done the lawn work, fixed the cars, and so on, and women have for years cleaned the house, cooked the meals, and so on. In other words, John is doing man's work, and Veronica is doing woman's work.

© COMSTOCK IMAGES/JUPITER IMAGES

Maybe they have followed gender lines, but the question remains why certain tasks became man's work and others became woman's work. Moreover, their arrangement doesn't explain why John and Veronica don't split every task evenly. In other words, why doesn't John clean half the house and Veronica clean half the house? Why doesn't Veronica mow the lawn on the second and fourth week of every month and John mow the lawn every first and third week of the month?

The law of comparative advantage may be the answer to all these questions. Consider two tasks: cleaning the house and mowing the lawn. The following table shows how long John and Veronica take to complete the two tasks individually.

	Time to Clean the House	Time to Mow the Lawn
John	120 minutes	50 minutes
Veronica	60 minutes	100 minutes

Here is the opportunity cost of each task for each person.

	Opportunity Cost of Cleaning the House	Opportunity Cost of Mowing the Lawn
John	2.40 mowed lawns	0.42 clean houses
Veronica	0.60 mowed lawns	1.67 clean houses

In other words, John has a comparative advantage in mowing the lawn, and Veronica has a comparative advantage in cleaning the house.

Now let's compare two settings. In setting 1, John and Veronica each do half of each task. In setting 2, John only mows the lawn and Veronica only cleans the house.

In setting 1, John spends 60 minutes cleaning half of the house and 25 minutes mowing half of the lawn, for a total of 85 minutes; Veronica spends 30 minutes cleaning half of the house and 50 minutes mowing half of the lawn, for a total of 80 minutes. The total time spent by Veronica and John cleaning the house and mowing the lawn is 165 minutes.

In setting 2, John spends 50 minutes mowing the lawn, and Veronica spends 60 minutes cleaning the house. The total time spent by Veronica and John cleaning the house and mowing the lawn is 110 minutes.

In which setting are Veronica and John better off? John works 85 minutes in setting 1 and 50 minutes in setting 2; so he is better off in setting 2. Veronica works 80 minutes in setting 1 and 60 minutes in setting 2; so Veronica is also better off in setting 2. Together, John and Veronica spend 55 fewer minutes in setting 2 than in setting 1. Getting the job done in 55 fewer minutes is the benefit of specializing in various duties around the house. Given our numbers, we would expect that John will mow the lawn (and do nothing else) and Veronica will clean the house (and do nothing else).

exporting perfume to the United States. Just as the pure theory predicts, individuals in the two countries specialize in and trade the good in which they have a comparative advantage. The outcome is brought about spontaneously through the actions of individuals trying to make themselves better off; they are simply trying to gain through trade.

Thinking like An Economist

The Benefits of Searching for Profit

I s the desire to earn profit useful to society at large? Henri's desire for profit ended up moving both the United States and France toward specializing in and trading the good in which they had a comparative advantage. As we showed earlier in the chapter, when countries specialize and trade, they are better off than when they do neither.

SELF-TEST

(Answers to Self-Test questions are in the Self-Test Appendix.)

1. Suppose the United States can produce 120 units of X at an opportunity cost of 20 units of Y, and Great Britain can produce 40 units of X at an opportunity cost of 80 units of Y. Identify favorable terms of trade for the two countries.

2. If a country can produce more of all goods than any other country, would it benefit from specializing and trading? Explain your answer.

3. Do government officials analyze data to determine what their country can produce at a comparative advantage?

TRADE RESTRICTIONS

International trade theory shows that countries gain from free international trade, that is, from specializing in the production of the goods in which they have a comparative advantage and trading those goods for other goods. In the real world, however, the numerous types of trade restrictions give rise to the question: If countries gain from international trade, why are there trade restrictions? The answer requires an analysis of costs and benefits; specifically, we need to determine who benefits and who loses when trade is restricted. But first, we need to explain some pertinent background information.

The Distributional Effects of International Trade

The previous section explained that specialization and international trade benefit individuals in different countries, but this benefit occurs on net. Not every individual person may gain.

To illustrate, Pam Dickson lives and works in the United States making clock radios. She produces and sells 12,000 clock radios per year at a price of $40 each. As the situation stands, there is no international trade. Individuals in other countries who make clock radios do not sell them in the United States.

Then one day, the U.S. market is opened to clock radios from China. Chinese manufacturers seem to have a comparative advantage in the production of clock radios because they sell their clock radios in the United States for $25 each. Pam realizes that she cannot compete at this price. Her sales drop to such a degree that she goes out of business. Thus, the introduction of international trade in this instance has harmed Pam personally.

Consumers' and Producers' Surpluses

The preceding example raises the issue of the distributional effects of free trade. The benefits of international trade are not equally distributed to all individuals in the

economics 24/7

YOU'RE GETTING BETTER BECAUSE OTHERS ARE GETTING BETTER

Smith can produce X in 30 minutes, and Y in 60 minutes. Jones can produce X in 2 hours and Y in 3 hours. Initially:

- Smith can produce X in 30 minutes and Y in 60 minutes.
- Jones can produce X in 2 hours and Y in 3 hours.

Smith is better at producing X and Y than Jones. Suppose that Smith gets even better at producing X. He can produce X in 15 minutes as opposed to 30 minutes.

- Smith can produce X in 15 minutes and Y in 60 minutes.
- Jones can produce X in 2 hours and Y in 3 hours.

Will Smith's getting better at producing X cause Jones to get better at producing Y? The quick and obvious answer is no. Smith's ability to produce X in 15 minutes instead of 30 minutes doesn't change the time it takes Jones to produce X and Y. It still takes Jones 2 hours to produce X and 3 hours to produce Y.

But look at things in terms of opportunity cost. Initially the opportunity cost for Smith of producing 1 X is ½ Y and the opportunity cost of producing 1 Y is 2 X. For Jones, the opportunity cost of producing 1 X is ²/₃ Y and the opportunity cost of producing 1 Y is 1½ X. Given these opportunity costs, Smith has a comparative advantage in producing X, and Jones has a comparative advantage in producing Y.

When Smith gets better at doing X, his opportunity cost of producing 1 X now *falls* to ¼ Y and his opportunity cost of doing 1 Y *rises* to 4 Y. In other words, Smith's becoming better at producing X makes him relatively worse at producing Y.

As for Jones, because Smith has become relatively better at producing X, Jones has becoming relatively better at producing Y. We reach this conclusion by comparing Jones's opportunity cost of producing Y *before* and *after* Smith gets better at producing X. Before Smith gets better at producing X, Jones gives up 1½ X to get 1 Y whereas Smith has to give up 2 X to get 1 Y.

- Jones gives up 1½ X to get 1 Y.
- Smith gives up 2 X to get 1 Y.

We might say that Jones has only a *slight* comparative advantage over Smith when it comes to producing Y. But after Smith gets better at producing X, Jones gives up 1½ X to get 1 Y, whereas Smith gives up 4 X to get 1 Y.

- Jones gives up 1½ X to get 1 Y.
- Smith gives up 4 X to get 1 Y.

Jones now has a *substantial* comparative advantage over Smith when it comes to producing Y.

Suppose X is being a lawyer and Y is being a farmer. When Smith becomes better as a lawyer, Jones automatically becomes a better farmer (or a relatively lower low-cost farmer). If we change things and say that X is being an accountant and Y is driving a truck, then as Smith becomes a better accountant, Jones automatically becomes a better trucker.

Looking at things in terms of opportunity cost provides us with an insight into our world. Namely, as some people become better at what they do, they naturally make other people better at what they do. Become a better mathematician, singer, or teacher, and you naturally make others better (a lower low-cost producer) at what they do.

---

population. Therefore relevant to our discussion are the topics of consumers' and producers' surpluses, which were first discussed in Chapter 3.

Consumers' surplus is the difference between the maximum price a buyer is willing and able to pay for a good or service and the price actually paid.

Consumers' surplus = Maximum buying price − Price paid

Consumers' surplus is a dollar measure of the benefit gained by being able to purchase a unit of a good for less than one is willing to pay for it. For example, if Yakov would have paid $10 to see the movie at the Cinemax but paid only $4, his consumer surplus is $6. Consumers' surplus is the consumers' net gain from trade.

Producers' surplus (or sellers' surplus) is the difference between the price sellers receive for a good and the minimum or lowest price for which they would have sold the good.

Producers' surplus = Price received − Minimum selling price

Producers' surplus is a dollar measure of the benefit gained by being able to sell a unit of output for more than one is willing to sell it. For example, if Joan sold her knit sweaters for $24 each but would have sold them for as low as (but no lower than) $14 each, her producer surplus is $10 per sweater. Producers' surplus is the producers' net gain from trade.

Both consumers' and producers' surplus are represented in Exhibit 3. In part (a), the shaded triangle represents consumers' surplus. This triangle includes the area under the demand curve and above the equilibrium price. In part (b), the shaded triangle represents producers' surplus. This triangle includes the area above the supply curve and under the equilibrium price.

Finding ECONOMICS

While Negotiating the Price of a House

Robin is negotiating the price of the house she wants to buy from Yakov. Her last offer for the house was $478,000 and he countered with $485,000. She is thinking about offering $481,000. Where is the economics?

Obviously, in this negotiation each person is trying to increase his or her surplus at the expense of the other. Specifically, the lower the price Robin pays, the higher her consumers' surplus will be and the lower Yakov's producers' surplus. Alternatively, the higher the price Yakov receives, the higher his producers' surplus will be and the lower Robin's consumers' surplus.

exhibit 3

Consumers' and Producers' Surplus

(a) Consumers' surplus. As the shaded area indicates, the difference between the maximum or highest amount consumers would be willing to pay and the price they actually pay is consumers' surplus. (b) Producers' surplus. As the shaded area indicates, the difference between the price sellers receive for the good and the minimum or lowest price they would be willing to sell the good for is producers' surplus.

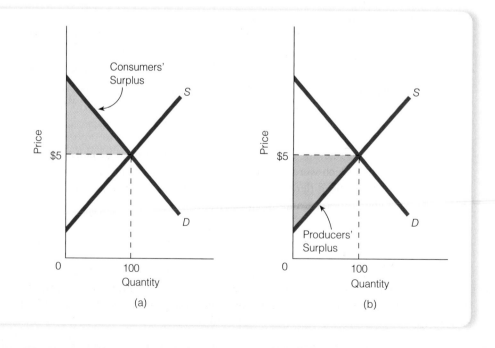

exhibit 4

The Effects of a Tariff

A tariff raises the price of cars from P_W to $P_W + T$, decreases consumers' surplus, increases producers' surplus, and generates tariff revenue. Because consumers lose more than producers and government gain, there is a net loss due to the tariff.

	Consumers' Surplus	Producers' Surplus	Government Tariff Revenue
Free trade (No tariff)	1 + 2 + 3 + 4 + 5 + 6	7	None
Tariff	1 + 2	3 + 7	5
Loss or Gain	− (3 + 4 + 5 + 6)	+3	+5

Result of Tariff = Loss to consumers + Gain to producers + Tariff revenue
$$= -(3 + 4 + 5 + 6) \quad\quad +3 \quad\quad\quad +5$$
$$= -(4 + 6)$$

(a) World Market

(b) Domestic (U.S.) Market

The Benefits and Costs of Trade Restrictions

Of the numerous ways to restrict international trade, tariffs and quotas are two of the more common. We discuss these two methods using the tools of supply and demand concentrating on two groups: U.S. consumers and U.S. producers.

TARIFFS A **tariff** is a tax on imports. The primary effect of a tariff is to raise the price of the imported good for the domestic consumer. Exhibit 4 illustrates the effects of a tariff on cars imported into the United States. The world price for cars is P_W, as shown in Exhibit 4(a). At this price in the domestic U.S. market, U.S. consumers buy Q_2 cars, as shown in part (b). They buy Q_1 from U.S. producers and the difference between Q_2 and Q_1 $(Q_2 - Q_1)$ from foreign producers. In other words, U.S. imports at P_W are $Q_2 - Q_1$.

In this situation, consumers' surplus is the area under the demand curve and above the world price, P_W. This is the sum of the areas 1, 2, 3, 4, 5, and 6 [see Exhibit 4(b)]. Producers' surplus is the area above the supply curve and below the world price, P_W. This is area 7.

Tariff
A tax on imports.

Now suppose a tariff is imposed. The price for imported cars in the U.S. market rises to $P_W + T$ (the world price plus the tariff). At this price, U.S. consumers buy Q_4 cars: Q_3 from U.S. producers and $Q_4 - Q_3$ from foreign producers. U.S. imports are $Q_4 - Q_3$, which is a smaller number of imports than at the pretariff price. An effect of tariffs, then, is to reduce imports. After the tariff has been imposed, at price $P_W + T$, consumers' surplus consists of areas 1 and 2, and producers' surplus consists of areas 3 and 7.

Thus consumers receive more consumers' surplus when tariffs do not exist and less when they do exist. In our example, consumers received areas 1 through 6 in consumers' surplus when the tariff did not exist but only areas 1 and 2 when the tariff did exist. Because of the tariff, consumers' surplus was reduced by an amount equal to areas 3, 4, 5, and 6.

Producers, though, receive less producers' surplus when tariffs do not exist and more when they do exist. In our example, producers received producers' surplus equal to area 7 when the tariff did not exist, but they received producers' surplus equal to areas 3 and 7 with the tariff. Because of the tariff, producers' surplus increased by an amount equal to area 3.

The government collects tariff revenue equal to area 5. This area is obtained by multiplying the number of imports $(Q_4 - Q_3)$ by the tariff, which is the difference between $P_W + T$ and P_W.[1]

In conclusion, the effects of the tariff are a decrease in consumers' surplus, an increase in producers' surplus, and tariff revenue for government. Because the loss to consumers (areas 3, 4, 5, and 6) is greater than the gain to producers (area 3) plus the gain to government (area 5), *a tariff results in a net loss.* The net loss is areas 4 and 6.

Quota

A legal limit on the amount of a good that may be imported.

QUOTAS A **quota** is a legal limit on the amount of a good that may be imported. For example, the government may decide to allow no more than 100,000 foreign cars to be imported, or 10 million barrels of OPEC oil, or 30,000 Japanese television sets. A quota reduces the supply of a good and raises the price of imported goods for domestic consumers (Exhibit 5).

Once again, we consider the situation in the U.S. car market. At a price of P_W (established in the world market for cars), U.S. consumers buy Q_1 cars from U.S. producers and $Q_2 - Q_1$ cars from foreign producers. Consumers' surplus is equal to areas 1, 2, 3, 4, 5, and 6. Producers' surplus is equal to area 7.

Suppose now that the U.S. government sets a quota equal to $Q_4 - Q_3$. Because this is the number of foreign cars U.S. consumers imported when the tariff was imposed (see Exhibit 4), the price of cars rises to P_Q in Exhibit 5 (which is equal to $P_W + T$ in Exhibit 4). At P_Q, consumers' surplus is equal to areas 1 and 2, and producers' surplus consists of areas 3 and 7. The decrease in consumers' surplus due to the quota is equal to areas 3, 4, 5, and 6; the increase in producers' surplus is equal to area 3.

But what about area 5? This area is not transferred to government, as was the case when a tariff was imposed. Rather, it represents the additional revenue earned by the importers (and sellers) of $Q_4 - Q_3$. Before the quota, importers were importing $Q_2 - Q_1$, but only part of this total amount $(Q_4 - Q_3)$ is relevant because this is the amount of imports now that the quota has been established. Before the quota was established, the dollar amount that the importers received for $Q_4 - Q_3$ was $P_W \times (Q_4 - Q_3)$, or area 8. Because of the quota, the price rises to P_Q, and they now receive $P_Q \times (Q_4 - Q_3)$, or areas 5 and 8. The difference between the total revenues on $Q_4 - Q_3$ with a quota and without a quota is area 5.

---

1. For example, if the tariff is $100 and the number of imports is 50,000, then the tariff is $5 million.

exhibit 5

	Consumers' Surplus	Producers' Surplus	Revenue of Importers
Free trade (No quota)	$1 + 2 + 3 + 4 + 5 + 6$	7	8
Quota	$1 + 2$	$3 + 7$	$5 + 8$
Loss or Gain	$- (3 + 4 + 5 + 6)$	$+3$	$+5$

Result of Quota = Loss to consumers + Gain to producers + Gain to importers
$$= - (3 + 4 + 5 + 6) \qquad +3 \qquad\qquad +5$$
$$= - (4 + 6)$$

The Effects of a Quota

A quota that sets the legal limit of imports at $Q_4 - Q_3$ causes the price of cars to increase from P_w to P_Q. A quota raises price, decreases consumers' surplus, increases producers' surplus, and increases the total revenue importers earn. Because consumers lose more than producers and importers gain, there is a net loss due to the quota.

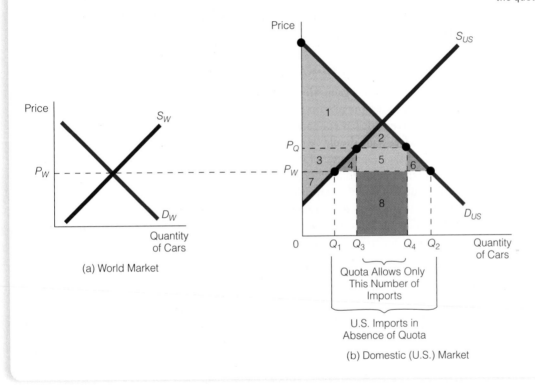

(a) World Market

(b) Domestic (U.S.) Market

In conclusion, the effects of a quota are a decrease in consumers' surplus, an increase in producers' surplus, and an increase in total revenue for the importers who sell the allowed number of imported units. Because the loss to consumers (areas 3, 4, 5, and 6) is greater than the increase in producers' surplus (area 3) plus the gain to importers (area 5), there is a *net loss as a result of the quota*. The net loss is equal to areas 4 and 6.[2]

2. It is perhaps incorrect to imply that government receives nothing from a quota. Although it receives nothing directly, it may gain indirectly. Economists generally argue that because government officials are likely to be the persons who decide which importers will get to satisfy the quota, importers will naturally lobby them. Thus, government officials will likely receive something, if only dinner at an expensive restaurant while the lobbyist makes his or her pitch. In short, in the course of the lobbying, resources will be spent by lobbyists as they curry favor with government officials or politicians who have the power to decide who gets to sell the limited number of imported goods. In economics, lobbyists' activities geared toward obtaining special privileges are referred to as rent seeking.

Finding ECONOMICS

In a Policy Debate

There is a debate tonight at the college Irina attends. There will be four people on either side of the issue: Should the United States practice free trade? Irina attends the debate and comes away thinking that both sides made good points during the debate. The no-free-trade side argued that because other countries do not always practice free trade, neither should the United States. The pro-free-trade side argued that free trade leads to lower prices for U.S. consumers. Where is the economics?

Most of the debate, we believe, will fit into our discussion of Exhibits 4 and 5. These two exhibits show what happens to consumers and producers, and to society as a whole, as the result of both free and prohibited trade. The diagrams show (1) the benefits of prohibited free trade to domestic producers, (2) the costs of prohibited trade to domestic consumers, (3) tariff revenue to government, if it exists, and (4) the overall net costs to prohibited trade.

Why Nations Sometimes Restrict Trade

If free trade results in net gain, why do nations sometimes restrict trade? Based on the analysis in this chapter so far, the case for free trade (no tariffs or quotas) appears to be a strong one. The case for free trade has not gone unchallenged, however. Some persons maintain that at certain times free trade should be restricted or suspended. In almost all cases, they argue that doing so is in the best interest of the public or country as a whole. In a word, they advance a public interest argument. Other persons contend that the public interest argument is only superficial; down deep, they say, it is a special interest argument clothed in pretty words. As you might guess, the debate between the two groups is often heated.

The following sections describe some arguments that have been advanced for trade restrictions.

THE NATIONAL DEFENSE ARGUMENT It is often stated that certain industries—such as aircraft, petroleum, chemicals, and weapons—are necessary to the national defense. Suppose the United States has a comparative advantage in the production of wheat and country X has a comparative advantage in the production of weapons. Many Americans feel that the United States should not specialize in the production of wheat and then trade wheat to country X in exchange for weapons. Leaving weapons production to another country, they maintain, is too dangerous.

The national defense argument may have some validity, but even valid arguments may be abused. Industries that are not really necessary to the national defense may maintain otherwise. In the past, the national defense argument has been used by some firms in the following industries: pens, pottery, peanuts, papers, candles, thumbtacks, tuna fishing, and pencils.

THE INFANT INDUSTRY ARGUMENT Alexander Hamilton, the first U.S. secretary of the treasury, argued that so-called infant, or new, industries often need protection from older, established foreign competitors until they are mature enough to compete on an equal basis. Today, some persons voice the same argument. The infant industry argument is clearly an argument for temporary protection. Critics charge, however, that after an industry is protected from foreign competition, removing the protection is almost impossible; the once infant industry will continue to maintain that it isn't old enough to go it alone. Critics of the infant industry argument say that political realities make it unlikely that a benefit, once bestowed, will be removed.

Finally, the infant industry argument, like the national defense argument, may be abused. All new industries, whether they could currently compete successfully with foreign producers or not, would argue for protection on infant industry grounds.

OFFSHORE OUTSOURCING, OR OFFSHORING

Outsourcing is the term used to describe work done for a company by another company or by people other than the original company's employees. It entails purchasing a product or process from an outside supplier rather than producing it in house. To illustrate, suppose company X has, in the past, hired employees for personnel, accounting, and payroll services. Currently, though, these duties are performed by a company in another state. Company X has outsourced these work activities.

When a company outsources certain work activities to individuals in another country, it is said to be engaged in offshore outsourcing, or offshoring. Consider a few examples. A New York securities firm replaces 800 software engineering employees with a team of software engineers in India. A computer company replaces 200 on-call technicians in its headquarters in Texas with 150 on-call technicians in India.

The benefits of offshoring for a U.S. firm are obvious; it pays lower wages to individuals in other countries for the same work that U.S. employees do for higher wages. Benefits also flow to the employees hired in the foreign countries. The costs of offshoring are said to fall on persons who lose their jobs as a result, such as the software engineer in New York or the on-call computer technician in Texas. Some have argued that offshoring will soon become a major political issue and that it could bring with it a wave of protectionism.

©AFP/GETTY IMAGES

There will undoubtedly be both proponents of and opponents to offshoring. On net, however, are there more benefits than costs or more costs than benefits? Consider a U.S. company that currently employs Jones as a software engineer, paying her x a year. Then, one day, the company tells Jones that it has to let her go; it is replacing her with a software engineer in India who will work for z a year (where z is less than x).

Some have asked why Jones doesn't simply agree to work for z, the same wage as that agreed to by the Indian software engineer? Obviously, Jones can work elsewhere for some wage between x and z. Assume this wage is y. Thus, even though offshoring has moved Jones from earning x to earning y, y is still more than z.

In short, the U.S. company is able to lower its costs from x to z, and Jones's income falls from x to y. The U.S. company lowers its costs more than Jones's income falls because the difference between x and z is greater than the difference between x and y.

If the U.S. company operates within a competitive environment, its lower costs will shift its supply curve to the right and end up lowering prices. In other words, offshoring can end up reducing prices for U.S. consumers. The political fallout from offshoring might, in the end, depend on how visible, to the average American, the employment effects of offshoring are relative to the price reduction effect.

THE ANTIDUMPING ARGUMENT **Dumping** is the sale of goods abroad at a price below their cost and below the price charged in the domestic market. If a French firm sells wine in the United States for a price below the cost of producing the wine and below the price charged in France, it is dumping wine in the United States. Critics of dumping maintain that it is an unfair trade practice that puts domestic producers of substitute goods at a disadvantage.

In addition, critics charge that dumpers seek only to penetrate a market and drive out domestic competitors, only to raise prices. However, some economists point to the infeasibility of this strategy. After the dumpers have driven out their competition and raised prices, their competition is likely to return. For their efforts, the dumpers, in turn, would have incurred only a string of losses (owing to their selling below cost). Opponents of the antidumping argument also point out that domestic consumers benefit from dumping because they pay lower prices.

Dumping
The sale of goods abroad at a price below their cost and below the price charged in the domestic market.

THE FOREIGN EXPORT SUBSIDIES ARGUMENT Some governments subsidize firms that export goods. If a country offers a below-market (interest rate) loan to a company, it is often argued, the government subsidizes the production of the good the firm produces. If, in turn, the firm exports the good to a foreign country, that country's producers of substitute goods call foul. They complain that the foreign firm has been given an unfair advantage that they should be protected against.[3]

Others say that consumers should not turn their backs on a gift (in the form of lower prices). If foreign governments want to subsidize their exports and thus give a gift to foreign consumers at the expense of their own taxpayers, then the recipients should not complain. Of course, the recipients are usually not the ones who are complaining. Usually, the one's complaining are the domestic producers who can't sell their goods at as high a price because of the gift domestic consumers are receiving from foreign governments.

THE LOW FOREIGN WAGES ARGUMENT It is sometimes argued that American producers can't compete with foreign producers because American producers pay high wages to their workers and foreign producers pay low wages to their workers. The American producers insist that international trade must be restricted, or they will be ruined. However, the argument overlooks why American wages are high and foreign wages are low in the first place: productivity. High productivity and high wages are usually linked, as are low productivity and low wages. If an American worker, who receives $20 per hour, can produce (on average) 100 units of X per hour, working with numerous capital goods, then the cost per unit may be lower than when a foreign worker, who receives $2 per hour, produces (on average) 5 units of X per hour, working by hand. In short, a country's high-wage disadvantage may be offset by its productivity advantage, and a country's low-wage advantage may be offset by its productivity disadvantage. High wages do not necessarily mean high costs when productivity and the costs of nonlabor resources are included.

THE SAVING DOMESTIC JOBS ARGUMENT Sometimes, the argument against completely free trade is made in terms of saving domestic jobs. Actually, we have already discussed this argument in its different guises. For example, the low foreign wages argument is one form of it: If domestic producers cannot compete with foreign producers because foreign producers pay low wages and domestic producers pay high wages, domestic producers will go out of business and domestic jobs will be lost. The foreign export subsidies argument is another form of this argument: If foreign government subsidies give a competitive edge to foreign producers, not only will domestic producers fail, but as a result of their failure, domestic jobs will be lost. Critics of the saving domestic jobs argument (in all its guises) often assert that if a domestic producer is being outcompeted by foreign producers and if domestic jobs in an industry are being lost as a result, the world market is signaling that those labor resources could be put to better use in an industry in which the country holds a comparative advantage.

 Thinking like AN ECONOMIST

Economics Versus Politics

International trade often becomes a battleground between economics and politics. The simple tools of supply and demand and consumers' and producers' surpluses show that free trade leads to net gains. On the whole, tariffs and quotas make living standards lower than they would be if free trade were permitted.

(continued)

---

3. Words are important in this debate. For example, domestic producers who claim that foreign governments have subsidized foreign firms say that they are not asking for economic protectionism, but only retaliation, or reciprocity, or simply tit for tat—words that have less negative connotation than those their opponents use.

> *Thinking Like An Economist* (continued)
>
> On the other side, though, are the realities of business and politics. Domestic producers may advocate quotas and tariffs to make themselves better off, giving little thought to the negative effects felt by foreign producers or domestic consumers.
>
> Perhaps the battle over international trade comes down to this: Policies are largely advocated, argued, and lobbied for based more on their distributional effects than on their aggregate or overall effects. On an aggregate level, free trade produces a net gain for society, whereas restricted trade produces a net loss. But economists understand that even if free trade in the aggregate produces a net gain, not every single person will benefit more from free trade than from restricted trade. We have just shown how a subset of the population (producers) gains more, in a particular instance, from restricted trade than from free trade. In short, economists realize that the crucial question in determining real-world policies is more often, "How does it affect me?" than "How does it affect us?"

WORLD TRADE ORGANIZATION (WTO)

The international trade organization, the *World Trade Organization (WTO)*, came into existence on January 1, 1995. It is the successor to the General Agreement on Tariffs and Trade (GATT), which was set up in 1947. Today, 151 countries in the world are members of the WTO.

According to the WTO, its "overriding objective is to help trade flow smoothly, freely, fairly, and predictably." It does this by administering trade agreements, acting as a forum for trade negotiations, settling trade disputes, reviewing national trade policies, assisting developing countries in trade policy issues, and cooperating with other international organizations. Perhaps its most useful and controversial role is adjudicating trade disputes. For example, suppose the United States claims that the Canadian government is preventing U.S. producers from openly selling their goods in Canada. The WTO will look at the matter, consult with trade experts, and then decide the issue. A country that is found engaging in unfair trade can either desist from this practice or face appropriate retaliation from the injured country.

In theory, at least, the WTO is supposed to lead to freer international trade, and there is some evidence that it has done so. The critics of the WTO often say that it has achieved this objective at some cost to a nation's sovereignty. For example, in some past trade disputes between the United States and other countries, the WTO has decided against the United States.

Also, some critics of the WTO often argue that the member countries often put trade issues above environmental issues and do not do enough to help the poor in the world. In the past, some of the critics of the WTO have taken to the streets to demonstrate against it. In a few cases, riots have broken out.

SELF-TEST

1. Who benefits and who loses from tariffs? Explain your answer.

2. Identify the directional change in consumers' surplus and producers' surplus when we move from free trade to tariffs. Is the change in consumers' surplus greater than, less than, or equal to the change in producers' surplus?

3. What is a major difference between the effects of a quota and the effects of a tariff?

4. Outline the details of the infant industry argument for trade restriction.

"SHOULD WE IMPOSE TARIFFS IF THEY IMPOSE TARIFFS?"

Student:

Here is a problem I have with our discussion of free and prohibited trade. Essentially, I am in favor of free international trade, but I think the United States should have free trade with those countries that practice free trade with it. In other words, if country X practices free trade with the United States, then the United States should practice free trade with it. But if country Y places tariffs on U.S. goods entering the country, then the United States ought to place tariffs on country Y's goods entering this country.

Instructor:

Many people feel the same way you do, but this opinion overlooks something that we showed in both Exhibits 4 and 5: the losses of moving from free trade to prohibited trade (where either tariffs or quotas exist) are greater than the gains. Remember? There is a net loss to society.

Student:

I just think it is only fair that other countries get what they give. If they give free trade to us, then we ought to give free trade back to them. If they place tariffs and quotas on our goods, then we ought to do the same to their goods.

Instructor:

You need to keep in mind the price the United States has to pay for this policy of tit for tat.

Student:

What do you mean? What price does the United States have to pay?

Instructor:

It has to incur the net loss illustrated in Exhibits 4 and 5. If you look back at Exhibit 4, for example, you will notice that moving from free trade to prohibited trade does the following: (1) decreases consumers' surplus, (2) increases producers' surplus, and (3) raises tariff revenue. But when we count up all the gains of prohibited trade and compare them with all the losses, we conclude that the losses are greater than the gains. In other words, there is a net loss to prohibited trade.

Student:

But suppose our practicing tit for tat (giving free trade for free trade and prohibited trade for prohibited trade) forces other countries to move away from prohibited trade. In other words, what I am saying is this: We need to look at this issue of free versus prohibited trade over time. Maybe the United States has to practice prohibited trade today (with those countries that impose tariffs on quotas on the United States) in order to force those countries to practice free trade tomorrow. Couldn't it work out that way?

Instructor:

It could work out that way. Or, then, things could escalate toward greater prohibited trade. In other words, country A imposes tariffs and quotas on country B, and then country B raises its tariffs and quotas even higher on country A; so country A retaliates and raises its tariffs and quotas on country B, and so on.

Student:

So what is your point? Is it that free trade is the best policy to practice no matter what other countries do?

Instuctor:

That is what many economists would say, but that is not really the point I am making here. I am simply making two points with respect to the discussion. First, in response to your position that that United States ought to practice tit for tat (give free trade for free trade, tariffs for tariffs, quotas for quotas), I am simply drawing your attention to the net loss Americans incur if they practice prohibited trade—no matter what other countries are doing. In other words, there is a net loss for Americans even if other countries are practicing free trade or prohibited trade. Second, with respect to your second point, about prohibited trade leading to free trade tomorrow, I am saying that we can't be sure that prohibited trade today won't lead to greater prohibitions on trade tomorrow. This is not to say you can't be right: It is possible for prohibited trade today to lead to less prohibited trade tomorrow.

Points to Remember

1. There is a net loss to a country that imposes tariffs or quotas on imported goods. This net loss exists no matter what another country is doing—whether it is practicing free or prohibited trade.

2. We cannot easily predict the outcome of the United States practicing tit for tat in international trade.

a reader asks | Why Does the Government Impose Tariffs and Quotas?

If tariffs and quotas result in higher prices for U.S. consumers, then why does the government impose them?

The answer is that government is sometimes more responsive to producer interests than to consumer interests. But then we have to wonder why. To explain, consider the following example.

Suppose there are 100 U.S. producers of good X and 20 million U.S. consumers of it. The producers want to protect themselves from foreign competition; so they lobby for and receive a quota on foreign goods that compete with good X. As a result, consumers must pay higher prices. For simplicity's sake, let's say that consumers must pay $40 million more. Thus, producers receive $40 million more for good X than they would have if the quota had not been imposed. If the $40 million received is divided equally among the 100 producers, each producer receives $400,000 more as a result of the quota. If the additional $40 million paid is divided equally among the 20 million consumers, each customer pays $2 more as a result of the quota.

A producer is likely to think, "I should lobby for the quota because if I'm effective, I'll receive $400,000." A consumer is likely to think, "Why

should I lobby against the quota? If I'm effective, I'll save only $2. Saving $2 isn't worth the time and trouble my lobbying would take."

In short, the benefits of quotas are concentrated on relatively few producers, and the costs of quotas are spread out over relatively many consumers. Thus, each producer's gain is relatively large compared with each consumer's loss. We predict that producers will lobby government to obtain the relatively large gains from quotas but that consumers will not lobby government to keep from paying the small additional cost due to quotas.

Politicians are in the awkward position of hearing from people who want the quotas but not hearing from people who are against them. It is likely politicians will respond to the vocal interests. Politicians may mistakenly assume that consumers' silence means that they accept the quota policy, when in fact they may not. Consumers may simply not find it worthwhile to do anything to fight the policy.

Chapter Summary

SPECIALIZATION AND TRADE

- A country has a comparative advantage in the production of a good if it can produce the good at a lower opportunity cost than another country can.

- Individuals in countries that specialize and trade have a higher standard of living than would be the case if their countries did not specialize and trade.

- Government officials do not analyze cost data to determine what their country should specialize in and trade. Instead, the desire to earn a dollar, peso, or euro guides individuals' actions and produces the unintended consequence that countries specialize in and trade the good(s) in which they have a comparative advantage. However, trade restrictions can change this outcome.

TARIFFS AND QUOTAS

- A tariff is a tax on imports. A quota is a legal limit on the amount of a good that may be imported.

- Both tariffs and quotas raise the price of imports.

- Tariffs lead to a decrease in consumers' surplus, an increase in producers' surplus, and tariff revenue for the government. Consumers lose more through tariffs than producers and government (together) gain.

- Quotas lead to a decrease in consumers' surplus, an increase in producers' surplus, and additional revenue for the importers who sell the amount specified by the quota. Consumers lose more through quotas than producers and importers (together) gain.

ARGUMENTS FOR TRADE RESTRICTIONS

- The national defense argument states that certain goods—such as aircraft, petroleum, chemicals, and weapons—are necessary to the national defense and should be produced domestically whether the country has a comparative advantage in their production or not.

- The infant industry argument states that infant, or new, industries should be protected from free (foreign) trade so that they have time to develop and compete on an equal basis with older, more established foreign industries.

- The antidumping argument states that domestic producers should not have to compete (on an unequal basis) with foreign producers that sell products below cost and below the prices they charge in their domestic markets.

- The foreign export subsidies argument states that domestic producers should not have to compete (on an unequal basis) with foreign producers that have been subsidized by their governments.

- The low foreign wages argument states that domestic producers cannot compete with foreign producers that pay low wages to their employees when domestic producers pay high wages to their employees. For high-paying domestic firms to survive, limits on free trade are proposed.

- The saving domestic jobs argument states that through low foreign wages or government subsidies (or dumping, etc.), foreign producers will be able to outcompete domestic producers and that therefore domestic jobs will be lost. For domestic firms to survive and domestic jobs not to be lost, limits on free trade are proposed.

- Everyone does not accept the arguments for trade restrictions as valid. Critics often maintain that the arguments can be and are abused and that in most cases they are motivated by self-interest.

Key Terms and Concepts

Comparative Advantage	Tariff	Quota	Dumping

Questions and Problems

1 Although a production possibilities frontier is usually drawn for a country, one could be drawn for the world. Picture the world's production possibilities frontier. Is the world positioned at a point on the PPF or below it? Give a reason for your answer.

2 If country A is better than country B at producing all goods, will country A still be made better off by specializing and trading? Explain your answer. (Hint: Look at Exhibit 1.)

3 The desire for profit can end up pushing countries toward producing goods in which they have a comparative advantage. Do you agree or disagree? Explain your answer.

4 "Whatever can be done by a tariff can be done by a quota." Discuss.

5 Neither free trade nor prohibited trade comes with just benefits. Both come with benefits and costs. Therefore, free trade is neither better nor worse than prohibited trade. Comment.

6 Consider two groups of domestic producers: those that compete with imports and those that export goods. Suppose the domestic producers that compete with imports convince the legislature to impose a high tariff on imports—so high, in fact, that almost all imports are eliminated. Does this policy in any way adversely affect domestic producers that export goods? If so, how?

7 Suppose the U.S. government wants to curtail imports. Would it be likely to favor a tariff or a quota to accomplish its objective? Why?

8 Suppose the landmass known to you as the United States of America had been composed, since the nation's founding, of separate countries instead of separate states. Would you expect the standard of living of the people who inhabit this landmass to be higher, lower, or equal to what it is today? Why?

9 Even though Jeremy is a better gardener and novelist than Bill is, Jeremy still hires Bill as his gardener. Why?

10 Suppose that a constitutional convention is called tomorrow and that you are chosen as one of the delegates from your state. You and the other delegates must decide whether it will be constitutional or unconstitutional for the federal government to impose tariffs and quotas or to restrict international trade in any way. What would be your position?

11 Some economists have argued that because domestic consumers gain more from free trade than domestic producers gain from (import) tariffs and quotas, consumers should buy out domestic producers and rid themselves of costly tariffs and quotas. For example, if consumers save $400 million from free trade (through paying lower prices) and producers gain $100 million from tariffs and quotas, consumers can pay producers something more than $100 million but less than $400 million and get producers to favor free trade too. Assuming this scheme were feasible, what do you think of it?

12 If there is a net loss to society from tariffs, why do tariffs exist?

Working with Numbers and Graphs

1 Using the data in the table, answer the following questions:

a. For which good does Canada have a comparative advantage?

b. For which good does Italy have a comparative advantage?

c. What might be a set of favorable terms of trade for the two countries?

d. Prove that both countries would be better off in the specialization-trade case than in the no-specialization–no-trade case.

Points on Production Possibilities Frontier	Canada		Italy	
	Good X	Good Y	Good X	Good Y
A	150	0	90	0
B	100	25	60	60
C	50	50	30	120
D	0	75	0	180

2 In the following figure, P_W is the world price and $P_W + T$ is the world price plus a tariff. Identify the following:

a. The level of imports at P_W.

b. The level of imports at $P_W + T$.

c. The loss in consumers' surplus as a result of a tariff.

d. The gain in producers' surplus as a result of a tariff.

e. The tariff revenue as the result of a tariff.

f. The net loss to society as a result of a tariff.

g. The net benefit to society of moving from a tariff situation to a no-tariff situation.

CHAPTER 19

INTERNATIONAL FINANCE

© PETER MENZEL/PHOTO RESEARCHERS

Introduction When people travel to a foreign country, they buy goods and services in the country, whose prices are quoted in yen, pounds, euros, pesos, or some other currency. For example, a U.S. tourist in Mexico might want to buy a good priced in pesos and to know what the good costs in dollars and cents. The answer depends on the current exchange rate between the dollar and the peso, but what determines the exchange rate? This is just one of the many questions answered in this chapter.

THE BALANCE OF PAYMENTS

Countries keep track of their domestic level of production by calculating their gross domestic product (GDP). Similarly, they keep track of the flow of their international trade (receipts and expenditures) by calculating their balance of payments. The **balance of payments** is a periodic (usually annual) statement of the money value of all transactions between residents of one country and residents of all other countries. The balance of payments provides information about a nation's imports and exports, domestic residents' earnings on assets located abroad, foreign earnings on domestic assets, gifts to and from foreign countries (including foreign aid), exchange of assets, and official transactions by governments and central banks.

Balance of payments accounts record both debits and credits. A debit is indicated by a minus (−) sign, and a credit is indicated by a plus (+) sign. *Any transaction that supplies the country's currency in the foreign exchange market is recorded as a* **debit**. (The **foreign exchange market** is the market in which currencies of different countries are exchanged.) For example, a U.S. retailer wants to buy Japanese television sets so that he can sell them in his stores in the United States. To buy the TV sets from the Japanese, the retailer first has to supply U.S. dollars (in the foreign exchange market) in return for Japanese yen. Then he will turn over the yen to the Japanese in exchange for the television sets.

Balance of Payments
A periodic (usually annual) statement of the money value of all transactions between residents of one country and the residents of all other countries.

Debit
In the balance of payments, any transaction that supplies the country's currency in the foreign exchange market.

Foreign Exchange Market
The market in which currencies of different countries are exchanged.

exhibit 1

Debits and Credits

Item	Definition	Example
Debit (−)	Any transaction that supplies the country's currency.	Jim, an American, supplies dollars in exchange for yen so that he can use the yen to buy Japanese goods.
Credit (+)	Any transaction that creates a demand for the country's currency.	Svetlana, who is Russian and living in Russia, supplies rubles in order to demand dollars so that she can use the dollars to buy U.S. goods.

Any transaction that creates a demand for the country's currency in the foreign exchange market is recorded as a **credit**. For example, a Russian retailer wants to buy computers from U.S. computer producers. To pay the U.S. producers, who want U.S. dollars, the Russian retailer must supply rubles (in the foreign exchange market) in return for dollars. Then she will turn over the dollars to the U.S. producers in exchange for the computers. Exhibit 1 presents a summary of debits and credits.

The international transactions that are summarized in the balance of payments can be grouped into three categories, or three accounts—the current account, the capital account, and the official reserve account—and a statistical discrepancy. Exhibit 2 illustrates a U.S. balance of payments account for year Z. The data in the exhibit are hypothetical (to make the calculations simpler) but not unrealistic. In this section, we describe and explain each of the items in the balance of payments using the data in Exhibit 2 for our calculations.

Credit
In the balance of payments, any transaction that creates a demand for the country's currency in the foreign exchange market.

Current Account

The **current account** includes all payments related to the purchase and sale of goods and services. The current account has three major components: exports of goods and services, imports of goods and services, and net unilateral transfers abroad.

Current Account
The account in the balance of payments that includes all payments related to the purchase and sale of goods and services. Components of the account include exports, imports, and net unilateral transfers abroad.

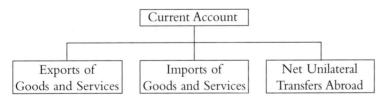

EXPORTS OF GOODS AND SERVICES Americans export goods (e.g., cars), they export services (e.g., insurance, banking, transportation, and tourism), and they receive income on assets they own abroad. All three activities increase the demand for U.S. dollars while increasing the supply of foreign currencies in the foreign exchange market; thus, they are recorded as credits (+). For example, if a foreigner buys a U.S. computer, payment must ultimately be made in U.S. dollars. Thus, she is required to supply her country's currency when she demands U.S. dollars. (We use *foreigner* in this chapter to refer to a resident of a foreign country.)

IMPORTS OF GOODS AND SERVICES Americans import goods and services, and foreigners receive income on assets they own in the United States. These activities increase the demand for foreign currencies while increasing the supply of U.S. dollars to the foreign exchange market; thus, they are recorded as debits (−). For example, if an

exhibit 2

U.S. Balance of Payments, Year Z

The data in this exhibit are hypothetical, but not unrealistic. All numbers are in billions of dollars. The plus and minus signs in the exhibit should be viewed as operational signs.

CURRENT ACCOUNT

1. EXPORTS OF GOODS AND SERVICES   +340
    a. Merchandise exports (including military sales)   +220
    b. Services   +30
    c. Income from U.S. assets abroad   +90
2. IMPORTS OF GOODS AND SERVICES   −390
    a. Merchandise imports (including military purchases) −300
    b. Services   −40
    c. Income from foreign assets in U.S.   −50

Merchandise Trade Balance
Difference between value of merchandise exports (item 1a)
and value of merchandise imports (item 2a): +220 − 300 = −80

3. NET UNILATERAL TRANSFERS ABROAD   −11

Current Account Balance
Items 1, 2, 3: +340 − 390 − 11 = ⟶ −61

CAPITAL ACCOUNT

4. OUTFLOW OF U.S. CAPITAL   −16
5. INFLOW OF FOREIGN CAPITAL   +60

Capital Account Balance
Items 4 and 5: −16 + 60 = ⟶ +44

OFFICIAL RESERVE ACCOUNT

6. INCREASE (−) IN U.S. OFFICIAL RESERVE ASSETS   −4
7. INCREASE (+) IN FOREIGN OFFICIAL ASSETS IN U.S.   +3

Official Reserve Balance
Items 6 and 7: −4 + 3 = ⟶ −1

STATISTICAL DISCREPANCY   +18

TOTAL $0 $0
                                                         (always zero)

BALANCE OF PAYMENTS =

Summary statistic of all ⟨⟩ items (items 1−7 and the statistical discrepancy)

+$340 − $390 − $11 − $16 + $60 − $4 + $3 + $18 = $0

or

Summary statistic of all ☐ items (current account balance, capital account balance, official reserve balance, and the statistical discrepancy)

−$61 + $44 − $1 + $18 = $0

Note: The pluses (+) and the minuses (−) in the exhibit serve two purposes. First, they distinguish between credits and debits. A plus is always placed before a credit, and a minus is always placed before a debit. Second, in terms of the calculations, the pluses and minuses are viewed as operational signs. In other words, if a number has a plus in front of it, it is added to the total. If a number has a minus in front of it, it is subtracted from the total.

American buys a Japanese car, payment must ultimately be made in Japanese yen. Thus, he is required to supply U.S. dollars when he demands Japanese yen.

In Exhibit 2, exports of goods and services total +$340 billion in year Z, and imports of goods and services total −$390 billion.[1] Before discussing the third component of the

---

1. In everyday language, people do not say, "Exports are a positive $X billion and imports are a negative $Y billion." Placing a plus sign (+) in front of exports and a minus sign (−) in front of imports simply reinforces the essential point that exports are credits and imports are debits. This will be useful later when we calculate certain account balances.

current account—net unilateral transfers abroad—we define some important relationships between exports and imports.

Look at the difference between the *value of merchandise exports* (1a in Exhibit 2) and the *value of merchandise imports* (2a in the exhibit). This difference is the merchandise trade balance or the balance of trade. Specifically, the **merchandise trade balance** is the difference between the value of merchandise exports and the value of merchandise imports. In year Z, the merchandise trade balance is $220 billion − $300 billion = −$80 billion.

$$\text{Merchandise trade balance} = \text{Value of merchandise exports}$$
$$- \text{Value of merchandise imports}$$

If the value of a country's merchandise exports is less than the value of its merchandise imports, it is said to have a **merchandise trade deficit**.

$$\text{Merchandise trade deficit} = \text{Value of merchandise exports}$$
$$< \text{Value of merchandise imports}$$

If the value of a country's merchandise exports is greater than the value of its merchandise imports, it is said to have a **merchandise trade surplus**.

$$\text{Merchandise trade surplus} = \text{Value of merchandise exports}$$
$$> \text{Value of merchandise imports}$$

Exhibit 3 shows the U.S. merchandise trade balance from 1995 to 2007. Notice that there has been a merchandise trade deficit in each of these years.

NET UNILATERAL TRANSFERS ABROAD Unilateral transfers are one-way money payments. They can go from Americans or the U.S. government to foreigners or foreign governments. If an American sends money to a relative in a foreign country, if the U.S. government gives money to a foreign country as a gift or grant, or if an American retires in a foreign country and receives a Social Security check there, all these transactions are referred to as unilateral transfers. If an American or the U.S. government makes a unilateral transfer abroad, this gives rise to a demand for foreign currency and a supply of U.S. dollars; thus, it is entered as a debit item in the U.S. balance of payments accounts.

Unilateral transfers can also go from foreigners or foreign governments to Americans or to the U.S. government. If a foreign citizen sends money to a relative living in the United States, this is a unilateral transfer. If a foreigner makes a unilateral transfer to an American, this gives rise to a supply of foreign currency and a demand for U.S. dollars; thus, it is entered as a credit item in the U.S. balance of payments accounts.

Net unilateral transfers abroad include both types of transfers—from the United States to foreign countries and from foreign countries to the United States. The dollar amount of net unilateral transfers is negative if U.S. transfers are greater than foreign transfers. It is positive if foreign transfers are greater than U.S. transfers.

For year Z in Exhibit 2, we have assumed that unilateral transfers made by Americans to foreign citizens are greater than unilateral transfers made by foreign citizens to Americans. Thus, there is a *negative* net dollar amount, −$11 billion.

Items 1, 2, and 3 in Exhibit 2—exports of goods and services, imports of goods and services, and net unilateral transfers abroad—comprise the current account. The **current account balance** is the summary statistic for these three items. In year Z, it is −$61 billion. The news media sometimes call the current account balance the balance of payments. To an economist, this reference is incorrect; the balance of payments includes several more items.

Merchandise Trade Balance
The difference between the value of merchandise exports and the value of merchandise imports.

Merchandise Trade Deficit
The situation when the value of merchandise exports is less than the value of merchandise imports.

Merchandise Trade Surplus
The situation when the value of merchandise exports is greater than the value of merchandise imports.

Current Account Balance
In the balance of payments, the summary statistic for exports of goods and services, imports of goods and services, and net unilateral transfers abroad.

exhibit 3

U.S. Merchandise Trade Balance

In each of the years shown, 1995–2007, a merchandise trade deficit has existed.

Source: U.S. Department of Commerce, Bureau of Economic Analysis.

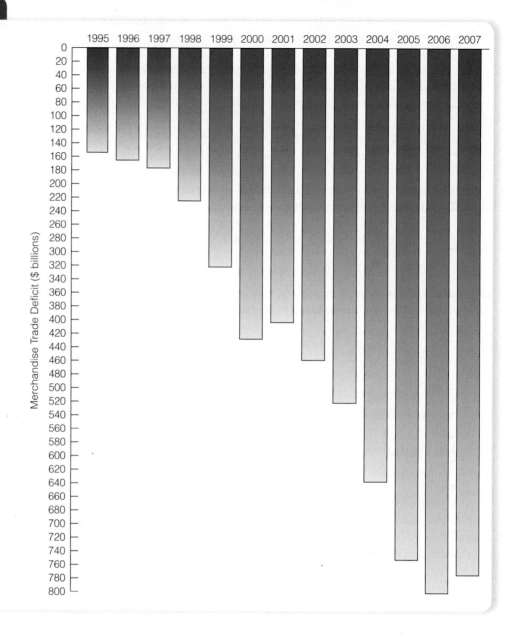

Capital Account

The **capital account** includes all payments related to the purchase and sale of assets and to borrowing and lending activities. Its major components are outflow of U.S. capital and inflow of foreign capital.

Capital Account
The account in the balance of payments that includes all payments related to the purchase and sale of assets and to borrowing and lending activities. Components include outflow of U.S. capital and inflow of foreign capital.

OUTFLOW OF U.S. CAPITAL American purchases of foreign assets and U.S. loans to foreigners are outflows of U.S. capital. As such, they give rise to a demand for foreign currency and a supply of U.S. dollars on the foreign exchange market. Hence, they are considered a debit. For example, if an American wants to buy land in Japan, U.S. dollars must be supplied to purchase (demand) Japanese yen.

INFLOW OF FOREIGN CAPITAL Foreign purchases of U.S. assets and foreign loans to Americans are inflows of foreign capital. As such, they give rise to a demand for U.S. dollars and to a supply of foreign currency on the foreign exchange market. Hence, they are considered a credit. For example, if a Japanese citizen buys a U.S. Treasury bill, Japanese yen must be supplied to purchase (demand) U.S. dollars.

Items 4 and 5 in Exhibit 2—outflow of U.S. capital and inflow of foreign capital—comprise the capital account. The **capital account balance** is the summary statistic for these two items. It is equal to the difference between the outflow of U.S. capital and the inflow of foreign capital. In year Z, it is $44 billion.

Official Reserve Account

A government possesses official reserve balances in the form of foreign currencies, gold, its reserve position in the **International Monetary Fund (IMF)**, and **special drawing rights (SDRs)**. Countries that have a deficit in their combined current and capital accounts can draw on their reserves. For example, if the United States has a deficit in its combined current and capital accounts of $5 billion, it can draw down its official reserves to meet this deficit.

Item 6 in Exhibit 2 shows that the United States increased its reserve assets by $4 billion in year Z. This is a debit item because if the United States acquires official reserves (say, through the purchase of a foreign currency), it has increased the demand for the foreign currency and supplied dollars. Thus, an increase in official reserves is like an outflow of capital in the capital account and appears as a payment with a negative sign. Therefore, an increase in foreign official assets in the United States is a credit item.

Statistical Discrepancy

If someone buys a U.S. dollar with, say, Japanese yen, someone must sell a U.S. dollar. Thus, dollars purchased equal dollars sold.

In all the transactions discussed so far—exporting goods, importing goods, sending money to relatives in foreign countries, buying land in foreign countries—dollars were bought and sold. The total number of dollars sold must always equal the total number of dollars purchased. However, balance of payments accountants do not have complete information; they can record only the credits and debits they observe. There may be more debits or credits than those observed in a given year.

Suppose in year Z, all debits are observed and recorded, but not all credits—perhaps because of smuggling activities, secret bank accounts, people living in more than one country, and so on. To adjust for this lack of information, balance of payments accountants use the *statistical discrepancy,* which is the part of the balance of payments that adjusts for missing information. In Exhibit 2, the statistical discrepancy is +$18 billion. This means that $18 billion worth of credits (+) went unobserved in year Z. There may have been some hidden exports and unrecorded capital inflows that year.

What the Balance of Payments Equals

The balance of payments is the summary statistic for:

- Exports of goods and services (item 1 in Exhibit 2).
- Imports of goods and services (item 2).

Capital Account Balance
The summary statistic for the outflow of U.S. capital equal to the difference between the outflow of U.S. capital and the inflow of foreign capital.

International Monetary Fund (IMF)
An international organization created to oversee the international monetary system. The IMF does not control the world's money supply, but it does hold currency reserves for member nations and make loans to central banks.

Special Drawing Right (SDR)
An international money, created by the IMF, in the form of bookkeeping entries; like gold and currencies, it can be used by nations to settle international accounts.

economics 24/7

MERCHANDISE TRADE DEFICIT, WE THOUGHT WE KNEW THEE

You read in the newspaper that the United States has a merchandise trade deficit; that is, the value of merchandise exports for the United States is *less than* the value of merchandise imports. In terms of Exhibit 2, 1a is less than 2a. For example, Americans exported $600 billion worth of goods and imported $800 billion worth of goods. The merchandise trade deficit is $200 billion.

The word *deficit* has a negative connotation to many people, who think of a trade deficit as something bad. It's bad, some people say, "Because it means Americans owe money to foreigners. Specifically, Americans are 'in debt' to foreigners to the tune of $200 billion."

Other people say that, because Americans are increasing demand for foreign-produced goods by more ($200 billion more, to be exact) than foreigners are increasing demand for U.S.-produced goods, demand is "leaving the country."

However, neither sentiment is correct. Americans do not owe foreigners anything and demand is not leaving the country.

The reason is obvious: Americans have already paid this $200 billion to foreigners. The $200 billion is part of the overall $800 billion that Americans spent on imported goods.

Still, even if Americans don't owe $200 billion to foreigners, isn't the $200 billion gone forever, never to return to the United States? That's not

true either. Foreigners may have those dollars, but they're not going to burn them. They're not going to eat them. They're not going to give them away. What they are going to do with those dollars—in fact, the only thing they can do with those dollars—is use them to buy "something American."[2]

They could buy real estate in the United States. For example, a Brazilian man with dollars might end up buying an apartment in downtown Manhattan. In other words, the dollars that we thought would leave the country for good are coming back home.

A foreign firm with U.S. dollars could hire a construction company to build a factory in the United States—Tennessee, Virginia, or South Dakota—so that it can produce some of its goods in the United States and thus lower its transportation costs. An American might end up working at that factory and thus be paid with some of the dollars that once were held by foreigners. (And the American worker is likely to spend those dollars to buy U.S. goods and services.)

The main point is simple: The dollars that foreigners initially hold because of the merchandise trade deficit will begin to return to the United States. They're not gone forever.

_____
2. If you are thinking that the foreigners who have the $200 billion can trade those dollars for other currencies, you are right. A Frenchman might trade some of his dollars for pesos, euros, or yen, but now someone else has the dollars the Frenchman once had, and we then have to ask what this new person will do with the dollars.

- Net unilateral transfers abroad (item 3).
- Outflow of U.S. capital (item 4).
- Inflow of foreign capital (item 5).
- Increase in U.S. official reserve assets (item 6).
- Increase in foreign official assets in the United States (item 7).
- Statistical discrepancy.

Calculating the balance of payments in year Z using these items, we have (in billions of dollars) $+340 - 390 - 11 - 16 + 60 - 4 + 3 + 18 = 0$.

Alternatively, the balance of payments is the summary statistic for:

- Current account balance.
- Capital account balance.
- Official reserve balance.
- Statistical discrepancy.

Calculating the balance of payments in year Z using these items, we have (in billions of dollars) − 61 + 44 − 1 + 18 = 0. The balance of payments for the United States in year Z equals zero.

Common MISCONCEPTIONS

About the Balance of Payments

There is a tendency to think that the balance of payments can be in deficit or surplus, but it is neither. The balance of payments always equals zero because the three accounts that comprise the balance of payments, taken together, plus the statistical discrepancy, include all of the sources and all of the uses of dollars in international transactions. Also, every dollar used must have a source, adding the sources (+) to the uses (−) necessarily gives us zero.

SELF-TEST

(Answers to Self-Test questions are in the Self-Test Appendix.)

1. If an American retailer buys Japanese cars from a Japanese manufacturer, is this transaction recorded as a debit or a credit? Explain your answer.

2. Exports of goods and services equal $200 billion and imports of goods and services equal $300 billion. What is the merchandise trade balance?

3. What is the difference between the merchandise trade balance and the current account balance?

THE FOREIGN EXCHANGE MARKET

If a U.S. buyer wants to purchase a good from a U.S. seller, the buyer simply gives the required number of U.S. dollars to the seller. If, however, a U.S. buyer wants to purchase a good from a seller in Mexico, the U.S. buyer must first exchange her U.S. dollars for Mexican pesos. Then, with the pesos, she buys the good from the Mexican seller. As explained, currencies of different countries are exchanged in the foreign exchange market. In this market, currencies are bought and sold for a price—the **exchange rate**. For instance, it might take $1.23 to buy a euro, 10 cents to buy a Mexican peso, and 13 cents to buy a Danish krone.

In this section, we explain why currencies are demanded and supplied in the foreign exchange market. Then we discuss how the exchange rate expresses the relationship between the demand for and the supply of currencies.

Exchange Rate
The price of one currency in terms of another currency.

The Demand for Goods

To simplify our analysis, we assume that there are only two countries in the world: the United States and Mexico. Thus there are only two currencies in the world: the U.S. dollar (USD) and the Mexican peso (MXN). We want to answer the following two questions:

1. What creates the demand for and the supply of dollars on the foreign exchange market?

2. What creates the demand for and the supply of pesos on the foreign exchange market?

Suppose an American wants to buy a couch from a Mexican producer. Before he can purchase the couch, the American must buy Mexican pesos; hence, Mexican pesos

exhibit 4

The Demand for Goods and the Supply of Currencies

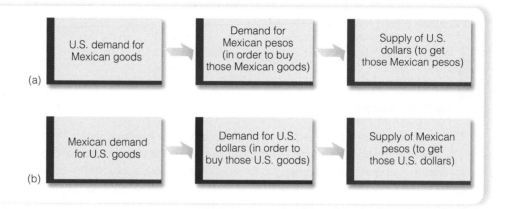

are demanded. The American buys Mexican pesos with U.S. dollars; that is, he supplies U.S. dollars to the foreign exchange market to demand Mexican pesos. We conclude that *the U.S. demand for Mexican goods leads to (1) a demand for Mexican pesos and (2) a supply of U.S. dollars on the foreign exchange market* [see Exhibit 4(a)]. Thus, the demand for pesos and the supply of dollars are linked:

Demand for pesos ↔ Supply of dollars

The result is similar for a Mexican who wants to buy a computer from a U.S. producer. Before she can purchase the computer, the Mexican must buy U.S. dollars; hence, U.S. dollars are demanded. The Mexican buys the U.S. dollars with Mexican pesos. We conclude that *the Mexican demand for U.S. goods leads to (1) a demand for U.S. dollars and (2) a supply of Mexican pesos on the foreign exchange market* [see Exhibit 4(b)]. Thus, the demand for dollars and the supply of pesos are linked:

Demand for dollars ↔ Supply of pesos

 Finding ECONOMICS

In a Trip to Ireland

Billy has just graduated from college and is planning a trip to Ireland. Where is the economics here? Obviously Billy cannot use dollars to buy goods and services in Ireland. He must use euros. He will have to buy euros with his dollars, and, in so doing, he supplies U.S. dollars.

The Demand for and Supply of Currencies

Exhibit 5 shows the markets for pesos and dollars. Part (a) shows the market for Mexican pesos. The quantity of pesos is on the horizontal axis, and the exchange rate—stated in terms of the dollar price per peso—is on the vertical axis. Exhibit 5(b) shows the market for U.S. dollars, which mirrors what is happening in the market for Mexican pesos. Notice that the exchange rates in (a) and (b) are reciprocals of each other. If 0.10 USD = 1 MXN, then 10 MXN = 1 USD.

exhibit 5

Translating U.S. Demand for Pesos into U.S. Supply of Dollars and Mexican Demand for Dollars into Mexican Supply of Pesos

(a) The market for pesos. (b) The market for dollars. The demand for pesos in (a) is linked to the supply of dollars in (b): When Americans demand pesos, they supply dollars. The supply of pesos in (a) is linked to the demand for

dollars in (b): When Mexicans demand dollars, they supply pesos. In (a), the exchange rate is 0.10 USD = 1 MXN, which is equal to 10 MXN = 1 USD in (b). Exchange rates are reciprocals of each other.

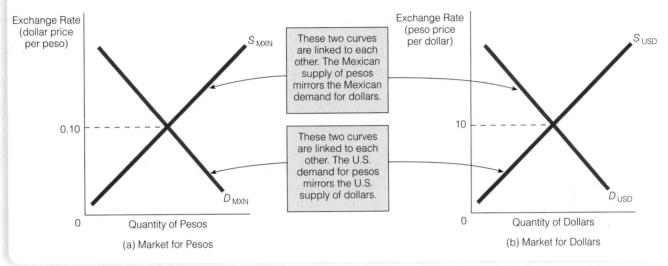

(a) Market for Pesos

(b) Market for Dollars

In Exhibit 5(a), the demand curve for pesos is downward sloping, indicating that, as the dollar price per peso increases, Americans buy fewer pesos and that, as the dollar price per peso decreases, Americans buy more pesos.

Dollar price per peso ↑   Americans buy fewer pesos.

Dollar price per peso ↓   Americans buy more pesos.

For example, if it takes $0.10 to buy a peso, Americans will buy more pesos than they would if it takes $0.20 to buy a peso. (It is analogous to buyers purchasing more soft drinks at $3 a six-pack than at $5 a six-pack.) Simply put, the higher the dollar price per peso, the more expensive Mexican goods are for Americans and the fewer Mexican goods Americans will buy. Thus, a smaller quantity of pesos is demanded.

The supply curve for pesos in Exhibit 5(a) is upward sloping. It is easy to understand why when we recall that the supply of Mexican pesos is linked to the Mexican demand for U.S. goods and U.S. dollars. Consider a price of $0.20 for 1 peso compared with a price of $0.10 for 1 peso. At 0.10 USD = 1 MXN, a Mexican buyer gives up 1 peso and receives 10 cents in return. But at 0.20 USD = 1 MXN, a Mexican buyer gives up 1 peso and receives 20 cents in return. Thus, U.S. goods are cheaper for Mexicans at the exchange rate of 0.20 USD = 1 MXN.

To illustrate, suppose a U.S. computer has a price tag of $1,000. At an exchange rate of 0.20 USD = 1 MXN, a Mexican will have to pay 5,000 pesos to buy the American computer; but at an exchange rate of 0.10 USD = 1 MXN, a Mexican will have to pay 10,000 pesos for the computer:

$$0.20 \text{ USD} = 1 \text{ MXN} \qquad\qquad 0.10 \text{ USD} = 1 \text{ MXN}$$

$$1 \text{ USD} = (1 \div 0.20) \text{ MXN} \qquad\qquad 1 \text{ USD} = (1 \div 0.10) \text{ MXN}$$

$$1,000 \text{ USD} = (1,000 \div 0.20) \text{ MXN} \qquad 1,000 \text{ USD} = (1,000 \div 0.10) \text{ MXN}$$

$$= 5,000 \text{ MXN} \qquad\qquad\qquad = 10,000 \text{ MXN}$$

To a Mexican buyer, the American computer is cheaper at the exchange rate of $0.20 per peso than at $0.10 per peso.

Exchange Rate	Dollar Price	Peso Price
0.20 USD = 1 MXN	1,000 USD	5,000 MXN [(1,000 ÷ 0.20) MXN]
0.10 USD = 1 MXN	1,000 USD	10,000 MXN [(1,000 ÷ 0.10) MXN]

Therefore, the higher the dollar price is per peso, the greater will be the quantity demanded of dollars by Mexicans (because U.S. goods will be cheaper) and hence the greater the quantity supplied of pesos to the foreign exchange market. The upward-sloping supply curve for pesos illustrates this.

FLEXIBLE EXCHANGE RATES

In this section, we discuss how exchange rates are determined in the foreign exchange market when the forces of supply and demand are allowed to rule. Economists refer to this as a **flexible exchange rate system**. In the next section, we discuss how exchange rates are determined under a fixed exchange rate system.

The Equilibrium Exchange Rate

In a completely flexible exchange rate system, the forces of supply and demand determine the exchange rate. In our two-country–two-currency world, suppose the equilibrium exchange rate (dollar price per peso) is 0.10 USD = 1 MXN, as shown in Exhibit 6. At this dollar price per peso, the quantity demanded of pesos equals the quantity supplied of pesos. There are no shortages or surpluses of pesos. At any other exchange rate, however, either an excess demand for pesos or an excess supply of pesos exists.

At the exchange rate of 0.12 USD = 1 MXN, a surplus of pesos exists. As a result, downward pressure will be placed on the dollar price of a peso (just as downward pressure will be placed on the dollar price of an apple if there is a surplus of apples). At the exchange rate of 0.08 USD = 1 MXN, there is a shortage of pesos, and upward pressure will be placed on the dollar price of a peso.

Flexible Exchange Rate System
The system whereby exchange rates are determined by the forces of supply and demand for a currency.

exhibit 6

A Flexible Exchange Rate System

The demand curve for pesos is downward sloping. The higher the dollar price for pesos, the fewer pesos will be demanded; the lower the dollar price for pesos, the more pesos will be demanded. At 0.12 USD = 1 MXN, there is a surplus of pesos, placing downward pressure on the exchange rate. At 0.08 USD = 1 MXN, there is a shortage of pesos, placing upward pressure on the exchange rate. At the equilibrium exchange rate, 0.10 USD = 1 MXN, the quantity demanded of pesos equals the quantity supplied of pesos.

Thinking like AN ECONOMIST

Linkages

The demand for dollars is linked to the supply of pesos, and the demand for pesos is linked to the supply of dollars. Economists often think in terms of one activity being linked to another because economics, after all, is about exchange. In an exchange, one gives (supply) and one gets (demand): John supplies $25 to demand the new book from the shopkeeper; the shopkeeper supplies the new book so that he may demand the $25. The diagram for such a transaction usually represents the demand for and supply of the new book, but it could also represent the demand for and supply of the money. Of course, in international exchange, where monies are bought and sold before goods are bought and sold, the diagrams reflect both.

Changes in the Equilibrium Exchange Rate

Chapter 3 explains that a change in the demand for a good, in the supply of a good, or in both will change the good's equilibrium price. The same holds true for the price of currencies. A change in the demand for pesos, in the supply of pesos, or in both will change the equilibrium dollar price per peso. If the dollar price per peso rises—say, from 0.10 USD = 1 MXN to 0.12 USD = 1 MXN—the peso is said to have **appreciated** and the dollar to have **depreciated**. A currency has appreciated in value if it takes more of a foreign currency to buy it. A currency has depreciated in value if it takes more of it to buy a foreign currency.

For example, a movement in the exchange rate from 0.10 USD = 1 MXN to 0.12 USD = 1 MXN means that it now takes 12 cents instead of 10 cents to buy a peso, so the dollar has depreciated. The other side of the coin, so to speak, is that it takes fewer pesos to buy a dollar; so the peso has appreciated. That is, at an exchange rate of 0.10 USD = 1 MXN, it takes 10 pesos to buy $1, but at an exchange rate of 0.12 USD = 1 MXN, it takes only 8.33 pesos to buy $1.

Appreciation
An increase in the value of one currency relative to other currencies.

Depreciation
A decrease in the value of one currency relative to other currencies.

Factors That Affect the Equilibrium Exchange Rate

If the equilibrium exchange rate can change owing to a change in the demand for and supply of a currency, then it is important to understand what factors can change demand and supply. This section presents three.

A DIFFERENCE IN INCOME GROWTH RATES An increase in a nation's income will usually cause the nation's residents to buy more of both domestic and foreign goods. The increased demand for imports will result in an increased demand for foreign currency.

Suppose U.S. residents experience an increase in income, but Mexican residents do not. As a result, the demand curve for pesos shifts rightward, as illustrated in Exhibit 7. This causes the equilibrium exchange rate to rise from 0.10 USD = 1 MXN to 0.12 USD = 1 MXN. *Ceteris paribus,* if one nation's income grows and another's lags behind, the currency of the higher-growth-rate country *depreciates,* and the currency of the lower-growth-rate country *appreciates.* To many persons, this seems paradoxical; nevertheless, it is true.

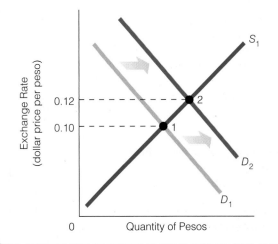

exhibit 7

The Growth Rate of Income and the Exchange Rate

If U.S. residents experience a growth in income but Mexican residents do not, U.S. demand for Mexican goods will increase, and with it, the demand for pesos. As a result, the exchange rate will change; the dollar price of pesos will rise. The dollar depreciates, the peso appreciates.

economics 24/7

BACK TO THE FUTURES

Meet (the fictional) Bill Whatley, owner of a Toyota dealership in Tulsa, Oklahoma. It is May, and Bill is thinking about a shipment of Toyotas he plans to buy in August. He knows that he must buy the Toyotas from Japan with yen, but he has a problem. The current price of ¥1 is $0.008. Bill wonders what the dollar price of a yen will be in August when he plans to make his purchase. If the price of ¥1 rises to $0.010, then, instead of paying $20,000 for a Toyota priced at ¥2.5 million, he will have to pay $25,000.[3] This difference of $5,000 may be enough to erase his profit on the sale of the Toyotas.

Bill can, however, purchase a futures contract today for the needed quantity of yen in August. A futures contract is a contract in which the seller agrees to provide a good (in this example, a currency) to the buyer on a specified future date at an agreed-on price. In short, Bill can buy yen today at a specified dollar price and take delivery of the yen at a later date (in August). Problem solved.

But if the price of ¥1 falls to $0.007 in August, Bill would have to pay only $17,500 (instead of $20,000) for a Toyota priced at ¥2.5 million. Although he could increase his profit in this case, Bill, like other car dealers, might not be interested in assuming the risk associated with changes in exchange rates. He may prefer to lock in a sure thing.

Who would sell yen to Bill? The answer is someone who is willing to assume the risk of changes in the value of currencies. For example, Julie Jackson thinks that the dollar price of a yen will go down between now and August. Therefore, she'll enter into a contract with Bill requiring her to give him ¥2.5 million in August for $20,000—the exchange rate specified in the contract being 1 JPY = 0.008 USD. If she's right and the actual exchange rate in August is 1 JPY = 0.007 USD, then she can purchase the ¥2.5 million for $17,500 and fulfill the contract with Bill by turning the yen over to him for $20,000. She walks away with $2,500 in profit.

Many economists argue that futures contracts offer people a way of dealing with the risk associated with a flexible exchange rate system. If a person doesn't know what next month's exchange rate will be and doesn't want to take the risk of waiting to see, then he can enter into a futures contract and effectively shift the risk to someone who voluntarily assumes it.

---

3. If ¥1 equals $0.008, then a Toyota with a price of ¥2.5 million costs $20,000 because ¥2.5 million × $0.008 = $20,000. If ¥1 equals $0.010, then a Toyota with a price of ¥2.5 million costs $25,000 dollars because ¥2.5 million × $0.010 equals $25,000.

Purchasing Power Parity (PPP) Theory

Theory stating that exchange rates between any two currencies will adjust to reflect changes in the relative price levels of the two countries.

DIFFERENCES IN RELATIVE INFLATION RATES Suppose the U.S. price level rises 10 percent at a time when Mexico experiences stable prices. An increase in the U.S. price level will make Mexican goods relatively less expensive for Americans and U.S. goods relatively more expensive for Mexicans. As a result, the U.S. demand for Mexican goods will increase, and the Mexican demand for U.S. goods will decrease.

In turn, the demand for and the supply of Mexican pesos are affected. As shown in Exhibit 8, the demand for Mexican pesos will increase; Mexican goods are relatively cheaper than they were before the U.S. price level rose. The supply of Mexican pesos will decrease; American goods are relatively more expensive, and so Mexicans will buy fewer American goods; thus, they demand fewer U.S. dollars and supply fewer Mexican pesos.

As Exhibit 8 shows, the result of an increase in the demand for Mexican pesos and a decrease in their supply constitutes an *appreciation* in the peso and a *depreciation* in the dollar. It takes 11 cents instead of 10 cents to buy 1 peso (dollar depreciation); it takes 9.09 pesos instead of 10 pesos to buy $1 (peso appreciation).

An important question is how much will the U.S. dollar depreciate as a result of the rise in the U.S. price level? (Recall that there is no change in Mexico's price level.) The **purchasing power parity (PPP) theory** predicts that the U.S. dollar will depreciate by 10 percent as a result of the 10 percent rise in the U.S. price level. This requires the dollar price of a peso to rise to 11 cents (10 percent of 10 cents is 1 cent, and 10 cents plus 1 cent

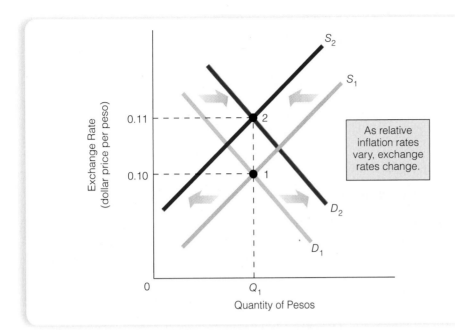

exhibit 8

Inflation, Exchange Rates, and Purchasing Power Parity (PPP)

If the price level in the United States increases by 10 percent while the price level in Mexico remains constant, then the U.S. demand for Mexican goods (and therefore pesos) will increase and the supply of pesos will decrease. As a result, the exchange rate will change; the dollar price of pesos will rise. The dollar depreciates, and the peso appreciates. PPP theory predicts that the dollar will depreciate in the foreign exchange market until the original price (in pesos) of American goods to Mexican customers is restored. In this example, this requires the dollar to depreciate 10 percent.

equals 11 cents). A 10 percent depreciation in the dollar restores the *original relative prices of American goods to Mexican customers.*

Consider a U.S. car with a price tag of $20,000. If the exchange rate is 0.10 USD = 1 MXN, a Mexican buyer of the car will pay 200,000 pesos. If the car price increases by 10 percent to $22,000 and the dollar depreciates 10 percent (to 0.11 USD = 1 MXN), the Mexican buyer of the car will still pay only 200,000 pesos.

Exchange Rate	Dollar Price	Peso Price
0.10 USD = 1 MXN	20,000 USD	200,000 MXN [(20,000/0.10) MXN]
0.11 USD = 1 MXN	22,000 USD	200,000 MXN [(22,000/0.11) MXN]

In short, the PPP theory predicts that *changes in the relative price levels of two countries will affect the exchange rate in such a way that 1 unit of a country's currency will continue to buy the same amount of foreign goods* as it did before the change in the relative price levels. In our example, the higher U.S. inflation rate causes a change in the equilibrium exchange rate and leads to a depreciated dollar, but 1 peso continues to have the same purchasing power it previously did.

On some occasions, the PPP theory of exchange rates has predicted accurately, but not on others. Many economists suggest that the theory does not always predict accurately because the demand for and the supply of a currency are affected *by more than the difference in inflation rates between countries.* For example, as noted, different income growth rates affect the demand for a currency and therefore the exchange rate. In the *long run,* however, and particularly when there is a *large difference in inflation rates across countries,* the PPP theory does predict exchange rates accurately.

CHANGES IN REAL INTEREST RATES As shown in the U.S. balance of payments in Exhibit 2, more than goods flow between countries. Financial capital also moves between countries. The flow of financial capital depends on different countries' *real interest rates*—interest rates adjusted for inflation.

To illustrate, suppose initially that the real interest rate is 3 percent in both the United States and Mexico. Then the real interest rate in the United States increases to 4.5 percent. As a result, Mexicans will want to purchase financial assets in the United States that pay a higher real interest rate than do financial assets in Mexico. The Mexican demand for dollars will increase, and therefore Mexicans will supply more pesos. As the supply of pesos increases on the foreign exchange market, the exchange rate (the dollar price per peso) will change; fewer dollars will be needed to buy pesos. In short, the dollar will appreciate, and the peso will depreciate.

Finding ECONOMICS

In the President Speaking to an Economic Advisor

The president of the United States is speaking to an economic advisor. The president asks, "What are the effects of the rather large budget deficits?" In response, the advisor might say that large budget deficits can affect interest rates, the value of the dollar, exports and imports, and the merchandise trade balance. "How so?" the president asks. Big deficits, the advisor says, mean that the federal government will have to borrow funds, which will increase the demand for credit. This will push up the interest rate. As the U.S. interest rate rises relative to interest rates in other countries, foreigners will want to purchase financial assets in the United States that pay a higher return. This will increase the demand for dollars, the dollar will appreciate, and foreign currencies will depreciate. In turn, this will affect both import and export spending, and thus it will affect the merchandise trade balance.

SELF-TEST

1. In the foreign exchange market, how is the demand for dollars linked to the supply of pesos?

2. What could cause the U.S. dollar to appreciate against the Mexican peso on the foreign exchange market?

3. Suppose that the U.S. economy grows and that the Swiss economy does not. How will this affect the exchange rate between the dollar and the Swiss franc? Why?

4. What does the purchasing power parity theory say? Give an example to illustrate your answer.

FIXED EXCHANGE RATES

Fixed Exchange Rate System
The system whereby a nation's currency is set at a fixed rate relative to all other currencies, and central banks intervene in the foreign exchange market to maintain the fixed rate.

The major alternative to the flexible exchange rate system is the **fixed exchange rate system**, which works the way it sounds. Exchange rates are fixed; they are not allowed to fluctuate freely in response to the forces of supply and demand. Central banks buy and sell currencies to maintain agreed-on exchange rates. The workings of the fixed exchange rate system are described in this section.

Fixed Exchange Rates and Overvalued/Undervalued Currency

Once again, we assume a two-country–two-currency world, but this time the United States and Mexico agree to fix the exchange rate of their currencies. Instead of letting the dollar depreciate or appreciate relative to the peso, the two countries agree to set the price of 1 peso at $0.12; that is, they agree to the exchange rate of 0.12 USD = 1 MXN. Generally, we call this the fixed exchange rate or the *official price* of a peso.[4] We will deal

---

4. If the price of 1 peso is $0.12, the price of $1 is approximately 8.33 pesos. Thus, setting the official price of a peso in terms of dollars automatically sets the official price of a dollar in terms of pesos.

exhibit 9

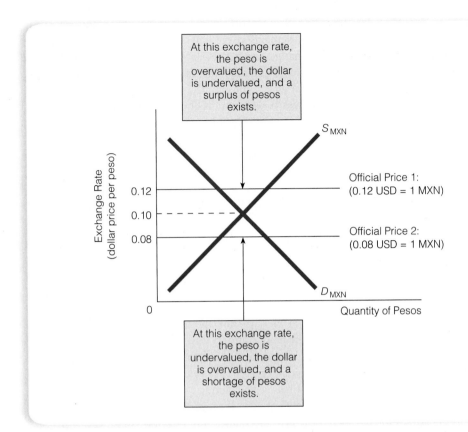

At this exchange rate, the peso is overvalued, the dollar is undervalued, and a surplus of pesos exists.

At this exchange rate, the peso is undervalued, the dollar is overvalued, and a shortage of pesos exists.

Official Price 1: (0.12 USD = 1 MXN)

Official Price 2: (0.08 USD = 1 MXN)

S_{MXN}

D_{MXN}

Exchange Rate (dollar price per peso)

Quantity of Pesos

A Fixed Exchange Rate System

In a fixed exchange rate system, the exchange rate is fixed—and it may not be fixed at the equilibrium exchange rate. The exhibit shows two cases. (1) If the exchange rate is fixed at official price 1, the peso is over-valued, the dollar is undervalued, and a surplus of pesos exists. (2) If the exchange rate is fixed at official price 2, the peso is undervalued, the dollar is overvalued, and a shortage of pesos exists.

with more than one official price in our discussion; so we refer to 0.12 USD = 1 MXN as official price 1 (Exhibit 9).

If the dollar price of pesos is above its equilibrium level (which is the case at official price 1), a surplus of pesos exists, and the peso is said to be **overvalued**. In other words, the peso is fetching more dollars than it would at equilibrium. For example, if in equilibrium, 1 peso trades for $0.10, but at the official exchange rate 1 peso trades for $0.12, then the peso is said to be overvalued.

Therefore, if the peso is overvalued, the dollar is undervalued; that is, it is fetching fewer pesos than it would at equilibrium. For example, if in equilibrium, $1 trades for 10 pesos, but at the official exchange rate, $1 trades for 8.33 pesos, then the dollar is undervalued.

Similarly, if the dollar price of pesos is below its equilibrium level (which is the case at official price 2 in Exhibit 9), a shortage of pesos exists, and the peso is **undervalued**; the peso is not fetching as many dollars as it would at equilibrium. Therefore, if the peso is undervalued, the dollar must be overvalued.

Overvalued
A currency is overvalued if its price in terms of other currencies is above the equilibrium price.

Undervalued
A currency is undervalued if its price in terms of other currencies is below the equilibrium price.

Overvalued peso ↔ Undervalued dollar

Undervalued peso ↔ Overvalued dollar

What Is So Bad About an Overvalued Dollar?

You read in the newspaper that the dollar is overvalued and that economists are concerned about the overvalued dollar. Why would economists be concerned?

Economists are concerned because the exchange rate—and hence the value of the dollar in terms of other currencies—affects the amount of U.S. exports and imports. Because it affects exports and imports, it naturally affects the merchandise trade balance.

Fixed Exchange Rates and an Overvalued Dollar

Initially, the demand for and supply of pesos are represented by D_1 and S_1, respectively. The equilibrium exchange rate is 0.10 USD = 1 MXN, which also happens to be the official (fixed) exchange rate.

In time, the demand for pesos rises to D_2, and the equilibrium exchange rate rises to 0.12 USD = 1 MXN. The official exchange rate is fixed, however, so the dollar will be overvalued. As explained in the text, this can lead to a trade deficit.

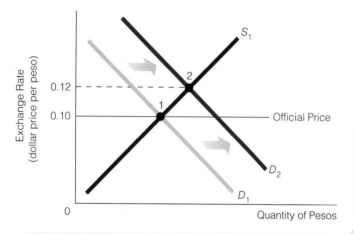

To illustrate, suppose the demand for and supply of pesos are represented by D_1 and S_1 in Exhibit 10. With this demand curve and supply curve, the equilibrium exchange rate is 0.10 USD = 1 MXN. Let's also suppose the exchange rate is fixed at this exchange rate. In other words, the equilibrium exchange rate and the fixed exchange rate are initially the same.

Time passes and eventually the demand curve for pesos shifts to the right, from D_1 to D_2. Under a flexible exchange rate system, the exchange rate would rise to 0.12 USD = 1 MXN. But a fixed exchange rate is in effect—not a flexible one. The exchange rate stays fixed at 0.10 USD = 1 MXN. This means that the fixed exchange rate (0.10 USD = 1 MXN) is below the new equilibrium exchange rate (0.12 USD = 1 MXN).

Recall that when the dollar price per peso is below its equilibrium level (which is the case), the peso is under-valued and the dollar is overvalued. At equilibrium (point 2 in Exhibit 10), 1 peso would trade for $0.12, but at its fixed rate (point 1), it trades for only $0.10; so the peso is undervalued. At equilibrium (point 2), $1 would trade for 8.33 pesos, but at its fixed rate (point 1), it trades for 10 pesos; so the dollar is overvalued.

What is bad about an overvalued dollar is that it makes U.S. goods more expensive for foreigners to buy, possibly affecting the U.S. merchandise trade balance. For example, suppose a U.S. good costs $100. At the equilibrium exchange rate (0.12 USD = 1 MXN), a Mexican would pay 833 pesos for the good, but at the fixed exchange rate (0.10 USD = 1 MXN), he will pay 1,000 pesos.

Exchange Rate	Dollar Price	Peso Price
0.12 USD = 1 MXN (equilibrium)	100 USD	833 MXN [(100 ÷ 0.12) MXN]
0.10 USD = 1 MXN (fixed)	100 USD	1,000 MXN [(100 ÷ 0.10) MXN]

The higher the prices are of U.S. goods (exports), the fewer of those goods Mexicans will buy, and, as just shown, an overvalued dollar makes U.S. export goods higher in price.

Ultimately, an overvalued dollar can affect the U.S. merchandise trade balance. As U.S. exports become more expensive for Mexicans, they buy fewer U.S. exports. If exports fall below imports, the result is a U.S. trade deficit.[5]

Government Involvement in a Fixed Exchange Rate System

In Exhibit 9, suppose the governments of Mexico and the United States agree to fix the exchange rate at 0.12 USD = 1 MXN. At this exchange rate, a surplus of pesos exists. To maintain the exchange rate at 0.12 USD = 1 MXN, the Federal Reserve System (the Fed) could buy the surplus of pesos with dollars. Consequently, the demand for pesos

---

5. The other side of the coin, so to speak, is that if the dollar is overvalued, the peso must be undervalued. An undervalued peso makes Mexican goods cheaper for Americans. So while the overvalued dollar is causing Mexicans to buy fewer U.S. exports, the undervalued peso is causing Americans to import more goods from Mexico. In conclusion, U.S. exports fall, U.S. imports rise, and we move closer to a trade deficit, or, if one already exists, it becomes larger.

BIG MAC ECONOMICS

In an earlier chapter, we explained why goods that can be easily transported from one location to another usually sell for the same price in all locations. For example, if a candy bar can be moved from Atlanta to Seattle, we would expect the candy bar to sell for the same price in both locations. The reason is that, if the candy bar is priced higher in Seattle than Atlanta, people will move candy bars from Atlanta (where the price is relatively low) to Seattle to fetch the higher price. In other words, the supply of candy bars will rise in Seattle and fall in Atlanta. These changes in supply in the two locations affect the price of the candy bars in the two locations. In Seattle the price will fall, and in Atlanta the price will rise. This price movement will stop when the price of a candy bar is the same in the two locations.

© CHARLES PERTWEE/BLOOMBERG NEWS/LANDOV

Now consider a good that is sold all over the world: McDonald's Big Mac. Suppose the exchange rate between the dollar and the yen is $1 = ¥100 and the price of a Big Mac in New York City is $3 and ¥400 in Tokyo. Given the exchange rate, a Big Mac is not selling for the same price in the two cities. In New York, it is $3, but in Tokyo it is $4 (the price in Tokyo is ¥400, and $1 = ¥100). Stated differently, in New York, $1 buys one-third of a Big Mac, but in Tokyo, $1 buys only one-fourth of a Big Mac.

However, Big Macs won't be shipped from New York to Tokyo to fetch the higher price. Instead, the exchange rate is likely to adjust in such a way that the price of a Big Mac is the same in both cities.

Now ask yourself what the exchange rate has to be between the dollar and yen before the Big Mac is the same dollar price in New York and Tokyo. Of the three following exchange rates, pick the correct one:

1. $1 = ¥133.33
2. $1 = ¥150.00
3. $1 = ¥89.00

The answer is the first one: $1 = ¥133.33. At this exchange rate, a Big Mac in New York is $3, and a Big Mac in Tokyo that is ¥400 is $3 (once we have computed its price in dollars). At the exchange rate of $1 = ¥133.33, ¥1 equals $0.0075, and $0.0075 times ¥400 is $3.

The *purchasing power parity theory* in economics predicts that the exchange rate between two currencies will adjust so that, in the end, $1 buys the same amount of a given good in all places around the world. Thus, if the exchange rate is initially $1 = ¥100 when a Big Mac is $3 in New York and ¥400 in Tokyo, it will change to become $1 = ¥133.33. That is, the dollar will soon appreciate relative to the yen.

The Economist, a well-known economics magazine, publishes what it calls the Big Mac index each year. It shows current exchange rates and the cost of a Big Mac in different countries (just as we did here). Then it predicts which currencies will appreciate and depreciate based on this information. *The Economist* does not always predict accurately, but it does do so in many cases.

If you want to predict whether the euro, pound, or peso is going to appreciate or depreciate in the next few months, looking at exchange rates in terms of the price of a Big Mac will be a useful approach.

will increase, and the demand curve will shift to the right, ideally, by enough to raise the equilibrium rate to the current fixed exchange rate.

Alternatively, instead of the Fed's buying pesos (to mop up the excess supply of pesos), the Banco de Mexico (the central bank of Mexico) could buy pesos with some of its reserve dollars. (It doesn't buy pesos with pesos because using pesos would not reduce the surplus of pesos on the market.) This action by the Banco de Mexico will also increase the demand for pesos and raise the equilibrium rate.

Finally, the two actions could be combined; that is, both the Fed and the Banco de Mexico could buy pesos.

Options Under a Fixed Exchange Rate System

Suppose there is a surplus of pesos in the foreign exchange market, indicating that the peso is overvalued and the dollar is undervalued. Suppose also that, although the Fed and the Banco de Mexico each attempt to rectify this situation by buying pesos, this combined action is not successful. The surplus of pesos persists for weeks, along with an overvalued peso and an undervalued dollar. A few options are available to pursue.

Devaluation

A government action that changes the exchange rate by lowering the official price of a currency.

Revaluation

A government action that changes the exchange rate by raising the official price of a currency.

DEVALUATION AND REVALUATION Mexico and the United States could agree to reset the official price of the dollar and the peso. Doing so entails *devaluation* and *revaluation*. A **devaluation** occurs when the official price of a currency is lowered. A **revaluation** occurs when the official price of a currency is raised.

For example, suppose the first official price of a peso is 0.10 USD = 1 MXN, and the first official price of $1 is 10 pesos. Mexico and the United States agree to change the official price of their currencies. The second official price is 0.12 USD = 1 MXN, and the second official price of $1 is 8.33 pesos.

Moving from the first official price to the second, the peso has been revalued because it takes *more dollars to buy a peso* (12 cents instead of 10). Of course, moving from the first official price to the second means the dollar has been devalued because it takes *fewer pesos to buy a dollar* (8.33 pesos instead of 10).

One country might want to devalue its currency, but another country might not want to revalue its currency. For example, if Mexico wants to devalue its currency relative to the U.S. dollar, U.S. authorities might not always willingly comply. To see why, we have to understand that the United States will not sell as many goods to Mexico if the dollar is revalued. As explained earlier, revaluing the dollar means Mexicans have to pay more for it; instead of paying, say, 8.33 pesos for $1, Mexicans might have to pay 10 pesos. At a revalued dollar (a higher peso price for a dollar), Mexicans will find U.S. goods more expensive and not want to buy as many. Americans who produce goods to sell to Mexico may see that a revalued dollar will hurt their pocketbooks, and so they will argue against it.

PROTECTIONIST TRADE POLICY (QUOTAS AND TARIFFS) Recall that an overvalued dollar can bring on or widen a trade deficit. To deal with both the trade deficit and the overvalued dollar at the same time, some say a country can impose quotas and tariffs to reduce domestic consumption of foreign goods. (Chapter 18 explains how both tariffs and quotas meet this objective.) A drop in the domestic consumption of foreign goods goes hand in hand with a decrease in the demand for foreign currencies. In turn, this decrease can affect the value of the country's currency on the foreign exchange market. In this case, it can get rid of an overvalued dollar.

Economists are quick to point out, though, that trade deficits and overvalued currencies are sometimes used as an excuse to promote trade restrictions, many of which simply benefit special interests (e.g., U.S. producers that compete for sales with foreign producers in the U.S. market).

CHANGES IN MONETARY POLICY Sometimes, a nation can use monetary policy to support the exchange rate or the official price of its currency. Suppose the United States is continually running a merchandise trade deficit; year after year, imports are outstripping exports. To remedy this, the United States might enact a tight monetary policy to retard inflation and drive up interest rates (at least in the short run). The tight monetary policy will reduce the U.S. rate of inflation and thereby lower U.S. prices relative to prices in other nations. This effect will make U.S. goods relatively cheaper than they were before (assuming other nations don't also enact a tight monetary policy) and promote U.S. exports and discourage foreign imports. It will also generate a flow of investment funds into the United States in search of higher real interest rates.

Some economists argue against fixed exchange rates because they think it unwise for a nation to adopt a particular monetary policy simply to maintain an international exchange rate. Instead, they believe domestic monetary policies should be used to meet domestic economic goals, such as price stability, low unemployment, low and stable interest rates, and so forth.

The Gold Standard

If nations adopt the gold standard, they *automatically fix* their exchange rates. Suppose the United States defines a dollar as equal to 1/10 of an ounce of gold and Mexico defines a peso as equal to 1/100 of an ounce of gold. Therefore, 1 ounce of gold could be bought with either 10 dollars or 100 pesos. The fixed exchange rate between dollars and pesos is 10 MXN = 1 USD or 0.10 USD = 1 MXN.

To have an international gold standard, countries must do the following:

1. Define their currencies in terms of gold.

2. Stand ready and willing to convert gold into paper money and paper money into gold at the rate specified (e.g., the United States would buy and sell gold at $10 an ounce).

3. Link their money supplies to their holdings of gold.

With this last point in mind, consider how a gold standard would work. Initially assume that the gold standard (fixed) exchange rate of 0.10 USD = 1 MXN is the equilibrium exchange rate. Then a change occurs: Inflation in Mexico raises prices there by 100 percent. A Mexican table that was priced at 2,000 pesos before the inflation is now priced at 4,000 pesos. At the gold standard (fixed) exchange rate, Americans now have to pay $400 (4,000 pesos ÷ 10 pesos per dollar) to buy the table, whereas before the inflation Americans had to pay only $200 (2,000 pesos ÷ 10 pesos per dollar) for the table. As a result, Americans buy fewer Mexican tables; Americans import less from Mexico.

At the same time, Mexicans import more from the United States because American prices are now relatively lower than before inflation hit Mexico. As a quick example, suppose that before inflation hit Mexico, an American pair of shoes cost $200 and that, as before, a Mexican table cost 2,000 pesos. At 0.10 USD = 1 MXN, the $200 American shoes cost 2,000 pesos and the 2,000-peso Mexican table cost $200. In other words, 1 pair of American shoes traded for (or equaled) 1 Mexican table.

Then inflation raised the price of the Mexican table to 4,000 pesos, or $400. Because the American shoes are still $200 (there has been no inflation in the United States) and the exchange rate is still fixed at 0.10 USD = 1 MXN, 1 pair of American shoes no longer equals 1 Mexican table; instead, it equals 1/2 of a Mexican table. In short, the inflation in Mexico has made U.S. goods *relatively cheaper* for Mexicans. As a result, Mexicans buy more U.S. goods; they import more from the United States.

To summarize, the inflation in Mexico has caused Americans to buy fewer goods from Mexico and Mexicans to buy more goods from the United States. In terms of the merchandise trade balance for each country, in the United States, imports decline (Americans are buying less from Mexico) and exports rise (Mexicans are buying more from the United States); so the U.S. trade balance is likely to move into surplus. Contrarily, in Mexico, exports decline (Americans are buying less from Mexico) and imports rise (Mexicans are buying more from the United States); so Mexico's trade balance is likely to move into deficit.

On a gold standard, Mexicans have to pay for the difference between their imports and exports with gold. Gold is therefore shipped to the United States. An increase in the supply of gold in the United States expands the U.S. money supply. A decrease in the supply of gold in Mexico contracts the Mexican money supply. Prices are affected in both countries. In the United States, prices begin to rise; in Mexico, they begin to fall.

As U.S. prices go up and Mexican prices go down, the earlier situation begins to reverse itself. American goods look more expensive to Mexicans, and they begin to buy less, whereas Mexican goods look cheaper to Americans, and they begin to buy more. Consequently, American imports begin to rise and exports begin to fall; Mexican imports begin to fall and exports begin to rise. Thus, by changing domestic money supplies and price levels, the gold standard begins to correct the initial trade balance disequilibrium.

The change in the money supply that the gold standard sometimes requires has prompted some economists to voice the same charge against the gold standard that is often heard against the fixed exchange rate system: It subjects domestic monetary policy to international instead of domestic considerations. In fact, many economists cite this as part of the reason many nations abandoned the gold standard in the 1930s. At a time when unemployment was unusually high, many nations with trade deficits felt that matters would only get worse if they contracted their money supplies to live by the edicts of the gold standard.

SELF-TEST

1. Under a fixed exchange rate system, if one currency is overvalued, then another currency must be undervalued. Explain why this statement is true.

2. How does an overvalued dollar affect U.S. exports and imports?

3. In each of the following cases, identify whether the U.S. dollar is overvalued or undervalued:

    a. The fixed exchange rate is $2 = £1, and the equilibrium exchange rate is $3 = £1.

    b. The fixed exchange rate is $1.25 = €1, and the equilibrium exchange rate is $1.10 = €1.

    c. The fixed exchange rate is $1 = 10 pesos, and the equilibrium exchange rate is $1 = 14 pesos.

4. Under a fixed exchange rate system, why might the United States want to devalue its currency?

FIXED EXCHANGE RATES VERSUS FLEXIBLE EXCHANGE RATES

As in many economic situations, any exchange rate system has both its costs and its benefits. This section discusses some of the arguments and issues surrounding fixed exchange rates and flexible exchange rates.

Promoting International Trade

Which are better at promoting international trade: fixed or flexible exchange rates? This section presents the case for each.

THE CASE FOR FIXED EXCHANGE RATES   Proponents of a fixed exchange rate system often argue that fixed exchange rates promote international trade, whereas flexible exchange rates stifle it. A major advantage of fixed exchange rates is certainty. Individuals in different countries know from day to day the value of their nation's currency. With flexible exchange rates, individuals are less likely to engage in international trade because of the added risk of not knowing from one day to the next how many dollars, euros, or yen they will have to trade for other currencies. Certainty is a necessary ingredient in international trade; flexible exchange rates promote uncertainty, which hampers international trade.

Economist Charles Kindleberger, a proponent of fixed exchange rates, believes that having fixed exchange rates is analogous to having a single currency for the entire United States instead of having a different currency for each of the 50 states. One currency in the United States promotes trade, whereas 50 different currencies would hamper it. In Kindleberger's view:

> The main case against flexible exchange rates is that they break up the world market. . . . Imagine trying to conduct interstate trade in the USA if there were fifty different state monies, none of which was dominant. This is akin to barter, the inefficiency of which is explained time and again by textbooks.[6]

THE CASE FOR FLEXIBLE EXCHANGE RATES Advocates of flexible exchange rates, as noted, maintain that it is better for a nation to adopt policies to meet domestic economic goals than to sacrifice domestic economic goals to maintain an exchange rate. Also, the chance is too great that the fixed exchange rate will diverge greatly from the equilibrium exchange rate, creating persistent balance of trade problems leading deficit nations to impose trade restrictions (tariffs and quotas) that hinder international trade.

Optimal Currency Areas

As of 2008, the European Union (EU) consists of 27 member states. According to the European Union, its ultimate goal is "an ever closer union among the peoples of Europe, in which decisions are taken as closely as possible to the citizen." As part of meeting this goal, the EU established its own currency—the euro—on January 1, 1999.[7] Although euro notes and coins were not issued until January 1, 2002, certain business transactions were made in euros beginning January 1, 1999.

The European Union and the euro are relevant to a discussion of an *optimal currency area.* An **optimal currency area** is a geographic area in which exchange rates can be fixed or a *common currency* used without sacrificing domestic economic goals, such as low unemployment. The concept of an optimal currency area originated in the debate over whether fixed or flexible exchange rates are better. Most of the pioneering work on optimal currency areas was done by Robert Mundell, the winner of the 1999 Nobel Prize in Economics.

Before discussing an optimal currency area, we need to look at the relationships among labor mobility, trade, and exchange rates. *Labor mobility* means that it is easy for the residents of one country to move to another country.

Optimal Currency Area
A geographic area in which exchange rates can be fixed or a common currency used without sacrificing domestic economic goals, such as low unemployment.

TRADE AND LABOR MOBILITY Suppose there are only two countries: the United States and Canada. The United States produces calculators and soft drinks, and Canada produces bread and muffins. Currently, the two countries trade with each other, and there is complete labor mobility between them.

One day, the residents of both countries reduce their demand for bread and muffins and increase their demand for calculators and soft drinks. In other words, relative demand changes. Demand increases for U.S. goods and falls for Canadian goods. Business firms in Canada lay off employees because their sales have plummeted. Incomes in Canada begin to fall, and the unemployment rate begins to rise. In the United States, prices initially rise because of the increased demand for calculators and soft drinks. In response to the higher demand for their products, U.S. business firms begin to hire more workers and increase their production. Their efforts to hire more workers drive wages up and reduce the unemployment rate.

Because labor is mobile, some of the newly unemployed Canadian workers move to the United States to find work, easing the economic situation in both countries. The

---

6. Charles Kindleberger, *International Money* (London: Allen and Unwin, 1981), p. 174.

7. So far, 15 of the 27 member states have adopted the euro as their official currency.

movement of labor will reduce some of the unemployment problems in Canada, and, with more workers in the United States, more output will be produced, thus dampening upward price pressures on calculators and soft drinks. Thus, changes in relative demand pose no major economic problems for either country if labor is mobile.

TRADE AND LABOR IMMOBILITY Now let's suppose that relative demand has changed but that labor is *not* mobile between the United States and Canada. We assume labor immobility, perhaps due to either political or cultural barriers to people moving between the two countries. If people cannot move, what happens in the economies of the two countries depends largely on whether exchange rates are fixed or flexible.

If exchange rates are flexible, the value of U.S. currency changes vis-à-vis Canadian currency. If Canadians want to buy more U.S. goods, they will have to exchange their domestic currency for U.S. currency. This increases the demand for U.S. currency on the foreign exchange market at the same time that it increases the supply of Canadian currency. Consequently, U.S. currency appreciates and Canadian currency depreciates. Because Canadian currency depreciates, U.S. goods become relatively more expensive for Canadians; so they buy fewer. And because U.S. currency appreciates, Canadian goods become relatively cheaper for Americans; so they buy more. Canadian business firms begin to sell more goods; so they hire more workers, the unemployment rate drops, and the bad economic times in Canada begin to disappear.

If exchange rates are fixed, however, U.S. goods will not become relatively more expensive for Canadians, and Canadian goods will not become relatively cheaper for Americans. Consequently, the bad economic times in Canada (high unemployment) might last for a long time indeed instead of beginning to reverse. Thus, if labor is immobile, changes in relative demand may pose major economic problems when exchange rates are fixed but not when they are flexible.

COSTS, BENEFITS, AND OPTIMAL CURRENCY AREAS Flexible exchange rates have both benefits (just discussed) and costs. The costs include the cost of exchanging one currency for another (there is a charge to exchange, say, U.S. dollars for Canadian dollars or U.S. dollars for Japanese yen) and the added risk of not knowing what the value of one's currency will be on the foreign exchange market on any given day. For many countries, the benefits outweigh the costs, and so they have flexible exchange rate systems.

Suppose some of the costs of flexible exchange rates could be eliminated, while maintaining the benefits. Two countries could have a fixed exchange rate or adopt a common currency and retain the benefits of flexible exchange rates when labor is mobile between the two countries. Then there is no reason to have separate currencies that float against each other because resources (labor) can move easily and quickly in response to changes in relative demand. The two countries can either fix exchange rates or adopt the same currency.

When labor in countries within a certain geographic area is mobile enough to move easily and quickly in response to changes in relative demand, the countries are said to constitute an *optimal currency area*. Countries in such an area can either fix their currencies or adopt the same currency and thus keep all the benefits of flexible exchange rates without any of the costs.

It is commonly argued that the states within the United States constitute an optimal currency area. Labor can move easily and quickly between, say, North Carolina and South Carolina in response to relative demand changes. Some economists argue that the countries that compose the European Union are within an optimal currency area and that adopting a common currency—the euro—will benefit these countries. Other economists disagree. They argue that, although labor is somewhat more mobile in Europe today than in the past, certain language and cultural differences make labor mobility less than sufficient to truly constitute an optimal currency area.

THE CURRENT INTERNATIONAL MONETARY SYSTEM

Today's international monetary system is best described as a managed flexible exchange rate system, sometimes referred to more casually as a **managed float**. In a way, this system is a rough compromise between the fixed and flexible exchange rate systems. The current system operates under flexible exchange rates, but not completely. Nations now and then intervene to adjust their official reserve holdings to moderate major swings in exchange rates.

Proponents of the managed float system stress the following advantages:

1. *It allows nations to pursue independent monetary policies.* Under a (strictly) fixed exchange rate system, fixed either by agreement or by gold, a nation with a merchandise trade deficit might have to enact a tight monetary policy to retard inflation and to promote its exports. This type of action is not needed with the managed float, whose proponents argue that solving trade imbalances by adjusting one price—the exchange rate—is better than adjusting the price level.

2. *It solves trade problems without trade restrictions.* As stated earlier, under a fixed exchange rate system, nations sometimes impose tariffs and quotas to solve trade imbalances. For example, a deficit nation might impose import quotas so that exports and imports of goods will be more in line. Under the current system, trade imbalances are usually solved through changes in exchange rates.

3. *It is flexible and therefore can easily adjust to shocks.* In 1973–1974, the OPEC nations dramatically raised the price of oil, resulting in trade deficits for many oil-importing nations. A fixed exchange rate system would have had a hard time accommodating such a major change in oil prices, but the current system had little trouble. Exchange rates took much of the shock (there were large changes in exchange rates), thus allowing most nations' economies to weather the storm with a minimum of difficulty.

Opponents of the current international monetary system stress the following disadvantages:

1. *It promotes exchange rate volatility and uncertainty and results in less international trade than would be the case under fixed exchange rates.* Under a flexible exchange rate system, volatile exchange rates make conducting business riskier for importers and exporters. As a result, there is less international trade than there would be under a fixed exchange rate system. Proponents respond that the futures market in currencies allows importers and exporters to shift the risk of fluctuations in exchange rates to others. For example, if an American company wants to buy a quantity of a good from a Japanese company three months from today, it can contract today for the desired quantity of yen that it will need at a specified price. It will not have to worry about a change in the dollar price of yen during the next three months. Purchasing a futures contract has a cost, but it is usually modest.

2. *It promotes inflation.* As we have seen, the monetary policies of different nations are not independent of one another under a fixed exchange rate system. For example, a nation with a merchandise trade deficit is somewhat restrained from inflating its currency because this will worsen the deficit problem. The deficit will make the nation's goods more expensive relative to foreign goods and promote the purchase of imports. In its attempt to maintain the exchange rate, a nation with a merchandise trade deficit would have to enact a tight monetary policy. Under the current system, a nation with a merchandise trade deficit does not have to maintain exchange rates or try to solve its deficit problem through changes in its money supply. Opponents of the current system argue that this frees nations to inflate, predicting that more inflation will result than would occur under a fixed exchange rate system.

Managed Float
A managed flexible exchange rate system, under which nations now and then intervene to adjust their official reserve holdings to moderate major swings in exchange rates.

3. *Changes in exchange rates alter trade balances in the desired direction only after a long time; in the short run, a depreciation in a currency can make the situation worse instead of better.* It is often argued that soon after a depreciation in a trade-deficit nation's currency, the trade deficit will increase (not decrease, as hoped). The reason is that import demand is inelastic in the short run: Imports are not very responsive to a change in price. For example, suppose Mexico is running a trade deficit with the United States at the present exchange rate of 0.12 USD = 1 MXN. At this exchange rate, the peso is overvalued. Mexico buys 2,000 television sets from the United States, each with a price tag of $500. Assume Mexico therefore spends 8.33 million pesos on imports of American television sets. Now suppose that the overvalued peso begins to depreciate, say, to 0.11 USD = 1 MXN and that, in the short run, Mexican customers buy only 100 fewer American television sets; that is, they import 1,900 television sets. At a price of $500 each and an exchange rate of 0.11 USD = 1 MXN, Mexicans now spend 8.63 million pesos on imports of American television sets. In the short run, then, a depreciation in the peso has widened the trade deficit because imports fell by only 5 percent, whereas the price of imports (in terms of pesos) increased by 9.09 percent. As time passes, imports will fall off more (it takes time for Mexican buyers to shift from higher-priced American goods to lower-priced Mexican goods), and the deficit will shrink.

SELF-TEST

1. What is an optimal currency area?

2. Country 1 produces good X, and country 2 produces good Y. People in both countries begin to demand more of good X and less of good Y. Assume that there is no labor mobility between the two countries and that a flexible exchange rate system exists. What will happen to the unemployment rate in country 2? Explain your answer.

3. How important is labor mobility in determining whether an area is an optimal currency area?

"WHY IS THE DEPRECIATION OF ONE CURRENCY TIED TO THE APPRECIATION OF ANOTHER CURRENCY?"

Student:

I know that when the dollar depreciates, some other currency appreciates. Is this just the way it is? For example, if $1 equals €1, and then $1.25 equals €1, the arithmetic of exchange rates tells me that now $1 will only fetch €0.8. Is that all there is to it?

Instructor:

Not exactly. You are focusing on the arithmetic (of exchange rates) to the exclusion of the economics. There is an economic reason why dollar appreciation is linked to euro appreciation.

Student:

What is that economic reason?

Instructor:

Think of what can lead to the dollar's depreciating. Let's suppose that you want to travel to Germany where the euro is used. You take your dollars and buy euros with them. In other words, you do two things: You (1) buy euros by (2) supplying dollars.

Now think of how you are affecting the market for euros and the market for dollars. You are increasing the *demand for euros* in the market for euros, and you are increasing the *supply of dollars* in the market for dollars. Remember in Exhibit 5 how we linked the demand for one currency with the supply of another? That is happening here: Your demand for euros is linked to your supply of dollars. So, if you increase the demand for euros, you are automatically increasing the supply of dollars.

Student:

I'm used to thinking that my action of buying something affects only one market. For instance, when I buy more books, this action affects only the market for books. You seem to be telling me that this is not the case when I buy a currency, such as the euro. To buy euros is to supply dollars.

Instructor:

That's right. So when you increase the demand for euros, you automatically increase the supply of dollars. And then we have to ask ourselves, what happens in each of the two markets—the market for euros and the market for dollars?

Student:

Well, if I increase the demand for euros, the price of a euro in terms of dollars will rise. Also, if I increase the supply of dollars, the price of a dollar in terms of euros will fall.

Instructor:

And what do you call it when the price of a euro has risen in terms of dollars?

Student:

We say the dollar has depreciated because it now takes more dollars and cents to buy a euro.

Instructor:

And what do you call it when the price of a dollar has fallen in terms of euros?

Student:

We say the euro has appreciated because it now takes fewer euros to buy a dollar.

Instructor:

So let's go back to your original query. You wondered whether the dollar's depreciating and the euro's appreciating were just matters of arithmetic. Now we know that they aren't. They are a matter of curves shifting in different markets.

Points to Remember

1. To buy a currency is to affect two markets, not just one. If you buy euros, you affect the euro market. But by selling dollars to buy euros, you also affect the dollar market.

2. The fact that when one currency depreciates another appreciates is a matter of curves shifting in two currency markets.

a reader asks | How Do I Convert Currencies?

I plan to travel to several different countries during the summer. How do I convert prices of products in other countries into dollars?

Here is the general formula to use:

$$\text{Price of the product in dollars} = \text{Price of the product in foreign currency} \times \text{Price of the foreign currency in dollars}$$

For example, suppose you travel to Mexico and see something priced at 100 pesos. You'd change the general formula into a specific one:

$$\text{Price of the product in dollars} = \text{Price of the product in pesos} \times \text{Price of a peso in dollars}$$

If the dollar price of a peso is, say, $0.12, then the dollar price of the product is $12. Here is the calculation:

$$\text{Price of the product in dollars} = 100 \times 0.12 = 12$$

Or suppose you are in Tokyo and you see a product for ¥10,000. What is the price in dollars? At the exchange rate of 0.008 USD = 1 JPY, it is $80.

$$\text{Price of the product in dollars} = 10,000 \times 0.008 = 80$$

Now let's suppose you are in Russia and you don't know the exchange rate between dollars and rubles. You pick up a newspaper to find out (often, exchange rates are quoted in the newspaper). But instead of finding the exchange rate quoted in terms of the dollar price of a ruble (e.g., $0.0318 for 1 ruble), you find the ruble price of a dollar (31.4190 rubles for $1). What do you do now?

Perhaps the easiest thing to do is first convert rubles per dollar into dollars per ruble and then use the earlier formula to find the price of the Russian product in dollars. Recall that exchange rates are reciprocals, so:

$$\text{Dollars per ruble} = \frac{1}{\text{Rubles per dollar}}$$

To illustrate, if it takes 31.4190 rubles to purchase $1, then it takes 0.0318 dollars to buy 1 ruble. Here is the computation:

$$\text{Dollars per ruble} = \frac{1}{31.41990} = 0.0318$$

Now, because you know that $0.0318 = 1 ruble, then if, say, a Russian coat costs 10,000 rubles, it costs $318:

$$\text{Price of the product in dollars} = 10,000 \times 0.0318 = 318$$

Chapter Summary

BALANCE OF PAYMENTS

- The balance of payments provides information about a nation's imports and exports, domestic residents' earnings on assets located abroad, foreign earnings on domestic assets, gifts to and from foreign countries, and official transactions by governments and central banks.

- In a nation's balance of payments, any transaction that supplies the country's currency in the foreign exchange market is recorded as a debit ($-$). Any transaction that creates a demand for the country's currency is recorded as a credit ($+$).

- The three main accounts of the balance of payments are the current account, the capital account, and the official reserve account.

- The current account includes all payments related to the purchase and sale of goods and services. The three major components of the account are exports of goods and services, imports of goods and services, and net unilateral transfers abroad.

- The capital account includes all payments related to the purchase and sale of assets and to borrowing and lending activities. The major components are outflow of U.S. capital and inflow of foreign capital.

- The official reserve account includes transactions by the central banks of various countries.

- The merchandise trade balance is the difference between the value of merchandise exports and the value of merchandise imports. If exports are greater than imports, a nation has a trade surplus; if imports are greater than exports, a nation has a trade deficit.

- The balance of payments equals Current account balance + Capital account balance + Official reserve balance + Statistical discrepancy.

THE FOREIGN EXCHANGE MARKET

- The market in which currencies of different countries are exchanged is called the foreign exchange market. In this market, currencies are bought and sold for a price: the exchange rate.

- When the residents of a nation demand a foreign currency, they must supply their own currency. For example, if Americans demand Mexican goods, they also demand Mexican pesos and supply U.S. dollars. If Mexicans demand American goods, they also demand U.S. dollars and supply Mexican pesos.

FLEXIBLE EXCHANGE RATES

- Under flexible exchange rates, the foreign exchange market will equilibrate at the exchange rate where the quantity demanded of a currency equals the quantity supplied of the currency; for example, the quantity demanded of U.S. dollars equals the quantity supplied of U.S. dollars.

- If the price of a nation's currency increases relative to a foreign currency, the nation's currency is said to have appreciated. For example, if the price of a peso rises from 0.10 USD = 1 MXN to 0.15 USD = 1 MXN, the peso has appreciated. If the price of a nation's currency decreases relative to a foreign currency, the nation's currency is said to have depreciated. For example, if the price of a dollar falls from 10 MXN = 1 USD to 8 MXN = 1 USD, the dollar has depreciated.

- Under a flexible exchange rate system, the equilibrium exchange rate is affected by a difference in income growth rates between countries, a difference in inflation rates between countries, and a change in (real) interest rates between countries.

FIXED EXCHANGE RATES

- Under a fixed exchange rate system, countries agree to fix the price of their currencies. The central banks of the countries must then buy and sell currencies to maintain the agreed-on exchange rate.

- If a persistent deficit or surplus in a nation's combined current and capital account exists at a fixed exchange rate, the nation has a few options to deal with the problem: devalue or revalue its currency, enact protectionist trade policies (in the case of a deficit), or change its monetary policy.

- A gold standard automatically fixes exchange rates. To have an international gold standard, nations must do the following: (1) define their currencies in terms of gold, (2) stand ready and willing to convert gold into paper money and paper money into gold at a specified rate, and (3) link their money supplies to their holdings of gold. The change in the money supply that the gold standard sometimes requires has prompted some economists to voice the same charge against the gold standard that is often heard against the fixed exchange rate system: It subjects domestic monetary policy to international instead of domestic considerations.

THE CURRENT INTERNATIONAL MONETARY SYSTEM

- Today's international monetary system is described as a managed flexible exchange rate system, or managed float. For the most part, the exchange rate system is flexible, although nations periodically intervene in the foreign exchange market to adjust rates. Because it is a managed float system, it is difficult to tell whether nations will emphasize the float part or the managed part in the future.

- Proponents of the managed flexible exchange rate system believe it offers several advantages: (1) It allows nations to pursue independent monetary policies. (2) It solves trade problems without trade restrictions. (3) It is flexible and therefore can easily adjust to shocks.

- Opponents of the managed flexible exchange rate system believe it has several disadvantages: (1) It promotes exchange rate volatility and uncertainty and results in less international trade than would be the case under fixed exchange rates. (2) It promotes inflation. (3) It corrects trade deficits only a long time after a depreciation in the currency; in the interim, it can make matters worse.

Key Terms and Concepts

Balance of Payments	Merchandise Trade	Exchange Rate	Overvalued
Debit	Surplus	Flexible Exchange Rate	Undervalued
Foreign Exchange Market	Current Account Balance	System	Devaluation
Credit	Capital Account	Appreciation	Revaluation
Current Account	Capital Account Balance	Depreciation	Optimal Currency Area
Merchandise Trade	International Monetary Fund	Purchasing Power Parity	Managed Float
Balance	(IMF)	(PPP) Theory	
Merchandise Trade Deficit	Special Drawing Right (SDR)	Fixed Exchange Rate System	

Questions and Problems

1 Suppose the United States and Japan have a flexible exchange rate system. Explain whether each of the following events will lead to an appreciation or depreciation in the U.S. dollar and Japanese yen.

   a. U.S. real interest rates rise above Japanese real interest rates.

   b. The Japanese inflation rate rises relative to the U.S. inflation rate.

   c. Japan imposes a quota on imports of American radios.

2 Give an example that illustrates how a change in the exchange rate changes the relative price of domestic goods in terms of foreign goods.

3 Suppose the media report that the United States has a deficit in its current account. What does this imply about the U.S. capital account balance and official reserve account balance?

4 Suppose Canada has a merchandise trade deficit and Mexico has a merchandise trade surplus. The two countries have a flexible exchange rate system; so the Mexican peso appreciates and the Canadian dollar depreciates. However, soon after the depreciation of the Canadian dollar, Canada's trade deficit grows instead of shrinks. Why might this occur?

5 What are the strong and weak points of the flexible exchange rate system? What are the strong and weak points of the fixed exchange rate system?

6 Individuals do not keep a written account of their balance of trade with other individuals. For example, John doesn't keep an account of how much he sells to Alice and how much he buys from her. In addition, neither cities nor any of the 50 states calculate their balance of trade with all other cities and states. However, nations do calculate their merchandise trade balance with other nations. If nations do it, should individuals, cities, and states do it? Why or why not?

7 Every nation's balance of payments equals zero. Therefore, is each nation on an equal footing in international trade and finance with every other nation? Explain your answer.

8 Suppose your objective is to predict whether the euro (the currency of the European Union) and the U.S. dollar will appreciate or depreciate on the foreign exchange market in the next two months. What information would you need to help make your prediction? Specifically, how would this information help you predict the direction of the foreign exchange value of the euro and dollar? Next, explain how a person who could accurately predict exchange rates could become extremely rich in a short time.

9 Suppose the price of a Big Mac always rises by the percentage rise in the price level of the country in which it is sold. According to the purchasing power parity (PPP) theory, we would expect the price of a Big Mac to be the same everywhere in the world. Why?

10 If everyone in the world spoke the same language, would the world be closer to or further from being an optimal currency area? Explain your answer.

Working with Numbers and Graphs

1 The following foreign exchange information appeared in a newspaper:

	U.S. Dollar Equivalent		Currency per U.S. Dollar	
	Thurs.	**Fri.**	**Thurs.**	**Fri.**
Russia (ruble)	0.0318	0.0317	31.4190	31.5290
Brazil (real)	0.3569	0.3623	2.8020	2.7601
India (rupee)	0.0204	0.0208	48.9100	47.8521

   a. Between Thursday and Friday, did the U.S. dollar appreciate or depreciate against the Russian ruble?

   b. Between Thursday and Friday, did the U.S. dollar appreciate or depreciate against the Brazilian real?

   c. Between Thursday and Friday, did the U.S. dollar appreciate or depreciate against the Indian rupee?

2 If $1 equals ¥0.0093, what does ¥1 equal?

3 If $1 equals 7.7 krone (Danish), what does 1 krone equal?

4 If $1 equals 31 rubles, what does 1 ruble equal?

5 If the current account is −$45 billion, the capital account is +$55 billion, and the official reserve balance is −$1 billion, what does the statistical discrepancy equal?

6 Why does the balance of payments always equal zero?

CHAPTER **20**

GLOBALIZATION AND INTERNATIONAL IMPACTS ON THE ECONOMY

Introduction In the world in which we live, we hear much of *globalization*. In this chapter we discuss what globalization is, the causes of it, the costs and benefits of it, and its future. We then return to a framework of analysis we first used in the macroeconomics part of this text—aggregate demand and aggregate supply (*AD-AS*)—and we use *AD-AS* to discuss some of the effects of globalization on a national economy.

WHAT IS GLOBALIZATION?

Many economists define **globalization** as one of two things:

1. A phenomenon by which individuals and businesses in any part of the world are much more affected by events elsewhere in the world than before.
2. The growing integration of the national economies of the world to the degree that we may be witnessing the emergence and operation of a single worldwide economy.

These factors—people and businesses across the world having greater impact on each other, creating a smaller world, and the movement toward a worldwide economy—are repeated in the many different definitions of globalization. Let's take a closer look at these key features.

A Smaller World

The first definition emphasizes that economic agents in any given part of the world are affected by events elsewhere in the world. If you live in the United States, you are not affected only by what happens in the United States but also by what happens in Brazil, Russia, and China. For example, in recent years, the Chinese government was taking much of the money it earned in trade with the United States and buying bonds issued by the U.S. government. As a result of the Chinese purchases of U.S. bonds, interest rates in the United States ended up being lower than they would have been. Because of lower

Globalization
A phenomenon by which economic agents in any given part of the world are more affected by events elsewhere in the world than before; the growing integration of the national economies of the world to the degree that we may be witnessing the emergence and operation of a single worldwide economy.

interest rates, some people were able to take out mortgage loans to buy houses that they would not be eligible for otherwise. Some people took out car loans to buy cars that they otherwise would not have been able to buy.

But can you see how, in a sense, globalization makes the world smaller? China hasn't moved physically; it isn't any closer to the United States (in terms of distance) than it was 100 years ago. Still, because of globalization, what happens in distant China today has an effect on you, just as, in the past, what happened in locations only 10 miles or 100 miles away would affect you. For all practical purposes, we live in a smaller world today than people did 100 years ago.

Finding ECONOMICS

In a Clothing Store

Brandon is at a clothing store buying a number of items—shirts, sweaters, trousers, etc. He doesn't check to see in which country each of these items was produced. Instead, he just checks out the item and its price, and he decides whether to buy it. Where is the economics?

Many of the items Brandon buys were very likely produced in other countries. To Brandon, buying an item of clothing produced in China, Brazil, or India is really no different from buying an item of clothing in a factory 10 miles away. For Brandon, China, Brazil, or India might as well be down the street. In some ways, the world Brandon lives in is a small world, one in which distance doesn't matter as much as it used to; it is one in which trades between people living in different countries are becoming increasingly more common.

A World Economy

Globalization is closely aligned with a movement toward more free enterprise, freer markets, and more freedom of movement for people and goods. Thomas Friedman, author of several books on globalization, states that "globalization means the spread of free-market capitalism in the world." Economic globalization is essentially a free enterprise activity, and to the degree that many countries are globalizing, they are moving toward greater free enterprise practices. Much of this globalization and much of the movement toward freer markets are occurring in the world today.

With globalization, the world is moving from hundreds of national economies toward *one large world economy.* In this world economy, speaking about *different* economic systems does not make as much sense as it once did. Speaking about *the* economic system for that one world economy does make sense. And, as explained, the economic system that best describes what is happening in the world economy is free enterprise or capitalism.

Finding ECONOMICS

In The Economist

"Mr. Bhattacharjee is not the first leader to preach socialism while practising capitalism." Mr. Bhattacharjee is the chief minister of the Indian state, West Bengal. The statement about him was made in *The Economist* (a news magazine that covers economic issues in particular) in November 2007. Where is the economics? The statement gives us a glimpse into the what is happening in the world today with respect to the adoption of economic systems—specifically, the movement is toward capitalism.

SHOULD YOU LEAVE A TIP?

In the United States, tipping in restaurants is common, amounting to $16 billion a year. Yet 24 percent of the individuals in one study said that they thought tipping was unfair to customers. In the past, some states prohibited tipping. For example, in the early 1900s, Arkansas, Mississippi, Iowa, South Carolina, Tennessee, and Washington passed laws to prohibit tipping.

Of all the people in the rest of the world, some have the same tipping practices as Americans, but certainly not all. For example, adding an automatic service charge to a restaurant bill is increasingly customary in European restaurants, rather than tipping the server. Little tipping of any sort goes on in Argentina and Vietnam. Much less tipping occurs (i.e., fewer service providers expect tips) in Australia, New Zealand, and Italy than in the United States, and more tipping goes on in Mexico and Egypt than in the United States.

In several studies, researchers looked at the number of different service providers (out of a total of 33) for which tipping is customary in a given country. The more service providers it was customary to tip in a country, the higher the country's so-called prevalence of tipping. For example, if it was customary to tip 31 different service providers in country A but only 15 in country B, then country A would have a higher prevalence of tipping than country B.

© MOODBOARD/ALAMY

The conclusion of these studies is that countries where success and materialism were highly valued had a higher prevalence of tipping than countries where caring and personal relationships were highly valued. In addition, the prevalence of tipping increased as the national need for achievement and recognition rose. In one study, tipping was more prevalent in countries with lower taxes than in countries with higher taxes.

If it becomes increasingly relevant to speak of a world economy instead of hundreds of national economies, will tipping practices around the world become more common? If they do become more common, toward what degree of tipping will they gravitate? Because we do not know the answer to these questions, why ask? The answer is twofold: First, the questions get us to think about what changes we are likely to see in our everyday lives and, as globalization continues, whether the changes will be only in the economic realm (e.g., we can buy more clothes from China), or whether they will disperse outward into the social and cultural realms. Second, the questions force us to separate into categories things that are so deeply embedded in the character of a people (and therefore unlikely to change) from things that are somewhat superficial (and therefore more likely to change). Which is a rock (incapable of absorbing), and which is a sponge (capable of absorbing)?

TWO WAYS TO SEE GLOBALIZATION

Sometimes, a definition is not as good a description or explanation as a picture. Let's create two mental pictures that should give you a good idea of what globalization is about. The first picture is of a world without any barriers to trade, where the cost of dealing with anyone in the world is essentially the same.

No Barriers

Suppose land was not divided into nation states—no United States, no China, no Russia. Also suppose physical, economic, or political barriers to trade did not exist. Essentially, then, you could trade with anyone, no matter where in the world this person lived. You could trade with a person living 5,000 miles away as easily as you could trade with your next-door neighbor.

In this pretend world, businesses could hire workers and set up factories anywhere in the world. People could open savings accounts in banks 7,000 miles away or buy stock in companies located on the other side of the globe.

Now, in a sense, our world—the world that we live in today—is moving in this direction. As this movement proceeds, a nation's economy (e.g., the U.S. economy) becomes more and more a part of the world economy. As this process continues, speaking about a world or global economy, rather than about the Russian, U.S., or Chinese economy, becomes increasingly relevant.

A Union of States

The second way to see globalization is familiar to people who reside in the United States, made up as it is of 50 states. Today, moving goods and services among these states is easy. A person can produce goods in, say, North Carolina and then transport them (with only a few exceptions) for sale to every state in the country. In addition, a person living anywhere in the United States can move to any state and work, save, purchase, sell, and so on. In other words, within the United States, free movement of people and goods is possible.

Some people will argue today that economic globalization is, in a way, similar to changing countries (of the world) into states of one country. It is similar to making independent countries such as the United States, Russia, China, Brazil, and Japan into the United States of the World.

GLOBALIZATION FACTS

How do you know globalization is occurring? You need to see certain things happening in the world before you can say that globalization is taking place.

You need to see:

- Countries in the world opening up to more trade with each other.
- People in one country investing some of their money in other countries.
- Companies in one country hiring people in other countries.

Essentially, you need to see people in the world acting more like they once acted only within their individual countries. Some evidence suggests that all these things are happening.

International Trade

Tariff
A tax on imports.

The average **tariff** rate in the United States was 40 percent in 1946. The average tariff today is today is about 1.6 percent. Also, federal government revenue from tariffs in the early 1900s accounted for half of all federal government revenues, whereas today tariffs account for less than 2 percent. Exhibit 1 presents average tariff rates in the United States during the period 1930–2007.

The decline in tariff rates in the United States has also been accompanied by similar declines in countries such as India, China, Brazil, and many others. For example, in 2000, the average tariff rate in China was 18.7 percent; one year later, it was 12.8 percent. In 2000, the average tariff rate in India was 30.2 percent; one year later, it was 21 percent. Furthermore, both India and China are trading more with other countries. For example, 15 years ago, China did not trade much with the countries of Europe. Today, for most European countries, China is one of their top five trading partners.

exhibit 1

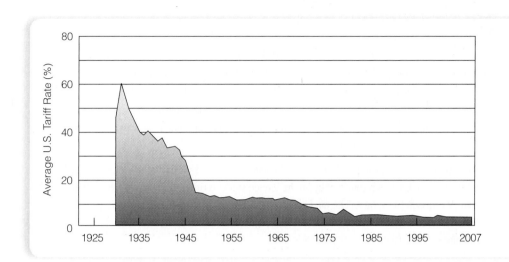

As further evidence of globalization, between 1973 and 2007, countries exported and imported more goods. Exports became a larger percentage of a country's total output. To explain these changes, think of an analogy. Suppose you produce computers. Last year, all the computers you produced were purchased by residents of the country in which you live. This year, residents of your country purchase half the computers you produced, and persons who live in foreign countries purchased the other half. In 2007, U.S. exports and imports were more like the second scenario; in 1973, things were closer to the first scenario.

Foreign Exchange Trading

When people of one country want to trade with people of another country or invest in a foreign company, they have to buy the currency used in the other country. So if globalization occurs, we would expect a lot more currency exchanges to take place. In economics, *foreign exchange trading* is a term that means buying and selling foreign currencies. In 1995, daily foreign exchange trading was 60 times higher than it was in 1977. In 1992, daily foreign exchange trading amounted to $820 billion. In 1998, this amount had risen to $1.5 trillion, close to doubling in just 6 years. In 2007, foreign exchange trading had risen to over $3 trillion.

Foreign Direct Investment

If a U.S. company wants to invest in a company in, say, Russia, it undertakes what is called *foreign direct investment.* The more foreign direct investment there is, the more likely the process of globalization is at work. In 1975, foreign direct investment amounted to $23 billion. In 1997, it had risen to $644 billion, a 30-fold increase. Between 1984 and 2003, U.S. investment holdings in foreign companies tripled, and foreign investment in the U.S. increased six-fold.

Personal Investments

Many people in the United States own stocks. If you own a number of stocks, you are said to have a stock portfolio. In 1980, these stock portfolios were comprised of no more than 2 percent of foreign stocks. Today, it is 14 percent. Thus, Americans are increasingly buying stock in foreign companies.

Finding ECONOMICS

In a Foreign Stock Transaction

Two years ago Jake bought a few foreign stocks. Specifically, he bought 1,000 shares of an Irish firm's stock and 400 shares of a French firm's stock. In both Ireland and France the currency used is the euro. In recent months, the value of the dollar in relationship to the euro has been falling. In other words, it now takes more dollars and cents to buy a euro than it did when Jake bought the stock. Where is the economics?

The economics appears in two places. First, buying foreign stocks is part of the overall globalization picture. Second, Jake's return for buying the foreign stocks is rising as the dollar falls. When Jake sells the foreign stock, he will be paid in euros, and euros are rising in value relative to the dollar. So, when he exchanges the euros for dollars, he will get more dollars now than he would have before the dollar fell in value (in relation to the euro).

The World Trade Organization

The World Trade Organization (WTO) is an international organization whose mission is to promote international free trade (trade between countries). In 1948, only 23 countries of the world chose to be members of the precursor to the WTO, GATT (General Agreement on Tariffs and Trade); in mid-2008, that number had risen to 151 countries.

Business Practices

More and more, Americans are working for foreign companies that have offices in the United States. For example, the number of Americans working for foreign companies (with offices in the United States) grew from 4.9 million in 1991 to 6.5 million in 2001, an increase of 1.6 million.

MOVEMENT TOWARD GLOBALIZATION

How did we come to live in a global economy? Did someone push a button years ago to start the process? Globalization has been on the world stage for longer than the past two decades. In fact, the world has gone through different globalization periods. For example, globalization was occurring during the period from the mid-1800s to the late 1920s. Some people today refer to it as the First Era of Globalization. In some ways, when it came to the movement of people, the world then was freer than the world today, as evidenced by the fact that many people moved from country to country without a passport, which was not required.

The First Era of Globalization was largely ended by World Wars I and II and the Great Depression. Even though the Great Depression and the world wars were over by 1945, globalization did not start anew. The Cold War essentially divided the world into different camps (free versus unfree, capitalist versus communist), which led to relatively high political and economic barriers. The visible symbol of these barriers—the Berlin Wall—separated not only East from West Germany but one group of countries living under one political and economic system from another group of countries living under a different political and economic system.

The more recent period of globalization of today has several causal factors. Not everyone agrees as to what all the factors are, and not everyone agrees on the weight one assigns to each of the factors. For example, some people will argue that one factor means more

economics 24/7

PROPER BUSINESS ETIQUETTE AROUND THE WORLD

Customs and traditions differ among countries, sometimes when it comes to conducting business. Not knowing how business is done in a country can act as a stumbling block to getting business done. What follows is a list of countries and certain rules of business etiquette in the different countries.[1]

Beijing, China
- If someone offers you his or her business card, accept with both hands, read it immediately, and then present your business card to the person.
- In business, men normally wear a suit and tie.

Berlin, Germany
- When out with German business associates, try not to talk about sports. Many businesspeople believe that sports talk is the domain of the uneducated.
- Drinking before all have raised their glasses together is considered impolite.

Dubai, United Arab Emirates
- Do not arrange appointments on Friday because it is Dubai's day of prayer and rest.

- Business slows down during the month of Ramadan (when Muslims fast). Foreign businesspeople are expected to observe the slower pace.

Hong Kong
- Running out of business cards is considered impolite.

Mexico City
- Having business cards printed in English on one side and in Spanish on the other is considered good form.
- Business clothing is fairly formal.

Sydney, Australia
- Knowing about the latest sports matches is important.
- Don't take yourself too seriously.

Tokyo, Japan
- Remove your shoes when entering a Japanese home.

Zurich, Switzerland
- People often greet each other when entering an office or shop. Try to do the same, even if your greeting is in your own language.
- Talking about money or personal wealth is frowned upon.

---

1. The reference guide is *The Economist*'s City Guide.

---

to globalization than another factor. Still, it is important that you are aware of the causal factors of globalization most often mentioned.

The End of the Cold War

The Cold War intensified after World War II and, most agree, ended with the visible fall of the Berlin Wall in 1989. This event, although historic in and of itself, occurred at the time when the Soviet empire was beginning to crumble, and many of the communist East European countries were breaking away from the Soviet Union. As some explain the event, the end of the Cold War resulted in turning two different worlds (the capitalist and communist worlds) into one. It resulted in a thawing of not only political but economic relations between former enemies. You might not trade with your enemy, but once that person or country is no longer your enemy, you don't feel the same need to exclude him or it from your political and economic life.

At the beginning of this section, we asked you to imagine a world where no barriers affected your trading with anyone in the world. The barriers might be distance, culture, politics, or anything else. The Cold War acted as a political barrier between certain groups of countries; once it ended, one barrier standing in the way of trade disappeared.

One way to view the current period of economic liberalization (freer markets, lower tariffs) and globalization is to ask whether it would be occurring as it is today if the United States and the Soviet Union were still engaged in the Cold War. This is doubtful. Even though the end of the Cold War might not be the full and only cause for the current period of globalization, if the Cold War had not ended, globalization would probably not be accelerating at the pace it is today.

Advancing Technology

In the past, innovations such as the internal combustion engine, steamship, telephone, and telegraph led to increased trade between people in different countries. All of these inventions led to lower transportation or communication costs, and lower costs mean fewer barriers to trade. What technology often does is lower the hindrances (of physical distance) that act as stumbling blocks to trade. For example, the cost of a 3-minute telephone call from New York to London in 1930 was $250. In 1960, it was $60.42; in 1980, it was $6.32; and in 2000, it was 40 cents. Today, the cost is even less. As the costs of communicating continue to fall, in some sense, the hindrance of physical distance (to trade) is overcome. Businesspeople in the United States, for example, can more cheaply talk with businesspeople in China.

Now consider the price of a computer over the years. The cost of a computer in 1960—one comparable to the desktop computer that many people today have on their desks at home—was $1.8 million. That computer was $199,983 in 1970, $27,938 in 1980, $7,275 in 1990, and only $1,000 in 2000. People today not only use computers for their work, but they communicate with others via the Internet. The personal computer and Internet technology make it possible for people to communicate with others over long distances, thus increasing the probability that they will trade with each other, such as on eBay or craigslist.

Today, even farmers in poor developing countries can have access to people and information that they didn't have access to only a few years ago. A farmer in the Ivory Coast can check agricultural prices in the world with a cell phone—something that was unheard of a decade ago. Or consider such innovations as online banking. Years ago, it was common to have your bank just down the road from you. Today, it is possible to open up an account with an online bank, many of which are located nowhere near you.

Policy Changes

Governments have the power to slow down the process of globalization if they want. Suppose two countries, A and B, have free economic relations with each other. Neither country imposes tariffs on the goods of the other. Neither country prevents its citizens from going to the other country to live and work. Neither country hampers its citizens from investing in the other country. Then, one day, for whatever reason, the government of country A decides to impose tariffs on the goods of country B and limit its citizens from traveling to and investing in country B. In other words, the government of country A decides to close its political and economic doors. Just as a government of one country can close the door on another, it can open the door too, and it can do so a little, more than a little, or a lot. In recent decades, governments of many countries have been opening their doors to other countries. China has opened its door, India has opened its door, and Russia has opened its door.

The driving forces of this most recent period of globalization have been (1) the end of the Cold War, (2) technological changes that lower the costs of transporting goods and communicating with people, and (3) government policy changes that express an openness toward freer markets and long-distance trade.

SELF-TEST

(Answers to Self-Test questions are in the Self-Test Appendix.)

1. Some have said that the end of the Cold War has led to greater globalization. Explain the reasoning.

2. What is globalization?

3. How might advancing technology lead to increased globalization?

BENEFITS AND COSTS OF GLOBALIZATION

Some people believe that globalization is, in general, a good thing and that its benefits outweigh its costs. Other people take the opposite view that the costs of globalization are greater than the benefits. Let's look at what those who favor globalization say are its benefits and what those who oppose it say are its costs. As you read, you will probably begin to form your own opinion.

The Benefits

TRADE To say that the world is undergoing globalization is really no more than saying that people are trading with more people, at greater distances, than they once did. They are trading different things: money for goods, their labor services for money, their savings for expected returns, and so on. Expanding trade—which is what globalization is about—is no more than extending the benefits of trading to people you might not have traded with earlier.

Economist David Friedman compared free international trade to a technology. He says that you can produce, say, cars in two ways. You can set up factories in Detroit, Michigan, and produce cars. Or you can harvest wheat in the Midwest, load it on ships and send it to Japan, and then wait for the ships to return with cars.

Looking at things the second way sometimes brings out the magic of trade. After all, with free trade across countries, wheat gets turned into cars, an accomplishment that really is magical. The lesson Friedman is trying to communicate is that we all think a technological improvement is a good thing because it often leads to a higher standard of living. So trading with people across the world really is nothing more than a technology of sorts; it is a way to turn wheat into cars. The more we trade with others, the more magic we witness.

INCOME PER PERSON Now let's consider the benefits of globalization in a slightly more concrete way. As both India and China opened up their economies to globalization in recent decades, they experienced increases in income per person. For example, between 1980 and 2000, income per person doubled in India. Between 1940 and 2000, income per person increased by 400 percent in China, much of this increase coming in recent years. According to the International Monetary Fund, these dramatic increases in income per person accompanied the expansion of free international trade (which is a key component of globalization).

PRICES Numerous studies have established a link between lower prices and the degree of international trade and globalization. Simply put, international trade (a key component of globalization) lowers prices. For example, Exhibit 2 shows the CPI (consumer price index) and an import price index for the period 1990–2004. The CPI (which contains domestic goods and imported goods) rose faster than the import price index (which contains only imported goods). Also, between 1977 and 2004, the inflation-adjusted prices for an array of goods traded between countries fell, while the inflation-adjusted prices for an array of goods not traded between countries actually increased. Some of the traded

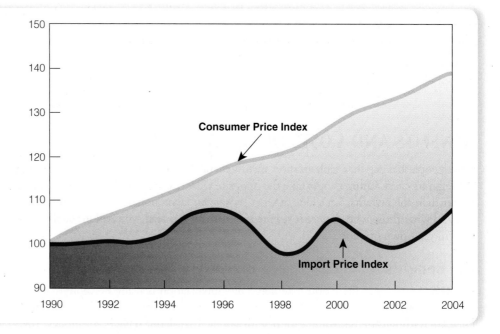

exhibit 2

CPI and Import Price Index, 1990–2004

The CPI increased at a faster rate during the period 1990–2004 than the import price index (which both increased and decreased during the period).

Source: Bureau of Labor Statistics.

goods whose prices fell include audio equipment (26 percent), TV sets (51 percent), toys (34 percent), and clothing (9 percent); some of the nontraded goods whose prices increased include whole milk (28 percent), butter (23 percent), ice cream (18 percent), and peanut butter (9 percent).

PRODUCTIVITY AND INNOVATION Firms that face global competition are often pushed to increase their productivity and to innovate more. According to the 2006 *Economic Report of the President,* "Studies show that firms exposed to the world's best practices demonstrate higher productivity through many channels, such as learning from these best practices, and also creating new products and processes in response to this exposure." For example, one study from the United Kingdom showed that almost 3 times as many firms that faced global competition reported product or process innovations than firms that did not face global competition.

Or consider the extreme case of North and South Korea. The two countries share a people and a culture, but North Korea avoided the process of globalization during the period in which South Korea embraced it. What we observe is that South Koreans enjoy a much higher standard of living than North Koreans.

The Costs

INCREASED INCOME INEQUALITY Globalization's critics often point out that globalization seems to go hand in hand with increased income inequality between rich and poor countries in the world. In fact, income inequality has increased. For example, 100 years ago, people in rich countries had about 10 times more income than people in poor countries. Today, they have about 75 times more income. Without a doubt, globalization and income inequality are strongly correlated. The question, though, is whether globalization causes the inequality. The critics of globalization say it does, whereas the supporters say it does not.

The supporters of globalization argue that it is much like a train. Economic systems that get on the train will benefit (and reach their economic destinies faster), but those that don't will get left increasingly farther behind. In other words, it may not be globalization that delivers greater income inequality but rather a combination of some countries globalizing while others are not. (If everyone is walking, some faster than others, then some will always be in front of others. If those who are walking fast start to run while the others continue their slow walking pace, the gap between the ones in front and the ones in back will grow.)

Of course, getting on the globalization train is not always a matter of choice. Sometimes, a conductor on the train doesn't let some people on. Some rich countries work against some poor countries when it comes to the poor countries' globalization efforts. For example, tariffs on goods imported from the poor, developing world are 30 percent above the global average for all tariffs.

LOSING AMERICAN JOBS Many critics of globalization argue that globalization can result in Americans losing certain jobs. Suppose a U.S. company hires engineers in India to do jobs once done by Americans. This practice of hiring people in other countries is often called **offshoring**.

Some Americans may lose their jobs to workers in other countries due to globalization. It has already happened. Over the past few years, a major New York securities firm replaced its team of 800 American software engineers, who earned about $150,000 per year, with an equally competent team in India earning an average of about $20,000 a year. Additionally, the number of radiologists in the United States is expected to fall significantly because it is now possible to send the data (that U.S. radiologists analyze) over the Internet to Asian radiologists, who can analyze the data at a fraction of the cost.

Keep in mind, though, that offshoring is a two-way street: The United States might offshore certain jobs to, say, India or China, but foreign countries around the world offshore jobs to the United States too. Although some Americans lose jobs due to globalization efforts, jobs are always being lost (and found) in a dynamic economy that is responding to market changes. Even if the degree of offshoring in the United States were zero, people would still be losing old jobs and getting new jobs every day.

Offshoring
Work done for a company by persons other than the original company's employees in a country other than the one in which the company is located.

MORE POWER TO BIG CORPORATIONS Many critics of globalization argue that the process will simply hand over the world (and especially the developing countries) to large Western corporations (headquartered in the United States, the United Kingdom, Canada, etc.). In fact, in the minds of many people, globalization is not defined as in this chapter, but rather as the process of *corporatizing* the world. Instead of governments deciding what will and will not be done, large corporations will assume the responsibility.

The proponents of globalization often point out a major difference between a corporation and a government. First, a government can force people to do certain things (such as pay taxes or join the military). No corporation can do the same; instead, corporations can simply produce goods that they hope customers will buy. Additionally, the proponents of globalization often argue that the critics overestimate the influence and reach of large transnational companies. For example, in 2000, the top 100 transnational companies produced only 4.3 percent of the entire world's output, which is about as much as what one country, the United Kingdom, produced in 2000.

Common MISCONCEPTIONS

About Offshoring

Some people talk as if globalization is only about offshoring. In other words, with globalization, jobs leave the United States for other countries. However, globalization involves not only offshoring, but *inshoring* too. As an example, a foreign country sets up an operation in the United States and employs Americans. By one estimate, in 2004, the United States had outsourced 10 million jobs, but it had insourced 6.5 million jobs.

economics 24/7

WILL GLOBALIZATION CHANGE THE SOUND OF MUSIC?

Suppose you had only 100 people to whom you could sell a good. Given this small number, you had better sell something that some of the 100 people want to buy. For example, if the 100 people don't like fruit salad, then you better not produce and offer to sell fruit salad; if some of them like bread, then perhaps you should produce and offer to sell bread.

Now increase the number of people from 100 to 1 million. A group of 1 million is much more likely than a group of 100 to contain people who like fruit salad. In other words, as the size of the potential customer base increases, the number of things you can sell increases too. In a world of 100 people, you can sell only bread, but in a world of 1 million people, you can sell fruit salad or bread.

The point is simple: The larger the size of the potential customer base (the more people you can possibly sell to), the greater the variety of goods is likely to be. Globalization is, to a large degree, expanding everyone's ability to potentially sell to more people. American companies aren't limited to selling only to Americans; they can sell to others in the world too. Chinese firms aren't limited to selling only to Chinese; they can sell to others in the world too.

As a musician, you can play different styles of music: jazz, pop, classical, hard rock, metal, hip-hop, and so on. If you are limited to selling your music to the people of a single state of the United States, you can offer to sell fewer styles of music than if you could sell your music to the people who reside throughout the United States.

More specifically, consider the musician in the United States who is experimenting with a new style of music. With a population (305 million) of only the United States as a potential customer base, the musician might not yet have enough actual customers to make it worth producing and offering to sell this particular, unique, and narrowly defined music. However, if the musician can draw on the population of the world (6.6 billion), then she might be able to find enough people who are willing to buy her new type of music.

As we move toward a world economy, we see a greater variety within almost every category of goods: a greater variety of music to listen to, books to read, types of television shows to watch, and so on. Today, the greater variety of goods you see in your world is an effect of globalization.

THE CONTINUING GLOBALIZATION DEBATE

Many (but certainly not all) economists argue that the worldwide benefits of globalization are likely to be greater than the worldwide costs. Of course, not everyone is going to see the beneficial side of globalization. To a large degree, whether people support or criticize globalization seems to depend on where they are sitting. Globalization doesn't affect everyone in the same way, and often *how* it affects *you* determines how you feel about it. For example, suppose Sanders, an American worker residing in New York, loses his job to an Indian worker in New Delhi, India, who will do Sanders' job for less pay. In this case, Sanders incurs real costs, but for Sanders' company, the change means lower costs and higher profits. For the company's customers, the change might mean lower prices. So in this case, Sanders is probably a strong opponent of offshoring, but his company and its customers are probably supporters.

Seeing the benefits of globalization is often much more difficult than seeing its costs. For example, the supporters of globalization argue that it brings greater economic wealth, lower prices (than would otherwise exist), more innovation, less poverty, and so on. Yet seeing all these benefits is sometimes difficult. When you buy cheaper goods or different goods because of globalization, you probably never say, "Wow, I can't believe all the benefits I get from globalization!" In fact, you might not even connect the lower-priced goods with globalization at all. The benefits of globalization tend to be difficult to perceive, partly because they are so widely dispersed.

The costs of globalization, in contrast, are more visible, often because they are so concentrated. A person who loses a job because of freer international trade in the world knows exactly what is to blame for his predicament. He surely could receive some benefits from globalization (in the role of a consumer), but he also could, for a time, incur some rather high costs (in the role of an unemployed worker). This person is likely to know of the costs but be unaware of the benefits.

In the end, the people who receive only benefits from globalization might not be able to see the benefits or to connect them with globalization. The people who receive benefits and costs from globalization may be aware only of the costs. This one-sided view could create strong antiglobalization sentiment in a country.

MORE OR LESS GLOBALIZATION: A TUG OF WAR?

Is increased globalization inevitable? Will the day come when all countries in the world are similar to the 50 states in the United States—part of one global economy with easy movement of people, resources, financial capital, goods, and services among the countries? Or will the conditions that prevented globalization reappear and reverse the recent trend?

Think of this struggle as a tug of war. The forces of globalization pull in one direction, and the forces of antiglobalization pull in the other. As of today, the forces of globalization are moving things in their direction. The trend may not continue uninterrupted. Surely, at any time, the forces of antiglobalization could put on a burst of energy and make an extra strong tug on the rope.

To help answer the question about the future of globalization, recall what we said about the driving forces of the most recent era of globalization: the end of the Cold War, changes in technology (which lowered the costs of transportation and communication), and policy changes that opened up countries' economies to each other.

Less Globalization

INCREASED POLITICAL TENSION The end of the Cold War is a historical fact that we cannot undo, but we could enter a period when political tensions among countries or among groups of countries emerge. We are not suggesting that such a period of tension will happen, only that it could. If it did, it could slow down globalization or, depending on the severity of the tension, even reverse it.

Terrorism Another inhibiting factor to globalization is global terrorism. Global terrorism tends to motivate certain countries into closing borders and into being much more careful about the people and goods crossing their borders.

Technology We cannot undo our technology. We cannot go from a world with the Internet to one without it. So it is unlikely that anything on the technological front will slow down or reverse globalization.

Government Policies Policy changes can slow down or reverse globalization. Governments of countries that opened up their economies to others could reverse their course; doors that opened to others can be closed. We cannot say whether this sort of isolationism will happen in the future.

More Globalization

Some still argue that, even with the forces of antiglobalization looming on the horizon, the forces of globalization are stronger. In the end, these individuals say, the forces of globalization will win the tug of war. They believe that in the long run, economics influences politics, not the other way around. As some proof of that assertion, they often point to the former Soviet Union and to China. Both were strongly communist countries. Both countries saw, in the end, that they were worse off by holding themselves outside the orbit of free market forces. You might say that they found themselves out of step with the economic forces that were loudly playing on the world stage.

Many economists argue that globalization is not just a passing trend. They argue that the basic globalization force that will probably not be overcome—no matter how strong the political forces may be against it—is the human inclination that the founder of modern economics, Adam Smith, noticed more than 200 years ago. Smith said that human beings want to trade with each other. In fact, the desire to trade separates us from all other species, he says. In his words, "Man is an animal that makes bargains: no other animal does this—no dog exchanges bones with another."

We want to trade with people: our next-door neighbor, the person down the street, the person on the other side of town, the person in the next state, the person on the other side of the country, and ultimately the person on the other side of the world. Some economists go on to suggest that our trading inclination is a good thing in that, when we trade with people, we not only tolerate them but we have much less reason to fight with them. Robert Wright, a visiting scholar at the University of Pennsylvania, argues that it is not a coincidence that religious toleration is high in the United States, a country that is open to trade and globalization. We often see, he argues, that people who live in countries that trade with other people—people who live in countries that are open to other people—are people who tolerate others.

In a similar vein, Thomas Friedman advanced his "Golden Arches theory of conflict prevention," which says that "no two countries that both had McDonald's had fought a war against each other since each got its McDonald's." The United States will not fight Germany because both countries have McDonald's. France won't fight Mexico because both countries have McDonald's. Certainly, it is not the sheer presence of a McDonald's that prevents people from fighting with other people. McDonald's is symbolic of certain things being present in the country. For Friedman, the franchise is a symbol for a certain degree of economic globalization and a level of economic development sufficient enough to support a large middle class.

SELF-TEST

1. Identify some of the benefits of globalization.
2. Identify some of the costs of globalization.

INTERNATIONAL FACTORS AND AGGREGATE DEMAND

In a world that is undergoing globalization, what happens in one country can affect events in another country. Simply put, changes in other countries can influence the U.S. economy. In this first section we discuss two international factors that can affect the U.S. economy by first affecting U.S. aggregate demand: net exports and the J-curve.

Net Exports

In an earlier chapter, net exports are defined as the difference between exports (*EX*) and imports (*IM*). For example, if exports are $80 billion and imports are $60 billion, then net exports are $20 billion. Also, recall that if net exports rise, the *AD* curve shifts to the right; if net exports fall, the *AD* curve shifts to the left.

Now we discuss two factors that can change net exports: (1) foreign Real GDP and (2) the exchange rate. To simplify matters, we assume there are only two countries in the world: the United States and Japan. With respect to these two countries, let's consider the two factors.

FOREIGN REAL GDP (OR FOREIGN REAL NATIONAL INCOME) As Japan's Real GDP (or real national income) rises, the Japanese buy more U.S. goods; so U.S. exports rise. As a result, U.S. net exports rise, and the *AD* curve shifts to the right. As Japan's Real GDP falls, the Japanese buy fewer U.S. goods; so U.S. exports fall. As a result, U.S. net exports fall, and the *AD* curve shifts to the left.

This is how economic expansions and contractions in other countries are felt in the United States. Given a contraction in Japan, with a lower Real GDP in Japan, the Japanese buy fewer U.S. goods. U.S. exports fall, and so do net exports. As a result, the *AD* curve in the United States shifts to the left. Because the *AD* curve shifts to the left, Real GDP in the United States falls.

EXCHANGE RATE Recall that the exchange rate is the price of one country's currency in terms of another country's currency. If a country's currency *appreciates*, it takes less of that country's currency to buy the other currency. On the other hand, if a country's currency *depreciates*, it takes more of that country's country to buy the other currency.

Appreciation and depreciation affect the prices of a country's goods. If, say, the U.S. dollar depreciates relative to the Japanese yen, U.S. residents have to pay more dollars to buy Japanese goods. To illustrate, suppose the dollar price of a yen is $0.012 and that a Toyota is priced at ¥2 million. At this exchange rate, a U.S. resident pays $24,000 for a Toyota ($0.012 × ¥20 million = $24,000). If the dollar depreciates to $0.018 for ¥1, then the U.S. resident will have to pay $36,000 for a Toyota.

As the dollar depreciates, Japanese goods become more expensive for U.S. residents; so they buy fewer Japanese goods. Thus, U.S. imports decline.[2] The other side of the coin is that, as the dollar depreciates relative to the yen, the yen appreciates relative to the dollar. Thus U.S. goods become less expensive for the Japanese, and they buy more U.S. goods; so U.S. exports rise.

In summary, a depreciation in the dollar and an appreciation in the yen will raise U.S. exports, lower U.S. imports, and therefore raise U.S. net exports. This shifts the U.S. *AD* curve to the right, leading to a rise in the U.S. Real GDP level.

The series of events are symmetrical if the U.S. dollar appreciates relative to the Japanese yen. In this case, U.S. goods become more expensive for the Japanese, causing them to buy fewer U.S. goods; so U.S. exports fall. And Japanese goods become cheaper for U.S. residents, causing them to buy more Japanese goods; so U.S. imports rise. A decline in U.S. exports, along with a rise in U.S. imports, will cause U.S. net exports to fall. The U.S. *AD* curve shifts to the left, leading to a decline in U.S. Real GDP.

For a quick review of the international factors that can shift the U.S. *AD* curve, see Exhibit 3.

The J-Curve

So far, we have assumed that if the dollar depreciates relative to the Japanese yen, U.S. residents and the Japanese will buy more U.S. goods and fewer Japanese goods. Thus, U.S. exports rise, U.S. imports fall, and therefore U.S. net exports rise.

---

2. Throughout this chapter, unless otherwise explicitly stated, we assume that if the physical quantity of exports rises (falls), the total spending on exports rises (falls). Also, if the physical quantity of imports rises (falls), the total spending on imports rises (falls). Because of this assumption, it is not necessary to differentiate constantly between the physical quantity of imports and the total spending on imports. Given our assumption, they go up and down together. One place we explicitly drop this assumption is in the discussion of the J-curve.

HOW HARD WILL IT BE TO GET INTO HARVARD IN 2025?

The Indian Institute of Technology (in India) is one of the hardest universities in the world to be admitted to, largely because of its reputation. It has been compared to putting Harvard, MIT (Massachusetts Institute of Technology), and Princeton together.

In an average year, about 178,000 high school seniors in India take the exam necessary to apply to the Indian Institute of Technology. Just over 3,500 students (only 1.96 percent of all applicants) are admitted. In comparison, the admission rate of Harvard University is nearly 10 percent. Often, students from India who are admitted to MIT, Princeton, and Cal Tech (all of which are listed in the top 10 of U.S. colleges and universities) cannot gain admission to the Indian Institute of Technology.

Other highly prestigious U.S. universities and colleges—such as Brown, Columbia, Cornell, Dartmouth, Harvard, the University of Pennsylvania, Princeton, Yale, Stanford, Northwestern, and Duke—have some of the most selective admission criteria of all colleges and universities in the country. Each year, students who have the grade point average and standardized test scores to be considered for admission are turned away.

This phenomenon has been occurring at the same time that college tuition in this country has been increasing rapidly. For example, during the period 1990–2003, college tuition went up by 130 percent, considerably more than medical care costs, the price of housing, food, gasoline, cars, and so on.

If we look around the world at other prestigious institutions of higher learning, we see the same theme: The admission rate is usually low, and the cost is usually high.

Consider how grades (one major criterion) and money actually function in admissions: They are rationing devices. We know that because of scarcity, some mechanism has to ration the available resources, goods, and

© INDEX STOCK IMAGERY/JUPITER IMAGES

services. Still we have to ask why these two rationing devices—grades and money—have become stiffer when it comes to being admitted to the top universities in the world. Why must grades be ever higher and ever more money required?

The answer is twofold. First, the population of the world increased while the number of Harvards did not. Harvard cannot clone itself; nor can Yale, the Indian Institute of Technology, or MIT. To a large degree, the world has only one Harvard, Oxford (in the United Kingdom), and Indian Institute of Technology. We can produce more computers, houses, and dining room chairs as the population of the world increases, but producing more Harvards seems to be much more difficult. So, over time, top-notch, one-of-a-kind educational institutions become scarce. As a result, the rationing devices for such institutions must do more work to ration, and it will become harder and more expensive to get admitted to such places.

The second reason involves globalization. One of things that pays a high dividend in a global economy is education. Brains seem to matter more than brawn, increasing the overall demand for a college education—not just at Harvard but at all levels of higher education (from community colleges to four-year state and private universities). So, will the premium placed on education in a global economy cause the demand at the most prestigious educational establishments to rise at a faster rate than at other colleges? That question is like asking, if the premium for playing music were to rise, would the demand to be at Juilliard (one of the premier music institutions in the world) rise faster than the demand to study with the local piano teacher down the street? The likely answer is yes. With a growing world population, and with the global economy paying a high premium to those who are educated (compared to those who are not), we can expect it to get increasingly difficult and more expensive to be admitted to the world's best institutions of higher learning.

But this scenario may not happen initially. There may be a difference between what *initially* happens and what *ultimately* happens. To illustrate, suppose U.S. residents are currently buying 100,000 cars from the Japanese, the average Japanese car sells for ¥2 million, and the exchange rate is currently $0.012 per yen. This means U.S. residents are

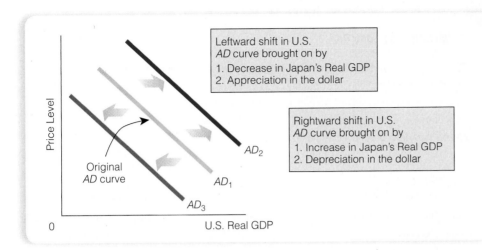

exhibit 3

International Impacts on the U.S. AD Curve

Anything that increases U.S. net exports shifts the U.S. AD curve to the right. This includes an increase in Japan's Real GDP (in a two-country world, where the two countries are Japan and the United States) and a depreciation in the dollar. Anything that decreases U.S. net exports shifts the U.S. AD curve to the left. This includes a decrease in Japan's Real GDP and an appreciation in the dollar.

exhibit 4

The J-Curve

The United States starts with net exports of –$40 billion. As the dollar depreciates, net exports increase to –$60 bil-lion. With time, net exports become $0. If we follow the course of net exports, we map out a J. This is called the J-curve.

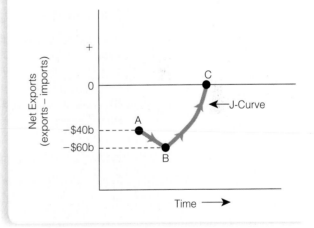

spending an average of $24,000 a car for 100,000 cars. Thus, a total of $2.4 billion is spent on imported Japanese cars.

Now suppose the exchange rate changes, and the dollar depreciates to $0.018 per yen, causing the average price of a Japanese car to be $36,000. At this higher price, U.S. residents buy fewer Japanese cars, but they don't buy that many fewer initially. Instead of buying 100,000 cars, they initially buy 90,000 cars. Now a total of $3.24 billion is spent on imported Japanese cars. Instead of declining after a depreciation in the dollar, U.S. spending on imports has initially risen. If we assume U.S. exports have not changed yet, a rise in U.S. imports will lead to a fall in U.S. net exports and cause the U.S. AD curve to shift to the left.

But this situation is not likely to last. In time, U.S. residents will switch from the higher-priced Japanese goods to lower-priced U.S. goods. For example, in time, U.S. residents purchase only 60,000 Japanese cars. At this number, with the exchange rate of $0.018 per yen, U.S. spending on imported Japanese cars is $2.16 billion. In time, too, U.S. exports will rise, and the combination of rising exports and falling imports will lead to an increase in net exports. The U.S. AD curve will shift to the right.

This phenomenon in which import spending initially rises after a depreciation and then later falls is summarized in the **J-curve**, so-called because a curve showing the change in net exports due to a currency depreciation has the shape of a J. In Exhibit 4, the United States initially has negative net exports of –$40 billion (its imports of $130 billion are greater than its exports of $90 billion). This position is represented by point A in the exhibit.

Next, the dollar depreciates relative to the yen. Total spending on imports rises to, say, $150 billion; so net exports rise to –$60 billion. This is represented by point B. In time, though, exports rise to, say, $100 billion and imports fall to, say, $100 billion, making net exports equal to zero. This is represented by point C.

If we start at point A and draw a line to point B and then to point C, we have a J-curve. This is the route that net exports may take after a depreciation in a country's currency.

J-Curve

The curve that shows a short-run worsening in net exports after a currency depreciation, followed by an improvement.

Thinking like AN ECONOMIST

Short Run and Long Run

The discussion of the J-curve points out that economists sometimes think in terms of both the short run and the long run. Does the depreciation of a country's currency lead to an increase or a decrease in import spending? According to the J-curve theory, the answer is that both an increase and a decrease result. Imports increase initially, but in the long run they decrease. An economist's answers may differ depending on the time horizon under consideration.

SELF-TEST

1. Explain how an economic boom in one country can be felt in another country.
2. Predict and explain what will happen to U.S. Real GDP if the dollar appreciates relative to the Japanese yen.

INTERNATIONAL FACTORS AND AGGREGATE SUPPLY

Just as international factors can affect the demand side of the U.S. economy, certain international factors can affect the supply side. This section discusses a few international factors that can shift the U.S. aggregate supply curve.

Foreign Input Prices

In an earlier chapter, we stated that a change in the price of inputs will shift the short-run aggregate supply (*SRAS*) curve. For example, if the price of labor (wage rate) rises, the *SRAS* curve shifts leftward.

American producers buy inputs not only from other Americans but also from foreigners. A rise in the price of foreign inputs leads to a leftward shift in the U.S. *SRAS* curve. A fall in the price of foreign inputs leads to a rightward shift in the U.S. *SRAS* curve.

Why Foreign Input Prices Change

Supply and demand in the input market in the foreign country could change, possibly causing a rise in the price of foreign inputs. For example, suppose U.S. producers buy input X from Japan. The supply of X in Japan could fall, or the demand for X in Japan could rise. Either or both changes would increase the price of X for U.S. producers.

THE EXCHANGE RATE A change in the exchange rate between the dollar and the yen could change the price for a foreign input. For example, a depreciation in the dollar relative to the yen would make input X more expensive for U.S. producers. An appreciation in the dollar would make input X less expensive for U.S. producers. Exhibit 5 presents a summary of the points in this section.

FACTORS THAT AFFECT BOTH AGGREGATE DEMAND AND AGGREGATE SUPPLY

Changes in some international factors can affect both aggregate demand and short-run aggregate supply in the United States. Two of these factors are the exchange rate and relative interest rates.

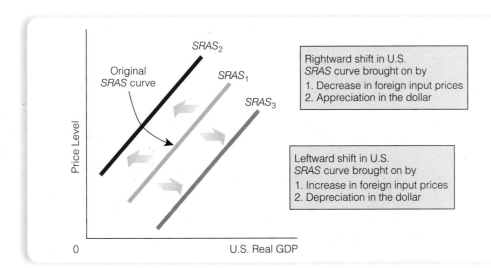

exhibit 5

International Impacts on the U.S. *SRAS* Curve

The U.S. *SRAS* curve shifts if foreign input prices change. If foreign input prices rise, the U.S. *SRAS* curve shifts leftward; if foreign input prices fall, the *SRAS* curve shifts rightward. Similarly, if the dollar depreciates, foreign inputs become more expensive and the *SRAS* curve shifts leftward. If the dollar appreciates, foreign inputs become cheaper and the *SRAS* curve shifts rightward.

The Exchange Rate

As discussed, changes in exchange rates affect both the *AD* and *SRAS* curves. The overall, or net, effect on Real GDP depends on how much the *AD* curve shifts relative to the shift in the *SRAS* curve. We consider two cases: dollar depreciation and dollar appreciation.

DOLLAR DEPRECIATION As the dollar depreciates, the *AD* curve shifts rightward and the *SRAS* curve leftward. If the *AD* curve shifts rightward by more than the *SRAS* curve shifts leftward, Real GDP rises [see Exhibit 6(a)]. If the *AD* curve shifts rightward by less than the SRAS curve shifts leftward, Real GDP falls [see Exhibit 6(b)]. If the *AD* curve shifts rightward by the same amount that the *SRAS* curve shifts leftward, Real GDP does not change [see Exhibit 6(c)]. In each of these three cases, the price level rises. In summary, dollar depreciation raises the price level and may accompany an increasing, decreasing, or constant Real GDP.

DOLLAR APPRECIATION As the dollar appreciates, the *AD* curve shifts leftward and the *SRAS* curve rightward. Once again, what happens to Real GDP depends on the relative shifts of the two curves. If the *AD* curve shifts leftward by more than the *SRAS* curve shifts rightward, Real GDP falls. If the *AD* curve shifts leftward by less than the *SRAS* curve shifts rightward, Real GDP rises. If the *AD* curve shifts leftward by the same amount that the *SRAS* curve shifts rightward, Real GDP does not change. In each case, though, the price level falls. In summary, dollar appreciation lowers the price level and may accompany an increasing, decreasing, or constant Real GDP.

The Role That Interest Rates Play

In a two-country world with only the United States and Japan, real interest rates rise in the United States and remain constant in Japan. The higher real interest rates in the United States will attract foreign capital (in search of the highest return possible). Because foreigners will be interested in dollar-denominated assets that pay interest, they will have to exchange their country's currency for U.S. dollars. This will increase the demand for U.S. dollars and lead to an appreciation in the dollar.

Then, if the dollar appreciates, we know that both the U.S. *AD* and *SRAS* curves are affected. The *AD* curve shifts leftward and the *SRAS* curve shifts rightward. As explained earlier, the effect on Real GDP depends on the relative shifts in the two curves. Many

exhibit 6

Depreciation in the Dollar: Effects on the Price Level and Real GDP

A change in exchange rates affects both aggregate demand and short-run aggregate supply. If the dollar depreciates,

the *AD* curve shifts rightward and the *SRAS* curve shifts leftward. The overall impact on Real GDP—up, down, or unchanged—depends on whether the *AD* curve shifts rightward by (a) more,

(b) less, or (c) an amount equal to the leftward shift in the *SRAS* curve. In all three cases, dollar depreciation leads to a higher price level.

(a)

(b)

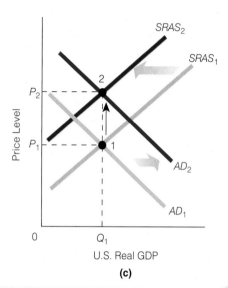

(c)

economists argue, however, that given the interest rate differential, the *AD* curve typically tends to shift leftward by more than the *SRAS* curve shifts rightward, and thus Real GDP falls [see Exhibit 7(a)]. In summary, typically, a rise in real interest rates in the United States relative to foreign interest rates tends to decrease U.S. Real GDP.

Now suppose real interest rates fall in the United States relative to interest rates in Japan. The higher real interest rate in Japan attracts capital to Japan. The demand for yen rises, and as a result the yen appreciates and the dollar depreciates. A depreciated dollar shifts the U.S. *AD* curve rightward and the *SRAS* curve leftward [see Exhibit 7(b)]. Many economists argue that given the interest rate differential discussed here, the *AD* curve typically tends to shift rightward by more than the *SRAS* curve shifts leftward, and thus Real GDP rises. In summary, typically a fall in real interest rates in the United States relative to foreign interest rates tends to increase U.S. Real GDP.

SELF-TEST

1. How do foreign input prices affect the U.S. *SRAS* curve?

2. What is the effect on the U.S. price level of lower real interest rates in Japan than in the United States? Explain your answer.

DEFICITS: INTERNATIONAL EFFECTS AND DOMESTIC FEEDBACK

Deficits in the United States—both budget and trade deficits—affect the U.S. economy. Earlier chapters explored how the budget deficit can directly affect the U.S. economy. However, the budget deficit can also have international effects, and these international effects can have domestic feedback that also affects the U.S. economy. This section looks

exhibit 7

International Interest Rates, Exchange Rates, and Real GDP

(a) If the U.S. real interest rate is higher than the Japanese real interest rate, capital will flow from Japan to the United States. In the process, the demand for the dollar rises, and the dollar appreciates. Dollar appreciation causes the *AD* curve to shift leftward by more than the *SRAS* curve shifts rightward, which is typical given the initial event. As a result, U.S. Real GDP falls.

(b) If the U.S. real interest rate is lower than the Japanese real interest rate, capital will flow from the United States to Japan. In the process, the demand for yen rises, the supply of dollars rises, and the yen appreciates and the dollar depreciates. Dollar depreciation causes the *AD* curve to shift rightward and the *SRAS* curve to shift leftward. We have drawn the *AD* curve shifting rightward by more than the *SRAS* curve shifts leftward, which is typical given the initial event. As a result, U.S. Real GDP rises.

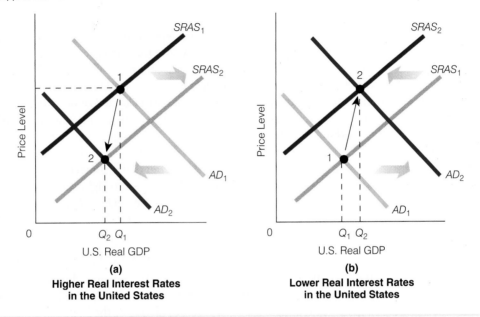

(a) **Higher Real Interest Rates in the United States**

(b) **Lower Real Interest Rates in the United States**

at the possibilities of international feedback effects and the relationship between the budget deficit and the trade deficit.

The Budget Deficit and Expansionary Fiscal Policy

Suppose North Dakotans want their elected representatives in Congress to push for a particular spending program that will assist them and no one else—and their elected representatives oblige them. Congress passes the spending program but does not raise the taxes necessary to pay for it. This domestic action can affect the international economic scene, and here is a scenario to show how.

Even with a budget deficit, Congress passes the spending program to help North Dakotans but neither raises taxes to finance the program nor cuts any other spending programs on the books. As a result of these actions—one more spending program, no fewer spending programs, and no more taxes—the budget deficit grows. To finance the growing budget deficit, the U.S. Treasury borrows more funds in the credit (or loanable funds) market than it would have borrowed if the latest spending program had not been passed. The increased demand for credit raises the real interest rate. The higher U.S. interest rate attracts foreign capital. The demand for dollars in the foreign exchange market rises, and the dollar appreciates.

As this happens, the U.S. *AD* curve shifts leftward, and the *SRAS* curve shifts rightward. The *AD* curve shifts leftward by more than the *SRAS* curve shifts rightward, putting downward pressure on Real GDP.

But Real GDP might not *actually* decrease. We have discussed only how a rising budget deficit affects the exchange rate (via the interest rate) and feeds back in the domestic economy. The direct effect of the rising budget deficit on the domestic economy also needs to be considered. Under certain conditions (e.g., zero crowding out), expansionary fiscal policy can raise aggregate demand and is effective at raising Real GDP. So:

1. The rising budget deficit affects the domestic economy directly and pushes *Real GDP upward.*

2. But increased deficit financing raises U.S. interest rates and prompts increased foreign capital inflows, an increased demand for dollars, and dollar appreciation. Under typical conditions, an appreciated dollar feeds back into the domestic economy and pushes *Real GDP downward.*

Obviously, what happens *on net* depends on how strong the international feedback effects are on the domestic economy. Are they strong enough to offset the initial expansionary push (upward) in Real GDP? Even if not, and Real GDP rises on net, we can still conclude that expansionary fiscal policy raises Real GDP more in a **closed economy** than in an **open economy**. The reason is that, in a closed economy, the international feedback effects that reduce Real GDP are absent (see the second point in the preceding list).

Exhibit 8(a) illustrates the point. With zero crowding out, expansionary fiscal policy shifts the aggregate demand curve from AD_1 to AD_2. But because of the higher interest rates, increased foreign capital inflows, and dollar appreciation, the AD curve shifts leftward from AD_2 to AD_3, and the $SRAS$ curve shifts rightward from $SRAS_1$ to $SRAS_2$.

In a closed economy, Real GDP rises from Q_1 to Q_2. In an open economy, where international feedback effects play a role, Real GDP ends up at a lower level, Q_3.

The Budget Deficit and Contractionary Fiscal Policy

If expansionary fiscal policy raises Real GDP more in a closed economy than in an open economy, what are the effects of contractionary fiscal policy in a closed or open economy? Suppose reduced government spending decreases the budget deficit. With a diminished budget deficit, the U.S. Treasury borrows fewer funds in the credit market than it would have borrowed if government spending had not been reduced. The decreased demand for loanable funds lowers the real interest rate (relative to foreign interest rates), making foreign assets seem more desirable. The demand for foreign currencies increases, and the dollar depreciates in value.

As this happens, the U.S. AD curve shifts to the right, and the $SRAS$ curve shifts to the left. The AD curve shifts rightward by more than the $SRAS$ curve shifts leftward, putting upward pressure on Real GDP. However, Real GDP might not *actually* increase because we haven't yet considered the effect of the lower budget deficit (due to the reduction in government spending) on the domestic economy. Under certain conditions, a cut in government spending reduces aggregate demand and therefore reduces Real GDP. So:

1. The cut in government spending reduces the budget deficit and affects the domestic economy directly, pushing *Real GDP downward.*

2. But reduced deficit financing lowers U.S. interest rates and prompts increased capital outflows, increased demand for foreign currencies, and dollar depreciation. Under typical conditions, a depreciated dollar feeds back into the domestic economy and pushes *Real GDP upward.*

What happens *on net* depends on whether the international feedback effects on the domestic economy are strong enough to offset the initial contractionary push in Real GDP.

Even if the international feedback effects on the domestic economy do not outweigh the initial contractionary push (downward) in Real GDP, and Real GDP falls on net, we can still conclude that contractionary fiscal policy lowers Real GDP more in a closed economy than in an open economy.

Closed Economy
An economy that does not trade goods and services with other countries.

Open Economy
An economy that trades goods and services with other countries.

exhibit 8

Expansionary and Contractionary Fiscal Policy in Open and Closed Economies

(a) The consequences of expansionary fiscal policy for both open and closed economies. Congress passes a spending program without raising taxes, and the AD curve shifts from AD_1 to AD_2. To finance the growing budget deficit, the Treasury borrows more funds in the loanable funds market, and the interest rate rises. The higher interest rate attracts foreign capital and causes the dollar to appreciate. As the dollar appreciates, the AD curve shifts from AD_2 to AD_3, and the SRAS curve shifts from $SRAS_1$ to $SRAS_2$. Real GDP goes from Q_1 to Q_2 in a closed economy, and from Q_1 to Q_3 in an open economy. Expansionary fiscal policy raises Real GDP more in a closed economy than in an open economy. (b) Contractionary fiscal policy lowers Real GDP more in a closed economy than in an open economy.

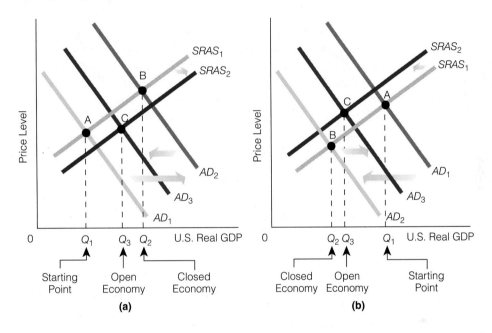

(a)   (b)

Exhibit 8(b) illustrates our point. The cut in government spending shifts the AD curve from AD_1 to AD_2. But because of the lower interest rates, increased capital outflows, and dollar depreciation, the AD curve shifts rightward from AD_2 to AD_3, and the SRAS curve shifts leftward from $SRAS_1$ to $SRAS_2$.

In a closed economy, Real GDP falls from Q_1 to Q_2. In an open economy, where international feedback effects play a role, Real GDP ends up at a higher level, Q_3.

The Effects of Monetary Policy

Monetary policy certainly affects international economic factors that feed back to the United States. Here we consider both expansionary and contractionary monetary policy.

EXPANSIONARY MONETARY POLICY Suppose the Federal Reserve increases the money supply. In Exhibit 9(a), the increase causes the AD curve to shift rightward from AD_1 to AD_2 and Real GDP to rise from Q_1 to Q_2.

An increase in the money supply also has international effects. Expansionary monetary policy causes interest rates to fall in the short run (the liquidity effect), leading to an outflow of capital from the United States. Americans begin to supply more dollars on the foreign exchange market so that they can purchase foreign assets. As the supply of dollars rises, the dollar depreciates.

Dollar depreciation affects both U.S. aggregate demand and U.S. short-run aggregate supply. As noted, it shifts the AD curve to the right and the SRAS curve to the left. In

exhibit 9

Expansionary and Contractionary Monetary Policy in Open and Closed Economies

(a) The consequences of expansionary monetary policy for both open and closed economies. The Fed increases the money supply, and the AD curve shifts from AD_1 to AD_2. Real GDP rises from Q_1 to Q_2. The increased money supply leads to lower interest rates in the short run, promoting U.S. capital outflow and a depreciated dollar, which raises U.S. exports, lowers U.S. imports, and raises U.S. net exports. Higher net exports shift the AD curve rightward from AD_2 to AD_3. The depreciated dollar shifts the $SRAS$ curve leftward from $SRAS_1$ to $SRAS_2$. Real GDP ends up at Q_3. Expansionary monetary policy raises Real GDP more in an open economy than in a closed economy. (b) Contractionary monetary policy lowers Real GDP more in an open economy than in a closed economy.

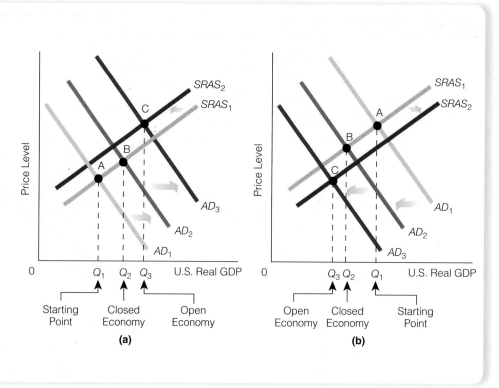

(a)

(b)

Exhibit 9(a), the AD curve shifts to the right (from AD_2 to AD_3) and the $SRAS$ curve shifts to the left (from $SRAS_1$ to $SRAS_2$). Consequently, Real GDP rises from Q_2 to Q_3.

Therefore, expansionary monetary policy raises Real GDP more in an open economy than in a closed economy.

CONTRACTIONARY MONETARY POLICY If the Federal Reserve contracts the money supply, in the AD-AS framework, the AD curve shifts leftward from AD_1 to AD_2, and Real GDP falls from Q_1 to Q_2 [see Exhibit 9(b)].

There are also international effects of a decrease in the money supply. Contractionary monetary policy causes interest rates to rise, leading to an inflow of foreign capital into the United States. The demand for dollars rises on the foreign exchange market, and the dollar appreciates. Dollar appreciation affects both U.S. aggregate demand and U.S. short-run aggregate supply. As we know, dollar appreciation shifts the AD curve to the left and the $SRAS$ curve to the right. In Exhibit 9(b), the AD curve shifts from AD_2 to AD_3, and the $SRAS$ curve shifts from $SRAS_1$ to $SRAS_2$. Consequently, Real GDP falls from Q_2 to Q_3.

Therefore, contractionary monetary policy lowers Real GDP more in an open economy than in a closed economy.

SELF-TEST

1. Explain how expansionary monetary policy works in an open economy.

2. Explain how expansionary fiscal policy works in an open economy.

"WHY DO SOME PEOPLE FAVOR GLOBALIZATION AND OTHERS DO NOT?"

Student:

One of the things I have noticed about globalization is that some people in the United States seem to be in favor of it and others seem to be against it. Why is this?

Instructor:

It probably has much to do with how the benefits and costs of globalization are distributed across the population. People in one location might receive mainly the benefits, and people in some other location might incur mostly the costs.

Student:

Do any real world examples illustrate your point?

Instructor:

A while back *The New York Times* reported about two cities in Michigan: Holland and Greenville.[3] In Holland, a factory was losing business and firing workers. Then a German company bought it. Today the factory is shipping wastewater treatment equipment to countries in the Middle East and in Asia. Also, it is operating with twice as many workers as it did before the German company bought it. The people in Holland, Michigan, see this as a benefit of globalization.

But only 60 miles away from Holland, in Greenville, Michigan, the story is different. In Greenville, a Swedish company shut down what had been the largest refrigerator factory in the country and eliminated about 2,700 jobs in the town. For the people of Greenville, globalization seemed to come with costs.

Student:

What do most economists say about globalization? Do think that for the country as a whole globalization comes with net benefits (more benefits than costs) or net costs (more costs than benefits)?

Instructor:

Most economists seem to think that globalization comes with net benefits.

Student:

But economic policy isn't always determined by what economists think, is it?

Instructor:

You're right about that. Economic policy does not get made in a political vacuum. Politics plays a role in deciding which economic policies get adopted and implemented. Think about this in terms of our Michigan cities example. Suppose we went to Greenville, where jobs had been lost, and tell the residents of the city that globalization, on net, is good for the country. Suppose we said that, for the country as a whole, there are more benefits from globalization than costs. What would the residents of Greenville say? They might say that is all well and good, but globalization hasn't been that good to them and that is what matters. As a result, their vote, to the extent that they have one on the issue, is *against* globalization.

Student:

I see. In other words, sometimes what might be beneficial for the country (as a whole) is not beneficial for some part of the country.

Instructor:

That is the way some things turn out.

Points to Remember

1. Globalization can come with net benefits for a country, but not everyone in the country necessarily benefits from globalization.

2. The benefits and costs of globalization are not evenly spread throughout a country. The benefits may fall on some people and the costs on others.

3. See Peter S. Goodman, "2 Outcomes when Foreigners Buy Factories," *New York Times*, April 7, 2008.

a reader asks | Will My Job Be Sent Overseas?

One hears much these days about outsourcing or offshoring jobs. Are some jobs more likely to be sent overseas than others?

When it comes to some jobs, location matters. With others, location doesn't seem to matter. First, let's look at some jobs where location matters.

If you are sick and need a doctor, you prefer to have a doctor close to you. If you live in Ithaca, New York, you will probably want a doctor who works in Ithaca, New York, not in Bangkok, 8,553 miles away.

If you need a plumber, you will probably want a plumber close by, not one on the other side of the world. If you want to go out to eat, you will most likely go to a restaurant near where you live, not one on the other side of the world.

Now when it comes to buying a book, location may not matter. Where the bookseller resides may not matter, as long as you can get the book fairly quickly. When it comes to someone answering your technical computer questions, it may not matter where the technician is situated. As long as the technician speaks your language, listens well, and gives clear and concise instructions, you probably don't care where he or she is located.

In short, when a provider's (supplier's, worker's) location is important to you, the job that the provider performs will probably not be offshored to another country. When a provider's location is not important to you, the probability of the provider's job being offshored rises.

In 2004, *Forbes* magazine ran a story titled "Ten Professions Not Likely to Be Outsourced." Here is the list:

- Chief executive officer
- Physician and surgeon
- Pilot, copilot, and flight engineer
- Lawyer
- Computer and information systems manager
- Sales manager
- Pharmacist
- Chiropractor
- Physician's assistant
- Education administrator, elementary and secondary school

Chapter Summary

WHAT IS GLOBALIZATION?

- Globalization is a phenomenon by which individuals and businesses in any part of the world are much more affected by events elsewhere in the world than before; it is the growing integration of national economies of the world to the degree that we may be witnessing the emergence and operation of a single worldwide economy.

- Certain facts provide evidence that globalization is occurring. Some of these facts are (1) lower tariff rates in many countries, (2) many countries exporting and importing more goods than in the past, (3) greater foreign exchange trading, (4) more foreign direct investment, (5) many more people owning foreign stocks, (6) many more countries having joined the WTO in recent years, and (7) a greater number of Americans working for foreign companies that have offices in the United States.

MOVEMENT TOWARD GLOBALIZATION

- What has caused this most recent push toward globalization? In the chapter we identified (1) the end of the Cold War, (2) advancing technology, and (3) policy changes as causal factors.

BENEFITS AND COSTS OF GLOBALIZATION

- Some of the benefits of globalization include (1) benefits from increased international trade, (2) greater income per person, (3) lower prices for goods, (4) greater product variety, and (5) increased productivity and innovation.

- Some of the costs of globalization include (1) increased income inequality (although there is some debate), (2) offshoring, and (3) increased economic power for large corporations (although there is some debate here too).

- When it comes to globalization, it is often much more difficult to see the benefits than the costs. The benefits are largely dispersed over a large population, but the costs (e.g., offshoring) might be concentrated on relatively few.

THE FUTURE OF GLOBALIZATION

- The future of globalization is under debate. Some persons argue that globalization will continue; others say it will stall and (perhaps) backtrack.

NET EXPORTS AND AGGREGATE DEMAND

- An increase in net exports will shift the *AD* curve to the right. A decrease in net exports will shift the *AD* curve to the left.
- Two factors can change net exports: foreign Real GDP (or real national income) and exchange rates. For example, in a two-country world (Japan and the United States), an increase in Japan's Real GDP and a depreciation in the dollar will increase U.S. net exports and shift the U.S. *AD* curve to the right. Alternatively, a decrease in Japan's Real GDP and an appreciation in the dollar will decrease U.S. net exports and shift the U.S. *AD* curve to the left.

THE AGGREGATE SUPPLY CURVE AND INTERNATIONAL FACTORS

- A change in foreign input prices will impact the U.S. *SRAS* curve. For example, an increase in foreign input prices will shift the U.S. *SRAS* curve to the left. A decrease in foreign input prices will shift the U.S. *SRAS* curve to the right.
- A change in foreign input prices can be the result of changes in the input market in the foreign country.

- A change in foreign input prices (paid by U.S. producers) can be the result of a change in the exchange rate. For example, if the dollar depreciates, U.S. producers will pay higher prices for foreign inputs. If the dollar appreciates, U.S. producers will pay lower prices for foreign inputs.

INTERNATIONAL FACTORS AND AGGREGATE DEMAND AND SHORT-RUN AGGREGATE SUPPLY

- A change in the exchange rate will affect both the U.S. *AD* curve and the U.S. *SRAS* curve. For example, if the dollar depreciates, the *AD* curve will shift to the right, and the *SRAS* curve will shift to the left.
- A change in real interest rates will affect both the U.S. *AD* curve and the U.S. *SRAS* curve. To illustrate, suppose the U.S. real interest rate rises relative to the Japanese interest rate. Higher real interest rates in the United States will attract foreign capital. Foreigners, in search of U.S. assets that pay interest, will bid up the price of a dollar; thus, the dollar appreciates. If the dollar appreciates, the *AD* curve will shift to the left, and the *SRAS* curve will shift to the right. The U.S. price level will fall. What happens to the U.S. Real GDP depends on the relative shifts in the *AD* and *SRAS* curves. Typically, the *AD* curve shifts leftward by more than the *SRAS* curve shifts rightward, and so Real GDP falls.

FISCAL AND MONETARY POLICY IN CLOSED AND OPEN ECONOMIES

- Expansionary fiscal policy raises Real GDP more in a closed economy than in an open economy.
- Contractionary fiscal policy lowers Real GDP more in a closed economy than in an open economy.
- Expansionary monetary policy raises Real GDP more in an open economy than in a closed economy.
- Contractionary monetary policy lowers Real GDP more in an open economy than in a closed economy.

Key Terms and Concepts

Globalization	Offshoring	Closed Economy	Open Economy
Tariff	J-Curve		

Questions and Problems

1 Why might it be easier to recognize the costs of globalization than the benefits?

2 If globalization continues over the next few decades, how might your life be different?

3 How might governments impact globalization?

4 Identify and explain two of the benefits and two of the costs of globalization.

5 What effect might advancing technology have on globalization?

6 Some have argued that the end of the Cold War acted as a catalyst toward greater globalization. How so?

7 What is Thomas Friedman's "Golden Arches theory of conflict prevention"?

8 David Friedman said that free (international) trade is a technology. Explain what he means.

9 Will globalization lead to some people losing jobs? Explain your answer.

10 How do tariff rates in the United States today compare with 1946?

11 Assume a two-country world where the two countries are the United States and Japan. Note the impact on U.S. Real GDP of each of the following:

   a. A fall in the real interest rate in the United States relative to the real interest rate in Japan.

   b. An economic expansion in Japan.

12 Give a numerical example to illustrate what the depreciation of a country's currency does to the prices of its imports.

13 If Americans buy fewer units of good X, which is produced in Japan, will they necessarily spend less money overall on good X? Explain your answer.

14 "The discussion of the J-curve points out that economists sometimes think in terms of both the short run and the long run." Do you agree or disagree? Explain your answer.

15 Explain how a change in the exchange rate can change both the U.S. *AD* and *SRAS* curves.

16 Suppose country A undertakes a policy mix of contractionary fiscal policy and expansionary monetary policy. What do you predict would happen to real interest rates, the value of country A's currency, and net exports? Explain your answer.

17 Why might import spending rise in a country soon after a depreciation of its currency? Is import spending likely to fall over time? Explain your answers.

18 Explain why expansionary monetary policy is more likely to increase Real GDP in an open economy than in a closed economy.

19 Explain why contractionary fiscal policy is more likely to decrease Real GDP in a closed economy than in an open economy.

20 Explain why contractionary monetary policy lowers Real GDP more in an open economy than in a closed economy.

Working with Numbers and Graphs

1 Starting with an exchange rate of $1 = ¥114 and a price tag of ¥10,000 for a Japanese item, show what happens to the price of the Japanese item if the yen depreciates by 5 percent.

2 Graphically show and explain the domestic and feedback effects on Real GDP in the United States as a result of contractionary fiscal policy.

3 Graphically show and explain the domestic and feedback effects on Real GDP in the United States as a result of contractionary monetary policy.

CHAPTER 21

STOCKS, BONDS, FUTURES, AND OPTIONS

Introduction Economic and financial news is all around us. "The economy is headed toward recession." "The value of the dollar is falling." "The budget deficit is growing" "The stock market took a loss today." "Bonds are strong."

In much of this book we have talked about various economic news items. In this chapter we turn to the part of economics that deals with financial matters. In this chapter we discuss stocks, bonds, futures, and options.

FINANCIAL MARKETS

Everyone has heard of stocks and bonds, and everyone knows that stocks and bonds can be sold and purchased. But not everyone knows the economic purpose served by stocks and bonds.

Buying and selling stocks and bonds take place in financial markets, which serve the purpose of channeling money from some people to other people. To illustrate, Jones has saved $10,000 over two years, and Smith is just starting a new company. Smith needs money to get the new company up and running. On the other hand, Jones would like to invest the savings and receive a return. Jones and Smith may not know each other; in fact, they may live on opposite ends of the country. A financial market, however, can bring these two people together. It allows Jones either to invest in Smith's company or to lend Smith some money. For example, Jones might either buy stock in Smith's company or buy a bond that Smith's company is issuing. In this chapter, we discuss more about how people like Smith and Jones help each other through a financial market. Specifically, in this section, we discuss stocks, and in the next section, bonds.

Common MISCONCEPTIONS

About Financial Brokers

Smith has $10,000 to lend, and Jones wants to borrow $10,000. The problem is that Smith and Jones do not know each other. Enter the middleman, Brown, who stands between the Smiths and Joneses of the world. He is the person who brings the Smiths and Joneses together. For his services rendered, he is paid a fee. Some people will argue that Brown does not provide any worthwhile service to anyone, but they're wrong. His service is to bring Smith and Jones together. Without Brown, it is less likely that Smith will lend and Jones will borrow—that is, less likely that Smith and Jones will enter into a mutually advantageous trade.

STOCKS

What does it mean when someone tells you that she owns 100 shares of a stock? If Jane owns 100 shares of Yahoo! stock, she is a part owner in Yahoo!, Inc., which is a global Internet media company that offers a network of World Wide Web programming. A **stock** is a claim on the assets of a corporation that gives the purchaser a share in the corporation.

In our example, Jane is not an owner in the sense that she can walk into Yahoo! headquarters (in Santa Clara, California) and start issuing orders. She cannot hire or fire anyone, and she cannot decide what the company will or will not do over the next few months or years. But still she is an owner, and as an owner she can, if she wants, sell her ownership rights in Yahoo!. All she has to do is find a buyer for her 100 shares of stock. Most likely, she could do so in a matter of minutes, if not seconds.

Stock
A claim on the assets of a corporation that gives the purchaser a share of the corporation.

Finding ECONOMICS

At an Online Brokerage Website

Frank has an account with TD Ameritrade. He goes online one morning to see what price Yahoo! stock (symbol YHOO) is selling at. At 10:45 A.M. EDT, the stock is selling at $29.74 a share. One minute later it is selling for one cent less at $29.73. Where is the economics? Supply and demand are at work with respect to Yahoo! stock. The equilibrium price is changing fairly fast in this market. At 10:45 A.M. EDT the equilibrium price is $29.74. One minute later it has fallen to $29.73. Ten minutes later it has risen to $27.99. Think of how fast the market for Yahoo! stock equilibrates compared to some other markets (such as the housing market).

Where Are Stocks Bought and Sold?

Groceries are bought and sold at the grocery store. Clothes are bought and sold at the clothing store. But where are stocks bought and sold?

To answer that question, let's go back to 1792, when 24 men met under a buttonwood tree on what is now Wall Street in New York City. These men essentially bought and sold stock (for themselves and their customers) at this location. Someone might have said, "I want to sell 20 shares in company X. Are you willing to buy them for $2 a share?"

From this humble beginning came the New York Stock Exchange (NYSE). Every weekday (excluding holidays), men and women meet at the NYSE in New York City and buy and sell stock. For example, suppose you own 100 shares of a stock that is listed on the NYSE. You do not have to go to the NYSE in New York to sell it. You simply contact a stockbroker (either over the phone, in person, or online), who conveys your wishes to sell the stock to a person at the NYSE itself. That person at the NYSE then executes your order.

The NYSE is not the only exchange where stocks are bought and sold. For example, there are the American Stock Exchange (AMEX) and the NASDAQ stock market (NASDAQ is pronounced "NAS-dak" and stands for National Association of Securities Dealers Automated Quotations). Buying and selling stock on the NASDAQ do not take place in the same way as on the NYSE. Instead of the buying and selling taking place in a central location, the NASDAQ is an electronic stock market with trades executed through a sophisticated computer and telecommunications network. The NYSE might in fact change to this kind of market in the near future; instead of people meeting in one location to buy and sell stock, they could do it electronically.

Increasingly, Americans are not only buying and selling stocks on the U.S. stock exchanges and markets, but in foreign stock exchanges and markets too. For example, an American might buy a stock listed on the German Stock Exchange, the Montreal Stock Exchange, or the Swiss Exchange.

The Dow Jones Industrial Average (DJIA)

You may have heard news commentators say, "The Dow fell 302 points on heavy trading." They are talking about the **Dow Jones Industrial Average (DJIA)**, which first appeared on the scene more than 100 years ago, on May 26, 1896, and was devised by Charles H. Dow. Dow took 11 stocks, summed their prices on a particular day, and then divided by 11. The average price was the DJIA. (Some of the original companies included American Cotton Oil, Chicago Gas, National Lead, and U.S. Rubber.)

When Charles Dow first computed the DJIA, the stock market was not highly regarded in the United States. Prudent investors bought bonds, not stocks. Stocks were thought to be the arena for speculators and conniving Wall Street operators. It was thought back then that Wall Streeters managed stock prices to make themselves better off at the expense of others. There was a lot of gossip about what was and was not happening in the stock market.

Dow devised the DJIA to convey information about what was happening in the stock market. Before the DJIA, people had a hard time figuring out whether the stock market, on average, was rising or falling. Instead, they knew only that a particular stock went up or down by so many cents or dollars. The average price of a certain number of stocks, he thought, would largely mirror what was happening in the stock market as a whole. With this number, people could then have some sense of what the stock market was doing on any given day.

Today, the DJIA consists of 30 stocks that are widely held by individuals and institutional investors (see Exhibit 1, which shows the 30 stocks in the Dow Industrial Average as of February 19, 2008). The list can and does change from time to

Dow Jones Industrial Average (DJIA)
The most popular, widely cited indicator of day-to-day stock market activity. The DJIA is a weighted average of 30 widely traded stocks on the New York Stock Exchange.

---

exhibit 1

3M Co.	Home Depot Inc.
Alcoa Inc.	Intel Corp.
American Express Co.	International Business Machines Corp.
AT&T Inc.	Johnson & Johnson
Bank of America	JPMorgan Chase & Co.
Boeing Co.	Kraft Foods, Inc.
Caterpillar Inc.	McDonald's Corp.
Chevron	Merck & Co. Inc.
Citigroup Inc.	Microsoft Corp.
Coca-Cola Co.	Pfizer Inc.
E.I. DuPont de Nemours & Co.	Procter & Gamble Co.
ExxonMobil Corp.	United Technologies Corp.
General Electric Co.	Verizon Communications Inc.
General Motors Corp.	Wal-Mart Stores Inc.
Hewlett-Packard Co.	Walt Disney Co.

The 30 Stocks of the Dow Jones Industrial Average (DJIA)

Here are the 30 stocks that comprise the Dow Jones Industrial Average.

exhibit 2

DJIA, January 1, 2004–October 13, 2008

Here we show the ups and downs of the DJIA from January 1, 2004, to October 13, 2008.

time, as determined by the editors of *The Wall Street Journal.* And the DJIA is no longer computed simply by summing the prices of stocks and dividing by 30. A special divisor is used to avoid distortions that can occur, such as companies splitting their stock shares. Exhibit 2 shows the Dow Jones Industrial Average during the period of January 1, 2004–October 13, 2008.

In addition to the DJIA, other prominent stock indexes are cited in the United States. A few include the NASDAQ Composite, the Standard & Poor's 500, the Russell 2000, and the Wilshire 5000. There are also prominent stock indexes around the world, such as the Hang Seng (in Hong Kong), the Bovespa (Brazil), IPC (Mexico), BSE 30 (India), CAC 40 (France), and others.

What causes the DJIA to go up? What causes it to go down? Economic consulting firms have attempted to find out what influences the Dow. According to many economists, the Dow is closely connected to changes in such things as consumer credit, business expectations, exports and imports, personal income, and the money supply. For example, increases in consumer credit are expected to push up the Dow, the thought being that when consumer credit rises, people will buy more goods and services, and this is good for the companies that sell goods and services. When consumer credit falls, the opposite effect occurs.

How the Stock Market Works

To raise money for investment in a new product or a new manufacturing technique, a company can do one of three things. First, it can go to a bank and borrow the money. Second, it can borrow the money by issuing a bond (a promise to repay the borrowed money with interest; you will learn more about bonds later in the chapter). Third, it can sell or issue stock in the company or, put another way, sell part of the company. Stocks are also called *equity* because the buyer of the stock has part ownership of the company.

ARE SOME ECONOMISTS POOR INVESTORS?

You might think that economists would do pretty well in the stock market compared to the average person. After all, the job of economists is to understand how markets work and to study key economic indicators.

So how do you explain a May 11, 2005, article in the *Los Angeles Times* titled "Experts Are at a Loss on Investing"? The article looked at the investments of four economists—all Nobel Prize winners in economics. Not one of them said that he invests the way he should invest, and none of them seemed to be getting rich through their investments. Often, there seems to be a big difference between knowing what to do and doing it.

Harry M. Markowitz won the Nobel Prize in Economics in 1990 for his work in financial economics. He is known as the father of modern portfolio theory, the main idea being that people should diversify their investments.

Markowitz, however, did not follow his own advice. Most of his life, he put half of his money in a stock fund and the other half in a conservative, low-interest investment. Markowitz, age 77 at the time, says, "In retrospect, it would have been better to have been more in stocks when I was younger."

George Akerlof, who won the Nobel Prize in Economics in 2001, had invested most of his money in money market accounts, which tend to have relatively low interest rate returns but are safe. Akerlof, when confronted with this fact, said, "I know it's utterly stupid."

Clive Granger, who won the Nobel Prize in Economics in 2003, was asked about his investments. He said, "I would rather spend my time enjoying my income than bothering about investments."

Daniel Kahneman, who won the Nobel Prize in Economics in 2002, had this to say about his investments: "I think very little about my retirement savings, because I know that thinking could make me poorer or more miserable or both."

Almost every activity comes with both benefits and costs. There are certainly benefits to investing wisely, but there are costs too. It takes time to find out about various investments, to research them, and to keep informed on how they are doing.

The actions of our four Nobel Prize winners also point out something else. Many people think that economics is simply about money and money matters, but it is not. It is about utility and happiness and making oneself better off. Each of our four Nobel Prize winners might not have been doing the best thing for his wallet, but certainly each knew this and continued on the same path anyway. Each was willing to sacrifice some money to live a preferred lifestyle.

What is the lesson for you? Should you care nothing about your investments and hope that your financial future will take care of itself? Or should you spend all your time regularly watching, researching, and evaluating various investments that either you have made or plan to make? Neither extreme is sensible. You can learn enough about investments to protect yourself from the financial uncertainties of the future but not spend so much time worrying about the future that you don't enjoy the present.

When a company is initially formed, the owners set up a certain amount of stock, which is worth very little. The owners of the company try to find people (usually friends and associates) who would be willing to buy the stock (in the hopes that one day it will be worth something). In these early days of the company, anyone who owned stock would find it nearly impossible to sell it. For example, if Jones owned 100 shares of some new company that almost no one had heard of, hardly anyone would be willing to pay any money to buy the stock.

As the company grows and needs more money, it may decide to offer its stock on the open market. In other words, it offers its stock to anyone who wants to buy it. By this time, the company may be known well enough that some people are willing to buy it. The company makes what is called an **initial public offering (IPO)** of its stock. The process is quite simple. Usually, an **investment bank** sells the stock for the company for an initial

Initial Public Offering (IPO)
A company's first offering of stock to the public.

Investment Bank
A firm that acts as an intermediary between the company that issues the stock and the public that wishes to buy the stock.

price—say, $10 a share. How do you find out about an IPO? They are announced in *The Wall Street Journal.*

For example, suppose that William Welch started a company in 1895 and that, through the years, the company was passed down to family members. In 2009, the family members running the company want to expand it to two, three, or four times its current size. To get the money to do this, one way is to sell shares in the company—that is, by issuing stock. Once they have issued shares in the company to the public, the company is no longer solely family owned. Now many of the public own part of it too.

Once there is an IPO, the stock is usually traded on a stock exchange or in an electronic stock market. Sometimes, the stock that initially sold for $10 will rise in price, and sometimes it will fall like a rock. Its success or failure all depends on what people in the stock market think the issuing company will do in the future. If they think the company is destined for big earnings, the stock will likely rise in price. If they think the company is destined for losses, or only marginal earnings, the stock will likely fall in price.

In a way, you can think of trading stock in much the same way as trading baseball cards, paintings, or anything else. The price depends on the forces of supply and demand. If demand rises and supply is constant, then the price of the stock will rise. If demand falls and supply is constant, then the price of the stock will fall.

Why Do People Buy Stock?

Millions of people in the United States, and in countries all over the world, buy stock every day. Sometimes, people buy a stock because they hear that others are buying it and because they think the stock is hot. In other words, the stock is very popular and everyone wants it. In the 1990s, some of the Internet stocks fit this description. People bought stocks such as Yahoo!, Amazon.com, and eBay just because they thought the Internet was the wave of the future and almost anything connected with the Internet was destined for great profit.

More often, though, people buy a stock because they think the earnings of the company that initially issued the stock are likely to rise. (Remember that a share of stock represents ownership in a company.) The more profitable that company is expected to be, the more likely people are going to want to own that company, and therefore the greater the demand for the company's stock.

Dividend
A share of the profits of a corporation distributed to stockholders.

Most people therefore buy stock for a couple of typical reasons. Some people buy stocks for the **dividends**, which are payments made to stockholders based on a company's profits. For example, suppose company X has issued one million shares of stock that are owned by investors. Each year, the company tabulates its profit and loss, and, if there is a profit, it distributes some of the profit among the owners of the company as dividends. This year's dividend might be $1 for each share of stock a person owns. So if Jones owns 50,000 shares of stock, she will receive a dividend check for $50,000.

The other reason to buy stock is for the expected gain in its price. Stockholders can make money if they buy shares at a lower price and sell at a higher price. For example, Smith buys 100 shares of Microsoft stock today. He thinks that the company is going to do well and that a year from now he can sell it for as much as $50 more a share than he purchased it. In other words, he hopes to earn $5,000 on his stock purchase.

People also sell stock for many reasons. Smith might sell his 100 shares of IBM because he needs the money, perhaps to help his son pay for college or to put together a down payment for a house. Another common reason for selling stock is that the stockholder thinks the stock is likely to go down in price soon. It is better today to sell at $25 a share than to sell one week from now at $18 a share.

Common MISCONCEPTIONS

About Stocks

Someone buys a stock at $100 a share, and five weeks later the stock is selling for $86 a share. The person decides not to sell the stock because, he says, "I can't take the loss." That response signifies that the person thinks the share price of the stock will rise. ("I can't sell today because I can't take the loss. I have to wait until the price rises so that I won't have to take a loss.") But the price that has gone down is not guaranteed to go up. In fact, a misconception is that a stock's price has gone so low that it has nowhere to go but up. The share price of a stock can start at, say, $500, and continue to go down until no one is willing to pay anything for the stock. In other words, the share price of a stock can fall to zero.

How to Buy and Sell Stock

Buying and selling stock are relatively easy. You can buy or sell stock through a full-service stockbrokerage firm, a discount broker, or an online broker. With all varieties of brokers, you usually open an account by depositing a certain dollar amount, commonly between $1,000 and $2,500. Once you have opened an account, you can begin to trade (buy and sell stock).

With a full-service broker, you may call up on the phone and ask your broker to recommend a good stock. Your broker, usually called an *account representative,* might say that you should buy X, Y, or Z stock. When you ask why these are good stocks to buy, the representative may say that the firm's research department has looked closely at them and believes they are headed for good times based on the current economic situation in the country, the level of exports, the new technology that is coming to market, and other factors.

If you do not require help selecting stocks, you can go either to a discount broker or to an online broker. You can call up a discount broker, as you did a full-service broker, and say you want to buy or sell so many shares of a given stock. The broker will execute the trade for you but not offer any advice.

You can do the same thing online. You go to your broker's website, log in, enter your username and password, and then buy or sell stock. You may, for example, submit an order to buy 100 shares of stock X. Your online broker will register your buy request and then advise you when it has been executed. Your account, easily visible online, will show how much cash you have in it, how many shares of a stock you hold, and so on.

Buying Stocks or Buying the Market

You can use various methods to decide which stocks to purchase. The first way is to buy shares of stock that you think are going to rise in price. So you might buy 50 shares of Microsoft, 100 shares of General Electric, and 500 shares of Amazon.com.

Another way is to invest in a stock mutual fund, which is a collection of stocks that is managed by a fund manager who works for a mutual fund company. For example, Smith may operate Mutual Fund Z at Mutual Fund Company Z. If you put, say, $10,000 into Mutual Fund Z, you are in effect buying stocks in that fund. If the fund consists of stocks A, B, C, W, and X, the fund manager may, on any given day, buy more of A and sell some of B or sell all of C and add stock D to the fund portfolio. Thus, as a buyer of the fund, you put your money into the manager's hands, and the fund manager does what he or she thinks is best to maximize the overall returns from the fund.

Mutual fund companies often advertise the records of their fund managers. They might say, "Our fund managers have the best record on Wall Street. Invest with us and get the highest returns you can." You may be prompted to put your money in the hands of the experts because you feel they know better than you which stocks to buy and sell and when to do each.

You could use another strategy, though, and buy the stocks that make up a stock index. For example, the DJIA, a stock index, gives us information on the performance of the 30 stocks that make up the Dow. Other indexes are made up differently. The Standard & Poor's 500 index is a broad index of stock market activity because it is made up of 500 of the largest U.S. companies. Another broad-based stock index is the Wilshire 5000, which consists of the stocks of about 6,500 firms. (Yes, even though it consists of more than 5,000 firms, it is still called the Wilshire 5000.) So, instead of buying a mutual fund that consists of various stocks picked by the so-called experts, you can buy a mutual fund that consists of the stocks that make up a particular index.

An easy way to do this is to buy what are called Spyders. The term *Spyders* comes from SPDRs, which stands for Standard & Poor's Depository Receipts. Spyders are securities that represent ownership in the SPDR Trust, which buys the stocks that make up the Standard & Poor's (S&P) 500 index, and that are traded under the symbol SPY. Spyders cost one-tenth of the S&P index (the total of the share prices of the stocks in the S&P). For example, if the S&P index is 1,350, then a Spyder will sell for $135.

When you buy Spyders, you are buying the stock of 500 companies. Because you are buying the stock of so many companies, you are said to be buying the market. For example, suppose Jack decides to buy the market instead of buying a few individual stocks. He opens an account with an online broker; that is, he goes online, opens an account, and sends the broker a check so that he can start trading (buying and selling stock). He then checks (at the online broker website) on the current price of Spyders, which is, say, $135 per share. He decides to buy 100 shares, for a total price of $13,500. (His online broker charges him a small commission for this stock purchase.) In a minute or less, he sees that he has purchased the 100 shares of Spyders. That's all there is to it.

How to Read the Stock Market Page

Once you have purchased some stock, you will want to find out how it is doing. Is it rising or falling in price? Is it paying a dividend? How many shares were traded today?

One of the places you can go to find the answers to these questions, as well as other information, is the newspaper. On the stock market page (keep in mind that many newspapers are online), you will see something similar to what you see in Exhibit 3. Let's look at each item in each column of the bottom line.

---

exhibit 3

How to Read the Stock Market Page of a Newspaper

We show here part of the stock market page of a newspaper. We explain how to read the page in the text.

(1) 52W high	(2) 52W low	(3) Stock	(4) Ticker	(5) Div	(6) Yield %	(7) P/E	(8) Vol 00s	(9) High	(10) Low	(11) Close	(12) Net chg
45.39	19.75	ResMed	RMD			57.5	3831	42.00	39.51	41.50	-1.90
11.63	3.55	Revlon A	REV				162	6.09	5.90	6.09	+0.12
77.25	55.13	RioTinto	RTP	2.30	3.2		168	72.75	71.84	72.74	+0.03
31.31	16.63	RitchieBr	RBA			20.9	15	24.49	24.29	24.49	-0.01
8.44	1.75	RiteAid	RAD				31028	4.50	4.20	4.31	+0.21
38.63	18.81	RobtHall	RHI			26.5	6517	27.15	26.50	26.50	+0.14
51.25	**27.69**	**Rockwell**	**ROK**	**1.02**	**2.1**	**14.5**	**6412**	**47.99**	**47.00**	**47.54**	**+0.24**

52W High This stands for the high price of the stock over the past 52 weeks. For this stock, you see the number 51.25, which is $51.25.

52W Low This stands for the low price of the stock over the past 52 weeks. For this stock, you see the number 27.69, which is $27.69.

Stock In this column, you see Rockwell. This is either an abbreviation of the name or the full name of the company whose stock we are investigating. The company here is Rockwell Automation Incorporated.

Ticker ROK is the stock or ticker symbol for Rockwell Automation Incorporated.

Div This stands for dividend. You see the number 1.02 on the bottom line, which means that the last annual dividend per share of stock was $1.02. For example, a person who owned 5,000 shares of Rockwell Automation stock would have received $1.02 per share or $5,100 in dividends. (A blank means the company does not currently pay out dividends.)

Yield % The yield of a stock is the dividend divided by the closing price.

$$\text{Yield} = \frac{\text{Dividend per share}}{\text{Closing price per share}}$$

The closing price of the stock (shown in the one of the later columns) is 47.54 ($47.54). If we divide the dividend ($1.02) by the closing price ($47.54), we get a yield of 2.1 percent. The higher the yield, the better the prospects are for the stock, *ceteris paribus.* For example, a stock that yields 5 percent is better than a stock that yields 3 percent, if all other things between the two stocks are the same.

P/E This stands for P/E ratio, or price-earnings ratio. The number here, 14.5, is obtained by taking the latest closing price per share and dividing it by the latest available net earnings per share.

$$\text{P/E} = \frac{\text{Closing price per share}}{\text{Net earnings per share}}$$

A stock with a P/E ratio of 14.5 means that the stock is selling for a share price that is 14.5 times its earnings per share.

A high P/E ratio usually indicates that people believe there will be higher-than-average growth in earnings. Suppose that most stocks have a P/E ratio of 14.5, that is, they sell for a share price that is 14.5 times their earnings per share. Also suppose that stock X has a P/E ratio of, say, 50. What would make stock X have a P/E ratio so much higher than most stocks? Obviously, the people buying stock X expect that its future earnings will somehow warrant the higher prices they are paying for the stock today. Whether or not they are right remains to be seen.

Vol 00s This stands for volume in the hundreds. The number 6412 translates to 641,200. It means that 641,200 shares of this stock were traded (bought and sold) on this day.

High This stands for the high price the stock traded for on this day. The number is 47.99 ($47.99).

Low This stands for the low price the stock traded for on this particular day. The number is 47.00 ($47.00).

Close This is the share price of the stock when trading stopped on this day: 47.54 ($47.54).

Net Chg. This stands for net change: +0.24 (+$0.24). The price of the stock on this particular day closed 24 cents higher than it did the day before.

Common MISCONCEPTIONS

About the DJIA

Some people seem to think that if they don't own any of the stocks making up the DJIA, the ups and downs in the index don't affect them. But this is not exactly true. Many economists say that what happens in the stock market—or to the DJIA—is a forerunner of future economic events. So if the DJIA goes down over time, it is indicating that the economic future is somewhat depressed; if it goes up over time, it is indicating that the economic future looks good. The economic future—good or bad—is something that does affect you. It affects what prices you pay, how easy or hard it is to get a job, how large or small an increase in income you get, and so on.

SELF-TEST

(Answers to Self-Test questions are in the Self-Test Appendix.)

1. How many stocks does the DJIA consist of?
2. Why do people buy stocks?
3. What does the yield of a stock equal?
4. What does a P/E ratio of 23 mean?

BONDS

If a company in St. Louis wants to build a new factory, how can it get the necessary money? Recall that companies use three principal ways to raise money. First, they can go to banks and take out loans. Second, they can issue stock, or sell ownership rights in the company. Third, they can issue bonds. A **bond** is simply an IOU, or a promise to pay. Typically, companies, governments, or government agencies issue bonds. In each case, the purpose of issuing a bond is to borrow money. The issuer of a bond is a borrower, and the person who buys the bond is a lender.

Bond
An IOU, or promise to pay.

The Components of a Bond

There are three major components of a bond: face (par) value, maturity date, and coupon rate.

Face Value (Par Value)
Dollar amount specified on a bond, the total amount the issuer of the bond will repay to the buyer of the bond.

FACE VALUE The **face value**, or **par value**, of a bond is the total amount the issuer of the bond will repay to the buyer of the bond. For example, suppose Smith buys a bond from Company Z, and the face value of the bond is $1,000. Company Z promises to pay Smith $1,000 at some point in the future.

economics 24/7

$1.3 QUADRILLION

At the close of the 20th century, the editors of the financial magazine *The Economist* identified the highest-returning investments for each year, beginning in 1900 and ending in 1999. For example, the highest returning investment in 1974 was gold, in 1902 it was U.S. Treasury bills, and in 1979 it was silver.

© NONSTOCK/JUPITER IMAGES

The editors then asked how much income a person would have earned at the end of 1999, if she had invested $1 in the highest-returning investment in 1900, and then taken the returns from that investment and invested it in the highest-returning investment in 1901, and so on for each year during the century. After taxes and dealer costs, she would have earned $1.3 quadrillion. (Quadrillion comes after trillion. In 2008, Warren Buffet, the richest person in the world, had $62 billion; so $1.3 quadrillion is 20,967 times what Warren Buffet had at the time.) So, with perfect foresight (or with a crystal ball that always correctly tells you what the highest-returning investment of the year will be), you could be rich beyond your imagination.

After the editors ran their experiment, they changed it. They went back and asked themselves what one would have earned over the 20th century if, instead of investing in the highest returning investment in a given year, she invested in it one year late. That is, if X is the best investment in 1956, then invest in it in 1957.

The editors made this change in the belief that many people invest in a hot investment only when it is too late. By the time they hear about it, investing in it at that point is usually too late. (Think of an investment as a mountain: Going up the mountain is comparable to increasing returns on the investment, and going down the mountain is comparable to decreasing returns. It's only when the investment is near its peak that many people hear about it. But then it's too late. There is no place to go but down.)

To put this into context, the person with the crystal ball or with perfect foresight would have invested in the Polish stock market in 1993, when no one was talking about it, and he would have reaped a 754 percent gain. The typical investor would have invested in it one year later, in 1994, when everyone was talking about it. The problem is that the Polish stock market fell by 55 percent in 1994.

So the person who invested always one year late over the 20th century would have earned, after taxes and dealer costs, $290.

What are the economic lessons? First, the best investments are often the ones that you don't hear about until it is too late. Second, ignoring the first lesson—thinking that a popular investment is necessarily a good investment—is often the way to low returns.

MATURITY DATE The maturity date is the day that the issuer of the bond must pay the buyer the face value; it is the date the bond is said to come due. For example, suppose Smith buys a bond with a face value of $1,000 that matures on December 31, 2015. On December 31, 2015, he receives $1,000 from the issuer of the bond.

COUPON RATE The coupon rate is the percentage of the face value that the bond-holder receives each year until the bond matures. For example, suppose Smith buys a bond with a face value of $1,000 that matures in 5 years and has a coupon rate of 10 percent. He receives a coupon payment of $100 each year for 5 years.

To illustrate, Jorge buys a bond with a face value of $1,000 and a coupon rate of 7 percent. The maturity date of the bond is 10 years from today. Each year, for the next 10 years, Jorge receives 7 percent of $1,000 from the issuer, which amounts to $70 a year for each of 10 years. In the 10th year, he also receives $1,000 from the bond issuer. This bond has a maturity date in 10 years, a coupon rate of 7 percent, and a face value of $1,000.

Bond Ratings

Bonds are rated or evaluated. The more likely it is that the bond issuer will pay the face value of the bond at maturity and meet all scheduled coupon payments, the higher the bond's rating will be. Two of the best-known ratings are Standard & Poor's and Moody's. If a bond gets a rating of AAA from Standard & Poor's or a rating of Aaa from Moody's, it has received the highest rating possible. You can be sure that it is one of the securest bonds you can buy; there is little doubt that the bond issuer will pay the face value of the bond at maturity and meet all scheduled coupon payments.

Bonds rated in the B to D category are of lower quality than those in the A category. A bond in the C category may be in default (the issuer of the bond cannot pay off the bond), and those in the D category are definitely in default.

Bond Prices and Yields (or Interest Rates)

The price that a person pays for a bond depends on market conditions. The greater the demand is for the bond relative to the supply, the higher the price will be. The price is important because it determines the yield, or interest rate, that the bondholder receives on the bond. (In everyday language, the yield is referred to as the interest rate on the bond. For example, someone might ask what interest rate is that bond paying? We could easily substitute the term *yield* for the term *interest rate* and give an answer of something like "5.26 percent.")

Let's suppose that Gupta is the owner of a bond with a face value of $1,000 and a coupon rate of 5 percent. He decides to sell this bond to Jones for $950. Now we know that the coupon payment on this bond will be 5 percent of $1,000 each year, or $50; so Jones can expect to receive $50 each year. But the **yield** on the bond is the coupon payment divided by the price paid for the bond.

Yield
Equal to the annual coupon payment divided by the price paid for the bond.

$$\text{Yield (or interest rate)} = \frac{\text{Annual coupon payment}}{\text{Price paid for the bond}}$$

In this example, it is $50 ÷ $950 = 5.26 percent. For the bond buyer, the higher the yield is, the better the deal is.

As another example, suppose Robin buys a bond with the face value of $1,000 for $900. The coupon rate on the bond is 4 percent. Because the coupon rate is 4 percent, Robin receives 4 percent of $1,000 (the face value of the bond) each year through the time the bond matures: $40 a year. Because Robin bought the bond for a price lower than the face value, her yield will be higher than the coupon rate. To find the yield, divide the annual coupon payment of $40 by the price of the bond ($900). This gives Robin a yield of 4.4 percent.

Now suppose Robin had paid $1,100 for the bond instead of $900. In this case, the yield would be 3.6 percent, which is lower than the coupon rate. In other words, as the price paid for the bond rises, the yield declines.

Finally, the coupon rate and the yield are the same when the price paid for the bond equals the face value. For example, a bond with a face value of $1,000 and a coupon rate of 5 percent is purchased for $1,000. The yield ($50 ÷ $1,000) is 5 percent, which is equal to the coupon rate.

Common MISCONCEPTIONS

About the Coupon Rate and Yield (Interest Rate)

Many people seem to think that the coupon rate of a bond is the yield that the bond earns. This is not true. The yield (or interest rate) and the coupon rate are two different things. Only when the price of the bond equals the face value of the bond does the yield (interest rate) equal the coupon rate. When the price of the bond is lower the face value of the bond, the yield will be greater than the coupon rate; when the price of the bond is greater than the face of the bond, the yield will be less than the coupon rate.

Types of Bonds

This section briefly describes some of the many types of bonds issued by companies, governments, and government agencies.

CORPORATE BONDS A corporate bond is issued by a private corporation. Corporate bonds may sell for a price above or below face value depending on current supply-and-demand conditions. The interest that corporate bonds pay is fully taxable.

MUNICIPAL BONDS Municipal bonds are issued by state and local governments. States may issue bonds to help pay for a new highway. Local governments may issue bonds to finance a civic auditorium or a sports stadium. Many people purchase municipal bonds because the interest paid on the bonds is not subject to federal taxes.

TREASURY BILLS, NOTES, AND BONDS When the federal government wants to borrow funds, it can issue Treasury bills (T-bills), notes, or bonds. These securities differ only in their time to maturity. Although called by different names, all are bonds. Treasury bills mature in 13, 26, or 52 weeks. Treasury notes mature in 2 to 10 years, and Treasury bonds mature in more than 10 to 30 years. Treasury bills, notes, and bonds are considered very safe investments because it is unlikely the federal government will default on its bond obligations. After all, the federal government has the power to tax to pay off bondholders.

INFLATION-INDEXED TREASURY BONDS In 1997, the federal government began to issue inflation-indexed bonds. The first indexed Treasury bonds that were issued matured in 10 years and were available at face values as small as $1,000.

What is the difference between an inflation-indexed Treasury bond and a Treasury bond that is not indexed? An inflation-indexed Treasury bond guarantees the purchaser a certain real rate of return, but a nonindexed Treasury bond does not. For example, suppose you purchase an inflation-indexed, 10-year, $1,000 bond that pays a 4 percent coupon rate. If there is no inflation, the annual interest payment will be $40. But if the inflation rate is, say, 3 percent, the government will mark up the value of the bond by 3 percent—from $1,000 to $1,030. Then it will pay 4 percent on this higher dollar amount. So instead of paying $40 each year, it pays $41.20. By increasing the monetary value of the security by the rate of inflation, the government guarantees the bondholder a real return of 4 percent.

How to Read the Bond Market Page

On the bond market page of the newspaper, you can find information about the different types of bonds. Here we discuss how to read the information that relates to both corporate bonds and Treasury bonds. First, let's look at corporate bonds.

CORPORATE BONDS Not all publications will present corporate bond information in exactly the same format. The format we show you here is common, though.

(1) Bonds	(2) Cur Yld	(3) Vol	(4) Close	(5) Net Chg
AT&T 6 5/8 34	6.7	115	99 1/2	−3/4

Bonds This column presents three pieces of information: (1) the abbreviation for the company that issued the bond—AT&T, a telecommunications company; (2) the coupon rate of the bond, 6 5/8; and (3) the year the bond matures, 2034.

Cur Yld In this column, you find the current yield. (We showed how to compute the yield on a bond.) If the bond is purchased today (hence the word *current*), it will provide a yield of 6.7 percent.

Vol. In this column is the volume, 115. The dollar volume today is $115,000.

Close In this column, you find the closing price for the bond on this day, 99 1/2. Bond prices are quoted in points and fractions, and each point is $10. Thus, 99 1/2 is $999.50: 99.5 × 10 = $999.50.

Net Chg. In this column, you find the net change for the day. Here, it is −3/4, which means the price on this day was $7.50 lower than it was the previous day.

TREASURY BONDS Not all publications will present Treasury bond information in exactly the same format. The format we show you here is common, though.

(1) Rate	(2) Maturity	(3) Bid	(4) Ask	(5) Chg	(6) Yield
7 3/4	Feb. 09	105:12	105:14	−1	5.50

Rate In this column, you find the coupon rate of the bond. This Treasury bond pays 7 3/4 percent of the face value of the bond in annual interest payments.

Maturity In this column, you find when the bond matures. This Treasury bond matures in February 2009.

Bid In this column, you find how much the buyer is willing to pay for the bond (or the price you will receive if you sell the bond): 105:12. The number after the colon stands for 32nds of $10. Therefore, 105:12 is $1,053.75. First, multiply 105 × $10 = $1,050. Second, turn 12/32 into 0.375, and multiply by $10, giving you $3.75. Then add $3.75 to $1,050 to get $1,053.75.

Ask In this column, you find how much the seller is asking for to sell the bond. This is the price you will pay if you buy the bond: $1,054.37.

Chg. In this column, you find the change in the price of the bond from the previous trading day, expressed in 32nds. Therefore, −1 means that the price of the bond fell by 1/32nd of $10, or approximately 32 cents from the previous day.

Yield In this column, you find the yield, which is based on the ask price. Someone who buys the bond today (at the ask price) and holds it to maturity will reap a return of 5.50 percent.

Risk and Return

Whether buying stocks or bonds, the common denominator is that people buy them for the return. Simply stated, they hope to make money. How much money people can hope to make is tied directly to the different risk and return factors of stocks and bonds. For example, buying stock in a new company might be much riskier than buying a Treasury bond issued by the U.S. Treasury. You can be fairly sure that the U.S. Treasury is going to pay off that bond because the U.S. government has the ability to tax people. But you can't be so sure of a positive return on the stock you buy in the new company. You might buy the stock for $10 one day, and three days later it falls to $1 and stays at that price (or thereabouts) for 10 years.

In Chapter 1, we said there was a well-known principle in economics: There is no such thing as a free lunch. Applied to stocks and bonds (or any investment), that principle means you never get something for nothing. In short, higher returns come with higher risks, and lower returns come with lower risks. Treasury bonds, for example, will often pay (relatively) low returns because they are so safe (risk-free).

SELF-TEST

1. What is a bond?
2. If the coupon payment on a bond is $400 a year and the coupon rate is 7 percent, then what is the face value?
3. If the annual coupon payment for a bond is $1,000 and the price paid for the bond was $9,500, then what is the yield or interest rate?
4. What is the difference between a municipal bond and a Treasury bond?

FUTURES AND OPTIONS

In this section, we discuss both futures and options.

Futures

Myers is a miller. He buys wheat from the wheat farmer, turns the wheat into flour, and then sells the flour to the baker. Obviously, he wants to earn a profit for what he does. How much, if any, profit he earns depends on the price at which he can buy the wheat and the price at which he can sell the flour.

Myers decides to buy a futures contract in wheat. A **futures contract** is a contract in which the seller agrees to provide a good (in this case, wheat) to the buyer on a specified future date at an agreed-on price. For example, Myers might buy bushels of wheat now, for a price of $3 a bushel, to be delivered to him in six months.

But who would sell him the futures contract? A likely possibility is a speculator, someone who buys and sells commodities to profit from changes in the market. A speculator assumes risk in the hope of making a gain.

Futures Contract
An agreement to buy or sell a specific amount of something (commodity, currency, financial instrument) at an agreed-on price on a stipulated future date.

Suppose Smith, a speculator, believes that the price of wheat six months from now is going to be lower than it is today. She may look at things this way: "The price of wheat today is $3 a bushel. I think the price of wheat in six months will be close to $2 a bushel. Why not promise the miller that I will deliver him as much wheat as he wants in six months if, in return, he agrees today to pay me $3 a bushel for it. Then, in six months, I will buy the wheat for $2 a bushel, sell it to the miller for $3 a bushel, and earn myself $1 profit per bushel." So Myers, the miller, and Smith, the speculator, enter into a futures contract. Myers buys 200 bushels of wheat for delivery in six months; Smith sells 200 bushels of wheat for delivery in six months.

Each party gets something out of the deal. Myers, the miller, gets peace of mind. He knows that he will be able to buy the wheat at a price that will let him earn a profit on his deal with the baker. Smith takes a chance, which she is willing to take, for the chance of earning a profit.

As another example, Wilson is a farmer who grows primarily corn. The current price of corn is $3.34 a bushel. Wilson doesn't have any corn to sell right now, but he will in two months. He hopes that between now and two months, the price of corn won't fall to, say, something under $3. He decides to enter into a futures contract in corn. He promises to deliver 5,000 bushels of corn two months from now for $3.34 a bushel. Leung, a speculator in corn, decides that this is a good deal for him because he believes that in two months the price of a bushel of corn will have risen to $3.94. So Wilson and Leung enter into a futures contract. Two months pass and the price of corn has dropped to $3.10. Leung turned out to be wrong about the price rising. So farmer Wilson delivers 5,000 bushels of corn to speculator Leung, for which Leung pays Wilson $3.34 a bushel (for a total of $16,700), as agreed. Then Leung turns around and sells the corn for $3.10 a bushel (receiving $15,500), losing $1,200 on the deal.

CURRENCY FUTURES A futures contract can be written for wheat, as we have seen, or for a currency, a stock index, or even bonds. Here is how a currency futures contract works.

You check the dollar price of a euro today and find that it is $1.20. Thus, for every $1.20, you get 1 euro in return. You expect that, in three months, you will have to pay $1.50 to buy a euro. With this in mind, you enter into a futures contract. Essentially, you say that you are willing to buy $10 million worth of euros three months from now for $1.20 a euro. Who might be willing to enter into this contract with you? Anyone who thinks the dollar price of a euro will be lower (not higher) in three months. Suppose you and Werner enter a contract. You promise to buy $10 million worth of euros in three months (at $1.20 a euro), and Werner promises to sell you $10 million worth of euros in three months (at $1.20 a euro).

Three months pass, and it now takes $1.30 to buy a euro. Werner has to buy $10 million worth of euros at an exchange rate of $1.30 per euro. For $10 million, he gets 7,692,307 euros, which he turns over to you for $1.20 each, leaving him with $9,230,768. Obviously, Werner has taken a loss; he spent $10 million to get $9,230,768 in return, for a loss of $769,232.

On the other side of the deal, you now have 7,692,307 euros, for which you paid $9,230,768. If you sell them all, because you get $1.30 for every euro, you will get approximately $10 million. You are better off by $769,232.

Option

A contract that gives the owner the right, but not the obligation, to buy or sell shares of a stock at a specified price on or before a specified date.

Options

An **option** is a contract that gives the owner of the option the right, but not the obligation, to buy or sell shares of a stock at a specified price on or before a specified date. There are two types of options: calls and puts.

CALL OPTION Call options give the owner of the option the right to *buy* shares of a stock at a specified price within the time limits of the contract. The specified price at which the buyer can buy shares of a stock is called the *strike price*. For example, Brown buys a call option for $20. The call option specifies that he can buy 100 shares of IBM stock at a strike price of $150 within the next month. If the price of IBM stocks falls below $150, Brown doesn't exercise his call option. He simply tears it up and accepts the fact that he has lost $20. If he still wants to buy IBM stock, he can do so through his stockbroker as he normally does and pay the going price, which is lower than $150. But if the price rises above $150, he exercises his call option, buys the stock at $150 a share, and then sells it for the higher market price. He has made a profit.

If Brown buys a call option, then there has to be someone who sells it to him. Anyone who would sell Brown a call option is a person who thought the option wouldn't be exercised. For example, if Jones believed that the price of IBM was going to fall below $150, then he would gladly sell a call option to Brown for $20, thinking that the option would never be exercised. That's $20 in his pocket.

PUT OPTIONS Put options give the owner the right, but not the obligation, to *sell* (rather than buy, as in a call option) shares of a stock at a strike price during some period of time. For example, suppose Martin buys a put option to sell 100 shares of IBM stock at $130 during the next month. If the share price rises above $130, Martin will not exercise his put option. He will simply tear it up and sell the stock for more than $130. On the other hand, if the price drops below $130, then he will exercise his option to sell the stock for $130 a share.

People who think the price of the stock is going to decline buy put options. Obviously, the people who think the price of the stock is going to rise sell put options. Why not sell a put option for, say, $20, if you expect the price of the stock to rise? The buyer is not going to exercise the option.

HOW YOU CAN USE CALL AND PUT OPTIONS You can use call and put options in a number of ways. Suppose you think a stock, currently selling for $250 a share, is going to rise in price during the next few months. You don't have enough money to buy many shares of stock, but you would like to benefit from the rise in the price of the stock. In such a case, you can buy a call option, which will sell for a fraction of the cost of the stock. So with limited resources, you decide to buy the call option, which gives you the right to buy, say, 100 shares of the stock at $250 anytime during the next three months.

A natural question is, if you don't have the money to buy the stock at $250 a share now, how are you going to buy it at $250 in a few months? You don't have to buy the stock. If you are right that the price of the stock will rise, then your call option will become worth more to people. In other words, if you bought the option when the price of the stock was $250 and the stock rises to $300, then your call option has become more valuable. You can sell it and benefit from the uptick in the price of the stock.

Alternatively, let's say you expect the price of the stock to fall. Then you can buy a put option. In other words, you buy the right to sell the stock for $250 any time during the next three months. If the price does fall, your option becomes more valuable. In fact, the farther the price falls, the more valuable your put option becomes. People who have the stock and want to sell it for a price higher than it currently fetches on the market will be willing to buy your put option from you for some price higher than the price you paid.

As an example, the current price of a call option for AT&T stock is $10, and the current price of the AT&T stock is $100. Ginny decides to buy a call option for $10, giving her the right to buy AT&T at a price of $100. Five months pass, and the price of AT&T shares has risen to $150. If Ginny wants, she can exercise her call option to buy AT&T stock at $100 (which is $50 less than the current price of $150). In other words, she can spend $100 to buy a share of stock, which she can turn around and immediately sell for $150, making a profit of $50 per share.

SELF-TEST

1. What is a futures contract?

2. You expect that a stock will rise in the next few months, but you do not have enough money to buy many shares of the stock. What can you do instead?

3. What is a put option?

"I HAVE THREE QUESTIONS."

Student:

Can a firm that issues a bond set the coupon rate at any rate it wants?

Instructor:

No. To illustrate, suppose company A needs to borrow $10 million and decides to issue $1,000 bonds. The only way anyone would be willing to buy one of these bonds (lend the company $10,000) is if the company promised the buyers a rate of return comparable to the interest rate they could get if they simply put the money in a savings account. The company has to set the coupon rate in such a way that it attracts people to its bonds. If people are earning, say, 5 percent on their savings accounts, they will not lend money to the company unless the company pays a coupon rate of at least 5 percent. In short, the coupon rate is set at a competitive level— not just any level the company wants to set it at.

Student:

Is it a good idea to buy stock?

Instructor:

A lot depends on such factors as your age (are you at the beginning of your work career or near the end), your income, and how much you can afford to invest in the stock market. There is no guarantee that the stock you buy will go up in price. For example, consider what happened to the DJIA over the 1930s. At the beginning of 1930, the Dow stood around 250, but at the end of 1939, it was around 150. Over the decade of the 1930s, the Dow went down by 40 percent.

However, having said this, stock prices have gone up over the long run. For example, suppose we look at the S&P Index during the period 1926–2004. The data show that you would have had a 70 percent likelihood of earning a positive investment return over a 1-year period, but that would have risen to 86.5 percent chance of a positive investment return if you had held the stocks in the index over a 5-year period. The probability of a positive return goes up to 97.1 percent if you had held the stocks for 10 years.

Student:

Last question: Suppose I buy 100 shares of stock at a price of $40 a share. The stock goes down in price to $32. Shouldn't I wait until the share price rises to $40 or higher before I sell it?

Instructor:

When it comes to stock, what goes down is not guaranteed to go up. Even if the stock's price has gone down by $8, it might go down more. You want always to look forward, to the future (not backward, to the past), when deciding whether to sell a stock. if you think there is a reason for the price to fall even farther, it is better to sell at $32 (and take an $8 per share loss) than to sell at $25 and take a bigger loss. If you think there is a reason for the price to rise, then hold on to the stock.

Points to Remember

1. A company that issues bonds cannot set the coupon rate at whatever rate it wants.

2. Based on the period 1926–2004, the longer a person would have held stocks, the higher the probability he or she would have received a positive return.

3. Stocks that go down in price are not guaranteed to go up in price.

a reader asks | Is There a Financial Language All Its Own?

Sometimes, when I watch the financial news, I hear people using unfamiliar terms. Some of the terms they use seem to be peculiar to their field of financial expertise. What are some of these terms and what do they mean?

Here are some of the terms, followed by what they mean:

After the Bell
After the close of the stock market.

Air Pocket Stock
A stock that plunges fast and furiously, much like an airplane that hits an air pocket.

Big Board
A nickname for the New York Stock Exchange.

Bo Derek
A perfect stock or investment, named after the movie actress who starred in the 1979 movie *10*.

Bear Market
A market in which prices are expected to fall.

Bull Market
A market in which prices are expected to rise. The terms *bull* and *bear* come from how these animals attack their opponents. The bull puts its horns up in the air, and a bear moves its paws down (across its opponent).

Casino Finance
An investment strategy that is considered extremely risky.

Deer Market
A flat market in which not much is happening and investors are usually timid; neither a bull nor a bear market.

Eat Well, Sleep Well
A phrase that expresses the idea that, when it comes to investing, no one gets anything for nothing. If you want a high return, you usually have to assume some risk. If you don't want to take on much risk, then you will likely have a low return. In short, high risk comes with high return, and low risk comes with low return. Do you want a risky investment that may end up feeding you well, or do you want a safe investment that lets you sleep at night?

Falling Knife
A stock whose price has fallen significantly in a short time—"Don't try to catch a falling knife" (you can hurt yourself).

Goldilocks Economy
An economy that is not too hot or too cold but just right. People often referred to the economy in the mid- to late 1990s in the United States as the Goldilocks economy.

Lemon
A disappointing investment.

Love Money
Money given by family or friends to a person to start a business.

Nervous Nellie
An investor who isn't comfortable with investing, mainly because of the risks.

Sandwich Generation
People, usually of middle age, who are sandwiched, in a sense, between their children and their parents. They are said to have to take care of two groups of people, one on either side of them.

Santa Claus Rally
A jump in the price of stocks that often occurs the week between Christmas and New Year.

Short Selling
A technique used by investors who are trying to benefit from a falling stock price. To illustrate, Brian, who believes that stock X will soon fall in price, borrows the stock from someone who currently owns it and promises to return it later. He then sells the stock, hoping to buy it back later at a lower price.

War Babies
The name given to stocks issued by companies that produce military hardware (e.g., tanks, airplanes, etc.).

Chapter Summary

STOCKS

- A stock is a claim on the assets of a corporation that gives the purchaser a share (ownership) in the corporation. Stocks are sometimes called equity because the buyer of the stock has part ownership of the company that initially issued the stock.

- Stocks are bought and sold on exchanges and markets such as the New York Stock Exchange.

- Some people buy stocks for the dividends, which are payments made to stockholders based on a company's profits; others attempt to make money by buying shares at a lower price and selling at a higher price.

- Today, 30 stocks make up the Dow Jones Industrial Average (DJIA). The DJIA was devised by Charles Dow to convey information about what was happening in the stock market.
- A stock index fund consists of the stocks that make up an index.
- The yield (or interest rate) of a stock is equal to the dividend divided by the closing price of the stock.
- The P/E ratio for a stock is equal to the closing price per share (of the stock) divided by the net earnings per share. A stock with a P/E ratio of, say, 15 means that the stock is selling for a share price that is 15 times its earnings per share.

BONDS

- A bond is an IOU, or a promise to pay, typically issued by companies, governments, or government agencies.
- The three major components of a bond are face or par value, maturity date, and coupon rate.

- The price that a person pays for a bond depends on market conditions: The greater the demand is for the bond relative to the supply, the higher the price will be.
- The yield on the bond is the coupon payment divided by the price paid for the bond.
- Bonds are rated or evaluated. The more likely it is that the bond issuer will pay the face value of the bond at maturity and meet all scheduled coupon payments, the higher the bond's rating will be.
- The price of a bond and its yield (or interest rate) are inversely related.

FUTURES AND OPTIONS

- In a futures contract, a seller agrees to provide a good to the buyer on a specified future date at an agreed-on price.
- An option is a contract giving the owner the right, but not the obligation, to buy or sell a particular good at a specified price on or before a specified date.

Key Terms and Concepts

Stock	Initial Public Offering	Dividend	Yield
Dow Jones Industrial	(IPO)	Bond	Futures Contract
Average (DJIA)	Investment Bank	Face Value (Par Value)	Option

Questions and Problems

1. What is the purpose of financial markets?
2. What does it mean if the Dow Jones Industrial Average rises by, say, 100 points in a day?
3. What does it mean to buy the market?
4. What does it mean if someone invests in a mutual fund? in a stock market fund?
5. If the share price of each of 500 stocks rises on Monday, does everyone in the stock market believe that stocks are headed even higher? (No one will buy a stock if he or she thought share prices were headed lower.)
6. Which of the two stocks has a bigger gap between its closing price and net earnings per share: Stock A with a P/E ratio of 15 or Stock B with a P/E ratio of 44? Explain your answer.
7. "An issuer of a bond is a borrower." Do you agree or disagree? Explain your answer.

8. If the face value of a bond is $10,900 and the annual coupon payment is $600, what is the coupon rate?
9. Why might a person purchase an inflation-indexed Treasury bond?
10. "If you can predict interest rates, then you can earn a fortune buying and selling bonds." Do you agree or disagree? Explain your answer.
11. Why might a person buy a futures contract?
12. Why might a person buy a call option?
13. "The currency speculator who sells futures contracts assumes the risk that someone else doesn't want to assume." Do you agree or disagree? Explain your answer.
14. If you thought the share price of a stock was going to fall, would you buy a call option or a put option?

Working with Numbers and Graphs

1. You own 1,250 shares of stock X, and you read in the newspaper that the dividend for the stock is 3.88. What did you earn in dividends?
2. The closing price of a stock is 90.25, and the dividend is 3.50. What is the yield of the stock?
3. The closing price of the stock is $66.40, and the net earnings per share are $2.50. What is the stock's P/E ratio?

4. The face value of a bond is $10,000, and the annual coupon payment is $850. What is the coupon rate?
5. A person buys a bond that matures in 10 years and pays a coupon rate of 10 percent. The face value of the bond is $10,000. How much money will the bondholder receive in the tenth year?

SELF-TEST APPENDIX

Chapter 1

CHAPTER 1, PAGE 5

1 False. It takes two things for scarcity to exist: finite resources and infinite wants. If people's wants were equal to or less than the finite resources available to satisfy their wants, there would be no scarcity. Scarcity exists only because people's wants are greater than the resources available to satisfy their wants. Scarcity is the condition of infinite wants clashing with finite resources.

2 Because of scarcity, there is a need for a rationing device. People will compete for the rationing device. For example, if dollar price is the rationing device, people will compete for dollars.

3 Because our unlimited wants are greater than our limited resources—that is, because scarcity exists—some wants must go unsatisfied. We must choose which wants we will satisfy and which we will not.

CHAPTER 1, PAGE 13

1 Every time a person is late to history class, the instructor subtracts one-tenth of a point from the person's final grade. If the instructor raised the opportunity cost of being late to class—by subtracting one point from the person's final grade—economists predict there would be fewer persons late to class. In summary, the higher the opportunity cost of being late to class, the less likely people will be late to class.

2 Yes. To illustrate, suppose the marginal benefits and marginal costs (in dollars) are as follows for various hours of studying.

Hour	Marginal Benefits	Marginal Costs
First hour	$20.00	$10.00
Second hour	$14.00	$11.00
Third hour	$13.00	$12.00
Fourth hour	$12.10	$12.09
Fifth hour	$11.00	$13.00

Clearly, you will study the first hour because the marginal benefits are greater than the marginal costs. Stated differently, there is a net benefit of $10 (the difference between the marginal benefits of $20 and the marginal costs of $10) for studying the first hour. If you stop studying after the first hour and do not proceed to the second, then you will forfeit the net benefit of $3 for the second hour. To maximize your net benefits of studying, you must proceed until the marginal benefits and the marginal costs are as close to equal as possible. (In the extreme, this is an epsilon away from equality. However, economists simply speak of "equality" between the two for convenience.) In this case, you will study through the fourth hour. You will not study the fifth hour because it is not worth it; the marginal benefits of

studying the fifth hour are less than the marginal costs. In short, there is a net cost to studying the fifth hour.

3 You might feel sleepy the next day, you might be less alert while driving, and so on.

Chapter 2

CHAPTER 2, PAGE 39

1 A straight-line PPF represents constant opportunity costs between two goods. For example, for every unit of X produced, one unit of Y is forfeited. A bowed-outward PPF represents increasing opportunity costs. For example, we may have to forfeit one unit of X to produce the eleventh unit of Y, but we have to forfeit two units of X to produce the one hundredth unit of Y.

2 A bowed-outward PPF is representative of increasing costs. In short, the PPF would not be bowed outward if increasing costs did not exist. To prove this, look back at Exhibits 1 and 2. In Exhibit 1, costs are constant (not increasing), and the PPF is a straight line. In Exhibit 2, costs are increasing, and the PPF is bowed outward.

3 The first condition is that the economy is currently operating *below* its PPF. It is possible to move from a point below the PPF to a point on the PPF and get more of all goods. The second condition is that the economy's PPF shifts outward.

4 False. Take a look at Exhibit 5. There are numerous productive efficient points, all of which lie on the PPF.

CHAPTER 2, PAGE 44

1 Transaction costs are the costs associated with the time and effort needed to search out, negotiate, and consummate a trade. The transaction costs are likely to be higher for buying a house than for buying a car because buying a house is a more detailed and complex process.

2 Under certain conditions, Smith will buy good X from Jones. For example, suppose Smith and Jones agree on a price of, say, $260, and neither person incurs transaction costs greater than $40. If transaction costs are zero for each person, then each person benefits $40 from the trade. Specifically, Smith buys the good for $40 less than his maximum price, and Jones sells the good for $40 more than his minimum price. But suppose each person incurs a transaction cost of, say, $50. Smith would be unwilling to pay $260 to Jones and $50 in transaction costs (for a total of $310) when he is only willing to pay a maximum price of $300 for good X. Similarly, Jones would be unwilling to sell good X for $260 and incur $50 in transaction costs (leaving him with only $210, or $10 less than his minimum selling price).

3 Answers will vary. Sample answer: John buys a magazine and reads it. There is no third-party effect. Sally asks a rock band to play at a party. Sally's next-door neighbor (a third party) is disturbed by the loud music.

CHAPTER 2, PAGE 48

1 If George goes from producing 5X to 10X, he gives up 5Y. This means the opportunity cost of 5 more X is 5 fewer Y. It follows that the opportunity cost of 1X is 1Y. Conclusion: The opportunity cost of 1X is 1Y.

2 If Harriet produces 10 more X she gives up 15Y. It follows that the opportunity cost of 1X is 1.5Y, and the opportunity cost of 1Y is 0.67X. If Bill produces 10 more X, he gives up 20Y. It follows that the opportunity cost of 1X is 2Y, and the opportunity cost of 1Y is 0.5X. Harriet is the lower cost producer of X, and Bill is the lower cost producer of Y. In short, Harriet has the comparative advantage in the production of X; Bill has the comparative advantage in the production of Y.

Chapter 3

CHAPTER 3, PAGE 66

1 Popcorn is a normal good for Sandi. Prepaid telephone cards are an inferior good for Mark.

2 Asking why demand curves are downward sloping is the same as asking why price and quantity demanded are inversely related (as one rises, the other falls). There are two reasons mentioned in this section: (1) as price rises, people substitute lower priced goods for higher priced goods, and (2) because individuals receive less utility from an additional unit of a good they consume, they are only willing to pay less for the additional unit. The second reason is a reflection of the law of diminishing marginal utility.

3 Suppose only two people, Bob and Alice, have a demand for good X. At a price of $7, Bob buys 10 units and Alice buys 3 units; at a price of $6, Bob buys 12 units and Alice buys 5 units. One point on the market demand curve represents a price of $7 and a quantity demanded of 13 units; another point represents $6 and 17 units. A market demand curve is derived by adding the quantities demanded at each price.

4 A change in income, preferences, prices of related goods, number of buyers, and expectations of future price can change demand. A change in the price of the good changes the quantity demanded of the good. For example, a change in *income* can change the *demand* for oranges, but only a change in the *price* of oranges can directly change the *quantity demanded* of oranges.

CHAPTER 3, PAGE 71

1 It would be difficult to increase the quantity supplied of houses over the next ten hours, so the supply curve in (a) is vertical, as in Exhibit 8. It is possible to increase the quantity supplied of houses over the next three months, however, so the supply curve in (b) is upward sloping.

2 a. The supply curve shifts to the left.
   b. The supply curve shifts to the left.
   c. The supply curve shifts to the right.

3 False. If the price of apples rises, the *quantity supplied* of apples will rise—not the *supply* of apples. We are talking about a *movement* from one point on a supply curve to a point higher up on the supply curve and not about a shift in the supply curve.

CHAPTER 3, PAGE 82

1 Disagree. In the text, we plainly saw how supply and demand work at an auction. Supply and demand are at work in the grocery store, too, although no auctioneer is present. The essence of the auction example is the auctioneer raising the price when there was a shortage and lowering the price when there was a surplus. The same thing happens at the grocery store. For example, if there is a surplus of corn flakes, the manager of the store is likely to have a sale (lower prices) on corn flakes. Many markets without auctioneers act *as if* there are auctioneers raising and lowering prices in response to shortages and surpluses.

2 No. It could be the result of a higher supply of computers. Either a decrease in demand or an increase in supply will lower price.

3 a. Lower price and quantity
   b. Lower price and higher quantity
   c. Higher price and lower quantity
   d. Lower price and quantity

4 At equilibrium quantity, the maximum buying price and the minimum selling price are the same. For example, in Exhibit 15, both prices are $40 at the equilibrium quantity 4. Equilibrium quantity is the only quantity at which the maximum buying price and the minimum selling price are the same.

5 $44; $34.

CHAPTER 3, PAGE 85

1 Yes, if nothing else changes—that is, yes, *ceteris paribus.* If some other things change, though, they may not. For example, if the government imposes an effective price ceiling on gasoline, Jamie may pay lower gas prices at the pump but have to wait in line to buy the gas (due to first come, first served trying to ration the shortage). It is not clear if Jamie is better off paying a higher price and not waiting in line or paying a lower price and waiting in line. The point, however, is that buyers don't necessarily prefer lower prices to higher prices unless everything else (quality, wait, service, etc.) stays the same.

2 Disagree. Both long-lasting shortages and long lines are caused by price ceilings. First, the price ceiling is imposed, creating the shortage; then, the rationing device first come, first served emerges because price isn't permitted to fully ration the good. There are shortages every day that don't cause long lines to form. Instead, buyers bid up price, output and price move to equilibrium, and there is no shortage.

3 Buyers might argue for price ceilings on the goods they buy—especially if they don't know that price ceilings have some effects they may not like (e.g., fewer exchanges, FCFS used as a rationing device). Sellers might argue for price floors on the goods they sell—especially if they expect their profits to rise. Employees might argue for a wage floor on the labor services they sell—especially if they don't know that they may lose their jobs or have their hours cut back as a result.

Chapter 4

CHAPTER 4, PAGE 94

1 The price of food will rise along with the premium for food insurance.

2 The new demand curve would be between D_1 and D_2.

CHAPTER 4, PAGE 95

1 City 2

2 City 2

CHAPTER 4, PAGE 96

1 If supply and tuition are constant and demand rises, the shortage of openings at the university will become greater. The university will continue to use its nonprice rationing devices (GPA, SAT scores, ACT scores) but will have to raise the standards of admission. Instead of requiring a GPA of, say, 3.5 for admission, it may raise the requirement to 3.8.

2 Not likely. A university that didn't make admission easier in the face of a surplus of openings might not be around much longer. When tuition cannot be adjusted directly—in other words, when the rationing device of price cannot be adjusted—it is likely that the nonprice rationing device (standards) will be.

CHAPTER 4, PAGE 97

1 Any price above 70 cents.

2 Assuming that tolls are not used, freeway congestion will worsen. An increase in driving population simply shifts the demand curve for driving to the right.

CHAPTER 4, PAGE 99

1 Agree. At any price below equilibrium price, a shortage exists: The quantity demanded of kidneys is greater than the quantity supplied of kidneys. As price rises toward its equilibrium level, quantity supplied rises and quantity demanded falls until the two are equal.

2 It depends on whether or not $0 is the equilibrium price of kidneys. If it is—that is, if the kidney demand and supply curves intersect at $0—then there is no shortage of kidneys. But if, at $0, the quantity demanded of kidneys is greater than the quantity supplied, then a shortage exists.

CHAPTER 4, PAGE 101

1 Yes. At the equilibrium wage rate, the quantity demanded of labor equals the quantity supplied. At a higher wage (the minimum wage), the quantity supplied stays constant (given the vertical supply curve), but the quantity demanded falls. Thus, a surplus results.

2 The person is assuming that the labor demand curve is vertical (no matter what the wage rate is the quantity demanded of labor is always the same).

CHAPTER 4, PAGE 102

1 Look at the demand curve and the supply curve between Q_2 and Q_1. Notice that the demand curve lies *above* the supply curve in this area. This means that buyers are willing to pay more for each of the units between Q_2 and Q_2 (more, say, for the $Q_2 + 1$ unit) than sellers need to receive for them to place these units on the market. In short, moving from an equilibrium price to a price floor lowers the number of mutually beneficial trades that will be made. As discussed in Chapter 3, price floors lead to fewer exchanges.

2 It is likely that producers care more about how a change affects them than how it affects society. At the price floor, they receive more producers' surplus than they receive at the equilibrium price, even though consumers lose, in terms of consumers' surplus, more than producers gain. Look at it like this: Producers gain $10 and consumers lose $12. The sum of positive $10 and negative $12 is negative $2. Producers may not care about the sum ($-$2); they care about their $10 gain.

CHAPTER 4, PAGE 104

1 Moving from a system where patients cannot sue their HMOs to one where they can gives patients something they didn't have before (the right to sue) at a higher price (higher charges for health care coverage). The "free lunch"—the right to sue—isn't free after all.

2 If the students get the extra week and nothing else changes, then the students will probably say they are better off. In other words, more of one thing (time) and no less of anything else makes one better off. But if because of the extra week, the professor grades their papers harder than she would have otherwise, then some or all of the students may say that they weren't made better off by the extra week.

CHAPTER 4, PAGE 105

1 One possible answer is: There are two cities, one with clean air and the other with dirty air. The demand to live in the clean-air city is higher than the demand to live in the dirty-air city. As a result, housing prices are higher in the clean-air city than in the dirty-air city.

2 Ultimately, the person who owns the land in the good-weather city receives the payment. Look at it this way: People have a higher demand for houses in good-weather cities than they do for houses in bad-weather cities. As a result, house builders receive higher prices for houses built and sold in good-weather cities. Because of the higher house prices in good-weather cities, house builders have a higher demand for land in good-weather cities. In the end, higher demand for land translates into higher land prices or land rents for landowners.

CHAPTER 4, PAGE 107

1 Suppose University X gives a full scholarship to every one of its football players (all of whom are superathletes). In addition, suppose that the full scholarship (translated into wages) is far below the equilibrium wage of each of the football players. (Think of it this way: Each football player gets a wage, or full scholarship, of $10,000 a year, when his equilibrium wage is $40,000 a year.) Paying lower than the equilibrium wage will end up transferring dollars and other benefits from the football players to the university to the

new field house and track and perhaps to you if you use the track for exercise.

2 If paying student athletes (a wage above the full scholarship) lowers consumers' demand for college athletics, then the equilibrium wage for college athletes is not as high as shown in Exhibit 10.

CHAPTER 4, PAGE 108

1 Answers will vary. Students sometimes say that it is "fairer" if everyone is charged the same price. Is it unfair then that movie goers pay less if they go to the 2 p.m. movie than if they go to the 8 p.m. movie?

2 In the application dealing with the kidney market, there was a price ceiling that resulted in a shortage of kidneys. In the application dealing with the 10 a.m. class, the university charged a below-equilibrium price for the 10 a.m. class, leading to a shortage of such classes.

Chapter 5

CHAPTER 5, PAGE 123

1 $E_d = 1.44$.

2 If there is a change in price, quantity demanded will change (in the opposite direction) by 0.39 times the percentage change in price. For example, if price rises 10 percent, then quantity demanded will fall 3.9 percent. If price rises 20 percent, then quantity demanded will fall 7.8 percent.

3 a. Total revenue falls.

b. Total revenue falls.

c. Total revenue remains constant.

d. Total revenue rises.

e. Total revenue rises.

4 Alexi is implicitly assuming that demand is inelastic. If, however, she is wrong and demand is elastic, then a rise in price will actually lower total revenue.

CHAPTER 5, PAGE 126

1 No. Moving from 7 to 9 substitutes doesn't necessarily change demand from being inelastic to elastic. It simply leads to a rise in price elasticity of demand, *ceteris paribus*. For example, if price elasticity of demand is 0.45 when there are 7 substitutes, it will be higher when there are 9 substitutes, *ceteris paribus*. Higher could be 0.67. If this is the case, demand is still inelastic (but less so than before).

2 a. Dell computers.

b. Heinz ketchup.

c. Perrier water.

In all three cases, the good with the higher price elasticity of demand is the more specific of the two goods; therefore, it has more substitutes.

CHAPTER 5, PAGE 135

1 The good in question is a normal good, and it is income elastic; that is, as income rises, the quantity demanded rises by a greater percentage. In this case, quantity demanded rises by 1.33 times the percentage change in income. If income rises by 10 percent, the quantity demanded of the good will rise by 13.3 percent.

2 A change in price does not change quantity supplied.

3 Tax revenue is equal to the tax times the quantity sold. If demand is inelastic, there will be a smaller cutback in quantity sold due to the higher price brought about by the tax.

4 Under the condition that the demand for computers is perfectly inelastic or that the supply of computers is perfectly elastic.

Chapter 6

CHAPTER 6, PAGE 145

1 The paradox is that water, which is essential to life, is cheap, and diamonds, which are not essential to life, are expensive. The solution to the paradox depends on knowing the difference between total and marginal utility and the law of diminishing marginal utility. By saying that water is essential to life and that diamonds are not essential to life, we signify that water gives us high total utility relative to diamonds. But then, if water gives us greater total utility than diamonds do, why isn't the price of water greater than that of diamonds. Price isn't a reflection of total utility; it is a reflection of marginal utility. The marginal utility of water is less than that of diamonds. This answer raises another question: How can the total utility of water be greater than that of diamonds, but the marginal utility of water be less than that of diamonds? The answer is based on the fact that water is plentiful and diamonds are not and on the law of diminishing marginal utility. There is so much more water than diamonds that the next (additional) unit of water gives us less utility (lower marginal utility) than the next unit of diamonds.

2 If total utility declines, marginal utility must be negative. For example, if total utility is 30 utils when Lydia consumes 3 apples and 25 utils when she consumes 4 apples, it must be because the fourth apple had a marginal utility of −5 utils. Chapter 1 explains that something that takes utility away from us (or gives us disutility) is called a *bad*. For Lydia, the fourth apple is a bad, not a good.

3 The total utility and the marginal utility of a good are the same for the first unit of the good consumed. For example, before Tomas eats his first apple, he receives no utility or disutility from apples. Eating the first apple, he receives 15 utils. So the total utility (*TU*) for 1 apple is 15 utils, and the marginal utility (*MU*) for the first apple is 15 utils. Exhibit 1 shows that *TU* and *MU* are the same for the first unit of good X.

CHAPTER 6, PAGE 149

1 Alesandro is not in consumer equilibrium because the marginal utility per dollar of X is 16 utils, and the marginal utility per dollar of Y is 13.14 utils. To be in equilibrium, a consumer has to receive the same marginal utility per dollar for each good consumed.

2 The marginal utility-to-price ratio for one of the goods is higher than the ratio for the other good.

CHAPTER 6, PAGE 155

1 Yes, Brandon is compartmentalizing. He is treating $100 that comes from his grandmother differently from $100 that comes from his father.

2 The endowment effect relates to individuals valuing X more highly when they possess it than when they don't have it but are thinking of acquiring it. Friedman argues that if we go back in time to a hunter-gatherer society when there were no well established property rights (no rules as to what is mine and thine), if some individuals would fight hard to keep what they possessed but wouldn't fight as hard to acquire what they did not possess, they would have a higher probability of surviving than individuals who would fight hard at both times. Thus, those who would fight hard only to keep what they possessed would have a higher probability of reproductive success. The characteristic of holding on to what you have has been passed down from generation to generation, and, although it may not be as important today as it was in a hunter-gatherer society, it still influences behavior.

Chapter 7

CHAPTER 7, PAGE 171

1 No. Individuals will form teams or firms only when the sum of what they can produce as a team (or firm) is greater than the sum of what they can produce working alone.

2 The person earning the low salary has lower implicit costs and so is more likely to start a business. She gives up less to start a business.

3 Accounting profit is larger. Only explicit costs are subtracted from total revenue in computing accounting profit, but both explicit and implicit costs are subtracted from total revenue in computing economic profit. If implicit costs are zero, then accounting profit and economic profit are the same. Economic profit is never greater than accounting profit.

4 A business owner can be earning a profit but not covering costs when he is earning (positive) accounting profit but his total revenue does not cover the sum of his explicit and implicit costs. For example, suppose Brad earns total revenue of $100,000 and has explicit costs of $40,000 and implicit costs of $70,000. His accounting profit is $60,000, but his total revenue of $100,000 is not large enough to cover the sum of his explicit and implicit costs ($110,000). Brad's economic profit is a negative $10,000. In other words, although Brad earns an accounting profit, he takes an economic loss.

CHAPTER 7, PAGE 178

1 No. The short run and the long run are not lengths of time. The short run is that period of time when some inputs are fixed and therefore the firm has fixed costs. The long run is any period of time when no inputs are fixed (i.e., all inputs are variable) and thus all costs are variable costs. The short run can be, say, six months, and the long run can be a much shorter period of time. In other words, the time period when there are no fixed inputs can be shorter than the time period when there are fixed inputs.

2 The law of diminishing marginal returns holds only when we add more of one input to a given (fixed) quantity of another input. The statement does not identify one input as fixed (it says that both increase), and so the law of diminishing marginal returns is not relevant in this situation.

3 When MC is declining, MPP is rising; when MC is constant, MPP is constant; and when MC is rising, MPP is falling.

CHAPTER 7, PAGE 187

1 $ATC = TC/Q$ and $ATC = AFC + AVC$.

2 Yes. Suppose a business incurs a cost of $10 to make a product. Before it can sell the product, though, the demand for it falls and moves the market price from $15 to $6. Does the owner of the business say, "I can't sell the product for $6 because I'd be taking a loss"? If she does, she chooses to let a sunk cost affect her current decision. Instead, she should ask herself, "Do I think the market price of the product will rise or fall?" If she thinks it will fall, she should sell the product today for $6.

3 Unit costs are another name for average total costs (ATC); so the question is what happens to ATC as MC rises? You might be inclined to say that as MC rises, so does ATC, but this is not necessarily so [see region 1 in Exhibit 5(b)]. What matters is whether MC is greater than ATC. If it is, then ATC will rise. If it is not, then ATC will decline. This is a trick question of sorts. There is a tendency to misinterpret the average-marginal rule and to believe that as marginal cost rises, average total cost rises and that as marginal cost falls, average total cost falls. But the average-marginal rule actually says that when MC is above ATC, ATC rises, and when MC is below ATC, ATC falls.

4 Yes. As marginal physical product (MPP) rises, marginal cost (MC) falls. If MC falls enough to move below unit cost (which is the same as average total cost), then unit cost declines. Similarly, as MPP falls, MC rises. If MC rises enough to move above unit cost, then unit cost rises.

CHAPTER 7, PAGE 191

1 It currently takes 10 units of X and 10 units of Y to produce 50 units of good Z. Let both X and Y double to 20 units each. As a result, the output of Z more than doubles—say, to 150 units. When inputs are increased by some percentage and output increases by a greater percentage, then economies of scale are said to exist. When economies of scale exist, unit costs fall, and another name for unit costs is average total costs.

2 The $LRATC$ curve would be horizontal. When there are constant returns to scale, output doubles if inputs double. If this happens, unit costs stay constant. In other words, they don't rise and they don't fall; so the $LRATC$ curve is horizontal.

3 Unit costs must have been lower when it produced 200 units than when it produced 100 units. That is, there were economies of scale between 100 units and 200 units. To explain further, profit per unit is the difference between price per unit and cost per unit (or unit costs): Profit per unit = Price per unit − Cost per unit. Suppose the unit cost is $3 when the price is $4—giving a profit per unit of $1. Next, there are economies of scale as the firm raises output from 100 units to 200 units. Unit costs must fall—let's say to $2 per unit. If price is $3, then there is still a $1 per-unit profit.

Chapter 8

CHAPTER 8, PAGE 201

1   The firm cannot change the price of the product it sells by its actions. For example, if firm A cuts back on the supply of what it produces and the price of its product does not change, then we'd say that the firm cannot control the price of the product it sells. In other words, if price is independent of a firm's actions, the firm does not have any control over price.

2   The easy and incomplete answer is that a perfectly competitive firm is a price taker because it is in a market where it cannot control the price of the product it sells. But this simply leads to the question, why can't it control the price? The answer is that it is in a market where its supply is small relative to the total market supply, it sells a homogeneous good, and all buyers and sellers have all relevant information.

3   If a perfectly competitive firm tries to charge a price higher than equilibrium price, all buyers will know this (assumption 3). These buyers will then simply buy from another firm that sells the same (homogeneous) product (assumption 2).

4   No. A market doesn't have to perfectly match all assumptions of the theory of perfect competition for it to be labeled a perfectly competitive market. What is important is whether it acts *as if* it is perfectly competitive. "If it walks like a duck and it quacks like a duck, it's a duck." Well, if it acts like a perfectly competitive market, it's a perfectly competitive market.

CHAPTER 8, PAGE 209

1   No. Whether a firm earns profits depends on the relationship between price (P) and average total cost (ATC). If $P > ATC$, then the firm earns profits. To understand this, remember that profits exist when total revenue (TR) minus total cost (TC) is a positive number. Total revenue is simply price times quantity ($TR = P \times Q$), and total cost is average total cost times quantity ($TC = ATC \times Q$). Because quantity (Q) is common to both TR and TC, if $P > ATC$, then $TR > TC$, and the firm earns profits.

2   In the short run, whether a firm should shut down operations depends on the relationship between price and average variable cost (AVC), not between price and ATC. It depends on whether price is greater than or less than average variable cost. If $P > AVC$, the firm should continue to produce; if $P < AVC$, it should shut down.

3   As long as $MR > MC$—for example, $MR = \$6$ and $MC = \$4$—the firm should produce and sell additional units of a good because this adds more to TR than it does to TC. It's adding $\$6$ to TR and $\$4$ to TC. Whenever you add more to TR than you do to TC, the gap between the two becomes larger.

4   We start with the upward-sloping market supply curve and work backward. First, market supply curves are upward sloping because they are the addition of individual firms' supply curves—which are upward sloping. Second, individual firms' supply curves are upward sloping because they are the portion of their marginal cost curves above their average variable cost curves, and this portion of the MC curve is upward sloping. Third, marginal cost curves have upward-sloping portions because of the law of diminishing marginal returns. In conclusion, market supply curves are upward sloping because of the law of diminishing marginal returns.

CHAPTER 8, PAGE 217

1   According to the theory of perfect competition, the profits will draw new firms into the market. As these new firms enter the market, the market supply curve will shift to the right. As a result of a larger supply, price will fall. As price declines, profit will decline until firms in the market are earning (only) normal (or zero economic) profit. When there is zero economic profit, there is no longer an incentive for firms to enter the market.

2   No. The market is only in long-run competitive equilibrium when (1) there is no incentive for firms to enter or exit the industry, (2) there is no incentive for firms to produce more or less output, and (3) there is no incentive for firms to change their plant size. If any of these conditions is not met, then the market is not in long-run equilibrium.

3   Initially, price will rise. Recall from Chapter 3 that, when demand increases, *ceteris paribus*, price rises. In time, though, price will drop because new firms will enter the industry due to the positive economic profits generated by the higher price. How far the price drops depends on whether the firms are in a constant-cost, an increasing-cost, or a decreasing-cost industry. In a constant-cost industry, price will return to its original level; in an increasing-cost industry, price will return to a level above its original level; and in a decreasing-cost industry, price will return to a level below its original level.

4   Maybe initially, but probably not after certain adjustments are made. If firm A really has a genius on its payroll and, as a result, earns higher profits than firm B, then firm B might try to hire the genius away from firm A by offering a higher income. To keep the genius, firm A will have to match the offer. As a result, the costs of firm A will rise, and, if nothing else changes, its profits will decline.

CHAPTER 8, PAGE 218

1   Higher prices depend on how many firms in the market witness higher costs. If only one has increased costs, then the market supply curve is not likely to shift enough to bring about a higher price. If, however, many firms in the market witness higher costs, then the market supply curve will shift left, and price will rise.

2   No. Perfectly competitive firms that sell homogeneous products won't advertise individually, but the industry could advertise in the hope of pushing the market (industry) demand curve (for their product) to the right.

Chapter 9

CHAPTER 9, PAGE 226

1   Let's assume the statement is right—that there are always some close substitutes for the product a firm sells. The question, however, is how close does the substitute have to be before the theory of monopoly is not useful? For example,

a slightly close substitute for a seller's product may not be close enough to matter. The theory of monopoly may still be useful in predicting a firm's behavior.

2 Economies of scale exist when a firm doubles inputs and its output more than doubles, lowering its unit costs (average total costs) in the process. If economies of scale exist only when a firm produces a large quantity of output and one firm is already producing this output, then new firms (that initially produce less output) will have higher unit costs than those of the established firm. Some economists argue that this will make the new firms uncompetitive when compared to the established firm. In other words, economies of scale act as a barrier to entry, effectively preventing firms from entering the industry and competing with the established firm.

3 In a monopoly, there is a single seller of a good for which there are no close substitutes, and there are extremely high barriers to competing with the single seller. If a movie superstar has so much talent that the moviegoing public puts her in a class by herself, she might be considered a monopolist. Can anyone compete with her? They can try, but she may have such great talent (relative to everyone else) that no one will be able to effectively compete with her. Her immense talent acts as a barrier to entry in the sense that even if others try to compete with her, they won't be a close enough substitute for her.

CHAPTER 9, PAGE 233

1 The single-price monopolist has to lower price to sell an additional unit of its good (as a downward-sloping demand curve necessitates). As long as it has to lower price to sell an additional unit, its marginal revenue will be below its price. A demand curve plots price (P) and quantity (Q), and a marginal revenue curve plots marginal revenue (MR) and quantity (Q). Because $P > MR$ for a monopolist, its demand curve will lie above its marginal revenue curve.

2 No. Profit depends on whether price is greater than average total cost. A monopolist can produce the quantity of output at which $MR = MC$, charge the highest price per unit possible for the output, and still have its unit costs (ATC) greater than price. If this is the case, the monopolist incurs losses; it does not earn profits.

3 No. The last chapter explains that a firm is resource allocative efficient when it charges a price equal to its marginal cost ($P = MC$). The monopolist does not do this; it charges a price above marginal cost. Profit maximization ($MR = MC$) does not lead to resource allocative efficiency ($P = MC$) because for the monopolist $P > MR$. This is not the case for the perfectly competitive firm, where $P = MR$.

4 A monopolist is searching for the highest price at which it can sell its product. In contrast, the perfectly competitive firm doesn't have to search; it simply takes the equilibrium price established in the market. For example, suppose Nancy is a wheat farmer. She gets up one morning and wants to know at what price she should sell her wheat. She simply turns on the radio, listens to the farm report, and finds out that the equilibrium price per bushel of wheat is, say, $5. Being a price taker, she knows she can't sell her wheat for a penny more than this ($5 is the highest price), and she won't want to sell her wheat for a penny less. The monopoly firm doesn't know the highest price for its product. It has to search for it; it has to experiment with different prices before it finds the so-called highest price.

CHAPTER 9, PAGE 243

1 There are three in particular: (1) A monopoly firm produces too little output relative to a perfectly competitive firm; this causes the deadweight loss of monopoly. (2) The profits of the monopoly are sometimes subject to rent-seeking behavior. Rent seeking, while rational for an individual firm, wastes society's resources. Society receives no benefit if one firm expends resources to take over the monopoly position of another firm. Resources that could have been used to produce goods (e.g., computers, software, shoes, houses, etc.) are instead used to transfer profits from one firm to another. (3) A monopolist may not produce its products at the lowest possible cost. Again, this wastes society's resources.

2 As an example, suppose a perfectly competitive firm would produce 100 units of good X, but a monopoly firm would produce only 70, for a difference of 30 units. Buyers value these 30 units by more than it would cost the monopoly firm to produce them, yet the monopoly firm chooses not to produce them. The net benefit (benefits to buyers minus costs to the monopolist) of producing these 30 units is said to be the deadweight loss of monopoly. It represents how much buyers lose because the monopolist chooses to produce less than the perfectly competitive firm.

3 A seller who is not a price searcher is a price taker. A price taker can sell a product at only one price, the market equilibrium price.

Chapter 10

CHAPTER 10, PAGE 250

1 A monopolistic competitor is like a monopolist in that it faces a downward-sloping demand curve; it is a price searcher, $P > MR$; and it is not resource allocative efficient. It is like a perfect competitor in that it sells to many buyers and competes with many sellers, and there is easy entry into and exit from the market.

2 Essentially, monopolistic competitors face downward-sloping demand curves. Because the demand curve is downward sloping, it cannot be tangent to the lowest point on a U-shaped ATC curve (see Exhibit 3).

CHAPTER 10, PAGE 258

1 The incentive in both cases is the same: profit. Firms have an incentive to form a cartel to increase their profits. After the cartel is formed, however, each firm has an incentive to break the cartel to increase its profits even further, as illustrated in Exhibit 5. If there is no cartel agreement, the firm is earning zero profits by producing q_1. After the cartel is formed, it earns CP_CAB in profits by producing q_C. But it can earn even higher profits (FP_CDE) by cheating on the cartel and producing q_{CC}.

2 The kink occurs because the demand curve for an oligopolist is more elastic above the kink than it is below it. The difference in elasticity is based on the assumption that rival

(oligopoly) firms will not match a price hike but will match a price decline. Thus, if a given oligopolist raises product price, it is assumed that its quantity demanded will fall a lot, but if it lowers price, its quantity demanded will not rise much.

3 The dominant firm tries to figure out the price that would exist if it were not in the market. If this price is $10, the dominant firm figures out how much it would supply at this price (the answer is zero) and at all prices lower than this. For example, suppose the firm supplies 0 units at $10, 20 units at $9, and 30 units at $8. These, then, are three points on the dominant firm's demand curve—sometimes called the residual demand curve. Next, the dominant firm produces the level of output at which $MR = MC$ and charges the highest price per unit consistent with this output.

Chapter 11

CHAPTER 11, PAGE 284

1 How a market is defined helps determine whether a firm is considered a monopoly. If a market is defined broadly, it will include more substitute goods, and so the firm is less likely to be considered a monopolist. If a market is defined narrowly, it will include fewer substitute goods, and so the firm is more likely to be considered a monopolist.

2 The four-firm concentration ratio is 20 percent; the Herfindahl index is 500. The formulas in Exhibit 1 show how each is computed.

3 The Herfindahl index provides information about the dispersion of firm size in an industry. For example, suppose the top four firms in an industry have 15 percent, 10 percent, 9 percent, and 8 percent market shares. The four-firm concentration ratio will be the same for an industry with 15 firms as it is for an industry with 150 firms. The Herfindahl index will be different in the two situations.

CHAPTER 11, PAGE 290

1 Average cost pricing is the same as profit regulation. The regulators state that the natural monopolist must charge a price equal to its average total costs ($P = ATC$). Under this pricing policy, there is no incentive for the natural monopolist to keep costs down. In fact, there may be an incentive to deliberately push costs up. Higher costs—in the form of higher salaries or more luxurious offices—simply mean higher prices to cover the higher costs.

2 No matter what the motive is for initially regulating an industry, eventually the regulating agency will be captured by the special interests (the firms) in the industry. In the end, the regulatory body will not so much regulate the industry as serve the interests of the firms in the industry.

3 According to the capture theory, the outcomes of the regulatory process will favor the regulated firms. According to the public choice theory, the outcomes of the regulatory process will favor the regulators.

4 Sometimes they favor regulation, and at other times they do not. Economists make the point that regulation involves both costs and benefits, and whether the particular regulation in question is worthwhile depends on whether the costs are greater or less than the benefits.

Chapter 12

CHAPTER 12, PAGE 302

1 $MRP = MR \times MPP$. For a perfectly competitive firm, $MR = P$, so MR is $10. MPP in this case is 19 units. It follows that $MRP = \$190$.

2 There is no difference between MRP and VMP if the firm is perfectly competitive. In this situation, $P = MR$, and because $MRP = MR \times MPP$ and $VMP = P \times MPP$, the two are the same. If the firm is a price searcher—monopolist, monopolistic competitor, or oligopolist—$P > MR$; therefore, $VMP > MRP$.

3 A factor price taker can buy all it wants of a factor at the equilibrium price, and it will not cause factor price to rise. For example, if firm X is a factor price taker in the labor market, it can buy all the labor it wants at the equilibrium wage, and it will not cause this wage to rise.

4 A firm should buy that quantity at which MRP of labor = MFC of labor.

CHAPTER 12, PAGE 314

1 The MRP curve is the firm's factor demand curve. $MRP = P \times MPP$ for a perfectly competitive firm; so if either the price of the product that labor produces rises or the MPP of labor rises (reflected in a shift in the MPP curve), the factor demand curve shifts rightward.

2 It means that for every 1 percent change in the wage rate, the quantity demanded of labor changes by 3 times this percentage. For example, if wage rates rise 10 percent, then the quantity demanded of labor falls 30 percent.

3 The short answer is because supply-and-demand conditions differ among markets. But this answer raises the question, why do supply-and-demand conditions differ? This question is answered in Exhibit 11.

4 We can't answer this question specifically without more information. We know that under four conditions, wage rates would not differ: (1) The demand for every type of labor is the same; (2) there are no special nonpecuniary aspects to any job; (3) all labor is ultimately homogeneous and can costlessly be trained for different types of employment; and (4) all labor is mobile at zero cost. For wage rates to differ, one or more of these conditions is not being met. For example, perhaps labor is not mobile at zero cost.

Chapter 13

CHAPTER 13, PAGE 326

1 The demand for union labor is lowered by (a) a decline in the demand for the product that union labor produces, (b) a decline in the price of substitute factors, and (c) a decline in the marginal physical product of union labor.

2 A closed shop requires an employee to be a member of the union before he or she can be hired; a union shop does not. The union shop requires employees to join the union within a certain period of time after becoming employed.

3   The objective of a strike is to prove to management that union members will not work for a wage rate that is lower than the rate specified by the union. In terms of Exhibit 3, it is to prove that union members will not work for less than W_2.

CHAPTER 13, PAGE 334

1   A monopsonist cannot buy additional units of a factor without increasing the price it pays for the factor. A factor price taker can.

2   A minimum wage will increase the number of people working when (1) the firm hiring the labor is a monopsonist, and (2) the minimum wage is above the wage it is already paying and below the wage that corresponds to the point where $MFC = MRP$. To understand this completely, look at Exhibit 4(c). Suppose the firm is currently purchasing Q_1 labor and paying W_1. Then W_2 becomes the minimum wage the monopsonist can pay to workers. Now it hires Q_2 workers. Notice, however, that if the monopsonist had to pay a wage higher than the wage that equates MFC and MRP, it would employ fewer workers than Q_1.

3   If the higher wage rate reduces the number of people working in the unionized sector and the people who lose their jobs in the unionized sector move to the nonunionized sector, then the supply of labor will increase in the nonunionized sector and wage rates will fall, as illustrated in Exhibit 6.

Chapter 14

CHAPTER 14, PAGE 344

1   Government can change the distribution of income through transfer payments and taxes. Look at this equation:

$$\text{Individual income} = \text{Labor income} + \text{Asset income} + \text{Transfer payments} - \text{Taxes}$$

By increasing one person's taxes and increasing another person's transfer payments, government can change people's incomes.

2   The statement is true. For example, two people can have unequal incomes at any one point in time and still earn the same incomes over time. For example, in year 1, Patrick earns $40,000 and Moisha earns $20,000. In year 2, Moisha earns $40,000 and Patrick earns $20,000. In each year, there is income inequality, but over the two years, Patrick and Moisha earn the same income ($60,000).

3   No. Individual income = Labor income + Asset income + Transfer payments − Taxes. It is possible for Smith's income to come entirely from labor income and Jones's income to come entirely from asset income. The same dollar income does not necessitate the same source of income.

CHAPTER 14, PAGE 347

1   No. The income shares total 105 percent.

2   A Gini coefficient of 0 represents perfect income equality and a Gini coefficient of 1 represents complete income inequality, so we are sure that country A has neither perfect income equality nor complete income inequality. Beyond this, it is difficult to say anything. Usually, the Gini coefficient is used

as a comparative measure. For example, if country A's Gini coefficient is 0.45 and country B's is 0.60, we could then conclude that country A has a more equal (less unequal) distribution of income than country B has.

CHAPTER 14, PAGE 349

1   The simple fact that Jack earns more than Harry is not evidence of wage discrimination. We lack the information necessary to know whether wage discrimination exists. For example, we don't know whether Jack and Harry work the same job, we don't know how productive each person is, and so on.

2   Increased risk could affect income negatively or positively. There is a higher probability of both higher and lower income if a person assumes a lot of risk than if she simply plays it safe. To illustrate, suppose Nancy has decided she wants to be an actress, even though her parents want her to be an accountant. The chances of her being successful in acting are small, but if she is successful, she will earn a much higher income than if she had been an accountant (a top actress earns more than a top accountant). Of course, if she isn't successful, she will earn less income as an actress than she would have as an accountant (the average actress earns less than the average accountant).

CHAPTER 14, PAGE 357

1   Whether poor people always exist depends on how we define being poor. If we define it in relative terms and if we assume that there is no absolute income equality, then some people must fall into, say, the lowest 10 percent of income earners. We could refer to these persons as poor. Remember, though, that these persons are relatively poor—they earn less than a large percentage of the income earners in the country—but we do not know anything about their absolute incomes. In a world of multimillion-dollar income earners, a person who earns $100,000 might be considered poor.

2   12.3 percent.

3   An African American or Hispanic female who is the head of a large family and who is young and has little education.

Chapter 15

CHAPTER 15, PAGE 369

1   The price for loanable funds tends to equal the return on capital goods because there is a monetary incentive for them to be equal. Suppose the return on capital is 12 percent, and the price for loanable funds is 10 percent. In this case, a person could borrow loanable funds at 10 percent and invest in capital goods to earn the 12 percent return. As this happens, though, the amount of capital increases and its return falls. If the interest rates are reversed and the return on capital is lower than the price for a loanable fund, no one will borrow to invest in capital goods. Over time, then, the stock of capital will diminish and its return will rise.

2   The real interest rate, and not the nominal interest rate, matters to borrowers and lenders because the real interest rate is the rate paid by borrowers and received by lenders. For example, if a person borrows funds at a 12 percent interest

rate and the inflation rate is 4 percent, he will be paying only an 8 percent (real) interest rate to the lender. Stated differently, the lender has 8 percent, not 12 percent, more buying power because he made the loan.

3 $907.03. The formula is $PV = \$1,000/(1 + 0.05)^2$.

4 No. The present value of $2,000 a year for 4 years at an 8 percent interest rate is $6,624.25. [$PV = \$2,000/(1 + 0.08)^1 + \$2,000/(1 + 0.08)^2 + \$2,000/(1 + 0.08)^3 + \$2,000/(1 + 0.08)^4$]. The present value is less than the cost of the capital good, so it is not worth purchasing.

CHAPTER 15, PAGE 372

1 Jones earns $2 million a year as a news anchor for KNBC. His next best alternative in the news industry is earning $1.9 million a year as a news anchor for KABC. If Jones were not working in the news industry, his next best alternative would be as a journalism professor earning $100,000 a year. Within the news industry, Jones earns $100,000 economic rent (the difference between $2 million and $1.9 million). If we move beyond the news industry, Jones earns $1.9 million economic rent (the difference between $2 million and $100,000).

2 It is $0.

3 When a firm competes for artificial rents, it expends resources to simply transfer economic rent from another firm to itself. In other words, resources are used only to bring about a transfer; no additional goods and services are produced. But when a firm competes for real rents, resources are used to produce additional goods and services.

CHAPTER 15, PAGE 375

1 A probability cannot be assigned to uncertainty; a probability can be assigned to risk.

2 There are many different theories that purport to explain profit. One theory states that profit exists because uncertainty exists. No uncertainty, no profit. Another theory states that profit exists because arbitrage opportunities exist (the opportunities to buy low and sell high), and some people are alert to these opportunities. Still another theory states that profit exists because some people (called entrepreneurs) are capable of creating profit opportunities by devising a new product, production process, or marketing strategy.

3 Profit can be a signal, especially if the profit is earned in a competitive market. Specifically, profit signals that buyers value a good (as evidenced by the price they are willing and able to pay for the good) by more than the factors that go to make the good.

Chapter 16

CHAPTER 16, PAGE 386

1 The market output does not reflect or adjust for either external costs (in the case of a negative externality) or external benefits (in the case of a positive externality). The socially optimal output does.

2 An economist certainly prefers the socially optimal output to the market output if no costs are incurred by moving from the market output to the socially optimal output. But this isn't likely to be the case. The economist considers whether the benefits of moving to the socially optimal output are greater than or less than the costs of moving to the socially optimal output. If the benefits are greater, then the answer is yes; if the benefits are less than the costs, then it is no.

CHAPTER 16, PAGE 391

1 To internalize an externality means to adjust the private cost by the external cost. To illustrate, suppose someone's private cost is $10 and the external cost is $2. If the person internalizes the externality, the external cost becomes his cost, which is now $12.

2 Transaction costs are associated with the time and effort needed to search out, negotiate, and consummate an exchange. These costs are higher for buying a house than they are for buying a hamburger. It takes more time and effort to search out a house to buy, negotiate a price, and consummate the deal than it takes to search out and buy a hamburger.

3 Under certain conditions, the property rights assignment does not matter to the resource allocative outcome. Specifically, if transaction costs are zero or trivial, the property rights assignment that a court makes is irrelevant. Of course, if transaction costs are not zero or trivial, then the property rights assignment does matter.

4 Given a negative externality, there is a marginal external cost. The marginal external cost (MEC) plus the marginal private cost (MPC) equals the marginal social cost (MSC): $MSC = MPC + MEC$. If a corrective tax (t) is to correctly adjust for the marginal external cost associated with the negative externality, it must be equal to the marginal external cost—in other words, $t = MEC$. With this condition fulfilled, $MPC + t = MSC = MPC + MEC$.

CHAPTER 16, PAGE 394

1 All other things held constant, less pollution is preferable to more pollution. Zero pollution is the least amount of pollution possible; therefore, zero pollution is best. But in reality, all other things are not held constant. Sometimes, when we reduce pollution, we also eliminate some of the things we want. The economist wants to eliminate pollution as long as the benefits of eliminating pollution are greater than the costs. When the benefits equal the costs, the economist would stop eliminating pollution. If society has eliminated so much pollution that the costs of eliminating it are greater than the benefits, then society has gone too far. It has eliminated too much pollution. Some units of pollution were simply not worth eliminating.

2 Under market environmentalism, the entities that can eliminate pollution at the lowest cost are the ones that eliminate the pollution. This is not the case under standards, where both the low-cost and high-cost eliminators of pollution must reduce pollution.

3 The dollar price of the pollution permits is a cost for firm Z, but it is not a cost to society. As far as society is concerned, firm Z simply paid $660 to firms X and Y. Firm Z ended up with $660 less, and firms X and Y ended up with $660 more;

the amounts offset each other. Only when resources are used in eliminating pollution is the dollar cost of those resources counted as a cost to society of eliminating pollution.

CHAPTER 16, PAGE 396

1 After a nonexcludable public good is produced, the individual or firm that produced it wouldn't be able to collect payment for it. When a nonexcludable public good is provided to one person, it is provided to everyone. Because an individual can consume the good without paying for it, he or she is likely to take a free ride. Another way of answering this question is simply to say, "The market fails to produce nonexcludable public goods because of the free-rider problem."

2 a. A composition notebook is a private good. It is rivalrous in consumption; if one person is using it, someone else cannot.

   b. A Shakespearean play performed in a summer theater is an excludable public good. It is nonrivalrous in consumption (everyone in the theater can see the play) but excludable (a person must pay to get into the theater).

   c. An apple is a private good. It is rivalrous in consumption; if one person eats it, someone else cannot.

   d. A telephone service is a private good. One person using the phone (e.g., in your house) prevents someone else from using it.

   e. Sunshine is a nonexcludable public good. It is nonrivalrous in consumption (one person's consumption of it doesn't reduce its consumption by others) and nonexcludable (it is impossible to exclude free people from consuming the sunshine).

3 A concert is an example. One person consuming the concert does not take away from others consuming it to the same degree. However, people can be excluded from consuming it.

CHAPTER 16, PAGE 401

1. The sellers of product X know that the good could, under certain conditions, cause health problems, but they do not release this information to buyers. Consequently, the demand for good X is likely to be greater than it would be if there were symmetric information. The quantity consumed of good X is likely to be higher when there is asymmetric information than when there is symmetric information.

2. To illustrate, consider the used car market discussed in the text. If there are two types of used cars—good used cars and lemons—and asymmetric information, the market price for a used car may understate the value of a good used car and overstate the value of a lemon. This condition induces sellers of lemons to enter the market and sellers of good cars to leave it. (The owners of good used cars will not want to sell their cars for less than their cars are worth.) In theory, the used car market may eventually consist of nothing but lemons; that is, a used car market for good cars would not exist.

3. A college professor tells her students that she does not believe in giving grades of D or F. As a result, her students do not take as many measures to guard against receiving low grades. Does your example have the characteristic of this example—namely, one person's assurance affects another person's incentive?

Chapter 17
CHAPTER 17, PAGE 414

1 No. The model doesn't say every politician has to behave this way; it simply predicts that politicians who do these things have an increased chance of winning the election in a two-person race.

2 Voters may want more information from politicians, but supplying that information is not always in the best interests of politicians. When they speak in specific terms, politicians are often labeled as being at one end or the other of the political spectrum. But politicians don't win elections by being in the right wing or left wing; they win elections by being in the middle.

3 Yes. In the cost equation of voting, we included (1) the cost of driving to the polls, (2) the cost of standing in line, and (3) the cost of filling out the ballot. Bad weather (heavy rain, snow, or ice) would likely raise the cost of driving to the polls and the cost of standing in line, therefore raising the cost of voting. The higher the cost of voting, the less likely people will vote, *ceteris paribus*.

CHAPTER 17, PAGE 416

1 2 units.

2 In Example 2 with equal taxes, 1 unit received a simple majority of the votes. Person C was made worse off because his *MPB* for the first unit of good Y was $100, but he ended up paying a tax of $120 and was worse off by $20.

CHAPTER 17, PAGE 420

1 Both farmers and consumers are affected by federal agricultural policy—but not in the same way and not to the same degree. Federal agricultural policy directly affects farmers' incomes, usually by a large amount. It indirectly affects consumers' costs, but not as much as it does farmers' incomes. Simply put, farmers have more at stake than consumers when it comes to federal agricultural policy. People tend to be better informed about matters that mean more to them.

2 The legislation is more likely to pass when group A includes 10 million persons because the wider the dispersal is of the costs of the legislation, the greater the likelihood is of passage. When costs are widely dispersed, the cost to any one individual is so small that she or he is unlikely to lobby against the legislation.

3 Examples are teachers saying that more money for education will help the country compete in the global marketplace, domestic car manufacturers saying that tariffs on foreign imports will save American jobs and U.S. manufacturing, and farmers saying that subsidies to farmers will preserve the "American" farm and a way of life that Americans cherish. Whether any of these groups is right or wrong is not the point. The point is that special interest groups are likely to advance their arguments (good or bad) with public interest talk.

4 Rent seeking is socially wasteful because the resources that are used to seek rent could instead be used to produce goods and services.

Chapter 18

CHAPTER 18, PAGE 432

1 For the United States, 1X = 1/6Y or 1Y = 6X. For England, 1X = 2Y or 1Y = 1/2X. Let's focus on the opportunity cost of 1X in each country. In the United States, 1X = 1/6Y, and in Great Britain, 1X = 2Y. Terms of trade that are between these two end points would be favorable for the two countries. For example, 1X = 1Y is good for the United States because it would prefer to give up 1X and get 1Y in trade than to give up 1X and only get 1/6Y (without trade). Similarly, Great Britain would prefer to give up 1Y and get 1X in trade than to give up 1Y and get only 1/2X (without trade). Any terms of trade between 1X = 1/6Y and 1X = 2Y will be favorable to the two countries.

2 Yes, this is what the theory of comparative advantage shows. Exhibit 1 shows that the United States could produce more of both food and clothing than Japan. Still, the United States benefits from specialization and trade, as shown in Exhibit 2. In column 5 of this exhibit, the United States can consume 10 more units of food by specializing and trading.

3 No. Individuals' desire to buy low and sell high (earn a profit) pushes countries into producing and trading at a comparative advantage. Government officials do not collect cost data and then issue orders to firms in the country to produce X, Y, or Z. We have not drawn the PPFs in this chapter and identified the cost differences between countries to show what countries actually do in the real world. We described things technically to simply show how countries benefit from specialization and trade.

CHAPTER 18, PAGE 441

1 Domestic producers benefit from tariffs because producers' surplus rises; domestic consumers lose because consumers' surplus falls. Also, government benefits in that it receives the tariff revenue. Moreover, consumers lose more than producers and government gains, so that there is a net loss resulting from tariffs.

2 Consumers' surplus falls more than producers' surplus rises.

3 With a tariff, the government receives tariff revenue. With a quota, it does not. In the latter case, the revenue that would have gone to government goes instead to the importers who get to satisfy the quota.

4 Infant or new domestic industries need to be protected from older, more established competitors until they are mature enough to compete on an equal basis. Tariffs and quotas provide these infant industries the time they need.

Chapter 19

CHAPTER 19, PAGE 453

1 A debit. When an American enters into a transaction in which he has to supply U.S. dollars in the foreign exchange market (to demand a foreign currency), the transaction is recorded as a debit.

2 We do not have enough information to answer this question. The merchandise trade balance is the difference between the value of *merchandise* exports and *merchandise* imports. The question gives only the value of exports and imports. *Exports* is a more inclusive term than merchandise exports. Exports include (a) merchandise exports, (b) services, and (c) income from U.S. assets abroad (see Exhibit 2). Similarly, *imports* is a more inclusive term than merchandise imports. It includes (a) merchandise imports, (b) services, and (c) income from foreign assets in the United States.

3 The merchandise trade balance includes fewer transactions than are included in the current account balance. The merchandise trade balance is the summary statistic for merchandise exports and merchandise imports. The current account balance is the summary statistic for exports of goods and services (which include merchandise exports), imports of goods and services (which include merchandise imports), and net unilateral transfers abroad (see Exhibit 2).

CHAPTER 19, PAGE 460

1 As the demand for dollars increases, the supply of pesos increases. For example, suppose someone in Mexico wants to buy something produced in the United States. The American wants to be paid in dollars, but the Mexican doesn't have any dollars; she has pesos. So she has to buy dollars with pesos; in other words, she has to supply pesos to buy dollars. Thus, as she demands more dollars, she will necessarily have to supply more pesos.

2 The dollar is said to have appreciated (against the peso) when it takes more pesos to buy a dollar and fewer dollars to buy a peso. For this to occur, either the demand for dollars must increase (i.e., the supply of pesos increases) or the supply of dollars must decrease (i.e., the demand for pesos decreases). To see this graphically, look at Exhibit 5(b). The only way for the peso price per dollar to rise (on the vertical axis) is for either the demand curve for dollars to shift to the right or the supply curve of dollars to shift to the left. Each of these occurrences is mirrored in the market for pesos in part (a) of the exhibit.

3 *Ceteris paribus,* the dollar will depreciate relative to the franc. As incomes for Americans rise, the demand for Swiss goods rises. This increases the demand for francs and the supply of dollars on the foreign exchange market. In turn, this leads to a depreciated dollar and an appreciated franc.

4 The purchasing power parity (PPP) theory states that the exchange rate between any two currencies will adjust to reflect changes in the relative price levels of the two countries. For example, suppose the U.S. price level rises 5 percent and Mexico's price level remains constant. According to the PPP theory, the U.S. dollar will depreciate 5 percent relative to the Mexican peso.

CHAPTER 19, PAGE 466

1 The terms *overvalued* and *undervalued* refer to the equilibrium exchange rate: the exchange rate at which the quantity demanded and quantity supplied of a currency are the same in the foreign exchange market. Let's suppose the equilibrium exchange rate is 0.10 USD = 1 MXN. This is the same as saying that 10 pesos = $1. If the exchange rate is fixed at 0.12 USD = 1 MXN (which is the same as 8.33 pesos = $1),

the peso is overvalued and the dollar is undervalued. Specifically, a currency is overvalued if 1 unit of it fetches more of another currency than it would in equilibrium; a currency is undervalued if 1 unit of it fetches less of another currency than it would in equilibrium. In equilibrium, 1 peso would fetch $0.10, and at the current exchange rate it fetches 0.12 dollars; so the peso is overvalued. In equilibrium, $1 would fetch 10 pesos, and at the current exchange rate, it fetches only 8.33 pesos; so the dollar is undervalued.

2 An overvalued dollar means some other currency, say the Japanese yen, is undervalued. An overvalued dollar makes U.S. goods more expensive for the Japanese; so they buy fewer U.S. goods, thus reducing U.S. exports. On the other hand, an undervalued yen makes Japanese goods cheaper for Americans; so they buy more Japanese goods, and the U.S. imports more. Thus, an overvalued dollar reduces U.S. exports and raises U.S. imports.

3 a. Dollar is overvalued.

   b. Dollar is undervalued.

   c. Dollar is undervalued.

4 The devaluation of a country's currency makes it cheaper for foreigners to buy the country's products.

CHAPTER 19, PAGE 470

1 An optimal currency area is a geographic area in which exchange rates can be fixed or a common currency used without sacrificing any domestic economic goals.

2 As the demand for good Y falls, the unemployment rate in country 2 will rise. This increase in the unemployment rate is likely to be temporary, though. The increased demand for good X (produced by country 1) will increase the demand for country 1's currency, leading to an appreciation in country 1's currency and a depreciation in country 2's currency. Country 1's good (good X) will become more expensive for the residents of country 2, and they will buy less. Country 2's good (good Y) will become less expensive for the residents of country 1, and they will buy more. As a result of the additional purchases of good Y, country 2's unemployment rate will begin to decline.

3 Labor mobility is very important to determining whether or not an area is an optimal currency area. If there is little or no labor mobility, an area is not likely to be an optimal currency area. If there is labor mobility, an area is likely to be an optimal currency area.

Chapter 20

CHAPTER 20, PAGE 483

1 As some explain it, the end of the Cold War resulted in turning two different worlds (the capitalist and communist worlds) into one. It resulted in a thawing of not only political but economic relations between former enemies. You might not trade with your enemy, but once that person or country is no longer your enemy, you don't feel the same need to exclude him or it from your political and economic life.

2 Globalization is the phenomenon by which individuals and businesses in any part of the world are much more affected than before by events elsewhere in the world; it is the growing integration of the national economies of the world to the degree that we may be witnessing the emergence and operation of a single worldwide economy.

3 Advancing technology can reduce both transportation and communication costs, making it less costly to trade with people around the world.

CHAPTER 20, PAGE 488

1 Benefits identified in the section include (a) benefits from increased international trade, (b) higher income per person, (c) lower prices for goods, (d) greater product variety, and (e) increased productivity and innovation.

2 Costs identified in the section include (a) increased income inequality, (b) offshoring, and (c) more power for big corporations.

CHAPTER 20, PAGE 492

1 In country A, there is an economic expansion, and real income in the country rises. As a result, residents of the country buy more imports from country B. In country B, exports rise relative to imports, thus increasing net exports. As net exports in country B rise, the *AD* curve for country B shifts to the right, increasing Real GDP.

2 If the dollar appreciates, the Japanese yen depreciates. U.S. products become more expensive for the Japanese, and Japanese products become cheaper for Americans. U.S. imports will rise, U.S. exports will fall, and consequently U.S. net exports will fall. As a result, the *AD* curve in the United States will shift leftward, pushing down Real GDP.

CHAPTER 20, PAGE 494

1 Foreign input prices can change directly as a result of supply conditions in the foreign country, or they can change indirectly as a result of a change in the exchange rate. In either case, as foreign input prices rise—either directly or as a result of a depreciated dollar—the U.S. *SRAS* curve shifts leftward. If foreign input prices fall—either directly or as a result of an appreciated dollar—the *SRAS* curve shifts rightward.

2 The higher real interest rates in the United States attract capital to the United States, increasing the demand for the dollar. As a result, the dollar appreciates and the yen depreciates. An appreciated dollar shifts the U.S. *AD* curve leftward and the U.S. *SRAS* curve rightward. The *AD* curve shifts leftward by more than the *SRAS* curve shifts rightward; so the price level falls.

CHAPTER 20, PAGE 498

1 When the money supply is raised, the *AD* curve shifts rightward, pushing up Real GDP. Also, as a result of the increased money supply, interest rates may decline in the short run. This promotes U.S. capital outflow and a depreciated dollar. As a result of the depreciated dollar, imports become more expensive for Americans, and U.S. exports become cheaper for foreigners. Imports fall and exports rise, thereby increasing net exports and *again* shifting the *AD* curve to the right. Real GDP rises.

2 Expansionary fiscal policy pushes the *AD* curve rightward and (under certain conditions) raises Real GDP. If the expansionary fiscal policy causes a deficit, then the government will have to borrow to finance the deficit, and interest rates will be pushed upward. As a result of the higher interest rates, foreign capital inflows and dollar appreciation increase, thus pushing the *AD* curve leftward and the *SRAS* curve rightward.

Chapter 21

CHAPTER 21, PAGE 512

1 30.

2 Stocks are purchased either for the dividends that the stocks may pay, the expected gain in price (of the stock), or both.

3 The yield of a stock is the dividend per share (of the stock) divided by the closing price per share.

4 A P/E ratio of 23 means that the stock is selling for a share price that is 23 times its earnings per share.

CHAPTER 21, PAGE 517

1 A bond is an IOU or a promise to pay. The issuer of a bond is borrowing funds and promising to pay back those funds (with interest) at a later date.

2 $0.07x = \$400$, so $x = \$400/0.07$, or $\$5,714.29$.

3 $\$1,000/\$9,500 = 10.53$ percent.

4 Municipal bonds are issued by state and local governments, and a Treasury bond is issued by the federal government.

CHAPTER 21, PAGE 520

1 A futures contract is a contract in which the seller agrees to provide a good to the buyer on a specified future date at an agreed-on price.

2 You can buy a call option, which sells for a fraction of the cost of the stock. A call option gives the owner of the option the right to buy shares of a stock at a specified price within the time limits of the contract.

3 A put option gives the owner the right, but not the obligation, to *sell* (rather than buy, as in a call option) shares of a stock at a strike price during some period of time.

Web Chapter 22

CHAPTER 22, PAGE 528

1 A farmer protects herself through the futures market. Specifically, she enters into a futures contract with someone who will guarantee to take delivery of her foodstuff (in the future) for a stated price. Then, if the price goes up or down between the present and the future, the farmer does not have to worry. She has locked in the price of her foodstuff.

2 If the farmer faces an inelastic demand curve, the order of preference would be (b), (a), (c). That is, he prefers (b) to (a) and (a) to (c). In (b), if all farmers except himself have bad weather, then the market supply curve of the individual farmer's product shifts to the left, bringing about a higher price. But the individual farmer's supply curve doesn't shift to the left; it stays where it is. Thus, the individual farmer sells the same amount of output at the higher price. Consequently, his total revenue rises. In (a), both the market supply curve and the individual farmer's supply curve shift left; so the farmer has less to sell at a higher price. Again, if the demand is inelastic, the individual farmer will increase his total revenue but not as much as in (b), where the individual farmer's output did not fall. Finally, in (c), the market supply curve shifts to the right, lowering price. If demand is inelastic, this lowers total revenue.

3 Increased productivity will lead to higher total revenue when demand is elastic. To illustrate, increased productivity shifts the supply curve to the right. This lowers price. If demand is elastic, then the percentage rise in quantity sold is greater than the percentage fall in price; therefore, total revenue rises. In summary, increased productivity leads to higher total revenue when demand is elastic.

CHAPTER 22, PAGE 532

1 Because the deficiency payment is the difference between the target price and the market price, the answer depends on the market price. If the market price is, say, $4, and the target price is $7, then the deficiency payment is $3.

2 A farmer pledges a certain number of bushels of foodstuff to obtain a loan—say, 500 bushels. He receives a loan equal to the number of bushels times the designated loan rate per bushel. For example, if the loan rate is $2 per bushel and 500 bushels are pledged, then the loan is $1,000. The farmer either pays back the loan with interest or keeps the loan and forfeits the bushels. Which course of action the farmer takes depends on the market price of the crop. If the market price is higher than the loan rate, the farmer pays back the loan and sells the crop. If the market price is less than the loan rate, the farmer forfeits the crop. A nonrecourse loan guarantees that the farmer will not receive less than the loan rate for each bushel of the crop.

3 The effects of a price support are (a) a surplus, (b) fewer exchanges (less bought by private citizens), (c) higher prices paid by consumers of the crop (on which the support exists), and (d) government purchase and storage of the surplus crop (for which taxpayers pay).

GLOSSARY

Absolute (Money) Price The price of a good in money terms.

Accounting Profit The difference between total revenue and explicit costs.

Adverse Selection A phenomenon that occurs when the parties on one side of the market, who have information not known to others, self-select in a way that adversely affects the parties on the other side of the market.

Antitrust Law Legislation passed for the stated purpose of controlling monopoly power and preserving and promoting competition.

Appreciation An increase in the value of one currency relative to other currencies.

Arbitrage Buying a good at a low price and selling it for a higher price.

Asymmetric Information Information that either the buyer or the seller in a market exchange has and that the other does not have.

Average Fixed Cost (AFC) Total fixed cost divided by quantity of output: $AFC = TFC/Q$.

Average Total Cost (ATC), or Unit Cost Total cost divided by quantity of output: $ATC = TC/Q$.

Average Variable Cost (AVC) Total variable cost divided by quantity of output: $AVC = TVC/Q$.

Average-Marginal Rule When the marginal magnitude is above the average magnitude, the average magnitude rises; when the marginal magnitude is below the average magnitude, the average magnitude falls.

Bad Anything from which individuals receive disutility or dissatisfaction.

Balance of Payments A periodic (usually annual) statement of the money value of all transactions between residents of one country and the residents of all other countries.

Bond An IOU, or promise to pay.

Budget Constraint All the combinations or bundles of two goods a person can purchase, given a certain money income and prices for the two goods.

Business Firm An entity that employs factors of production (resources) to produce goods and services to be sold to consumers, other firms, or the government.

Capital Produced goods that can be used as inputs for further production, such as factories, machinery, tools, computers, and buildings.

Capital Account The account in the balance of payments that includes all payments related to the purchase and sale of assets and to borrowing and lending activities. Components include outflow of U.S. capital and inflow of foreign capital.

Capital Account Balance The summary statistic for the outflow of U.S. capital equal to the difference between the outflow of U.S. capital and the inflow of foreign capital.

Capture Theory of Regulation A theory holding that no matter what the motive is for the initial regulation and the establishment of the regulatory agency, eventually the agency will be captured (controlled) by the special interests of the industry being regulated.

Cartel An organization of firms that reduces output and increases price in an effort to increase joint profits.

Cartel Theory In this theory of oligopoly, oligopolistic firms act as if there were only one firm in the industry.

Ceteris Paribus A Latin term meaning "all other things constant" or "nothing else changes."

Closed Economy An economy that does not trade goods and services with other countries.

Closed Shop An organization in which an employee must belong to the union before he or she can be hired.

Coase Theorem In the case of trivial or zero transaction costs, the property rights assignment does not matter to the resource allocative outcome.

Collective Bargaining The process whereby wage rates and other issues are determined by a union bargaining with management on behalf of all union members.

Comparative Advantage The situation where someone or a country can produce a good at lower opportunity cost than someone else or another country can.

Complements Two goods that are used jointly in consumption. If two goods are complements, the demand for one rises as the price of the other falls (or the demand for one falls as the price of the other rises).

Concentration Ratio The percentage of industry sales (or assets, output, labor force, or some other factor) accounted for by x number of firms in the industry.

Conglomerate Merger A merger between companies in different industries.

Constant Returns to Scale The condition when inputs are increased by some percentage and output increases by an equal percentage, causing unit costs to remain constant.

Constant-Cost Industry An industry in which average total costs do not change as (industry) output increases or decreases when firms enter or exit the industry, respectively.

Consumer Equilibrium Equilibrium that occurs when the consumer has spent all income and the marginal utilities per dollar spent on each good purchased are equal: $MU_A/P_A = MU_B/P_B = \ldots = MU_Z/P_Z$, where the letters A–Z represent all the goods a person buys.

Consumers' Surplus (CS) The difference between the maximum price a buyer is willing and able to pay for a good or service and the price actually paid. $CS =$ Maximum buying price – Price paid

Contestable Market A market in which entry is easy and exit is costless, new firms can produce the product at the same cost as current firms, and exiting firms can easily dispose of their fixed assets by selling them.

Craft (Trade) Union A union whose membership is made up of individuals who practice the same craft or trade.

Credit In the balance of payments, any transaction that creates a demand for the country's currency in the foreign exchange market.

Cross Elasticity of Demand A measure of the responsiveness in quantity demanded of one good to changes in the price of another good.

Current Account The account in the balance of payments that includes all payments related to the purchase and sale of goods and services. Components of the account include exports, imports, and net unilateral transfers abroad.

Current Account Balance In the balance of payments, the summary statistic for exports of goods and services, imports of goods and services, and net unilateral transfers abroad.

Deadweight Loss The loss to society of not producing the competitive, or supply-and-demand-determined, level of output.

Deadweight Loss of Monopoly The net value (value to buyers over and above costs to suppliers) of the difference between the monopoly quantity of output (where $P > MC$) and the competitive quantity of output (where $P = MC$). The loss of not producing the competitive quantity of output.

Debit In the balance of payments, any transaction that supplies the country's currency in the foreign exchange market.

Decisions at the Margin Decision making characterized by weighing the additional (marginal) benefits of a change against the additional (marginal) costs of a change with respect to current conditions.

Decreasing-Cost Industry An industry in which average total costs decrease as output increases and increase as output decreases when firms enter and exit the industry, respectively.

Demand The willingness and ability of buyers to purchase different quantities of a good at different prices during a specific time period.

Demand Curve The graphical representation of the law of demand.

Demand Schedule The numerical tabulation of the quantity demanded of a good at different prices. A demand schedule is the numerical representation of the law of demand.

Depreciation A decrease in the value of one currency relative to other currencies.

Derived Demand Demand that is the result of some other demand. For example, factor demand is the result of the demand for the products that the factors go to produce.

Devaluation A government action that changes the exchange rate by lowering the official price of a currency.

Diamond-Water Paradox The observation that things with the greatest value in use sometimes have little value in exchange and things with little value in use sometimes have the greatest value in exchange.

Diseconomies of Scale The condition when inputs are increased by some percentage and output increases by a smaller percentage, causing unit costs to rise.

Disequilibrium A state of either surplus or shortage in a market.

Disequilibrium Price A price other than equilibrium price. A price at which quantity demanded does not equal quantity supplied.

Disutility The dissatisfaction one receives from a bad.

Dividend A share of the profits of a corporation distributed to stockholders.

Dow Jones Industrial Average (DJIA) The most popular, widely cited indicator of day-to-day stock market activity. The DJIA is a weighted average of 30 widely traded stocks on the New York Stock Exchange.

Dumping The sale of goods abroad at a price below their cost and below the price charged in the domestic market.

Economic Profit The difference between total revenue and total cost, including both explicit and implicit costs.

Economic Rent Payment in excess of opportunity costs.

Economics The science of scarcity; the science of how individuals and societies deal with the fact that wants are greater than the limited resources available to satisfy those wants.

Economies of Scale Economies that exist when inputs are increased by some percentage and output increases by a greater percentage, causing unit costs to fall.

Efficiency Exists when marginal benefits equal marginal costs.

Elastic Demand The demand when the percentage change in quantity demanded is greater than the percentage change in price. Quantity demanded changes proportionately more than price changes.

Elasticity of Demand for Labor The percentage change in the quantity demanded of labor divided by the percentage change in the wage rate.

Employee Association An organization whose members belong to a particular profession.

Entrepreneurship The particular talent that some people have for organizing the resources of land, labor, and capital to produce goods, seek new business opportunities, and develop new ways of doing things.

Equilibrium Equilibrium means "at rest." Equilibrium in a market is the price quantity combination from which there is no tendency for buyers or sellers to move away. Graphically, equilibrium is the intersection point of the supply and demand curves.

Equilibrium Price (Market-Clearing Price) The price at which quantity demanded of the good equals quantity supplied.

Equilibrium Quantity The quantity that corresponds to equilibrium price. The quantity at which the amount of the good that buyers are willing and able to buy equals

the amount that sellers are willing and able to sell, and both equal the amount actually bought and sold.

Ex Ante Phrase that means "before," as in before a trade.

Excess Capacity Theorem Theorem that a monopolistic competitor in equilibrium produces an output smaller than the one that would minimize its costs of production.

Exchange (Trade) The process of giving up one thing for something else.

Exchange Rate The price of one currency in terms of another currency.

Excludable A characteristic of a good whereby it is possible, or not prohibitively costly, to exclude someone from receiving the benefits of the good after it has been produced.

Explicit Cost A cost incurred when an actual (monetary) payment is made.

Ex Post Phrase that means "after," as in after a trade.

Externality A side effect of an action that affects the well-being of third parties.

Face Value (Par Value) Dollar amount specified on a bond, the total amount the issuer of the bond will repay to the buyer of the bond.

Factor Price Taker A firm that can buy all of a factor it wants at the equilibrium price. It faces a horizontal (flat, perfectly elastic) supply curve of factors.

Fixed Costs Costs that do not vary with output; the costs associated with fixed inputs.

Fixed Exchange Rate System The system whereby a nation's currency is set at a fixed rate relative to all other currencies, and central banks intervene in the foreign exchange market to maintain the fixed rate.

Fixed Input An input whose quantity cannot be changed as output changes.

Flexible Exchange Rate System The system whereby exchange rates are determined by the forces of supply and demand for a currency.

Foreign Exchange Market The market in which currencies of different countries are exchanged.

Free Rider Anyone who receives the benefits of a good without paying for it.

Futures Contract An agreement to buy or sell a specific amount of something (commodity, currency, financial instrument) at an agreed-on price on a stipulated future date.

Game Theory A mathematical technique used to analyze the behavior of decision makers who try to reach an optimal position for themselves through game playing or the use of strategic behavior, who are fully aware of the interactive nature of the process at hand, and who anticipate the moves of other decision makers.

Gini Coefficient A measure of the degree of inequality in the income distribution.

Globalization A phenomenon by which economic agents in any given part of the world are more affected by events elsewhere in the world than before; the growing integration of the national economies of the world to the degree that we may be witnessing the emergence and operation of a single worldwide economy.

Good Anything from which individuals receive utility or satisfaction.

Government Bureaucrat An unelected person who works in a government bureau and who is assigned a special task relating to a law or program passed by the legislature.

Herfindahl Index Index that measures the degree of concentration in an industry, equal to the sum of the squares of the market shares of each firm in the industry.

Horizontal Merger A merger between firms that are selling similar products in the same market.

Human Capital Education, development of skills, and anything else that is particular to the individual and that increases personal productivity.

Implicit Cost A cost that represents the value of resources used in production for which no actual (monetary) payment is made.

Income Elastic The condition when the percentage change in quantity demanded of a good is greater than the percentage change in income.

Income Elasticity of Demand A measure of the responsiveness of quantity demanded to changes in income.

Income Inelastic The condition when the percentage change in quantity demanded of a good is less than the percentage change in income.

Income Unit Elastic The condition when the percentage change in quantity demanded of a good is equal to the percentage change in income.

Increasing-Cost Industry An industry in which average total costs increase as output increases and decrease as output decreases when firms enter and exit the industry, respectively.

Indifference Curve The curve that represents an indifference set and that shows all the bundles of two goods giving an individual equal total utility.

Indifference Curve Map Represents a number of indifference curves for a given individual with reference to two goods.

Indifference Set Group of bundles of two goods that give an individual equal total utility.

Industrial Union A union whose membership is made up of individuals who work in the same firm or industry but do not all practice the same craft or trade.

Inelastic Demand The demand when the percentage change in quantity demanded is less than the percentage change in price. Quantity demanded changes proportionately less than price changes.

Inferior Good A good the demand for which falls (rises) as income rises (falls).

Initial Public Offering (IPO) A company's first offering of stock to the public.

In-Kind Transfer Payments Transfer payments, such as food stamps, medical assistance, and subsidized housing, that are made in a specific good or service rather than in cash.

Internalizing Externalities An externality is internalized if the persons or group that generated the externality incorporate into their own private or internal cost-benefit calculations the external benefits (in the case of a positive externality) or the external costs (in the case of a negative externality) that third parties bear.

International Monetary Fund (IMF) An international organization created to oversee the international monetary system. The IMF does not control the world's money supply, but it does hold currency reserves for member nations and make loans to central banks.

Interpersonal Utility Comparison Comparing the utility one person receives from a good, service, or activity with the utility another person receives from the same good, service, or activity.

Investment Bank A firm that acts as an intermediary between the company that issues the stock and the public that wishes to buy the stock.

J-Curve The curve that shows a short-run worsening in net exports after a currency depreciation, followed by an improvement.

Kinked Demand Curve Theory A theory of oligopoly that assumes that if a single firm in the industry cuts prices, other firms will do likewise, but if it raises price, other firms will not follow suit. The theory predicts price stickiness or rigidity.

Labor The physical and mental talents people contribute to the production process.

Land All natural resources, such as minerals, forests, water, and unimproved land.

Law of Demand As the price of a good rises, the quantity demanded of the good falls, and as the price of a good falls, the quantity demanded of the good rises, *ceteris paribus.*

Law of Diminishing Marginal Returns As ever larger amounts of a variable input are combined with fixed inputs, eventually the marginal physical product of the variable input will decline.

Law of Diminishing Marginal Utility For a given time period, the marginal (additional) utility or satisfaction gained by consuming equal successive units of a good will decline as the amount consumed increases.

Law of Increasing Opportunity Costs As more of a good is produced, the opportunity costs of producing that good increase.

Law of Supply As the price of a good rises, the quantity supplied of the good rises, and as the price of a good falls, the quantity supplied of the good falls, *ceteris paribus.*

Least-Cost Rule Rule that specifies the combination of factors that minimizes costs. This requires that the following condition be met: $MPP_1/P_1 = MPP_2/P_2 = \ldots = MPP_N/P_N$, where the numbers stand for the different factors.

Loanable Funds Funds that someone borrows and another person lends, for which the borrower pays an interest rate to the lender.

Lock-In Effect The situation when a particular product or technology becomes the standard and is difficult or impossible to dislodge as the standard.

Logrolling The exchange of votes to gain support for legislation.

Long Run A period of time in which all inputs in the production process can be varied (no inputs are fixed).

Long-Run Average Total Cost (*LRATC*) Curve A curve that shows the lowest (unit) cost at which the firm can produce any given level of output.

Long-Run Competitive Equilibrium The condition where $P = MC = SRATC = LRATC$. There are zero economic profits, firms are producing the quantity of output at which price is equal to marginal cost, and no firm has an incentive to change its plant size.

Long-Run (Industry) Supply (LRS) Curve Graphic representation of the quantities of output that the industry is prepared to supply at different prices after the entry and exit of firms are completed.

Lorenz Curve A graph of the income distribution that expresses the relationship between the cumulative percentage of households and the cumulative percentage of income.

Macroeconomics The branch of economics that deals with human behavior and choices as they relate to highly aggregate markets (e.g., the goods and services market) or the entire economy.

Managed Float A managed flexible exchange rate system, under which nations now and then intervene to adjust their official reserve holdings to moderate major swings in exchange rates.

Managerial Coordination The process in which managers direct employees to perform certain tasks.

Marginal Benefits Additional benefits. The benefits connected to consuming an additional unit of a good or undertaking one more unit of an activity.

Marginal Cost (MC) The change in total cost that results from a change in output: $MC = \Delta TC/\Delta Q$.

Marginal Costs Additional costs. The costs connected to consuming an additional unit of a good or undertaking one more unit of an activity.

Marginal Factor Cost (MFC) The additional cost incurred by employing an additional factor unit.

Marginal Physical Product (MPP) The change in output that results from changing the variable input by one unit, holding all other inputs fixed.

Marginal Productivity Theory Theory stating that firms in competitive or perfect product and factor markets pay factors their marginal revenue products.

Marginal Rate of Substitution The amount of one good an individual is willing to give up to obtain an additional unit of another good and maintain equal total utility.

Marginal Revenue (MR) The change in total revenue that results from selling one additional unit of output.

Marginal Revenue Product (MRP) The additional revenue generated by employing an additional factor unit.

Marginal Social Benefits (MSB) The sum of marginal private benefits (MPB) and marginal external benefits (MEB): $MSB = MPB + MEB$.

Marginal Social Costs (MSC) The sum of marginal private costs (MPC) and marginal external costs (MEC): $MSC = MPC + MEC$.

Marginal Utility The additional utility a person receives from consuming an additional unit of a good.

Market Any place people come together to trade.

Market Coordination The process in which individuals perform tasks, such as producing certain quantities of goods, based on changes in market forces, such as supply, demand, and price.

Market Failure A situation in which the market does not provide the ideal or optimal amount of a good.

Market Structure The particular environment of a firm, the characteristics of which influence the firm's pricing and output decisions.

Median Voter Model A model suggesting that candidates in a two-person political race will move toward matching the preferences of the median voter (i.e., the person whose preferences are at the center, or in the middle, of the political spectrum).

Merchandise Trade Balance The difference between the value of merchandise exports and the value of merchandise imports.

Merchandise Trade Deficit The situation when the value of merchandise exports is less than the value of merchandise imports.

Merchandise Trade Surplus The situation when the value of merchandise exports is greater than the value of merchandise imports.

Microeconomics The branch of economics that deals with human behavior and choices as they relate to relatively small units—an individual, a firm, an industry, a single market.

Minimum Efficient Scale The lowest output level at which average total costs are minimized.

Monitor A person in a business firm who coordinates team production and reduces shirking.

Monopolistic Competition A theory of market structure based on three assumptions: many sellers and buyers, firms producing and selling slightly differentiated products, and easy entry and exit.

Monopoly A theory of market structure based on three assumptions: There is one seller, it sells a product for which no close substitutes exist, and there are extremely high barriers to entry.

Monopsony A single buyer in a factor market.

Moral Hazard A condition that exists when one party to a transaction changes his or her behavior in a way that is hidden from and costly to the other party.

Natural Monopoly The condition where economies of scale are so pronounced that only one firm can survive.

Negative Externality The condition that exists when a person's or group's actions cause a cost (adverse side effect) to be felt by others.

Network Good A good whose value increases as the expected number of units sold increases.

Neutral Good A good the demand for which does not change as income rises or falls.

Nominal Interest Rate The interest rate determined by the forces of supply and demand in the loanable funds market. The interest rate actually charged (or paid) in the market; the market interest rate. Nominal interest rate = Real interest rate + Expected inflation rate.

Nonexcludable A characteristic of a good whereby it is impossible, or prohibitively costly, to exclude someone from receiving the benefits of the good after it has been produced.

Nonrivalrous in Consumption A good is nonrivalrous in consumption if its consumption by one person does not reduce its consumption by others.

Normal Good A good the demand for which rises (falls) as income rises (falls).

Normal Profit Zero economic profit. A firm that earns normal profit is earning revenue equal to its total costs (explicit plus implicit costs). This is the level of profit necessary to keep resources employed in the firm.

Normative Economics The study of "what should be" in economic matters.

Offshoring Work done for a company by persons other than the original company's employees in a country other than the one in which the company is located.

Oligopoly A theory of market structure based on three assumptions: few sellers and many buyers, firms producing either homogeneous or differentiated products, and significant barriers to entry.

Open Economy An economy that trades goods and services with other countries.

Opportunity Cost The most highly valued opportunity or alternative forfeited when a choice is made.

Optimal Currency Area A geographic area in which exchange rates can be fixed or a common currency used without sacrificing domestic economic goals, such as low unemployment.

Option A contract that gives the owner the right, but not the obligation, to buy or sell shares of a stock at a specified price on or before a specified date.

Overvalued A currency is overvalued if its price in terms of other currencies is above the equilibrium price.

Own Price The price of a good. For example, if the price of oranges is $1, this is its own price.

Perfect Competition A theory of market structure based on four assumptions: (1) There are many sellers and buyers, (2) sellers sell a homogeneous good, (3) buyers and sellers have all relevant information, and (4) entry into or exit from the market is easy.

Perfect Price Discrimination A price structure in which the seller charges the highest price that each consumer is willing to pay for the product rather than go without it.

Perfectly Elastic Demand The demand when a small percentage change in price causes an extremely large percentage change in quantity demanded (from buying all to buying nothing).

Perfectly Inelastic Demand The demand when the quantity demanded does not change as price changes.

Positive Economics The study of "what is" in economic matters.

Positive Externality The condition that exists when a person's or group's actions cause a benefit (beneficial side effect) to be felt by others.

Positive Rate of Time Preference Preference for earlier over later availability of goods.

Poverty Income Threshold (Poverty Line) Income level below which people are considered to be living in poverty.

Present Value The current worth of some future dollar amount of income or receipts.

Price Ceiling A government-mandated maximum price above which legal trades cannot be made.

Price Discrimination A price structure in which the seller charges different prices for the product it sells and the price differences do not reflect cost differences.

Price Elasticity of Demand A measure of the responsiveness of quantity demanded to changes in price.

Price Elasticity of Supply A measure of the responsiveness of quantity supplied to changes in price.

Price Floor A government-mandated minimum price below which legal trades cannot be made.

Price Leadership Theory In this theory of oligopoly, the dominant firm in the industry determines price, and all other firms take their price as given.

Price Searcher A seller that has the ability to control to some degree the price of the product it sells.

Price Support A government-mandated minimum price for agricultural products; an example of a price floor.

Price Taker A seller that does not have the ability to control the price of the product it sells; the seller takes the price determined in the market.

Producers' (Sellers') Surplus (PS) The difference between the price sellers receive for a good and the minimum or lowest price for which they would have sold the good. PS = Price received – Minimum selling price

Production Possibilities Frontier (PPF) Represents the possible combinations of two goods that can be produced in a certain period of time under the conditions of a given state of technology and fully employed resources.

Productive Efficiency The situation that exists when a firm produces its output at the lowest possible per-unit cost (lowest ATC).

Productive Inefficiency The condition where less than the maximum output is produced with given resources and technology. Productive inefficiency implies that more of one good can be produced without any less of another good being produced.

Profit The difference between total revenue and total cost.

Profit-Maximization Rule The rule that profit is maximized by producing the quantity of output at which $MR = MC$.

Public Choice The branch of economics that deals with the application of economic principles and tools to public sector decision making.

Public Choice Theory of Regulation A theory holding that regulators are seeking to do—and will do through regulation—what is in their best interest (specifically to enhance their power and the size and budget of their regulatory agencies).

Public Employee Union A union whose membership is made up of individuals who work for the local, state, or federal government.

Public Franchise A right granted to a firm by government that permits the firm to provide a particular good or service and that excludes all others from doing the same.

Public Good A good the consumption of which by one person does not reduce the consumption by another person—that is, a public good is characterized by nonrivalry in consumption. There are both excludable and nonexcludable public goods. An excludable public good, while nonrivalrous in consumption, can be denied to a person who does not pay for it. A nonexcludable public good is nonrivalrous in consumption and cannot be denied to a person who does not pay for it.

Public Interest Theory of Regulation A theory holding that regulators are seeking to do—and will do through regulation—what is in the best interest of the public or society at large.

Purchasing Power Parity (PPP) Theory Theory stating that exchange rates between any two currencies will adjust to reflect changes in the relative price levels of the two countries.

Pure Economic Rent A category of economic rent where the payment is to a factor that is in fixed supply, implying that it has zero opportunity costs.

Quota A legal limit on the amount of a good that may be imported.

Rational Ignorance The state of not acquiring information because the costs of acquiring it are greater than the benefits.

Rationing Device A means for deciding who gets what of available resources and goods.

Real Interest Rate The nominal interest rate adjusted for expected inflation—that is, the nominal interest rate minus the expected inflation rate. When the expected inflation rate is zero, the real interest rate equals the nominal interest rate.

Regulatory Lag The time period between when a natural monopoly's costs change and when the regulatory agency adjusts prices for it.

Relative Price The price of a good in terms of another good.

Rent Seeking Actions of individuals and groups who spend resources to influence public policy in the hope of redistributing (transferring) income to themselves from others.

Residual Claimants Persons who share in the profits of a business firm.

Resource Allocative Efficiency The situation when firms produce the quantity of output at which price equals marginal cost: $P = MC$.

Revaluation A government action that changes the exchange rate by raising the official price of a currency.

Rivalrous in Consumption A good is rivalrous in consumption if its consumption by one person reduces its consumption by others.

Roundabout Method of Production The production of capital goods that enhance productive capabilities to ultimately bring about increased consumption.

Scarcity The condition in which our wants are greater than the limited resources available to satisfy those wants.

Screening The process employers use to increase the probability of choosing good employees based on certain criteria.

Second-Degree Price Discrimination A price structure in which the seller charges a uniform price per unit for one specific quantity, a lower price for an additional quantity, and so on.

Shirking The behavior of a worker who is putting forth less than the agreed-on effort.

Short Run A period of time in which some inputs in the production process are fixed.

Shortage (Excess Demand) A condition in which quantity demanded is greater than quantity supplied. Shortages occur only at prices below equilibrium price.

Short-Run (Firm) Supply Curve The portion of the firm's marginal cost curve that lies above the average variable cost curve.

Short-Run Market (Industry) Supply Curve The horizontal addition of all existing firms' short-run supply curves.

Socially Optimal Amount (Output) An amount that takes into account and adjusts for all benefits (external and private) and all costs (external and private). The socially optimal amount is the amount at which $MSB = MSC$. Sometimes, the socially optimal amount is referred to as the efficient amount.

Special Drawing Right (SDR) An international money, created by the IMF, in the form of bookkeeping entries; like gold and currencies, it can be used by nations to settle international accounts.

Special Interest Groups Subsets of the general population that hold (usually) intense preferences for or against a particular government service, activity, or policy. Often, special interest groups gain from public policies that may not be in accord with the interests of the general public.

Stock A claim on the assets of a corporation that gives the purchaser a share of the corporation.

Strike The situation in which union employees refuse to work at a certain wage or under certain conditions.

Subsidy A monetary payment by government to a producer of a good or service.

Substitutes Two goods that satisfy similar needs or desires. If two goods are substitutes, the demand for one rises as the price of the other rises (or the demand for one falls as the price of the other falls).

Sunk Cost A cost incurred in the past that cannot be changed by current decisions and therefore cannot be recovered.

Supply The willingness and ability of sellers to produce and offer to sell different quantities of a good at different prices during a specific time period.

Supply Curve The graphical representation of the law of supply.

Supply Schedule The numerical tabulation of the quantity supplied of a good at different prices. A supply schedule is the numerical representation of the law of supply.

Surplus (Excess Supply) A condition in which quantity supplied is greater than quantity demanded. Surpluses occur only at prices above equilibrium price.

Target Price A guaranteed price; if the market price is below the target price, the farmer receives a deficiency payment equal to the difference between the market price and the target price.

Tariff A tax on imports.

Technology The body of skills and knowledge concerning the use of resources in production. An advance in technology commonly refers to the ability to produce more output with a fixed amount of resources or the ability to produce the same output with fewer resources.

Terms of Trade How much of one thing is given up for how much of something else.

Theory An abstract representation of the real world designed with the intent to better understand the world.

Third-Degree Price Discrimination A price structure in which the seller charges different prices in different markets or charges a different price to different segments of the buying population.

Tie-In Sale A sale whereby one good can be purchased only if another good is also purchased.

Total Cost (TC) The sum of fixed costs and variable costs.

Total Revenue (TR) Price times quantity sold.

Total Surplus (TS) The sum of consumers' surplus and producers' surplus: $TS = CS + PS$.

Total Utility The total satisfaction a person receives from consuming a particular quantity of a good.

Transaction Costs The costs associated with the time and effort needed to search out, negotiate, and consummate an exchange.

Transfer Payments Payments to persons that are not made in return for goods and services currently supplied.

Transitivity The principle whereby if A is preferred to B, and B is preferred to C, then A is preferred to C.

Trust A combination of firms that come together to act as a monopolist.

Undervalued A currency is undervalued if its price in terms of other currencies is below the equilibrium price.

Union Shop An organization in which a worker is not required to be a member of the union to be hired but must become a member within a certain period of time after being employed.

Unit Elastic Demand The demand when the percentage change in quantity demanded is equal to the percentage change in price. Quantity demanded changes proportionately to price changes.

Util An artificial construct used to measure utility.

Utility A measure of the satisfaction, happiness, or benefit that results from the consumption of a good.

Value Marginal Product (VMP) The price of the good multiplied by the marginal physical product of the factor: $VMP = P \times MPP$.

Variable Costs Costs that vary with output; the costs associated with variable inputs.

Variable Input An input whose quantity can be changed as output changes.

Veil of Ignorance The imaginary veil or curtain behind which a person does not know his or her position in the income distribution.

Vertical Merger A merger between companies in the same industry but at different stages of the production process.

Wage Discrimination The situation that exists when individuals of equal ability and productivity (as measured by their contribution to output) are paid different wage rates.

X-Inefficiency The increase in costs and organizational slack in a monopoly resulting from the lack of competitive pressure to push costs down to their lowest possible level.

Yield Equal to the annual coupon payment divided by the price paid for the bond.

INDEX